D1542975

The Spirit
and Origins
of American
Protestantism

Books by Rev. John A. Hardon, S.J.

The Protestant Churches of America
All My Liberty
Christianity in Conflict
Religions of the World
The Hungry Generation

THE SPIRIT AND ORIGINS OF AMERICAN PROTESTANTISM

A Source Book in Its Creeds

John A. Hardon, S.J.
Bellarmine School of Theology
Loyola University in Chicago

PFLAUM PRESS  DAYTON, OHIO 1968

BT
990
.H18
c. 2

Imprimi Potest: Robert F. Harvanek, S.J.
Provincial
Chicago Province, Society of Jesus

Nihil Obstat: Thomas G. Doran
Censor Deputatus

Imprimatur: ✠ Loras T. Lane, D.D.
Bishop of Rockford, Illinois
May 10, 1968

The *Nihil Obstat* and *Imprimatur* are official declarations that a book or pamphlet is free of doctrinal or moral error. No implication is contained therein that those who have granted the *Nihil Obstat* and *Imprimatur* agree with the contents, opinions or statements expressed.

Library of Congress Catalog Card Number: 68-21241

Copyright © 1968 by John A. Hardon, S.J.

Printed in the United States of America

PREFACE

An educational purpose of importance is furthered by this new book from Father Hardon. Among Roman Catholics it has often been the practice to generalize about "protestantism" as if there were no significant differences between the Protestant churches. Of course, Catholics have been aware that liturgical practices differ among Protestants, but they have not been so aware of doctrinal variations between Protestant communions.

Undoubtedly the right place to begin is with the confessions if an understanding is wanted of historic and continuing differences among Protestants. The confessions trace for us the place of the various churches in the course of historical developments within Christianity. The confessions show us how the several communities have understood and confessed the faith and how they understood their relation to one another and to the Roman Catholic Church.

A warning is in order. Comparing the confessions may give the unwary the mistaken impression that Protestant churches are static and unchanging institutions. While it is clear that institutions generally, including the churches, resist change, one positive aspect of belief common to all Protestant churches is that the Church must always be open to the judging and renewing activity of God. Confessions are subject to renewal along with other institutions of the Church. Thus a continuous process of rethinking of the faith goes on in Protestant churches, rethinking which today is informed by the ecumenical movement and takes account of the thinking of Catholic theologians.

The Roman Catholic Church, through its official conversations in the United States and elsewhere with individual Protestant churches, is becoming better acquainted with each of these heritages. This familiarity must be extended, however, so that Prot-

OCT 16 1968

estant and Catholic laity and clergy generally may meet the doctrines of other churches as they are lived in their members. This book can be used as a resource for dialogue locally about our variant understandings of the common faith.

While not all Protestants and Anglicans will agree precisely with the interpretations of their confessional positions given by Father Hardon, few will deny the value of the explanations and none will deny the value of an accessible collection of the original texts.

Today the historic confessional differences are not the only, perhaps they are not even the primary, differences among the churches. Yet they persist and we cannot escape dealing with them. Patience and resolution are needed to resolve the differences, or they will return to plague us. As the Christian churches labor and live together more and more, they will have to discover the way also to bring to an end their confessional differences by confessing afresh the one true faith.

William A. Norgren
Executive Director
Department of Faith and Order
National Council of the Churches of Christ
in the United States of America

Table of Contents

Introduction

There is a legitimate sense in which Protestantism refers to all Christian movements, other than the Roman Catholic Church, that share the heritage of Western Christianity. But this is an extension of a term which has historical rootage. Protestantism as a type of the Christian religion stems from the Reformation and especially from the work of Luther and Calvin. Four hundred years have changed many things in Protestantism, but they have not effaced the spirit and theological emphasis first created by the Reformers in the sixteenth century.

It is this spirit and emphasis that the reader will see reflected in detail in the confessions of faith that form the present volume. Yet some background and explanation are needed to understand better what these confessions are meant to teach, and some apologia should be given for dividing, as I did, the whole sweep of Protestantism into two principal categories—the Reformation creeds and the Post-Reformation professions of faith, and each of these into further classifications according to historical lineage or doctrinal presupposition.

The first part of the book deals with the main lines of historic Protestantism which traced its origins to the Reformation. The second part gives the creeds (or their equivalent) of those religious bodies which are connected somehow with the Reformation but whose main principles are indigenous to America, as based on revelations purportedly received since apostolic times (like the Latter Day Saints), or as traceable to ideas that antedate the Reformation (like the Adventists), or as professing a complete reinterpretation of the Gospels (like Christian Science), or as favoring a pragmatic concept of religion (like Ethical Culture and the Unity School of Christianity).

It was only after serious consideration of other alternatives that a decision was reached to comprehend both forms of religious profession under a single title—*The Spirit and Origins of Ameri-can Protestantism*—and after it became clear that standard lexicographers accept the term "Protestant" in both a historical (Reformation) and transhistorical (Post-Reformation) sense that allow wide latitude of meaning.

The writing of this book was first prompted by the growing need in the ecumenical movement for easy access to the doctrinal positions of the principal religious bodies in Protestantism.

Ecumenism is now moving into its second and more serious stage, beyond the removal of barriers that for so long had sepa-rated the inheritors of the Reformation and those who gave alle-giance to Rome. But this deeper dialogue will be only as mean-ingful as each side understands the other, which presupposes adequate and accurate knowledge of the sources of their respec-tive faiths.

Among these sources none are more valuable (and valid) than the carefully worked out professions of belief that correspond, on the Catholic side, to the declarations of general councils or the pronouncements of the Holy See.

Some are called symbols of faith, as the Augsburg Confession among the Lutherans, and adherence to these symbols is a mark of orthodoxy. Departure in any substantial degree means to cut oneself off from the church which professes the creed. Others are statements of faith, as among churches in the Congregational family, where formal creedalism is discouraged while some agree-ment in doctrine is expected among those who join together in a covenanted community. Still others, exemplified in the Disciples of Christ and the Christian Scientists, subscribe to the principles of their founders whom they regard as pacesetters in giving direc-tion to religious thought rather than formulators of a mandatory creed.

No matter what their binding power, even when it is minimal (as for the Baptists), professions of faith are the single most cohesive force that gives internal unity to a Christian religious body. The same does not hold in other religious cultures like Hinduism and Buddhism. But in Christianity, which presumes the acceptance on faith of certain premises of revelation, the very concept of a church implies some uniformity of belief expressed in concrete symbols to which all who belong to the church are somehow supposed to subscribe. So true is this that as a religious group reduces these premises to the vanishing point or couches them in language that is consciously ambivalent, other churches charge it with diluting the teachings of Christ and often proceed to write another confessional document to meet what they consider heresy.

It should not come as a surprise, therefore, that no organized religious body in Christendom is without its own confessional center. The word "confessional" may not be used, and mandatory belief may not be required. But the irreducible minimum stands: in order to have an intelligible basis for existing as a church and to give rational grounds for its distinctive character, a more or less elaborate declaration of faith is of the essence of Christian ecclesiology.

This is the reason why merger efforts in the United States are so concerned with drafting plans of union and principles of coalition. There is always the underlying assumption that, when Christian bodies join in organic fusion, they have melted their superficial differences and are now a new creation that finds visible expression in a new profession of faith.

The problem of selection among the various confessions of faith was not an easy one in the compilation of this volume. Churches in the Reformed tradition alone have over sixty different creeds. It is estimated that in the United States there are about two hundred churches that qualify as Pentecostal, and each has its own distinctive beliefs. Today the Baptists number about thirty denominations in the country, and each has certain distinctive features that might qualify as creedal. Although the United Methodist Church is the largest Wesleyan body in America, it has twenty competitive denominations—all Methodist and all professing a more or less different faith.

It was clearly impossible to give all or even most of these doctrinal statements in one book. A single denomination like the Associate Reformed Presbyterian Church, with a membership under forty thousand, has a published confession of faith that runs to two hundred pages.

Some norms of selectivity had to be followed, and I wish to

share them briefly with the reader because they will help to appreciate the creedal documents that were included and facilitate their use beyond the immediate denomination from which they came.

The first rule I set myself was that certain doctrinal statements are so well established and have been accepted for so many years that they may properly be regarded as classic expressions of the Protestant faith. In this class belong the Augsburg Confession, the Westminster Confession and the Thirty-nine Articles.

Other professions have also stood the test of time, in spite of American religious fluidity, and consequently they promise to remain in possession for generations to come. The Philadelphia and New Hampshire Confessions of Baptist faith are typical. Both were drafted in the nineteenth century and today are as generally acceptable as when first formulated. Here the norm is not so much long duration as survival in a kind of Darwinian struggle among competitors.

Still other documents are more recent productions, but based on years of planning. The 1967 Presbyterian Confession is a case in point. It represents the mature thinking of the ablest minds in that denomination, striving to update their religious position without compromising on what they hold to be essentials. Another example is the latest Mennonite Creed, which was twenty years in the making and shows a remarkable awareness of modern trends while remaining faithful to Menno Simons and his interpretation of Christianity.

Longevity, however, and survival are not the only test of worth, whether in how long a doctrinal profession has been used, or how long it took to produce it, or even how successfully it managed to survive competition. Equally important is the influence it had on the development of Protestantism. By this standard, Thomas Campbell's *Declaration and Address* is among the most significant religious productions of the past century. His own Campbellites have since changed their names several times; and the derivative Disciples of Christ and Churches of Christ are not the largest churches in the United States. But what Campbell so painstakingly wrote in 1809 has affected the whole course of Protestant history in America.

A final norm I followed was to choose by preference that confessional statement which seemed most representative of a cluster
of churches within a given religious tradition. In some cases this
was obvious. All Lutherans subscribe to the Augsburg Confession
and Luther's Catechism; all Presbyterians accept the Westminster Confession; and all Baptists recognize the Philadelphia
and New Hampshire documents. In other cases it was more difficult to choose. Among groups of the Free Church ancestry, the
Congregationalists are certainly typical, in spite of their practical
absorption since the birth of the United Church of Christ. But,
then, which other bodies should also be included? Those chosen
were the largest in affiliated membership, or their leaders have
been outstanding in the progress of religious thought.

Moreover, after reading through several thousand pages of confessional writing, one conclusion became clear. Not more than
half a dozen major professions of faith represent the collective
belief of four-fifths of American Protestantism.

I have purposely included several religious groups that only
loosely qualify as churches—certainly Ethical Culture and the
Unity School of Christianity. They could not be omitted without
distorting the picture of our national religious culture. Much of it
is unstructured, unecclesiastical, and, in a true sense, unchurched.
It is America, however, and more widespread than most people
realize. Some would say over forty million belong to this post-
Protestant, nondenominational society.

What deserves to be better known is that, for all their amor-
phous character, these quasi-churches are not disorganized. Quite
the contrary. There is more efficiency in the mail-order methods
of the Unity School of Christianity than in many large churches
with recognized ecclesiastical status. Part of their organization is
to have a rather definite body of principles and a clear idea of
how these principles should be carried into practice.

In order to give the confessional statements a historical context,
I have introduced each of the main religious families with some
background on what distinguishes their tradition and how it
differs from other forms of Protestantism. Included in these intro-
ductions, or in another prefatory essay, is a short analysis of the
creed itself.

Some readers may wonder why a book on Protestant confessions of faith should be published by a Catholic author. The immediate reason was the recommendation of the Second Vatican Council.

> We must get to know the outlook of our separated brethren. Study is absolutely required for this, and it should be pursued in fidelity to truth and with a spirit of good will. Catholics, who already have a proper grounding, need to acquire a more adequate understanding of the respective doctrines of our separated brethren, their history, their spiritual and liturgical life, their religious psychology and cultural background (*Degree on Ecumenism*, II, 9).

Another reason was the need that Catholics have for understanding the differences between what their faith demands and what those who are called Protestants believe. Ecumenism does not mean blurring these differences but rather exploring them and, with divine grace, working towards their solution. Some are proposing the very changes in Catholic doctrine and practice that originally separated the Reformers from Rome in the sixteenth century, for example, in papal and episcopal authority, celibacy of priests and religious life under vows, the Mass as sacrifice and the bodily presence of Christ in the Eucharist, the Church's right to make laws binding in conscience and the indissolubility of Christian marriage.

No one who reads the confessional statements in this volume can have any doubt that Catholicism is not Protestantism. Any attempt to make the one into the other is to turn back the pages of history and to do an injustice to both religious traditions.

My hope is that when this book is used together with its companion volume, the revised *Protestant Churches of America*, the reader will find what the author has learned from experience, that American Protestantism is more vital than ever before in its history. To know this vitality and cooperate with its efforts to help this nation grow in religious conviction is to promote ecumenism where it counts the most, in the minds of those who believe in the Son of God.

PART ONE
CHURCHES OF REFORMATION ORIGIN

Historians are divided in their analysis of what factors were ultimately responsible for the Reformation in the sixteenth century. In one sense everything that preceded the Reformation contributed to its development and everyone who urged a much-needed reform in the Church's "head and members" was its precursor.

Yet the true father of the Reformation was Martin Luther whose genius alone, it has been said, laid the foundations of that *via moderna* in Christianity that has so deeply affected the thinking and culture of the Western world.

The birthday of Protestantism is commonly dated October 31, 1517, when Martin Luther nailed his ninety-five theses to the church door of the castle at Wittenberg. Within ten years, every major difference from the parent Roman Catholicism had been stated by Luther, and whatever subsequent development took place only built on the foundations he laid with a clarity and vigor that prompted his friend Melanchthon to say that "Luther is a miracle among men. What he says and writes grips the heart and leaves a marvelous deep impression behind."

His basic principle was an appeal to conscience, personally enlightened by the Spirit, against what he called the accretions of human ingenuity. Standing before the Diet of Worms in 1521, and charged by the Empire with promoting heresy, Luther replied in a statement that has become famous. The imperial judges asked him for a plain reply to this accusation; in a word, was he prepared to recant or not.

> Your Imperial Majesty and Your Lordships demand a simple answer. Here it is, plain and unvarnished. Unless I am convicted of error by the testimony of Scripture or—since I put no trust in the unsupported authority of Pope or of councils, since it is plain that they have often erred and often contradicted themselves— by manifest reasoning I stand convicted by the Scriptures to which I have appealed, and my conscience is taken captive by God's word. I cannot and will not recant anything, for to act against our conscience is neither safe for us, nor open to us.
>
> On this I take my stand. I can do no other. God help me. Amen.[1]

[1] Martin Luther, *Opera Latina*, VI, 8.

3

During the next twenty-five years, until his death in 1546, Luther elaborated this theory of conscience to include the whole construct of the Reformation. The conscience, he taught, is bound up with the Word of God in the Scriptures. Therefore, instead of popes and councils, Scripture alone (*sola Scriptura*) became the source of religious knowledge. By the time of the Formula of Concord (1577), this had been canonized into an article of faith, that "Holy Scripture alone is acknowledged as the only judge, norm, and rule, according to which, as by the only touchstone, all doctrines are to be examined and judged, as to whether they are godly or ungodly, true or false." [2] Language could not be clearer on the Scriptures as the fountainhead of all doctrine and the only standard of Christian belief.

However, Scriptures themselves need an interpreter. Since ecclesiastical authority was ruled out, the alternative was the indwelling Spirit of God. Both the antecedent question of which books of the Bible are inspired and the problem of determining what a given passage means, are subject not to the whims of a human institution (like the Church) but to the ever present divine light in the soul. If this idea was thematic in Luther, it was systematized by John Calvin in his *Institutes of the Christian Religion,* first published in 1536, to become the greatest single legacy of the Reformation and the *Summa Theologica* of Protestantism.

Accordingly, the principle that by the Spirit alone (*solo Spiritu*) do we understand the Scriptures was axiomatic. "The testimony of the Spirit is more excellent than all reason. For as God alone is a fit witness of Himself in His Word, so also the Word will not find acceptance in men's hearts before it is sealed by the inward testimony of the Spirit." So that "those whom the Holy Spirit has inwardly taught truly rest upon Scripture," and "the certainty it deserves with us, it attains by the testimony of the Spirit. For even if it wins reverence for itself by its own majesty, it seriously affects us only when it is sealed upon our hearts through the Spirit. Therefore, illumined by His power, we believe neither by our own nor by any one else's judgment that Scripture is from God," or that a given meaning attached to a biblical text is divinely true. "But above human judgment we affirm with utter

2 *Formula of Concord,* "De Compendiaria Regula Atque Norma," 3.

certainty, just as if we were gazing upon the majesty of God Himself, that it has flowed to us from the very mouth of God." [3]

Among the verities that Luther and Calvin were convinced the Spirit had taught them by the ministry of the Word was the complete depravity of human nature since the fall, and consequently that whatever good we do or hope we have of heaven comes only from grace (*sola gratia*) and not at all from the effort or good works of man.

Basic to the Reformation theology of grace was the principle that original justice was due to human nature by a strict right of essence. "Original justice," wrote Luther, "was part of man's nature." [4] As a result, when Adam fell and lost the righteousness he possessed, his nature became essentially corrupt and his faculties were intrinsically vitiated. Nothing in the literature of historic Protestantism is more emphatically asserted against the "scholastic innovators" who misinterpreted revelation and the teaching of St. Augustine.

"See what follows," urged Luther, "if you maintain that original righteousness was not a part of nature but a sort of superfluous or superadded gift. When you declare that righteousness was not a part of the essence of man, does it not also follow that sin, which took its place, is not part of the essence of man either?" [5] If this were so, "there was no purpose in sending Christ the Redeemer," whose unique function was to win the grace we need to supply for our complete helplessness and inability to do any good. If, then, we are saved, all the credit belongs to God and none to us; grace alone accounts for man's salvation and not in any sense the works of man, whose corruption is capable of nothing but sin and whose freedom, in Luther's phrase, is "only an empty phrase." To God alone the glory, therefore, and to His grace the thanks.

One final element belongs to the foundations of Reformation thought, the doctrine that by faith alone (*sola fide*) are we saved, namely, by an absolute trust in God's mercy that in spite of our sinfulness the merits of His Son will hide our sins and spare us from the hellfire that we justly deserve. In the words of the Augsburg Confession (1530), "Our works cannot reconcile us to God

[3] John Calvin, *Institutes of the Christian Religion*, I, 7, 4-5.
[4] Luther, *Commentary on Genesis*, III, 7.
[5] *Ibid.*

or merit remission of sins and grace and justification. This we obtain only by faith, when we believe that we are received into grace on account of Christ." And to make sure there is no mistaking this trust for the dogmatic faith of Catholics, who made acceptance of revealed truths the first requisite for salvation, "Men are warned that the word *faith* does not signify the knowledge of an event—the devils and impious men have that—but it signifies a faith which believes not in an event merely, but also in the effect of an event, namely this article, the remission of sins, i.e., that we have, through Christ, grace, righteousness, and remission of sins." [6]

Thus we have the full complement of principles on which the structure of classic Protestantism was built, likened to the pillars of a massive building: the interior conscience instead of external authority, the Scriptures in place of ecclesiastical tradition, the interior Spirit supplying for the pope and councils, divine grace making up for the innate deficiency of will, and confident trust relying on the promise of the Savior, "because consciences cannot be quieted by any good works, but by faith alone, when they believe assuredly that they have a God who is propitiated for the sake of Christ." [7]

In the four centuries since these concepts were propounded, they have undergone much development and seen applications that Luther and Calvin never suspected, but their original spirit has not been lost. This spirit has remained fairly constant and still serves to unite what is externally the most fragmented form of Christianity in existence, whose very beginnings were marked by cleavage and division. For although it is true that Luther was the first of the Protestant Reformers, the churches of the Reformation really had four beginnings: under Luther, Calvin, Henry VIII and the Anabaptists, all within a generation of that Eve of All Saints in Wittenberg. Each prototype has since grown into a multitude of churches and denominations that, in spite of mergers and overlappings, still retain characteristic elements that are traceable to their respective ancestry, along with the common features that first marked the origins of Protestantism.

[6] *The Augsburg Confession,* 20.
[7] *Ibid.,* 18.

1. Lutheranism

The religious crisis which Luther and his followers precipitated in Germany occasioned a series of conferences which became landmarks in the history of Protestantism. Summoned by Charles V to the Diet of Worms, Luther refused to submit and was condemned as an outlaw, but taken by the Elector of Saxony into protective custody. Eight years later, at the Diet of Speyer (1529), the Lutheran princes refused to agree that Catholic worship should be free everywhere and the new religion be allowed only in places where it already had some followers.

Their "protest" at Speyer became symbolic of the whole movement and gave the name by which the Churches of the Reformation have since become known. When the Diet of Speyer proved inoperative, the Emperor called the Diet of Augsburg (1530) to effect a reconciliation between Catholics and Reformers. While this attempt failed, a compromise was reached among the factions in the Protestant camp, and the agreement was stabilized in the Confession of Augsburg, for which Melanchthon wrote an Apology after the creedal statement was challenged by the Catholics. Both documents are now doctrinal standards in Churches of the Lutheran tradition.

Luther's productivity was phenomenal. There were four Weimar editions of his writings, amounting to eighty-three volumes. The current English translation will run to fifty-five volumes in octavo. His two catechisms, a larger and smaller, were originally intended "for the improperly indoctrinated Roman clergy who had joined the evangelicals and to the teachers of the parochial schools." They have since been recognized as the most unique of his writings and the most influential, in marked contrast with the polemic tracts he was forced to compose to meet the steady opposition from leaders of the Reformation.

After Luther's death, the area of conflict widened between his own evangelical disciples and the followers of Calvin and Zwingli. Questions of sin and grace, justification and free will, the ministry and the Lord's Supper, baptism and predestination, divided the different groups, even among the Lutherans, who were partially reconciled by the Formula of Concord, which is the last of their fundamental confessions of faith.

By the middle of the seventeenth century, Lutheranism had been established not only in Germany and Central Europe, but in Denmark—where the Church was organized in 1536 with the king as ruling prelate—Sweden, East Prussia, Iceland, Hungary, Silesia, Poland and Transylvania. The first Lutherans to make a permanent settlement in America came from Holland to the Dutch New Netherlands (Manhattan) in 1623.

Doctrine and Worship. Justification by faith alone lies at the heart of Lutheranism, which strenuously opposes any kind of synergism (Greek *syn,* "with," and *ergon,* "work"), that in the act of conversion the human will can cooperate with the Holy Spirit and God's grace. Its emphasis is always on God's sole activity in the process of salvation.

Unlike the Reformed Churches, however, Lutheran bodies abstain from examining too closely the mystery of predestination which is painfully raised by the denial of freedom in contact with grace. They concentrate on the confidence we should have in God's mercy and the gratitude we owe Him for his promised redemption. In the Evangelical tradition, therefore, God has done everything for us; we need only accept his benefit with appreciation. He has already come to us in the person of the Savior; so that nothing can separate us from this treasury of goodness.

Lutheran Churches retain in large measure the pre-Reformation idea of the Atonement as something objective, and not merely personal to each individual. One modification, however, is that they do not consider the sufferings of Christ a satisfaction for sin but a punishment which Christ underwent vicariously on our behalf. This concept of the Atonement is a prominent feature of Lutheran preaching and liturgical hymns.

No area of Lutheran theology more clearly distinguishes it from others, notably the Calvinist, than the doctrine of the Eucharist. Lutherans repudiate any idea of the presence of Christ in the Eucharist in a purely spiritual manner. They hold that He is present in a bodily way, and the communicants partake physically of his body and blood, along with the visible elements. "The body and blood of Christ are received with the bread and wine, not only spiritually by faith, but also orally, in a supernatural and celestial way, because of the sacramental union. He who eats this bread eats the body of Christ." [1] Unlike the Catholic belief, there is no transubstantiation but a kind of impanation (inbreadness) in which Christ's presence exists alongside the substance and accidents of bread and wine; the union between elements and Christ being called sacramental. In the Formula of Concord, the body and blood are said to be present "in, with and under" the bread and wine. Technically the doctrine is consubstantiation.

Behind this theory is the application of a principle of Christology, adapted from the teaching of Chalcedon, that the two natures in Christ are not commingled or confused, yet are inseparably united. The Reformed Churches maintained that after the Ascension Christ's human nature was on the right hand of the heavenly Father, and therefore only His divinity was really present in the Eucharist, together with a virtual (but not bodily) presence of His humanity. Lutherans objected that such separation is impossible, so that wherever Christ is present, He is there both as God and man, hence also in the Eucharist.

Upholding the ancient faith that Christ is true God and man, Lutherans made the miracle of the Incarnation central in their tradition and the focus of all their teaching. It was particularly concerned to preserve such fundamental doctrines as the divinity of Christ that Lutheran Churches the world over have promoted Christian day schools and, at great sacrifice, built an impressive system of religion-centered education. When civil pressures threatened the parochial schools, they were quick to defend their educational policy.

> Whereas the Word of God, our rule of life, enjoins upon all Christian parents the duty of bringing up their children in the nurture and admonition of the Lord; therefore all Christians who educate their children in schools are in duty bound to entrust their children to such schools only as secure the education of children

[1] Arthur C. Piepkorn, *What the Symbolical Books of the Lutheran Church Have to Say About Worship and the Sacraments*, St. Louis, 1952, p. 30.

in the nurture and admonition of the Lord, while at the same time it is with us self-understood that we are willing to make good citizens of our children, to the utmost of our ability.[2]

In the development of Lutheran forms of worship, the basic structure was the Roman Catholic Mass. Among the major changes, the most important was the removal of sacrificial prayers from the Canon of the Mass. Luther himself carried out this reform. His idea was to give expression to the doctrine of the Eucharistic Presence without the concept of sacrifice of propitiation for the living and the dead.

The normal sequence of the Canon is the Preface, Sanctus, Lord's Prayer, Words of Institution, Pax Domini, Agnus Dei, and distribution of Holy Communion. In giving the elements to the faithful, the minister says, "Take, eat; this is the true body (blood) of our Lord and Savior Jesus Christ, given into death for (shed for the remission of) your sins. May this strengthen and preserve you in the true faith unto life everlasting."

Another change was to make the sermon an essential part of the Eucharistic service. The Word of God, in the sense of the word that is preached, remains to this day a prominent feature of Lutheranism. Orders of worship prescribe the sermon after the Nicene Creed and before the Offertory.

An innovation that has since become part of most other Protestant churches was the singing of hymns by the congregation during the Communion service. As early as 1526 Luther composed his German Mass (*Deutsche Messe*), in which the *Credo* and *Agnus Dei* were replaced by German hymns so that the whole congregation could sing together. He also replaced the Latin Introit by a hymn in the vernacular and added a prescriptive hymn after the Epistle in place of the Gradual. Luther's love of music was proverbial, and faithful to his memory the churches have made religious songs almost coextensive with divine worship.

Customs differ greatly in different countries. In Germany, for instance, the liturgical heritage of Lutheranism has been much reduced; in the United States it is growing at a pace so rapid that

---

[2] Resolution of Missouri Synod (1890), *A Century of Grace*, St. Louis, 1947, p. 207.

concern has been expressed over the "ritualistic movement." Comparable to the High and Low Church types in Anglicanism, Lutheran bodies closer to the Reformation spirit have altars, altar candles, vestments, and order of worship that are remarkably Catholic in external form.

Recent Developments. All principal Lutheran Churches of Reformation times were established institutions following the norm of the Augsburg Treaty of 1555, *cujus regio, ejus religio,* which meant that civil rulers determined the religious affiliation of their subjects. To this day, Lutheranism is the state religion of Norway, Sweden, Denmark and Finland. In Germany the Lutheran Churches continued to be established bodies until the Weimar Constitution of 1919, when Church and State were declared separated throughout the country.

In Scandinavia, the national bodies are supported financially by the civil authorities and administered by a ministry of ecclesiastical affairs, which is a joint Ministry of Church and Education in Norway and Sweden. Except for assistant pastors, bishops and clergy are appointed by the Crown; and Parliament acts as the Church's highest legislative body, in spite of the fact that members of Parliament need not belong to the Lutheran Church.

The European trend has been in the direction of emancipating the Church from political control and giving it independence in purely spiritual matters. Sweden has a national Church Assembly that can vote on ecclesiastical issues, present recommendations to Parliament, and exercise a kind of veto; but the legal competence of the assembly is naturally limited as long as the Church is officially established. In the United States the congregation is the basic unit of Lutheran church government, with no semblance of the close tie-in with civil powers as in Europe.

During the nineteenth century, two competing theological trends in Lutheranism struggled for mastery in Europe, with heavy overtones in America. In 1821, Friedrich Schleiermacher (1768-1834) published his *Christian Faith* which dates an epoch in the history of modern theology. While rationalists and supernaturalists carried on their fight in schools of divinity, Schleiermacher took the ground from under their contention by removing its main premise. The Christian faith, he claimed, does not consist in any kind of doctrinal propositions. It is a condition of devout feeling and, like all other internal experience, simply an object to be described.

Against the supernaturalists Schleiermacher maintained that Christianity is not something to be received on authority from without, but an inward state of our own self-consciousness. Against the rationalists he said religion is not a product of rational thinking, but an emotion of the heart, a feeling which occurs independently of the mind.

The net result of this emphasis on the subjective experience was to usher Low Church mentality into Lutheran circles, with an undervaluation of the sacraments and a new stress on revivalism. There was a correlative downgrading of church authority and the development of an ecclesiastical structure built along Free Church and Congregational lines.

In the opposite direction, Lutheran confessionalism reacted against the liberal tendencies of the Enlightenment and the "religion of feeling" to inaugurate what can only be called a Lutheran Renascence. Since the beginning of the present century, interest in Luther's theology and Reformation thought has become the dominant characteristic of the Evangelical Churches. German and Swedish scholars have been the mainstay of the movement, but supported by Danish and Flemish theologians.

One effect of this renascence has been the discovery in Reformation sources of doctrinal principles that lay hidden for centuries, principles that are being exploited in the current drive for Christian unity.

AUGSBURG CONFESSION

Lutheranism is unique among the inheritors of the Reformation in having a strong sense of loyalty to established confessions of faith. It is further unique in having gathered together at an early date the fundamental professions on which, it was held, the faith of the Evangelical Church depends. The *Book of Concord*, published in 1580, sought to resolve whatever conflicts had arisen in the first fifty years since Wittenberg and to this day remains the mainstay of Lutheran belief.

Before giving what are called the "Symbolical (Creedal) Documents" of Lutheranism, the *Book of Concord* states the three universal Creeds—Apostles', Nicene and Athanasian, with minor variants from their Roman Catholic versions. Thus the Apostles' Creed has the German *christlich* to translate the Latin *catholica* in the article, "I believe in the Holy Spirit, the holy Christian Church." In the same way, wherever "Catholic" occurs in the Athanasian Creed, the authors of the *Book of Concord* changed it to "Christian."

After the three major Creeds, the *Book of Concord* includes the Augsburg Confession (1531), the Apology of the Augsburg Confession (1531), the Smalcald Articles (1537), Treatise on the Power and Primacy of the Pope (1537), Luther's Small and Large Catechisms (1529), and the Formula of Concord (1577).

Among these documents the Confession of Augsburg and Luther's Small Catechism are the most significant; the first because of its detailed exposition of the Evangelical faith and the second because it remains to this day the most popular manual of Lutheran belief.

The Confession of Augsburg is literally the *Grundbekenntnis* (basic creed) of the Lutheran Church, but not only because it outlines the main doctrines professed by believing Lutherans. It reflects the mood of their approach to Christianity. Lutheran commentators view it as an expression of theological conservatism in contrast to radicalism, where the radical were Anabaptists and others who broke with the mainstream of the Reformation within a few years of its beginning on the continent. The Confession also shows the Lutheran concern for historic continuity and apostolicity, in contrast to what they call novelty and modernism.

Although fundamental to any understanding of world Lutheranism, the Confession of Augsburg is not a complete confession of faith. It passes by in silence such controversial issues as purgatory, the worship of saints, and especially papal authority. Luther himself recognized these "omissions," and yet sanctioned them in the interest of religious concord. To this day, the Confession is a tribute to the ecumenical spirit which characterizes the Evangelical tradition in Protestantism. Whatever dialectic the document reveals is mainly on the side of excluding the Anabaptist tendency to take "salvation by faith alone" with absolute literalness.

and the Zwinglian view of the sacraments as purely symbolic and in no sense effective of the grace they signify.

More than any other document of the Reformation, the Confession of Augsburg has remained unchanged in over four hundred years. The massiveness of its Evangelical message, joined to an ecumenical approach founded on Scripture, has kept its influence alive.

Melanchthon, Luther's confidant and adviser, is the principal author of the Confession. Correspondence between the two men shows that Luther approved the document, of which he wrote in a letter that "it pleases me very much." The 1531 edition, however, must not be confused with the 1540 version, also written by Melanchthon, commonly called the *Confessio Variata* (The Varied Confession). Although substantially the same, it contains significant changes made to satisfy the demands of the Swiss followers of Calvin, notably on the subject of the Eucharist. Thus the original Confession of Augsburg teaches that "the true body and blood of Christ are really present in the Supper of our Lord under the form of bread and wine and are there distributed and received. The contrary doctrine is therefore rejected" (Article X). Whereas the *Variata* deleted the words "that the true body and blood of Christ are really present," as well as the rejection of the contrary belief. For these was substituted: "Together with the bread and wine in the Supper the communicants are shown (*exhibeantur* instead of the former *adsint et distribuantur*) the body and blood of Christ." In this way, both Calvin's spiritual presence in the Eucharist and Zwingli's symbolism could be read into the altered Confession of Augsburg.

Only the 1531 version is authentic, and as such is universally accepted in Lutheran Churches. It is generally placed immediately after the three ecumenical creeds in official listings of the symbolical documents of Lutheranism.

I. *God.* We unanimously hold and teach, in accordance with the decree of the Council of Nicaea, that there is one divine essence, which is called and which is truly God, and that there are three persons in this one divine essence, equal in power and alike eternal: God the Father, God the Son, God the Holy Spirit. All three are one divine essence, eternal, without division, without end, of infinite power, wisdom, and goodness, one creator and preserver of all things visible and invisible. The word "person" is to be understood as the Fathers employed the term in this connection, not as a part or a property of another but as that which exists of itself.

Therefore all the heresies which are contrary to this article are rejected. Among these are the heresy of the Manichaeans, who assert that there are two gods, one good and one evil; also that of the Valentinians, Arians, Eunomians, Mohammedans, and others like them; also that of the Samosatenes, old and new, who hold that there is only one person and sophistically assert that the other two, the Word and the Holy Spirit, are not necessarily distinct persons but that the Word signifies a physical word or voice and that the Holy Spirit is a movement induced in creatures.

II. *Original Sin.* It is also taught among us that since the fall of Adam all men who are born according to the course of nature are conceived and born in sin. That is, all men are full of evil lust and inclinations from their mothers' wombs and are unable by nature to have true fear of God and true faith in God. Moreover, this inborn sickness and hereditary sin is truly sin and condemns to the eternal wrath of God all those who are not born again through Baptism and the Holy Spirit.

Rejected in this connection are the Pelagians and others who deny that original sin is sin, for they hold that natural man is made righteous by his own powers, thus disparaging the sufferings and merit of Christ.

III. *The Son of God.* It is also taught among us that God the Son became man, born of the Virgin Mary, and that the two natures, divine and human, are so inseparably united in one person that there is one Christ, true God and true man, who was truly born, suffered, was crucified, died, and was buried in order to be a sacrifice not only for original sin but also for all other sins and to propitiate God's wrath. The same Christ also descended into hell, truly rose from the dead on the third day, ascended into heaven, and sits on the right hand of God, that he may eternally rule and have dominion over all creatures, that through the Holy Spirit he may sanctify, purify, strengthen, and comfort all who believe in him, that he may bestow on them life and every grace and blessing, and that he may protect and defend them against the devil and against sin. The same Lord Christ will return openly to judge the living and the dead, as stated in the Apostles' Creed.

IV. *Justification.* It is also taught among us that we cannot obtain forgiveness of sin and righteousness before God by our own merits, works, or satisfaction, but that we receive forgiveness of sin and become righteous before God by grace, for Christ's sake, through faith, when we believe that Christ suffered for us and that for his sake our sin is forgiven and righteousness and eternal life are given to us. For God will regard and reckon this faith as righteousness, as Paul says in Romans 3:21-26 and 4:5.

V. *The Office of the Ministry.* To obtain such faith God instituted the office of the ministry, that is, provided the Gospel and the sacraments. Through these, as through means, he gives the Holy Spirit, who works faith, when and where he pleases, in those who hear the Gospel. And the Gospel teaches that we have a gracious God, not by our own merits but by the merit of Christ, when we believe this.

Condemned are the Anabaptists and others who teach that the Holy Spirit comes to us through our own preparations, thoughts, and works without the external word of the Gospel.

VI. *The New Obedience.* It is also taught among us that such faith should produce good fruits and good works and that we must do all such good works as God has commanded, but we should do them for God's sake and not place our trust in them as if thereby to merit favor before God. For we receive forgiveness of sin and righteousness through faith in Christ, as Christ himself says, "So you also, when you have done all that is commanded you, say, 'We are unworthy servants'" (Luke 17:10). The Fathers also teach thus, for Ambrose says, "It is ordained of God that whoever believes in Christ shall be saved, and he shall have forgiveness of sins, not through works but through faith alone, without merit."

VII. *The Church.* It is also taught among us that one holy Christian church will be and remain forever. This is the assembly of all believers among whom the Gospel is preached in its purity and the holy sacraments are administered according to the Gospel. For it is sufficient for the true unity of the Christian church that the Gospel be preached in conformity with a pure understanding of it and that the sacraments be administered in accordance with the divine Word. It is not necessary for the true unity of the Christian church that ceremonies, instituted by men, should be observed uniformly in all places. It is as Paul says in Eph. 4:4, 5, "There is one body and one Spirit, just as you were called to the one hope that belongs to your call, one Lord, one faith, one baptism."

VIII. *What the Church Is.* Again, although the Christian church, properly speaking, is nothing else than the assembly of all believers and saints, yet because in this life many false Christians, hypocrites, and even open sinners remain among the godly, the sacraments are efficacious even if the priests who administer them are wicked men, for as Christ himself indicated, "The Pharisees sit on Moses' seat" (Matt. 23:2).

Accordingly the Donatists and all others who hold contrary views are condemned.

IX. *Baptism.* It is taught among us that Baptism is necessary and that grace is offered through it. Children, too, should be baptized, for in Baptism they are committed to God and become acceptable to him.

On this account the Anabaptists who teach that infant Baptism is not right are rejected.

X. *The Holy Supper of Our Lord.* It is taught among us that the true body and blood of Christ are really present in the Supper of our Lord under the form of bread and wine and are there distributed and received. The contrary doctrine is therefore rejected.

XI. *Confession.* It is taught among us that private absolution should be retained and not allowed to fall into disuse. However, in confession it is not necessary to enumerate all trespasses and sins, for this is impossible. Ps. 19:12, "Who can discern his errors?"

XII. *Repentance.* It is taught among us that those who sin after Baptism receive forgiveness of sin whenever they come to repentance, and absolution should not be denied them by the church. Properly speaking, true repentance is nothing else than to have contrition and sorrow, or terror, on account of sin, and yet at the same time to believe the Gospel and absolution (namely, that sin has been forgiven and grace has been obtained through Christ), and this faith will comfort the heart and again set it at rest. Amendment of life and the forsaking of sin should then follow, for these must be the fruits of repentance, as John says, "Bear fruit that befits repentance" (Matt. 3:8).

Rejected here are those who teach that persons who have once become godly cannot fall again.

Condemned on the other hand are the Novatians who denied absolution to such as had sinned after Baptism.

Rejected also are those who teach that forgiveness of sin is not obtained through faith but through the satisfactions made by man.

XIII. *The Use of the Sacraments.* It is taught among us that the sacraments were instituted not only to be signs by which people might be identified outwardly as Christians, but that they are signs and testimonies of God's will toward us for the purpose of awakening and strengthening our faith. For this reason they require faith, and they are rightly used when they are received in faith and for the purpose of strengthening faith.

XIV. *Order in the Church.* It is taught among us that nobody should publicly teach or preach or administer the sacraments in the church without a regular call.

XV. *Church Usages.* With regard to church usages that have been established by men, it is taught among us that those usages are to be observed which may be observed without sin and which contribute to peace and good order in the church, among them being certain holy days, festivals, and the like. Yet we accompany these observances with instruction so that consciences may not be burdened by the notion that such things are necessary for salvation. Moreover it is taught that all ordinances and traditions instituted by men for the purpose of propitiating God and earning grace are contrary to the Gospel and the teaching about faith in Christ. Accordingly monastic vows and other traditions concerning distinctions of foods, days, etc., by which it is intended to earn grace and make satisfaction for sin, are useless and contrary to the Gospel.

XVI. *Civil Government.* It is taught among us that all government in the world and all established rule and laws were instituted and ordained by God for the sake of good order, and that Christians may without sin occupy civil offices or serve as princes and judges, render decisions and pass sentence according to imperial and other existing laws, punish evildoers with the sword, engage in just wars, serve as soldiers, buy and sell, take required oaths, possess property, be married, etc.

Condemned here are the Anabaptists who teach that none of the things indicated above is Christian.

Also condemned are those who teach that Christian perfection requires the forsaking of house and home, wife and child, and the renunciation of such activities as are mentioned above. Actually, true perfection consists alone of proper fear of God and real faith in God, for the Gospel does not teach an outward and temporal but an inward and eternal mode of existence and righteousness of the heart. The Gospel does not overthrow civil authority, the state, and marriage but requires that all these be kept as true orders of God and that everyone, each according to his own calling, manifest Christian love and genuine good works in his station of life. Accordingly Christians are obliged to be subject to civil authority and obey its commands and laws in all that can be done without sin. But when commands of the civil authority cannot be obeyed without sin, we must obey God rather than men (Acts 5:29).

XVII. *The Return of Christ to Judgment.* It is also taught among us that our Lord Jesus Christ will return on the last day for judgment and will raise up all the dead, to give eternal life and everlasting joy to believers and the elect but to condemn ungodly men and the devil to hell and eternal punishment.

Rejected, therefore, are the Anabaptists who teach that the devil and condemned men will not suffer eternal pain and torment.

Rejected, too, are certain Jewish opinions which are even now making an appearance and which teach that, before the resurrection of the dead, saints and godly men will possess a worldly kingdom and annihilate all the godless.

XVIII. *Freedom of the Will.* It is also taught among us that man possesses some measure of freedom of the will which enables him to live an outwardly honorable life and to make choices among the things that reason comprehends. But without the grace, help, and activity of the Holy Spirit man is not capable of making himself acceptable to God, of fearing God and believing in God with his whole heart, or of expelling inborn evil lusts from the heart. This is accomplished by the Holy Spirit, who is given through the Word of God, for Paul says in 1 Cor. 2:14, "Natural man does not receive the gifts of the Spirit of God."

In order that it may be evident that this teaching is no novelty, the clear words of Augustine on free will are here quoted from the third book of his *Hypognosticon:* "We concede that all men have a free will, for all have a natural, innate understanding and reason. However, this does not enable them to act in matters pertaining to God (such as loving God with their whole heart or fearing him), for it is only in the outward acts of this life that they have freedom to choose good or evil. By good I mean what they are capable of by nature: whether or not to labor in the fields, whether or not to eat or drink or visit a friend, whether to dress or undress, whether to build a house, take a wife, engage in a trade, or do whatever else may be good and profitable. None of these is or exists without God, but all things are from him and through him. On the other hand, by his own choice man can also undertake evil, as when he wills to kneel before an idol, commit murder, etc."

XIX. *The Cause of Sin.* It is taught among us that although almighty God has created and still preserves nature, yet sin is caused in all wicked men and despisers of God by the perverted will. This is the will of the devil and of all ungodly men; as soon as God withdraws his support, the will turns away from God to evil. It is as Christ says in John 8:44, "When the devil lies, he speaks according to his own nature."

XX. *Faith and Good Works.* Our teachers have been falsely accused of forbidding good works. Their writings on the Ten Commandments, and other writings as well, show that they have given good and profitable accounts and instructions concerning true Christian estates and works. About these little was taught in former times, when for the most part sermons were concerned with childish and useless works like rosaries, the cult of saints, monasticism, pilgrimages, appointed fasts, holy days, brotherhoods, etc. Our opponents no longer praise these useless works so highly as they once did, and they have also learned to speak now of faith, about which they did not preach at all in former times. They do not teach now that we become righteous before God by our works alone, but they add faith in Christ and say that faith and works make us righteous before God. This teaching may offer a little more comfort than the teaching that we are to rely solely on our works.

Since the teaching about faith, which is the chief article in the Christian life, has been neglected so long (as all must admit) while nothing but works was preached everywhere, our people have been instructed as follows:

We begin by teaching that our works cannot reconcile us with God or obtain grace for us, for this happens only through faith, that is, when we believe that our sins are forgiven for Christ's sake, who alone is the mediator who reconciles the Father. Whoever imagines that he can accomplish this by works, or that he can merit grace, despises Christ and seeks his own way to God, contrary to the Gospel.

This teaching about faith is plainly and clearly treated by Paul in many passages, especially in Eph. 2:8, 9, "For by grace you have been saved through faith; and this is not your own doing, it is the gift of God—not because of works, lest any man should boast," etc.

That no new interpretation is here introduced can be demonstrated from Augustine, who discusses this question thoroughly and teaches the same thing, namely, that we obtain grace and are justified before God through faith in Christ and not through works. His whole book, *De spiritu et littera,* proves this.

Although this teaching is held in great contempt among untried people, yet it is a matter of experience that weak and terrified consciences find it most comforting and salutary. The conscience cannot come to rest and peace through works, but only through faith, that is, when it is assured and knows that for Christ's sake it has a gracious God, as Paul says in Rom. 5:1, "Since we are justified by faith, we have peace with God."

In former times this comfort was not heard in preaching, but poor consciences were driven to rely on their own efforts, and all sorts of works were undertaken. Some were driven by their conscience into monasteries in the hope that there they might merit grace through monastic life. Others devised other works for the purpose of earning grace and making satisfaction for sins. Many of them discovered that they did not obtain peace by such means. It was therefore necessary to preach this doctrine about faith in Christ and diligently to apply it in order that men may know that the grace of God is appropriated without merits, through faith alone.

Instruction is also given among us to show that the faith here spoken of is not that possessed by the devil and the ungodly, who also believe the history of Christ's suffering and his resurrection from the dead, but we mean such true faith as believes that we receive grace and forgiveness of sin through Christ.

Whoever knows that in Christ he has a gracious God, truly knows God, calls upon him, and is not, like the heathen, without God. For the devil and the ungodly do not believe this article concerning the forgiveness of sin, and so they are at enmity with God, cannot call upon him, and have no hope of receiving good from him. Therefore, as has just been indicated, the Scriptures speak of faith but do not mean by it such knowledge as the devil and ungodly men possess. Heb. 11:1 teaches about faith in such a way as to make it clear that faith is not merely a knowledge of historical events but is a confidence in God and in the fulfillment of his promises. Augustine also reminds us that we should understand the word "faith" in the Scriptures to mean confidence in God, assurance that God is gracious to us, and not merely such a knowledge of historical events as the devil also possesses.

It is also taught among us that good works should and must be done, not that we are to rely on them to earn grace but that we may do God's will and glorify him. It is always faith alone that apprehends grace and forgiveness of sin. When through faith the Holy Spirit is given, the heart is moved to do good works. Before that, when it is without the Holy Spirit, the heart is too weak. Moreover, it is in the power of the devil, who drives poor human beings into many sins. We see this in the philosophers who undertook to lead honorable and blameless lives; they failed to accomplish this, and instead fell into many great and open sins. This is what happens when a man is without true faith and the Holy Spirit and governs himself by his own human strength alone.

Consequently this teaching concerning faith is not to be accused of forbidding good works but is rather to be praised for teaching that good works are to be done and for offering help as to how they may be done. For without faith and without Christ human nature and human strength are much too weak to do good works, call upon God, have patience in suffering, love one's neighbor, diligently engage in callings which are commanded, render obedience, avoid evil lusts, etc. Such great and genuine works cannot be done without the help of Christ, as he himself says in John 15:5, "Apart from me you can do nothing."

XXI. *The Cult of Saints.* It is also taught among us that saints should be kept in remembrance so that our faith may be strengthened when we see what grace they received and how they were sustained by faith. Moreover, their good works are to be an example for us, each of us in his own calling. So His Imperial Majesty may in salutary and godly fashion imitate the example of David in making war on the Turk, for both are incumbents of a royal office which demands the defense and protection of their subjects.

However, it cannot be proved from the Scriptures that we are to invoke saints or seek help from them. "For there is one mediator between God and men, Christ Jesus" (1 Tim. 2:5), who is the only saviour, the only highpriest, advocate, and intercessor before God (Rom. 8:34). He alone has promised to hear our prayers. Moreover, according to the Scriptures, the highest form of divine service is sincerely to seek and call upon this same Jesus Christ in every time of need. "If anyone sins, we have an advocate with the Father, Jesus Christ the righteous" (I John 2:1).

This is just about a summary of the doctrines that are preached and taught in our churches for proper Christian instruction, the consolation of consciences, and the amendment of believers. Certainly we should not wish to put our own souls and consciences in grave peril before God by misusing his name or Word, nor should we wish to bequeath to our children and posterity any other teaching than that which agrees with the pure Word of God and Christian truth. Since this teaching is grounded clearly on the Holy Scriptures and is not contrary or opposed to that of the universal Christian church, or even of the Roman church (in so far as the latter's teaching is reflected in the writings of the Fathers), we think that our opponents cannot disagree with us in the articles set forth above. Therefore, those who presume to reject, avoid, and separate from our churches as if our teaching were heretical, act in an unkind and hasty fashion, contrary to all Christian unity and love, and do so without any solid basis of divine command or Scripture. The dispute and dissension are concerned chiefly with various traditions and abuses. Since, then, there is nothing unfounded or defective in the principal articles and since this our confession is seen to be godly and Christian, the bishops should in all fairness act more leniently, even if there were some defect among us in regard to traditions, although we hope to offer firm grounds and reasons why we have changed certain traditions and abuses.

ARTICLES ABOUT MATTERS IN DISPUTE, IN WHICH AN ACCOUNT IS GIVEN OF THE ABUSES WHICH HAVE BEEN CORRECTED

From the above it is manifest that nothing is taught in our churches concerning articles of faith that is contrary to the Holy Scriptures or what is common to the Christian church. However, inasmuch as some abuses have been corrected (some of the abuses having crept in over the years and others of them having been introduced with violence), we are obliged by our circumstances to give an account of them and to indicate our reasons for permitting changes in these cases in order that Your Imperial Majesty may perceive that we have not acted in an unchristian and frivolous manner but have been compelled by God's command (which is rightly to be regarded as above all custom) to allow such changes.

XXII. *Both Kinds in the Sacrament.* Among us both kinds are given to laymen in the sacrament. The reason is that there is a clear command and order of Christ, "Drink of it, all of you" (Matt. 26:27). Concerning the chalice Christ here commands with clear words that all should drink of it.

In order that no one might question these words and interpret them as if they apply only to priests, Paul shows in I Cor. 11:20 ff. that the whole assembly of the congregation in Corinth received both kinds. This usage continued in the church for a long time, as can be demonstrated from history and from writings of the Fathers. In several places Cyprian mentions that the cup was given to laymen in his time. St. Jerome also states that the priests who administered the sacrament distributed the blood of Christ to the people. Pope Gelasius himself ordered that the sacrament was not to be divided. Not a single canon can be found which requires the reception of only one kind. Nobody knows when or through whom this custom of receiving only one kind was introduced, although Cardinal Cusanus mentions when the use was approved. It is evident that such a custom, introduced contrary to

God's command and also contrary to the ancient canons, is unjust. Accordingly it is not proper to burden the consciences of those who desire to observe the sacrament according to Christ's institution or to compel them to act contrary to the arrangement of our Lord Christ. Because the division of the sacrament is contrary to the institution of Christ, the customary carrying about of the sacrament in processions is also omitted by us.

XXIII. *The Marriage of Priests.* Among all people, both of high and of low degree, there has been loud complaint throughout the world concerning the flagrant immorality and the dissolute life of priests who were not able to remain continent and who went so far as to engage in abominable vices. In order to avoid such unbecoming offense, adultery, and other lechery, some of our priests have entered the married state. They have given as their reason that they have been impelled and moved to take this step by the great distress of their consciences, especially since the Scriptures clearly assert that the estate of marriage was instituted by the Lord God to avoid immorality, for Paul says, "Because of the temptation to immorality, each man should have his own wife" (I Cor. 7-3), and again, "It is better to marry than to be aflame with passion" (I Cor. 7:9). Moreover, when Christ said in Matt. 19:11, "Not all men can receive this precept," he indicated that few people have the gift of living in celibacy, and he certainly knew man's nature. God created man as male and female according to Gen. 1:27. Experience has made it all too manifest whether or not it lies in human power and ability to improve or change the creation of God, the supreme Majesty, by means of human resolutions or vows without a special gift or grace of God. What good has resulted? What honest and chaste manner of life, what Christian, upright, and honorable sort of conduct has resulted in many cases? It is well-known what terrible torment and frightful disturbance of conscience many have experienced on their death-beds on this account, and many have themselves acknowledged this. Since God's Word and command cannot be altered by any human vows or laws, our priests and other clergy have taken wives to themselves for these and other reasons and causes.

It can be demonstrated from history and from the writings of the Fathers that it was customary for priests and deacons to marry in the Christian church of former times. Paul therefore said in I Tim. 3:2, "A bishop must be above reproach, married only once." It was only four hundred years ago that the priests in Germany were compelled by force to take the vows of celibacy. At that time there was such serious and strong resistance that an archbishop of Mayence who had published the new papal decree was almost killed during an uprising of the entire body of priests. The decree concerning celibacy was at once enforced so hastily and indecently that the pope at the time not only forbade future marriages of priests but also broke up the marriages which were of long standing. This was of course not only contrary to all divine, natural and civil law, but was also utterly opposed and contrary to the canons which the popes had themselves made and to the decisions of the most renowned councils.

Many devout and intelligent people in high station have expressed similar opinions and the misgiving that such enforced celibacy and such prohibition of marriage (which God himself instituted and left free to man) never produced any good but rather gave occasion for many great and evil vices and much scandal. As his biography shows, even one of the popes, Pius II, often said and allowed himself to be quoted as saying that while there may well have been some reasons for prohibiting the marriage of clergymen, there were now more important, better, and weightier reasons for permitting them to be married. There is no doubt that Pope Pius, as a prudent and intelligent man, made this statement because of grave misgivings.

In loyalty to Your Imperial Majesty we therefore feel confident that, as a most renowned Christian emperor, Your Majesty will graciously take into account the fact that, in these last times of which the Scriptures prophesy, the world is growing worse and men are becoming weaker and more infirm.

Therefore it is most necessary, profitable, and Christian to recognize this fact in order that the prohibition of marriage may not cause worse and more disgraceful lewdness and vice to prevail in German lands. No one is able to alter or arrange such matters in a better or wiser way than God himself, who instituted marriage to aid human infirmity and prevent unchastity.

The old canons also state that it is sometimes necessary to relax severity and rigor for the sake of human weakness and to prevent and avoid greater offense.

In this case relaxation would certainly be both Christian and very necessary. How would the marriage of priests and clergy, and especially of the pastors and others who are to minister to the church, be of disadvantage to the Christian church as a whole? If this hard prohibition of marriage is to continue longer, there may be a shortage of priests and pastors in the future.

As we have observed, the assertion that priests and clergymen may marry is based on God's Word and command. Besides, history demonstrates both that priests were married and that the vow of celibacy has been the cause of so much frightful and unchristian offense, so much adultery, and such terrible, shocking immorality and abominable vice that even some honest men among the cathedral clergy and some of the courtiers in Rome have often acknowledged this and have complained that such vices among the clergy would, on account of their abomination and prevalence, arouse the wrath of God. It is therefore deplorable that Christian marriage has not only been forbidden but has in many places been swiftly punished, as if it were a crime, in spite of the fact that in the Holy Scriptures God commanded that marriage be held in honor. Marriage has also been highly praised in the imperial laws and in all states in which there have been laws and justice. Only in our time does one begin to persecute innocent people simply because they are married—and especially priests, who above all others should be spared—although this is done contrary not only to divine law but also to canon law. In I Tim. 4:1, 3 the apostle Paul calls the teaching that forbids marriage a doctrine of the devil. Christ himself asserts that the devil is a murderer from the beginning (John 8:44). These two statements fit together well, for it must be a doctrine of the devil to forbid marriage and then to be so bold as to maintain such a teaching with the shedding of blood.

However, just as no human law can alter or abolish a command of God, neither can any vow alter a command of God. St. Cyprian therefore offered the counsel that women who were unable to keep their vows of chastity should marry. He wrote in his eleventh letter, "If they are unwilling or unable to keep their chastity, it is better for them to marry than to fall into the fire through their lusts, and they should see to it that they do not give their brothers and sisters occasion for offense."

In addition, all the canons show great leniency and fairness toward those who have made vows in their youth—and most of the priests and monks entered into their estates ignorantly when they were young.

XXIV. *The Mass.* We are unjustly accused of having abolished the Mass. Without boasting, it is manifest that the Mass is observed among us with greater devotion and more earnestness than among our opponents. Moreover, the people are instructed often and with great diligence concerning the holy sacrament, why it was instituted, and how it is to be used (namely, as a comfort for terrified consciences) in order that the people may be drawn to the Communion and Mass. The people are also given instruction about other false teachings concerning the sacrament. Meanwhile no conspicuous changes have been made in the public ceremonies of the Mass, except that in certain places German hymns are sung in addition to the Latin responses for the instruction and exercise of the people. After all, the chief purpose of all ceremonies is to teach the people what they need to know about Christ.

Before our time, however, the Mass came to be misused in many ways, as is well-known, by turning it into a sort of fair, by buying and selling it, and by observing it in almost all churches for a monetary consideration. Such abuses were often condemned by learned and devout men even before our time. Then when our preachers preached about these things and the priests were reminded of the terrible responsibility which should properly concern every Christian (namely, that whoever uses the sacrament unworthily is guilty of the body and blood of Christ), such mercenary Masses and private Masses, which had hitherto been held under compulsion for the sake of revenues and stipends, were discontinued in our churches.

At the same time the abominable error was condemned according to which it was taught that our Lord Christ had by his death made satisfaction only for original sin, and had instituted the Mass as a sacrifice for other sins. This transformed the Mass into a sacrifice for the living and the dead, a sacrifice by means of which sin was taken away and God was reconciled. Thereupon followed a debate as to whether one Mass held for many people merited as much as a special Mass held for an individual. Out of this grew the countless multiplication of Masses, by the performance of which men expected to get everything they needed from God. Meanwhile faith in Christ and true service of God were forgotten.

Demanded without doubt by the necessity of such circumstances, instruction was given so that our people might know how the sacrament is to be used rightly. They were taught, first of all, that the Scriptures show in many places that there is no sacrifice for original sin, or for any other sin, except the one death of Christ. For it is written in the Epistle to the Hebrews that Christ offered himself once and by this offering made satisfaction for all sin. It is an unprecedented novelty in church doctrine that Christ's death should have made satisfaction only for original sin and not for other sins as well. Accordingly it is to be hoped that everyone will understand that this error is not unjustly condemned.

In the second place, St. Paul taught that we obtain grace before God through faith and not through works. Manifestly contrary to this teaching is the misuse of the Mass by those who think that grace is obtained through the performance of this work, for it is well-known that the Mass is used to remove sin and obtain grace and all sorts of benefits from God, not only for the priest himself but also for the whole world and for others, both living and dead.

In the third place, the holy sacrament was not instituted to make provision for a sacrifice for sin—for the sacrifice has already taken place—but to awaken our faith and comfort our consciences when we perceive that through the sacrament grace and forgiveness of sin are promised us by Christ. Accordingly the sacrament requires faith, and without faith it is used in vain.

Inasmuch, then, as the Mass is not a sacrifice to remove the sins of others, whether living or dead, but should be a Communion in which the priest and others receive the sacrament for themselves, it is observed among us in the following manner: On holy days, and at other times when communicants are present, Mass is held and those who desire it are communicated. Thus the Mass is preserved among us in its proper use, the use which was formerly observed in the church and which can be proved by St. Paul's statement in I Cor. 11:20 ff. and by many statements of the Fathers. For Chrysostom reports how the priest stood every day, inviting some to Communion and forbidding others to approach. The ancient canons also indicate that one man officiated and communicated the other priests and deacons, for the words of the Nicene canon read, "After the priests the deacons shall receive the sacrament in order from the bishop or priest."

Since, therefore, no novelty has been introduced which did not exist in the church from ancient times, and since no conspicuous change has been made in the public ceremonies of the Mass except that other unnecessary Masses which were held in addition to the parochial Mass, probably through abuse, have been discontinued, this manner of holding Mass ought not in fairness be condemned as heretical or unchristian. In times past, even in large churches where there were many people, Mass was not held on every day that the people assembled, for according to the Tripartite History, Book 9, on Wednesday and Friday the Scriptures were read and expounded in Alexandria, and otherwise these services were held without Mass.

XXV. *Confession.* Confession has not been abolished by the preachers on our side. The custom has been retained among us of not administering the sacrament to those who have not previously been examined and absolved. At the same time the people are carefully instructed concerning the consolation of the Word of absolution so that they may esteem absolution as a great and precious thing. It is not the voice or word of the man who speaks it, but it is the Word of God, who forgives sin, for it is spoken in God's stead and by God's command. We teach with great diligence about this command and power of keys and how comforting and necessary it is for terrified consciences. We also teach that God requires us to believe this absolution as much as if we heard God's voice from heaven, that we should joyfully comfort ourselves with absolution, and that we should know that through such faith we obtain forgiveness of sins. In former times the preachers who taught much about confession never mentioned a word concerning these necessary matters but only tormented consciences with long enumerations of sins, with satisfactions, with indulgences, with pilgrimages and the like. Many of our opponents themselves acknowledge that we have written about and treated of true Christian repentance in a more fitting fashion than had been done for a long time.

Concerning confession we teach that no one should be compelled to recount sins in detail, for this is impossible. As the psalmist says, "Who can discern his errors?" Jeremiah also says, "The heart is desperately corrupt; who can understand it?" Our wretched human nature is so deeply submerged in sins that it is unable to perceive or know them all, and if we were to be absolved only from those which we can enumerate we would be helped but little. On this account there is no need to compel people to give a detailed account of their sins. That this was also the view of the Fathers can be seen in Dist. I, *De poenitentia,* where these words of Chrysostom are quoted: "I do not say that you should expose yourself in public or should accuse yourself before others, but obey the prophet who says, 'Show your way to the Lord.' Therefore confess to the Lord God, the true judge, in your prayer, telling him of your sins not with your tongue but in your conscience." Here it can be clearly seen that Chrysostom does not require a detailed enumeration of sins. The marginal note in *De poenitentia,* Dist. 5, also teaches that such confession is not commanded by the Scriptures but was instituted by the church. Yet the preachers on our side diligently teach that confession is to be retained for the sake of absolution (which is its chief and most important part), for the consolation of terrified consciences, and also for other reasons.

XXVI. *The Distinction of Foods.* In former times men taught, preached, and wrote that distinctions among foods and similar traditions which had been instituted by men serve to earn grace and make satisfaction for sin. For this reason new fasts, new ceremonies, new orders, and the like were invented daily, and were ardently and urgently promoted, as if these were a necessary service of God by means of which grace would be earned if they were observed and a great sin committed if they were omitted. Many harmful errors in the church have resulted from this.

In the first place, the grace of Christ and the teaching concerning faith are thereby obscured, and yet the Gospel earnestly urges them upon us and strongly insists that we regard the merit of Christ as something great and precious and know that faith in Christ is to be esteemed far above all works. On this account St. Paul contended mightily against the law of Moses and against human tradition so that we should learn that we do not become good in God's sight by our works but that it is only through faith in Christ that we obtain grace for Christ's sake. This teaching has been almost completely extinguished by those who have taught that grace is to be earned by prescribed fasts, distinctions among foods, vestments, etc.

In the second place, such traditions have also obscured the commands of God, for these traditions were exalted far above God's commands. This also was regarded as Christian life: whoever observed festivals in this way, prayed in this way, fasted in this way, and dressed in this way was said to live a spiritual and Christian life. On the other hand, other necessary good works were considered secular and unspiritual: the works which everybody is obliged to do according to his calling—for example, that a husband should labor to support his wife and children and bring them up in the fear of God, that a wife should bear children and care for them, that a prince and magistrates should govern land and people, etc. Such works, commanded by God, were to be regarded as secular and imperfect, while traditions were to be given the glamorous title of alone being holy and perfect works. Accordingly there was no end or limit to the making of such traditions.

In the third place, such traditions have turned out to be a grievous burden to consciences, for it was not possible to keep all the traditions, and yet the people were of the opinion that they were a necessary service of God. Gerson writes that many fell into despair on this account, and some even committed suicide, because they had not heard anything of the consolation of the grace of Christ. We can see in the writings of the summists and canonists how consciences have been confused, for they undertook to collate the traditions and sought mitigations to relieve consciences, but they were so occupied with such efforts that they neglected all wholesome Christian teachings about more important things, such as faith, consolation in severe trials, and the like. Many devout and learned people before our time have also complained that such traditions caused so much strife in the church that godly people were thereby hindered from coming to a right knowledge of Christ. Gerson and others have complained bitterly about this. In fact, Augustine was also displeased that consciences were burdened with so many traditions, and he taught in this connection that they were not to be considered necessary observances.

Our teachers have not taught concerning these matters out of malice or contempt of spiritual authority, but dire need has compelled them to give instruction about the aforementioned errors which have arisen from a wrong estimation of tradition. The Gospel demands that the teaching about faith should and must be emphasized in the church, but this teaching cannot be understood if it is supposed that grace is earned through self-chosen works.

It is therefore taught that grace cannot be earned, God cannot be reconciled, and sin cannot be atoned for by observing the said human traditions. Accordingly they should not be made into a necessary service of God. Reasons for this shall be cited from the Scriptures. In Matt. 15:1-20 Christ defends the apostles for not observing the customary traditions, and he adds, "In vain do they worship me, teaching as doctrines the precepts of men" (Matt. 15:9). Since he calls them vain service, they must not be necessary. Thereupon Christ says, "Not what goes into the mouth defiles a man." Paul also says in Rom. 14:17, "The kingdom of God does not mean food and drink," and in Col. 2:16 he says, "Let no one pass judgment on you in questions of food and drink or with regard to a festival," etc. In Acts 15:10,11 Peter says, "Why do you make trial of God by putting a yoke upon the neck of the disciples which neither our fathers nor we have been able to bear? But we believe that we shall be saved through the grace of the Lord Jesus, just as they will." Here Peter forbids the burdening of consciences with additional outward ceremonies, whether of Moses or of another. In I Tim. 4:1,3 such prohibitions as forbid food or marriage are called a doctrine of the devil, for it is diametrically opposed to the Gospel to institute or practice such works for the purpose of earning forgiveness of sin or with the notion that nobody is a Christian unless he performs such services.

Although our teachers are, like Jovinian, accused of forbidding mortification and discipline, their writings reveal something quite different. They have always taught concerning the holy cross that Christians are obliged to suffer, and this is true and real rather than invented mortification.

They also teach that everybody is under obligation to conduct himself, with reference to such bodily exercise as fasting and other discipline, so that he does not give occasion to sin, but not as if he earned grace by such works. Such bodily exercise should not be limited to certain specified days but should be practiced continually. Christ speaks of this in Luke 21:34, "Take heed to yourselves lest your hearts be weighed down with dissipation," and again, "This kind of demon cannot be driven out by anything but fasting and prayer." Paul said that he pommeled his body and subdued it, and by this he indicated that it is not the purpose of mortification to merit grace but to keep the body in such condition that one can perform the duties required by one's calling. Thus fasting in itself is not rejected, but what is rejected is making a necessary service of fasts on prescribed days and with specified foods, for this confuses consciences.

We on our part also retain many ceremonies and traditions (such as the liturgy of the Mass and various canticles, festivals, and the like) which serve to preserve order in the church. At the same time, however, the people are instructed that such outward forms of service do not make us righteous before God and that they are to be observed without burdening consciences, which is to say that it is not a sin to omit them if this is done without causing scandal. The ancient Fathers maintained such liberty with respect to outward ceremonies, for in the East they kept Easter at a time different from that of Rome. When some regarded this difference as divisive of the church, they were admonished by others that it was not necessary to maintain uniformity in such customs. Irenaeus said, "Disagreement in fasting does not destroy unity in faith," and there is a statement in Dist. 12 that such disagreement in human ordinances is not in conflict with the unity of Christendom. Moreover, the Tripartite History, Book 9, gathers many examples of dissimilar church usages and adds the profitable Christian observation, "It was not the intention of the apostles to institute holy days but to teach faith and love."

XXVII. *Monastic Vows.* In discussing monastic vows it is necessary to begin by considering what opinions have hitherto been held concerning them, what kind of life was lived in the monasteries, and how many of the daily observances in them were contrary not only to the Word of God but also to papal canons. In the days of St. Augustine monastic life was voluntary. Later, when true discipline and doctrine had become corrupted, monastic vows were invented, and the attempt was made to restore discipline by means of these vows as if in a well conceived prison.

In addition to monastic vows many other requirements were imposed, and such fetters and burdens were laid on many before they had attained an appropriate age.

Many persons also entered monastic life ignorantly, for although they were not too young, they had not sufficiently appreciated or understood their strength. All of those who were thus ensnared and entangled were pressed and compelled to remain, in spite of the fact that even the papal canons might have set many of them free. The practice was stricter in women's convents than in those of men, though it would have been seemly to show more consideration to women as the weaker sex. Such severity and rigor displeased many devout people in the past, for they must have seen that both boys and girls were thrust into monasteries to provide for their maintenance. They must also have seen what evils came from this arrangement, what scandals and burdened consciences resulted. Many people complained that in such a momentous matter the canons were not strictly adhered to. Besides, monastic vows gained such a reputation, as is well known, that many monks with even a little understanding were displeased.

It was claimed that monastic vows were equal to Baptism, and that by monastic life one could earn forgiveness of sin and justification before God. What is more, they added that monastic life not only earned righteousness and godliness, but also that by means of this life both the precepts and the counsels included in the Gospel were kept, and so monastic vows were praised more highly than Baptism. They also claimed that more merit could be obtained by monastic life than by all other states of life instituted by God—whether the office of pastor and preacher, of ruler, prince, lord, or the like, all of whom serve in their appointed calling according to God's Word and command without invented spirituality. None of these things can be denied, for they are found in their own books.

Furthermore, those who were thus ensnared and inveigled into a monastery learned little about Christ. Formerly the monasteries had conducted schools of Holy Scripture and other branches of learning which are profitable to the Christian church, so that pastors and bishops were taken from monasteries. But now the picture is changed. In former times people gathered and adopted monastic life for the purpose of learning the Scriptures, but now it is claimed that monastic life is of such a nature that thereby God's grace and righteousness before God are earned. In fact, it is called a state of perfection and is regarded as far superior to the other estates instituted by God. All this is mentioned, without misrepresentation, in order that one may better grasp and understand what our teachers teach and preach.

For one thing, it is taught among us with regard to those who desire to marry that all those who are not suited for celibacy have the power, right, and authority to marry, for vows cannot nullify God's order and command. God's command in I Cor. 7:2 reads, "Because of the temptation to immorality, each man should have his own wife and each woman her own husband." It is not alone God's command that urges, drives, and compels us to do this, but God's creation and order also direct all to marriage who are not endowed with the gift of virginity by a special act of God. This appears from God's own words in Gen. 2:18, "It is not good that the man should be alone; I will make him a helper fit for him."

What objection may be raised to this? No matter how much one extols the vow and the obligation, no matter how highly one exalts them, it is still impossible to abrogate God's command. Learned men say that a vow made contrary to papal canons is not binding. How much less must be their obligation, lawfulness, and power when they are contrary to God's command!

If there were no reasons which allowed annulment of the obligation of a vow, the popes could not have dispensed and released men from such obligation, for no man has the right to cancel an obligation which is derived from divine law. Consequently the popes were well aware that some amelioration ought to be exercised in connection with this obligation and have often given dispensations, as in the case of the king of Aragon and many others. If dispensations were granted for the maintenance of temporal interests, how much more should dispensations be granted for necessities of men's souls!

Why, then, do our opponents insist so strongly that vows must be kept without first ascertaining whether a vow is of the proper sort? For a vow must involve what is possible and voluntary and must be uncoerced. Yet it is commonly known to what an extent perpetual chastity lies within human power and ability, and there are few, whether men or women, who have taken monastic vows of themselves, willingly, and after due consideration. Before they came to a right understanding they were persuaded to take monastic vows, and sometimes they have been compelled and forced to do so. Accordingly it is not right to argue so rashly and insistently about the obligation of vows inasmuch as it is generally conceded that it belongs to the very nature and character of a vow that it should be voluntary and should be assumed only after due consideration and counsel.

Several canons and papal regulations annul vows that are made under the age of fifteen years. They hold that before this age one does not possess sufficient understanding to determine or arrange the order of one's whole future life. Another canon concedes still more years to human frailty, for it prohibits the taking of monastic vows before the eighteenth year. On the basis of this provision most monastics have excuse and reason for leaving their monasteries inasmuch as a majority of them entered the cloister in their childhood, before attaining such age.

Finally, although the breaking of monastic vows might be censured, it would not follow that the marriage of those who broke them should be dissolved. For St. Augustine says in his *Nuptiarum,* Question 27, Chapter I, that such a marriage should not be dissolved, and St. Augustine is no inconsiderable authority in the Christian church, even though some have subsequently differed from him.

Although God's command concerning marriage frees and releases many from monastic vows, our teachers offer still more reasons why monastic vows are null and void. For all service of God that is chosen and instituted by men to obtain righteousness and God's grace without the command and authority of God is opposed to God and the holy Gospel and contrary to God's command. So Christ himself says in Matt. 15:9, "In vain do they worship me, teaching as doctrines the precepts of men." St. Paul also teaches everywhere that one is not to seek for righteousness in the precepts and services invented by men but that righteousness and godliness in God's sight come from faith and trust when we believe that God receives us into favor for the sake of Christ, his only Son.

It is quite evident that the monks have taught and preached that their invented spiritual life makes satisfaction for sin and obtains God's grace and righteousness. What is this but to diminish the glory and honor of the grace of Christ and deny the righteousness of faith? It follows from this that the customary vows were an improper and false service of God. Therefore they are not binding, for an ungodly vow, made contrary to God's command, is null and void. Even the canons teach that an oath should not be an obligation to sin.

St. Paul says in Gal. 5:4, "You are severed from Christ, you who would be justified by the law; you have fallen away from grace." In the same way, those who would be justified by vows are severed from Christ and have fallen away from God's grace, for they rob Christ, who alone justifies, of his honor and bestow this honor on their vows and monastic life.

One cannot deny that the monks have taught and preached that they were justified and earned forgiveness of sins by their vows and their monastic life and observances. In fact, they have invented a still more indecent and absurd claim, namely, that they could apply their good works to others. If one were inclined to count up all these claims for the purpose of casting them into their teeth, how many items could be assembled which the monks themselves are now ashamed of and wish had never occurred! Besides all this, they persuaded the people that the invented spiritual estate of the orders was Christian perfection. Certainly this is exaltation of works as a means of attaining justification. Now, it is no small offense in the Christian church that the people should be presented with such a service of God, invented by men without the command of God, and should be taught that such a service would make men good and righteous before God. For righteousness of faith, which should be emphasized above all else in the Christian church, is obscured when man's eyes are dazzled with this curious angelic spirituality and sham of poverty, humility, and chastity.

Besides, the commands of God and true and proper service of God are obscured when people are told that monks alone are in a state of perfection. For this is Christian perfection: that we fear God honestly with our whole hearts, and yet have sincere confidence, faith, and trust that for Christ's sake we have a gracious, merciful God; that we may and should ask and pray God for those things of which we have need, and confidently expect help from him in every affliction connected with our particular calling and station in life; and that meanwhile we do good works for others and diligently attend to our calling. True perfection and right service of God consist of these things and not of mendicancy or wearing a black or gray cowl, etc. However, the common people, hearing the state of celibacy praised above all measure, draw many harmful conclusions from such false exaltation of monastic life, for it follows that their consciences are troubled because they are married. When the common man hears that only mendicants are perfect, he is uncertain whether he can keep his possessions and engage in business without sin. When the people hear that it is only a counsel not to take revenge, it is natural that some should conclude that it is not sinful to take revenge outside of the exercise of their office. Still others think that it is not right at all for Christians, even in the government, to avenge wrong.

Many instances are also recorded of men who forsook wife and child, and also their civil office, to take shelter in a monastery. This, they said, is fleeing from the world and seeking a life more pleasing to God than the other. They were unable to understand that one is to serve God by observing the commands God has given and not by keeping the commands invented by men. That is a good and perfect state of life which has God's command to support it; on the other hand, that is a dangerous state of life which does not have God's command behind it. About such matters it was necessary to give the people proper instruction.

In former times Gerson censured the error of the monks concerning perfection and indicated that it was an innovation of his time to speak of monastic life as a state of perfection.

Thus there are many godless opinions and errors associated with monastic vows: that they justify and render men righteous before God, that they constitute Christian perfection, that they are the means of fulfilling both evangelical counsels and precepts, and that they furnish the works of supererogation which we are not obligated to render to God. Inasmuch as all these things are false, useless, and invented, monastic vows are null and void.

XXVIII. *The Power of Bishops.* Many and various things have been written in former times about the power of bishops, and some have improperly confused the power of bishops with the temporal sword. Out of this careless confusion many serious wars, tumults, and uprisings have resulted because the bishops, under pretext of the power given them by Christ, have not only introduced new forms of worship and burdened consciences with reserved cases and violent use of the ban, but have also presumed to set up and depose kings and emperors according to their pleasure. Such outrage has long since been condemned by learned and devout people in Christendom. On this account our teachers have been compelled, for the sake of comforting consciences, to point out the difference between spiritual and temporal power, sword, and authority, and they have taught that because of God's command both authorities and powers are to be honored and esteemed with all reverence as the two highest gifts of God on earth.

Our teachers assert that according to the Gospel the power of keys or the power of bishops is a power and command of God to preach the Gospel, to forgive and retain sins, and to administer and distribute the sacraments. For Christ sent out the apostles with this command, "As the Father has sent me, even so I send you. Receive the Holy Spirit. If you forgive the sins of any, they are forgiven; if you retain the sins of any, they are retained" (John 20:21-23).

This power of keys or of bishops is used and exercised only by teaching and preaching the Word of God and by administering the sacraments (to many persons or to individuals, depending on one's calling). In this way are imparted not bodily but eternal things and gifts, namely, eternal righteousness, the Holy Spirit, and eternal life. These gifts cannot be obtained except through the office of preaching and of administering the holy sacraments, for St. Paul says, "The gospel is the power of God for salvation to everyone who has faith." Inasmuch as the power of the church or of bishops bestows eternal gifts and is used and exercised only through the office of preaching, it does not interfere at all with government or temporal authority. Temporal authority is concerned with matters altogether different from the Gospel. Temporal power does not protect the soul, but with the sword and physical penalties it protects body and goods from the power of others.

Therefore, the two authorities, the spiritual and the temporal, are not to be mingled or confused, for the spiritual power has its commission to preach the Gospel and administer the sacraments. Hence it should not invade the function of the other, should not set up and depose kings, should not annul temporal laws or undermine obedience to government, should not make or prescribe to the temporal power laws concerning worldly matters. Christ himself said, "My kingship is not of this world," and again, "Who made me a judge or divider over you?" Paul also wrote in Phil. 3:20, "Our commonwealth is in heaven," and in II Cor. 10:4,5, "The weapons of our warfare are not worldly but have divine power to destroy strongholds and every proud obstacle to the knowledge of God."

Thus our teachers distinguish the two authorities and the functions of the two powers, directing that both be held in honor as the highest gifts of God on earth.

In cases where bishops possess temporal authority and the sword, they possess it not as bishop by divine right, but by human, imperial right, bestowed by Roman emperors and kings for the temporal administration of their lands. Such authority has nothing at all to do with the office of the Gospel.

According to divine right, therefore, it is the office of the bishop to preach the Gospel, forgive sins, judge doctrine and condemn doctrine that is contrary to the Gospel, and exclude from the Christian community the ungodly whose wicked conduct is manifest. All this is to be done not by human power but by God's Word alone. On this account parish ministers and churches are bound to be obedient to the bishops according to the saying of Christ in Luke 10:16, "He who hears you hears me." On the other hand, if they teach, introduce, or institute anything contrary to the Gospel, we have God's command not to be obedient in such cases, for Christ says in Matt. 7:15, "Beware of false prophets." St. Paul also writes in Gal. 1:8, "Even if we, or an angel from heaven, should preach to you a gospel contrary to that which we preached to you, let him be accursed," and in II Cor. 13:8, "We cannot do anything against the truth, but only for the truth." Again Paul refers to "the authority which the Lord has given me for building up and not for tearing down." Canon law requires the same in Part II, Question 7, in the chapters "Sacerdotes" and "Oves."

St. Augustine also writes in his reply to the letters of Petilian that one should not obey even regularly elected bishops if they err or if they teach or command something contrary to the divine Holy Scriptures.

Whatever other power and jurisdiction bishops may have in various matters (for example, in matrimonial cases and in tithes), they have these by virtue of human right. However, when bishops are negligent in the performance of such duties, the princes are obliged, whether they like to or not, to administer justice to their subjects for the sake of peace and to prevent discord and great disorder in their lands.

Besides, there is dispute as to whether bishops have the power to introduce ceremonies in the church or establish regulations concerning foods, holy days, and the different orders of the clergy. Those who attribute such power to bishops cite Christ's saying in John 16:12,13, "I have yet many things to say to you, but you cannot bear them now. When the Spirit of truth comes, he will guide you into all the truth." They also cite the example in Acts 15:20,29, where the eating of blood and what is strangled was forbidden. Besides, they appeal to the fact that the Sabbath was changed to Sunday—contrary, as they say, to the Ten Commandments. No case is appealed to and urged so insistently as the change of the Sabbath, for thereby they wish to maintain that the power of the church is indeed great because the church has dispensed from the altered part of the Ten Commandments.

Concerning this question our teachers assert that bishops do not have power to institute or establish anything contrary to the Gospel, as has been indicated above and as is taught by canon law throughout the whole of the ninth Distinction. It is patently contrary to God's command and Word to make laws out of opinions or to require that they be observed in order to make satisfaction for sins and obtain grace, for the glory of Christ's merit is blasphemed when we presume to earn grace by such ordinances. It is also apparent that because of this notion human ordinances have multiplied beyond calculation while the teaching concerning faith and righteousness of faith has almost been suppressed. Almost every day new holy days and new fasts have been prescribed, new ceremonies and new venerations of saints have been instituted in order that by such works grace and everything good might be earned from God.

Again, those who institute human ordinances also act contrary to God's command when they attach sin to foods, days, and similar things and burden Christendom with the bondage of the law, as if in order to earn God's grace there had to be a service of God among Christians like the Levitical service, and as if God had commanded the apostles and bishops to institute it, as some have written. It is quite believable that some bishops were misled by the example of the law of Moses. The result was that countless regulations came into being—for example, that it is a mortal sin to do manual work on holy days (even when it does not give offense to others), that it is a mortal sin to omit the seven hours, that some foods defile the conscience, that fasting is a work by which God is reconciled, that in a reserved case sin is not forgiven unless forgiveness is secured from the person for whom the case is reserved, in spite of the fact that canon law says nothing of the reservation of guilt but speaks only about the reservation of ecclesiastical penalties.

Where did the bishops get the right and power to impose such requirements on Christendom to ensnare men's consciences? In Acts 15:10 St. Peter forbids putting a yoke on the neck of the disciples. And St. Paul said in II Cor. 10:8 that authority was given for building up and not for tearing down. Why, then, do they multiply sins with such requirements?

Yet there are clear passages of divine Scripture which forbid the establishment of such regulations for the purpose of earning God's grace or as if they were necessary for salvation. Thus St. Paul says in Col. 2:16, "Let no one pass judgment on you in questions of food and drink or with regard to a festival or a new moon or a sabbath. These are only a shadow of what is to come; but the substance belongs to Christ." Again in Col. 2:20-23, "If with Christ you died to the regulations of the world, why do you live as if you still belonged to the world? Why do you submit to regulations, 'Do not handle, Do not taste, Do not touch' (referring to things which all perish as they are used), according to human precepts and doctrines? These have an appearance of wisdom." In Tit. 1:14 St. Paul also forbids giving heed to Jewish myths or to commands of men who reject the truth.

Christ himself says concerning those who urge human ordinances on people, "Let them alone; they are blind guides" (Matt. 15:14). He rejects such service of God and says, "Every plant which my heavenly Father has not planted will be rooted up" (Matt. 15:13).

If, then, bishops have the power to burden the churches with countless requirements and thus ensnare consciences, why does the divine Scripture so frequently forbid the making and keeping of human regulations? Why does it call them doctrines of the devil? Is it possible that the Holy Spirit warned against them for nothing?

Inasmuch as such regulations as have been instituted as necessary to propitiate God and merit grace are contrary to the Gospel, it is not at all proper for the bishops to require such services of God. It is necessary to preserve the teaching of Christian liberty in Christendom, namely, that bondage to the law is not necessary for justification, as St. Paul writes in Gal. 5:1, "For freedom Christ has set us free; stand fast, therefore, and do not submit again to a yoke of slavery." For the chief article of the Gospel must be maintained, namely, that we obtain the grace of God through faith in Christ without our merits; we do not merit it by services of God instituted by men.

What are we to say, then, about Sunday and other similar church ordinances and ceremonies? To this our teachers reply that bishops or pastors may make regulations so that everything in the churches is done in good order, but not as a means of obtaining God's grace or making satisfaction for sins, nor in order to bind men's consciences by considering these things necessary services of God and counting it a sin to omit their observance even when this is done without offense. So St. Paul directed in I Cor. 11:5 that women should cover their heads in the assembly. He also directed that in the assembly preachers should not all speak at once, but one after another, in order.

It is proper for the Christian assembly to keep such ordinances for the sake of love and peace, to be obedient to the bishops and parish ministers in such matters, and to observe the regulations in such a way that one does not give offense to another and so that there may be no disorder or unbecoming conduct in the church. However, consciences should not be burdened by contending that such things are necessary for salvation or that it is a sin to omit them, even when no offense is given to others, just as no one would say that a woman commits a sin if without offense to others she goes out with uncovered head.

Of like character is the observance of Sunday, Easter, Pentecost, and similar holy days and usages. Those who consider the appointments of Sunday in place of the Sabbath as a necessary institution are very much mistaken, for the Holy Scriptures have abrogated the Sabbath and teach that after the revelation of the Gospel all ceremonies of the old law may be omitted. Nevertheless, because it was necessary to appoint a certain day so that the people might know when they ought to assemble, the Christian church appointed Sunday for this purpose, and it was the more inclined and pleased to do this in order that the people might have an example of Christian liberty and might know that the keeping neither of the Sabbath nor of any other day is necessary.

There are many faulty discussions of the transformation of the law, of the ceremonies of the New Testament, and of the change of the Sabbath, all of which have arisen from the false and erroneous opinion that in Christendom one must have services of God like the Levitical or Jewish services and that Christ commanded the apostles and bishops to devise new ceremonies which would be necessary for salvation. Such errors were introduced into Christendom when the righteousness of faith was no longer taught and preached with clarity and purity. Some argue that although Sunday must not be kept as of divine obligation, it must nevertheless be kept as almost of divine obligation, and they prescribe the kind and amount of work that may be done on the day of rest. What are such discussions but snares of the conscience? For although they undertake to lighten and mitigate human regulations, yet there can be no moderation or mitigation as long as the opinion remains and prevails that their observance is necessary. And this opinion will remain as long as there is no understanding of the righteousness of faith and Christian liberty.

The apostles directed that one should abstain from blood and from what is strangled. Who observes this prohibition now? Those who do not observe it commit no sin, for the apostles did not wish to burden consciences with such bondage but forbade such eating for a time to avoid offense. One must pay attention to the chief article of Christian doctrine, and this is not abrogated by the decree.

Scarcely any of the ancient canons are observed according to the letter, and many of the regulations fall into disuse from day to day even among those who observe such ordinances most jealously. It is impossible to give counsel or help to consciences unless this mitigation is practiced, that one recognizes that such rules are not to be deemed necessary and that disregard of them does not injure consciences.

The bishops might easily retain the obedience of men if they did not insist on the observance of regulations which cannot be kept without sin. Now, however, they administer the sacrament in one kind and prohibit administration in both kinds. Again, they forbid clergymen to marry and admit no one to the ministry unless he first swears an oath that he will not preach this doctrine, although there is no doubt that it is in accord with the holy Gospel. Our churches do not ask that the bishops should restore peace and unity at the expense of their honor and dignity (though it is incumbent on the bishops to do this, too, in case of need), but they ask only that the bishops relax certain unreasonable burdens which did not exist in the church in former times and which were introduced contrary to the custom of the universal Christian church. Perhaps there was some reason for introducing them, but they are not adapted to our times. Nor can it be denied that some regulations were adopted from want of understanding. Accordingly the bishops ought to be so gracious as to temper these regulations inasmuch as such changes do not destroy the unity of Christian churches. For many regulations devised by men have with the passing of time fallen into disuse and are not obligatory, as papal law itself testifies. If, however, this is impossible and they cannot be persuaded to mitigate or abrogate human regulations which are not to be observed without sin, we are bound to follow the apostolic rule which commands us to obey God rather than men.

St. Peter forbids the bishops to exercise lordship as if they had power to coerce the churches according to their will. It is not our intention to find ways of reducing the bishops' power, but we desire and pray that they may not coerce our consciences to sin. If they are unwilling to do this and ignore our petition, let them consider how they will answer for it in God's sight, inasmuch as by their obstinacy they offer occasion for division and schism, which they should in truth help to prevent.

(Conclusion)

These are the chief articles that are regarded as controversial. Although we could have mentioned many more abuses and wrongs, to avoid prolixity and undue length we have indicated only the principal ones. The others can readily be weighed in the light of these. In the past there have been grave complaints about indulgences, pilgrimages, and misuse of the ban. Parish ministers also had endless quarrels with monks about the hearing of confessions, about burials, about sermons on special occasions, and about countless other matters. All these things we have discreetly passed over for the common good in order that the chief points at issue may better be perceived.

It must not be thought that anything has been said or introduced out of hatred or for the purpose of injuring anybody, but we have related only matters which we have considered it necessary to adduce and mention in order that it may be made very clear that we have introduced nothing, either in doctrine or in ceremonies, that is contrary to Holy Scripture or the universal Christian church. For it is manifest and evident (to speak without boasting) that we have diligently and with God's help prevented any new and godless teaching from creeping into our churches and gaining the upper hand in them.

In keeping with the summons, we have desired to present the above articles as a declaration of our confession and the teaching of our preachers. If anyone should consider that it is lacking in some respect, we are ready to present further information on the basis of the divine Holy Scripture.

Your Imperial Majesty's most obedient servants:

> JOHN, *duke of Saxony, elector*
> GEORGE, *margrave of Brandenburg*
> ERNEST, *duke of Luneburg*
> PHILIP, *landgrave of Hesse*
> JOHN FREDERICK, *duke of Saxony*
> FRANCIS, *duke of Luneburg*
> WOLFGANG, *prince of Anhalt*
> *Mayor and council of Nuremberg*
> *Mayor and council of Reutlingen*

LUTHER'S CATECHISM

Luther wrote two catechisms, commonly distinguished as the Small Catechism for the laity, and the Large Catechism (originally the German Catechism) for the clergy. Both were first published in 1529. The difference between them is not only their relative size. The catechism for the clergy is more theological and polemic. It enters into details of the moral law and is more a series of homilies than a book of catechetical instruction.

Actually the Small Catechism was also intended for pastors and preachers, but mainly to be used by them for teaching the plain people. Their ignorance of the faith, according to Luther, was so appalling that he felt constrained to write a short outline of the Christian religion. His preface to the catechism is an eloquent description of the state of the times and of the need for some kind of manual to help pastors and people acquire at least the rudiments of religious knowledge.

Once the faithful have mastered the essentials, they are exhorted to take up the Large Catechism. But in all this, compulsion should not be used. Instruction and persuasion are to replace ecclesiastical law. Once a person realizes the gravity of his sinful condition and his inability to do any good of himself, he will readily submit to the teachings of Christ and—above all—approach the sacrament of the Lord's Supper for the grace he needs to be saved.

Grace, mercy, and peace in Jesus Christ, our Lord, from Martin Luther to all faithful, godly pastors and preachers.

The deplorable conditions which I recently encountered when I was a visitor constrained me to prepare this brief and simple catechism or statement of Christian teaching. Good God, what wretchedness I beheld! The common people, especially those who live in the country, have no knowledge whatever of Christian teaching, and unfortunately many pastors are quite incompetent and unfitted for teaching. Although the people are supposed to be Christian, are baptized, and receive the holy sacrament, they do not know the Lord's Prayer, the Creed, or the Ten Commandments, they live as if they were pigs and irrational beasts, and now that the Gospel has been restored they have mastered the fine art of abusing liberty.

How will you bishops answer for it before Christ that you have so shamefully neglected the people and paid no attention at all to the duties of your office? May you escape punishment for this! You withhold the cup in the Lord's Supper and insist on the observance of human laws, yet you do not take the slightest interest in teaching the people the Lord's Prayer, the Creed, the Ten Commandments, or a single part of the Word of God. Woe to you forever!

I therefore beg of you for God's sake, my beloved brethren who are pastors and preachers, that you take the duties of your office seriously, that you have pity on the people who are entrusted to your care, and that you help me to teach the catechism to the people, especially those who are young. Let those who lack the qualifications to do better at least take this booklet and these forms and read them to the people word for word in this manner:

In the first place, the preacher should take the utmost care to avoid changes or variations in the text and wording of the Ten Command-ments, the Creed, the Lord's Prayer, the sacraments, etc. On the con-trary, he should adopt one form, adhere to it, and use it repeatedly year after year. Young and inexperienced people must be instructed on the basis of a uniform, fixed text and form. They are easily confused if a teacher employs one form now and another form—perhaps with the intention of making improvements—later on. In this way all the time and labor will be lost.

This was well understood by our good fathers, who were accustomed to use the same form in teaching the Lord's Prayer, the Creed, and the Ten Commandments. We, too, should teach these things to the young and unlearned in such a way that we do not alter a single syllable or recite the catechism differently from year to year. Choose the form that pleases you, therefore, and adhere to it henceforth. When you preach to intelligent and educated people, you are at liberty to exhibit your learning and to discuss these topics from different angles and in such a variety of ways as you may be capable of. But when you are teaching the young, adhere to a fixed and unchanging form and method. Begin by teaching them the Ten Commandments, the Creed, the Lord's Prayer, etc., following the text word for word so that the young may repeat these things after you and retain them in their memory.

If any refuse to receive your instructions, tell them that they deny Christ and are no Christians. They should not be admitted to the sacrament, be accepted as sponsors in Baptism, or be allowed to partic-ipate in any Christian privileges. On the contrary, they should be turned over to the pope and his officials, and even to the devil himself. In addition, parents and employers should refuse to furnish them with food and drink and should notify them that the prince is disposed to banish such rude people from his land.

Although we cannot and should not compel anyone to believe, we should nevertheless insist that the people learn to know how to distinguish between right and wrong according to the standards of those among whom they live and make their living. For anyone who desires to reside in a city is bound to know and observe the laws under whose protection he lives, no matter whether he is a believer or, at heart, a scoundrel or knave.

In the second place, after the people have become familiar with the text, teach them what it means. For this purpose, take the explanations in this booklet, or choose any other brief and fixed explanations which you may prefer, and adhere to them without changing a single syllable, as stated above with reference to the text. Moreover, allow yourself ample time, for it is not necessary to take up all the parts at once. They can be presented one at a time. When the learners have a proper understanding of the First Commandment, proceed to the Second Commandment, and so on. Otherwise they will be so overwhelmed that they will hardly remember anything at all.

In the third place, after you have thus taught this brief catechism, take up a large catechism so that the people may have a richer and fuller understanding. Expound every commandment, petition, and part, pointing out their respective obligations, benefits, dangers, advantages, and disadvantages, as you will find all of this treated at length in the many books written for this purpose. Lay the greatest weight on those commandments or other parts which seem to require special attention among the people where you are. For example, the Seventh Commandment, which treats of stealing, must be emphasized when instructing laborers and shopkeepers, and even farmers and servants, for many of these are guilty of dishonesty and thievery. So, too, the Fourth Commandment must be stressed when instructing children and the common people in order that they may be encouraged to be orderly, faithful, obedient, and peaceful. Always adduce many examples from the Scriptures to show how God punished and blessed.

You should also take pains to urge governing authorities and parents to rule wisely and educate their children. They must be shown that they are obliged to do so, and that they are guilty of damnable sin if they do not do so, for by such neglect they undermine and lay waste both the kingdom of God and the kingdom of the world and are the worst enemies of God and man. Make very plain to them the shocking evils they introduce when they refuse their aid in the training of children to become pastors, preachers, notaries, etc., and tell them that

God will inflict awful punishments on them for these sins. It is necessary to preach about such things. The extent to which parents and governing authorities sin in this respect is beyond telling. The devil also has a horrible purpose in mind.

Finally, now that the people are freed from the tyranny of the pope, they are unwilling to receive the sacrament and they treat it with contempt. Here, too, there is need of exhortation, but with this understanding: No one is to be compelled to believe or to receive the sacrament, no law is to be made concerning it, and no time or place should be appointed for it. We should so preach that, of their own accord and without any law, the people will desire the sacrament and, as it were, compel us pastors to administer it to them. This can be done by telling them: It is to be feared that anyone who does not desire to receive the sacrament at least three or four times a year despises the sacrament and is no Christian, just as he is no Christian who does not hear and believe the Gospel. Christ did not say, "Omit this," or Despise this," but he said, "Do this, as often as you drink it," etc. Surely he wishes that this be done and not that it be omitted and despised. "*Do* this," he said.

He who does not highly esteem the sacrament suggests thereby that he has no sin, no flesh, no devil, no world, no death, no hell. That is to say, he believes in none of these, although he is deeply immersed in them and is held captive by the devil. On the other hand, he suggests that he needs no grace, no life, no paradise, no heaven, no Christ, no God, nothing good at all. For if he believed that he was involved in so much that is evil and was in need of so much that is good, he would not neglect the sacrament in which aid is afforded against such evil and in which such good is bestowed. It is not necessary to compel him by any law to receive the sacrament, for he will hasten to it of his own accord, he will feel constrained to receive it, he will insist that you administer it to him.

Accordingly you are not to make a law of this, as the pope has done. All you need to do is clearly to set forth the advantage and disadvantage, the benefit and loss, the blessing and danger connected with this sacrament. Then the people will come of their own accord and without compulsion on your part. But if they refuse to come, let them be, and tell them that those who do not feel and acknowledge their great need and God's gracious help belong to the devil. If you do not give such admonitions, or if you adopt odious laws on the subject, it is your own fault if the people treat the sacrament with contempt. How can they be other than negligent if you fail to do your duty and remain silent. So it is up to you, dear pastor and preacher! Our office has become something different from what it was under the pope. It is now a ministry of grace and salvation. It subjects us to greater burdens and labors, dangers and temptations, with little reward or gratitude from the world. But Christ himself will be our reward if we labor faithfully. The Father of all grace grant it! To him be praise and thanks forever, through Christ, our Lord. Amen.

I

THE TEN COMMANDMENTS

in the plain form in which the head of the family shall teach it to his household

THE FIRST
"You shall have no other gods."
What does this mean?
Answer: We should fear, love, and trust in God above all things.

THE SECOND
"You shall not take the name of the Lord your God in vain."
What does this mean?
Answer: We should fear and love God, and so we should not use his name to curse, swear, practice magic, lie, or deceive, but in every time of need call upon him, pray to him, praise him, and give him thanks.

THE THIRD
"Remember the Sabbath day, to keep it holy."
What does this mean?
Answer: We should fear and love God, and so we should not despise his Word and the preaching of the same, but deem it holy and gladly hear and learn it.

THE FOURTH
"Honor your father and your mother."
What does this mean?
Answer: We should fear and love God, and so we should not despise our parents and superiors, nor provoke them to anger, but honor, serve, obey, love, and esteem them.

THE FIFTH
"You shall not kill."
What does this mean?
Aswer: We should fear and love God, and so we should not endan-

ger our neighbor's life, nor cause him any harm, but help and befriend him in every necessity of life.

THE SIXTH

"You shall not commit adultery."

What does this mean?

Answer: We should fear and love God, and so we should lead a chaste and pure life in word and deed, each one loving and honoring his wife or her husband.

THE SEVENTH

"You shall not steal."

What does this mean?

Answer: We should fear and love God, and so we should not rob our neighbor of his money or property, nor bring them into our possession by dishonest trade or by dealing in shoddy wares, but help him to improve and protect this income and property.

THE EIGHTH

"You shall not bear false witness against your neighbor."

What does this mean?

Answer: We should fear and love God, and so we should not tell lies about our neighbor, nor betray, slander, or defame him, but should apologize for him, speak well of him, and interpret charitably all that he does.

THE NINTH

"You shall not covet your neighbor's house."

What does this mean?

Answer: We should fear and love God, and so we should not seek by craftiness to gain possession of our neighbor's inheritance or home, nor to obtain them under pretext of legal right, but be of service and help to him so that he may keep what is his.

THE TENTH

"You shall not covet your neighbor's wife, or his manservant, or his maidservant, or his ox, or his ass, or anything that is your neighbor's."

What does this mean?

Answer: We should fear and love God, and so we should not abduct, estrange, or entice away our neighbor's wife, servants, or cattle, but encourage them to remain and discharge their duty to him.

(Conclusion)

What does God declare concerning all these commandments?

Answer: He says, "I the Lord your God am a jealous God, visiting the iniquity of the fathers upon the children to the third and the fourth generation of those who hate me, but showing steadfast love to thousands of those who love me and keep my commandments."

What does this mean?

Answer: God threatens to punish all who transgress these commandments. We should therefore fear his wrath and not disobey these commandments. On the other hand, he promises grace and every blessing to all who keep them. We should therefore love him, trust in him, and cheerfully do what he has commanded.

II

THE CREED

in the plain form in which the head of the family shall teach it to his household

THE FIRST ARTICLE: CREATION

"I believe in God, the Father almighty, maker of heaven and earth."

What does this mean?

Answer: I believe that God has created me and all that exists; that he has given me and still sustains my body and soul, all my limbs and senses, my reason and all the faculties of my mind, together with food and clothing, house and home, family and property; that he provides me daily and abundantly with all the necessities of life, protects me from all danger, and preserves me from all evil. All this he does out of his pure, fatherly, and divine goodness and mercy, without any merit or worthiness on my part. For all of this I am bound to thank, praise, serve, and obey him. This is most certainly true.

THE SECOND ARTICLE: REDEMPTION

"And in Jesus Christ, his only son, our Lord; who was conceived by the Holy Spirit, born of the virgin Mary, suffered under Pontius Pilate, was crucified, dead, and buried: he descended into hell, the third day he rose from the dead, he ascended into heaven, and is seated on the right hand of God, the Father almighty, whence he shall come to judge the living and the dead."

What does this mean?

Answer: I believe that Jesus Christ, true God, begotten of the Father from eternity, and also true man, born of the virgin Mary, is my Lord, who has redeemed me, a lost and condemned creature, delivered me and freed me from all sins, from death, and from the power of the devil, not with silver and gold but with his holy and precious blood and with his innocent sufferings and death, in order that I may be his, live under him in his kingdom, and serve him in everlasting righteousness, innocence, and blessedness, even as he is risen from the dead, and lives and reigns to all eternity. This is most certainly true.

THE THIRD ARTICLE: SANCTIFICATION

"I believe in the Holy Spirit, the holy Christian church, the communion of saints, the forgiveness of sins, the resurrection of the body, and the life everlasting. Amen."

What does this mean?

Answer: I believe that by my own reason or strength I cannot believe in Jesus Christ, my Lord, or come to him. But the Holy Spirit has called me with his gifts, and sanctified and preserved me in true faith, just as he calls, gathers, enlightens, and sanctifies the whole Christian church on earth and preserves it in union with Jesus Christ in the one true faith. In this Christian Church he daily and abundantly forgives all my sins, and the sins of all believers, and on the last day he will raise me and all the dead and will grant eternal life to me and to all who believe in Christ. This is most certainly true.

III

THE LORD'S PRAYER

in the plain form in which the head of the family shall teach it to his household

(INTRODUCTION)

"Our Father who art in Heaven."

What does this mean?

Answer: Here God would encourage us to believe that he is truly our Father and we are truly his children in order that we may approach him boldly and confidently in prayer, even as beloved children approach their dear father.

THE FIRST PETITION

"Hallowed be thy name."

What does this mean?

Answer: To be sure, God's name is holy in itself, but we pray in this petition that it may also be holy for us.

How is this done?

Answer: When the Word of God is taught clearly and purely and we, as children of God, lead holy lives in accordance with it. Help us to do this, dear Father in heaven! But whoever teaches and lives otherwise than as the Word of God teaches, profanes the name of God among us. From this preserve us, heavenly Father!

DUQUESNE UNIVERSITY LIBRARY

THE SECOND PETITION

"Thy kingdom come."

What does this mean?

Answer: To be sure, the kingdom of God comes of itself, without our prayer, but we pray in this petition that it may also come to us.

How is this done?

Answer: When the heavenly Father gives us his Holy Spirit so that by his grace we may believe his holy Word and live a godly life, both here in time and hereafter forever.

THE THIRD PETITION

"Thy will be done, on earth as it is in heaven."

What does this mean?

Answer: To be sure, the good and gracious will of God is done without our prayer, but we pray in this petition that it may also be done by us.

How is this done?

Answer: When God curbs and destroys every evil counsel and purpose of the devil, of the world, and of our flesh which would hinder us from hallowing his name and prevent the coming of his kingdom, and when he strengthens us and keeps us steadfast in his Word and in faith even to the end. This is his good and gracious will.

THE FOURTH PETITION

"Give us this day our daily bread."

What does this mean?

Answer: To be sure, God provides daily bread, even to the wicked, without our prayer, but we pray in this petition that God may make us aware of his gifts and enable us to receive our daily bread with thanksgiving.

What is meant by daily bread?

Answer: Everything required to satisfy our bodily needs, such as food and clothing, house and home, fields and flocks, money and property; a pious spouse and good children, trustworthy servants, godly and faithful rulers, good government; seasonable weather, peace and health, order and honor; true friends, faithful neighbors, and the like.

THE FIFTH PETITION

"And forgive us our debts, as we also have forgiven our debtors."

What does this mean?

Answer: We pray in this petition that our heavenly Father may not look upon our sins, and on their account deny our prayers, for we neither merit nor deserve those things for which we pray. Although we

DUQUESNE UNIVERSITY LIBRARY

sin daily and deserve nothing but punishment, we nevertheless pray that God may grant us all things by his grace. And assuredly we on our part will heartily forgive and cheerfully do good to those who may sin against us.

THE SIXTH PETITION

"And lead us not into temptation."

What does this mean?

Answer: God tempts no one to sin, but we pray in this petition that God may so guard and preserve us that the devil, the world, and our flesh may not deceive us or mislead us into unbelief, despair, and other great and shameful sins, but that, although we may be so tempted, we may finally prevail and gain the victory.

THE SEVENTH PETITION

"But deliver us from evil."

What does this mean?

Answer: We pray in this petition, as in a summary, that our Father in heaven may deliver us from all manner of evil, whether it affect body or soul, property or reputation, and that at last, when the hour of death comes, he may grant us a blessed end and graciously take us from this world of sorrow to himself in heaven.

(Conclusion)

"Amen."

What does this mean?

Answer: It means that I should be assured that such petitions are acceptable to our heavenly Father and are heard by him, for he himself commanded us to pray like this and promised to hear us. "Amen, amen" means "Yes, yes, it shall be so."

IV

THE SACRAMENT OF HOLY BAPTISM

in the plain form in which the head of the family shall teach it to his household

FIRST

What is Baptism?

Answer: Baptism is not merely water, but it is water used according to God's command and connected with God's Word.

What is this Word of God?

Answer: As recorded in Matthew 28:19, our Lord Christ said, "Go therefore and make disciples of all nations, baptizing them in the name of the Father and of the Son and of the Holy Spirit."

SECOND

What gifts or benefits does Baptism bestow?

Answer: It effects forgiveness of sins, delivers from death and the devil, and grants eternal salvation to all who believe, as the Word and promise of God declare.

What is the Word and promise of God?

Answer: As recorded in Mark 16:16, our Lord Christ said, "He who believes and is baptized will be saved; but he who does not believe will be condemned."

THIRD

How can water produce such great effects?

Answer: It is not the water that produces these effects, but the Word of God connected with the water, and our faith which relies on the Word of God connected with the water. For without the Word of God the water is merely water and no Baptism. But when connected with the Word of God it is a Baptism, that is, a gracious water of life and a washing of regeneration in the Holy Spirit, as St. Paul wrote to Titus (3:5-8), "He saved us by the washing of regeneration and renewal in the Holy Spirit, which he poured out upon us richly through Jesus Christ our Saviour, so that we might be justified by his grace and become heirs in hope of eternal life. The saying is sure."

FOURTH

What does such baptizing with water signify?

Answer: It signifies that the old Adam in us, together with all sins and evil lusts, should be drowned by daily sorrow and repentance and be put to death, and that the new man should come forth daily and rise up, cleansed and righteous, to live forever in God's presence.

Where is this written?

Answer: In Romans 6:4, St. Paul wrote, "We were buried therefore with him by baptism into death, so that as Christ was raised from the dead by the glory of the Father, we too might walk in newness of life."

V

(CONFESSION AND ABSOLUTION)

How Plain People Are to Be Taught to Confess

What is confession?

Answer: Confession consists of two parts. One is that we confess our sins. The other is that we receive absolution or forgiveness from the confessor as from God himself, by no means doubting but firmly believing that our sins are thereby forgiven before God in heaven.

What sins should we confess?

Answer: Before God we should acknowledge that we are guilty of all manner of sins, even those of which we are not aware, as we do in the Lord's Prayer. Before the confessor, however, we should confess only those sins of which we have knowledge and which trouble us.

What are such sins?

Answer: Reflect on your condition in the light of the Ten Commandments: whether you are a father or mother, a son or daughter, a master or servant; whether you have been disobedient, unfaithful, lazy, ill-tempered, or quarrelsome; whether you have harmed anyone by word or deed; and whether you have stolen, neglected, or wasted anything, or done other evil.

Please give me a brief form of confession.

Answer: You should say to the confessor: "Dear Pastor, please hear my confession and declare that my sins are forgiven for God's sake."

"Proceed."

"I, a poor sinner, confess before God that I am guilty of all sins. In particular I confess in your presence that, as a manservant or maidservant, etc., I am unfaithful to my master, for here and there I have not done what I was told. I have made my master angry, caused him to curse, neglected to do my duty, and caused him to suffer loss. I have also been immodest in word and deed. I have quarreled with my equals. I have grumbled and sworn at my mistress, etc. For all this I am sorry and pray for grace. I mean to do better."

A master or mistress may say: "In particular I confess in your presence that I have not been faithful in training my children, servants, and wife to the glory of God. I have cursed. I have set a bad example by my immodest language and actions. I have injured my neighbor by speaking evil of him, overcharging him, giving him inferior goods and short measure." Masters and mistresses should add whatever else they have done contrary to God's commandments and to their action in life, etc.

If, however, anyone does not feel that his conscience is burdened by such or by greater sins, he should not worry, nor should he search for and invent other sins, for this would turn confession into torture; he should simply mention one or two sins of which he is aware. For example, "In particular I confess that I once cursed. On one occasion I also spoke indecently. And I neglected this or that," etc. Let this suffice.

If you have knowledge of no sin at all (which is quite unlikely), you should mention none in particular, but receive forgiveness upon the general confession which you make to God in the presence of the confessor.

Then the confessor shall say: "God be merciful to you and strengthen your faith. Amen."

Again he shall say: "Do you believe that the forgiveness I declare is the forgiveness of God?"

Answer: "Yes, I do."

Then he shall say: "Be it done for you as you have believed. According to the command of our Lord Jesus Christ, I forgive you your sins in the name of the Father and of the Son and of the Holy Spirit. Amen. Go in peace."

A confessor will know additional passages of the Scriptures with which to comfort and to strengthen the faith of those whose consciences are heavily burdened or who are distressed and sorely tried. This is intended simply as an ordinary form of confession for plain people.

VI

THE SACRAMENT OF THE ALTAR

in the plain form in which the head of the family shall teach it to his household

What is the Sacrament of the Altar?

Answer: Instituted by Christ himself, it is the true body and blood of our Lord Jesus Christ, under the bread and wine, given to us Christians to eat and to drink.

Where is this written?

Answer: The holy evangelists Matthew, Mark, and Luke, and also St. Paul, write thus: "Our Lord Jesus Christ, on the night when he was betrayed, took bread, and when he had given thanks, he broke it, and gave it to the disciples and said, 'Take, eat; this is my body which is given for you. Do this in remembrance of me.' In the same way also he took the cup, after supper, and when he had given thanks he gave it to them, saying, 'Drink of it, all of you. This cup is the new covenant in my blood, which is poured out for many for the forgiveness of sins. Do this, as often as you drink it, in remembrance of me.' "

What is the benefit of such eating and drinking?

Answer: We are told in the words "for you" and "for the forgiveness of sins." By these words the forgiveness of sins, life and salvation are given to us in the sacrament, for where there is forgiveness of sins, there are also life and salvation.

How can bodily eating and drinking produce such great effects?

Answer: The eating and drinking do not in themselves produce them, but the words "for you" and "for the forgiveness of sins." These words, when accompanied by the bodily eating and drinking, are the chief thing in the sacrament, and he who believes these words has what they say and declare: the forgiveness of sins.

Who, then, receives this sacrament worthily?

Answer: Fasting and bodily preparation are a good external discipline, but he is truly worthy and well prepared who believes these words: "for you" and "for the forgiveness of sins." On the other hand, he who does not believe these words, or doubts them, is unworthy and unprepared, for the words "for you" require truly believing hearts.

VII

(MORNING AND EVENING PRAYERS)

How the head of the family shall teach his household to say
morning and evening prayers

In the morning, when you rise, make the sign of the cross and say, "In the name of God, the Father, the Son, and the Holy Spirit. Amen."

Then, kneeling or standing, say the Apostles' Creed and the Lord's Prayer. Then you may say this prayer:

"I give Thee thanks, heavenly Father, through thy dear Son Jesus Christ, that Thou hast protected me through the night from all harm and danger. I beseech Thee to keep me this day, too, from all sin and evil, that in all my thoughts, words, and deeds I may please Thee. Into thy hands I commend my body and soul and all that is mine. Let thy holy angel have charge of me, that the wicked one may have no power over me. Amen."

After singing a hymn (possibly a hymn on the Ten Commandments) or whatever your devotion may suggest, you should go to your work joyfully.

In the evening, when you retire, make the sign of the cross and say, "In the name of God, the Father, the Son, and the Holy Spirit. Amen."

Then, kneeling or standing, say the Apostles' Creed and the Lord's Prayer. Then you may say this prayer:

"I give Thee thanks, heavenly Father, through thy dear Son Jesus Christ, that Thou hast this day graciously protected me. I beseech Thee to forgive all my sin and the wrong which I have done. Graciously protect me during the coming night. Into thy hands I commend my body and soul and all that is mine. Let thy holy angels have charge of me, that the wicked one may have no power over me. Amen."

Then quickly lie down and sleep in peace.

VIII
(GRACE AT TABLE)

*How the head of the family shall teach his household to offer
blessing and thanksgiving at table*

(BLESSING BEFORE EATING)

When the children and the whole household gather at the table, they should reverently fold their hands and say:

"The eyes of all look to Thee, O Lord, and Thou givest them their food in due season. Thou openest thy hand; Thou satisfieth the desire of every living thing."

(It is to be observed that "satisfying the desire of every living thing" means that all creatures receive enough to eat to make them joyful and of good cheer. Greed and anxiety about food prevent such satisfaction.)

Then the Lord's Prayer should be said, and afterwards this prayer:

"Lord God, heavenly Father, bless us, and these thy gifts which of thy bountiful goodness Thou hast bestowed on us, through Jesus Christ our Lord. Amen."

(THANKSGIVING AFTER EATING)

After eating, likewise, they should fold their hands reverently and say:

"O give thanks to the Lord, for he is good; for his steadfast love endures forever. He gives to the beasts their food, and to the young ravens which cry. His delight is not in the strength of the horse, nor his pleasure in the legs of a man; but the Lord takes pleasure in those who fear him, in those who hope in his steadfast love."

Then the Lord's Prayer should be said, and afterwards this prayer:

"We give Thee thanks, Lord God, our Father, for all thy benefits, through Jesus Christ our Lord, who lives and reigns forever. Amen."

IX
TABLE OF DUTIES

*consisting of certain passages of the Scriptures, selected for
various estates and conditions of men, by which they may be
admonished to do their respective duties*
(OMITTED)

2. Calvinism and the Reformed Tradition

Reformed Protestantism took its rise from two distinct but similar expressions of the Protestant spirit. The first was led by Ulrich Zwingli (1484-1531), who died when Luther was in mid-career, and before the Counter-Reformation began. This movement was confined for the most part to the German cantons of Switzerland. The second was started by John Calvin (1509-1564), who had never known Zwingli and who was active in French-speaking Switzerland.

The two Reformers had much in common, besides the geographical coincidence of centering their activity in Switzerland. Zwingli's headquarters were at Zurich, while Calvin's were centered at Geneva. They each favored a more intransigent type of Reform than characterized Lutheranism, with more stress on theological principles, less dependence on established traditions, and more freedom from the ritual customs of the Church prevalent in the sixteenth century.

Historians are divided on the precise influence exerted by Zwingli and Calvin in the shaping of the Reformed tradition. They agree, however, that Calvin supplied the clarity and theological insight, and systematized this tradition in a way that makes him the true father of a distinctive form of Protestantism. Yet Zwingli's contribution was indispensable as coming earlier, laying the groundwork among the Swiss people, and supplying a scriptural erudition that has ever since typified the Reformed churches.

While the extant writing of Zwingli, for example his commentaries on the New Testament, have little more than historical interest, Calvin's *Institutes of the Christian Religion* remain the single most significant theological work of the Reformation. It is

59

nothing less than a *Summa Theologica* of Protestantism and has no counterpart for depth and sharpness of thought among the Reformers. Although it is not a confession of faith, it has so deeply influenced all the Reformed statements of doctrine that they cannot properly be understood without reference to the *Institutes.*

If the relative roles of Zwingli and Calvin are now mostly of speculative value, the corresponding function of Continental and British Reformed traditions is still profoundly relevant. The founder of the Anglo-Saxon branch was John Knox (1513-1572), a Scot who visited Calvin at Geneva and returned to his country to produce what has since become known as Presbyterianism. The name has remained typical in English-speaking countries for groups that stem from John Knox, whereas churches that go back to Zwingli and Calvin directly are called Reformed, both in Europe and the Americas.

Distinctive Features. The guiding motif of churches in the Reformed tradition is the affirmation of God's sovereign majesty. Every phase of doctrine, worship and church policy is affected by this stress. Where Lutheranism might be described as anthropological, because its central doctrine is man's salvation, Calvinism is theocentric in that its governing principle is the service and glory due to God from His creatures.

Confessional standards repeatedly speak of the Glory of God which is man's universal purpose in existence. Thus the Genevan Catechism begins with the statement that "God has created us, and put us into this world in order that He might be glorified by us," and the first response of the Shorter Westminster Catechism reads, "Man's chief end is to glorify God."

Consistent with this accent, the distance between God and man is brought out in the strongest terms. In the Westminster Catechism, it is said "the distance between God and the creature is so great that although reasonable creatures do owe obedience unto Him, as their Creator, yet they could never have any fruition of Him, as their blessedness and reward, but by some voluntary condescension of God's part, which He hath been pleased to express by way of covenant."

Predestination and Election are organically connected with this notion of sovereignty. Since man's salvation is due entirely to God, and man contributes nothing, all the praise is due to the Creator, even when He condemns the damned to the eternal sufferings.

Unexpectedly the Reformed doctrine on grace has not paralyzed human activity. If anything it stimulates action, though of a particular kind. Predestination serves the function of an ethical motive, on the assumption that those who reflect on this mystery are all chosen to heavenly glory. Armed with the conviction that they are predestined, believers can afford to rejoice at their happy lot and go about life's affairs with a nonchalance that might scandalize less hardy Christians.

Reformed teaching on the sacraments is distinctive. God is not bound by the sacramental instruments of grace, and, in any case, they are effectual only to the elect. They are "holy signs and seals of the covenant of grace," whose efficacy somehow depends "upon the work of the Spirit, and the word of institution, which contains, together with a precept authorizing the use thereof, a promise of benefit to worthy receivers."

Baptism does not remit sin, but signifies becoming "ingrafted into Christ," and though it does not effect regeneration, yet infant baptism is retained. The Eucharistic doctrine has been the focus of controversy with Evangelical Protestantism since Reformation times and, like the Calvinist position on Predestination, has been much modified through tension. Present-day Reformed theology steers a middle course between the purely symbolic conception of Zwingli, who limited the sacrament to a commemorative meal and a confession of faith in Christ, and the Lutheran idea of a bodily presence and oral participation. Christ is in the Eucharist, they say, really but not bodily; and only the believers partake of Him. Familiar terms are "dynamic presence" and "virtual presence," whereby the communicant receives "the sacrificial virtue or effects of the death of Christ on the Cross."

Most characteristic of Anglo-Saxon Reformed churches is their unitary concept of the governing ministry. There is only one type of authority, the presbytery, but four kinds of office: pastors, teachers, elders and deacons. Presbyteries are usually organized on a geographical basis, but some exist to care for separate language groups or racial minorities. Although there are two grades of jurisdiction technically higher than the presbytery, the latter is the principal ruling body. Presbyteries consist of clerical and lay representatives within a given district, with power to receive and issue appeals or complaints, examine and license candidates for the ministry, resolve questions of doctrine and discipline, unite and divide congregations, and, in general, care for whatever pertains to the spiritual welfare of the churches within the presbytery. It is more than coincidental that the only layman among the major Reformers in the sixteenth century, John Calvin, should have developed a form of polity that gives the laity equal share with the clergy in church government. This idea was soon borrowed by other religious bodies and is now practically universal in Protestantism.

Reformed bodies derived from the continental tradition have a church government that stands midway between the Anglican and Presbyterian. It has been called modified Presbyterianism. The local church is governed by a consistory, made up of elders, deacons and the pastor. Elders have charge of the spiritual guidance, and deacons of the benevolent side of the congregation. Churches in a given area are grouped into a classis, composed of all the ministers in the territory and an elder from each consistory. Classes in turn are organized into synods, meeting annually and composed equally of ministers and elders from each classis. At the head of the denomination is a general synod, also with equal minister-elder representation and constituting the highest legislative and judicial body in the church.

Confessions of Faith. It is customary to distinguish Reformed confessional documents from their Lutheran equivalents by saying that the former are less important because Scripture has always held the towering position in Calvinism. This is only partially correct, as the history of Protestantism shows, to the extent that Lutheran articles of faith generally reflect a more creedal approach to Christianity where the Calvinist are more doctrinal. Reformed bodies have produced several times as many confessions of faith as the Lutherans, with new forms for different countries and with major revisions that are going on to the present day. This is in marked contrast with the Evangelical symbols of faith which have not substantially changed since the Book of Concord in the sixteenth century, and they are practically uniform for all countries where Lutherans have established themselves.

In Switzerland the most important confessional statements are the two Helvetic Confessions of 1536 and 1566, and the *Consensus Tigurinus* of 1549. Whereas the Confessions are strongly Zwinglian, the *Consensus* is a compromise document drawn up by Calvin. A feature of all three is the doctrine of the Eucharist, which oscillates between the pure symbolism of Zwingli and the Calvinist theory that Christ is present in Holy Communion "for all who truly believe."

In France the composition of Calvin, *Confessio Gallicana,* first drafted in 1559 at a general synod of St. Germain, is still the confessional document of the French Reformed Church. Predestination is lucidly expounded in a long article and the Eucharist is said to be received by the communicant *spirituellement.* Germany produced a parallel statement of faith in the Heidelberg Catechism of 1563, a practical and edifying work with a moderate Eucharistic and Christological doctrine. In order to avoid offending the Lutherans, there is no express mention of Predestination, but a strongly anti-Catholic tone pervades the document. The Heidelberg Catechism has become popular also in Switzerland, Hungary and Poland. In 1566 the Netherlands adopted their *Confessio Belgica,* approved by a synod held at Antwerp, as the last continental document of this type compiled during the Reformation.

The Reformed faith was recognized as the national religion by the Scottish Parliament in 1560. In the same year the *Confessio Scoticana* was published. It is mildly Calvinist, with an almost Lutheran doctrine of the Eucharist and an ambivalent expression of the doctrine of Predestination.

However, the most significant statement of Calvinist teaching is not a Confessio but a set of Canons formulated (1619) by the Synod of Dortrecht (Dort) in the Dutch Reformed Church. The document arose out of a heated controversy on the question of Predestination. Most ministers and theologians in Holland held the doctrine in its full severity. God had from eternity arbitrarily chosen some persons for heaven and predestined others to damnation, irrespective of their faith or good works and dependent solely on the inscrutable will of God.

A less absolute tendency was advocated by the Arminian party, named after Jacob Arminius (1560-1609), professor at Leyden

Under adverse pressure from the orthodox clergy, the Arminians submitted a *Remonstrance* to the government in which they stated five theses that favored Catholic teachings on grace and became the subject of a celebrated controversy. God's predestination, they stated, rests upon His foreknowledge that certain people will persevere to the end; Christ died for all men, although only believers share in His merits; divine grace is not irresistible and it is possible for a person once in grace to lose the friendship of God.

In view of its importance, the synod invited Reformed representatives from other countries, including delegates from England. In its one hundred and thirty-seventh session, the Arminians were declared heretics, and a detailed statement of orthodox Calvinism was compiled. It said in substance, that the election of the predestined depends solely on God, Christ died only for the predestined, grace cannot be resisted, and those who have received the irresistible grace cannot subsequently fall away.

The Westminster Confession was formulated in 1646, to become the standard of doctrine for Presbyterian churches in the British Isles and America.

Most recently the United Presbyterian Church U.S.A. (Northern) adopted a new Confession of Faith that drastically changed the Westminster Confession which is still normative for other Presbyterian bodies in America and Europe.

AMERICAN REFORMED CHURCHES

Although their historical origins are the same, Reformed churches properly so-called differ considerably from their Anglo-Saxon counterparts or Presbyterians. These differences are reflected in their respective confessions of faith, which will be separately treated: first the symbolic documents of continental Calvinism and then those of its Anglo-American parallel.

Churches of Calvinist beginnings, from outside of Britain, are relatively small in the United States compared with Presbyterian denominations. Their influence, however, has been beyond all proportion to their size, notably in keeping the principles of

Zwingli and Calvin doctrinally alive in a culture that tends to be religiously neutral.

Among the American denominations that are counted as Reformed churches, two of them account for the majority of Reformed membership: the Reformed Church in America and the Christian Reformed Church.

Both bodies subscribe to the same basic doctrinal standards, namely the Heidelberg Catechism, the Belgic Confession and the Canons of the Synod of Dort. They differ in their interpretation of these dogmatic positions.

The Reformed Church in America came into existence as a direct result of the migration of Calvinists from Holland under the sponsorship of the Dutch East India Company. The colonists settled along the Hudson River and in 1628 organized at New Amsterdam (now New York) what was to become the oldest church in America with an uninterrupted ministry. Several additional churches were in operation when the English took over the Dutch colony in 1664, and in 1792 they broke away from the parent body in Holland. Efforts to unite with the German Reformed bodies failed because the Dutch objected to the Heidelberg Confession as being too Lutheran. They wanted to include the Dordrecht Articles of the Mennonites, with their emphasis on God's primacy in human life, and the Belgic Confession with its "mild and gentle spirit."

One of the notable features of the Reformed Church in America is its strong ecumenism. It has long been a member of the National and World Councils of Churches, and has also made a practice of exchanging its ministers with other denominations.

The Christian Reformed Church is an offshoot of the Reformed Church in America. It was organized in 1857 by members who objected to a trend in the older church toward doctrinal liberalism and the use of English in liturgical services. Originally known as the Holland Reformed Church, it almost died out in the early years after secession, until immigrants from Europe and anti-Masonic critics from the Reformed Church gave it new recruits.

Later on the name was changed to its present form and English was accepted for preaching and the liturgy. In doctrinal matters, however, the Christian Reformed have remained staunchly faithful to what they regard as essentials of the faith. Most of the church-affiliated elementary and secondary schools sponsored by the Reformed groups in America belong to this denomination.

THE HEIDELBERG CATECHISM

The earliest confessional document in common use among Reformed churches was written during the lifetime of Calvin. Known as the Heidelberg Catechism, from the place of its composition, it was the joint effort of two young theologians at the University of Heidelberg. Zacharias Ursinus (1534-1583), a pupil of Melanchthon, and Casper Olevian (1536-1587), a follower of John Calvin. Frederick III, Elector of the Palatinate, had ordered the Catechism in order to reconcile the contending factions in his territory. Frederick defended the Augsburg Confession as modified by Melanchthon, but he inclined towards the Reformed point of view, insisting on the self-sufficiency of Scripture and "repelled by the bigotry and intolerance of the ultra-Lutherans."

Published in 1563, the Heidelberg Catechism combined in a remarkable manner the conciliatory spirit of Melanchthon, friend and assistant of Luther, and the practicality of Zwingli and Calvin.

In some churches of the Reformed persuasion, the Heidelberg Catechism is the only doctrinal standard required to be explicitly taught in the denomination. The plan of the Catechism corresponds to the development of religious life through the experiences of repentance, faith and love. Older Reformation catechisms usually followed the outline of the Creed, Decalogue, Lord's Prayer, Baptism and the Lord's Supper. In the Heidelberg document these are worked into an organic system.

Christianity is thus represented not as a commanding law, nor as an intellectual scheme, but in its evangelical, practical and attractive aspect as the source of peace and comfort in life and death.

The Catechism is a work of religious enthusiasm, based on the principles of Calvin and Zwingli, interpreted by Bullinger and Melanchthon. It is remarkably free from polemical zeal or intolerance, and should be classed along with Luther's Small Catechism as the most popular and influential compendium of doctrine produced by the Reformation. Its subject matter follows the sequence of St. Paul's letter to the Romans (except for chapters 9 to 11) and reflects to a marked degree the apostle's concern for the salvation of sinners through the passion and death of Christ.

Question 1. What is your only comfort, in life and in death?

Answer: That I belong—body and soul, in life and in death—not to myself but to my faithful Savior, Jesus Christ, who at the cost of his own blood has fully paid for all my sins and has completely freed me from the dominion of the devil; that he protects me so well that without the will of my Father in heaven not a hair can fall from my head; indeed, that everything must fit his purpose for my salvation. Therefore, by his Holy Spirit, he also assures me of eternal life, and makes me wholeheartedly willing and ready from now on to live for him.

Question 2. How many things must you know that you may live and die in the blessedness of this comfort?

Answer: Three. First, the greatness of my sin and wretchedness. Second, how I am freed from all my sins and their wretched consequences. Third, what gratitude I owe to God for such redemption.

PART I
Of Man's Misery

Question 3. Where do you learn of your sin and its wretched consequences?

Answer: From the Law of God.

Question 4. What does the Law of God require of us?

Answer: Jesus Christ teaches this in a summary in Matthew 22:37-40: "You shall love the Lord your God with all your heart, and with all your soul, and with all your mind. This is the great and first commandment. And a second is like it, you shall love your neighbor as yourself. On these two commandments depend all the law and the prophets." (Cf. Luke 10-27.)

Question 5. Can you keep all this perfectly?

Answer: No, for by nature I am prone to hate God and my neighbor.

Question 6. Did God create man evil and perverse like this?

Answer: No. On the contrary, God created man good and in his image, that is, in true righteousness and holiness, so that he might rightly know God his Creator, love him with his whole heart, and live with him in eternal blessedness, praising and glorifying him.

Question 7. Where, then, does this corruption of human nature come from?

Answer: From the fall and disobedience of our first parents, Adam and Eve, in the Garden of Eden; whereby our human life is so poisoned that we are all conceived and born in the state of sin.

Question 8. But are we so perverted that we are altogether unable to do good and prone to do evil?

Answer: Yes, unless we are born again through the Spirit of God.

Question 9. Is not God unjust in requiring of man in his Law what he cannot do?

Answer: No, for God so created man that he could do it. But man, upon the instigation of the devil, by deliberate disobedience, has cheated himself and all his descendants out of these gifts.

Question 10. Will God let man get by with such disobedience and defection?

Answer: Certainly not, for the wrath of God is revealed from heaven, both against our inborn sinfulness and our actual sins, and he will punish them according to his righteous judgment in time and in eternity, as he has declared: "Cursed be everyone who does not abide by all things written in the book of the Law, and do them."

Question 11. But is not God also merciful?

Answer: God is indeed merciful and gracious, but he is also righteous. It is his righteousness which requires that sin committed against the supreme majesty of God be punished with extreme, that is, with eternal punishment of body and soul.

PART II
Of Man's Redemption

Question 12. Since, then, by the righteous judgment of God we have deserved temporal and eternal punishment, how may we escape this punishment, come again to grace, and be reconciled to God?

Answer: God wills that his righteousness be satisfied; therefore, payment in full must be made to his righteousness, either by ourselves or by another.

Question 13. Can we make this payment ourselves?

Answer: By no means. On the contrary, we increase our debt each day.

Question 14. Can any mere creature make the payment for us?

Answer: No one. First of all, God does not want to punish any other creature for man's debt. Moreover, no mere creature can bear the burden of God's eternal wrath against sin and redeem others from it.

Question 15. Then, what kind of mediator and redeemer must we seek?

Answer: One who is a true and righteous man and yet more powerful than all creatures, that is, one who is at the same time true God.

Question 16. Why must he be a true and righteous man?

Answer: Because God's righteousness requires that man who has sinned should make reparation for sin, but the man who is himself a sinner cannot pay for others.

Question 17. Why must he at the same time be true God?

Answer: So that by the power of his divinity he might bear as a man the burden of God's wrath, and recover for us and restore to us righteousness and life.

Question 18. Who is this mediator who is at the same time true God and a true and perfectly righteous man?

Answer: Our Lord Jesus Christ, who is freely given to us for complete redemption and righteousness.

Question 19. Whence do you know this?

Answer: From the holy gospel, which God himself revealed in the beginning in the Garden of Eden, afterward proclaimed through the holy patriarchs and prophets and foreshadowed through the sacrifices and other rites of the Old Covenant, and finally fulfilled through his own well-beloved Son.

Question 20. Will all men, then, be saved through Christ as they became lost through Adam?

Answer: No. Only those who, by true faith, are incorporated into him and accept all his benefits.

Question 21. What is true faith?

Answer: It is not only a certain knowledge by which I accept as true all that God has revealed to us in his Word, but also a wholehearted trust which the Holy Spirit creates in me through the gospel, that, not only to others, but to me also God has given the forgiveness of sins, everlasting righteousness and salvation, out of sheer grace solely for the sake of Christ's saving work.

Question 22. What, then, must a Christian believe?

Answer: All that is promised us in the gospel, a summary of which is taught us in the articles of the Apostles' Creed, our universally acknowledged confession of faith.

Question 23. What are these articles?

Answer: I believe in God the Father Almighty, Maker of Heaven and earth;

And in Jesus Christ, his only-begotten Son, our Lord; who was conceived by the Holy Spirit, born of the Virgin Mary; suffered under Pontius Pilate, was crucified, dead, and buried; he descended into hell; the third day he rose again from the dead; he ascended into heaven, and sits at the right hand of God the Father Almighty; from thence he shall come to judge the living and the dead.

I believe in the Holy Spirit; the holy catholic Church; the communion of saints; the forgiveness of sins; the resurrection of the body; and the life everlasting.

Question 24. How are these articles divided?

Answer: Into three parts: The first concerns God *the Father* and our *creation;* the second, God *the Son* and our *redemption;* and the third, God *the Holy Spirit* and our *sanctification.*

Question 25. Since there is only one Divine Being, why do you speak of three, Father, Son, and Holy Spirit?

Answer: Because God has thus revealed himself in his Word, that these three distinct persons are the one, true, eternal God.

Of God the Father

Question 26. What do you believe when you say: "I believe in God the Father Almighty, Maker of heaven and earth"?

Answer: That the eternal Father of our Lord Jesus Christ, who out of nothing created heaven and earth with all that is in them, who also upholds and governs them by his eternal counsel and providence, is for the sake of Christ his Son my God and my Father. I trust in him so completely that I have no doubt that he will provide me with all things necessary for body and soul. Moreover, whatever evil he sends upon me in this troubled life he will turn to my good, for he is able to do it, being almighty God, and is determined to do it, being a faithful Father.

Question 27. What do you understand by the providence of God?

Answer: The almighty and ever-present power of God whereby he still upholds, as it were by his own hand, heaven and earth together with all creatures, and rules in such a way that leaves and grass, rain and drought, fruitful and unfruitful years, food and drink, health and sickness, riches and poverty, and everything else, come to us not by chance but by his fatherly hand.

Question 28. What advantage comes from acknowledging God's creation and providence?

Answer: We learn that we are to be patient in adversity, grateful in the midst of blessing, and to trust our faithful God and Father for the future, assured that no creature shall separate us from his love, since all creatures are so completely in his hand that without his will they cannot even move.

Of God the Son

Question 29. Why is the Son of God called JESUS, which means SAVIOR?

Answer: Because he saves us from our sins, and because salvation is to be sought or found in no other.

Question 30. Do those who seek their salvation and well-being from saints, by their own efforts, or by other means really believe in the only Savior Jesus?

Answer: No. Rather, by such actions they deny Jesus, the only Savior and Redeemer, even though they boast of belonging to him. It therefore follows that either Jesus is not a perfect Savior, or those who receive this Savior with true faith must possess in him all that is necessary for their salvation.

Question 31. Why is he called CHRIST, that is, the ANOINTED ONE?

Answer: Because he is ordained by God the Father and anointed with the Holy Spirit to be our *chief Prophet* and *Teacher,* fully revealing to us the secret purpose and will of God concerning our redemption; to be *our only High Priest,* having redeemed us by the one sacrifice of his body and ever interceding for us with the Father; and to be *our eternal King,* governing us by his Word and Spirit, and defending and sustaining us in the redemption he has won for us.

Question 32. But why are you called a Christian?

Answer: Because through faith I share in Christ and thus in his anointing, so that I may confess his name, offer myself a living sacrifice of gratitude to him, and fight against sin and the devil with a free and good conscience throughout this life and hereafter with him in eternity over all creatures.

Question 33. Why is he called GOD'S ONLY-BEGOTTEN SON, since we also are God's children?

Answer: Because Christ alone is God's own eternal Son, whereas we are accepted for his sake as children of God by grace.

Question 34. Why do you call him OUR LORD?

Answer: Because, not with gold or silver but at the cost of his blood, he has redeemed us body and soul from sin and all the dominion of the devil, and has bought us for his very own.

Question 35. What is the meaning of: "Conceived by the Holy Spirit, born of the Virgin Mary"?

Answer: That the eternal Son of God, who is and remains true and eternal God, took upon himself our true manhood from the flesh and blood of the Virgin Mary through the action of the Holy Spirit, so that he might also be the true seed of David, like his fellow men in all things, except for sin.

Question 36. What benefit do you receive from the holy conception and birth of Christ?

Answer: That he is our Mediator, and that, in God's sight, he covers over with his innocence and perfect holiness the sinfulness in which I have been conceived.

Question 37. What do you understand by the word "suffered"?

Answer: That throughout his life on earth, but especially at the end of it, he bore in body and soul the wrath of God against the sin of the whole human race, so that by his suffering, as the only expiatory sacrifice, he might redeem our body and soul from everlasting damnation, and might obtain for us God's grace, righteousness, and eternal life.

Question 38. Why did he suffer "under Pontius Pilate" as his judge?

Answer: That he, being innocent, might be condemned by an earthly judge, and thereby set us free from the judgment of God which, in all its severity, ought to fall upon us.

Question 39. Is there something more in his having been crucified than if he had died some other death?

Answer: Yes, for by this I am assured that he took upon himself the curse which lay upon me, because the death of the cross was cursed by God.

Question 40. Why did Christ have to suffer "death"?

Answer: Because the righteousness and truth of God are such that nothing else could make reparation for our sins except the death of the Son of God.

Question 41. Why was he "buried"?

Answer: To confirm the fact that he was really dead.

Question 42. Since, then, Christ died for us, why must we also die?

Answer: Our death is not a reparation for our sins, but only a dying to sin and an entering into eternal life.

Question 43. What further benefit do we receive from the sacrifice and death of Christ on the cross?

Answer: That by his power our old self is crucified, put to death, and buried with him, so that the evil passions of our mortal bodies may reign in us no more, but that we may offer ourselves to him as a sacrifice of thanksgiving.

Question 44. Why is there added: "He descended into hell"?

Answer: That in my severest tribulations I may be assured that Christ my Lord has redeemed me from hellish anxieties and torment by the unspeakable anguish, pains, and terrors which he suffered in his soul both on the cross and before.

Question 45. What benefit do we receive from "the resurrection" of Christ?

Answer: First, by his resurrection he has overcome death that he might make us share in the righteousness which he has obtained for us through his death. Second, we too are now raised by his power to a new life. Third, the resurrection of Christ is a sure pledge to us of our blessed resurrection.

Question 46. How do you understand the words: "He ascended into heaven"?

Answer: That Christ was taken up from the earth into heaven before the eyes of his disciples and remains there on our behalf until he comes again to judge the living and the dead.

Question 47. Then, is not Christ with us unto the end of the world, as he has promised us?

Answer: Christ is true man and true God. As a man he is no longer on earth, but in his divinity, majesty, grace, and Spirit, he is never absent from us.

Question 48. But are not the two natures in Christ separated from each other in this way, if the humanity is not wherever the divinity is?

Answer: Not at all; for since divinity is incomprehensible and everywhere present, it must follow that the divinity is indeed beyond the bounds of the humanity which it has assumed, and is nonetheless ever in that humanity as well, and remains personally united to it.

Question 49. What benefit do we receive from Christ's ascension into heaven?

Answer: First, that he is our Advocate in the presence of his Father in heaven. Second, that we have our flesh in heaven as a sure pledge that he, as the Head, will also take us, his members, up to himself. Third, that he sends us his Spirit as a counterpledge by whose power we seek what is above, where Christ is, sitting at the right hand of God, and not things that are on earth.

Question 50. Why is there added: "And sits at the right hand of God"?

Answer: Because Christ ascended into heaven so that he might manifest himself there as the Head of his Church, through whom the Father governs all things.

Question 51. What benefit do we receive from this glory of Christ, our Head?

Answer: First, that through his Holy Spirit he pours out heavenly gifts upon us, his members. Second, that by his power he defends and supports us against all our enemies.

Question 52. What comfort does the return of Christ "to judge the living and the dead" give you?

Answer: That in all affliction and persecution I may await with head held high the very Judge from heaven who has already submitted himself to the judgment of God for me and has removed all the curse from me; that he will cast all his enemies and mine into everlasting condemnation, but he shall take me, together with all his elect, to himself into heavenly joy and glory.

The Holy Spirit

Question 53. What do you believe concerning "the Holy Spirit"?

Answer: First, that, with the Father and the Son, he is equally eternal God; second, that God's Spirit is also given to me, preparing me through a true faith to share in Christ and all his benefits, that he comforts me and will abide with me forever.

Question 54. What do you believe concerning "the Holy Catholic Church"?

Answer: I believe that, from the beginning to the end of the world, and from among the whole human race, the Son of God, by his Spirit and his Word, gathers, protects, and preserves for himself, in the unity of the true faith, a congregation chosen for eternal life. Moreover, I believe that I am and forever will remain a living member of it.

Question 55. What do you understand by "the communion of saints"?

Answer: First, that believers one and all, as partakers of the Lord Christ, and all his treasures and gifts, shall share in one fellowship. Second, that each one ought to know that he is obliged to use his gifts freely and with joy for the benefit and welfare of other members.

Question 56. What do you believe concerning "the forgiveness of sins"?

Answer: That, for the sake of Christ's reconciling work, God will no more remember my sins or the sinfulness with which I have to struggle all my life long; but that he graciously imparts to me the righteousness of Christ so that I may never come into condemnation.

Question 57. What comfort does "the resurrection of the body" give you?

Answer: That after this life my soul shall be immediately taken up to Christ, its Head, and that this flesh of mine, raised by the power of Christ, shall be reunited with my soul, and be conformed to the glorious body of Christ.

Question 58. What comfort does the article concerning "the life everlasting" give you?

Answer: That, since I now feel in my heart the beginning of eternal joy, I shall possess, after this life, perfect blessedness, which no eye has seen, nor ear heard, nor the heart of man conceived, and thereby praise God forever.

Question 59. But how does it help you now that you believe all this?

Answer: That I am righteous in Christ before God, and an heir of eternal life.

Question 60. How are you righteous before God?

Answer: Only by true faith in Jesus Christ. In spite of the fact that my conscience accuses me that I have grievously sinned against all the commandments of God, and have not kept any one of them, and that I am still ever prone to all that is evil, nevertheless, God, without any merit of my own, out of pure grace, grants me the benefits of the perfect expiation of Christ, imputing to me his righteousness and holiness as if I had never committed a single sin or had ever been sinful, having fulfilled myself all the obedience which Christ has carried out for me, if only I accept such favor with a trusting heart.

Question 61. Why do you say that you are righteous by faith alone?

Answer: Not because I please God by virtue of the worthiness of my faith, but because the satisfaction, righteousness, and holiness of Christ alone are my righteousness before God, and because I can accept it and make it mine in no other way than by faith alone.

Question 62. But why cannot our good works be our righteousness before God, or at least a part of it?

Answer: Because the righteousness which can stand before the judgment of God must be absolutely perfect and wholly in conformity with the divine Law. But even our best works in this life are all imperfect and defiled with sin.

Question 63. Will our good works merit nothing, even when it is God's purpose to reward them in this life, and in the future life as well?

Answer: This reward is not given because of merit, but out of grace.

Question 64. But does not this teaching make people careless and sinful?

Answer: No, for it is impossible for those who are ingrafted into Christ by true faith not to bring forth the fruit of gratitude.

The Holy Sacraments

Question 65. Since, then, faith alone makes us share in Christ and all his benefits, where does such faith originate?

Answer: The Holy Spirit creates it in our hearts by the preaching of the holy gospel, and confirms it by the use of the holy Sacraments.

Question 66. What are the Sacraments?

Answer: They are visible, holy signs and seals instituted by God in order that by their use he may the more fully disclose and seal to us the promise of the gospel, namely, that because of the one sacrifice of Christ accomplished on the cross he graciously grants us the forgiveness of sins and eternal life.

Question 67. Are both the Word and the Sacraments designed to direct our faith to the one sacrifice of Jesus Christ on the cross as the only ground of our salvation?

Answer: Yes, indeed, for the Holy Spirit teaches in the gospel and confirms by the holy Sacraments that our whole salvation is rooted in the one sacrifice of Christ offered for us on the cross.

Question 68. How many Sacraments has Christ instituted in the New Testament?

Answer: Two, holy Baptism and the holy Supper.

Holy Baptism

Question 69. How does holy Baptism remind and assure you that the one sacrifice of Christ on the cross avails for you?

Answer: In this way: Christ has instituted this external washing with water and by it has promised that I am as certainly washed with his blood and Spirit from the uncleanness of my soul and from all my sins, as I am washed externally with water which is used to remove the dirt from my body.

Question 70. What does it mean to be washed with the blood and Spirit of Christ?

Answer: It means to have the forgiveness of sins from God, through grace, for the sake of Christ's blood which he shed for us in his sacrifice on the cross, and also to be renewed by the Holy Spirit and sanctified as members of Christ, so that we may more and more die unto sin and live in a consecrated and blameless way.

Question 71. Where has Christ promised that we are as certainly washed with his blood and Spirit as with the water of Baptism?

Answer: In the institution of Baptism which runs thus: "Go therefore and make disciples of all nations, baptizing them in the name of the Father and of the Son and of the Holy Spirit." "He who believes and is baptized will be saved: but he who does not believe will be condemned." This promise is also repeated where the Scriptures call baptism "the water of rebirth" and the washing away of sins.

Question 72. Does merely the outward washing with water itself wash away sins?

Answer: No; for only the blood of Jesus Christ and the Holy Spirit cleanse us from all sins.

Question 73. Then why does the Holy Spirit call Baptism the water of rebirth and the washing away of sins?

Answer: God does not speak in this way except for a strong reason. Not only does he teach us by Baptism that just as the dirt of the body is taken away by water, so our sins are removed by the blood and Spirit of Christ; but more important still, by the divine pledge and sign he wishes to assure us that we are just as truly washed from our sins spiritually as our bodies are washed with water.

Question 74. Are infants also to be baptized?

Answer: Yes, because they, as well as their parents, are included in the covenant and belong to the people of God. Since both redemption from sin through the blood of Christ and the gift of faith from the Holy Spirit are promised to these children no less than to their parents, infants are also by Baptism, as a sign of the covenant, to be incorporated into the Christian church and distinguished from the children of unbelievers. This was done in the Old Covenant by circumcision. In the New Covenant Baptism has been instituted to take its place.

The Holy Supper

Question 75. How are you reminded and assured in the holy Supper that you participate in the one sacrifice of Christ on the cross and in all his benefits?

Answer: In this way: Christ has commanded me and all believers to eat of this broken bread, and to drink of this cup in remembrance of him. He has thereby promised that his body was offered and broken on the cross for me, and his blood was shed for me, as surely as I see with my eyes that the bread of the Lord is broken for me, and that the cup is shared with me. Also, he has promised that he himself as certainly feeds and nourishes my soul to everlasting life with his crucified body and shed blood as I receive from the hand of the minister and actually taste the bread and the cup of the Lord which are given to me as sure signs of the body and blood of Christ.

Question 76. What does it mean to eat the crucified body of Christ and to drink his shed blood?

Answer: It is not only to embrace with a trusting heart the whole passion and death of Christ, and by it to receive the forgiveness of sins and eternal life. In addition, it is to be so united more and more to his blessed body by the Holy Spirit dwelling both in Christ and in us that, although he is in heaven and we are on earth, we are nevertheless flesh of his flesh and bone of his bone, always living and being governed by one Spirit, as the members of our bodies are governed by one soul.

Question 77. Where has Christ promised that he will feed and nourish believers with his body and blood just as surely as they eat of this broken bread and drink of this cup?

Answer: In the institution of the holy Supper which reads: The Lord Jesus on the night when he was betrayed took bread, and when he had given thanks, he broke it, and said, "this is my body which is for you. Do this in remembrance of me." In the same way also the cup, after supper, saying, "this cup is the new covenant in my blood. Do this, as often as you drink it, in remembrance of me." For as often as you eat this bread and drink the cup, you proclaim the Lord's death until he comes.

This promise is also repeated by the apostle Paul: When we bless "the cup of blessing," is it not a means of sharing in the blood of Christ? When we break the bread, is it not a means of sharing the body of Christ? Because there is one loaf, we, many as we are, are one body; for it is one loaf of which we all partake.

Question 78. Do the bread and wine become the very body and blood of Christ?

Answer: No, for as the water in Baptism is not changed into the blood of Christ, nor becomes the washing away of sins by itself, but is only a divine sign and confirmation of it, so also in the Lord's Supper the sacred bread does not become the body of Christ itself, although, in accordance with the nature and usage of sacraments, it is called the body of Christ.

Question 79. Then why does Christ call the bread his body, and the cup his blood, or the New Covenant in his blood, and why does the apostle Paul call the Supper "a means of sharing" in the body and blood of Christ?

Answer: Christ does not speak in this way except for a strong reason. He wishes to teach us by it that as bread and wine sustain this temporal life so his crucified body and shed blood are the true food and drink of our souls for eternal life. Even more, he wishes to assure us by this visible sign and pledge that we come to share in his true body and blood through the working of the Holy Spirit as surely as we receive with our mouth these holy tokens in remembrance of him, and that all his sufferings and his death are our own as certainly as if we had ourselves suffered and rendered satisfaction in our own persons.

Question 80. What difference is there between the Lord's Supper and the papal Mass?

Answer: The Lord's Supper testifies to us that we have complete forgiveness of all our sins through the one sacrifice of Jesus Christ which he himself has accomplished on the cross once for all; (and that through the Holy Spirit we are incorporated into Christ, who is now in heaven with his true body at the right hand of the Father and is there to be worshiped). But the Mass teaches that the living and the dead do not have forgiveness of sins through the sufferings of Christ unless Christ is again offered for them daily by the priest (and that Christ is bodily under the form of bread and wine and is therefore to be worshiped in them). Therefore the Mass is fundamentally a complete denial of the once for all sacrifice and passion of Jesus Christ (and as such an idolatry to be condemned).

Question 81. Who ought to come to the table of the Lord?

Answer: Those who are displeased with themselves for their sins, and who nevertheless trust that these sins have been forgiven them and that their remaining weakness is covered by the passion and death of Christ, and who also desire more and more to strengthen their faith and improve their life. The impenitent and hypocrites, however, eat and drink judgment to themselves.

Question 82. Should those who show themselves to be unbelievers and enemies of God by their confession and life be admitted to this Supper?

Answer: No, for then the covenant of God would be profaned and his wrath provoked against the whole congregation. According to the ordinance of Christ and his apostles, therefore, the Christian church is under obligation, by the office of the keys, to exclude such persons until they amend their lives.

Question 83. What is the office of the keys?

Answer: The preaching of the holy gospel and Christian discipline. By these two means the kingdom of heaven is opened to believers and shut against unbelievers.

Question 84. How is the kingdom of heaven opened and shut by the preaching of the holy gospel?

Answer: In this way: The kingdom of heaven is opened when it is proclaimed and openly testified to believers, one and all, according to the command of Christ, that as often as they accept the promise of the gospel with true faith all their sins are truly forgiven them by God for the sake of Christ's gracious work. On the contrary, the wrath of God and eternal condemnation fall upon all unbelievers and hypocrites as long as they do not repent. It is according to this witness of the gospel that God will judge the one and the other in this life to come.

Question 85. How is the kingdom of heaven shut and opened by Christian discipline?

Answer: In this way: Christ commanded that those who bear the Christian name in an unchristian way either in doctrine or in life should be given brotherly admonition. If they do not give up their errors or evil ways, notification is given to the church or to those ordained for this by the church. Then, if they do not change after this warning, they are forbidden to partake of the holy Sacraments and are thus excluded from the communion of the church and by God himself from the kingdom of Christ. However, if they promise and show real amendment, they are received again as members of Christ and of the church.

PART III
Thankfulness

Question 86. Since we are redeemed from our sin and its wretched consequences by grace through Christ without any merit of our own, why must we do good works?

Answer: Because just as Christ has redeemed us with his blood he also renews us through his Holy Spirit according to his own image, so that with our whole life we may show ourselves grateful to God for his goodness and that he may be glorified through us; and further, so that we ourselves may be assured of our faith by its fruits and by our reverent behavior may win our neighbors to Christ.

Question 87. Can those who do not turn to God from their ungrateful impenitent life be saved?

Answer: Certainly not! Scripture says, "Surely you know that the unjust will never come into possession of the kingdom of God." Make no mistake: no fornicator or idolater, none who are guilty either of adultery or of homosexual perversion, no thieves or grabbers or drunkards or slanderers or swindlers, will possess the kingdom of God.

Question 88. How many parts are there to the true repentance or conversion of man?

Answer: Two: the dying of the old self and the birth of the new.

Question 89. What is the dying of the old self?

Answer: Sincere sorrow over our sins and more and more to hate them and to flee from them.

Question 90. What is the birth of the new self?

Answer: Complete joy in God through Christ and a strong desire to live according to the will of God in all good works.

Question 91. But what are good works?

Answer: Only those which are done out of true faith, in accordance with the Law of God, and for his glory, and not those based on our own opinion or on the traditions of men.

Question 92. What is the Law of God?

Answer: God spoke all these words saying:

FIRST COMMANDMENT

"I am the Lord your God, who brought you out of the land of Egypt, out of the house of bondage. You shall have no other gods before Me."

SECOND COMMANDMENT

"You shall not make yourself a graven image, or any likeness of anything that is in heaven above, or that is in the earth beneath, or that is in the water under the earth; you shall not bow down to them or serve them; for I the Lord your God am a jealous God, visiting the iniquity of the fathers upon the children to the third and the fourth generation of those who hate Me, but showing steadfast love to thousands of those who love Me and keep My commandments."

THIRD COMMANDMENT

"You shall not take the name of the Lord your God in vain; for the Lord will not hold him guiltless who takes His name in vain."

FOURTH COMMANDMENT

"Remember the sabbath day, to keep it holy. Six days you shall labor, and do all your work; but the seventh day is a sabbath to the Lord your God; in it you shall not do any work, you, or your son, or your daughter, your manservant, or your maidservant, or your cattle, or the sojourner who is within your gates; for in six days the Lord made heaven and earth, the sea, and all that is in them, and rested the seventh day; therefore the Lord blessed the sabbath day and hallowed it."

FIFTH COMMANDMENT

"Honor your father and your mother, that your days may be long in the land which the Lord your God gives you."

SIXTH COMMANDMENT

"You shall not kill."

SEVENTH COMMANDMENT

"You shall not commit adultery."

EIGHTH COMMANDMENT

"You shall not steal."

NINTH COMMANDMENT

"You shall not bear false witness against your neighbor."

TENTH COMMANDMENT

"You shall not covet your neighbor's house; you shall not covet your neighbor's wife, or his manservant, or his maidservant, or his ox, or his ass, or anything that is your neighbor's."

Question 93. How are these commandments divided?

Answer: Into two tables, the first of which teaches us in four commandments how we ought to live in relation to God: the other, in six commandments, what we owe to our neighbor.

Question 94. What does the Lord require in the first commandment?

Answer: That I must avoid and flee all idolatry, sorcery, enchantments, invocation of saints or other creatures because of the risk of losing my salvation. Indeed, I ought properly to acknowledge the only true God, trust in him alone, in humility and patience expect all good from him only, and love, fear and honor him with my whole heart. In short, I should rather turn my back on all creatures than do the least thing against his will.

Question 95. What is idolatry?

Answer: It is to imagine or possess something in which to put one's trust, in place of or beside the one true God who has revealed himself in his Word.

Question 96. What does God require in the second commandment?

Answer: That we should not represent him or worship him in any other manner than he has commanded in his Word.

Question 97. Should we, then, not make any images at all?

Answer: God cannot and should not be pictured in any way. As for creatures, although they may indeed be portrayed, God forbids making or having any likeness of them in order to worship them, or to use them to serve him.

Question 98. But may not pictures be tolerated in churches in place of books for unlearned people?

Answer: No, for we must not try to be wiser than God who does not want his people to be taught by means of lifeless idols, but through the living preaching of his Word.

Question 99. What is required in the third commandment?

Answer: That we must not profane or abuse the name of God by cursing, by perjury, or by unnecessary oaths. Nor are we to participate in such horrible sins by keeping quiet and thus giving silent consent. In a word, we must not use the holy name of God except with fear and reverence so that he may be rightly confessed and addressed by us, and be glorified in all our words and works.

Question 100. Is it, therefore, so great a sin to blaspheme God's name by cursing and swearing that God is also angry with those who do not try to prevent and forbid it as much as they can?

Answer: Yes, indeed; for no sin is greater or provokes his wrath more than the profaning of his name. That is why he commanded it to be punished with death.

Question 101. But may we not swear oaths by the name of God in a devout manner?

Answer: Yes, when the civil authorities require it of their subjects, or when it is otherwise needed to maintain and promote fidelity and truth, to the glory of God and the welfare of our neighbor. Such oath-taking is grounded in God's Word and has therefore been rightly used by God's people under the Old and New Covenants.

Question 102. May we also swear by the saints or other creatures?

Answer: No; for a lawful oath is a calling upon God, as the only searcher of hearts, to bear witness to the truth, and to punish me if I swear falsely. No creature deserves such honor.

Question 103. What does God require in the fourth commandment?

Answer: First, that the ministry of the gospel and Christian education be maintained, and that I diligently attend church, especially on the Lord's day, to hear the Word of God, to participate in the holy Sacraments, to call publicly upon the Lord, and to give Christian service to those in need. Second, that I cease from my evil works all the days of my life, allow the Lord to work in me through his Spirit, and thus begin in this life the eternal Sabbath.

Question 104. What does God require in the fifth commandment?

Answer: That I show honor, love, and faithfulness to my father and mother and to all who are set in authority over me; that I submit myself with respectful obedience to all their careful instruction and discipline; and that I also bear patiently their failures, since it is God's will to govern us by their hand.

Question 105. What does God require in the sixth commandment?

Answer: That I am not to abuse, hate, injure, or kill my neighbor, either with thought, or by word or gesture, much less by deed, whether by myself or through another, but to lay aside all desire for revenge; and that I do not harm myself or willfully expose myself to danger. This is why the authorities are armed with the means to prevent murder.

Question 106. But does this commandment speak only of killing?

Answer: In forbidding murder God means to teach us that he abhors the root of murder, which is envy, hatred, anger, and desire for revenge, and that he regards all these as hidden murder.

Question 107. Is it enough, then, if we do not kill our neighbor in any of these ways?

Answer: No; for when God condemns envy, hatred, and anger, he requires us to love our neighbor as ourselves, to show patience, peace, gentleness, mercy, and friendliness towards him, to prevent injury to him as much as we can, also to do good to our enemies.

Question 108. What does the seventh commandment teach us?

Answer: That all unchastity is condemned by God, and that we should therefore detest it from the heart, and live chaste and disciplined lives, whether in holy wedlock or in single life.

Question 109. Does God forbid nothing more than adultery and such gross sins in this commandment?

Answer: Since both our body and soul are a temple of the Holy Spirit, it is his will that we keep both pure and holy. Therefore he forbids all unchaste actions, gestures, words, thoughts, desires and whatever may excite another person to them.

Question 110. What does God forbid in the eighth commandment?

Answer: He forbids not only the theft and robbery which civil authorities punish, but God also labels as theft all wicked tricks and schemes by which we seek to get for ourselves our neighbor's goods, whether by force or under the pretext of right, such as false weights and measures, deceptive advertising or merchandising, counterfeit money, exorbitant interest, or any other means forbidden by God. He also forbids all greed and misuse and waste of his gifts.

Question 111. But what does God require of you in this commandment?

Answer: That I work for the good of my neighbor wherever I can and may, deal with him as I would have others deal with me, and do my work well so that I may be able to help the poor in their need.

Question 112. What is required in the ninth commandment?

Answer: That I do not bear false witness against anyone, twist anyone's words, be a gossip or a slanderer, or condemn anyone lightly without a hearing. Rather I am required to avoid, under penalty of God's wrath, all lying and deceit as the works of the devil himself. In judicial and all other matters I am to love the truth, and to speak and confess it honestly. In deed, insofar as I am able, I am to defend and promote my neighbor's good name.

Question 113. What is required in the tenth commandment?

Answer: That there should never enter our heart even the least inclination or thought contrary to any commandment of God, but that we should always hate sin with our whole heart and find satisfaction and joy in all righteousness.

Question 114. But can those who are converted to God keep these commandments perfectly?

Answer: No, for even the holiest of them make only a small beginning in obedience in this life. Nevertheless, they begin with serious purpose to conform not only to some, but to all the commandments of God.

Question 115. Why, then, does God have the ten commandments preached so strictly since no one can keep them in this life?

Answer: First, that all our life long we may become increasingly aware of our sinfulness, and therefore more eagerly seek forgiveness of sins and righteousness in Christ. Second, that we may constantly and diligently pray to God for the grace of the Holy Spirit, so that more and more we may be renewed in the image of God, until we attain the goal of full perfection after this life.

Prayer

Question 116. Why is prayer necessary for Christians?

Answer: Because it is the chief part of the gratitude which God requires of us, and because God will give his grace and Holy Spirit only to those who sincerely beseech him in prayer without ceasing, and who thank him for these gifts.

Question 117. What is contained in a prayer which pleases God and is heard by him?

Answer: First, that we sincerely call upon the one true God, who has revealed himself to us in his Word, for all that he has commanded us to ask of him. Then, that we thoroughly acknowledge our need and evil condition so that we may humble ourselves in the presence of his majesty. Third, that we rest assured that, in spite of our unworthiness, he will certainly hear our prayer for the sake of Christ our Lord, as he has promised us in his Word.

Question 118. What has God commanded us to ask of him?

Answer: All things necessary for soul and body which Christ the Lord has included in the prayer which he himself taught us.

Question 119. What is the Lord's Prayer?

Answer: "Our Father who art in heaven, hallowed be thy name. Thy kingdom come, thy will be done, on earth as it is in heaven. Give us this day our daily bread; and forgive us our debts, as we also have forgiven our debtors; and lead us not into temptation, but deliver us from evil, for thine is the kingdom and the power and the glory, forever. Amen."

Question 120. Why has Christ commanded us to address God: "Our Father"?

Answer: That at the very beginning of our prayer he may awaken in us the childlike reverence and trust toward God which should be the motivation of our prayer, which is that God has become our Father through Christ and will much less deny us what we ask him in faith than our human fathers will refuse us earthly things.

Question 121. Why is there added: "who art in heaven"?

Answer: That we may have no earthly conception of the heavenly majesty of God, but that we may expect from his almighty power all things that are needed for body and soul.

Question 122. What is the first petition?

Answer: "Hallowed be thy name." That is: help us first of all to know thee rightly, and to hallow, glorify, and praise thee in all thy works through which there shine thine almighty power, wisdom, goodness, righteousness, mercy, and truth. And so order our whole life in thought, word, and deed that thy name may never be blasphemed on our account, but may always be honored and praised.

Question 123. What is the second petition?

Answer: "Thy kingdom come." That is: so govern us by thy Word and Spirit that we may more and more submit ourselves unto thee. Uphold and increase thy church. Destroy the works of the devil, every power that raises itself against thee, and all wicked schemes thought up against thy holy Word, until the full coming of thy kingdom in which thou shalt be all in all.

Question 124. What is the third petition?

Answer: "Thy will be done, on earth, as it is in heaven." That is: grant that we and all men may renounce our own will and obey thy will, which alone is good, without grumbling, so that everyone may carry out his office and calling as willingly and faithfully as the angels in heaven.

Question 125. What is the fourth petition?

Answer: "Give us this day our daily bread." That is: be pleased to provide for all our bodily needs so that thereby we may acknowledge that thou art the only source of all that is good, and that without thy blessing neither our care and labor nor thy gifts can do us any good.

Therefore, may we withdraw our trust from all creatures and place it in thee alone.

Question 126. What is the fifth petition?

Answer: "And forgive us our debts, as we also have forgiven our debtors." That is: be pleased, for the sake of Christ's blood, not to charge to us, miserable sinners, our many transgressions, nor the evil which still clings to us. We also find this witness of thy grace in us, that it is our sincere intention heartily to forgive our neighbor.

Question 127. What is the sixth petition?

Answer: "And lead us not into temptation, but deliver us from evil." That is: since we are so weak that we cannot stand by ourselves for one moment, and besides, since our sworn enemies, the devil, the world, and our own sin, ceaselessly assail us, be pleased to preserve and strengthen us through the power of thy Holy Spirit so that we may stand firm against them, and not be defeated in this spiritual warfare, until at last we obtain complete victory.

Question 128. How do you close this prayer?

Answer: "For thine is the kingdom and the power and the glory, forever." That is: we ask all this of thee because, as our King, thou art willing and able to give us all that is good since thou hast power over all things, and that by this not we ourselves but thy holy name may be glorified forever.

Question 129. What is the meaning of the little word "Amen"?

Answer: Amen means: this shall truly and certainly be. For my prayer is much more certainly heard by God than I am persuaded in my heart that I desire such things from him.

THE BELGIC CONFESSION

The Belgic Confession was composed by Guy de Bres for the churches in Flanders and the Netherlands. Written in 1561, it was formally adopted at Emden in 1571 and at Dort in 1619. Once the Synod of Dort approved the document as one of the doctrinal standards of the Reformed churches, its future acceptance was assured.

There is more than theological significance to the Belgic Confession. De Bres wrote it as an apologia for his faith, and sent it in 1562 to Philip II of Spain, together with an address in which the petitioners declared that they were ready to obey the government in all lawful things, but they would "offer their backs to stripes, their tongues to knives, their mouths to gags, and their whole bodies to the fire," rather than deny the truth expressed in this Confession.

Authorities differ on the extent to which De Bres depended on Calvin for the Confession. It is certain that he had access to a doctrinal summary written by the latter for the Reformed churches of France, published two years earlier.

Candidates for the ministry and officeholders in the Reformed churches are expected to subscribe to this fundamental statement of faith.

I. *There Is Only One God.* We all believe with the heart and confess with the mouth that there is one only simple and spiritual Being, which we call God; and that He is eternal, incomprehensible, invisible, immutable, infinite, almighty, perfectly wise, just, good, and the overflowing fountain of all good.

II. *By What Means God Is Made Known unto Us.* We know Him by two means: First, by the creation, preservation, and government of the universe; which is before our eyes as a most elegant book wherein all creatures, great and small, are as so many characters leading us to *see clearly the invisible things of God, even his everlasting power and divinity,* as the apostle Paul says (Rom. 1:20). All which things are sufficient to convince men and leave them without excuse. Second, He makes Himself more clearly and fully known to us by His holy and divine Word, that is to say, as far as is necessary for us to know in this life, to His glory and our salvation.

III. *The Written Word of God.* We confess that this Word of God was not sent nor delivered by the will of man, but that *men spake from God, being moved by the Holy Spirit,* as the apostle Peter says; and that afterwards God, from a special care which He has for us and our salvation, commanded His servants, the prophets and apostles, to commit His revealed word to writing; and He himself wrote with His own finger the two tables of the law. Therefore we call such writings holy and divine Scripture.

IV. *Canonical Books of the Holy Scripture.* We believe that the Holy Scriptures are contained in two books, namely, the Old and the New Testament, which are canonical, against which nothing can be alleged. These are thus named in the Church of God.

The books of the Old Testament are the five books of Moses, to wit: Genesis, Exodus, Leviticus, Numbers, Deuteronomy; the book of Joshua, Judges, Ruth, the two books of Samuel, the two of the Kings, two books of the Chronicles, commonly called Paralipomenon, the first of Ezra, Nehemiah, Esther; Job, the Psalms of David, the three books of Solomon, namely, the Proverbs, Ecclesiastes, and the Song of Songs; the four great prophets: Isaiah, Jeremiah, Ezekiel, and Daniel; and the twelve lesser prophets, namely, Hosea, Joel, Amos, Obadiah, Jonah, Micah, Nahum, Habakkuk, Zephaniah, Haggai, Zechariah, and Malachi.

Those of the New Testament are the four evangelists, to wit: Matthew, Mark, Luke, and John; the Acts of the Apostles; the fourteen epistles of the apostle Paul, namely, one to the Romans, two to the Corinthians, one to the Galatians, one to the Ephesians, one to the Philippians, one to the Colossians, two to the Thessalonians, two to Timothy, one to Titus, one to Philemon, and one to the Hebrews; the seven epistles of the other apostles, namely, one of James, two of Peter, three of John, one of Jude; and the Revelation of the apostle John.

V. *Whence the Holy Scriptures Derive Their Dignity and Authority.* We receive all these books, and these only, as holy and canonical, for the regulation, foundation, and confirmation of our faith; believing without any doubt all things contained in them, not so much because the Church receives and approves them as such, but more especially because the Holy Spirit witnesses in our hearts that they are from God, and also because they carry the evidence thereof in themselves. For the very blind are able to perceive that the things foretold in them are being fulfilled.

VI. *The Difference between the Canonical and Apocryphal Books.* We distinguish those sacred books from the apocryphal, viz.: the third and fourth books of Esdras, the books of Tobit, Judith, Wisdom, Jesus Sirach, Baruch, the Appendix to the book of Esther, the Song of the Three Children in the Furnace, the History of Susannah, of Bell and the Dragon, the Prayer of Manasseh, and the two books of the Maccabees. All of which the Church may read and take instruction from, so far as they agree with the canonical books; but they are far from having such power and efficacy that we may from their testimony confirm any point of faith or of the Christian religion; much less may they be used to detract from the authority of the other, that is, the sacred books.

VII. *The Sufficiency of the Holy Scriptures to Be the Only Rule of Faith.* We believe that those Holy Scriptures fully contain the will of God, and that whatsoever man ought to believe unto salvation is sufficiently taught therein. For since the whole manner of worship which God requires of us is written in them at large, it is unlawful for any one, though an apostle, to teach otherwise than we are now taught in the Holy Scriptures: *nay, though it were an angel from heaven,* as the apostle Paul says. For since it is forbidden to *add unto or take away anything from the Word of God,* it does thereby evidently appear that the doctrine thereof is most perfect and complete in all respects.

Neither may we consider any writings of men, however holy these men may have been, of equal value with those divine Scriptures, nor ought we to consider custom, or the great multitude, or antiquity, or succession of times and persons, or councils, decrees or statutes, as of equal value with the truth of God, since the truth is above all; *for all men are of themselves liars, and more vain than vanity itself.* Therefore we reject with all our hearts whatsoever does not agree with this infallible rule, as the apostles have taught us, saying, *Prove the spirits, whether they are of God.* Likewise: *If any one cometh unto you, and bringeth not this teaching, receive him not into your house.*

VIII. *God Is One in Essence, yet Distinguished in Three Persons.* According to this truth and this Word of God, we believe in one only God, who is the one single essence, in which are three persons, really, truly, and eternally distinct according to their incommunicable properties; namely, the Father, and the Son, and the Holy Spirit. The Father is the cause, origin, and beginning of all things visible and invisible; the Son is the word, wisdom, and image of the Father; the Holy Spirit is the eternal power and might, proceeding from the Father and the Son. Nevertheless, God is not by this distinction divided into three, since the Holy Scriptures teach us that the Father, and the Son, and the Holy Spirit have each His personality, distinguished by Their properties; but in such wise that these three persons are but one only God.

Hence, then, it is evident that the Father is not the Son, nor the Son the Father, and likewise the Holy Spirit is neither the Father nor the Son. Nevertheless, these persons thus distinguished are not divided, nor intermixed; for the Father has not assumed the flesh, nor has the Holy Spirit, but the Son only. The Father has never been without His Son, or without His Holy Spirit. For They are all three co-essential. There is neither first nor last; for They are all three one, in truth, in power, in goodness, and in mercy.

IX. *The Proof of the Foregoing Article of the Trinity of Persons in One God.* All this we know as well from the testimonies of Holy Writ as from their operations, and chiefly by those we feel in ourselves. The testimonies of the Holy Scriptures that teach us to believe this Holy Trinity are written in many places of the Old Testament, which are not so necessary to enumerate as to choose them out with discretion and judgment.

In Genesis, chap. 1:26,27, God says: *Let us make man in our image, after our likeness,* etc. *And God created man in his own image, male and female created he them.* And Gen. 3:22, *Behold, the man is become as one of us.* From this saying, Let *us* make man in *our* image, it appears that there are more persons than one in the Godhead; and when He says, *God* created, He signifies the unity. It is true, He does not say how many persons there are, but that which appears to us somewhat obscure in the Old Testament is very plain in the New. For when our Lord was baptized in Jordan, the voice of the Father was heard, saying, *This is my beloved Son;* the Son was seen in the water, and the Holy Spirit appeared in the shape of a dove. This form is also instituted by Christ in the baptism of all believers: *Make disciples of all the nations, baptizing them into the name of the Father and of the Son and of the Holy Spirit.* In the Gospel of Luke the angel Gabriel thus addressed Mary, the mother of our Lord: *The Holy Spirit shall come upon thee, and the power of the Most High shall overshadow thee; wherefore also the holy thing which is begotten shall be called the Son of God.* Likewise: *The grace of the Lord Jesus Christ, and the love of God, and the communion of the Holy Spirit, be with you all.* And (A.V.): *There are three that bear record in heaven, the Father, the Word, and the Holy Ghost: and these three are one.*

In all these places we are fully taught that there are three persons in one only divine essence. And although this doctrine far surpasses all human understanding, nevertheless we now believe it by means of the Word of God, but expect hereafter to enjoy the perfect knowledge and benefit thereof in heaven.

Moreover, we must observe the particular offices and operations of these three persons towards us. The Father is called our Creator, by His power; the Son is our Savior and Redeemer, by His blood; the Holy Spirit is our Sanctifier, by His dwelling in our hearts.

This doctrine of the Holy Trinity has always been affirmed and maintained by the true Church since the time of the apostles to this very day against the Jews, Mohammedans, and some false Christians and heretics, as Marcion, Manes, Praxeas, Sebellius, Samosatenus, Arius, and such like, who have been justly condemned by the orthodox fathers. Therefore, in this point, we do willingly receive the three creeds, namely, that of the Apostles, of Nicea, and of Athanasius; likewise that which, conformable thereunto is agreed upon by the ancient fathers.

X. *Jesus Christ Is True and Eternal God.* We believe that Jesus Christ according to His divine nature is the only begotten Son of God, begotten from eternity, not made, nor created (for then He would be a creature), but co-essential and co-eternal with the Father, *the very image of his substance and the effulgence of his glory,* equal unto Him in all things. He is the Son of God, not only from the time that He assumed our nature but from all eternity, as these testimonies, when compared together, teach us. Moses says that God created the world; and St. John says that all things were made by that Word which he calls God. The apostle says that God made the world by His Son; likewise, that God created all things by Jesus Christ. Therefore it must needs follow that He who is called God, the Word, the Son, and Jesus Christ, did exist at that time when all things were created by Him. Therefore the prophet Micah says: *His goings forth are from of old, from everlasting.* And the apostle: *He hath neither beginning of days nor end of life.* He therefore is that true, eternal, and almighty God whom we invoke, worship, and serve.

XI. *The Holy Spirit Is True and Eternal God.* We believe and confess also that the Holy Spirit from eternity proceeds from the Father and the Son; and therefore neither is made, created, nor begotten, but only proceeds from both; who in order is the third person of the Holy Trinity; of one and the same essence, majesty, and glory with the Father and the Son; and therefore is the true and eternal God, as the Holy Scriptures teach us.

XII. *The Creation of All Things, Especially the Angels.* We believe that the Father by the Word, that is, by His Son, has created of nothing the heaven, the earth, and all creatures, when it seemed good unto Him, giving unto every creature its being, shape, form, and several offices to serve its Creator; that He also still upholds and governs them by His eternal providence and infinite power for the service of mankind, to the end that man may serve his God.

He also created the angels good, to be His messengers and to serve His elect; some of whom are fallen from that excellency in which God created them into everlasting perdition, and the others have by the grace of God remained stedfast and continued in their first state. The devils and evil spirits are so depraved that they are enemies of God and every good thing; to the utmost of their power as murderers watching to ruin the Church and every member thereof, and by their wicked stratagems to destroy all; and are, therefore, by their own wickedness adjudged to eternal damnation, daily expecting their horrible torments.

Therefore we reject and abhor the error of the Sadducees, who deny the existence of spirits and angels; and also that of the Manichees, who assert that the devils have their origin of themselves, and that they are wicked of their own nature, without having been corrupted.

XIII. *The Providence of God and His Government of All Things.* We believe that the same good God, after He had created all things, did not forsake them or give them up to fortune or chance, but that He rules and governs them according to His holy will, so that nothing happens in this world without His appointment; nevertheless, God neither is the Author of nor can be charged with the sins which are committed. For His power and goodness are so great and incomprehensible that He orders and executes His work in the most excellent and just manner, even then when devils and wicked men act unjustly. And as to what He does surpassing human understanding, we will not curiously inquire into farther than our capacity will admit of; but with the greatest humility and reverence adore the righteous judgments of God, which are hid from us, contenting ourselves that we are pupils of Christ, to learn only those things which He has revealed to us in His Word, without transgressing these limits.

This doctrine affords us unspeakable consolation, since we are taught thereby that nothing can befall us by chance, but by the direction of our most gracious and heavenly Father; who watches over us with a paternal care, keeping all creatures so under His power that *not a hair of our head (for they are all numbered), nor a sparrow can fall to the ground without the will of our Father,* in whom we do entirely trust; being persuaded that He so restrains the devil and all our enemies that without His will and permission they cannot hurt us.

And therefore we reject that damnable error of the Epicureans, who say that God regards nothing but leaves all things to chance.

XIV. *The Creation and Fall of Man, and His Incapacity to Perform What Is Truly Good.* We believe that God created man out of the dust of the earth, and made and formed him after His own image and likeness, good, righteous, and holy, capable in all things to will agreeably to the will of God. *But being in honor, he understood it not,* neither knew his excellency, but wilfully subjected himself to sin and consequently to death and the curse, giving ear to the words of the devil. For the commandment of life, which he had received, he transgressed; and by sin separated himself from God, who was his true life; having corrupted his whole nature; whereby he made himself liable to corporal and spiritual death. And being thus become wicked, perverse, and corrupt in all his ways, he has lost all his excellent gifts which he had received from God, and retained only small remains thereof, which, however, are sufficient to leave man without excuse; for all the light which is in us is changed into darkness, as the Scriptures teach us, saying: *The light shineth in the darkness, and the darkness apprehended it not;* where St. John calls men darkness.

Therefore we reject all that is taught repugnant to this concerning the free will of man, since man is but a slave to sin, and *can receive nothing, except it have been given him from heaven.* For who may presume to boast that he of himself can do any good, since Christ says: *No man can come to me, except the Father that sent me draw him?* Who will glory in his own will, who understands that *the mind of the flesh is enmity against God?* Who can speak of his knowledge, since *the natural man receiveth not the things of the Spirit of God?* In short, who dare suggest any thought, since he knows that *we are not sufficient of ourselves to account anything as of ourselves, but that our sufficiency is of God?* And therefore what the apostle says ought justly to be held sure and firm, that *God worketh in us both to will and to work, for his* good pleasure. For there is no understanding nor will conformable to the divine understanding and will but what Christ has wrought in man; which He teaches us, when He says: *Apart from me ye can do nothing.*

XV. *Original Sin.* We believe that through the disobedience of Adam original sin is extended to all mankind: which is a corruption of the whole nature and a hereditary disease, wherewith even infants in their mother's womb are infected, and which produces in man all sorts of sin, being in him as a root thereof, and therefore is so vile and abominable in the sight of God that it is sufficient to condemn all mankind. Nor is it altogether abolished or wholly eradicated even by baptism; since sin always issues forth from this woeful source, as water from a fountain; notwithstanding it is not imputed to the children of God unto condemnation, but by His grace and mercy is forgiven them. Not that they should rest securely in sin, but that a sense of this corruption should make believers often to sigh, desiring to be delivered from this body of death.

Wherefore we reject the error of the Pelagians, who assert that sin proceeds only from imitation.

XVI. *Eternal Election.* We believe that, all the posterity of Adam being thus fallen into perdition and ruin by the sin of our first parents, God then did manifest Himself such as He is; that is to say, merciful and just: merciful, since He delivers and preserves from this perdition all whom He in His eternal and unchangeable counsel of mere goodness has elected is Christ Jesus our Lord, without any respect to their works; just, in leaving others in the fall and perdition wherein they have involved themselves.

XVII. *The Recovery of Fallen Man.* We believe that our most gracious God, in His admirable wisdom and goodness, seeing that man had thus thrown himself into physical and spiritual death and made himself wholly miserable, was pleased to seek and comfort him, when he trembling fled from His presence, promising him that He would give His Son (who would be *born of a woman*) *to bruise the head of the serpent* and to make him blessed.

XVIII. *The Incarnation of Jesus Christ.* We confess, therefore, that God has fulfilled the promise which He made to the fathers by the mouth of His holy prophets, when He sent into the world, at the time appointed by Him, His own only-begotten and eternal Son, who *took upon Him the form of a servant* and *became like unto man*, really assuming the true human nature with all its infirmities, sin excepted; being conceived in the womb of the blessed virgin Mary by the power of the Holy Spirit without the means of man; and did not only assume human nature as to the body, but also a true human soul, that He might be a real man. For since the soul was lost as well as the body, it was necessary that He should take both upon Him, to save both.

Therefore we confess (in opposition to the heresy of the Anabaptists, who deny that Christ assumed human flesh of His mother) that Christ *partook of the flesh and blood of the children;* that He is a *fruit of the loins of David after the flesh; born of the seed of David according to the flesh; a fruit of the womb of Mary; born of a woman; a branch of David; a shoot of the root of Jesse; sprung from the tribe of Judah;* descended from the Jews according to the flesh; of the seed of Abraham, since (A.V.) *he took on him the seed of Abraham,* and *was made like unto his brethren in all things, sin excepted;* so that in truth He is our IMMANUEL, that is to say, *God with us.*

XIX. *The Union and Distinction of the Two Natures in the Person of Christ.* We believe that by this conception the person of the Son is inseparably united and connected with the human nature; so that there are not two Sons of God, nor two persons, but two natures united in one single person; yet each nature retains its own distinct properties. As, then, the divine nature has always remained uncreated, without beginning of days or end of life, filling heaven and earth, so also has the human nature not lost its properties but remained a creature, having beginning of days, being a finite nature, and retaining all the properties of a real body. And though He has by His resurrection given immortality to the same, nevertheless He has not changed the reality of His human nature; forasmuch as our salvation and resurrection also depend on the reality of His body.

But these two natures are so closely united in one person that they were not separated even by His death. Therefore that which He, when dying, commended into the hands of His Father, was a real human spirit, departing from His body. But in the meantime the divine nature always remained united with the human, even when He lay in the grave; and the Godhead did not cease to be in Him, any more than it did when He was an infant, though it did not so clearly manifest itself for a while. Wherefore we confess that He is very God and very man: very God by His power to conquer death; and very man that He might die for us according to the infirmity of His flesh.

XX. *God Has Manifested His Justice and Mercy in Christ.* We believe that God, who is perfectly merciful and just, sent His Son to assume that nature in which the disobedience was committed, to make satisfaction in the same, and to bear the punishment of sin by His most bitter passion and death. God therefore manifested His justice against His Son when He laid our iniquities upon Him, and poured forth His mercy and goodness on us, who were guilty and worthy of damnation, out of mere and perfect love, giving His Son unto death for us, and raising Him for our justification, that through Him we might obtain immortality and life eternal.

XXI. *The Satisfaction of Christ, Our Only High Priest, for Us.* We believe that Jesus Christ is ordained with an oath to be an everlasting High Priest, after the order of Melchizedek; and that He has presented Himself in our behalf before the Father, to appease His wrath by His full satisfaction, by offering Himself on the tree of the cross, and pouring out His precious blood to purge away our sins, as the prophets had foretold. For it is written: *He was wounded for our transgressions, he was bruised for our iniquities; the chastisement of our peace was upon him; and with his stripes we are healed. He was led as a lamb to the slaughter, and numbered with the transgressors;* and condemned by Pontius Pilate as a malefactor, though he had first declared Him innocent. Therefore, *He restored that which he took not away,* and *suffered, the righteous for the unrighteous,* as well in His body as in His soul, feeling the terrible punishment which our sins had merited; insomuch that *his sweat became as it were great drops of blood falling* down upon the ground. He called out: *My God, My God, why hast thou forsaken me?* and has suffered all this for the remission of our sins.

Wherefore we justly say with the apostle Paul that we know nothing *save Jesus Christ, and him crucified;* we *count all things but loss and refuse for the excellency of the knowledge of Christ Jesus our Lord,* in whose wounds we find all manner of consolation. Neither is it necessary to seek or invent any other means of being reconciled to God than this only sacrifice, once offered, by which *he hath perfected forever them that are sanctified.* This is also the reason why He was called by the angel of God, JESUS, that is to say, SAVIOR, because He would *save his people from their sins.*

XXII. *Our Justification through Faith in Jesus Christ.* We believe that, to attain the true knowledge of this great mystery, the Holy Spirit kindles in our hearts an upright faith, which embraces Jesus Christ with all His merits, appropriates Him, and seeks nothing more besides Him. For it must needs follow, either that all things which are requisite to our salvation are not in Jesus Christ, or if all things are in Him, that then those who possess Jesus Christ through faith have complete salvation in Him. Therefore, for any to assert that Christ is not sufficient, but that something more is required besides Him, would be too gross a blasphemy; for hence it would follow that Christ was but half a Savior.

Therefore we justly say with Paul, that we are *justified by faith alone, or by faith apart from works.* However, to speak more clearly, we do not mean that faith itself justifies us, for it is only an instrument with which we embrace Christ our righteousness. But Jesus Christ, imputing to us all His merits, and so many holy works which He has done for us and in our stead, is our righteousness. And faith is an instrument that keeps us in communion with Him in all His benefits, which, when they become ours, are more than sufficient to acquit us of our sins.

XXIII. *Wherein Our Justification before God Consists.* We believe that our salvation consists in the remission of our sins for Jesus Christ's sake, and that therein our righteousness before God is implied; as David and Paul teach us, declaring this to be the blessedness of man that *God imputes righteousness to him apart from works.* And the same apostle says that we are *justified freely by his grace, through the redemption that is in Christ Jesus.*

And therefore we always hold fast this foundation, ascribing all the glory to God, humbling ourselves before Him, and acknowledging ourselves to be such as we really are, without presuming to trust in any thing in ourselves, or in any merit of ours, relying and resting upon the obedience of Christ crucified alone, which becomes ours when we believe in Him. This is sufficient to cover all our iniquities, and to give us confidence in approaching to God; freeing the conscience of fear, terror, and dread, without following the example of our first father, Adam, who, trembling, attempted to cover himself with figleaves. And, verily, if we should appear before God, relying on ourselves or on any other creature, though ever so little, we should, alas! be consumed. And therefore every one must pray with David: *O Jehovah, enter not into judgment with thy servant; for in thy sight no man living is righteous.*

XXIV. *Man's Sanctification and Good Works.* We believe that this true faith, being wrought in man by the hearing of the Word of God and the operation of the Holy Spirit, regenerates him and makes him a new man, causing him to live a new life, and freeing him from the bondage of sin. Therefore it is so far from being true that this justifying faith makes men remiss in a pious and holy life, that on the contrary without it they would never do anything out of love to God, but only out of self-love or fear of damnation. Therefore it is impossible that this holy faith can be unfruitful in man; for we do not speak of a vain faith, but of such a faith which is called in Scripture a *faith working through love,* which excites man to the practice of those works which God has commanded in His Word.

These works, as they proceed from the good root of faith, are good and acceptable in the sight of God, forasmuch as they are all sanctified by His grace. Nevertheless they are of no account towards our justification, for it is by faith in Christ that we are justified, even before we do good works; otherwise they could not be good works, any more than the fruit of a tree can be good before the tree itself is good.

Therefore we do good works, but not to merit by them (for what can we merit?); nay, we are indebted to God for the good works we do, and not He to us, since it is He who *worketh in us both to will and to work, for his good pleasure.* Let us therefore attend to what is written: *When ye shall have done all the things that are commanded you, say, We are unprofitable servants; we have done that which it was our duty to do.* In the meantime we do not deny that God rewards good works, but it is through His grace that He crowns His gifts.

Moreover, though we do good works, we do not found our salvation upon them; for we can do no work but what is polluted by our flesh, and also punishable; and although we could perform such works, still the remembrance of one sin is sufficient to make God reject them. Thus, then, we would always be in doubt, tossed to and fro without any certainty, and our poor consciences would be continually vexed if they relied not on the merits of the suffering and death of our Savior.

XXV. *The Abolishing of the Ceremonial Law.* We believe that the ceremonies and symbols of the law ceased at the coming of Christ, and that all the shadows are accomplished; so that the use of them must be abolished among Christians; yet the truth and substance of them remain with us in Jesus Christ, in whom they have their completion. In the meantime we still use the testimonies taken out of the law and the prophets to confirm us in the doctrine of the gospel, and to regulate our life in all honorableness to the glory of God, according to His will.

XXVI. *Christ's Intercession.* We believe that we have no access unto God but alone through the only Mediator and Advocate, Jesus Christ the righteous; who therefore became man, having united in one person the divine and human natures, that we men might have access to the divine Majesty, which access would otherwise be barred against us. But this Mediator, whom the Father has appointed between Him and us, ought in no wise to affright us by His majesty, or cause us to seek another according to our fancy. For there is no creature, either in heaven or on earth, who loves us more than Jesus Christ; who, though *existing in the form of God,* yet *emptied himself, being made in the likeness of men and of a servant* for us, and *in all things was made like unto his brethren.* If, then, we should seek for another mediator who would be favorably inclined towards us, whom could we find who loved us more than He who laid down His life for us, even *while we were His enemies?* And if we seek for one who has power and majesty, who is there that has so much of both as He *who sits at the right hand of God* and *to whom hath been given all authority in heaven and on earth?* And who will sooner be heard than the own well beloved Son of God?

Therefore it was only through distrust that this practice of dishonoring, instead of honoring, the saints was introduced, doing that which they never have done nor required, but have on the contrary stedfastly rejected according to their bounden duty, as appears by their writings. Neither must we plead here our unworthiness; for the meaning is not that we should offer our prayers to God on the ground of our own worthiness, but only on the ground of the excellency and worthiness of the Lord Jesus Christ, whose righteousness is become ours by faith.

Therefore the apostle, to remove this foolish fear, or rather distrust, from us, rightly says that Jesus Christ *in all things was made like unto his brethren, that he might become a merciful* and *faithful high priest, to make propitiation for the sins of the people. For in that he himself hath suffered being tempted, he is able to succor them that are tempted.* And further to encourage us to go to Him, he says: *Having then a great high priest, who hath passed through the heavens, Jesus the Son of God, let us hold fast our confession. For we have not a high priest that cannot be touched with the feeling of our infirmities; but one that hath been in all points tempted like as we are, yet without sin. Let us therefore draw near with boldness unto the throne of grace, that we may receive mercy, and may find grace to help us in time of need.* The same apostle says: *Having boldness to enter into the holy place by the blood of Jesus, let us draw near with a true heart in fulness of faith,* etc. Likewise: Christ *hath his priesthood unchangeable; wherefore also he is able to save to the uttermost them that draw near unto God through him, seeing he ever liveth to make intercession for them.*

What more can be required? Since Christ Himself says: *I am the way, and the truth, and the life, no one cometh unto the Father but by me.* To what purpose should we, then, seek another advocate, since it has pleased God to give us His own Son as an Advocate? Let us not forsake Him to take another, or rather to seek after another, without ever being able to find him; for God well knew, when He gave Him to us, that we were sinners.

Therefore, according to the command of Christ, we call upon the heavenly Father through Jesus Christ our only Mediator, as we are taught in the Lord's Prayer; being assured that whatever we ask of the Father in His name will be granted us.

XXVII. *The Catholic Christian Church.* We believe and profess one catholic or universal Church, which is a holy congregation of true Christian believers, all expecting their salvation in Jesus Christ, being washed by His blood, sanctified and sealed by the Holy Spirit.

This Church has been from the beginning of the world, and will be to the end thereof; which is evident from this that Christ is an eternal King, which without subjects He cannot be. And this holy Church is preserved or supported by God against the rage of the whole world; though it sometimes for a while appears very small, and in the eyes of men to be reduced to nothing; as during the perilous reign of Ahab the Lord reserved unto Him seven thousand men who had not bowed their knees to Baal.

Furthermore, this holy Church is not confined, bound, or limited to a certain place or to certain persons, but is spread and dispersed over the whole world; and yet is joined and united with heart and will, by the power of faith, in one and the same Spirit.

XXVIII. *Every One Is Bound to Join Himself to the True Church.* We believe, since this holy congregation is an assembly of those who are saved, and outside of it there is no salvation, that no person of whatsoever state or condition he may be, ought to withdraw from it, content to be by himself; but that all men are in duty bound to join and unite themselves with it; maintaining the unity of the Church; submitting themselves to the doctrine and discipline thereof; bowing their necks under the yoke of Jesus Christ; and as mutual members of the same body, serving to the edification of the brethren, according to the talents God has given them.

And that this may be the more effectually observed, it is the duty of all believers, according to the Word of God, to separate themselves from all those who do not belong to the Church, and to join themselves to this congregation, wheresoever God has established it, even though the magistrates and edicts of princes were against it, yea, though they should suffer death or any other corporal punishment. Therefore all those who separate themselves from the same or do not join themselves to it act contrary to the ordinance of God.

XXIX. *The Marks of the True Church, and wherein It Differs from the False Church.* We believe that we ought diligently and circumspectly to discern from the Word of God which is the true Church, since all sects which are in the world assume to themselves the name of the Church. But we speak not here of hypocrites, who are mixed in the Church with the good, yet are not of the Church, though externally in it; but we say that the body and communion of the true Church must be distinguished from all sects that call themselves the Church.

The marks by which the true Church is known are these: If the pure doctrine of the gospel is preached therein; if it maintains the pure administration of the sacraments as instituted by Christ; if church discipline is exercised in punishing of sin; in short, if all things are managed according to the pure Word of God, all things contrary thereto rejected, and Jesus Christ acknowledged as the only Head of the Church. Hereby the true Church may certainly be known, from which no man has a right to separate himself.

With respect to those who are members of the Church, they may be known by the marks of Christians; namely, by faith, and when, having received Jesus Christ the only Savior, they avoid sin, follow after righteousness, love the true God and their neighbor, neither turn aside to the right or left, and crucify the flesh with the works thereof. But this is not to be understood as if there did not remain in them great infirmities; but they fight against them through the Spirit all the days of their life, continually taking their refuge in the blood, death, passion, and obedience of our Lord Jesus Christ, in whom they have remission of sins, through faith in Him.

As for the false Church, it ascribes more power and authority to itself and its ordinances than to the Word of God, and will not submit itself to the yoke of Christ. Neither does it administer the sacraments as appointed by Christ in His Word, but adds to and takes from them, as it thinks proper; it relies more upon men than upon Christ; and persecutes those who live holily according to the Word of God and rebuke it for its errors, covetousness, and idolatry.

These two Churches are easily known and distinguished from each other.

XXX. *The Government of the Church and Its Offices.* We believe that this true Church must be governed by that spiritual polity which our Lord has taught us in His Word; namely, that there must be ministers or pastors to preach the Word of God and to administer the sacraments; also elders and deacons, who, together with the pastors, form the council of the Church; that by these means the true religion may be preserved, and the true doctrine everywhere propagated, likewise transgressors punished and restrained by spiritual means; also that the poor and distressed may be relieved and comforted, according to their necessities. By these means everything will be carried on in the Church with good order and decency, when faithful men are chosen, according to the rule prescribed by St. Paul in his Epistle to Timothy.

XXXI. *The Ministers, Elders, and Deacons.* We believe that the ministers of God's Word, the elders, and the deacons ought to be chosen to their respective offices by a lawful election by the Church, with calling upon the name of the Lord, and in that order which the Word of God teaches. Therefore every one must take heed not to intrude himself by improper means, but is bound to wait till it shall please God to call him; that he may have testimony of his calling, and be certain and assured that it is of the Lord.

As for the ministers of God's Word, they have equally the same power and authority wheresoever they are, as they are all ministers of Christ, the only universal Bishop and the only Head of the Church.

Moreover, in order that this holy ordinance of God may not be violated or slighted, we say that every one ought to esteem the ministers of God's Word and the elders of the Church very highly for their work's sake, and be at peace with them without murmuring, strife, or contention, as much as possible.

XXXII. *The Order and Discipline of the Church.* In the meantime we believe, though it is useful and beneficial that those who are rulers of the Church institute and establish certain ordinances among themselves for maintaining the body of the Church, yet that they ought studiously to take care that they do not depart from those things which Christ, our only Master, has instituted. And therefore we reject all human inventions, and all laws which man would introduce into the worship of God, thereby to bind and compel the conscience in any manner whatever. Therefore we admit only of that which tends to nourish and preserve concord and unity, and to keep all men in obedience to God. For this purpose, excommunication or church discipline is requisite, with all that pertains to it, according to the Word of God.

XXXIII. *The Sacraments.* We believe that our gracious God, taking account of our weakness and infirmities, has ordained the sacraments, for us, thereby to seal unto us His promises, and to be pledges of the good will and grace of God towards us, and also to nourish and strengthen our faith; which He has joined to the Word of the gospel, the better to present to our senses both that which He declares to us by His Word and that which He works inwardly in our hearts, thereby confirming in us the salvation which He imparts to us. For they are visible signs and seals of an inward and invisible thing, by means whereof God works in us by the power of the Holy Spirit. Therefore the signs are not empty or meaningless, so as to deceive us. For Jesus Christ is the true object presented by them, without whom they would be of no moment.

Moreover, we are satisfied with the number of sacraments which Christ our Lord has instituted, which are two only, namely, the sacrament of baptism and the holy supper of our Lord Jesus Christ.

XXXIV. *Holy Baptism.* We believe and confess that Jesus Christ, who is the end of the law, has made an end, by the shedding of His blood, of all other sheddings of blood which men could or would make as a propitiation or satisfaction for sin; and that He, having abolished circumcision, which was done with blood, has instituted the sacrament of baptism instead thereof; by which we are received into the Church of God, and separated from all other people and strange religions, that we may wholly belong to Him whose mark and ensign we bear; and which serves as a testimony to us that He will forever be our gracious God and Father.

Therefore He has commanded all those who are His to be baptized with pure water, *into the name of the Father and of the Son and of the Holy Spirit,* thereby signifying to us, that as water washes away the filth of the body when poured upon it, and is seen on the body of the baptized when sprinkled upon him, so does the blood of Christ by the power of the Holy Spirit internally sprinkle the soul, cleanse it from its sins, and regenerate us from children of wrath unto children of God. Not that this is effected by the external water, but by the sprinkling of the precious blood of the Son of God; who is our Red Sea, through which we must pass to escape the tyranny of Pharaoh, that is, the devil, and to enter into the spiritual land of Canaan.

The ministers, therefore, on their part administer the sacrament and that which is visible, but our Lord gives that which is signified by the sacrament, namely, the gifts and invisible grace; washing, cleansing, and purging our souls of all filth and unrighteousness; renewing our hearts and filling them with all comfort; giving unto us a true assurance of His fatherly goodness; putting on us the new man, and putting off the old man with all his deeds.

We believe, therefore, that every man who is earnestly studious of obtaining life eternal ought to be baptized but once with this only baptism, without ever repeating the same, since we cannot be born twice. Neither does this baptism avail us only at the time when the water is poured upon us and received by us, but also through the whole course of our life.

Therefore we detest the error of the Anabaptists, who are not content with the one only baptism they have once received, and moreover condemn the baptism of the infants of believers, who we believe ought to be baptized and sealed with the sign of the covenant, as the children in Israel formerly were circumcised upon the same promises which are made unto our children. And indeed Christ shed His blood no less for the washing of the children of believers than for adult persons; and therefore they ought to receive the sign and sacrament of that which Christ has done for them; as the Lord commanded in the law that they should be made partakers of the sacrament of Christ's suffering and death shortly after they were born, by offering for them a lamb, which was a sacrament of Jesus Christ. Moreover, what circumcision was to the Jews, baptism is to our children. And for this reason St. Paul calls baptism the *circumcision of Christ*.

XXXV. *The Holy Supper of Our Lord Jesus Christ.* We believe and confess that our Savior Jesus Christ did ordain and institute the sacrament of the holy supper to nourish and support those whom He has already regenerated and incorporated into His family, which is His Church.

Now those who are regenerated have in them a twofold life, the one bodily and temporal, which they have from the first birth, and is common to all men; the other spiritual and heavenly, which is given them in their second birth, which is effected by the Word of the gospel, in the communion of the body of Christ; and this life is not common, but is peculiar to God's elect. In like manner God has given us, for the support of the bodily and earthly life, earthly and common bread, which is subservient thereto and is common to all men, even as life itself. But for the support of the spiritual and heavenly life which believers have He has sent a living bread, which descended from heaven, namely, Jesus Christ, who nourishes and strengthens the spiritual life of believers when they eat Him, that is to say, when they appropriate and receive Him by faith in the spirit.

In order that He might represent unto us this spiritual and heavenly bread, Christ has instituted an earthly and visible bread as a sacrament of His body, and wine as a sacrament of His blood, to testify by them unto us that, as certainly as we receive and hold this sacrament in our hands and eat and drink the same with our mouths, by which our life is afterwards nourished, we also do as certainly receive by faith (which is the hand and mouth of our soul) the true body and blood of Christ our only Savior in our souls, for the support of our spiritual life.

Now, as it is certain and beyond all doubt that Jesus Christ has not enjoined to us the use of His sacraments in vain, so He works in us all that He represents to us by these holy signs, though the manner surpasses our understanding and cannot be comprehended by us, as the operations of the Holy Spirit are hidden and incomprehensible. In the meantime we err not when we say that what is eaten and drunk by us is the proper and natural body and the proper blood of Christ. But the manner of our partaking of the same is not by the mouth, but by the spirit through faith. Thus, then, though Christ always sits at the right hand of His Father in the heavens, yet does He not therefore cease to make us partakers of Himself by faith. This feast is a spiritual table, at which Christ communicates Himself with all His benefits to us, and gives us there to enjoy both Himself and the merits of His sufferings and death: nourishing, strengthening, and comforting our poor comfortless souls by the eating of His flesh, quickening and refreshing them by the drink of His blood.

Further, though the sacraments are connected with the thing signified, nevertheless both are not received by all men. The ungodly indeed receives the sacrament to his condemnation, but he does not receive the truth of the sacrament, even as Judas and Simon the sorcerer both indeed received the sacrament but not Christ who was signified by it, of whom believers only are made partakers.

Lastly, we receive this holy sacrament in the assembly of the people of God, with humility and reverence, keeping up among us a holy remembrance of the death of Christ our Savior, with thanksgiving, making there confession of our faith and of the Christian religion. Therefore no one ought to come to this table without having previously rightly examined himself, lest by eating of this bread and drinking of this cup he eat and drink judgment to himself. In a word, we are moved by the use of this holy sacrament to a fervent love towards God and our neighbor.

Therefore we reject all mixtures and damnable inventions which men have added unto and blended with the sacraments, as profanations of them; and affirm that we ought to rest satisfied with the ordinance which Christ and His apostles have taught us, and that we must speak of them in the same manner as they have spoken.

XXXVI. *The Magistracy (Civil Government)*. We believe that our gracious God, because of the depravity of mankind, has appointed kings, princes, and magistrates; willing that the world should be governed by certain laws and policies; to the end that the dissoluteness of men might be restrained, and all things carried on among them with good order and decency. For this purpose He has invested the magistracy with *the sword for the punishment of evil-doers and for the protection of them that do well.*

Their office is not only to have regard unto and watch for the welfare of the civil state, but also to protect the sacred ministry,* that the kingdom of Christ may thus be promoted. They must therefore countenance the preaching of the Word of the gospel everywhere, that God may be honored and worshipped by every one, as He commands in His Word.

Moreover, it is the bounden duty of every one, of whatever state, quality, or condition he may be, to subject himself to the magistrates; to pay tribute, to show due honor and respect to them, and to obey them in all things which are not repugnant to the Word of God; to supplicate for them in their prayers that God may rule and guide them in all their ways, and *that we may lead a tranquil and quiet life in all godliness and gravity.*

Wherefore we detest the Anabaptists and other seditious people, and in general all those who reject the higher powers and magistrates and would subvert justice, introduce community of goods, and confound that decency and good order which God has established among men.

XXXVII. *The Last Judgment.* Finally, we believe, according to the Word of God, when the time appointed by the Lord (which is unknown to all creatures) is come and the number of the elect complete, that our Lord Jesus Christ will come from heaven, corporally and visibly, as He ascended, with great glory and majesty to declare Himself Judge of the living and the dead, burning this old world with fire and flame to cleanse it.

Then all men will personally appear before this great Judge, both men and women and children, that have been from the beginning of the world to the end thereof, being summoned by *the voice of the*

---

* In the original text this sentence read as follows: "Their office is not only to have regard unto and watch for the welfare of the civil state, but also that they protect the sacred ministry, and thus may remove and prevent all idolatry and false worship, that the kingdom of antichrist may be destroyed and the kingdom of Christ promoted." The Synod of 1910, recognizing the unbiblical teaching, contained in this sentence, concerning freedom of religion and concerning the duty of the State to suppress false religion, saw fit to add an explanatory footnote. The Synod of 1938, agreeing with the Synod of 1910 as to the unbiblical character of the teaching referred to, but recognizing a conflict between the objectionable clauses in the Article and its footnote, decided to eliminate the footnote and to make the change in the text of the Article which appears above, corresponding to the change adopted in 1905 by the General Synod of the *Gereformeerde Kerken in Nederland.* (See *Acts of Synod, 1910,* pp. 9, 104-105; also *Acts of Synod, 1938,* p. 17.)

archangel, and by the sound of the trump of God. For all the dead shall be raised out of the earth, and their souls joined and united with their proper bodies in which they formerly lived. As for those who shall then be living, they shall not die as the others, but be changed in the twinkling of an eye, and from corruptible become incorruptible. Then *the books* (that is to say, the consciences) *shall be opened, and the dead judged* according to what they shall have done in this world, whether it be good or evil. Nay, all men *shall give account of every idle word they have spoken,* which the world only counts amusement and jest; and then the secrets and hypocrisy of men shall be disclosed and laid open before all.

And therefore the consideration of this judgment is justly terrible and dreadful to the wicked and ungodly, but most desirable and comfortable to the righteous and elect; because then their full deliverance shall be perfected, and there they shall receive the fruits of their labor and trouble which they have borne. Their innocence shall be known to all, and they shall see the terrible vengeance which God shall execute on the wicked, who most cruelly persecuted, oppressed, and tormented them in this world, and who shall be convicted by the testimony of their own consciences, and shall become immortal, but only to be tormented in *the eternal fire which is prepared for the devil and his angels.*

But on the contrary, the faithful and elect shall be crowned with glory and honor; and the Son of God will confess their names before God His Father and His elect angels; all tears shall be wiped from their eyes; and their cause which is now condemned by many judges and magistrates as heretical and impious will then be known to be the cause of the Son of God. And for a gracious reward, the Lord will cause them to possess such a glory as never entered into the heart of man to conceive.

Therefore we expect that great day will be a most ardent desire, to the end that we may fully enjoy the promises of God in Christ Jesus our Lord. AMEN

Amen, come, Lord Jesus.—Rev. 22:20.

CANONS OF DORT

The Canons of Dort (or Dortrecht) are a product of the assembly of the Dutch Reformed Church, convened at Dort by the States-General to deal with the Arminian controversy. Arminius was a Dutch Calvinist who reacted against the deterministic logic of Calvinism.

Although primarily a national gathering of Dutch theologians, many foreign delegates from Switzerland, the Palatinate, Scotland, England and elsewhere took part. The Synod, which met in one hundred and fifty-four sessions, sat from November 13, 1618, to May 9, 1619, though the Arminians (Remonstrants) were not introduced until December 6, 1618.

John Bogerman, a strict Calvinist, was elected president. Supported by Prince Maurice of Orange, the Synod was set against the Arminians from the start, and its decisions were never in doubt.

Five sets of articles were passed on April 23, 1619, namely 1) unconditional election, 2) a limited atonement, 3) the total depravity of man, 4) the irresistibility of grace, and 5) the final perseverance of the saints. At a final session on May 9, 1619, the Synod drew up ninety-three canonical rules and confirmed the authority of the *Belgic Confession* and the *Heidelberg Catechism*.

This victory for Calvinist principles led to some two hundred Arminian clergy being deprived of their ministries and the eminent jurist, Hugo Grotius (1583-1645), being sentenced by the States-General to perpetual imprisonment. He escaped two years later when his wife managed to have him carried out of prison in a box of books. The same Synod led to some two hundred Arminian clergy being deprived of their positions and Johan van Oldenbarneveldt (1547-1619) being sentenced to capital punishment on a false charge of high treason. Oldenbarneveldt was the Dutch statesman whose support of William the Silent helped unify the people in their struggle against Spain.

As a rule the Reformed churches originating in continental Europe subscribe to the Confession of Faith and the Canons of Dort, without modification from their version in the seventeenth century. Presbyterian bodies treat the Dortrecht statements with reverence but do not generally include them among representative church creeds.

FIRST HEAD OF DOCTRINE.
Of Divine Predestination.

I. As all men have sinned in Adam, lie under the curse, and are obnoxious to eternal death, God would have done no injustice by leaving them all to perish, and delivering them over to condemnation on account of sin, according to the words of the Apostle, "that every mouth may be stopped, and all the world may become guilty before God:" "for all have sinned, and come short of the glory of God:" and "for the wages of sin is death."

II. But "in this the love of God was manifested, that he sent his only begotten Son into the world," "that whosoever believeth on him should not perish, but have everlasting life."

III. And that men may be brought to believe, God mercifully sends the messengers of these most joyful tidings, to whom he will, and at what time he pleaseth; by whose ministry men are called to repentance and faith in Christ crucified. "How then shall they call on him, in whom they have not believed? And how shall they believe in him of whom they have not heard? And how shall they hear without a preacher? And how shall they preach except they be sent?"

IV. The wrath of God abideth upon those who believe not this Gospel. But such as receive it, and embrace Jesus the Saviour by a true and living faith, are by him delivered from the wrath of God and from destruction, and have the gift of eternal life conferred upon them.

V. The cause or guilt of this unbelief as well as of all other sins, is no wise in God but in man himself; whereas faith in Jesus Christ, and salvation through him is the free gift of God, as it is written, "By grace ye are saved through faith, and that not of yourselves; it is the gift of God." "And unto you it is given on the behalf of Christ, not only to believe in him," &c. Phil. 1:29.

VI. That some receive the gift of faith from God, and others do not receive it proceeds from God's eternal decree, "For known unto God are all his works from the beginning of the world." Acts 15:18. Eph. 1:11. According to which decree, he graciously softens the hearts of the elect, however obstinate, and inclines them to believe; while he leaves the nonelect in his just judgment to their own wickedness and obduracy. And herein is especially displayed the profound, the merciful, and at the same time the righteous discrimination between men, equally involved in ruin; or that decree of election and reprobation, revealed in the word of God, which through men of perverse, impure and unstable minds, wrest it to their own destruction, yet to holy and pious souls affords unspeakable consolation.

VII. Election is the unchangeable purpose of God, whereby, before the foundation of the world, he hath, out of mere grace, according to the sovereign good pleasure of his own will, chosen, from the whole human race, which had fallen through their own fault, from their primitive state of rectitude, into sin and destruction, a certain number of persons to redemption in Christ, whom he from eternity appointed the Mediator and head of the elect, and the foundation of Salvation.

This elect number, though by nature neither better nor more deserving than others, but with them involved in one common misery, God hath decreed to give to Christ, to be saved by him, and effectually to call and draw them to his communion by his Word and Spirit, to bestow upon them true faith, justification and sanctification; and having powerfully preserved them in the fellowship of his Son, finally, to glorify them for the demonstration of his mercy, and for the praise of the riches of his glorious grace: as it is written, "According as he hath chosen us in him, before the foundation of the world, that we should be holy, and without blame before him in love; having predestinated us unto the adoption of children by Jesus Christ to himself, according to the good pleasure of his will, to the praise of the glory of his grace, wherein he hath made us accepted in the Beloved." And elsewhere, "Whom he did predestinate, them he also called; and whom he called, them he also justified; and whom he justified, them he also glorified." Rom. 8:20.

VIII. There are not various decrees of election, but one and the same decree respecting all those who shall be saved both under the Old and New Testament; since the Scripture declares the good pleasure, purpose and counsel of the divine will to be one, according to which he hath chosen us from eternity, both to grace and to glory, to salvation and the way of salvation, which he hath ordained that we should walk therein.

IX. This election was not founded upon foreseen faith, and the obedience of faith, holiness, or any other good quality or disposition in man, as the prerequisite, cause or condition on which it depended; but men chosen to faith and to the obedience of faith, holiness, etc. Therefore, election is the fountain of every saving good; from which proceed faith, holiness, and the other gifts of salvation, and finally eternal life itself, as its fruits and effects, according to that of the Apostle. "He hath chosen us (not because we were, but) that we should be holy and without blame before him in love." Eph. 1:4.

X. The good pleasure of God is the sole cause of this gracious election: which doth not consist herein, that God foreseeing all possible qualities of human actions, elected certain of these as a condition of salvation, but that he was pleased out of the common mass of sinners to adopt some certain persons as a peculiar people to himself, as it is written, "For the children being not yet born, neither having done any good or evil, etc., it was said (namely to Rebecca) the elder shall serve the younger; as it is written, Jacob have I loved, but Esau have I hated." "And as many as were ordained to eternal life believed." Acts 13:48.

XI. And as God himself is most wise, unchangeable, omniscient and omnipotent, so the election made by him can neither be interrupted nor changed, recalled nor annulled; neither can the elect be cast away, nor their number diminished.

XII. The elect, in due time, though in various degrees and in different measures, attain the assurance of this their eternal and unchangeable election, not by inquisitively prying into the secret and deep things of God; but by observing in themselves with a spiritual joy and holy pleasure, the infallible fruits of election pointed out in the Word of God; such as a true faith in Christ, filial fear, a godly sorrow for sin, a hungering and thirsting after righteousness, etc.

XIII. The sense and certainty of this election afford to the children of God additional matter for daily humiliation before him, for adoring the depth of his mercies, and rendering grateful returns of ardent love to him who first manifested so great love towards them. The consideration of this doctrine of election is so far from encouraging remissness in the observance of the divine commands, or from sinking men into carnal security, that these, in the just judgment of God, are the usual effects of rash presumption or of idle and wanton trifling with the grace of election, in those who refuse to walk in the ways of the elect.

XIV. As the doctrine of divine election by the most wise counsel of God, was declared by the prophets, by Christ himself, and by the apostles, and is clearly revealed in the Scriptures both of the Old and New Testament; so it is still to be published in due time and place in the Church of God, for which it was peculiarly designed, provided it be done with reverence, in the spirit of discretion and piety, for the glory of God's most holy name, and for enlivening and comforting his people, without vainly attempting to investigate the secret ways of the Most High.

XV. What peculiarly tends to illustrate and recommend to us the eternal and unmerited grace of election, is the express testimony of sacred Scripture, that not all, but some only, are elected, while others are passed by in the eternal decree; whom God, out of his sovereign, most just, irreprehensible and unchangeable good pleasure, hath decreed to leave in the common misery into which they have wilfully plunged themselves, and not to bestow upon them saving faith and the grace of conversion; but permitting them in his just judgment to follow their own way, at last for the declaration of his justice, to condemn and punish them for ever, not only on account of their unbelief, but also for all their other sins. And this is the decree of reprobation which by no means makes God the author of sin, (the very thought of which is blasphemy), but declares him to be an awful, irreprehensible, and righteous judge and avenger.

XVI. Those who do not yet experience a lively faith in Christ, an assured confidence of soul, peace of conscience, an earnest endeavour after filial obedience, and glorying in God through Christ, efficaciously wrought in them, and do nevertheless persist in the use of the means which God hath appointed for working these graces in us, ought not to be alarmed at the mention of reprobation, nor to rank themselves among the reprobate, but diligently to persevere in the use of means, and with ardent desires devoutly and humbly to wait for a season of richer grace. Much less cause have they to be terrified by the doctrine of reprobation, who, though they seriously desire to be turned to God, to please him only, and to be delivered from the body of death, cannot yet reach that measure of holiness and faith to which they aspire; since a merciful God has promised that he will not quench the smoking flax, nor break the bruised reed. But this doctrine is justly terrible to those, who, regardless of God, and of the Saviour Jesus Christ, have wholly given themselves up to the cares of the world, and the pleasures of the flesh, so long as they are not seriously converted to God.

XVII. Since we are to judge of the will of God, from his Word, which testifies that the children of believers are holy, not by nature, but in virtue of the covenant of grace, in which they together with the parents, are comprehended, godly parents have no reason to doubt of the election and salvation of their children whom it pleaseth God to call out of this life in their infancy.

XVIII. To those who murmur at the free grace of election, and just severity of reprobation, we answer with the Apostle: "Nay, but, O man, who art thou that repliest against God?" (Rom. 9:20); and quote the language of our Saviour, "Is it not lawful for me to do what I will with mine own?" And therefore with holy adoration of these mysteries, we exclaim in the words of the apostle: "O the depth of the riches both of the wisdom and knowledge of God! how unsearchable are his judgments, and his ways past finding out! For who hath known the mind of the Lord, or who hath been his counsellor? or who hath first given to him, and it shall be recompensed unto him again? For of him, and through him, and to him are all things: to whom be glory for ever. Amen."

SECOND HEAD OF DOCTRINE.
Of the death of Christ, and the redemption of men thereby.

I. God is not only supremely merciful, but also supremely just. And his justice requires (as he hath revealed himself in his Word) that our sins committed against his infinite majesty should be punished, not only with temporal, but with eternal punishments, both in body and soul; which we cannot escape, unless satisfaction be made to the justice of God.

II. Since therefore we are unable to make that satisfaction in our own persons, or to deliver ourselves from the wrath of God, he hath been pleased of his infinite mercy to give his only begotten Son, for our surety, who was made sin, and became a curse for us and in our stead, that he might make satisfaction to divine justice on our behalf.

III. The death of the Son of God is the only and most perfect sacrifice and satisfaction for sin; is of infinite worth and value, abundantly sufficient to expiate the sins of the whole world.

IV. This death derives its infinite value and dignity from these considerations; because the person who submitted to it was not only really man, and perfectly holy, but also the only begotten Son of God, of the same eternal and infinite essence with the Father and Holy Spirit, which qualifications were necessary to constitute him a Saviour for us; and because it was attended with a sense of the wrath and curse of God due to us for sin.

V. Moreover the promise of the Gospel is, that whosoever believeth in Christ crucified, shall not perish, but have everlasting life. This promise, together with the command to repent and believe, ought to be declared and published to all nations, and to all persons promiscuously and without distinction, to whom God out of his good pleasure sends the Gospel.

VI. And, whereas many who are called by the Gospel, do not repent nor believe in Christ, but perish in unbelief; this is not owing to any defect or insufficiency in the sacrifice offered by Christ upon the cross, but is wholly to be imputed to themselves.

VII. But as many as truly believe, and are delivered and saved from sin and destruction through the death of Christ, are indebted for this benefit solely to the grace of God given them in Christ from everlasting, and not to any merit of their own.

VIII. For this was the sovereign counsel and most gracious will and purpose of God the Father, that the quickening and saving efficacy of the most precious death of his Son, should extend to all the elect, for bestowing upon them alone the gift of justifying faith, thereby to bring them infallibly to salvation: that is, it was the will of God, that Christ by the blood of the cross, whereby he confirmed the new covenant, should effectually redeem out of every people, tribe, nation, and language, all those, and those only, who were from eternity chosen to salvation, and given to him by the Father; that he should confer upon them faith, which together with all the other saving gifts of the Holy Spirit, he purchased for them by his death; should purge them from all sin, both original and actual, whether committed before or after believing; and having faithfully preserved them even to the end, should at last bring them free from every spot and blemish to the enjoyment of glory in his own presence for ever.

IX. This purpose proceeding from everlasting love towards the elect, has from the beginning of the world to this day been powerfully accomplished, and will henceforward still continue to be accomplished, notwithstanding all the ineffectual opposition of the gates of hell: so that the elect in due time may be gathered together into one, and that there never may be wanting a Church composed of believers, the foundation of which is laid in the blood of Christ, which may steadfastly love and faithfully serve him as their Saviour, who as a bridegroom for his bride, laid down his life for them upon the cross; and which may celebrate his praises here and through all eternity.

THIRD AND FOURTH HEADS OF DOCTRINE.
Of the corruption of man,
his conversion to God, and the manner thereof.

I. Man was originally formed after the image of God. His understanding was adorned with a true and saving knowledge of his Creator, and of spiritual things; his heart and will were upright; all his affections pure; and the whole Man was holy: but revolting from God by the instigation of the devil, and abusing the freedom of his own will, he forfeited these excellent gifts: and on the contrary entailed on himself blindness of mind, horrible darkness, vanity and perverseness of judgment; became wicked, rebellious, and obdurate in heart and will, and impure in his affections.

II. Man after the fall begat children in his own likeness. A corrupt stock produced a corrupt offspring. Hence all the posterity of Adam, Christ only excepted, have derived corruption from their original parent, not by imitation, as the Pelagians of old asserted, but by the propagation of a vicious nature.

III. Therefore all men are conceived in sin, and are by nature children of wrath, incapable of any saving good, prone to evil, dead in sin, and in bondage thereto; and without the regenerating grace of the Holy Spirit, they are neither able nor willing to return to God, to reform the depravity of their nature, nor to dispose themselves to reformation.

IV. There remain, however, in man since the fall, the glimmerings of natural light, whereby he retains some knowledge of God, of natural things, and of the difference between good and evil, and discovers some regard for virtue, good order in society, and for maintaining an orderly external deportment. But so far is this light of nature from being sufficient to bring him to a saving knowledge of God, and to true conversion, that he is incapable of using it aright even in things natural and civil. Nay farther, this light, such as it is, man in various ways renders wholly polluted, and holds it in unrighteousness, by doing which he becomes inexcusable before God.

V. In the same light are we to consider the law of the decalogue, delivered by God to his peculiar people the Jews, by the hands of Moses. For though it discovers the greatness of sin, and more and more convinces man thereof, yet as it neither points out a remedy, nor imparts strength to extricate him from misery, and thus being weak through the flesh, leaves the transgressor under the curse, man cannot by this law obtain saving grace.

VI. What therefore neither the light of nature nor the law could do, that God performs by the operation of his Holy Spirit through the word or ministry of reconciliation: which is the glad tidings concerning the Messiah, by means whereof it hath pleased God to save such as believe, as well under the Old, as under the New Testament.

VII. This mystery of his will, God discovered to but a small number under the Old Testament; under the New, he reveals himself to many, without any distinction of people. The cause of this dispensation is not to be ascribed to the superior worth of one nation above another, nor to their making a better use of the light of nature, but results wholly from the sovereign good pleasure and unmerited love of God. Hence they, to whom so great and so gracious a blessing is communicated, above their desert, or rather notwithstanding their demerits, are bound to acknowledge it with humble and grateful hearts, and with the apostle to adore, not curiously to pry into the severity and justice of God's judgments displayed in others, to whom this grace is not given.

VIII. As many as are called by the Gospel, are unfeignedly called; for God hath most earnestly and truly declared in his word, what will be acceptable to him; namely, that all who are called, should comply with the invitation. He moreover seriously promises eternal life and rest, to as many as shall come to him, and believe in him.

IX. It is not the fault of the Gospel, nor of Christ offered therein, nor of God, who calls men by the Gospel, and confers upon them various gifts, that those who are called by the ministry of the Word, refuse to come and be converted. The fault lies in themselves; some of whom when called, regardless of their danger, reject the word of life; others, though they receive it, suffer it not to make a lasting impression on their heart; therefore, their joy, arising only from a temporary faith, soon vanishes, and they fall away; while others choke the seed of the word by perplexing cares, and the pleasures of this world, and produce no fruit. This our Saviour teaches in the parable of the sower. Matt. 13.

X. But that others who are called by the Gospel, obey the call and are converted, is not to be ascribed to the proper exercise of free will, whereby one distinguishes himself above others equally furnished with grace sufficient for faith and conversion, as the proud heresy of Pelagius maintains; but it must be wholly to God, who, as he hath chosen his own from eternity in Christ, so he confers upon them faith and repentance, rescues them from the power of darkness, and translates them into the kingdom of his own Son, that they may show forth the praises of him, who hath called them out of darkness into his marvellous light; and may glory not in themselves, but in the Lord, according to the testimony of the apostles in various places.

XI. But when God accomplishes his good pleasure in the elect, or works in them true conversion, he not only causes the Gospel to be externally preached to them, and powerfully illuminates their minds by his Holy Spirit, that they may rightly understand and discern the things of the Spirit of God; but by the efficacy of the same regenerating Spirit, he pervades the inmost recesses of the man; he opens the closed, and softens the hardened heart, and circumcises that which was uncircumcised; infuses new qualities into the will, which, though heretofore dead, he quickens; from being evil, disobedient, and refractory, he renders it good, obedient and pliable; actuates and strengthens it, that like a good tree, it may bring forth the fruits of good actions.

XII. And this is the regeneration so highly celebrated in Scripture and denominated a new creation; a resurrection from the dead: a making alive, which God works in us without our aid. But this is no wise effected merely by the external preaching of the Gospel, by moral suasion, or such a mode of operation, that after God has performed his part, it still remains in the power of man to be regenerated or not, to be converted or to continue unconverted; but it is evidently a supernatural work, most powerful, and at the same time most delightful, astonishing, mysterious and ineffable; not inferior in efficacy to creation or the resurrection from the dead, as the Scripture inspired by the author of this work declares; so that all in whose hearts God works in this marvellous manner, are certainly, infallibly and effectually regenerated, and do actually believe. Whereupon the will thus renewed, is not only actuated and influenced by God, but in consequence of this influence, becomes itself active. Wherefore also, man is himself rightly said to believe and repent, by virtue of that grace received.

XIII. The manner of this operation cannot be fully comprehended by believers in this life. Notwithstanding which, they rest satisfied with knowing and experiencing, that by this grace of God they are enabled to believe with the heart, and to love their Saviour.

XIV. Faith is therefore to be considered as the gift of God, not on account of its being offered by God to man, to be accepted or rejected at his pleasure; but because it is in reality conferred, breathed, and infused into him; nor even because God bestows the power or ability to believe, and then expects that man should, by the exercise of his own free will, consent to the terms of salvation, and actually believe in Christ; but because he who works in man both to will and to do, and indeed all things in all, produces both the will to believe and the act of believing also.

XV. God is under no obligation to confer this grace upon any; for how can he be indebted to man, who had no previous gift to bestow as a foundation for such recompense? Nay, who has nothing of his own but sin and falsehood? He therefore who becomes the subject of this grace, owes eternal gratitude to God, and gives him thanks for ever. Whoever is not made partaker thereof, is either altogether regardless of these spiritual gifts and satisfied with his own condition; or, is in no apprehension of danger, and vainly boasts the possession of that which he has not. With respect to those, who make an external profession of faith, and live regular lives, we are bound after the example of the Apostle to judge and speak of them in the most favourable manner; for the secret recesses of the heart are unknown to us. And as to others, who have not yet been called, it is our duty to pray for them to God, who calleth those things which be not, as though they were. But we are in no wise to conduct ourselves towards them with haughtiness, as if we had made ourselves to differ.

XVI. But as man by the fall did not cease to be a creature endowed with understanding and will, nor did sin, which pervaded the whole race of mankind, deprive him of the human nature, but brought upon him depravity, and spiritual death; so also this grace of regeneration, does not treat men as senseless stocks and blocks, nor takes away their will and its properties, neither does violence thereto; but spiritually quickens, heals, corrects, and at the same time sweetly and powerfully bends it: that where carnal rebellion and resistance formerly prevailed, a ready and sincere spiritual obedience begins to reign; in which the true and spiritual restoration and freedom of our will consist. Wherefore, unless the admirable author of every good work, wrought in us, man could have no hope of recovering from his fall by his own free will, by the abuse of which, in a state of innocence, he plunged himself into ruin.

XVII. As the almighty operation of God, whereby he prolongs and supports this our natural life, does not exclude, but requires the use of means, by which God of his infinite mercy and goodness hath chosen to exert his influence; so also the beforementioned supernatural operation of God, by which we are regenerated, in no wise excludes or subverts the use of the Gospel, which the most wise God has ordained to be the seed of regeneration, and food of the soul. Wherefore as the apostles, and the teachers who succeeded them, piously instructed the people concerning this grace of God, to his glory, and the abasement of all pride, and in the mean time, however, neglected not to keep them by the sacred precepts of the Gospel in the exercise of the Word, the sacraments and discipline: so even to this day, be it far from either instructors or instructed to presume to tempt God in the Church, by separating what he of his good pleasure hath most intimately joined together. For grace is conferred by means of admonitions; and the more readily we perform our duty, the more eminent usually is this blessing of God working in us, and the more directly is his work advanced; to whom alone all the glory both of means, and their saving fruit and efficacy, is for ever due. *Amen.*

FIFTH HEAD OF DOCTRINE.
Of the Perseverance of the Saints.

I. Whom God calls, according to his purpose, to the communion of his Son our Lord Jesus Christ, and regenerates by the Holy Spirit, he delivers also from the dominion and slavery of sin in this life; though not altogether from the body of sin and from the infirmities of the flesh, so long as they continue in this world.

II. Hence spring daily sins of infirmity, and hence spots adhere to the best works of the saints; which furnish them with constant matter for humiliation before God and flying for refuge to Christ crucified; for mortifying the flesh more and more by the spirit of prayer and by holy exercises of piety; and for pressing forward to the goal of perfection, till being at length delivered from this body of death, they are brought to reign with the Lamb of God in heaven.

III. By reason of these remains of indwelling sin, and the temptations of sin and of the world, those who are converted could not persevere in a state of grace, if left to their own strength. But God is faithful, who having conferred grace, mercifully confirms and powerfully preserves them therein, even to the end.

IV. Although the weakness of the flesh cannot prevail against the power of God, who confirms and preserves true believers in a state of grace, yet converts are not always so influenced and actuated by the Spirit of God, as not in some particular instances, sinfully to deviate from the guidance of divine grace, so as to be seduced by, and to comply with the lusts of the flesh; they must therefore be constant in watching and prayer, that they be not led into temptation. When these are neglected, they are not only liable to be drawn into great and heinous sins, by Satan, the world and the flesh, but sometimes by the righteous permission of God actually fall into these evils. This, the lamentable fall of David, Peter, and other saints described in Holy Scriptures, demonstrates.

V. By such enormous sins, however, they very highly offend God, incur a deadly guilt, grieve the Holy Spirit, interrupt the exercise of faith, very grievously wound their consciences, and sometimes lose the sense of God's favour, for a time, until on their returning into the right way by serious repentance, the light of God's fatherly countenance again shines upon them.

VI. But God, who is rich in mercy, according to his unchangeable purpose of election, does not wholly withdraw the Holy Spirit from his own people, even in their melancholy falls; nor suffer them to proceed so far as to lose the grace of adoption, and forfeit the state of justification, or to commit the sin unto death; nor does he permit them to be totally deserted, and to plunge themselves into everlasting destruction.

VII. For in the first place, in these falls he preserves in them the incorruptible seed of regeneration from perishing or being totally lost; and again, by his Word and Spirit, he certainly and effectually renews them to repentance, to a sincere and godly sorrow for their sins, that they may seek and obtain remission in the blood of the Mediator, may again experience the favour of a reconciled God, through faith adore his mercies, and henceforward more diligently work out their own salvation with fear and trembling.

VIII. Thus, it is not in consequence of their own merits or strength, but of God's free mercy, that they do not totally fall from faith and grace, nor continue and perish finally in their backslidings; which, with respect to themselves is not only possible, but would undoubtedly happen; but with respect to God, it is utterly impossible, since his counsel cannot be changed, nor his promise fail, neither can the call according to his purpose be revoked, nor the merit, intercession and preservation of Christ be rendered ineffectual, nor the sealing of the Holy Spirit be frustrated or obliterated.

IX. Of this preservation of the elect to salvation, and of their perseverance in the faith, true believers for themselves may and do obtain assurance according to the measure of their faith, whereby they arrive at the certain persuasion, that they ever will continue true and living members of the Church; and that they experience forgiveness of sins, and will at last inherit eternal life.

X. This assurance, however, is not produced by any peculiar revelation contrary to, or independent of the Word of God; but springs from faith in God's promises, which he has most abundantly revealed in his Word for our comfort; from the testimony of the Holy Spirit, witnessing with our spirit, that we are children and heirs of God (Rom. 8:16); and lastly, from a serious and holy desire to preserve a good conscience, and to perform good works. And if the elect of God were deprived of this solid comfort, that they shall finally obtain the victory; and of this infallible pledge or earnest of eternal glory, they would be of all men the most miserable.

XI. The Scripture moreover testifies, that believers in this life have to struggle with various carnal doubts, and that under grievous temptations they are not always sensible of this full assurance of faith, and certainty of persevering. But God, who is the Father of all consolation, does not suffer them to be tempted above that they are able; but will with the temptation also make a way to escape, that they may be able to bear it; (1 Cor. 10:13): and by the Holy Spirit again inspires them with the comfortable assurance of persevering.

XII. This certainty of perseverance, however, is so far from exciting in believers a spirit of pride, or of rendering them carnally secure, that on the contrary, it is the real source of humility, filial reverence, true piety, patience in every tribulation, fervent prayers, constancy in suffering, and in confessing the truth, and of solid rejoicing in God: so that the consideration of this benefit should serve as an incentive to the serious and constant practice of gratitude and good works, as appears from the testimonies of Scripture and the examples of the saints.

XIII. Neither does renewed confidence of persevering produce licentiousness or a disregard to piety, in those who are recovered from backsliding: but it renders them much more careful and solicitous to continue in the ways of the Lord, which he hath ordained, that they who walk therein may maintain an assurance of persevering; lest by abusing his Fatherly kindness, God should turn away his gracious countenance from them, to behold which is to the godly dearer than life; the withdrawing whereof is more bitter than death; and they in consequence hereof should fall into more grievous torments of conscience.

XIV. And as it hath pleased God, by the preaching of the Gospel, to begin this work of grace in us, so he preserves, continues, and perfects it by the hearing and reading of his Word, by meditation thereon, and by the exhortations, threatenings, and promises thereof, as well as by the use of the Sacraments.

XV. The carnal mind is unable to comprehend this doctrine of the perseverance of the saints, and the certainty thereof; which God hath most abundantly revealed in his Word, for the glory of his name, and the consolation of pious souls, and which he impresses upon the hearts of the faithful. Satan abhors it; the world ridicules it; the ignorant and hypocrite abuse, and heretics oppose it. But the spouse of Christ hath always most tenderly loved and constantly defended it, as an inestimable treasure: and God, against whom neither counsel nor strength can prevail, will dispose her to continue this conduct to the end. Now, TO THIS ONE GOD, FATHER, SON AND HOLY SPIRIT, BE HONOR AND GLORY, FOR EVER. *Amen.*

Conclusion

And this is the perspicuous, simple, and ingenuous declaration of the orthodox doctrine respecting the five articles which have been controverted in the Belgic churches; and the rejection of the errors, with which they have for some time been troubled. This doctrine, the Synod judges to be drawn from the Word of God, and to be agreeable to the confession of the Reformed Churches. Whence it clearly appears, that some, whom such conduct by no means became, have violated all truth, equity, and charity, in wishing to persuade the public:

"That the doctrine of the Reformed churches concerning predestination, and the points annexed to it, by its own genius and necessary tendency, leads off the minds of men from all piety and religion: that it is an opiate administered by the flesh and the devil; and the strong hold of Satan, where he lies in wait for all; and from which he wounds multitudes, and mortally strikes through many with the darts both of despair and security; that it makes God the author of sin, unjust, tyrannical, hypocritical: that it is nothing more than an interpolated Stoicism, Manicheism, Libertinism, Turkism: that it renders men carnally secure, since they are persuaded by it that nothing can hinder the salvation of the elect, let them live as they please; and therefore, that they may safely perpetrate every species of the most atrocious crimes; and that, if the reprobate should even perform truly all the works of the saints, their obedience would not in the least contribute to their salvation: that the same doctrine teaches, that God, by a mere arbitrary act of his will, without the least respect or view to any sin, has predestinated the greatest part of the world to eternal damnation; and has created them for this very purpose: that in the same manner in which the election is the fountain and cause of faith and good works, reprobation is the cause of unbelief and impiety: that many children of the faithful are torn, guiltless, from their mothers' breasts, and tyrannically plunged into hell; so that, neither baptism nor the prayers of the Church at their baptism, can at all profit them:" and many other things of the same kind, which the Reformed Churches not only do not acknowledge, but even detest with their whole soul.

Wherefore, this Synod of Dort, in the name of the Lord, conjures as many as piously call upon the name of our Saviour Jesus Christ, to judge of the faith of the Reformed Churches, not from the calumnies which, on every side, are heaped upon it; nor from the private expressions of a few among ancient and modern teachers, often dishonestly quoted, or corrupted and wrested to a meaning quite foreign to their intention; but from the public confessions of the churches themselves, and from this declaration of the orthodox doctrine, confirmed by the unanimous consent of all and each of the members of the whole Synod. Moreover, the Synod warns calumniators themselves, to consider the terrible judgment of God which awaits them, for bearing false witness against the confessions of so many churches; for distressing the consciences of the weak; and for labouring to render suspected the society of the truly faithful. Finally, this Synod exhorts all their brethren in the Gospel of Christ, to conduct themselves piously and religiously in handling this doctrine, both in the universities and churches; to direct it, as well in discourse as in writing, to the glory of the Divine Name, to holiness of life, and to the consolation of afflicted souls; to regulate, by the Scripture, according to the analogy of faith, not only their sentiments, but also their language; and, to abstain from all those phrases which exceed the limits necessary to be observed in ascertaining the genuine sense of the Holy Scriptures, and may furnish insolent sophists with a just pretext for violently assailing, or even vilifying, the doctrine of the Reformed Churches.

May Jesus Christ, the Son of God, who, seated at the Father's right hand, gives gifts to men, sanctify us in the truth; bring to the truth those who err; shut the mouths of the calumniators of sound doctrine, and endue the faithful ministers of his Word with the spirit of wisdom and discretion, that all their discourses may tend to the glory of God, and the edification of those who hear them. *Amen.*

That this is our faith and decision, we certify by subscribing our names.

Here follow the names, not only of PRESIDENT, ASSISTANT PRESIDENT, *and* SECRETARIES *of the Synod, and of the* PROFESSORS OF THEOLOGY *in the Dutch Churches; but all the* MEMBERS *who were deputed to the Synod, as the Representatives of their respective Churches; that is, of the Delegates from* Great Britain, the electoral Palatinate, Hessia, Switzerland, Wetteraw, the Republic and Church of Geneva, the Republic and Church of Bremen, the Republic and Church of Emden, the Duchy of Gelderland, and of Zutphen, South Holland, North Holland, Zealand, the province of Utrecht, Friesland, Transylvania, the State of Groningen and Omland, Drent, and the French Churches.

WESTMINSTER CONFESSION

The Westminster Confession is named after the Westminster Assembly which drafted it in 1646 under appointment by the Long Parliament to reform the English church. Originally the Assembly had been directed to revise the Thirty-nine Articles of the Church of England in a Puritan direction.

A bill passed on October 15, 1642, convening a body of divines having failed to receive the Royal Assent (Charles I), Parliament issued on June 12, 1643, an ordinance to the same effect. The conference consisted of one hundred and fifty-one nominated members—thirty lay assessors and one hundred and twenty-one divines. The ecclesiastics were carefully chosen from men of widely different views. They fell into four groups: Episcopalians, including four bishops; Presbyterians, who formed the largest group; a number of Independents with extraordinary influence because they were backed by Oliver Cromwell and the army; and a nucleus of Erastians who held without qualification that civil rulers held authority over the Church by divine right.

After the Assembly reached an impasse on the matter of uniformity of doctrine in England and Scotland, the Parliament under Scottish influence ordered a suspension of the revision on October 12, 1643, and the framing of "a Confession of Faith for the three Kingdoms (England, Scotland and Wales), according to the Solemn League and Covenant." This covenant was an agreement between the Scots and the English Parliament whose professed aims were the maintenance of the Presbyterian Church of Scotland, the reformation of the Church of England, the uniformity of the churches in the British Isles, the extirpation of popery and prelacy (episcopacy), the preservation of the rights of Parliaments and the liberties of the kingdoms, the defence of the King's just power, and the suppression of the malignants who sought to divide him from his people.

Under the impact of the Solemn League, the Westminster Assembly took a decidedly Presbyterian turn and set to work on the most ambitious revision of doctrine in the history of England. Its task occupied twenty-seven months of almost continuous labor and was completed on December 4, 1646. After revision it was finally approved by Parliament on June 20, 1648, but in the meantime the General Assembly at Edinburgh had ratified the Confession on August 27, 1647.

It is a masterpiece of thoroughness, expounding in thirty-three chapters all the leading articles of the Christian faith from the creation of the world to the last judgment. It taught emphatically the Calvinist doctrine of selective predestination, though it also recognized the freedom of the will (understood in Calvin's sense) and "the liberty or contingency of second causes" in the divine decrees.

No single document of Reformation faith has been more widely accepted by the adherents of John Calvin, although different groups required different degrees of adhesion to its principles. In 1690 the General Assembly in Scotland required "all entrants into the ministry and all other ministers and elders" to subscribe to it;

in 1694 each was required to declare it "the confession of his faith." American Congregationalist ministers were asked to accept the Westminster Confession with the words "freely and fully consent thereunto for the substance thereof." By the beginning of the eighteenth century, American Presbyterians could subscribe to the Confession with the qualified phrase "in all essential and necessary articles." Even the conservative United Presbyterian Church used the form, "an exhibition of the sense in which you understand the Holy Scriptures," which corresponds to the attitude of the more liberal United Presbyterian Church U.S.A.

As a rule, the Westminster Confession has remained intact over the centuries, with only minor changes made in the actual text. Perhaps the most drastic revision was made by the American General Synod in 1788, in the chapter on "The Civil Magistrate." More commonly modifications took the form of adopting declaratory statements. Thus the Free Church declared in 1846 that it regarded the Confession as "not favoring intolerance or persecution." Most recently the United Presbyterian Church U.S.A. adopted a concise profession of faith which some have interpreted as a repudiation of the Westminster Confession. Actually the Westminster document is accepted by the Church and forms part of its *Book of Confessions*. But the Confession of 1967 serves a declarative commentary to update the Westminster Confession.

CONFESSION OF FAITH.
CHAPTER I.
Of the Holy Scripture.

I. Although the light of nature, and the works of creation and providence, do so far manifest the goodness, wisdom, and power of God, as to leave men inexcusable; yet are they not sufficient to give that knowledge of God, and of his will, which is necessary unto salvation; therefore it pleased the Lord, at sundry times, and in divers manners, to reveal himself, and to declare that his will unto his Church; and afterwards, for the better preserving and propagating of the truth, and for the more sure establishment and comfort of the Church against the corruption of the flesh, and the malice of Satan and of the world, to commit the same wholly unto writing; which maketh the holy Scripture to be most necessary; those former ways of God's revealing his will unto his people being now ceased.

II. Under the name of holy Scripture, or the Word of God written, are now contained all the Books of the Old and New Testament, which are these:

Of the Old Testament.

Genesis.
Exodus.
Leviticus.
Numbers.
Deuteronomy.
Joshua.
Judges.
Ruth.
I. Samuel.
II. Samuel.
I. Kings.
II. Kings.
I. Chronicles.
II. Chronicles.
Ezra.
Nehemiah.
Esther.
Job.
Psalms.
Proverbs.

Ecclesiastes.
The Song of Songs.
Isaiah.
Jeremiah.
Lamentations.
Ezekiel.
Daniel.
Hosea.
Joel.
Amos.
Obadiah.
Jonah.
Micah.
Nahum.
Habakkuk.
Zephaniah.
Haggai.
Zechariah.
Malachi.

Of the New Testament.

The Gospels according to
Matthew.
Mark.
The Acts of the Apostles.
Paul's Epistle to the Romans.
Corinthians I.
Corinthians II.
Galatians.
Ephesians.
Philippians.
Colossians.
Thessalonians I.
Thessalonians II.
To Timothy I.

Luke.
John.
To Timothy II.
To Titus.
To Philemon.
The Epistle to the Hebrews.
The Epistle of James.
The First and Second Epistles of
Peter.
The First, Second, and Third
Epistles of John.
The Epistle of Jude.
The Revelation.

All which are given by inspiration of God, to be the rule of faith and life.

III. The books commonly called Apocrypha, not being of divine inspiration, are no part of the Canon of the Scripture; and therefore are of no authority in the Church of God, nor to be any otherwise approved, or made use of, than other human writings.

IV. The authority of the holy Scripture, for which it ought to be believed and obeyed, dependeth not upon the testimony of any man or church, but wholly upon God (who is truth itself), the Author thereof; and therefore it is to be received, because it is the Word of God.

V. We may be moved and induced by the testimony of the Church to an high and reverent esteem of the holy Scripture; and the heavenliness of the matter, the efficacy of the doctrine, the majesty of the style, the consent of all the parts, the scope of the whole (which is to give all glory to God), the full discovery it makes of the only way of man's salvation, the many other incomparable excellencies, and the entire perfection thereof, are arguments whereby it doth abundantly evidence itself to be the Word of God; yet, notwithstanding, our full persuasion and assurance of the infallible truth, and divine authority thereof, is from the inward work of the Holy Spirit, bearing witness by and with the Word in our hearts.

VI. The whole counsel of God, concerning all things necessary for his own glory, man's salvation, faith, and life, is either expressly set down in Scripture, or by good and necessary consequence may be deduced from Scripture: unto which nothing at any time is to be added, whether by new revelations of the Spirit, or traditions of men. Nevertheless we acknowledge the inward illumination of the Spirit of God to be necessary for the saving understanding of such things as are revealed in the Word; and that there are some circumstances concerning the worship of God, and government of the Church, common to human actions and societies, which are to be ordered by the light of nature and Christian prudence, according to the general rules of the Word, which are always to be observed.

VII. All things in Scripture are not alike plain in themselves, nor alike clear unto all; yet those things which are necessary to be known, believed, and observed, for salvation, are so clearly propounded and opened in some place of Scripture or other, that not only the learned, but the unlearned, in a due use of the ordinary means, may attain unto a sufficient understanding of them.

VIII. The Old Testament in Hebrew (which was the native language of the people of God of old), and the New Testament in Greek (which at the time of the writing of it was most generally known to the nations), being immediately inspired by God, and by his singular care and providence kept pure in all ages, are therefore authentical; so as in all controversies of religion the Church is finally to appeal unto them. But because these original tongues are not known to all the people of God who have right unto, and interest in the Scriptures, and are commanded, in the fear of God, to read and search them, therefore they are to be translated into the vulgar language of every nation unto which they come, that the Word of God dwelling plentifully in all, they may worship him in an acceptable manner, and, through patience and comfort of the Scriptures, may have hope.

IX. The infallible rule of interpretation of Scripture is the Scripture itself; and therefore, when there is a question about the true and full sense of any Scripture (which is not manifold, but one), it must be searched and known by other places that speak more clearly.

X. The Supreme Judge, by which all controversies of religion are to be determined, and all decrees of councils, opinions of ancient writers, doctrines of men, and private spirits, are to be examined, and in whose sentence we are to rest, can be no other but the Holy Spirit speaking in the Scripture.

CHAPTER II.
Of God, and of the Holy Trinity.

I. There is but one only living and true God, who is infinite in being and perfection, a most pure spirit, invisible, without body, parts, or passions, immutable, immense, eternal, incomprehensible, almighty, most wise, most holy, most free, most absolute, working all things according to the counsel of his own immutable and most righteous will, for his own glory; most loving, gracious, merciful, long-suffering, abundant in goodness and truth, forgiving iniquity, transgression, and sin; the rewarder of them that diligently seek him; and withal most just and terrible in his judgments; hating all sin, and who will by no means clear the guilty.

II. God hath all life, glory, goodness, blessedness, in and of himself; and is alone in and unto himself all-sufficient, not standing in need of any creatures which he hath made, nor deriving any glory from them, but only manifesting his own glory in, by, unto, and upon them: he is the alone foundation of all being, of whom, through whom, and to whom are all things; and hath most sovereign dominion over them, to do by them, for them, or upon them whatsoever himself pleaseth. In his sight all things are open and manifest; his knowledge is infinite, infallible, and independent upon the creature; so as nothing is to him contingent or uncertain. He is most holy in all his counsels, in all his works, and in all his commands. To him is due from angels and men, and every other creature, whatsoever worship, service, or obedience, he is pleased to require of them.

III. In the unity of the Godhead there be three persons, of one substance, power, and eternity: God the Father, God the Son, and God the Holy Ghost. The Father is of none, neither begotten nor proceeding; the Son is eternally begotten of the Father; the Holy Ghost eternally proceeding from the Father and the Son.

CHAPTER III.
Of God's Eternal Decree.

I. God from all eternity did, by the most wise and holy counsel of his own will, freely and unchangeably ordain whatsoever comes to pass; yet so as thereby neither is God the author of sin, nor is violence offered to the will of the creatures, nor is the liberty or contingency of second causes taken away, but rather established.

II. Although God knows whatsoever may or can come to pass upon all supposed conditions, yet hath he not decreed any thing because he foresaw it as future, or as that which would come to pass upon such conditions.

III. By the decree of God, for the manifestation of his glory, some men and angels are predestinated unto everlasting life, and others foreordained to everlasting death.

IV. These angels and men, thus predestinated and foreordained, are particularly and unchangeably designed; and their number is so certain and definite that it can not be either increased or diminished.

V. Those of mankind that are predestinated unto life, God, before the foundation of the world was laid, according to his eternal and immutable purpose, and the secret counsel and good pleasure of his will, hath chosen in Christ, unto everlasting glory, out of his mere free grace and love, without any foresight of faith or good works, or perseverance in either of them, or any other thing in the creature, as conditions, of causes moving him thereunto; and all to the praise of his glorious grace.

VI. As God hath appointed the elect unto glory, so hath he, by the eternal and most free purpose of his will, foreordained all the means thereunto. Wherefore they who are elected, being fallen in Adam, are redeemed by Christ, are effectually called unto faith in Christ by his Spirit working in due season; are justified, adopted, sanctified, and kept by his power through faith unto salvation. Neither are any other redeemed by Christ, effectually called, justified, adopted, sanctified, and saved, but the elect only.

VII. The rest of mankind God was pleased, according to the unsearchable counsel of his own will, whereby he extendeth or withholdeth mercy as he pleaseth, for the glory of his sovereign power over his creatures, to pass by, and to ordain them to dishonor and wrath for their sin, to the praise of his glorious justice.

VII. The doctrine of this high mystery of predestination is to be handled with special prudence and care, that men attending the will of God revealed in his Word, and yielding obedience thereunto, may, from the certainty of their effectual vocation, be assured of their eternal election. So shall this doctrine afford matter of praise, reverence, and admiration of God; and of humility, diligence, and abundant consolation to all that sincerely obey the gospel.

CHAPTER IV.
Of Creation.

I. It pleased God the Father, Son, and Holy Ghost, for the manifestation of the glory of his eternal power, wisdom, and goodness, in the beginning, to create or make of nothing the world, and all things therein, whether visible or invisible, in the space of six days, and all very good.

II. After God had made all other creatures, he created man, male and female, with reasonable and immortal souls, endued with knowledge, righteousness, and true holiness, after his own image, having the law of God written in their hearts, and power to fulfill it; and yet under a possibility of transgressing, being left to the liberty of their own will, which was subject unto change. Beside this law written in their hearts, they received a command not to eat of the tree of the knowledge of good and evil; which while they kept they were happy in their communion with God, and had dominion over the creatures.

CHAPTER V.
Of Providence.

I. God, the great Creator of all things, doth uphold, direct, dispose, and govern all creatures, actions, and things, from the greatest even to the least, by his most wise and holy providence, according to his infallible foreknowledge and the free and immutable counsel of his own will, to the praise of the glory of his wisdom, power, justice, goodness, and mercy.

II. Although in relation to the foreknowledge and decree of God, the first cause, all things come to pass immutably and infallibly, yet by the same providence he ordereth them to fall out, according to the nature of second causes, either necessarily, freely, or contingently.

III. God, in his ordinary providence, maketh use of means, yet is free to work without, above, and against them, at his pleasure.

IV. The almighty power, unsearchable wisdom, and infinite goodness of God so far manifest themselves in his providence that it extendeth itself even to the first fall, and all other sins of angels and men, and that not by a bare permission, but such as hath joined with it a most wise and powerful bounding, and otherwise ordering and governing of them, in a manifold dispensation, to his own holy ends; yet so as the sinfulness thereof proceedeth only from the creature, and not from God; who, being most holy and righteous, neither is nor can be the author or approver of sin.

V. The most wise, righteous, and gracious God doth oftentimes leave for a season his own children to manifold temptations and the corruption of their own hearts, to chastise them for their former sins, or to discover unto them the hidden strength of corruption and deceitfulness of their hearts, that they may be humbled; and to raise them to a more close and constant dependence for their support unto himself, and to make them more watchful against all future occasions of sin, and for sundry other just and holy ends.

VI. As for those wicked and ungodly men whom God, as a righteous judge, for former sins, doth blind and harden, from them he not only withholdeth his grace, whereby they might have been enlightened in their understandings and wrought upon in their hearts, but sometimes also withdraweth the gifts which they had, and exposeth them to such objects as their corruption makes occasion of sin; and withal, gives them over to their own lusts, the temptations of the world, and the power of Satan; whereby it comes to pass that they harden themselves, even under those means which God useth for the softening of others.

VII. As the providence of God doth, in general, reach to all creatures, so, after a most special manner, it taketh care of his Church, and disposeth all things to the good thereof.

CHAPTER VI.
Of the Fall of Man, of Sin, and of the Punishment thereof.

I. Our first parents, being seduced by the subtilty and temptation of Satan, sinned in eating the forbidden fruit. This their sin God was pleased, according to his wise and holy counsel, to permit, having purpose to order it to his own glory.

II. By this sin they fell from their original righteousness and communion with God, and so became dead in sin, and wholly defiled in all the faculties and parts of soul and body.

III. They being the root of all mankind, the guilt of this sin was imputed, and the same death in sin and corrupted nature conveyed to all their posterity descending from them by ordinary generation.

IV. From this original corruption, whereby we are utterly indisposed, disabled, and made opposite to all good, and wholly inclined to all evil, do proceed all actual transgressions.

V. This corruption of nature, during this life, doth remain in those that are regenerated; and although it be through Christ pardoned and mortified, yet both itself and all the motions thereof are truly and properly sin.

VI. Every sin, both original and actual, being a transgression of the righteous law of God, and contrary thereunto, doth, in its own nature, bring guilt upon the sinner, whereby he is bound over to the wrath of God and curse of the law, and so made subject to death, with all miseries spiritual, temporal, and eternal.

CHAPTER VII.
Of God's Covenant with Man.

I. The distance between God and the creature is so great that although reasonable creatures do owe obedience unto him as their Creator, yet they could never have any fruition of him as their blessedness and reward but by some voluntary condescension on God's part, which he hath been pleased to express by way of covenant.

II. The first covenant made with man was a covenant of works, wherein life was promised to Adam, and in him to his posterity, upon condition of perfect and personal obedience.

III. Man by his fall having made himself incapable of life by that covenant, the Lord was pleased to make a second, commonly called the covenant of grace: wherein he freely offered unto sinners life and salvation by Jesus Christ, requiring of them faith in him that they may be saved, and promising to give unto all those that are ordained unto life his Holy Spirit, to make them willing and able to believe.

IV. This covenant of grace is frequently set forth in the Scripture by the name of a testament, in reference to the death of Jesus Christ the testator, and to the everlasting inheritance, with all things belonging to it, therein bequeathed.

V. This covenant was differently administered in the time of the law and in the time of the gospel: under the law it was administered by promises, prophecies, sacrifices, circumcision, the paschal lamb, and other types and ordinances delivered to the people of the Jews, all fore-signifying Christ to come, which were for that time sufficient and efficacious, through the operation of the Spirit, to instruct and build up the elect in faith in the promised Messiah, by whom they had full remission of sins and eternal salvation; and is called the Old Testament.

VI. Under the gospel, when Christ the substance was exhibited, the ordinances in which this covenant is dispensed are the preaching of the word and the administration of the sacraments of Baptism and the Lord's Supper; which, though fewer in number, and administered with more simplicity and less outward glory, yet in them it is held forth in more fullness, evidence, and spiritual efficacy, to all nations, both Jews and Gentiles; and is called the New Testament. There are not, there-fore, two covenants of grace differing in substance, but one and the same under various dispensations.

CHAPTER VIII.
Of Christ the Mediator.

I. It pleased God, in his eternal purpose, to choose and ordain the Lord Jesus, his only-begotten Son, to be the Mediator between God and man, the Prophet, Priest, and King; the Head and Saviour of his Church, the Heir of all things, and Judge of the world; unto whom he did, from all eternity, give a people to be his seed, and to be by him in time redeemed, called, justified, sanctified, and glorified.

II. The Son of God, the second person in the Trinity, being very and eternal God, of one substance, and equal with the Father, did, when the fullness of time was come, take upon him man's nature, with all the essential properties and common infirmities thereof, yet without sin: being conceived by the power of the Holy Ghost in the womb of the Virgin Mary, of her substance. So that two whole, perfect, and distinct natures, the Godhead and the manhood, were inseparably joined together in one person, without conversion, composition, or confusion. Which person is very God and very man, yet one Christ, the only mediator between God and man.

III. The Lord Jesus, in his human nature thus united to the divine, was sanctified and anointed with the Holy Spirit above measure; having in him all the treasures of wisdom and knowledge, in whom it pleased the Father that all fullness should dwell; to the end that, being holy, harmless, undefiled, and full of grace and truth, he might be thoroughly furnished to execute the office of a mediator and surety. Which office he took not unto himself, but was thereunto called by his Father, who put all power and judgment into his hand, and gave him commandment to execute the same.

IV. This office the Lord Jesus did most willingly undertake, which, that he might discharge, he was made under the law, and did perfectly fulfill it; endured most grievous torments immediately in his soul, and most painful sufferings in his body; was crucified, and died; was buried, and remained under the power of death, yet saw no corruption. On the third day he arose from the dead, with the same body in which he suffered; with which also he ascended into heaven, and there sitteth at the right hand of his Father, making intercession; and shall return to judge men and angels at the end of the world.

V. The Lord Jesus, by his perfect obedience and sacrifice of himself, which he through the eternal Spirit once offered up unto God, hath fully satisfied the justice of his Father, and purchased not only reconciliation, but an everlasting inheritance in the kingdom of heaven, for all those whom the Father hath given unto him.

VI. Although the work of redemption was not actually wrought by Christ till after his incarnation, yet the virtue, efficacy, and benefits thereof were communicated unto the elect, in all ages successively from the beginning of the world, in and by those promises, types, and sacrifices, wherein he was revealed, and signified to be the seed of the woman which should bruise the serpent's head, and the lamb slain from the beginning of the world, being yesterday and to-day the same and forever.

VII. Christ, in the work of mediation, acteth according to both natures; by each nature doing that which is proper to itself, yet, by reason of the unity of the person, that which is proper to one nature is sometimes, in Scripture, attributed to the person denominated by the other nature.

VIII. To all those for whom Christ hath purchased redemption he doth certainly and effectually apply and communicate the same; making intercession for them, and revealing unto them, in and by the Word, the mysteries of salvation; effectually persuading them by his Spirit to believe and obey; and governing their hearts by his Word and Spirit; overcoming all their enemies by his almighty power and wisdom, in such manner and ways as are most consonant to his wonderful and unsearchable dispensation.

CHAPTER IX.
Of Free-will.

I. God hath endued the will of man with that natural liberty, that is neither forced nor by any absolute necessity of nature determined to good or evil.

II. Man, in his state of innocency, had freedom and power to will and to do that which is good and well-pleasing to God, but yet mutably, so that he might fall from it.

III. Man, by his fall into a state of sin, hath wholly lost all ability of will to any spiritual good accompanying salvation; so as a natural man, being altogether averse from that good, and dead in sin, is not able, by his own strength, to convert himself, or to prepare himself thereunto.

IV. When God converts a sinner, and translates him into the state of grace, he freeth him from his natural bondage under sin, and by his grace alone enables him freely to will and to do that which is spiritually good; yet so as that, by reason of his remaining corruption, he doth not perfectly, nor only, will that which is good, but doth also will that which is evil.

V. The will of man is made perfectly and immutably free to good alone, in the state of glory only.

CHAPTER X.
Of Effectual Calling.

I. All those whom God hath predestinated unto life, and those only, he is pleased, in his appointed and accepted time, effectually to call, by his Word and Spirit, out of that state of sin and death, in which they are by nature, to grace and salvation by Jesus Christ; enlightening their minds, spiritually and savingly, to understand the things of God; taking away their heart of stone, and giving unto them an heart of flesh; renewing their wills, and by his almighty power determining them to that which is good, and effectually drawing them to Jesus Christ; yet so as they come most freely, being made willing by his grace.

II. This effectual call is of God's free and special grace alone, not from any thing at all foreseen in man; who is altogether passive therein, until, being quickened and renewed by the Holy Spirit, he is thereby enabled to answer this call, and to embrace the grace offered and conveyed in it.

III. Elect infants, dying in infancy, are regenerated and saved by Christ through the Spirit, who worketh when, and where, and how he pleaseth. So also are all other elect persons, who are incapable of being outwardly called by the ministry of the Word.

IV. Others, not elected, although they may be called by the ministry of the Word, and may have some common operations of the Spirit, yet they never truly come unto Christ, and therefore can not be saved: much less can men, not professing the Christian religion, be saved in any other way whatsoever, be they never so diligent to frame their lives according to the light of nature and the law of that religion they do profess; and to assert and maintain that they may is very pernicious, and to be detested.

CHAPTER XI.
Of Justification.

I. Those whom God effectually calleth he also freely justifieth; not by infusing righteousness into them, but by pardoning their sins, and by accounting and accepting their persons as righteous: not for any thing wrought in them, or done by them, but for Christ's sake alone; nor by imputing faith itself, the act of believing, or any other evangelical obedience to them, as their righteousness; but by imputing the obedience and satisfaction of Christ unto them, they receiving and resting on him and his righteousness by faith; which faith they have not of themselves, it is the gift of God.

II. Faith, thus receiving and resting on Christ and his righteousness, is the alone instrument of justification; yet is it not alone in the person justified, but is ever accompanied with all other saving graces, and is no dead faith, but worketh by love.

III. Christ, by his obedience and death, did fully discharge the debt of all those that are thus justified, and did make a proper, real, and full satisfaction to his Father's justice in their behalf. Yet inasmuch as he was given by the Father for them, and his obedience and satisfaction accepted in their stead, and both freely, not for any thing in them, their justification is only of free grace; that both the exact justice and rich grace of God might be glorified in the justification of sinners.

IV. God did, from all eternity, decree to justify all the elect, and Christ did, in the fullness of time, die for their sins, and rise again for their justification: nevertheless, they are not justified until the Holy Spirit doth, in due time, actually apply Christ unto them.

V. God doth continue to forgive the sins of those that are justified; and although they can never fall from the state of justification, yet they may by their sins fall under God's fatherly displeasure, and not have the light of his countenance restored unto them, until they humble themselves, confess their sins, beg pardon, and renew their faith and repentance.

VI. The justification of believers under the Old Testament was, in all these respects, one and the same with the justification of believers under the New Testament.

CHAPTER XII.
Of Adoption.

All those that are justified God vouchsafeth, in and for his only Son Jesus Christ, to make partakers of the grace of adoption; by which they are taken into the number, and enjoy the liberties and privileges of the children of God; have his name put upon them; receive the Spirit of adoption; have access to the throne of grace with boldness; are enabled to cry, Abba, Father; are pitied, protected, provided for, and chastened by him as by a father; yet never cast off, but sealed to the day of redemption, and inherit the promises, as heirs of everlasting salvation.

CHAPTER XIII.
Of Sanctification.

I. They who are effectually called and regenerated, having a new heart, and a new spirit created in them, are further sanctified, really and personally, through the virtue of Christ's death and resurrection, by his Word and Spirit dwelling in them; the dominion of the whole body of sin is destroyed, and the several lusts thereof are more and more weakened and mortified, and they more and more quickened and strengthened, in all saving graces, to the practice of true holiness, without which no man shall see the Lord.

II. This sanctification is throughout in the whole man, yet imperfect in this life; there abideth still some remnants of corruption in every part, whence ariseth a continual and irreconcilable war, the flesh lusting against the spirit, and the spirit against the flesh.

III. In which war, although the remaining corruption for a time may much prevail, yet, through the continual supply of strength from the sanctifying Spirit of Christ, the regenerate part doth overcome; and so the saints grow in grace, perfecting holiness in the fear of God.

CHAPTER XIV.
Of Saving Faith.

I. The grace of faith, whereby the elect are enabled to believe to the saving of their souls, is the work of the Spirit of Christ in their hearts, and is ordinarily wrought by the ministry of the Word; by which also, and by the administration of the sacraments and prayer, it is increased and strengthened.

II. By this faith a Christian believeth to be true whatsoever is revealed in the Word, for the authority of God himself speaking therein; and acteth differently upon that which each particular passage thereof containeth; yielding obedience to the commands, trembling at the threatenings, and embracing the promises of God for this life and that which is to come. But the principal acts of saving faith are accepting, receiving, and resting upon Christ alone for justification, sanctification, and eternal life, by virtue of the covenant of grace.

III. This faith is different in degrees, weak or strong; may be often and many ways assailed and weakened, but gets the victory; growing up in many to the attainment of a full assurance through Christ, who is both the author and finisher of our faith.

CHAPTER XV.
Of Repentance unto Life.

I. Repentance unto life is an evangelical grace, the doctrine whereof is to be preached by every minister of the gospel, as well as that of faith in Christ.

II. By it a sinner, out of the sight and sense, not only of the danger, but also of the filthiness and odiousness of his sins, as contrary to the holy nature and righteous law of God, and upon the apprehension of his mercy in Christ to such as are penitent, so grieves for and hates his sins as to turn from them all unto God, purposing and endeavoring to walk with him in all the ways of his commandments.

III. Although repentance be not to be rested in as any satisfaction for sin, or any cause of the pardon thereof, which is the act of God's free grace in Christ; yet is it of such necessity to all sinners that none may expect pardon without it.

IV. As there is no sin so small but it deserves damnation, so there is no sin so great that it can bring damnation upon those who truly repent.

V. Men ought not to content themselves with a general repentance, but it is every man's duty to endeavor to repent of his particular sins particularly.

VI. As every man is bound to make private confession of his sins to God, praying for the pardon thereof, upon which, and the forsaking of them, he shall find mercy; so he that scandalizeth his brother, or the Church of Christ, ought to be willing, by a private or public confession and sorrow for his sin, to declare his repentance to those that are offended, who are thereupon to be reconciled to him, and in love to receive him.

CHAPTER XVI.
Of Good Works.

I. Good works are only such as God hath commanded in his holy Word, and not such as, without the warrant thereof, are devised by men out of blind zeal, or upon any pretense of good intention.

II. These good works done in obedience to God's commandments, are the fruits and evidences of a true and lively faith; and by them believers manifest their thankfulness, strengthen their assurance, edify their brethren, adorn the profession of the gospel, stop the mouths of the adversaries, and glorify God, whose workmanship they are, created in Christ Jesus thereunto, that, having their fruit unto holiness, they may have the end, eternal life.

III. Their ability to do good works is not at all of themselves, but wholly from the Spirit of Christ. And that they may be enabled thereunto, besides the graces they have already received, there is required an actual influence of the same Holy Spirit to work in them to will and to do of his good pleasure; yet are they not hereupon to grow negligent, as if they were not bound to perform any duty unless upon a special motion of the Spirit; but they ought to be diligent in stirring up the grace of God that is in them.

IV. They who in their obedience attain to the greatest height which is possible in this life, are so far from being able to supererogate and to do more than God requires, as that they fall short of much which in duty they are bound to do.

V. We can not, by our best works, merit pardon of sin, or eternal life at the hand of God, by reason of the great disproportion that is between us and God, whom by them we can neither profit nor satisfy for the debt of our former sins; but when we have done all we can, we have done but our duty, and are unprofitable servants; and because, as they are good, they proceed from his Spirit; and as they are wrought by us, they are defiled and mixed with so much weakness and imperfection that they can not endure the severity of God's judgment.

VI. Yet notwithstanding, the persons of believers being accepted through Christ, their good works also are accepted in him, not as though they were in this life wholly unblamable and unreprovable in God's sight; but that he, looking upon them in his Son, is pleased to accept and reward that which is sincere, although accompanied with many weaknesses and imperfections.

VII. Works done by unregenerate men, although for the matter of them they may be things which God commands, and of good use both to themselves and others; yet because they proceed not from a heart purified by faith, nor are done in a right manner, according to the Word, nor to a right end, the glory of God; they are therefore sinful, and can not please God, or make a man meet to receive grace from God. And yet their neglect of them is more sinful and displeasing unto God.

CHAPTER XVII.
Of the Perseverance of the Saints.

I. They whom God hath accepted in his Beloved, effectually called and sanctified by his Spirit, can neither totally nor finally fall away from the state of grace; but shall certainly persevere therein to the end, and be eternally saved.

II. This perseverance of the saints depends, not upon their own free-will, but upon the immutability of the decree of election, flowing from the free and unchangeable love of God the Father; upon the efficacy of the merit and intercession of Jesus Christ; the abiding of the Spirit and of the seed of God within them; and the nature of the covenant of grace: from all which ariseth also the certainty and infallibility thereof.

III. Nevertheless they may, through the temptations of Satan and of the world, the prevalency of corruption remaining in them, and the neglect of the means of their preservation, fall into grievous sins; and for a time continue therein: whereby they incur God's displeasure, and grieve his Holy Spirit; come to be deprived of some measure of their graces and comforts; have their hearts hardened, and their consciences wounded; hurt and scandalize others, and bring temporal judgments upon themselves.

CHAPTER XVIII.
Of the Assurance of Grace and Salvation.

I. Although hypocrites and other unregenerate men may vainly deceive themselves with false hopes and carnal presumptions of being in the favor of God and estate of salvation, which hope of theirs shall perish: yet such as truly believe in the Lord Jesus, and love him in sincerity, endeavoring to walk in all good conscience before him, may in this life be certainly assured that they are in a state of grace, and may rejoice in the hope of the glory of God, which hope shall never make them ashamed.

II. This certainty is not a bare conjectural and probable persuasion, grounded upon a fallible hope; but an infallible assurance of faith, founded upon the divine truth of the promises of salvation, the inward evidence of those graces unto which these promises are made, the testimony of the Spirit of adoption witnessing with our spirits that we are the children of God: which Spirit is the earnest of our inheritance, whereby we are sealed to the day of redemption.

III. This infallible assurance doth not so belong to the essence of faith, but that a true believer may wait long, and conflict with many difficulties before he be partaker of it: yet, being enabled by the Spirit to know the things which are freely given him of God, he may, without extraordinary revelation, in the right use of ordinary means, attain thereunto. And therefore it is the duty of every one to give all diligence to make his calling and election sure; that thereby his heart may be enlarged in peace and joy in the Holy Ghost, and in strength and cheerfulness in the duties of obedience, the proper fruits of this assurance: so far is it from inclining men to looseness.

IV. True believers may have the assurance of their salvation divers ways shaken, diminished, and intermitted; as, by negligence in preserving of it; by falling into some special sin, which woundeth the conscience, and grieveth the Spirit; by some sudden or vehement temptation; by God's withdrawing the light of his countenance, and suffering even such as fear him to walk in darkness and to have no light: yet are they never utterly destitute of that seed of God, and life of faith, that love of Christ and the brethren, that sincerity of heart and conscience of duty, out of which, by the operation of the Spirit, this assurance may in due time be revived, and by the which, in the mean time, they are supported from utter despair.

CHAPTER XIX.
Of the Law of God.

I. God gave to Adam a law, as a covenant of works, by which he bound him and all his posterity to personal, entire, exact, and perpetual obedience; promised life upon the fulfilling, and threatened death upon the breach of it; and endued him with power and ability to keep it.

II. This law, after his fall, continued to be a perfect rule of righteousness; and, as such, was delivered by God upon mount Sinai in ten commandments, and written in two tables; the first four commandments containing our duty towards God, and the other six our duty to man.

III. Beside this law, commonly called moral, God was pleased to give to the people of Israel, as a Church under age, ceremonial laws, containing several typical ordinances, partly of worship, prefiguring Christ, his graces, actions, sufferings, and benefits; and partly holding forth divers instructions of moral duties. All which ceremonial laws are now abrogated under the New Testament.

IV. To them also, as a body politic, he gave sundry judicial laws, which expired together with the state of that people, not obliging any other, now, further than the general equity thereof may require.

V. The moral law doth forever bind all, as well justified persons as others, to the obedience thereof; and that not only in regard of the matter contained in it, but also in respect of the authority of God the Creator who gave it. Neither doth Christ in the gospel any way dissolve, but much strengthen, this obligation.

VI. Although true believers be not under the law as a covenant of works, to be thereby justified or condemned; yet is it of great use to them, as well as to others; in that, as a rule of life, informing them of the will of God and their duty, it directs and binds them to walk accordingly; discovering also the sinful pollutions of their nature, hearts, and lives; so as, examining themselves thereby, they may come to further conviction of, humiliation for, and hatred against sin; together with a clearer sight of the need they have of Christ, and the perfection of his obedience. It is likewise of use to the regenerate, to restrain their corruptions, in that it forbids sin; and the threatenings of it serve to show what even their sins deserve, and what afflictions in this life they may expect for them, although freed from the curse thereof threatened in the law. The promises of it, in like manner, show them God's approbation of obedience, and what blessings they may expect upon the performance thereof; although not as due to them by the law as a covenant of words: so as a man's doing good, and refraining from evil, because the law encourageth to the one, and deterreth from the other, is no evidence of his being under the law, and not under grace.

VII. Neither are the forementioned uses of the law contrary to the grace of the gospel, but do sweetly comply with it: the Spirit of Christ subduing and enabling the will of man to do that freely and cheerfully which the will of God, revealed in the law, requireth to be done.

CHAPTER XX.
Of Christian Liberty, and Liberty of Conscience.

I. The liberty which Christ hath purchased for believers under the gospel consists in their freedom from the guilt of sin, the condemning wrath of God, the curse of the moral law; and in their being delivered from this present evil world, bondage to Satan, and dominion of sin, from the evil of afflictions, the sting of death, the victory of the grave, and everlasting damnation; as also in their free access to God, and their yielding obedience unto him, not out of slavish fear, but a child-like love and willing mind. All which were common also to believers under the law; but under the New Testament the liberty of Christians is further enlarged in their freedom from the yoke of the ceremonial law, to which the Jewish Church was subjected; and in greater boldness of access to the throne of grace, and in fuller communications of the free Spirit of God, than believers under the law did ordinarily partake of.

II. God alone is Lord of the conscience, and hath left it free from the doctrines and commandments of men which are in any thing contrary to his Word, or beside it in matters of faith or worship. So that to believe such doctrines, or to obey such commands out of conscience, is to betray true liberty of conscience; and the requiring of an implicit faith, and an absolute and blind obedience, is to destroy liberty of conscience, and reason also.

III. They who, upon pretense of Christian liberty, do practice any sin, or cherish any lust, do thereby destroy the end of Christian liberty; which is, that, being delivered out of the hands of our enemies, we might serve the Lord without fear, in holiness and righteousness before him, all the days of our life.

IV. And because the power which God hath ordained, and the liberty which Christ hath purchased, are not intended by God to destroy, but mutually to uphold and preserve one another; they who, upon pretense of Christian liberty, shall oppose any lawful power, or the lawful exercise of it, whether it be civil or ecclesiastical, resist the ordinance of God. And for their publishing of such opinions, or maintaining of such practices, as are contrary to the light of nature, or to the known principles of Christianity, whether concerning faith, worship, or conversation; or to the power of godliness; or such erroneous opinions or practices, as, either in their own nature, or in the manner of publishing or maintaining them, are destructive to the external peace and order which Christ hath established in the Church; they may lawfully be called to account, and proceeded against by the censures of the Church, and by the power of the Civil Magistrate.

CHAPTER XXI.
Of Religious Worship and the Sabbath-day.

I. The light of nature showeth that there is a God, who hath lordship and sovereignty over all; is good, and doeth good unto all; and is therefore to be feared, loved, praised, called upon, trusted in, and served with all the heart, and with all the soul, and with all the might. But the acceptable way of worshiping the true God is instituted by himself, and so limited to his own revealed will, that he may not be worshiped according to the imaginations and devices of men, or the suggestions of Satan, under any visible representations or any other way not prescribed in the Holy Scripture.

II. Religious worship is to be given to God, the Father, Son, and Holy Ghost; and to him alone: not to angels, saints, or any other creature: and since the fall, not without a Mediator; nor in the mediation of any other but of Christ alone.

III. Prayer with thanksgiving, being one special part of religious worship, is by God required of all men; and that it may be accepted, it is to be made in the name of the Son, by the help of his Spirit, according to his will, with understanding, reverence, humility, fervency, faith, love, and perseverance; and, if vocal, in a known tongue.

IV. Prayer is to be made for things lawful, and for all sorts of men living, or that shall live hereafter; but not for the dead, nor for those of whom it may be known that they have sinned the sin unto death.

V. The reading of the Scriptures with godly fear; the sound preaching; and conscionable hearing of the Word, in obedience unto God with understanding, faith, and reverence; singing of psalms with grace in the heart; as, also, the due administration and worthy receiving of the sacraments instituted by Christ; are all parts of the ordinary religious worship of God: besides religious oaths, vows, solemn fastings, and thanksgivings upon several occasions; which are, in their several times and seasons, to be used in an holy and religious manner.

VI. Neither prayer, nor any other part of religious worship, is now, under the gospel, either tied unto, or made more acceptable by any place in which it is performed, or towards which it is directed: but God is to be worshiped every where in spirit and truth; as in private families daily, and in secret each one by himself, so more solemnly in the public assemblies, which are not carelessly or willfully to be neglected or forsaken, when God, by his Word or providence, calleth thereunto.

VII. As it is of the law of nature, that, in general, a due proportion of time be set apart for the worship of God; so, in his Word, by a positive, moral, and perpetual commandment, binding all men in all ages, he hath particularly appointed one day in seven for a Sabbath, to be kept holy unto him: which, from the beginning of the world to the resurrection of Christ, was the last day of the week; and, from the resurrection of Christ, was changed into the first day of the week, which in Scripture is called the Lord's day, and is to be continued to the end of the world, as the Christian Sabbath.

VIII. This Sabbath is then kept holy unto the Lord, when men, after a due preparing of their hearts, and ordering of their common affairs beforehand, do not only observe an holy rest all the day from their own works, words, and thoughts, about their worldly employments and recreations; but also are taken up the whole time in the public and private exercises of his worship, and in the duties of necessity and mercy.

CHAPTER XXII.
Of Lawful Oaths and Vows.

I. A lawful oath is a part of religious worship, wherein, upon just occasion, the person swearing solemnly calleth God to witness what he asserteth or promiseth; and to judge him according to the truth or falsehood of what he sweareth.

II. The name of God only is that by which men ought to swear, and therein it is to be used with all holy fear and reverence; therefore to swear vainly or rashly by that glorious and dreadful name, or to swear at all by any other thing, is sinful, and to be abhorred. Yet as, in matters of weight and moment, an oath is warranted by the Word of God, under the New Testament, as well as under the Old, so a lawful oath, being imposed by lawful authority, in such matters ought to be taken.

III. Whosoever taketh an oath ought duly to consider the weightiness of so solemn an act, and therein to avouch nothing but what he is fully persuaded is the truth. Neither may any man bind himself by oath to any thing but what is good and just, and what he believeth so to be, and what he is able and resolved to perform. Yet it is a sin to refuse an oath touching any thing that is good and just, being imposed by lawful authority.

IV. An oath is to be taken in the plain and common sense of the words, without equivocation or mental reservation. It can not oblige to sin; but in any thing not sinful, being taken, it binds to performance, although to a man's own hurt: nor is it to be violated, although made to heretics or infidels.

V. A vow is of the like nature with a promissory oath, and ought to be made with the like religious care, and to be performed with the like faithfulness.

VI. It is not to be made to any creature, but to God alone: and that it may be accepted, it is to be made voluntarily, out of faith and conscience of duty, in way of thankfulness for mercy received, or for the obtaining of what we want; whereby we more strictly bind ourselves to necessary duties, or to other things, so far and so long as they may fitly conduce thereunto.

VII. No man may vow to do any thing forbidden in the Word of God, or what would hinder any duty therein commanded, or which is not in his own power, and for the performance whereof he hath no promise or ability from God. In which respect, popish monastical vows of perpetual single life, professed poverty, and regular obedience, are so far from being degrees of higher perfection, that they are superstitious and sinful snares, in which no Christian may entangle himself.

CHAPTER XXIII.
Of the Civil Magistrate.

I. God, the Supreme Lord and King of all the world, hath ordained civil magistrates to be under him, over the people, for his own glory and the public good, and to this end hath armed them with the power of the sword, for the defense and encouragement of them that are good, and for the punishment of evil-doers.

II. It is lawful for Christians to accept and execute the office of a magistrate when called thereunto; in the managing whereof, as they ought especially to maintain piety, justice, and peace, according to the wholesome laws of each commonwealth, so, for that end, they may lawfully, now under the New Testament, wage war upon just and necessary occasion.

III. The civil magistrate may not assume to himself the administration of the Word and Sacraments, or the power of the keys of the kingdom of heaven: yet he hath authority, and it is his duty to take order, that unity and peace be preserved in the Church, that the truth of God be kept pure and entire, that all blasphemies and heresies be suppressed, all corruptions and abuses in worship and discipline prevented or reformed, and all the ordinances of God duly settled, administered, and observed. For the better effecting whereof he hath power to call synods, to be present at them, and to provide that whatsoever is transacted in them be according to the mind of God.

The above section is changed in the American revision, and adapted to the separation of Church and State, as follows:

[III. *Civil magistrates may not assume to themselves the administration of the Word and Sacraments* (2 Chron. xxvi. 18); *or the power of the keys of the kingdom of heaven* (Matt. xvi. 19; 1 Cor. iv. 1, 2); *or, in the least, interfere in matters of faith* (John xviii. 36; Mal. ii. 7; Acts v. 29). *Yet as nursing fathers, it is the duty of civil magistrates to protect the Church of our common Lord, without giving the preference to any denomination of Christians above the rest, in such a manner that all ecclesiastical persons whatever shall enjoy the full, free, and unquestioned liberty of discharging every part of their sacred functions, without violence or danger* (Isa. xlix. 23). *And, as Jesus Christ hath appointed a regular government and discipline in his Church, no law of any commonwealth should interfere with, let, or hinder, the due exercise thereof, among the voluntary members of any denomination of Christians, according to their own profession and belief* (Psa. cv. 15; Acts xviii. 14-16). *It is the duty of civil magistrates to protect the person and good name of all their people, in such an effectual manner as that no person be suffered, either upon pretence of religion or infidelity, to offer any indignity, violence, abuse, or injury to any other person whatsoever: and to take order, that all religious and ecclesiastical assemblies be held without molestation or disturbance* (2 Sam. xxiii. 3; 1 Tim. ii. 1; Rom. xiii. 4).]

IV. It is the duty of people to pray for magistrates, to honor their persons, to pay them tribute and other dues, to obey their lawful commands, and to be subject to their authority, for conscience' sake. Infidelity or difference in religion doth not make void the magistrate's just and legal authority, nor free the people from their due obedience to him: from which ecclesiastical persons are not exempted; much less hath the Pope any power or jurisdiction over them in their dominions, or over any of their people; and least of all to deprive them of their dominions or lives, if he shall judge them to be heretics, or upon any other pretense whatsoever.

CHAPTER XXIV.
Of Marriage and Divorce.

I. Marriage is to be between one man and one woman: neither is it lawful for any man to have more than one wife, nor for any woman to have more that one husband at the same time.

II. Marriage was ordained for the mutual help of husband and wife; for the increase of mankind with a legitimate issue, and of the Church with an holy seed; and for preventing of uncleanness.

III. It is lawful for all sorts of people to marry who are able with judgment to give their consent. Yet it is the duty of Christians to marry only in the Lord. And, therefore, such as profess the true reformed religion should not marry with infidels, Papists, or other idolaters: neither should such as are godly be unequally yoked, by marrying with such as are notoriously wicked in their life, or maintain damnable heresies.

IV. Marriage ought not to be within the degrees of consanguinity or affinity forbidden in the Word; nor can such incestuous marriages ever be made lawful by any law of man, or consent of parties, so as those persons may live together, as man and wife. The man may not marry any of his wife's kindred nearer in blood than he may of his own, nor the woman of her husband's kindred nearer in blood than of her own.

V. Adultery or fornication, committed after a contract, being detected before marriage, giveth just occasion to the innocent party to dissolve that contract. In the case of adultery after marriage, it is lawful for the innocent party to sue out a divorce, and after the divorce to marry another, as if the offending party were dead.

VI. Although the corruption of man be such as is apt to study arguments, unduly to put asunder those whom God hath joined together in marriage; yet nothing but adultery, or such willful desertion as can no way be remedied by the Church or civil magistrate, is cause sufficient of dissolving the bond of marriage; wherein a public and orderly course of proceeding is to be observed; and the persons concerned in it, not left to their own wills and discretion in their own case.

CHAPTER XXV.
Of the Church.

I. The catholic or universal Church, which is invisible, consists of the whole number of the elect, that have been, are, or shall be gathered into one, under Christ the head thereof; and is the spouse, the body, the fullness of him that filleth all in all.

II. The visible Church, which is also catholic or universal under the gospel (not confined to one nation as before under the law) consists of all those, throughout the world, that profess the true religion, and of their children; and is the kingdom of the Lord Jesus Christ, the house and family of God, out of which there is no ordinary possibility of salvation.

III. Unto this catholic visible Church Christ hath given the ministry, oracles, and ordinances of God, for the gathering and perfecting of the saints, in this life, to the end of the world: and doth by his own presence and Spirit, according to his promise, make them effectual thereunto.

IV. This catholic Church hath been sometimes more, sometimes less visible. And particular churches, which are members thereof, are more or less pure, according as the doctrine of the gospel is taught and embraced, ordinances administered, and public worship performed more or less purely in them.

V. The purest churches under heaven are subject both to mixture and error; and some have so degenerated as to become no churches of Christ, but synagogues of Satan. Nevertheless, there shall be always a Church on earth to worship God according to his will.

VI. There is no other head of the Church but the Lord Jesus Christ: nor can the Pope of Rome, in any sense be head thereof; but is that Antichrist, that man of sin and son of perdition, that exalteth himself in the Church against Christ, and all that is called God.

CHAPTER XXVI.
Of the Communion of Saints.

I. All saints that are united to Jesus Christ their head, by his Spirit and by faith, have fellowship with him in his graces, sufferings, death, resurrection, and glory: and being united to one another in love, they have communion in each other's gifts and graces, and are obliged to the performance of such duties, public and private, as do conduce to their mutual good, both in the inward and outward man.

II. Saints, by profession, are bound to maintain an holy fellowship and communion in the worship of God, and in performing such other spiritual services as tend to their mutual edification; as also in relieving each other in outward things, according to their several abilities and necessities. Which communion, as God offereth opportunity, is to be extended unto all those who, in every place, call upon the name of the Lord Jesus.

III. This communion which the saints have with Christ, doth not make them in anywise partakers of the substance of his Godhead, or to be equal with Christ in any respect: either of which to affirm is impious and blasphemous. Nor doth their communion one with another, as saints, take away or infringe the title or propriety which each man hath in his goods and possessions.

CHAPTER XXVII.
Of the Sacraments.

I. Sacraments are holy signs and seals of the covenant of grace, immediately instituted by God, to represent Christ and his benefits, and to confirm our interest in him; as also to put a visible difference between those that belong unto the Church and the rest of the world; and solemnly to engage them to the service of God in Christ, according to his Word.

II. There is in every sacrament a spiritual relation or sacramental union, between the sign and the thing signified; whence it comes to pass that the names and the effects of the one are attributed to the other.

III. The grace which is exhibited in or by the sacraments, rightly used, is not conferred by any power in them; neither doth the efficacy of a sacrament depend upon the piety or intention of him that doth administer it, but upon the work of the Spirit, and the word of institution, which contains, together with a precept authorizing the use thereof, a promise of benefit to worthy receivers.

IV. There be only two sacraments ordained by Christ our Lord in the gospel, that is to say, Baptism and the Supper of the Lord: neither of which may be dispensed by any but by a minister of the Word lawfully ordained.

V. The sacraments of the Old Testament, in regard of the spiritual things thereby signified and exhibited, were, for substance, the same with those of the New.

CHAPTER XXVIII.
Of Baptism.

I. Baptism is a sacrament of the New Testament, ordained by Jesus Christ, not only for the solemn admission of the party baptized into the visible Church, but also to be unto him a sign and seal of the covenant of grace, of his ingrafting into Christ, of regeneration, of remission of sins, and of his giving up unto God, through Jesus Christ, to walk in newness of life: which sacrament is, by Christ's own appointment, to be continued in his Church until the end of the world.

II. The outward element to be used in this sacrament is water, wherewith the party is to be baptized in the name of the Father, and of the Son, and of the Holy Ghost, by a minister of the gospel lawfully called thereunto.

III. Dipping of the person into the water is not necessary; but baptism is rightly administered by pouring or sprinkling water upon the person.

IV. Not only those that do actually profess faith and obedience unto Christ, but also the infants of one or both believing parents are to be baptized.

V. Although it be a great sin to contemn or neglect this ordinance, yet grace and salvation are not so inseparably annexed unto it, as that no person can be regenerated or saved without it, or that all that are baptized are undoubtedly regenerated.

VI. The efficacy of baptism is not tied to that moment of time wherein it is administered; yet, notwithstanding, by the right use of this ordinance the grace promised is not only offered, but really exhibited and conferred by the Holy Ghost, to such (whether of age or infants) as that grace belongeth unto, according to the counsel of God's own will, in his appointed time.

VII. The sacrament of baptism is but once to be administered to any person.

CHAPTER XXIX.
Of the Lord's Supper.

I. Our Lord Jesus, in the night wherein he was betrayed, instituted the sacrament of his body and blood, called the Lord's Supper, to be observed in his Church, unto the end of the world; for the perpetual remembrance of the sacrifice of himself in his death, the sealing all benefits thereof unto true believers, their spiritual nourishment and growth in him, their further engagement in, and to all duties which they owe unto him; and to be a bond and pledge of their communion with him, and with each other, as members of his mystical body.

II. In this sacrament Christ is not offered up to his Father, nor any real sacrifice made at all for remission of sins of the quick or dead, but only a commemoration of that one offering up of himself, by himself, upon the cross, once for all, and a spiritual oblation of all possible praise unto God for the same; so that the Popish sacrifice of the mass, as they call it, is most abominably injurious to Christ's one only sacrifice, the alone propitiation for all the sins of the elect.

III. The Lord Jesus hath, in this ordinance, appointed his ministers to declare his word of institution to the people, to pray, and bless the elements of bread and wine, and thereby to set them apart from a common to an holy use; and to take and break the bread, to take the cup, and (they communicating also themselves) to give both to the communicants; but to none who are not then present in the congregation.

IV. Private masses, or receiving this sacrament by a priest, or any other, alone; as likewise the denial of the cup to the people; worshiping the elements, the lifting them up, or carrying them about for adoration, and the reserving them for any pretended religious use, are all contrary to the nature of this sacrament, and to the institution of Christ.

V. The outward elements in this sacrament, duly set apart to the uses ordained by Christ, have such relation to him crucified, as that truly, yet sacramentally only, they are sometimes called by the name of the things they represent, to wit, the body and blood of Christ; albeit, in substance and nature, they still remain truly, and only, bread and wine, as they were before.

VI. That doctrine which maintains a change of the substance of bread and wine, into the substance of Christ's body and blood (commonly called transubstantiation) by consecration of a priest, or by any other way, is repugnant, not to Scripture alone, but even to common-sense and reason; overthroweth the nature of the sacrament; and hath been, and is the cause of manifold superstitions, yea, of gross idolatries.

VII. Worthy receivers, outwardly partaking of the visible elements in this sacrament, do then also inwardly by faith, really and indeed, yet not carnally and corporally, but spiritually, receive and feed upon Christ crucified, and all benefits of his death: the body and blood of Christ being then not corporally or carnally in, with, or under the bread and wine; yet as really, but spiritually, present to the faith of believers in that ordinance, as the elements themselves are, to their outward senses.

VIII. Although ignorant and wicked men receive the outward elements in this sacrament, yet they receive not the thing signified thereby; but by their unworthy coming thereunto are guilty of the body and blood of the Lord, to their own damnation. Wherefore all ignorant and ungodly persons, as they are unfit to enjoy communion with him, so are they unworthy of the Lord's table, and can not, without great sin against Christ, while they remain such, partake of these holy mysteries, or be admitted thereunto.

CHAPTER XXX.
Of Church Censures.

I. The Lord Jesus, as king and head of his Church, hath therein appointed a government in the hand of Church officers, distinct from the civil magistrate.

II. To these officers the keys of the kingdom of heaven are committed, by virtue whereof they have power respectively to retain and remit sins, to shut that kingdom against the impenitent, both by the Word and censures; and to open it unto penitent sinners, by the ministry of the gospel, and by absolution from censures, as occasion shall require.

III. Church censures are necessary for the reclaiming and gaining of offending brethren; for deterring of others from the like offenses; for purging out of that leaven which might infect the whole lump; for vindicating the honor of Christ, and the holy profession of the gospel; and for preventing the wrath of God, which might justly fall upon the Church, if they should suffer his covenant, and the seals thereof, to be profaned by notorious and obstinate offenders.

IV. For the better attaining of these ends, the officers of the Church are to proceed by admonition, suspension from the Sacrament of the Lord's Supper for a season, and by excommunication from the Church, according to the nature of the crime and demerit of the person.

CHAPTER XXXI.
Of Synods and Councils.

I. For the better government and further edification of the Church, there ought to be such assemblies as are commonly called synods or councils.

The American edition here adds the following:

[*And it belongeth to the overseers and other rulers of the particular churches, by virtue of their office, and the power which Christ hath given them for edification, and not for destruction, to appoint such assemblies* (Acts xv.); *and to convene together in them, as often as they shall judge it expedient for the good of the Church* (Acts xv. 22, 23, 25).]

II. As magistrates may lawfully call a synod of ministers and other fit persons to consult and advise with about matters of religion; so, if magistrates be open enemies to the Church, the ministers of Christ, of themselves, by virtue of their office, or they, with other fit persons, upon delegation from their churches, may meet together in such assemblies.

III. [II.] It belongeth to synods and councils, ministerially, to determine controversies of faith, and cases of conscience; to set down rules and directions for the better ordering of the public worship of God, and government of his Church; to receive complaints in cases of maladministration, and authoritatively to determine the same: which decrees and determinations, if consonant to the Word of God, are to be received with reverence and submission, not only for their agreement with the Word, but also for the power whereby they are made, as being an ordinance of God, appointed thereunto in his Word.

IV. [III.] All synods or councils since the apostles' times, whether general or particular, may err, and many have erred; therefore they are not to be made the rule of faith or practice, but to be used as a help in both.

V. [IV.] Synods and councils are to handle or conclude nothing but that which is ecclesiastical: and are not to intermeddle with civil affairs which concern the commonwealth, unless by way of humble petition in cases extraordinary; or by way of advice for satisfaction of conscience, if they be thereunto required by the civil magistrate.

CHAPTER XXXII.
Of the State of Men after Death, and of the Resurrection of the Dead.

I. The bodies of men, after death, return to dust, and see corruption; but their souls (which neither die nor sleep), having an immortal subsistence, immediately return to God who gave them. The souls of the righteous, being then made perfect in holiness, are received into the highest heavens, where they behold the face of God in light and glory, waiting for the full redemption of their bodies: and the souls of the wicked are cast into hell, where they remain in torments and utter darkness, reserved to the judgment of the great day. Besides these two places for souls separated from their bodies, the Scripture acknowledgeth none.

II. At the last day, such as are found alive shall not die, but be changed; and all the dead shall be raised up with the self-same bodies, and none other, although with different qualities, which shall be united again to their souls forever.

III. The bodies of the unjust shall, by the power of Christ, be raised to dishonor; the bodies of the just, by his Spirit, unto honor, and be made conformable to his own glorious body.

CHAPTER XXXIII.
Of the Last Judgment.

I. God hath appointed a day wherein he will judge the world in righteousness by Jesus Christ, to whom all power and judgment is given of the Father. In which day, not only the apostate angels shall be judged, but likewise all persons, that have lived upon earth, shall appear before the tribunal of Christ, to give an account of their thoughts, words, and deeds; and to receive according to what they have done in the body, whether good or evil.

II. The end of God's appointing this day, is for the manifestation of the glory of his mercy in the eternal salvation of the elect; and of his justice in the damnation of the reprobate, who are wicked and disobedient. For then shall the righteous go into everlasting life, and receive that fullness of joy and refreshing which shall come from the presence of the Lord: but the wicked, who know not God, and obey not the gospel of Jesus Christ, shall be cast into eternal torments, and be punished with everlasting destruction from the presence of the Lord, and from the glory of his power.

III. As Christ would have us to be certainly persuaded that there shall be a day of judgment, both to deter all men from sin, and for the greater consolation of the godly in their adversity: so will he have that day unknown to men, that they may shake off all carnal security, and be always watchful, because they know not at what hour the Lord will come; and may be ever prepared to say, Come, Lord Jesus, come quickly. Amen.

> CHARLES HERLE, *Prolocutor.*
> CORNELIUS BURGES, *Assessor.*
> HERBERT PALMER, *Assessor.*
> HENRY ROBROUGHE, *Scriba.*
> ADONIRAM BYFIELD, *Scriba.*

PRESBYTERIAN CONFESSION OF 1967

The newest Reformed statement of doctrine is the Confession of 1967, drafted by the United Presbyterian Church U.S.A., itself a merger (1958) of the United Presbyterian Church of North America and The Presbyterian Church in the United States of America. In order to understand how the latest Confession came into being it will be useful to see something of the church which produced it.

Presbyterianism in the United States had three beginnings, all due to migrations from Europe. In 1623 the Dutch settled in New York as members of the Calvinist Reformed Church; in 1629 the Puritan refugees from England landed in Massachusetts at Salem, and although they first merged with the Pilgrims to form the Congregational Church, eventually many of them changed allegiance and became Presbyterians; and in 1685 Ulster men, or Scotch-Irish, arrived in New Jersey and Pennsylvania under the leadership of Francis Makemie, the father of American Presbyterianism.

The first milestone in American Presbyterianism was the Adopting Act of 1729, which decided that every minister and candidate for the ministry had to declare the Westminster Confession and Larger and Smaller Catechisms "in all essentials and necessary articles, good forms of sound words and systems of Christian doctrine." This was approved over the protests of those who questioned the Trinity and the divinity of Christ. To satisfy the latter, the concession was made that if any minister had scruples about any parts of these standards, he should propose them to the Synod who would then decide whether his difficulties involved anything "essential" that might warrant exclusion.

Apart from minor or temporary schisms in American Presbyterianism, two major breaks in unity occurred in the nineteenth century, neither of which has so far been healed.

In 1810 the Cumberland Presbytery seceded to form a separate denomination, known as the Cumberland Presbyterian Church. Its grievance was the Calvinist doctrine on predestination, which was rejected. In 1837 a more serious split took place over the slavery question. In that year several southern synods withdrew, to be joined in 1865 by forty-seven southern presbyteries and become the Presbyterian Church in the United States. Frequently called the Southern Presbyterian Church, its doctrinal position is notably conservative.

The northern denomination retained the name of Presbyterian Church in the U.S.A., adopted in 1821, and has the reputation of being more tolerant of theological liberalism. In 1958 it was joined by the United Presbyterian Church in North America, originally a group of Calvinists set up by secessionist missionaries from Scotland. It was this merger and prospects of further amalgamation with other bodies that occasioned the redrafting of a Confession of Faith.

The text of the Confession was approved by the 178th General Assembly of the Church (1966) as part of its proposal to revise the confessional position of the United Presbyterians in the U.S.A. Its purpose was not to replace the Westminster Confession, which the Assembly declared was a doctrinal guide, along with the Nicene and Apostles' Creeds. Rather it was "to call the church to that unity in confession and mission which is required of disciples today." The unity in question is both domestic, among Presbyterians, and outside the Reformed tradition. Presbyterians of the North and South are partners in a projected merger for upwards of twenty million American Protestants, including Methodists and Episcopalians. Architects of the planned union are leaders in the United Presbyterian Church in the U.S.A. Consciously irenic, the Confession of 1967 is well calculated to win adherents far beyond the Presbyterian fellowship.

The church confesses its faith when it bears a present witness to God's grace in Jesus Christ.

In every age the church has expressed its witness in words and deeds as the need of the time required. The earliest examples of confession are found within the Scriptures. Confessional statements have taken such varied forms as hymns, liturgical formulas, doctrinal definitions, catechisms, theological systems in summary, and declarations of purpose against threatening evil.

Confessions and declarations are subordinate standards in the church, subject to the authority of Jesus Christ, the Word of God, as the Scriptures bear witness to him. No one type of confession is exclusively valid, no one statement is irreformable. Obedience to Jesus Christ alone identifies the one universal church and supplies the continuity of its tradition. This obedience is the ground of the church's duty and freedom to reform itself in life and doctrine as new occasions, in God' providence, may demand.

The United Presbyterian Church in the United States of America acknowledges itself aided in understanding the gospel by the testimony of the church from earlier ages and from many lands. More especially it is guided by the Nicene and Apostles' Creeds from the time of the early church; the Scots Confession, the Heidelberg Catechism, and the Second Helvetic Confession from the era of the Reformation; the Westminster Confession and Shorter Catechism from the seventeenth century; and the Theological Declaration of Barmen from the twentieth century.

The purpose of the Confession of 1967 is to call the church to that unity in confession and mission which is required of disciples today. This Confession is not a "system of doctrine," nor does it include all the traditional topics of theology. For example, the Trinity and the Person of Christ are not redefined but are recognized and reaffirmed as forming the basis and determining the structure of the Christian faith.

God's reconciling work in Jesus Christ and the mission of reconciliation to which he has called his church are the heart of the gospel in any age. Our generation stands in peculiar need of reconciliation in Christ. Accordingly this Confession of 1967 is built upon that theme.

THE CONFESSION

In Jesus Christ God was reconciling the world to himself. Jesus Christ is God with man. He is the eternal Son of the Father, who became man and lived among us to fulfill the work of reconciliation. He is present in the church by the power of the Holy Spirit to continue and complete his mission. This work of God, the Father, Son, and Holy Spirit, is the foundation of all confessional statements about God, man, and the world. Therefore the church calls men to be reconciled to God and to one another.

PART I
GOD'S WORK OF RECONCILIATION
Section A. The Grace of Our Lord Jesus Christ
1. JESUS CHRIST

In Jesus of Nazareth true humanity was realized once for all. Jesus, a Palestinian Jew, lived among his own people and shared their needs, temptations, joys, and sorrows. He expressed the love of God in word and deed and became a brother to all kinds of sinful men. But his complete obedience led him into conflict with his people. His life and teaching judged their goodness, religious aspirations, and national hopes. Many rejected him and demanded his death. In giving himself freely for them he took upon himself the judgment under which all men stand convicted. God raised him from the dead, vindicating him as Messiah and Lord. The victim of sin became victor, and won the victory over sin and death for all men.

God's reconciling act in Jesus Christ is a mystery which the Scriptures describe in various ways. It is called the sacrifice of a lamb, a shepherd's life given for his sheep, atonement by a priest; again it is ransom of a slave, payment of debt, vicarious satisfaction of a legal penalty, and victory over the powers of evil. These are expressions of a truth which remains beyond the reach of all theory in the depths of God's love for man. They reveal the gravity, cost, and sure achievement of God's reconciling work.

The risen Christ is the savior for all men. Those joined to him by faith are set right with God and commissioned to serve as his reconciling community. Christ is head of this community, the church, which began with the apostles and continues through all generations.

The same Jesus Christ is the judge of all men. His judgment discloses the ultimate seriousness of life and gives promise of God's final victory over the power of sin and death. To receive life from the risen Lord is to have life eternal; to refuse life from him is to choose the death, which is separation from God. All who put their trust in Christ face divine judgment without fear, for the judge is their redeemer.

2. THE SIN OF MAN

The reconciling act of God in Jesus Christ exposes the evil in men as sin in the sight of God. In sin men claim mastery of their own lives, turn against God and their fellow men, and become exploiters and despoilers of the world. They lose their humanity in futile striving and are left in rebellion, despair, and isolation.

Wise and virtuous men through the ages have sought the highest good in devotion to freedom, justice, peace, truth, and beauty. Yet all human virtue, when seen in the light of God's love in Jesus Christ, is found to be infected by self-interest and hostility. All men, good and bad alike, are in the wrong before God and helpless without his forgiveness. Thus all men fall under God's judgment. No one is more subject to that judgment than the man who assumes that he is guiltless before God or morally superior to others.

God's love never changes. Against all who oppose him, God expresses his love in wrath. In the same love God took on himself judgment and shameful death in Jesus Christ, to bring men to repentance and new life.

Section B. The Love of God

God's sovereign love is a mystery beyond the reach of man's mind. Human thought ascribes to God superlatives of power, wisdom, and goodness. But God reveals his love in Jesus Christ by showing power in the form of a servant, wisdom in the folly of the cross, and goodness in receiving sinful men. The power of God's love in Christ to transform the world discloses that the Redeemer is the Lord and Creator who made all things to serve the purpose of his love.

God has created the world of space and time to be the sphere of his dealings with men. In its beauty and vastness, sublimity and awfulness, order and disorder, the world reflects to the eye of faith the majesty and mystery of its Creator.

God has created man in a personal relation with himself that man may respond to the love of the Creator. He has created male and female and given them a life which proceeds from birth to death in a succession of generations and in a wide complex of social relations. He has endowed man with capacities to make the world serve his needs and to enjoy its good things. Life is a gift to be received with gratitude and a task to be pursued with courage. Man is free to seek his life within the purpose of God: to develop and protect the resources of nature for the common welfare, to work for justice and peace in society, and in other ways to use his creative powers for the fulfillment of human life.

God expressed his love for all mankind through Israel, whom he chose to be his covenant people to serve him in love and faithfulness. When Israel was unfaithful, he disciplined the nation with his judgments and maintained his cause through prophets, priests, teachers, and true believers. These witnesses called all Israelites to a destiny in which they would serve God faithfully and become a light to the nations. The same witnesses proclaimed the coming of a new age, and a true servant of God in whom God's purpose for Israel and for mankind would be realized.

Out of Israel God in due time raised up Jesus. His faith and obedience were the response of the perfect child of God. He was the fulfillment of God's promise to Israel, the beginning of the new creation, and the pioneer of the new humanity. He gave history its meaning and direction and called the church to be his servant for the reconciliation of the world.

Section C. The Communion of the Holy Spirit

God the Holy Spirit fulfills the work of reconciliation in man. The Holy Spirit creates and renews the church as the community in which men are reconciled to God and to one another. He enables them to receive forgiveness as they forgive one another, and to enjoy the peace of God as they make peace among themselves. In spite of their sin, he gives them power to become representatives of Jesus Christ and his gospel of reconciliation to all men.

1. THE NEW LIFE

The reconciling work of Jesus was the supreme crisis in the life of mankind. His cross and resurrection become personal crisis and present hope for men when the gospel is proclaimed and believed. In this experience the Spirit brings God's forgiveness to men, moves them to respond in faith, repentance, and obedience, and initiates the new life in Christ.

The new life takes shape in a community in which men know that God loves and accepts them in spite of what they are. They therefore accept themselves and love others, knowing that no man has any ground on which to stand except God's grace.

The new life does not release a man from conflict with unbelief, pride, lust, fear. He still has to struggle with disheartening difficulties and problems. Nevertheless, as he matures in love and faithfulness in his life with Christ, he lives in freedom and good cheer, bearing witness on good days and evil days, confident that the new life is pleasing to God and helpful to others.

The new life finds its direction in the life of Jesus, his deeds and words, his struggles against temptation, his compassion, his anger, and his willingness to suffer death. The teaching of apostles and prophets guides men in living this life, and the Christian community nurtures and equips them for their ministries.

The members of the church are emissaries of peace and seek the good of man in cooperation with powers and authorities in politics, culture, and economics. But they have to fight against pretensions and injustices when these same powers endanger human welfare. Their strength is in their confidence that God's purpose rather than man's schemes will finally prevail.

Life in Christ is life eternal. The resurrection of Jesus is God's sign that he will consummate his work of creation and reconciliation beyond death and bring to fulfillment the new life begun in Christ.

2. THE BIBLE

The one sufficient revelation of God is Jesus Christ, the Word of God incarnate, to whom the Holy Spirit bears unique and authoritative witness through the Holy Scriptures, which are received and obeyed as the word of God written. The Scriptures are not a witness among others, but the witness without parallel. The church has received the books of the Old and New Testaments as prophetic and apostolic testimony in which it hears the Word of God and by which its faith and obedience are nourished and regulated.

The New Testament is the recorded testimony of apostles to the coming of the Messiah, Jesus of Nazareth, and the sending of the Holy Spirit to the Church. The Old Testament bears witness to God's faithfulness in his covenant with Israel and points the way to the fulfillment of his purpose in Christ. The Old Testament is indispensable to understanding the New, and is not itself fully understood without the New.

The Bible is to be interpreted in the light of its witness to God's work of reconciliation in Christ. The Scriptures, given under the guidance of the Holy Spirit, are nevertheless the words of men, conditioned by the language, thought forms, and literary fashions of the places and times at which they were written. They reflect views of life, history, and the cosmos which were then current. The church, therefore, has an obligation to approach the Scriptures with literary and historical understanding. As God has spoken his word in diverse cultural situations, the church is confident that he will continue to speak through the Scriptures in a changing world and in every form of human culture.

God's word is spoken to his church today where the Scriptures are faithfully preached and attentively read in dependence on the illumination of the Holy Spirit and with readiness to receive their truth and direction.

PART II
THE MINISTRY OF RECONCILIATION
Section A. The Mission of the Church
1. DIRECTION

To be reconciled to God is to be sent into the world as his reconciling community. This community, the church universal, is entrusted with God's message of reconciliation and shares his labor of healing the enmities which separate men from God and from each other. Christ has called the church to this mission and given it the gifts of the Holy Spirit. The church maintains continuity with the apostles and with Israel by faithful obedience to his call.

The life, death, resurrection, and promised coming of Jesus Christ has set the pattern for the church's mission. His life as man involves the church in the common life of men. His service to men commits the church to work for every form of human well-being. His suffering makes the church sensitive to all the sufferings of mankind so that it sees the face of Christ in the faces of men in every kind of need. His crucifixion discloses to the church God's judgment on man's inhumanity to man and the awful consequences of its own complicity in injustice. In the power of the risen Christ and the hope of his coming the church sees the promise of God's renewal of man's life in society and of God's victory over all wrong.

The church follows this pattern in the form of its life and in the method of its action. So to live and serve is to confess Christ as Lord.

2. FORMS AND ORDER

The institutions of the people of God change and vary as their mission requires in different times and places. The unity of the church is compatible with a wide variety of forms, but it is hidden and distorted when variant forms are allowed to harden into sectarian divisions, exclusive denominations, and rival factions.

Wherever the church exists, its members are both gathered in corporate life and dispersed in society for the sake of mission in the world.

The church gathers to praise God, to hear his word for mankind, to baptize and to join in the Lord's Supper, to pray for and present the world to him in worship, to enjoy fellowship, to receive instruction, strength, and comfort, to order and organize its own corporate life, to be tested, renewed, and reformed, and to speak and act in the world's affairs as may be appropriate to the needs of the time.

The church disperses to serve God wherever its members are, at work or play, in private or in the life of society. Their prayer and Bible study are part of the church's worship and theological reflection. Their witness is the church's evangelism. Their daily action in the world is the church in mission to the world. The quality of their relation with other persons is the measure of the church's fidelity.

Each member is the church in the world, endowed by the Spirit with some gift of ministry and is responsible for the integrity of his witness in his own particular situation. He is entitled to the guidance and support of the Christian community and is subject to its advice and correction. He in turn, in his own competence, helps to guide the church.

In recognition of special gifts of the Spirit and for the ordering of its life as a community, the church calls, trains, and authorizes certain members for leadership and oversight. The persons qualified for these duties in accordance with the polity of the church are set apart by ordination or other appropriate act and thus made responsible for their special ministries.

The church thus orders its life as an institution with a constitution, government, officers, finances, and administrative rules. These are instruments of mission, not ends in themselves. Different orders have served the gospel, and none can claim exclusive validity. A presbyterian polity recognizes the responsibility of all members for ministry and maintains the organic relation of all congregations in the church. It seeks to protect the church from exploitation by ecclesiastical or secular power and ambition. Every church order must be open to such reformation as may be required to make it a more effective instrument of the mission of reconciliation.

3. REVELATION AND RELIGION

The church in its mission encounters the religions of men and in that encounter becomes conscious of its own human character as a religion. God's revelation to Israel, expressed within Semitic culture, gave rise to the religion of the Hebrew people. God's revelation in Jesus Christ called forth the response of Jews and Greeks and came to expression within Judaism and Hellenism as the Christian religion. The Christian religion, as distinct from God's revelation of himself, has been shaped throughout its history by the cultural forms of its environment.

The Christian finds parallels between other religions and his own and must approach all religions with openness and respect. Repeatedly God has used the insight of non-Christians to challenge the church to renewal. But the reconciling word of the gospel is God's judgment upon all forms of religion, including the Christian. The gift of God in Christ is for all men. The church, therefore, is commissioned to carry the gospel to all men whatever their religion may be and even when they profess none.

4. RECONCILIATION IN SOCIETY

In each time and place there are particular problems and crises through which God calls the church to act. The church, guided by the Spirit, humbled by its own complicity and instructed by all attainable knowledge, seeks to discern the will of God and learn how to obey in these concrete situations. The following are particularly urgent at the present time.

a. God has created the peoples of the earth to be one universal family. In his reconciling love he overcomes the barriers between brothers and breaks down every form of discrimination based on racial or ethnic difference, real or imaginary. The church is called to bring all men to receive and uphold one another as persons in all relationships of life: in employment, housing, education, leisure, marriage, family, church, and the exercise of political rights. Therefore the church labors for the abolition of all racial discrimination and ministers to those injured by it. Congregations, individuals, or groups of Christians who exclude, dominate, or patronize their fellowmen, however subtly, resist the Spirit of God and bring contempt on the faith which they profess.

b. God's reconciliation in Jesus Christ is the ground of the peace, justice, and freedom among nations which all powers of government are called to serve and defend. The church, in its own life, is called to practice the forgiveness of enemies and to commend to the nations as practical politics the search for cooperation and peace. This requires the pursuit of fresh and responsible relations across every line of conflict, even at risk to national security, to reduce areas of strife and to broaden international understanding. Reconciliation among nations becomes peculiarly urgent as countries develop nuclear, chemical, and biological weapons, diverting their manpower and resources from constructive uses and risking the annihilation of mankind. Although nations may serve God's purposes in history, the church which identifies the sovereignty of any one nation or any one way of life with the cause of God denies the Lordship of Christ and betrays its calling.

c. The reconciliation of man through Jesus Christ makes it plain that enslaving poverty in a world of abundance is an intolerable violation of God's good creation. Because Jesus identified himself with the needy and exploited, the cause of the world's poor is the cause of his disciples. The church cannot condone poverty, whether it is the product of unjust social structures, exploitation of the defenseless, lack of national resources, absence of technological understanding, or rapid expansion of populations. The church calls every man to use his abilities, his possessions, and the fruits of technology as gifts entrusted to him by God for the maintenance of his family and the advancement of the common welfare. It encourages those forces in human society that raise men's hopes for better conditions and provide them with opportunity for a decent living. A church that is indifferent to poverty, or evades responsibility in economic affairs, or is open to one social class only, or expects gratitude for its beneficence makes a mockery of reconciliation and offers no acceptable worship to God.

d. The relationship between man and woman exemplifies in a basic way God's ordering of the interpersonal life for which he created mankind. Anarchy in sexual relationships is a symptom of man's alienation from God, his neighbor, and himself. Man's perennial confusion about the meaning of sex has been aggravated in our day by the availability of new means for birth control and the treatment of infection, by the pressures of urbanization, by the exploitation of sexual symbols in mass communication, and by world overpopulation. The church, as the household of God, is called to lead men out of this alienation into the responsible freedom of the new life in Christ. Reconciled to God, each person has joy in and respect for his own humanity and that of other persons; a man and woman are enabled to marry, to commit themselves to a mutually shared life, and to respond to each other in sensitive and lifelong concern; parents receive the grace to care for children in love and to nurture their individuality. The church comes under the judgment of God and invites rejection by man when it fails to lead men and women into the full meaning of life together, or withholds the compassion of Christ from those caught in the moral confusion of our time.

Section B. The Equipment of the Church

Jesus Christ has given the church preaching and teaching, praise and prayer, and Baptism and the Lord's Supper as means of fulfilling its service of God among men. These gifts remain, but the church is obliged to change the forms of its service in ways appropriate to different generations and cultures.

1. PREACHING AND TEACHING

God instructs his church and equips it for mission through preaching and teaching. By these, when they are carried on in fidelity to the Scriptures and dependence upon the Holy Spirit, the people hear the word of God and accept and follow Christ. The message is addressed to men in particular situations. Therefore effective preaching, teaching, and personal witness require disciplined study of both the Bible and the contemporary world. All acts of public worship should be conducive to men's hearing of the gospel in a particular time and place and responding with fitting obedience.

2. PRAISE AND PRAYER

The church responds to the message of reconciliation in praise and prayer. In that response it commits itself afresh to its mission, experiences a deepening of faith and obedience, and bears open testimony to the gospel. Adoration of God is acknowledgement of the Creator by the creation. Confession of sin is admission of all men's guilt before God and of their need for his forgiveness. Thanksgiving is rejoicing in God's goodness to all men and in giving for the needs of others. Petitions and intercessions are addressed to God for the continuation of his goodness, the healing of men's ills, and their deliverance from every form of oppression. The arts, especially music and architecture, contribute to the praise and prayer of a Christian congregation when they help men to look beyond themselves to God and to the world which is the object of his love.

3. BAPTISM

By humble submission to John's baptism Christ joined himself to men in their need and entered upon his ministry of reconciliation in the power of the Spirit. Christian baptism marks the receiving of the same Spirit by all his people. Baptism with water represents not only cleansing from sin but a dying Christ and a joyful rising with him to new life. It commits all Christians to die each day to sin and to live for righteousness. In baptism the church celebrates the renewal of the covenant with which God has bound his people to himself. By baptism individuals are publicly received into the church to share in its life and ministry, and the church becomes responsible for their training and support in Christian discipleship. When those baptized are infants the congregation, as well as the parents, has a special obligation to nurture them in the Christian life, leading them to make, by a public profession, a personal response to the love of God shown forth in their baptism.

4. THE LORD'S SUPPER

The Lord's Supper is a celebration of the reconciliation of men with God and with one another, in which they joyfully eat and drink together at the table of their Savior. Jesus Christ gave his church this remembrance of his dying for sinful men so that by participation in it they have communion with him and with all who shall be gathered to him. Partaking in him as they eat the bread and drink the wine in accordance with Christ's appointment, they receive from the risen and living Lord the benefits of his death and resurrection. They rejoice in the foretaste of the kingdom which he will bring to consummation at his promised coming, and go out from the Lord's Table with courage and hope for the service to which he has called them.

PART III
THE FULFILLMENT OF RECONCILIATION

God's redeeming work in Jesus Christ embraces the whole of man's life: social and cultural, economic and political, scientific and technological, individual and corporate. It includes man's natural environment as exploited and despoiled by sin. It is the will of God that his purpose for human life shall be fulfilled under the rule of Christ and all evil be banished from his creation.

Biblical visions and images of the rule of Christ such as a heavenly city, a father's house, a new heaven and earth, a marriage feast, and an unending day culminate in the image of the kingdom. The kingdom represents the triumph of God over all that resists his will and disrupts his creation. Already God's reign is present as a ferment in the world, stirring hope in men and preparing the world to receive its ultimate judgment and redemption.

With an urgency born of this hope the church applies itself to present tasks and strives for a better world. It does not identify limited progress with the kingdom of God on earth, nor does it despair in the face of disappointment and defeat. In steadfast hope the church looks beyond all partial achievement to the final triumph of God.

"Now to him who by the power at work within us is able to do far more abundantly than all we ask or think, to him be glory in the church and in Christ Jesus to all generations, forever and ever. Amen."

3. Anglicanism

The English Reformation had less doctrinal beginnings than its counterpart on the Continent. While the rulers of England had been restive about Rome for years before Henry VIII, the term *Ecclesia Anglicana* basically meant the Church in England. It was only when Tudor sovereigns in the sixteenth century decided to measure their strength with the Papacy that the situation changed.

Historians trace the origins of Anglicanism to a period covering thirty-six years, from 1527 when Henry VIII first proposed the annulment of his marriage to ecclesiastical authorities, to 1563 when his daughter, Queen Elizabeth I, promulgated the Thirty-Nine Articles under severe penalties. Between these dates the Church *in* England became the Church *of* England, with profound alterations in doctrine and religious practice.

Under pressure from Henry, the higher clergy disavowed the pope's spiritual jurisdiction in a famous "Abjuration of Papal Supremacy." At the Convocation of Canterbury in 1534, in reply to the question, "Whether the Roman Pontiff has any greater jurisdiction bestowed on him by God in the Holy Scriptures in this realm of England, than any other foreign (*externus*) bishop," they voted: Noes 34, Doubtful 1, Ayes 4. In the same year, the Convocation of York "unanimously and concordantly, with no dissentient," affirmed the same.

During the minority of Henry's son, Edward VI, the *Book of Common Prayer* was published in two editions (1549 and 1552), first along Lutheran and then Calvinist lines. A new *Ordinal* was issued (1550-1552) following a Lutheran pattern, in which every mention of a priesthood offering sacrifice was carefully omitted from the ordination ritual. However, the complete rupture with Catholicism did not come until 1563, when the Elizabethan Par-

169

liament made the Articles of Religion obligatory on all citizens under heavy penalties.

The main credit for establishing the English church should be given to Queen Elizabeth I (1533-1603) who inherited a religious problem at her accession and tried to solve it according to political expediency. When she became queen in 1558, the country as a whole was still predominantly Catholic, though with strong Calvinist undercurrents. Elizabeth disliked Catholics because they denied her legitimacy and spiritual supremacy, and the Calvinists because they abolished the episcopacy which she considered essential for the welfare of kings. Penal legislation was consistently directed against both elements. Among other laws, two acts of 1593 were a sweeping condemnation "of seditious sectaries and disloyal persons" who obstinately refused to attend Anglican church services, to be "committed to prison" and there to remain until they conform "according to Her Majesty's laws and statutes."

After a century of controversy against Catholics and Puritans, the English Church settled down from 1689 to a period of quiet. The Methodist departure in the eighteenth century and the Oxford movement in the nineteenth marked the critical stages in a new Anglicanism, whose main features are still rooted in the Reformation but whose present status in the English-speaking world is in the nature of a compromise between historical Protestantism and the Catholic Church.

Episcopalianism, as the English Church is known in America, was brought to the colonies in 1607 by a group of English settlers who founded what is now Jamestown, Virginia. The Episcopalians officially left the parent church at the time of the American Revolution, and proceeded to revise their juridical structure in a way compatible with a non-established denomination. They adopted the name Protestant Episcopal Church, which has been the subject of much discussion but emphasizes the unique character of American Episcopalianism: a democratic church united in spirit with the Anglican Communion throughout the world and committed to a poilcy of cooperation with other Protestant bodies, irrespective of their doctrinal traditions.

There is no easy way of describing the doctrinal position of Anglicanism or its Episcopalian segment in the United States. First a distinction should be made between the Anglican Communion and Anglicanism. The former represents the church in communion with and recognizing the leadership of the see of Canterbury, whether in England or elsewhere. Anglicanism properly applies to the system of doctrine and practice upheld by those Christians who may be very loosely affiliated with Canterbury but whose religious outlook claims to be distinct from that of other Christian communions both Catholic and Protestant.

By their own definition, Episcopalians belong to a church that is a member of the family known as the Anglican Churches. The term Anglican, however, does not imply adherence to the teachings of a religious leader as does "Lutheran" or "Calvinist." It means that Christian tradition which became the ethos of the Church of England and then spread to other countries. As expressed by the Anglican Congress in 1954, the Anglican Communion is a fellowship of churches at one and the same time catholic in seeking to do justice to the wholeness of Christian truth, in emphasizing continuity through the episcopate and in retaining the historic creeds and sacraments of undivided Christendom; and evangelical in its commission to proclaim the Gospel and in its emphasis on personal faith in Jesus Christ as Savior.

The accent between these contraries has produced three types of Episcopalian parishes, sometimes mistaken as separate denominations—the high, low and broad. In general a high parish stresses sacramental ritual, the supreme value of the Catholic tradition and a rather elaborate service of worship. At the other extreme, the low parish minimizes the liturgy; its services are simple and a stronger emphasis is placed on the Gospel and on personal religion. Between the two is the broad parish, which may be either high or low, but where the importance of a rational understanding of the Christian tradition is stressed, with a concern for "liberal" values.

In spite of these differences, there is a common core of beliefs and attitudes which Episcopalians regard as their special inheritance. This core is literally contained in the *Book of Common Prayer*, first compiled by Thomas Cranmer and others to produce in English a single comprehensive and authoritative guide for clergy and people. In 1549 Parliament had the first *Prayer Book* of Edward VI printed and by the first Act of Uniformity enforced it as the "national use." An *Ordinal* was issued in 1550.

Essentially a compromise volume between the Catholic and Reformed tendencies in the Church of England, the *Book of Common Prayer* was re-issued in 1552 with such major revisions as: omission of all references to Mass and altar, deletion of prayers for the dead. A year later, Queen Mary's Act of Repeal restored the ancient services. But with Elizabeth's accession to the throne, the *Book* was republished (1559) with only slight alterations and remained unchanged for the rest of the sixteenth century.

Puritan objections to the *Book of Common Prayer* and the political crises in England led to further revision. The 1662 edition has remained standard ever since, though a revised *Lectionary* was drawn up in 1871 and the Shortened Services Act (1872) allowed a more elastic interpretation of some of the rubrics.

Under suasion of the Oxford Movement, sentiment in favor of drastic revision built up to the point that a Royal Commission was appointed to undertake the task. No less than one hundred and eighteen meetings were held with the final decision to retain the 1662 *Book* and embody all changes in a new book, the use of which should be wholly permissive. Among other changes, it provided new rites for Baptism and Matrimony and reservation of the Sacrament was allowed.

Although passed in the Convocations and the Church Assembly by large majorities, Parliament turned down the new book in 1927 and again in 1928. Favored by the House of Lords, the Commons defeated the revision by a final vote of 266 to 220.

Without formal authority, the 1928 book was issued in England and continues to be used by many churches in a variety of editions. Its American equivalent went through a similar experience and also without formal approval by Parliament. The American *Book of Common Prayer* was thoroughly revised in 1928 along the same lines as in England. Most of the changes involved a recasting of the ultra-Protestant edition of 1552 and a return to that of 1549.

The doctrinal sections of the *Book of Common Prayer* are mainly the Thirty-Nine Articles, the Homilies referred to in Article 35, the Offices of Instruction, and the Catechism. Among these the Articles and the Episcopalian Catechism are of primary importance.

THIRTY-NINE ARTICLES

The best description of the Thirty-Nine Articles is to say that they are doctrinal formulae accepted by the Anglican Communion in the attempt to define its dogmatic position midway between Reformed Protestantism and Roman Catholicism. Their history of composition covered Ten Articles (1536), the Bishops' Book (1537), the Six Articles (1539), the King's Book (1543) and the Forty-Two Articles (1553). By a slight revision of the last-named, the Convocation of Bishops issued the first text of the Thirty-Nine Articles under Elizabeth.

A point commonly overlooked in treating of the Articles is that their definitive form was drafted during the sessions of the Council of Trent, and that, at least in several crucial places, the Articles were intended as a direct answer to Trent. Thus as early as 1546, Trent had declared that the canon of the Bible included the seven books dropped from the Old Testament by Luther and Calvin. The Articles responded by excising these books from the Scriptures. Again in 1547 the Council of Trent laid down that all seven sacraments were instituted by Christ. The Elizabethan Articles allow only two sacraments this institution.

On the other hand, the Articles avoided favoring an extreme Calvinism. They teach, for instance, that a man who has received the Holy Spirit and fallen into sin, "may rise again." The strict Calvinist would say "must rise again." In the same way one of the Articles lays down that "Christ died for all actual sins of men," where followers of the Synod of Dort would say that "Christ died only for the elect." If evidence is needed that the Articles are not Calvinistic, it is furnished by the repeated attempts made by the Puritans to alter or supplement them. The writing of the Westminster Confession, in fact, is the best witness that Reformed Protestantism in England was not satisfied with the Thirty-Nine Articles.

Church historians sometimes treat the Articles lightly and speak of them as archaisms which do not reflect the present-day spirit of Anglicanism. This is a mistake. No doubt they are not in the same category as the great ecumenical Creeds, and they tend to be more negative than positively dogmatic. Nevertheless they express the basic positions of faith of the Anglican Communion, to which numerous commentaries bear eloquent testimony. According to their most famous modern interpreter (Bicknell), "though certain Articles deal with questions that in their old form have no interest for the modern mind, the majority deal with those fundamental problems of theology that are debated anew in every age. Since in certain instances such Articles represent the typical attitude of the Church of England towards such problems, their statements have more than a bare historical interest."

As might be expected, the Articles are not perfectly identical as between England and the United States (or other countries). The strongly Erastian spirit of the English version, which places final authority over the Church in the hands of the sovereign, is softened or simply deleted in editions of the Articles outside the British Commonwealth.

I. *Of Faith in the Holy Trinity.* There is but one living and true God, everlasting, without body, parts, or passions; of infinite power, wisdom, and goodness; the Maker, and Preserver of all things both visible and invisible. And in unity of this Godhead there be three Persons, of one substance, power, and eternity; the Father, the Son, and the Holy Ghost.

II. *Of the Word or Son of God, which was made very Man.* The Son, which is the Word of the Father, begotten from everlasting of the Father, the very and eternal God, and of one substance with the Father, took Man's nature in the womb of the blessed Virgin, of her substance: so that two whole and perfect Natures, that is to say, the Godhead and Manhood, were joined together in one Person, never to be divided, whereof is one Christ, very God, and very Man; who truly suffered, was crucified, dead, and buried, to reconcile his Father to us, and to be a sacrifice, not only for original guilt, but also for actual sins of men.

III. *Of the going down of Christ into Hell.* As Christ died for us, and was buried; so also is it to be believed, that he went down into Hell.

IV. *Of the Resurrection of Christ.* Christ did truly rise again from death, and took again his body, with flesh, bones, and all things appertaining to the perfection of Man's nature; wherewith he ascended into Heaven, and there sitteth, until he return to judge all Men at the last day.

V. *Of the Holy Ghost.* The Holy Ghost, proceeding from the Father and the Son, is of one substance, majesty, and glory, with the Father and the Son, very and eternal God.

VI. *Of the Sufficiency of the Holy Scriptures for Salvation.* Holy Scripture containeth all things necessary to salvation: so that whatsoever is not read therein, nor may be proved thereby, is not to be required of any man, that it should be believed as an article of Faith, or be thought requisite or necessary to salvation. In the name of the Holy Scripture we do understand those canonical Books of the Old and New Testament, of whose authority was never any doubt in the Church.

Of the Names and Numbers of the Canonical Books.

Genesis,
Exodus,
Leviticus,
Numbers,
The First Book of Samuel,
The Second Book of Samuel,
The First Book of Kings,
The Second Book of Kings,
The First Book of Chronicles,
The Second Book of Chronicles,
The First Book of Esdras,
The Second Book of Esdras,
Deuteronomy,
Joshua,
Judges,
Ruth,
The Book of Esther,
The Book of Job,
The Psalms,
The Proverbs,
Ecclesiastes or Preacher,
Cantica, or Songs of Solomon,
Four Prophets the greater,
Twelve Prophets the less.

And the other Books (as Hierome saith) the Church doth read for example of life and instruction of manners; but yet doth it not apply them to establish any doctrine; such are these following:

The Third Book of Esdras,
The Fourth Book of Esdras,
The Book of Tobias,
The Book of Judith,
The rest of the Book of Esther,
The Book of Wisdom,
Jesus the Son of Sirach,
Baruch the Prophet,
The Song of the Three Children,
The Story of Susanna,
Of Bel and the Dragon,
The Prayer of Manasses,
The First Book of Maccabees,
The Second Book of Maccabees,

All the Books of the New Testament, as they are commonly received, we do receive, and account them Canonical.

VII. *Of the Old Testament.* The Old Testament is not contrary to the New: for both in the Old and New Testament everlasting life is offered to Mankind by Christ, who is the only Mediator between God and Man, being both God and Man. Wherefore they are not to be heard, which feign that the old Fathers did look only for transitory promises.

Although the Law given from God by Moses, as touching Ceremonies and Rites, do not bind Christian men, nor the Civil precepts thereof ought of necessity to be received in any commonwealth; yet notwithstanding, no Christian man whatsoever is free from the obedience of the Commandments which are called Moral.

VIII. *Of the Creeds.* The Nicene Creed, and that which is commonly called the Apostles' Creed, ought thoroughly to be received and believed: for they may be proved by most certain warrants of Holy Scripture.

IX. *Of Original or Birth-Sin.* Original Sin standeth not in the following of Adam, (as the Pelagians do vainly talk;) but it is the fault and corruption of the Nature of every man, that naturally is engendered of the offspring of Adam; whereby man is very far gone from original righteousness, and is of his own nature inclined to evil, so that the flesh lusteth always contrary to the Spirit; and therefore in every person born into this world, it deserveth God's wrath and damnation. And this infection of nature doth remain, yea in them that are regenerated; whereby the lust of the flesh, called in Greek φρόνημα φαρκός, (which some do expound the wisdom, some sensuality, some the affection, some the desire, of the flesh,) is not subject to the law of God. And although there is no condemnation for them that believe and are baptized; yet the Apostle doth confess, that concupiscence and lust hath of itself the nature of sin.

X. *Of Free-Will.* The condition of Man after the fall of Adam is such, that he cannot turn and prepare himself, by his own natural strength and good works, to faith, and calling upon God. Wherefore we have no power to do good works pleasant and acceptable to God, without the grace of God by Christ preventing us, that we may have a good will, and working with us, when we have that good will.

XI. *Of the Justification of Man.* We are accounted righteous before God, only for the merit of our Lord and Saviour Jesus Christ by Faith, and not for our own works or deservings. Wherefore, that we are justified by Faith only, is a most wholesome Doctrine, and very full of comfort, as more largely is expressed in the Homily of Justification.

XII. *Of Good Works.* Albeit that Good Works, which are the fruits of Faith, and follow after Justification, cannot put away our sins, and endure the severity of God's judgment; yet are they pleasing and acceptable to God in Christ, and do spring out necessarily of a true and lively Faith; insomuch that by them a lively Faith may be as evidently known as a tree discerned by the fruit.

XIII. *Of Works before Justification.* Works done before the grace of

Christ, and the Inspiration of his Spirit, are not pleasant to God, forasmuch as they spring not of faith in Jesus Christ; neither do they make men meet to receive grace, or (as the School-authors say) deserve grace of congruity: yea rather, for that they are not done as God hath willed and commanded them to be done, we doubt not but they have the nature of sin.

XIV. *Of Works of Supererogation.* Voluntary Works besides, over and above, God's Commandments, which they call Works of Supererogation, cannot be taught without arrogancy and impiety: for by them men do declare, that they do not only render unto God as much as they are bound to do, but that they do more for his sake, than of bounden duty is required: whereas Christ saith plainly, When ye have done all that are commanded to you, say, We are unprofitable servants.

XV. *Of Christ alone without Sin.* Christ in the truth of our nature was made like unto us in all things, sin only except, from which he was clearly void, both in his flesh, and in his spirit. He came to be the Lamb without spot, who, by sacrifice of himself once made, should take away the sins of the world; and sin (as Saint John saith) was not in him. But all we the rest, although baptized, and born again in Christ, yet offend in many things: and if we say we have no sin, we deceive ourselves, and the truth is not in us.

XVI. *Of Sin after Baptism.* Not every deadly sin willingly committed after Baptism is sin against the Holy Ghost, and unpardonable. Wherefore the grant of repentance is not to be denied to such as fall into sin after Baptism. After we have received the Holy Ghost, we may depart from grace given, and fall into sin, and by the grace of God we may arise again, and amend our lives. And therefore they are to be condemned, which say, they can no more sin as long as they live here, or deny the place of forgiveness to such as truly repent.

XVII. *Of Predestination and Election.* Predestination to Life is the everlasting purpose of God, whereby (before the foundations of the world were laid) he hath constantly decreed by his counsel secret to us, to deliver from curse and damnation those whom he hath chosen in Christ out of mankind, and to bring them by Christ to everlasting salvation, as vessels made to honour. Wherefore, they which be endued with so excellent a benefit of God, be called according to God's purpose by his Spirit working in due season: they through Grace obey the calling: they be justified freely: they be made sons of God by adoption: they be made like the image of his only-begotten Son Jesus Christ: they walk religiously in good works, and at length, by God's mercy, they attain to everlasting felicity.

As the godly consideration of Predestination, and our Election in Christ, is full of sweet, pleasant, and unspeakable comfort to godly persons, and such as feel in themselves the working of the Spirit of Christ, mortifying the works of the flesh, and their earthly members, and drawing up their mind to high and heavenly things, as well because it doth greatly establish and confirm their faith of eternal Salvation to be enjoyed through Christ, as because it doth fervently kindle their love towards God: So, for curious and carnal·persons, lacking the Spirit of Christ, to have continually before their eyes the sentence of God's Predestination, is a most dangerous downfall, whereby the Devil doth thrust them either into desperation, or into wretchlessness of most unclean living, no less perilous than desperation.

Furthermore, we must receive God's promises in such wise, as they be generally set forth to us in Holy Scripture: and, in our doings, that Will of God is to be followed, which we have expressly declared unto us in the Word of God.

XVIII. *Of obtaining eternal Salvation only by the Name of Christ.* They also are to be had accursed that presume to say, That every man shall be saved by the Law or Sect which he professeth, so that he be diligent to frame his life according to that Law, and the light of Nature. For Holy Scripture doth set out unto us only the Name of Jesus Christ, whereby men must be saved.

XIX. *Of the Church.* The visible Church of Christ is a congregation of faithful men, in the which the pure Word of God is preached, and the Sacraments be duly ministered according to Christ's ordinance, in all those things that of necessity are requisite to the same.

As the Church of Jerusalem, Alexandria, and Antioch, have erred; so also the Church of Rome hath erred, not only in their living and manner of Ceremonies, but also in matters of Faith.

XX. *Of the Authority of the Church.* The Church hath power to decree Rites or Ceremonies, and authority in Controversies of Faith: and yet it is not lawful for the Church to ordain any thing that is contrary to God's Word written, neither may it so expound one place of Scripture, that it be repugnant to another. Wherefore, although the Church be a witness and a keeper of Holy Writ, yet, as it ought not to decree any thing against the same, so besides the same ought it not to enforce any thing to be believed for necessity of Salvation.

XXI. *Of the Authority of General Councils.* (The Twenty-first of the former Articles is omitted; because it is partly of a local and civil nature, and is provided for, as to the remaining parts of it, in other Articles.)

XXII. *Of Purgatory.* The Romish Doctrine concerning Purgatory, Pardons, Worshipping and Adoration, as well of Images as of Relics, and also Invocation of Saints, is a fond thing, vainly invented, and grounded upon no warranty of Scripture, but rather repugnant to the Word of God.

XXIII. *Of Ministering in the Congregation.* It is not lawful for any man to take upon him the office of public preaching, or ministering the Sacraments in the Congregation, before he be lawfully called, and sent to execute the same. And those we ought to judge lawfully called and sent, which be chosen and called to this work by men who have public authority given unto them in the Congregation, to call and send Ministers into the Lord's vineyard.

XXIV. *Of Speaking in the Congregation in such a Tongue as the People understandeth.* It is a thing plainly repugnant to the Word of God, and the custom of the Primitive Church, to have public Prayer in the Church, or to minister the Sacraments, in a tongue not understanded of the people.

XXV. *Of the Sacraments.* Sacraments ordained of Christ be not only badges or tokens of Christian men's profession, but rather they be certain sure witnesses, and effectual signs of grace, and God's good will towards us, by the which he doth work invisibly in us, and doth not only quicken, but also strengthen and confirm our Faith in him.

There are two Sacraments ordained of Christ our Lord in the Gospel, that is to say, Baptism, and the Supper of the Lord.

Those five commonly called Sacraments, that is to say, Confirmation, Penance, Orders, Matrimony, and Extreme Unction, are not to be counted for Sacraments of the Gospel, being such as have grown partly of the corrupt following of the Apostles, partly are states of life allowed in the Scriptures; but yet have not like nature of Sacraments with Baptism, and the Lord's Supper, for that they have not any visible sign or ceremony ordained of God.

The Sacraments were not ordained of Christ to be gazed upon, or to be carried about, but that we should duly use them. And in such only as worthily receive the same, they have a wholesome effect or operation: but they that receive them unworthily, purchase to themselves damnation, as Saint Paul saith.

XXVI. *Of the Unworthiness of the Ministers, which hinders not the effect of the Sacraments.* Although in the visible Church the evil be ever mingled with the good, and sometimes the evil have chief authority in the Ministration of the Word and Sacraments, yet forasmuch as they do not the same in their own name, but in Christ's, and do minister by his commission and authority, we may use their Ministry, both in hearing the Word of God, and in receiving the Sacraments. Neither is the effect of Christ's ordinance taken away by their wickedness, nor the grace of God's gifts diminished from such as by faith, and rightly, do receive the Sacraments ministered unto them; which be effectual, because of Christ's institution and promise, although they be ministered by evil men.

Nevertheless, it appertaineth to the discipline of the Church, that inquiry be made of evil Ministers, and that they be accused by those that have knowledge of their offences; and finally, being found guilty, by just judgment be deposed.

XXVII. *Of Baptism.* Baptism is not only a sign of profession, and mark of difference, whereby Christian men are discerned from others that be not christened, but it is also a sign of Regeneration or New-Birth, whereby, as by an instrument, they that receive Baptism rightly are grafted into the Church; the promises of the forgiveness of sin, and of our adoption to be the sons of God by the Holy Ghost, are visibly signed and sealed; Faith is confirmed, and Grace increased by virtue of prayer unto God.

The Baptism of young Children is in any wise to be retained in the Church, as most agreeable with the institution of Christ.

XXVIII. *Of the Lord's Supper.* The Supper of the Lord is not only a sign of the love that Christians ought to have among themselves one to another; but rather it is a Sacrament of our Redemption by Christ's death: insomuch that to such as rightly, worthily, and with faith, receive the same, the Bread which we break is a partaking of the Body of Christ; and likewise the Cup of Blessing is a partaking of the Blood of Christ.

Transubstantiation (or the change of the substance of Bread and Wine) in the Supper of the Lord, cannot be proved by Holy Writ; but is repugnant to the plain words of Scripture, overthroweth the nature of a Sacrament, and hath given occasion to many superstitions.

The Body of Christ is given, taken, and eaten, in the Supper, only after an heavenly and spiritual manner. And the mean whereby the Body of Christ is received and eaten in the Supper, is Faith.

The Sacrament of the Lord's Supper was not by Christ's ordinance reserved, carried about, lifted up, or worshipped.

XXIX. *Of the Wicked, which eat not the Body of Christ in the use of the Lord's Supper.* The Wicked, and such as be void of a lively faith, although they do carnally and visibly press with their teeth (as Saint Augustine saith) the Sacrament of the Body and Blood of Christ; yet in no wise are they partakers of Christ: but rather, to their condemnation, do eat and drink the sign or Sacrament of so great a thing.

XXX. *Of both Kinds.* The Cup of the Lord is not to be denied to the Lay-people: for both the parts of the Lord's Sacrament, by Christ's ordinance and commandment, ought to be ministered to all Christian men alike.

XXXI. *Of the one Oblation of Christ finished upon the Cross.* The Offering of Christ once made is that perfect redemption, propitiation, and satisfaction for all sins of the whole world, both original and actual; and there is none other satisfaction for sin, but that alone. Wherefore the sacrifices of Masses, in the which it was commonly said, that the Priest did offer Christ for the quick and the dead, to have remission of pain or guilt, were blasphemous fables, and dangerous deceits.

XXXII. *Of the Marriage of Priests.* Bishops, Priests, and Deacons, are not commanded by God's Law, either to vow the estate of single life, or to abstain from marriage: therefore it is lawful for them, as for all other Christian men, to marry at their own discretion, as they shall judge the same to serve better to godliness.

XXXIII. *Of excommunicate Persons, how they are to be avoided.* That person which by open denunciation of the Church is rightly cut off from the unity of the Church, and excommunicated, ought to be taken of the whole multitude of the faithful, as an Heathen and Publican, until he be openly reconciled by penance, and received into the Church by a Judge that hath authority thereunto.

XXXIV. *Of the Traditions of the Church.* It is not necessary that Traditions and Ceremonies be in all places one, or utterly like; for at all times they have been divers, and may be changed according to the diversity of countries, times, and men's manners, so that nothing be ordained against God's Word. Whosoever, through his private judgment, willingly and purposely, doth openly break the Traditions and Ceremonies of the Church, which be not repugnant to the Word of God, and be ordained and approved by common authority, ought to be rebuked openly, (that others may fear to do the like,) as he that offendeth against the common order of the Church, and hurteth the authority of the Magistrate, and woundeth the consciences of the weak brethren.

Every particular or national Church hath authority to ordain, change, and abolish, Ceremonies or Rites of the Church ordained only by man's authority, so that all things be done to edifying.

XXXV. *Of the Homilies.* The Second Book of Homilies, the several titles whereof we have joined under this Article, doth contain a godly and wholesome Doctrine, and necessary for these times, as doth the former Book of Homilies, which were set forth in the time of Edward the Sixth; and therefore we judge them to be read in Churches by the Ministers, diligently and distinctly, that they may be understanded of the people.

Of the Names of the Homilies.

1. Of the right Use of the Church.
2. Against Peril of Idolatry.
3. Of repairing and keeping clean of Churches.
4. Of good Works: first of Fasting.
5. Against Gluttony and Drunkenness.
6. Against Excess of Apparel.
7. Of Prayer.
8. Of the Place and Time of Prayer.
9. That Common Prayers and Sacraments ought to be ministered in a known tongue.
10. Of the reverend Estimation of God's Word.
11. Of Alms-doing.
12. Of the Nativity of Christ.
13. Of the Passion of Christ.
14. Of the Resurrection of Christ.
15. Of the worthy receiving of the Sacrament of the Body and Blood of Christ.
16. Of the Gifts of the Holy Ghost.
17. For the Rogation-days.
18. Of the State of Matrimony.
19. Of Repentance.
20. Against Idleness.
21. Against Rebellion.

(This Article is received in this Church, so far as it declares the Books of Homilies to be an explication of Christian doctrine, and instructive in piety and morals. But all references to the constitution and laws of England are considered as inapplicable to the circumstances of this Church; which also suspends the order for the reading of said Homilies in churches, until a revision of them may be conveniently made, for the clearing of them, as well from obsolete words and phrases, as from the local references.)

XXXVI. *Of Consecration of Bishops and Ministers.* The Book of Consecration of Bishops, and Ordering of Priests and Deacons, as set forth by the General Convention of this Church in 1792, doth contain all things necessary to such Consecration and Ordering; neither hath it any thing that, of itself, is superstitious and ungodly. And, therefore, whosoever are consecrated or ordered according to said Form, we decree all such to be rightly, orderly, and lawfully consecrated and ordered.

XXXVII. *Of the Power of the Civil Magistrates.* The Power of the Civil Magistrate extendeth to all men, as well Clergy as Laity, in all things temporal; but hath no authority in things purely spiritual. And we hold it to be the duty of all men who are professors of the Gospel, to pay respectful obedience to the Civil Authority, regularly and legitimately constituted.

XXXVIII. *Of Christian Men's Goods, which are not common.* The Riches and Goods of Christians are not common, as touching the right, title, and possession of the same; as certain Anabaptists do falsely boast. Notwithstanding, every man ought, of such things as he possesseth, liberally to give alms to the poor, according to his ability.

XXXIX. *Of a Christian Man's Oath.* As we confess that vain and rash Swearing is forbidden Christian men by our Lord Jesus Christ, and James his Apostle, so we judge, that Christian Religion doth not prohibit, but that a man may swear when the Magistrate requireth, in a cause of faith and charity, so it be done according to the Prophet's teaching, in justice, judgment, and truth.

EPISCOPALIAN CATECHISM

The Prayer-Book Catechism dates from the earliest editions of the Book of Common Prayer. It is a short instruction in the form of a series of questions and answers, "to be learned by every person before he be brought to be confirmed by the bishop."

Essentially it consists of an exposition of the Baptismal covenant followed by a section on the sacraments of Baptism and the Eucharist. In former times it was strictly observed but nowadays such instruction is seldom given in the course of the service. Yet the doctrinal content of the Catechism is just as valid as it ever was.

Of special significance is the treatment of the Eucharist, which serves as an official commentary on the Articles which deal with the Lord's Supper. The questions were added to the Catechism at the urging of the Puritans for some clarification of this critical subject.

Question. What is your Name?

Answer. N. or N.N.

Question. Who gave you this Name?

Answer. My Sponsors in Baptism; wherein I was made a member of Christ, the child of God, and an inheritor of the kingdom of heaven.

Question. What did your Sponsors then for you?

Answer. They did promise and vow three things in my name: First, that I should renounce the devil and all his works, the pomps and vanity of this wicked world, and all the sinful lusts of the flesh; Secondly, that I should believe all the Articles of the Christian Faith; And Thirdly, that I should keep God's holy will and commandments, and walk in the same all the days of my life.

Question. Dost thou not think that thou art bound to believe, and to do, as they have promised for thee?

Answer. Yes, verily; and by God's help so I will. And I heartily thank our heavenly Father, that he hath called me to this state of salvation, through Jesus Christ our Saviour. And I pray unto God to give me his grace, that I may continue in the same unto my life's end.

Catechist. Rehearse the Articles of thy Belief.

Answer. I believe in God the Father Almighty, Maker of heaven and earth:

And in Jesus Christ his only Son our Lord: Who was conceived by the Holy Ghost, Born of the Virgin Mary: Suffered under Pontius Pilate, Was crucified, dead, and buried: He descended into hell; The third day he rose again from the dead: He ascended into heaven, And sitteth on the right hand of God the Father Almighty: From thence he shall come to judge the quick and the dead.

I believe in the Holy Ghost: The holy Catholic Church; The Communion of Saints: The Forgiveness of sins: The Resurrection of the body: And the Life everlasting. Amen.

Question. What dost thou chiefly learn in these Articles of thy Belief?

Answer. First, I learn to believe in God the Father, who hath made me, and all the world.

Secondly, in God the Son, who hath redeemed me, and all mankind.

Thirdly, in God the Holy Ghost, who sanctifieth me, and all the people of God.

Question. You said that your Sponsors did promise for you, that you should keep God's Commandments. Tell me how many there are?

Answer. Ten.

Question. Which are they?

Answer. The same which God spake in the twentieth Chapter of Exodus, saying, I am the Lord thy God, who brought thee out of the land of Egypt, out of the house of bondage.

I. Thou shalt have none other gods but me.

II. Thou shalt not make to thyself any graven image, nor the likeness of any thing that is in heaven above, or in the earth beneath, or in the water under the earth; thou shalt not bow down to them, nor worship them; for I the LORD thy God am a jealous God, and visit the sins of the fathers upon the children, unto the third and fourth generation of them that hate me; and show mercy unto thousands in them that love me and keep my commandments.

III. Thou shalt not take the Name of the LORD thy God in vain; for the LORD will not hold him guiltless, that taketh his Name in vain.

IV. Remember that thou keep holy the Sabbath-day. Six days shalt thou labour, and do all that thou hast to do; but the seventh day is the Sabbath of the LORD thy God. In it thou shalt do no manner of work; thou, and thy son, and thy daughter, thy man-servant, and thy maid-servant, thy cattle, and the stranger that is within thy gates. For in six days the LORD made heaven and earth, the sea, and all that in them is, and rested the seventh day, and hallowed it.

V. Honour thy father and thy mother; that thy days may be long in the land which the LORD thy God giveth thee.

VI. Thou shalt do no murder.

VII. Thou shalt not commit adultery.

VIII. Thou shalt not steal.

VIII. Thou shalt not bear false witness against thy neighbour.

IX. Thou shalt not covet thy neighbour's house, thou shalt not covet thy neighbour's wife, nor his servant, nor his maid, nor his ox, nor his ass, nor any thing that is his.

Question. What dost thou chiefly learn by these Commandments?

Answer. I learn two things; my duty towards God, and my duty towards my Neighbour.

Question. What is thy duty towards God?

Answer. My duty towards God is To believe in him, to fear him, And to love him with all my heart, with all my mind, with all my soul, and with all my strength: To worship him, to give him thanks: To put my whole trust in him, to call upon him: To honour his holy Name and his Word: And to serve him truly all the days of my life.

Question. What is thy duty towards thy Neighbour?

Answer. My duty towards my Neighbour is To love him as myself, and to do to all men as I would they should do unto me: To love, honour, and succour my father and mother: To honour and obey the civil authority: To submit myself to all my governors, teachers, spiritual pastors and masters: To order myself lowly and reverently to all my betters: To hurt nobody by word or deed: To be true and just in all my dealings: To bear no malice nor hatred in my heart: To keep my hands from picking and stealing, and my tongue from evil speaking, lying, and slandering: To keep my body in temperance, soberness, and chastity: Not to covet nor desire other men's goods; But to learn and labour truly to get mine own living, And to do my duty in that state of life unto which it shall please God to call me.

Catechist. My good Child, know this; that thou art not able to do these things of thyself, nor to walk in the Commandments of God, and to serve him, without his special grace; which thou must learn at all times to call for by diligent prayer. Let me hear, therefore, if thou canst say the Lord's Prayer.

Answer. Our Father, who art in heaven, Hallowed be thy Name. Thy kingdom come. Thy will be done, On earth as it is in heaven. Give us this day our daily bread. And forgive us our trespasses, As we forgive those who trespass against us. And lead us not into temptation, But deliver us from evil. Amen.

Question. What desirest thou of God in this Prayer?

Answer. I desire my Lord God, our heavenly Father, who is the giver of all goodness, to send his grace unto me, and to all people; that we may worship him, serve him, and obey him, as we ought to do. And I pray unto God, that he will send us all things that are needful both for our souls and bodies; and that he will be merciful unto us, and forgive us our sins; and that it will please him to save and defend us in all dangers both of soul and body; and that he will keep us from all sin and wickedness, and from our spiritual enemy, and from everlasting death. And this I trust he will do of his mercy and goodness, through our Lord Jesus Christ. And therefore I say, Amen. So be it.

Question. How many Sacraments hath Christ ordained in his Church?

Answer. Two only, as generally necessary to salvation; that is to say, Baptism, and the Supper of the Lord.

Question. What meanest thou by the word *Sacrament?*

Answer. I mean an outward and visible sign of an inward and spiritual grace given unto us; ordained by Christ himself, as a means whereby we receive the same, and a pledge to assure us thereof.

Question. How many parts are there in a Sacrament?

Answer. Two; the outward visible sign, and the inward spiritual grace.

Question. What is the outward visible sign or form in Baptism?

Answer. Water; wherein the person is baptized, In the Name of the Father, and of the Son, and of the Holy Ghost.

Question. What is the inward and spiritual grace?

Answer. A death unto sin, and a new birth unto righteousness: for being by nature born in sin, and the children of wrath, we are hereby made the children of grace.

Question. What is required of persons to be baptized?

Answer. Repentance, whereby they forsake sin; and Faith, whereby they stedfastly believe the promises of God made to them in that Sacrament.

Question. Why then are Infants baptized, when by reason of their tender age they cannot perform them?

Answer. Because they promise them both by their Sureties; which promise, when they come to age, themselves are bound to perform.

Question. Why was the Sacrament of the Lord's Supper ordained?

Answer. For the continual remembrance of the sacrifice of the death of Christ, and of the benefits which we receive thereby.

Question. What is the outward part or sign of the Lord's Supper?

Answer. Bread and Wine, which the Lord hath commanded to be received.

Question. What is the inward part, or thing signified?

Answer. The Body and Blood of Christ, which are spiritually taken and received by the faithful in the Lord's Supper.

Question. What are the benefits whereof we are partakers thereby?

Answer. The strengthening and refreshing of our souls by the Body and Blood of Christ, as our bodies are by the Bread and Wine.

Question. What is required of those who come to the Lord's Supper?

Answer. To examine themselves, whether they repent them truly of their former sins, stedfastly purposing to lead a new life; have a lively faith in God's mercy through Christ, with a thankful remembrance of his death; and be in charity with all men.

§ *The Minister of every Parish shall diligently, upon Sundays and Holy Days, or on some other convenient occasions, openly in the Church, instruct or examine so many Children of his Parish, sent unto him, as he shall think convenient, in some part of this Catechism.*

§ *And all Fathers, Mothers, Masters, and Mistresses, shall cause their Children, Servants, and Apprentices, who have not learned their Catechism, to come to the Church at the time appointed, and obediently to hear and to be ordered by the Minister, until such time as they have learned all that is here appointed for them to learn.*

§ *So soon as Children are come to a competent age, and can say the Creed, the Lord's Prayer, and the Ten Commandments, and can answer to the other questions of this short Catechism, they shall be brought to the Bishop.*

§ *And whensoever the Bishop shall give knowledge for Children to be brought unto him for their Confirmation, the Minister of every Parish shall either bring, or send in writing, with his hand subscribed thereunto, the Names of all such Persons within his Parish, as he shall think fit to be presented to the Bishop to be confirmed.*

THE LAMBETH-CHICAGO QUADRILATERAL

Increasing readiness to cooperate and explore the possibilities of reunion marked the temper of the Protestant Episcopal Church in the United States during the nineteenth century. The most natural form of cooperation was to promote closer relation with other branches of the Anglican Communion. The first impulse in that direction came in 1865 from a Synod of the Church of England in Canada, which sent a message to the Archbishop of Canterbury urging him to arrange a conference of all bishops of the Anglican Church.

In a short time Archbishop Longley responded favorably by inviting one hundred and forty-four bishops. Seventy-six prelates —nineteen from the United States—finally attended the first Lambeth Conference at the Lambeth Palace in London for five days in September, 1867.

Eleven years later, with Archbishop Tait presiding, a second Lambeth Conference was held, with one hundred bishops in attendance. The meeting was so successful that except for interruptions caused by wars, Lambeth Conferences every ten years have become an honored tradition. At these sessions varied topics have been discussed, including temperance, divorce, socialism, war, Christian education and such fundamental issues of faith and order as affect Anglicanism throughout the world.

Among the pronouncements emanating from Lambeth, none stands higher in practical importance than the declaration of the

Conference of 1888, when the Lambeth Quadrilateral was issued. It was the outcome of thought and of initiative in the American Church. Eighteen years earlier, William Huntington, then rector of All Saints Church in Worcester, Massachusetts, had written a book called *The Church-Idea, an Essay towards Unity*. In the book he presented the Episcopal Church as the best hope for promoting Church unity in the United States. Disavowing any intention of asking others to become Anglicans, he offered as a basis what he called the Anglican principles. "The true Anglican," he wrote, "like the city of God in the Apocalypse, may be said to be foursquare. Honestly to accept that position is to accept: 1) The Holy Scriptures as the Word of God, 2) The Primitive Church as the Rule of Faith, i.e., the Apostles' and Nicene Creeds, 3) The Two Sacraments Ordained by Christ Himself, and 4) The Episcopate as the Key-stone of Government Unity." *

Huntington's plea was to change the face of Anglicanism in America. "If our whole ambition," he urged, "be to continue as a small but respectable body of Christians, and to offer a refuge to people of refinement and sensibility . . . then let us say as much in plain terms, and frankly renounce any and all claim to Catholicity. We have only in such case, to wrap the robe of our dignity about us, and walk quietly along in a seclusion no one will take much trouble to disturb. Thus may we be a Church in name and a sect in deed. But if we aim at something nobler than this, if we would have our Communion become national in very truth—in other words, if we would bring the Church of Christ into the closest possible sympathy with the throbbing, sorrowing, sinning, repenting, aspiring heart of this great people—then let us press our reasonable claims to be the reconciler of a divided household, not in a spirit of arrogance . . . but with affectionate earnestness and an intelligent zeal." * *

In 1870 Huntington complained that sectarianism was the accepted norm in American Protestantism, and another sixteen years passed before the Episcopal Church took any responsive action. At the General Convention of 1886, held at Chicago, the House of Bishops received a memorial dealing with the subject of Church unity and signed by more than eleven hundred clergy

* W. R. Huntington, *The Church-Idea, an Essay towards Unity*, New York, 4th edition, 1870, p. 169.
* * *Ibid.*, p. 170.

and three thousand laymen. A committee appointed at once to consider "the matter of the reunion of Christendom" recommended a Declaration concerning Unity which was later adopted by the House of Bishops. This is not only the most important statement of the subject ever officially published by the Episcopal Church, but the historical beginning of the world ecumenical movement as we now know it. For it was this strong initial impulse by his Church that prompted the American prelate Charles Brent (1862-1929), as bishop in the Philippines, to lead the Edinburgh Mission Conference in 1910 towards the formation of what eventually became the World Council of Churches.

The Lambeth Quadrilateral of 1888 was nearly identical with that set forth at Chicago. The third and fourth pillars of Anglicanism were kept without rewording. Even the first two were only slightly changed to read: a) The Holy Scriptures of the Old and New Testaments, as "containing all things necessary to salvation," and as being the rule and ultimate standard of faith; b) The Apostles' Creed, as the Baptismal Symbol, and the Nicene Creed as the sufficient statement of the Christian faith.

To all whom it may concern, and especially our fellow-Christians of the different communions in our land, who, in their several spheres, have contended for the religion of Christ, the bishops declared:

1. Our earnest desire that the Saviour's prayer that we all may be one may, in its deepest and truest sense, be speedily fulfilled;

2. That we believe that all who have been duly baptized with water in the name of the Father, and of the Son, and of the Holy Ghost, are members of the Holy Catholic Church;

3. That in all things of human ordering or human choice relating to modes of worship and discipline, or to traditional customs, this Church is ready, in the spirit of love and humility, to forego all preferences of her own;

4. That this Church does not seek to absorb other communions, but rather, cooperating with them on the basis of a common faith and order, to discountenance schism, to heal the wounds of the body of Christ, and to promote the charity which is the chief of Christian graces and the visible manifestation of Christ to the world:

But furthermore, we do hereby affirm that the Christian unity now so earnestly desired by the memorialists can be restored only by the principles of unity exemplified by the undivided Catholic Church during the first ages of its existence, which principles we believe to be the substantial deposit of Christian faith and order committed by Christ and His Apostles to the Church unto the end of the world, and therefore incapable of compromise or surrender by those who have been ordained to be its stewards and trustees for the common and equal benefit of all men.

As inherent part of this sacred deposit, and therefore as essential to the restoration of unity among the divided branches of Christendom, we account the following, to wit:

I. The Holy Scriptures of the Old and New Testaments, as the revealed Word of God;

II. The Nicene Creed, as the sufficient statement of the Christian faith;

III. The two sacraments, Baptism and the Supper of the Lord, ministered with unfailing use of Christ's words of institution, and of the elements ordained by Him;

IV. The Historic Episcopate, locally adapted in the methods of its administration to the varying needs of the nations and peoples called of God into the unity of His Church.

Furthermore, deeply grieved by the sad divisions which afflict the Christian Church in our own land, we hereby declare our desire and readiness, so soon as there shall be any authorized response to this Declaration, to enter into brotherly conference with all or any Christian bodies seeking the restoration of the organic unity of the Church, with a view to the earnest study of the conditions under which so priceless a blessing might happily be brought to pass.

ANGLICAN ORDERS

Anglicanism is unique in its stress on the historical episcopate and presbyterate, which are believed to derive from Christ's ordination of the Apostles at the Last Supper.

Near the center of Anglican faith and polity, therefore, is the conviction that reception of orders somehow places a man in direct relationship with the bishop who ordains him; that the bishop confers on him what he in turn had received from the prelate who raised him to the episcopate—going back through history to the cenacle in Jerusalem.

If this emphasis on ordination has always been typical of the

Anglican tradition, it has not always been uniform. In fact the changes in the Ordinal are not only historically interesting but so important that, without some understanding of them, it is impossible to know the Church of England or its numerous Episcopalian counterparts. The present-day Ordinal is itself a mirror of the Church's belief in the one area of doctrine that touches most nearly on the essence of Anglicanism.

There have been four English ordinals, excluding the American edition incorporated into the *Book of Common Prayer* for the Protestant Episcopal Church in the United States, adopted in 1789.

The first Ordinal was published in 1550, and was the work of six Protestant bishops led by Thomas Cranmer, Archbishop of Canterbury. Its most significant feature was the formula at the imposition of hands, based on a revision drafted by Martin Bucer, the German Reformed theologian. It read: "Receive the Holy Ghost. Whose sins thou dost forgive they are forgiven; whose sins thou dost retain they are retained. And be thou a faithful dispenser of the Word of God and of His Holy Sacraments. In the name of the Father and of the Son and of the Holy Ghost. Amen." Corresponding to this pastoral concept of the ministry was the Bucerian admonition, to be recited by the bishop and still present in the Ordinal. The ordinands were exhorted to be mindful of their clerical dignity as messengers, watchmen, pastors, and stewards of the Lord. Bucer had earlier adopted this admonition for the ordination of his Strassburg presbyters, to replace the Catholic version which spoke of offering sacrifice.

In 1552 the second Ordinal appeared. It further changed the ceremony of ordination to the presbyterate along evangelical lines by omitting the ritual of handing the ordinand a chalice and host as symbolic of the eucharistic sacrifice. The omitted portion of the rubric is italicized: "The Bishop shall deliver to every one of them the Bible *in one hand and the Chalice or Cup with the Bread in the other hand* and saying, 'Take thou authority to preach the Word of God and to minister the holy Sacraments in the congregation where thou shalt be appointed.'"

Seven years later another Ordinal was published, but with only minor changes, except for the oath which demanded acknowledging the monarch spiritual head of the Church in England. This was introduced by Elizabeth, who had become queen the year before (1558), following the reign of the Catholic Mary Tudor. The controversial Matthew Parker was consecrated Archbishop of Canterbury under the new Ordinal late in 1559.

The final revision came in 1662, when the episcopacy and *Book of Common Prayer* were reinstated by Charles II after a decade of Puritanism under the Commonwealth. Two drastic modifications were made. The Preface to the Ordinal was revised so as to require henceforth that "no man shall be accounted or taken to be a lawful Bishop, Priest, or Deacon, in the Church of England, or suffered to execute any of the said Functions, except he be called, tried, examined, and admitted thereunto, according to the Form hereafter following, or hath had Episcopal Consecration or Ordination." The American version (1789) substituted "in this Church" for "in the Church of England."

Moreover, the formula of ordination was supplemented. While imposing hands on the neophyte, the bishop was to say, ". . . for the office and work of a priest in the Church of God, now committed unto thee by the imposition of our hands . . ." Various explanations have been given for this addition. A likely one was the reaction of an Anglicanism conscious of the historic priesthood and episcopacy as distinctive from the Presbyterian ministry, which the Puritan Parliament of 1648 had canonized in the Westminster Confession.

Again the American Ordinal differs from others, for example the Canadian, in giving the bishop an option. He may omit as part of the form of ordination the reference to forgiveness of sins, i.e., "Whose sins thou dost forgive, they are forgiven; and whose sins thou dost retain, they are retained."

PREFACE TO THE ORDINAL

It is evident unto all men, diligently reading Holy Scripture and ancient Authors, that from the Apostles' time there have been these Orders of Ministers in Christ's Church,—Bishops, Priests, and Deacons. Which Officers were evermore had in such reverend estimation, that no man might presume to execute any of them, except he were first called, tried, examined, and known to have such qualities as are requisite for the same; and also by public Prayer, with Imposition of Hands, were approved and admitted thereunto by lawful Authority. And therefore, to the intent that these Orders may be continued, and reverently used and esteemed in this Church, no man shall be accounted or taken to be a lawful Bishop, Priest, or Deacon, in this Church, or suffered to execute any of the said Functions, except he be called, tried, examined, and admitted thereunto, according to the Form hereafter following, or hath had Episcopal Consecration or Ordination.

And none shall be admitted a Deacon, Priest, or Bishop, except he be of the age which the Canon in that case provided may require.

And the Bishop, knowing either by himself, or by sufficient testimony, any Person to be a man of virtuous conversation, and without crime; and, after examination and trial, finding him sufficiently instructed in the Holy Scripture, and otherwise learned as the Canons require may, at the times appointed, or else, on urgent occasion, upon some other day, in the face of the Church, admit him a Deacon, in such manner and form as followeth.

THE FORM AND MANNER OF ORDERING PRIESTS

When the day appointed by the Bishop is come, there shall be a Sermon, or Exhortation, declaring the Duty and Office of such as come to be admitted Priests; how necessary that Order is in the Church of Christ, and also, how the People ought to esteem them in their Office.

A Priest shall present unto the Bishop, sitting in his chair near to the Holy Table, all those who are to receive the Order of Priesthood that day, each of them being decently habited, and shall say,

Reverend Father in God, I present unto you these persons present, to be admitted to the Order of Priesthood.

The Bishop.

Take heed that the persons, whom ye present unto us, be apt and meet, for their learning and godly conversation, to exercise their Ministry duly, to the honour of God, and the edifying of his Church.

The Priest shall answer,

I have inquired concerning them, and also examined them, and think them so to be.

Then the Bishop shall say unto the People,

Good People, these are they whom we purpose, God willing, to receive this day unto the holy Office of Priesthood; for, after due examination, we find not to the contrary, but that they are lawfully called to their Function and Ministry, and that they are persons meet for the same. But yet, if there be any of you who knoweth any Impediment, or notable Crime, in any of them, for that which he ought not to be received into this holy Ministry let him come forth in the Name of God, and show what the Crime or Impediment is.

And if any great Crime or Impediment be objected, the Bishop shall cease from Ordering that person, until such time as the party accused shall be found clear of that Crime.

Then the Bishop (commending such as shall be found meet to be Ordered, to the Prayers of the congregation) shall, with the Clergy and People present, say the Litany.

And Note, *That after the Suffrage, "That it may please thee to* illuminate all Bishops, etc.," *shall be said the following Suffrage:*

That it may please thee to bless these thy servants, now to be admitted to the Order of Priests, and to pour thy grace upon them; that they may duly exercise their Office, to the edifying of thy Church, and the glory of thy holy Name;

And Note *further, That in the discretion of the Bishop, instead of the Litany appointed, may be said the Litany for Ordinations.*

Then shall be said the Service for the Communion, with the Collect, Epistle, and Gospel, as followeth.

The Collect.

Almighty God, giver of all good things, who by thy Holy Spirit hast appointed divers Orders of Ministers in thy Church; Mercifully behold these thy servants now called to the Office of Priesthood; and so replenish them with the truth of thy doctrine, and adorn them with innocency of life, that, both by word and good example, they may faithfully serve thee in this Office, to the glory of thy Name, and the edification of thy Church; through the merits of our Saviour Jesus Christ, who liveth and reigneth with thee and the same Holy Spirit, world without end. Amen.

(Scripture Readings: Ephesians 4:7, Matthew 9:36 or John 10:1).

Then, the People being seated, the Bishop shall say unto those who are to be ordained Priests as followeth.

Ye have heard, Brethren, as well in your private examination, as in the exhortation which was now made to you, and in the holy Lessons taken out of the Gospel, and the writings of the Apostles, of what dignity, and of how great importance this Office is, whereunto ye are called. And now again we exhort you, in the Name of our Lord Jesus Christ, that ye have in remembrance, into how high a Dignity, and to how weighty an Office and Charge ye are called: that is to say, to be Messengers, Watchmen, and Stewards of the Lord; to teach, and to premonish, to feed and provide for the Lord's family; to seek for Christ's sheep that are dispersed abroad, and for his children who are in the midst of this naughty world, that they may be saved through Christ for ever.

Have always therefore printed in your remembrance, how great a treasure is committed to your charge. For they are the sheep of Christ, which he bought with his death, and for whom he shed his blood. The Church and Congregation whom you must serve, is his Spouse, and his Body. And if it shall happen that the same Church, or any Member thereof, do take any hurt or hindrance by reason of your negligence, ye know the greatness of the fault, and also the horrible punishment that will ensue. Wherefore consider with yourselves the end of the Ministry towards the children of God, towards the Spouse and Body of Christ; and see that ye never cease your labour, your care and diligence, until ye have done all that lieth in you, according to your bounden duty, to bring all such as are or shall be committed to your charge, unto that agreement in the faith and knowledge of God, and to that ripeness and perfectness of age in Christ, that there be no place left among you, either for error in religion, or for viciousness in life.

Forasmuch then as your Office is both of so great excellency, and of so great difficulty, ye see with how great care and study ye ought to apply yourselves, as well to show yourselves dutiful and thankful unto that Lord, who hath placed you in so high a dignity; as also to beware that neither you yourselves offend, nor be occasion that others offend. Howbeit, ye cannot have a mind and will thereto of yourselves; for that will and ability is given of God alone: therefore ye ought, and have need, to pray earnestly for his Holy Spirit. And seeing that ye cannot by any other means compass the doing of so weighty a work, pertaining to the salvation of man, but with doctrine and exhortation taken out of the Holy Scriptures, and with a life agreeable to the same; consider how studious ye ought to be in reading and learning the Scriptures, and in framing the manners both of yourselves, and of them that specially pertain unto you, according to the rule of the same Scriptures; and for this self-same cause, how ye ought to forsake and set aside, as much as ye may, all worldly cares and studies.

We have good hope that ye have well weighed these things with yourselves, long before this time; and that ye have clearly determined, by God's grace, to give yourselves wholly to this Office, whereunto it hath pleased God to call you: so that, as much as lieth in you, ye will apply yourselves wholly to this one thing, and draw all your cares and studies this way; and that ye will continually pray to God the Father, by the mediation of our only Saviour Jesus Christ, for the heavenly assistance of the Holy Ghost; that, by daily reading and weighing the Scriptures, ye may wax riper and stronger in your Ministry; and that ye may so endeavour yourselves, from time to time, to sanctify the lives of you and yours, and to fashion them after the Rule and Doctrine of Christ, that ye may be wholesome and godly examples and patterns for the people to follow.

And now, that this present Congregation of Christ may also understand your minds and wills in these things, and that this your promise may the more move you to do your duties; ye shall answer plainly to these things, which we, in the Name of God, and of his Church, shall demand of you touching the same.

Do you think in your heart, that you are truly called, according to the will of our Lord Jesus Christ, and according to the Canons of this Church, to the Order and Ministry of Priesthood?

Answer. I think it.

Bishop. Are you persuaded that the Holy Scriptures contain all Doctrine required as necessary for eternal salvation through faith in Jesus Christ? And are you determined, out of the said Scriptures to instruct the people committed to your charge; and to teach nothing, as necessary to eternal salvation, but that which you shall be persuaded may be concluded and proved by the Scripture?

Answer. I am so persuaded, and have so determined, by God's grace.

Bishop. Will you then give your faithful diligence always so to minister the Doctrine and Sacraments, and the Discipline of Christ, as the Lord hath commanded, and as this Church hath received the same, according to the Commandments of God, so that you may teach the people committed to your Cure and Charge with all diligence to keep and observe the same?

Answer. I will so do, by the help of the Lord.

Bishop. Will you be ready, with all faithful diligence, to banish and drive away from the Church all erroneous and strange doctrines contrary to God's Word; and to use both public and private monitions and exhortations, as well to the sick as to the whole, within your Cures, as need shall require, and occasion shall be given?

Answer. I will, the Lord being my helper.

Bishop. Will you be diligent in Prayers, and in reading the Holy Scriptures, and in such studies as help to the knowledge of the same, laying aside the study of the world and the flesh?

Answer. I will endeavour so to do, the Lord being my helper.

Bishop. Will you be diligent to frame and fashion your own selves, and your families, according to the Doctrine of Christ; and to make both yourselves and them, as much as in you lieth, wholesome examples and patterns to the flock of Christ?

Answer. I will apply myself thereto, the Lord being my helper.

Bishop. Will you maintain and set forwards, as much as lieth in you, quietness, peace, and love, among all Christian people, and especially among them that are or shall be committed to your charge?

Answer. I will so do, the Lord being my helper.

Bishop. Will you reverently obey your Bishop, and other chief Ministers, who, according to the Canons of the Church, may have the charge and government over you; following with a glad mind and will their godly admonitions, and submitting yourselves to their godly judgments?

Answer. I will so do, the Lord being my helper.

Then, all standing, shall the Bishop say,

Almighty God, who hath given you this will to do all these things; Grant also unto you strength and power to perform the same, that he may accomplish his work which he hath begun in you; through Jesus Christ our Lord. Amen.

After this, the Congregation shall be desired, secretly in their Prayers, to make their humble supplications to God for all these things; for the which Prayers there shall be silence kept for a space.

After which, the Persons to be ordained Priests kneeling, and others standing, the Bishop shall sing or say the Veni, Creator Spiritus; *the Bishop beginning, and the Priests, and others that are present, answering by verses, as followeth.*

(*Veni, Creator Spiritus.*)

That done, the Bishop shall pray in this wise, and say,

Let us pray.

Almighty God, and heavenly Father, who, of thine infinite love and goodness towards us, hast given to us thy only and most dearly beloved Son Jesus Christ, to be our Redeemer, and the Author of everlasting life; who, after he had made perfect our redemption by his death, and was ascended into heaven, sent abroad into the world his Apostles, Prophets, Evangelists, Doctors, and Pastors; by whose labour and ministry he gathered together a great flock in all parts of the world, to set forth the eternal praise of thy holy Name: For these so great benefits of thy eternal goodness, and for that thou hast vouchsafed to call these thy servants here present to the same Office and Ministry, appointed for the salvation of mankind, we render unto thee most hearty thanks, we praise and worship thee; and we humbly beseech thee, by the same thy blessed Son, to grant unto all, which either here or elsewhere call upon thy holy Name, that we may continue to show ourselves thankful unto thee for these and all thy other benefits; and that we may daily increase and go forwards in the knowledge and faith of thee and thy Son, by the Holy Spirit. So that as well by these thy Ministers, as by them over whom they shall be appointed thy Ministers, thy holy Name may be for ever glorified, and thy blessed kingdom enlarged; through the same thy Son Jesus Christ our Lord, who liveth and reigneth with thee in the unity of the same Holy Spirit, world without end. Amen.

When this Prayer is done, the Bishop with the Priests present, shall lay their Hands severally upon the Head of every one that receiveth the Order of Priesthood; the Receivers humbly kneeling, and the Bishop saying,

Receive the Holy Ghost for the Office and Work of a Priest in the Church of God, now committed unto thee by the Imposition of our hands. Whose sins thou dost forgive, they are forgiven; and whose sins thou dost retain, they are retained. And be thou a faithful Dispenser of the Word of God, and of his holy Sacraments; In the Name of the Father, and of the Son, and of the Holy Ghost. Amen.

Or this.

Take thou Authority to execute the Office of a Priest in the Church of God, now committed to thee by the Imposition of our hands. And be thou a faithful Dispenser of the Word of God, and of his holy Sacraments; In the Name of the Father, and of the Son, and of the Holy Ghost. Amen.

Then the Bishop shall deliver to every one of them kneeling, the Bible into his hand, saying,

Take thou Authority to preach the Word of God, and to minister the holy Sacraments in the Congregation, where thou shalt be lawfully appointed thereunto.

When this is done, the Nicene Creed shall be said, and the Bishop shall go on in the Service of the Communion, which all they who receive Orders shall take together, and remain in the same place where Hands were laid upon them, until such time as they have received the Communion.

The Communion being done, after the last Collect, and immediately before the Benediction, shall be said this Collect.

Most merciful Father, we beseech thee to send upon these thy servants thy heavenly blessing; that they may be clothed with righteousness, and that thy Word spoken by their mouths may have such success, that it may never be spoken in vain. Grant also, that we may have grace to hear and receive what they shall deliver out of thy most holy Word, or agreeable to the same, as the means of our salvation; that in all our words and deeds we may seek thy glory, and the increase of thy kingdom; through Jesus Christ our Lord. Amen.

The Peace of God, which passeth all understanding, keep your hearts and minds in the knowledge and love of God, and of his Son Jesus Christ our Lord: And the Blessing of God Almighty, the Father, the Son, and the Holy Ghost, be amongst you, and remain with you always. Amen.

And if, on the same day, the Order of Deacons be given to some, and the Order of Priesthood to others; the Deacons shall be first presented, and then the Priests; and it shall suffice that the Litany be once said for both. The Epistle shall be Ephesians iv. 7 to 13, as before in this Office. Immediately after which, they that are to be made Deacons, shall be examined and Ordained, as is above prescribed. Then one of them having read the Gospel (which shall be either Saint Matthew ix. 36 to 38, as before in this Office; or else Saint Luke xii, 35 to 38, as before in the Form for the Ordering of Deacons,) they that are to be made Priests shall likewise be examined and Ordained, as in this Office before appointed. The Collect shall be as followeth.

The Collect.

Almighty God, giver of all good things, who by thy Holy Spirit hast appointed divers Orders of Ministers in thy Church; Mercifully behold these thy servants now called to the Office of Deacon and these thy servants now called to the Office of Priest; and so replenish them with the truth of thy Doctrine, and adorn them with innocency of life, that, both by word and good example, they may faithfully serve thee in their Ministry, to the glory of thy Name and the edification of thy Church; through the merits of our Saviour Jesus Christ, who liveth and reigneth with thee and the same Holy Spirit, world without end. Amen.

ANGLO-CATHOLICISM

It is common knowledge that within the Anglican Communion there is a large proportion of clergy and laity who favor the Catholic side of their Church's faith and polity. The modern name for this more advanced section of the High Church movement is Anglo-Catholicism. From 1838 when the word first appeared its use has become general.

The Tractarian designation of their series of reprints of seventeenth century divines as the *Library of Anglo-Catholic Theology* (1841+) has sometimes led to the mistaken supposition that the word "Anglo-Catholic" was much older. Yet the Latin form *Anglo-Catholicus* does occur in the seventeenth century.

Anglo-Catholics emphasize the dogmatic and sacramental aspects of the Christian Creed and life, and the historic continuity of the existing Anglican Church with that of the Middle Ages; and they have generally wished to establish as close an agreement as possible without the sacrifice of essential principles between the doctrine of their Church and those of the Roman Catholic Church. Like other High Churchmen, they have always maintained that their principles alone rightly express the faith of the Church of England and its various national affiliates.

Among the expressions of belief published by Anglo-Catholics, one of the latest is that which occurs in *The People's Anglican Missal in the American Edition,* jointly issued in England and the United States. In the Introduction the authors state that "Loyalty to the Prayer-Book implies knowledge and sympathetic understanding of our liturgy. For the Prayer-Book is the result of a long evolution in worship, and that evolution still continues. When liturgy ceases to develop, as with any other living thing, it is dying or dead." *

They continue by explaining that the *Book of Common Prayer* should be treated as an "apocopated liturgy," which means that "our liturgy cannot be celebrated without the addition of material or knowledge which the Prayer-Book fails to supply. And when such supplementary material and the Prayer-Book Eucharistic formularies are published together as one book, the result is called a 'Missal.'" To be of wide service and provide ample scope of faith and ritual such a book "should be inclusive rather than exclusive, and those who believe in the guidance by the Holy Spirit of the Church will not doubt that the evolutionary process, which is so characteristic of the Western Liturgy, will surely, if slowly, eliminate that which is unworthy." **

The most extensive and widely used statement of doctrine of Anglo-Catholicism is given in the *Anglican Missal,* under the general heading of Eucharistic Worship. An adequate under-

---

* *The People's Anglican Missal in the American Edition,* New York: Frank Gavin Liturgical Foundation, 1962, p. i.

** *Ibid.*

standing of the Episcopalian way of life must take cognizance of this aspect of Anglicanism.

The Eucharist is celebrated in obedience to the divine command, Do this in remembrance of me. Hence it is an action carried out in imitation of what our Lord did and said. One of the ancient names for the essential part of the Eucharist is The Action. Liturgical prayer combines action, or ceremonial, with words, and even with silence, all of which makes one complete act of prayer.

The Action, which is also called the Anaphora (that is, the Offering), has from earliest times been preceded by a preparatory service known as the Proanaphora, or in the Anglican colloquial phrase, the "Ante-Communion Service." The Proanaphora seems to have originated as follows. In the first days of the Church, when paganism prevented any proper observance of the Lord's Day, most Christians could find no opportunity in daytime for corporate worship, and hence it was customary for them to assemble for corporate worship at night when other folk were asleep.

Necessity may have dictated the hours at which the early Christians worshipped, but if so, they made a virtue of that necessity by the explanation which they gave to it. The fact that in the midst of the night our Lord was born into the world, and rose again from the dead, and was, as he had said, to come again in judgement, seemed to the first Christians to make these hours of darkness a time of special grace. They therefore explained that they proposed to be in the midst of his worship if he came in judgement in their time, as he had foretold, like a thief in the night.

Hence, as early at night as possible on the last day of the week, they congregated for a vigil of prayer which issued in the celebration of The Action in the early morning hours of the morrow. From this vigil service, which was based upon the Jewish Synagogue service of prayer, Psalms, Scripture-reading and instruction, there developed the Proanaphora, which was designed to be a service of instruction for those who were looking forward to Baptism (that is, for the Catechumens), and as a means of preparation for the Faithful who alone were permitted to be present at the Anaphora to receive the Holy Communion.

Hence the Proanaphora came to be known as the Mass of the Catechumens and the Anaphora as the Mass of the Faithful, and the Catechumens were always dismissed, along with any of the baptized who were under discipline for sin, just before the Mass of the Faithful was begun.

These two divisions are obvious in our Prayer-Book rite. Our form of the Mass up to the Offertory consists of prayers of preparation, the reading of Scripture, and a Sermon or instruction, all which is the normal content of the Mass of the Catechumens in every part of the Church Catholic. Unfortunately, the Prayer-Book does not require the use of Psalms in the Eucharist, but in permitting the use of "hymns" it permits the use of Psalms which are the Church's first and greatest hymns.

The Mass of the Faithful consists of The Action, which is an imitation of what our Lord did and said in obedience to his divine command, Do this in remembrance of me. We read that he did four things, namely, took Bread, gave thanks, brake it, and gave it to them. During The Action the Church also does these four things.

First, he "took" the Bread and Wine which were to be used for the Offering. This is technically known as the Oblation and is accomplished at the Offertory. And it should be noted that the taking of a collection is not the real Offertory, but merely the People's share in it, whereby they provide the means of buying the Bread and Wine and of supporting the Church and the poor. In the earliest times the Bread and Wine were collected at this point, and what was not needed for the Mass was used for the relief of the poor and for the physical sustenance of those who served the Altar.

Secondly, our Lord "gave thanks." The Prayer-Book, following the Gregorian Canon, speaks of "this our Sacrifice of Praise and Thanksgiving." According to Jewish ideas, blessing or consecration was accomplished by a form of thanksgiving (that is, eucharist) wherein the worshipper identified himself with the One worshipped by praisng and thanking the Lord and by eating what had through sacrifice become in a peculiar sense the Lord's possession. For this reason the Consecration Prayer is eucharistic in tone. It begins with the Preface (*Let us give thanks unto our Lord God*) and continues in the form of thanksgiving. Identity with the One worshipped is asserted both in speech and action in the Words of Institution, wherein the Celebrant speaks in the Person of Christ (*This is my Body and This is my blood*), and even imitates the divine actions. Hence it is not strange that at this first point of conscious identification with our Lord in speech and action, and in praise and thanksgiving, we should think of the Consecration as being consummated. It is to be recognized that even though the essential thing about the Eucharist is obedience to our Lord in performing his Action, the use of the Words of Institution do constitute a conscious act of identity with him as almost nothing else does.

Thirdly, after our Lord had effected the Consecration by the successive acts of taking the bread and wine and blessing it in the form of thanksgiving, he "brake" the Bread. This action, known as the Fracture, came to be dramatized as a visible sign of the great sacrifice wherein he was broken on the Cross for us, and with which we must identify ourselves if that sacrifice is to be effective in our own souls. That is, sacrifice is a process whereby God makes use of us, for which reason this step in the Mass may well be named Utilization. Hence at this point we do well to think of the heartbreaks of suffering humanity and of our Lord's oneness with the sorrows of mankind, and of his being broken for us on the Cross, even as we must make of our own heart-breaks a loving union with his sacrifice. Only by such devotion can the agony of mankind become a part of Christ's agony, and be utilized in the process of divine redemption instead of being lost in ignorance of his love and rebellion against his compassion.

Fourthly, our Lord "gave" to his disciples this heavenly Food to be the food of their souls, and to consummate their union with him, and this Unification is, of course, the climax of the Mass of the Faithful, the act of Communion. Anything after this great act except the briefest of thanksgivings would seem to be an anticlimax.

The Offertory, the Consecration, the Fracture, and the Communion are the chief acts of The Action, and the Church joyfully emphasizes these by her ceremonial dramatization of them, in reverent obedience to the command, Do THIS. Anything less than a very careful carrying out of these acts is but a meagre obedience to the expressed wish of our great High Priest. Because the Prayer-Book does not make as much of the Fracture as of the others acts, many Priests re-inforce the present Prayer-Book usage by the addition of the ancient ceremonies thereof, as given in this Missal.

The Eucharist is sometimes defined as the making-present on the Altar of the eternal sacrifice offered once for all on Calvary, so that it becomes available to us as the means whereby we can, through our Communions, be identified with him in his sacrificial consecration to God. Liturgical prayer is thus different from other kinds of prayer. It is THE WORSHIP WHICH CHRIST OFFERED ON CALVARY made present on the Altar as the worship of the Church on earth, and through the union which each worshipper has with Christ, the individual is thus enabled to offer Christ's own perfect act of Worship. Hence the Mass can never be an act of private devotion. It is always the act of the whole Church, the mystical Body of Christ, which exists only in and through Christ, and which alone possesses Christ since Christ—its head and life—is also in possession of the Church, and of every soul therein which surrenders to him. He ordained the Eucharist as the means whereby we put ourselves into his possession and, in return, enter into possession of him. It is the Holy Communion of his broken Body and poured-out Blood. These words describe Christ as offered or sacrificed for us. That is, Holy Communion can only be a Communion because it is first of all a Sacrifice.

Hence the individual benefits thereby because he loses himself in that which Christ has ordained to be the corporate worship of all. Eucharistic worship is not a matter of personal edification but of self-forgetfulness. You go to Mass not to get but to give, for you can in this instance GET only by giving. "The price of love is thyself," says St. Augustine.

The individual ought therefore to exercise himself in certain acts during The Action. Four acts are indicated, as said above, conveniently known as OBLATION, CONSECRATION, UTILIZATION, and UNIFICATION, corresponding to the four acts of The Action.

First, consider Oblation. At the Offertory, when the Priest obeys the Prayer-Book Rubric, to "offer and place" upon the Holy Table, the Bread and the Wine, the worshipper may well remind himself that a gift should bring the giver with it—that just as his monetary offering, the fruit of his own labour, has helped provide this physical sustenance which is now offered and placed on the Altar, ready for consecration, so he should now complete the Offering, and give that which his Lord most desires. That is, at the Offertory he should offer and place himself in spirit upon the Altar, and thus make an oblation of himself at the time when the Priest offers thereon the physical sustenance of human life in the form of the Bread and Wine.

Secondly, there is Consecration. When, at the Preface, the Priest begins the Consecration, the individual should realize that he too is being consecrated to God along with his offering of himself and of this physical sustenance for human life. And when mere physical sustenance has become the Bread of Heaven, that is, when Christ has become sacramentally present, he should regard himself as a reasonable, holy, and living sacrifice, which has now become consecrate to God in union with Christ's sacrifice of himself. For in each Mass not only is the Bread and Wine consecrated but also each true worshipper.

Thirdly, there is Utilization. At the Fracture, when the Host is broken and the Particle is placed in the Chalice, the worshipper should, as it were, place his own sorrows, temptations, and aspirations in the Chalice, along with those of all of broken humanity, that the same may be lifted up to God in praise and thanksgiving. The language of love is pain. It was so for Christ. It must be so for us because we are sinners needing redemption through this great sacrifice. Thus through the Sacrifice of Praise and Thanksgiving is life sweetened and strengthened because it is surrendered to him in its joy and in its anguish to be used for his holy and happy purposes. And even if the Priest does not himself make the greater Fracture, but contents himself with the little Fracture which the Prayer-Book orders during the Words of Institution, at any rate the worshipper need not abstain from making the devotions appropriate to the Fracture at this point.

Our religion is a religion of redemption. Every soul, no matter how marred by evil, can be redeemed, that is, purified, utilized, and restored by the grace of the atoning sacrifice. All pain, sorrow, frustration, disease, death, can be mere wastage, or it can be utilized by God and made into something fine for all eternity. We who are to be co-redeemers with Christ must lift up broken humanity into union with the lifting up of the broken Christ upon the Cross, and we may do this at least in intention at the Fracture, as a prelude to the reception of the Blessed Sacrament which is the means of our intermingling of ourselves with Christ in his redemption of the world.

This idea needs emphasis. Consider it a moment. The English version of the Apostles Creed calls the Church *the Communion of the Saints*. But to go back to the original Greek and Latin forms of this Creed, in accordance with the Anglican principle of always going back to the sources in order to establish the proper interpretation, we find its literal meaning to be "the Communion of the Holy." This phrase must indicate at least all these things: (a) The Church is the fellowship of those who are in communion with, and who are therefore partakers of, the holiness of God; (b) all in the Church are therefore in communion with the Saints, i.e., those who are filled with God's holiness; but (c) holiness of dedication, according to the Jewish Scriptures, consists in being given over in sacrifice to God. This latter idea is the Jewish conception of holiness which our Lord accepted and taught. According to the Scriptures, holiness consists in being offered to God so as to be made by him fit and acceptable for his purposes. Christians are those who have accepted the Atonement (at-one-ment) made by Christ, which they can do only by entering into it and becoming part of it.

Thus the Holy Catholic Church is the Communion of the Holy (or, as we say, the Communion of the Saints) because it consists of all those souls, living and dead, who have been offered to God through the sacrifice of Christ. You are a Christian only because you are a part of the redemptive process which Christ made possible by his sacrifice of himself. The Eucharist is Communion (that is, close union) with Christ our Sacrifice. There could be no Communion in the Christian sense of the word if this service of worship were not first of all the making present and available for us of the eternal sacrifice of Calvary.

Thus fourthly, there is Unification. That is, the reception of our Lord in the act of Holy Communion, as said above, is an intermingling of ourselves with him, in such wise that we can achieve identity of purpose with him in his thoughts, desires, strength, and living. The reception of Holy Communion is the expression of all that is holy in our religion, and when the worshipper knows himself to be unfit or unprepared, he should content himself with an act of Spiritual Communion lest he "eat and drink condemnation to himself."

The method of assisting at Mass outlined above consists in making oneself a part of The Action at each step. Surely this is the best method of "following the service." Thereby each worshipper is able to experience the true inner meaning of the Eucharist. For therein we and ours, with praise and thanksgiving are offered to God through the eternal sacrifice on Calvary, which same is made present and available to us every time Mass is celebrated, and is the divinely ordained means of the renewal and of the maintenance of our union with Christ who is our Saviour because he is our Sacrifice.

To summarize:

1. OBLATION. At the Offertory offer yourself along with the People's gifts on the Altar.

2. CONSECRATION. From the Preface onwards suffer yourself, with praise and thanksgiving, to be consecrated to God's service.

3. UTILIZATION. At the Fracture will yourself to be a sacrifice in union with Christ's broken Body and poured-out Blood, to be used as he wills.

4. UNIFICATION. At the Communion give yourself to Christ, even as he gives himself to you, so that you may then go forth in union with him.

The phrase *Real Presence* does not mean that there can be an unreal presence. Rather, the words *Real Presence* reject the contrary idea of the real absence of Christ in favour of what every devout Communicant knows from experience, namely, that in this Sacrament Christ makes himself available to us in his humanity (which is the fundamental meaning of the phrase *Body* and *Blood*) as well as in his divinity. The real and whole Christ is here, after a fashion which enables us to receive him. He is present everywhere as God, but not in such a way as to enable us to receive him as our spiritual Food. In his humanity he is present only (a) in heaven where he continually makes intercession for us in the presentation of his eternal sacrifice; and (b) in the Sacrament which he has ordained to be the means whereby his heavenly presence and sacrifice is made available for us on earth.

4. Methodism

Methodism may be classified legitimately under Anglicanism as a historical descendant of the Reformation. So many things about the two types of systems of religious thought are related. Both had their origins on English soil; both profess to derive ultimately from a Church of England that was indigenous to the British Isles and independent of foreign domination; and both are striving to reunite on principles which they had in common before the rise of Methodism in the eighteenth century.

History and Principles. The founder of Methodism, John Wesley (1703-1791), was an ordained priest of the Church of England who until the day of his death insisted he did not want to sever connection with the Church in which he was reared. Yet even before he died, the principles he elaborated and the stress in church policy he advanced led him to organize a distinct denomination, whose current membership in the world compares favorably with Anglicanism and, in the United States, is about three times the size of the Protestant Episcopal Church.

It is not easy to describe Methodism in doctrinal terms because Wesley himself stressed the minimal importance of belief, in the sense of confessional doctrine, and described his followers in a passage that has since become classic.

> The distinguishing marks of a Methodist are not his opinions of any sort. His assenting to this or that scheme of religion, his embracing any particular set of notions, his espousing the judgment of one man or of another are all quite wide of the point. Whosoever, therefore, imagines that a Methodist is a man of such or such an opinion is grossly ignorant of the whole affair; he mistakes the truth totally.
>
> We believe indeed that "all scripture is given by inspiration of God;" and herein we are distinguished from Jews, Turks, and infidels. We believe the written word of God to be the only rule both of faith and practice; and herein we are fundamentally dis-

tinguished from those of the Roman Church. We believe Christ
to be eternal, the supreme God; and herein we are distinguished
from the Socinians and Arians. But as to all opinions which do
not strike at the root of Christianity, we think and let think.[1]

Among the "opinions which do not strike at the root of Christianity," and on which his followers were free to dissent, were the
character of the priesthood and the episcopate, the nature of
Christ's presence in the Eucharist, and the role of the sacraments
in the life of the Church.

But if Methodism allows considerable range in matters of doctrine, there is one element of its faith which not only distinguishes
Methodists from their Anglican forebears but from orthodox Protestantism in general. This is their teaching on sanctification,
which so closely resembles the Catholic doctrine on grace that
some have called Wesley a "papalist in disguise."

In his sermons and writings, Wesley constantly opposed the
Calvinist theory of predestination. Even when he affirmed that
God is the source of all human good, and that grace does not
depend on any power or merit in man, he labored to show the
untenability of any view that restricted salvation to the few who
are elected by the unsearchable decrees of an arbitrary God. "The
grace of God," he wrote "whence cometh our salvation, is free in
all, and free for all." [2]

When he revised the Thirty-Nine Articles of the Anglican creed
and sent them to America as a doctrinal basis for the new Methodist Episcopal Church, he eliminated the most extremely Calvinistic passages of Article nine, deleted the qualifying adverb
necessarily from Article twelve, which says that good works
"spring out necessarily of a true and lively faith," and entirely
dropped Article seventeen, with its unqualified statement of
predestinarianism.

Wesley's concern was mainly with the salvation of all men. He
was convinced that Christ came to seek and save that which was
lost, and the Church is commissioned to preach the Gospel of
redemption. But if predestinarianism is true, Christ's advent was
in vain and the whole task of evangelism a sham, because there is
no need (or possibility) of saving the unsaveable. Multitudes are

[1] John Wesley, "The Character of a Methodist," *Works*, London, vol. VIII, p. 31.
[2] John Wesley, "Free Grace," *Works*, vol. VII, p. 373.

beyond the love of God and nothing can be done to help them. He considered this a repudiation of the central truth of Christianity.

Methodism has since developed a well-integrated system of sanctification that rests on the prior belief that salvation is more than justification in the sense of removal (or hiding) of sin. It is a vital process that God intends to have grow with the passage of time and develop through man's cooperation. "Sanctification," according to the *Methodist Discipline*, "is that renewal of our fallen nature by the Holy Ghost, received through faith in Jesus Christ, whose blood of atonement cleanseth from all sin; whereby we are not only delivered from the guilt of sin, but are washed from its pollution, saved from its power, and are enabled, through grace, to love with all our hearts and to walk in His holy commandments blameless." [3]

Parallel with the Methodist teaching on sanctification is an emphasis on the Witness of the Spirit, who bears testimony to those who are reborn to God after a life of sin. By this witness is understood an inward impression on the soul, whereby the Spirit of God is believed immediately and directly to testify that a person is a child of God, that his sins are blotted out and that he is on the road to salvation.

This doctrine has inspired much of Methodist hymnology, composed by John Wesley's brother, Charles, in which the joyous experience of personal salvation is the dominant theme.

> No longer am I now afraid;
> Thy promise must take place.
> Perfect Thy strength in weakness made,
> Sufficient is Thy grace.
> Confident now of faith's increase,
> I all its fruits shall prove;
> Substantial joy, and settled peace,
> And everlasting love.
> Lord, I believe and rest secure
> In confidence divine
> Thy promise stands for ever sure
> And all Thou art is mine. [4]

Correlative with a stress on religion as personal experience has

[3] *Methodist Discipline*, num. 86.
[4] *Wesley's Prayers and Praises* (J. Alan Kay, editor), London Epworth Press, 1958, p. 79.

been the Methodist conviction that Christianity is essentially social. "Solitary religion," declared Wesley, "is not to be found" in the Gospel. " 'Holy solitaries' is a phrase no more consistent with the Gospel than holy adulterers. The Gospel of Christ knows no religion but social; no holiness, but social holiness." [5] This has deeply influenced Methodist thought and action, and stimulated what has since become a new religious dimension in the Western world. Wesley's followers were introduced into a fellowship in which moral, economic, and racial issues became an integral part of living the faith; Methodists became pioneers of the "Social Gospel" which has characterized so much of American (and Anglo-Saxon) Protestantism in modern times.

A typical area of Methodist social evangelism is the temperance movement. In the spirit of John Wesley, who forbade anyone even to touch "that liquid fire," Methodists have been leaders in opposing the sale and consumption of alcoholic beverages. Ministers are forbidden to indulge and may be penalized for proved breach of their abstinence pledge.

American Methodism. In 1967 the respective annual conferences of the Methodist Church and The Evangelical United Brethren Church voted to merge into a new denomination, to be called The United Methodist Church. Between these two churches, the Methodist partner is dominant to the point that it may properly be said that the Evangelical United Brethren are being absorbed into the Methodist family with such adjustments of their original ethos as may be necessary to produce a homogeneous denomination.

American Methodists account for about eighty percent of the world membership, and some eighty percent of Wesleyan affiliation in the United States belongs to The Methodist Church. Its codification, therefore, of belief and worship in the *Doctrines and Discipline of The Methodist Church* may be taken as fairly representative of the nature and function of American Methodism at the present day. Going back to the early days of the church's foundation in Colonial America, the *Discipline* has become an authoritative source book which the clergy urge the people to have "found in every Methodist home." It is revised every four years by the delegates to the General Conference.

[5] Wesley, *Works*, vol. I, p. XXII.

Two documents in the *Discipline* are essential to the under-standing of Methodism in America: the *Declaration of Union* formulated at the time of the merger, and the *Articles of Religion* which John Wesley sent to America in 1784 and which now hold the place of honor in the *Discipline*. Both deserve some explana-tion. In order to understand them, it is necessary to see something of the history of Methodism since the time of Francis Asbury, the first Methodist bishop to be ordained in America. Asbury's con-secrator was Thomas Coke, whom Wesley, in England, had or-dained to the episcopacy a few months before.

Francis Asbury was ordained elder and consecrated bishop during the Christmas Conference of 1784, at which time the offi-cial name of the church was adopted and included in the published acts under the title—*A Form of Discipline for the Ministers, Preachers and other Members of the Methodist Episcopal Church in America*. Asbury's genius in organizing lay preachers placed laymen into governing power in the church, and thus completely severed Methodism in the United States, both legally and doc-trinally, from the Church of England.

Three years after the church's American establishment oc-curred the first secession from the parent body. In 1787 a group of Negro Methodists met in Philadelphia to organize the African Methodist Episcopal Church. Their grievance was the discrimi-nation practiced against their brethren by the white members of the denomination. A few years later, in 1796, the African Method-ist Episcopal Zion Church was similarly started because of the racial discrimination in New York. Both bodies have flourishing congregations, mainly on the East coast, in the deep and Southern and Mid-Eastern states.

Within a dozen years of Asbury's death, lay representation in church policy contributed to the third major schism in American Methodism. In 1828 the Methodist Protestant Church seceded over the juridical question of appeal for restoration of expelled ministers, and the more basic issue of laymen and clergy in Church government.

In 1845 another division occurred over the slavery question, bisecting the Methodist Episcopal Church into the Methodist Episcopal Church, North, and the Methodist Episcopal Church, South.

Shortly after the Emancipation Declaration, the Methodist Episcopal Church, South, was faced with the problem of retaining in its body the thousands of liberated Negro slaves. On the Negroes' own initiative, the Colored Methodist Episcopal Church was founded in 1870. By an act of its General Conference, the name was changed in 1956 to the Christian Methodist Episcopal Church. Membership is concentrated in the Midwest and South.

Two principal mergers have changed the character of Methodism in America in the past generation: the 1939 coalition to form The Methodist Church and the 1967 union with the Evangelical United Brethren to create The United Methodist Church.

After years of negotiation, in 1939 a Plan of Union was adopted which joined the Methodist Episcopal Church, the Methodist Episcopal Church, South, and the Methodist Protestant Church. Their historical basis for fusion was that all three denominations "had their common origin in the organization of the Methodist Episcopal Church in America in 1784."

When the Evangelical United Brethren joined The Methodist Church in 1967, the Plan of Union corresponded to its namesake of thirty years before, but with a difference. Whereas in the nineteen-thirties the merger was really the healing of a long-standing schism, the latest was a new creation. The names of Otterbein, Boehm and Geeting for the Church of the United Brethren, and of Albright for the Evangelical Church (out of which the E.U.B. was formed in 1946) were not part of the Methodist tradition. Yet the religious body they finally produced had so much in common with Wesley's followers that early American history often referred to the Asbury groups as "English Methodists" and the Otterbein-Boehm-Albright groups as "German Methodists." What they had in common was dedication to the task of preaching the Gospel to their fellow countrymen.

> Since they were men deeply moved by a common faith and zeal, and held a like emphasis upon personal spiritual experience of salvation, it is no surprise to find them working in close fellowship with one another.[6]

The doctrinal traditions of both merging parties of The United

---

[6] *The Constitution for the United Methodist Church with Enabling Legislation and Other Historic Documents*, p. 6.

Methodist Church came from the evangelical revival of the eighteenth century. Their proposed Plan of Union builds on this inheritance.

When the American Methodists drafted their first Constitution in 1808, they placed a restrictive rule on irresponsible doctrinal changes, "contrary to our present existing and established standards of doctrine." This rule remained in force through numerous schisms and reunions, and bids fair to stay unchanged in the future. Though never really defined, the phrase "our present existing and established standards of doctrine" has come to mean three principal sources, all of Wesleyan origin: his *Sermons on Several Occasions, Explanatory Notes Upon the New Testament,* the *Articles of Religion* and revised version of the *Book of Common Prayer.*

In modern times the Methodists have become justly famous for their stress on the Social Gospel, and their application of the faith to social issues has made them representative (if not always typical) of American religion as "Christian Activism." An essential part of their newest merger includes a statement on *The Methodist Social Creed,* adopted in 1908, and since then become the basis for religious ethics across the whole spectrum of Protestant social thinking in the United States.

JOHN WESLEY'S ARTICLES OF RELIGION

I. *Of Faith in the Holy Trinity.* There is but one living and true God, everlasting, without body or parts, of infinite power, wisdom, and goodness; the maker and preserver of all things, visible and invisible. And in unity of this Godhead there are three persons, of one substance, power, and eternity—the Father, the Son, and the Holy Ghost.

II. *Of the Word, or Son of God, who was made very Man.* The Son, who is the Word of the Father, the very and eternal God, of one substance with the Father, took man's nature in the womb of the blessed Virgin; so that two whole and perfect natures, that is to say, the Godhead and Manhood, were joined together in one person, never to be divided; whereof is one Christ, very God and very Man, who truly suffered, was crucified, dead, and buried, to reconcile his Father to us, and to be a sacrifice, not only for original guilt, but also for the actual sins of man.

III. *Of the Resurrection of Christ.* Christ did truly rise again from the dead, and took again his body, with all things appertaining to the perfection of man's nature, wherewith he ascended into heaven, and there sitteth until he return to judge all men at the last day.

IV. *Of the Holy Ghost.* The Holy Ghost, proceeding from the Father and the Son, is of one substance, majesty, and glory with the Father and the Son, very and eternal God.

V. *Of the Sufficiency of the Holy Scriptures for Salvation.* The Holy Scriptures contain all things necessary to salvation; so that whatsoever is not read therein, nor may be proved thereby, is not to be required of any man that it should be believed as an article of faith, or be thought requisite or necessary to salvation. In the name of the Holy Scriptures we do understand those canonical books of the Old and New Testament of whose authority was never any doubt in the Church. The names of the canonical books are:

Genesis,	The First Book of Chronicles,
Exodus,	The Second Book of Chronicles,
Leviticus,	The Book of Ezra,
Numbers,	The Book of Nehemiah,
Deuteronomy,	The Book of Esther,
Joshua,	The Book of Job,
Judges,	The Psalms,
Ruth,	The Proverbs,
The First Book of Samuel,	Ecclesiastes or the Preacher,
The Second Book of Samuel,	Cantica or Song of Solomon,
The First Book of Kings,	Four Prophets the Greater,
The Second Book of Kings,	Twelve Prophets the Less.

All the books of the New Testament, as they are commonly received, we do receive and account canonical.

VI. *Of the Old Testament.* The Old Testament is not contrary to the New; for both in the Old and New Testament everlasting life is offered to mankind by Christ, who is the only Mediator between God and man, being both God and Man. Wherefore they are not to be heard who feign that the old fathers did look only for transitory promises. Although the law given from God by Moses as touching ceremonies and rites doth not bind Christians, nor ought the civil precepts thereof of necessity be received in any commonwealth; yet notwithstanding, no Christian whatsoever is free from obedience of the commandments which are called moral.

VII. *Of Original or Birth Sin.* Original sin standeth not in the following of Adam (as the Pelagians do vainly talk), but it is the corruption of the nature of every man, that naturally is engendered of the offspring of Adam, whereby man is very far gone from original righteousness, and of his own nature inclined to evil, and that continually.

VIII. *Of Free Will.* The condition of man after the fall of Adam is such that he cannot turn and prepare himself, by his own natural strength and works, to faith, and calling upon God; wherefore we have no power to do good works, pleasant and acceptable to God, without the grace of God by Christ preventing us, that we may have a good will, and working with us, when we have that good will.

IX. *Of the Justification of Man.* We are accounted righteous before God only for the merit of our Lord and Saviour Jesus Christ, by faith, and not for our own works or deservings. Wherefore, that we are justified by faith only is a most wholesome doctrine, and very full of comfort.

X. *Of Good Works.* Although good works, which are the fruits of faith, and follow after justification, cannot put away our sins, and endure the severity of God's judgment; yet are they pleasing and acceptable to God in Christ, and spring out of a true and lively faith, insomuch that by them a lively faith may be as evidently known as a tree is discerned by its fruit.

XI. *Of Works of Supererogation.* Voluntary works—besides, over and above God's commandments—which are called works of supererogation, cannot be taught without arrogancy and impiety. For by them men do declare that they do not only render unto God as much as they are bound to do, but that they do more for his sake than of bounden duty is required; whereas Christ saith plainly: When ye have done all that is commanded of you, say, We are unprofitable servants.

XII. *Of Sin after Justification.* Not every sin willingly committed after justification is the sin against the Holy Spirit, and unpardonable. Wherefore, the grant of repentance is not to be denied to such as fall into sin after justification: after we have received the Holy Spirit, we may depart from grace given, and fall into sin, and, by the grace of God, rise again and amend our lives. And therefore they are to be condemned who say they can no more sin as long as they live here; or deny the place of forgiveness to such as truly repent.

XIII. *Of the Church.* The visible Church of Christ is a congregation of faithful men in which the pure Word of God is preached, and the Sacraments duly administered according to Christ's ordinance, in all those things that of necessity are requisite to the same.

XIV. *Of Purgatory.* The Romish doctrine concerning purgatory, pardon, worshiping, and adoration, as well of images as of relics, and also invocation of saints, is a fond thing, vainly invented, and grounded upon no warrant of Scripture, but repugnant to the Word of God.

XV. *Of Speaking in the Congregation in such a Tongue as the People Understand.* It is a thing plainly repugnant to the Word of God, and the custom of the primitive Church, to have public prayer in the church, or to administer the Sacraments, in a tongue not understood by the people.

XVI. *Of the Sacraments.* Sacraments ordained of Christ are not only badges or tokens of Christian men's profession, but rather they are certain signs of grace, and God's good will toward us, by which he doth work invisibly in us, and doth not only quicken, but also strengthen and confirm, our faith in him.

There are two Sacraments ordained of Christ our Lord in the Gospel; that is to say, Baptism and the Supper of the Lord.

Those five commonly called sacraments, that is to say, confirmation, penance, orders, matrimony, and extreme unction, are not to be counted for Sacraments of the Gospel; being such as have partly grown out of the *corrupt* following of the apostles, and partly are states of life allowed in the Scriptures, but yet have not the like nature of Baptism and the Lord's Supper, because they have not any visible sign or ceremony ordained of God.

The Sacraments were not ordained of Christ to be gazed upon, or to be carried about; but that we should duly use them. And in such only as worthily receive the same they have a wholesome effect or operation; but they that receive them unworthily, purchase to themselves condemnation, as St. Paul saith, I Cor. 11:29.

XVII. *Of Baptism.* Baptism is not only a sign of profession and mark of difference whereby Christians are distinguished from others that are not baptized; but it is also a sign of regeneration or the new birth. The baptism of young children is to be retained in the church.

XVIII. *Of the Lord's Supper.* The Supper of the Lord is not only a sign of the love that Christians ought to have among themselves one to another, but rather is a sacrament of our redemption by Christ's death; insomuch that, to such as rightly, worthily, and with faith receive the same, the bread which we break is a partaking of the body of Christ; and likewise the cup of blessing is a partaking of the blood of Christ.

Transubstantiation, or the change of the substance of bread and wine in the Supper of our Lord, cannot be proved by Holy Writ, but is repugnant to the plain words of Scripture, overthroweth the nature of a sacrament, and hath given occasion to many superstitions.

The body of Christ is given, taken, and eaten in the Supper, only after a heavenly and spiritual manner. And the means whereby the body of Christ is received and eaten in the Supper is faith.

The Sacrament of the Lord's Supper was not by Christ's ordinance reserved, carried about, lifted up, or worshiped.

XIX. *Of Both Kinds.* The cup of the Lord is not to be denied to the lay people; for both the parts of the Lord's Supper, by Christ's ordinance and commandment, ought to be administered to all Christians alike.

XX. *Of the One Oblation of Christ, finished upon the Cross.* The offering of Christ, once made, is that perfect redemption, propitiation, and satisfaction for all the sins of the whole world, both original and actual; and there is none other satisfaction for sin but that alone. Wherefore the sacrifice of masses, in the which it is commonly said that the priest doth offer Christ for the quick and the dead, to have remission of pain or guilt, is a blasphemous fable and dangerous deceit.

XXI. *Of the Marriage of Ministers.* The ministers of Christ are not commanded by God's law either to vow the estate of single life, or to abstain from marriage; therefore it is lawful for them, as for all other Christians, to marry at their own discretion, as they shall judge the same to serve best to godliness.

XXII. *Of the Rites and Ceremonies of Churches.* It is not necessary that rites and ceremonies should in all places be the same, or exactly alike; for they have been always different, and may be changed according to the diversity of countries, times, and men's manners, so that nothing be ordained against God's Word. Whosoever, through his private judgment, willingly and purposely doth openly break the rites and ceremonies of the church to which he belongeth, which are not repugnant to the Word of God, and are ordained and approved by common authority, ought to be rebuked openly (that others may fear to do the like), as one that offendeth against the common order of the church, and woundeth the consciences of weak brethren.

Every particular church may ordain, change, or abolish rites and ceremonies, so that all things may be done to edification.

XXIII. *Of the Rulers of the United States of America.* The President, the Congress, the general assemblies, the governors, and the councils of state *as the delegates of the people,* are the rulers of the United States of America, according to the division of power made to them by the Constitution of the United States and by the constitutions of their respective states. And the said states are a sovereign and independent nation, and ought not to be subject to any foreign jurisdiction.

XXIV. *Of Christian Men's Goods.* The riches and goods of Christians are not common, as touching the right, title, and possession of the same, as some do falsely boast. Notwithstanding, every man ought, of such things as he possesseth, liberally to give alms to the poor, according to his ability.

XXV. *Of a Christian Man's Oath.* As we confess that vain and rash swearing is forbidden Christian men by our Lord Jesus Christ and James his apostle; so we judge that the Christian religion doth not prohibit, but that a man may swear when the magistrate requireth, in a cause of faith and charity, so it be done according to the prophet's teaching, in justice, judgment, and truth.

The following Article from the Methodist Protestant Discipline is placed here by the United Conference. It was not one of the Articles of Religion voted upon by the three churches.

XXVI. *Of Sanctification.* Sanctification is that renewal of our fallen nature by the Holy Ghost, received through faith in Jesus Christ, whose blood of atonement cleanseth from all sin; whereby we are not only delivered from the guilt of sin, but are washed from its pollution, saved from its power, and are enabled, through grace, to love God with all our hearts and to walk in his holy commandments blameless.

The following provision was adopted by the United Conference. This statement seeks to interpret to our churches in foreign lands Article XXIII of the Articles of Religion. It is a legislative enactment but is not a part of the Constitution.

XXVII. *Of the Duty of Christians to the Civil Authority.* It is the duty of all Christians, and especially of all Christian ministers, to observe and obey the laws and commands of the governing or supreme authority of the country of which they are citizens or subjects or in which they reside, and to use all laudable means to encourage and enjoin obedience to the powers that be.

EVANGELICAL UNITED BRETHREN CONFESSION OF FAITH

I. *God.* We believe in the one true, holy and living God, Eternal Spirit, who is Creator, Sovereign and Preserver of all things visible and invisible. He is infinite in power, wisdom, justice, goodness and love, and rules with gracious regard for the well-being and salvation of men, to the glory of his name. We believe the one God reveals himself as the Trinity; Father, Son and Holy Spirit, distinct but inseparable, eternally one in essence and power.

II. *Jesus Christ.* We believe in Jesus Christ, truly God and truly man, in whom the divine and human natures are perfectly and inseparably united. He is the eternal Word made flesh, the only begotten Son of the Father, born of the Virgin Mary by the power of the Holy Spirit. As ministering Servant he lived, suffered and died on the cross. He was buried, rose from the dead and ascended into heaven to be with the Father, from whence he shall return. He is eternal Savior and Mediator, who intercedes for us, and by him all men will be judged.

III. *The Holy Spirit.* We believe in the Holy Spirit who proceeds from and is one in being with the Father and the Son. He convinces the world of sin, of righteousness and of judgment. He leads men through faithful response to the gospel into the fellowship of the church. He comforts, sustains and empowers the faithful and guides them into all truth.

IV. *The Holy Bible.* We believe in the Holy Bible, Old and New Testaments, reveals the Word of God so far as it is necessary for our salvation. It is to be received through the Holy Spirit as the true rule and guide for faith and practice. Whatever is not revealed in or established by the Holy Scripture is not to be made an article of faith nor is it to be taught as essential to salvation.

V. *The Church.* We believe the Christian church is the community of all believers under the Lordship of Christ. We believe it is one, holy, apostolic and catholic. It is the redemptive fellowship in which the Word of God is preached by men divinely called, and the sacraments are duly administered according to Christ's own appointment. Under the discipline of the Holy Spirit the church exists for the maintenance of worship, the edification of believers and the redemption of the world.

VI. *The Sacraments.* We believe the sacraments, ordained by Christ, are symbols and pledges of the Christian's profession and of God's love toward us. They are means of grace by which God works invisibly in us, quickening, strengthening and confirming our faith in him. Two sacraments are ordained by Christ our Lord, namely, Baptism and the Lord's Supper.

We believe Baptism signifies entrance into the household of faith, and is a symbol of repentance and inner cleansing from sin, a representation of the new birth in Christ Jesus and a mark of Christian discipleship.

We believe children are under the atonement of Christ and as heirs of the Kingdom of God are acceptable subjects for Christian baptism. Children of believing parents through baptism become the special responsibility of the church. They should be nurtured and led to personal acceptance of Christ, and by profession of faith confirm their baptism.

We believe the Lord's Supper is a representation of our redemption, a memorial of the sufferings and death of Christ, and a token of love and union which Christians have with Christ and with one another. Those who rightly, worthily and in faith eat the broken bread and drink the blessed cup partake of the body and blood of Christ in a spiritual manner until he comes.

VII. *Sin and Free Will.* We believe man is fallen from righteousness and, apart from the grace of our Lord Jesus Christ, is destitute of holiness and inclined to evil. Except a man be born again, he cannot see the Kingdom of God. In his own strength, without divine grace, man cannot do good works pleasing and acceptable to God. We believe, however, man influenced and empowered by the Holy Spirit is responsible in freedom to exercise his will for good.

VIII. *Reconciliation Through Christ.* We believe God was in Christ reconciling the world to himself. The offering Christ freely made on the cross is the perfect and sufficient sacrifice for the sins of the whole world, redeeming man from all sin, so that no other satisfaction is required.

IX. *Justification and Regeneration.* We believe we are never accounted righteous before God through our works or merit, but that penitent sinners are justified or accounted righteous before God only by faith in our Lord Jesus Christ.

We believe regeneration is the renewal of man in righteousness through Jesus Christ, by the power of the Holy Spirit, whereby we are made partakers of the divine nature and experience newness of life. By this new birth the believer becomes reconciled to God and is enabled to serve him with the will and the affections.

We believe, although we have experienced regeneration, it is possible to depart from grace and fall into sin; and we may even then, by the grace of God, be renewed in righteousness.

X. *Good Works.* We believe good works are the necessary fruits of faith and follow regeneration but they do not have the virtue to remove our sins or to avert divine judgment. We believe good works, pleasing and acceptable to God in Christ, spring from a true and living faith, for through and by them faith is made evident.

XI. *Sanctification and Christian Perfection.* We believe sanctification is the work of God's grace through the Word and the Spirit, by which those who have been born again are cleansed from sin in their thoughts, words and acts, and are enabled to live in accordance with God's will, and to strive for holiness without which no one will see the Lord.

Entire sanctification is a state of perfect love, righteousness and true holiness which every regenerate believer may obtain by being delivered from the power of sin, by loving God with all the heart, soul, mind and strength, and by loving one's neighbor as one's self. Through faith in Jesus Christ this gracious gift may be received in this life both gradually and instantaneously, and should be sought earnestly by every child of God.

We believe this experience does not deliver us from the infirmities, ignorance and mistakes common to man, nor from the possibilities of further sin. The Christian must continue on guard against spiritual pride and seek to gain victory over every temptation to sin. He must respond wholly to the will of God so that sin will lose its power over him; and the world, the flesh and the devil are put under his feet. Thus he rules over these enemies with watchfulness through the power of the Holy Spirit.

XII. *The Judgment and the Future State.* We believe all men stand under the righteous judgment of Jesus Christ, both now and in the last day. We believe in the resurrection of the dead; the righteous to life eternal and the wicked to endless condemnation.

XIII. *Public Worship.* We believe divine worship is the duty and privilege of man who, in the presence of God, bows in adoration, humility and dedication. We believe divine worship is essential to the life of the church, and that the assembling of the people of God for such worship is necessary to Christian fellowship and spiritual growth.

We believe the order of public worship need not be the same in all places but may be modified by the church according to circumstances and the needs of men. It should be in a language and form understood by the people, consistent with the Holy Scriptures to the edification of all, and in accordance with the order and *Discipline* of the church.

XIV. *The Lord's Day.* We believe the Lord's Day is divinely ordained for private and public worship, for rest from unnecessary work, and should be devoted to spiritual improvement, Christian fellowship and service. It is commemorative of our Lord's resurrection and is an emblem of our eternal rest. It is essential to the permanence and growth of the Christian church, and important to the welfare of the civil community.

XV. *The Christian and Property.* We believe God is the owner of all things and that the individual holding of property is lawful and is a sacred trust under God. Private property is to be used for the manifestation of Christian love and liberality, and to support the church's mission in the world. All forms of property, whether private, corporate or public, are to be held in solemn trust and used responsibly for human good under the sovereignty of God.

XVI. *Civil Government.* We believe civil government derives its just powers from the sovereign God. As Christians we recognize the governments under whose protection we reside and believe such governments should be based on, and be responsible for, the recognition of human rights under God. We believe war and bloodshed are contrary to the gospel and spirit of Christ. We believe it is the duty of Christian citizens to give moral strength and purpose to their respective governments through sober, righteous and godly living.

METHODIST SOCIAL CREED

I. OUR HERITAGE.—The interest of The Methodist Church in social welfare springs from the gospel, and from the labors of John Wesley, who ministered to the physical, intellectual, and social needs of the people to whom he preached the gospel of personal redemption.

In our historic position we have sought to follow Christ in bringing the whole of life, with its activities, possessions, and relationships, into conformity with the will of God.

As Methodists we have an obligation to affirm our position on social and economic questions.

II. OUR THEOLOGICAL BASIS.—The Methodist Church must view the perplexing times and problems which we face today in the light of the life and teachings of Jesus. Jesus taught us to love our neighbors and seek justice for them as well as for ourselves. To be silent in the face of need, injustice, and exploitation is to deny him.

We believe that God is Father of all peoples and races, that Jesus Christ is his Son, that all men are brothers, and that each person is of infinite worth as a child of God.

We believe that "the earth is the Lord's and the fulness thereof." Our own capacities and all we possess are gifts of the Creator, and should be held and used in stewardship to him.

We believe that God in Christ is seeking to redeem all men and also society. This redemption is a continuing necessity.

We believe that the grace of God in Christ is available for redemption from individual and social sin as we seek in penitence and obedience to do his holy will.

We believe that all persons have supreme value in the sight of God, and ought to be so regarded by us. We test all institutions and practices by their effect upon persons. Since Jesus died for the redemption of all men, we believe we should live to help save man from sin and from every influence which would harm or destroy him.

III. OUR DECLARATION OF SOCIAL CONCERN.—Applying the foregoing principles, The Methodist Church declares itself as follows:

A. *The Family.*—We seek equal rights and justice for all persons; protection of the individual and the family by high standards of morality; Christian education for marriage, parenthood, and the home; adequate housing; improved marriage and divorce laws.

We believe that the church must be vitally concerned with the health and welfare needs of all people, first within the family, and, where necessary, through institutional care with high standards of scientific service and Christian dedication.

We believe that planned parenthood, practiced with respect for human life, fulfills rather than violates the will of God. It is the duty of each married couple prayerfully and responsibly to seek parenthood, avert it, or defer it, in accordance with the best expression of their Christian love. Families in all parts of the world should have available to them necessary information and medical assistance for birth control through public and private programs. This issue must be seen in reference to the pressing population problem now before the whole world.

We believe it is the plain responsibility of the family, as it is also the deep concern of the community, that the welfare of children whose mothers are employed outside the home be safeguarded. This responsibility includes provision for the protection, education, spiritual nurture, and wholesome recreation of every child, and for religious and educational programs which will secure these ends.

B. *Economic Life.*—1. *Christianity and the Economic Order.*—With full acknowledgment of stewardship under God and accountability to him, we stand for the acquisition of property by moral processes and the right to private ownership thereof. We refuse to identify Christianity with any economic system. We are under obligation to test each aspect of every economic order by the commands of Christ and judge its practices by the Christian gospel. We believe that it is our duty not only to bring Christ to the individual, but also to bring the increasingly technological society within which we live more nearly into conformity with the teachings of Christ. We believe that a free democratic way of life, influenced by Christian principles, can bring to mankind a society in which liberty is preserved, justice established, and brotherhood achieved.

We believe in the use of such opportunities for political action as are consistent with Christian principles. We urge Christians to view political responsibilities as an opportunity for Christian witness and service.

2. *Responsible Use of Power.*—The Christian point of view demands that concentrations of power in government, labor, business, and religious organizations be used responsibly. The task of the church in this regard is to help people in positions of power and the organizations which they serve to achieve and exercise a high level of social responsibility.

3. *Poverty and Unemployment.*—We believe that the economic development which makes possible material plenty for all imposes upon us great moral responsibility, in that the physical and spiritual development of millions of persons throughout the world is hindered by poverty. We therefore stand for the eradication of poverty everywhere.

We believe it is our Christian duty to provide opportunities for education and training for people to earn a living for themselves and their dependents, so that they may take advantage of new technology.

Lack of significant employment tends to destroy human self-respect. We believe that employable workers must be safeguarded from enforced unemployment.

4. *Wealth.*—We recognize the perils of prosperity. Our Lord has told us that we cannot serve God and mammon. As Christians we must examine earnestly before God our personal and business practices, lest we adopt the standards and assumptions of a materialistic society. Churches and their institutions as well as individuals own property, invest funds, and employ labor. In these areas practices and relationships must conform to the highest Christian standards.

5. *Working Conditions.*—We oppose all forms of social, economic, and moral waste. We urge the protection of the worker from dangerous and unsanitary working conditions, and from occupational diseases.

We stand for reasonable hours of labor, for just wages, for a fair day's work for a fair day's wages, for just working conditions, for periods of leisure, and for an equitable division of the product of industry.

We believe special protection should be provided for women and children, as well as migrant workers and others especially vulnerable to exploitation.

6. *Social Benefits for Workers.*—We stand for public and private programs of economic security for old age, for adequate insurance covering sickness and injury to the worker, and for increased protection against those preventable conditions which produce want.

7. *The Right to Organize for Collective Bargaining.*—We stand for the right of employees and employers alike to organize for collective bargaining, protection of both in the exercise of their right, the responsibility of both to bargain in good faith, and the obligation of both to work for the public good.

8. *Town and Country Life.*—We recognize the basic significance of town and country areas in relation to population supply, natural resources, community life, and Christian culture. We believe farmers, other agriculture workers, and those displaced by mechanization should have opportunity to earn a fair income.

Methodism, because of its large town and country membership and world-wide impact, must lead in developing an adequate Christian program in rural areas everywhere. This should pertain to people in their relationship to God, to the stewardship of the soil and the conservation of all natural resources, and to family, church, and community welfare.

9. *Urban Life.*—We believe the inner city to be a mission field crying out for bold new creative ways of witness. Here is emerging a pagan generation committed to values that run counter to those of the Christ. Therefore we call our urban congregations to a deeper involvement in neighborhood life. We call the Church to come into the city for Christ's sake, there to touch all forgotten persons with his compassion.

10. *Christian Vocation.*—We believe that every employable person so far as possible should be engaged in some vocation productive of common good. Every such vocation should be viewed as a Christian calling by those who pursue it as well as by those who receive its benefits, and our daily work should be regarded as a sphere of service to God. The creative use of leisure is also a major responsibility for the Christian.

C. *The Church and General Welfare.*—The Church is called to be a redeeming community of discerning Christian love—a fellowship of those who confess their sin, who rejoice in the love of God freely given, and who commit themselves continually to spiritual excellence in every facet of life.

1. *Alcohol Problems.*—We believe that the Christian principle of love for God and neighbor calls us to abstain from the use of alcoholic beverages and to minister to those victimized by their use. The use of beverage alcohol imperils the abundant life to which Christ calls. This is especially true in an organized and mechanized society. Individuals and families are destroyed by its use. We join with men of good conscience who seek to overcome the social, economic, and moral waste which this indulgence has created. The Church must become a healing and redemptive fellowship for those who suffer because of beverage alcohol.

2. *Crime and Rehabilitation.*—We stand for the application of the redemptive principle in treating law offenders and for study and action directed toward the improvement of laws, correctional facilities and services, and court procedures in order to facilitate rehabilitation. For this reason we deplore capital punishment.

We do not believe an individual should be excused from his personal responsibility to society; but we recognize that crime, and in particular juvenile delinquency leading to crime, is often a result of family failure and bad social conditions. Christian citizens and churches have a special opportunity and responsibility for creating those conditions of family life and social surroundings, wholesome recreation, vocational training, personal counseling, and social adjustment by which crime may be reduced, and offenders rehabilitated and redeemed by God's grace.

3. *Gambling.*—We stand for the achievement of community and personal standards which make unnecessary the resort to petty or commercial gambling as a recreation, escape, or producer of public or charitable revenue. As an act of faith and love, Christians should abstain from all gambling, and should participate in efforts to minister to those victimized by the practice, including compulsive gamblers.

4. *Mental Health and Medical Care.*—We stand for the provision of adequate medical care for all people, with special attention being given the aging, the young, and minority and low income groups. We support our government, individuals, and foundations in required research in public health; and we support legislation to meet these needs.

We believe that adequate facilities with professionally trained staff must be made available for the emotionally ill and the mentally retarded of every community. We also believe that churches may become spiritual centers of healing through worship, pastoral concern, and volunteer service for the emotionally ill.

5. *Drug Abuse.*—We seek to overcome those social and psychological forces which lead so large a part of our society to unhealthful dependence upon tobacco, alcohol, and drugs. The illicit traffic in drugs cannot be tolerated. Society must provide through public and private facilities for the treatment, rehabilitation, and after-care of narcotic addicts and other victims of drug abuse.

6. *Sex in Christian Life.*—We believe that sexual intercourse within holy matrimony with fidelity and love is a sacred experience and constitutes a needed expression of affection. We also believe that sexual intercourse outside the bonds of matrimony is contrary to the will of God. The outrageous exploitation of the strong forces underlying sexual experience is a destructive element of our culture. It not only distorts the meaning of sex experience but constitutes a blasphemous disregard of God's purpose for men and women. A case in point is the distribution of hard-core pornographic and other sex-exploitive material. We advocate thorough educational efforts in home, church, and school designed to elevate our whole understanding of the meaning of sexual experience.

7. *Social Welfare.*—We believe that meeting human need is both a private and a community responsibility. Adequate public assistance should be made available to all persons solely on the basis of need. Every individual should provide for his own needs, and share responsibility for the needs of others to the full extent of his ability, but we believe that no person in an affluent society should be demoralized because of unmet need.

D. *Human Rights.*—1. *Freedom from Discrimination.*—We stand for equal rights for all racial, cultural, and religious groups, and insist that the principles set forth in this creed apply to all alike. The right to choose a home, enter a school, secure employment, vote, and have access to public accommodations should be guaranteed to all regardless of race, culture, national origin, social class, or religion. Neither should any person be denied equal political, economic, or legal rights or opportunities because of sex.

That the Church should ever refuse access to worship or membership in its fellowship to any person because of race, color, or national origin is contrary to our fundamental Christian convictions.

2. *Civil Liberties and Civil Rights.*—We stand for freedom of speech, assembly, and press and broadcasting. The fundamental responsibility in the use of these freedoms and the justification of their exercise is adherence to the truth.

We stand for the right of all individuals and groups to advocate any peaceful and constitutional method for the solution of the problems that confront society.

E. *Peace and World Order.*—We believe that Christianity cannot be nationalistic; it must be universal in its outlook and appeal. The influence of the church must always be on the side of every effort seeking to remove those conditions of heart and mind, of social, economic, and international injustice, and of ideological conflict in which wars begin.

We must actively and constantly create the conditions of peace. We stand for the promotion of understanding, reconciliation, and good will; the relief of suffering, the lifting of living standards around the world; concern for the freedom and welfare of dependent and subject persons; the removal of racial tensions; the taking of steps toward disarmament; and the support of patient negotiations.

1. *International Organization.*—We believe that the United Nations is a working center of international cooperation which provides the most hopeful avenue leading to peace and world order. The United Nations with its related agencies should be strengthened through governmental cooperation and support. This effort deserves the support of all Christians. The Church itself, as a world fellowship, makes an important contribution to the development of world order.

2. *The Christian and Military Service.*—The Methodist Church, true to the principles of the New Testament, teaches respect for properly constituted civil authority. It encourages both love of country and love of all men. Believing that government rests upon the support of its conscientious citizens, it holds within its fellowship those who sincerely differ as to the Christian's duty in regard to military service. We ask and claim exemption by legal processes from all forms of military preparation or service for all religious conscientious objectors, as for those of the historic peace churches. We recognize the right of the individual to answer the call of his government according to the dictates of his Christian conscience. We also recognize that non-violent resistance can be a valid form of Christian witness. In all of these situations members of The Methodist Church have the authority and support of their church.

IV. OUR MANDATE: READ, STUDY, APPLY.—We recommend that this Social Creed be presented to our congregations orally or in printed form at least once a year, and that frequent references be made to it. Every local church shall encourage the study of the Social Creed and seek to apply its principles.

5. The Holiness Movement

Methodism has affected the religious thinking of many denominations outside its own immediate family. The Holiness movement stems from Wesley's doctrine on sanctification from which certain Methodist churches felt the general stream of his followers had departed. The result was a score of denominations, mainly in the United States, which are juridically distinct but united in professing a number of fundamental tenets of Protestant perfectionism.

There is no easy way of telling which specific churches belong to the Holiness tradition. But the more important include one or more of the following terms in their denominational title: Holiness, Nazarene, Church of God, Pentecostal, or Assemblies (of God).

They hold that, besides justification, there is a "second blessing" in which a person feels himself closely united with God. This is an emotional experience produced in the heart by the direct action of the Holy Spirit. While instantaneous in its effects, the "second blessing" may require years of preparation. It may also demand previous exorcism or driving out the evil spirit before the Spirit of God can enter a soul, commonly induced by the laying on of hands, by one who has already been sanctified.

As a group, Holiness bodies claim that the teachings and practices of the larger denominations have departed from the true faith and compromised with modernism. This stricture also applies to the Catholic Church. The favorite method of preaching is popular revivals, which used to be the regular mode of Methodist evangelism in colonial America. Most of the churches profess, without always stressing, the imminent second coming of Christ, which is to inaugurate a millenium of earthly peace and happiness before the last day.

The extreme left wing of the Holiness movement developed into the Pentecostal Churches. Some are similar to the Holiness Churches in admitting the fundamentalist principles of Christ's divinity, inerrancy of the Bible, the Virgin Birth and final resurrection for all the faithful, Christ's atonement and the early second coming or parousia. But a strong anti-trinitarian spirit has entered certain dominant Pentecostals, for example, those belonging to their largest denomination, the United Pentecostal Church.

The doctrinal foundation of the Holiness movement is concisely stated in John Wesley's *Plain Account of Christian Perfection*, which he wrote in 1766. Thomas A' Kempis, Jeremy Taylor, and William Law first led him to strive after that purity of intention which was the core of his later doctrine. He had taken a position already at Oxford, that perfection is "the humble, gentle, patient love of God and our neighbor ruling our tempers, words and actions." From this position he never departed, even when other phases of what later became Methodism occupied his attention.

When he told Dr. Gibson, the Bishop of London, what he meant by perfection, the prelate replied, "If this be all you mean, publish it to all the world. If any one then can confute what you say, he may have free leave." Wesley was thus led to write his classic treatise on Christian perfection. His purpose in writing the work was twofold: to defend himself against critics who charged him with teaching a kind of antinomianism or lawlessness in the name of sanctity, and to explain how Christianity can lead to great holiness if only the faithful give themselves generously to the following of Christ.

JOHN WESLEY'S
PLAIN ACCOUNT OF CHRISTIAN PERFECTION

Perhaps the general prejudice against Christian perfection may chiefly arise from a misapprehension of the nature of it. We willingly allow, and continually declare, there is no such perfection in this life as implies either a dispensation from doing good, and attending all the ordinances of God; or a freedom from ignorance, mistake, temptation, and a thousand infirmities necessarily connected with flesh and blood.

First, we not only allow, but earnestly contend, that there is no perfection in this life which implies any dispensation from attending all the ordinances of God; or from doing good unto all men while we have time, though "especially unto the household of faith." We believe that not only the babes in Christ, who have newly found redemption in His blood, but those also who are "grown up into perfect men," are indispensably obliged, as often as they have opportunity, to "eat bread and drink wine in remembrance of Him," and to "search the Scriptures," by fasting, as well as temperance, "to keep their bodies under, and bring them into subjection"; and, above all, to pour out their souls in prayer, both secretly, and in the great congregation.

We, secondly, believe that there is no such perfection in this life as implies an entire deliverance, either from ignorance or mistake, in things not essential to salvation, or from manifold temptations, or from numberless infirmities, wherewith the corruptible body more or less presses down the soul. We cannot find any ground in Scripture to suppose that any inhabitant of a house of clay is wholly exempt either from bodily infirmities, or from ignorance of many things; or to imagine any is incapable of mistake, or falling into divers temptations.

But whom then do you mean by "one that is *perfect?*" We mean one in "whom is the mind which was in Christ," and who so "walketh as Christ also walked"; a man "that hath clean hands and a pure heart," or that is "cleansed from all filthiness of flesh and spirit": one in whom is "no occasion of stumbling," and who accordingly "does not commit sin." To declare this a little more particularly: We understand by that scriptural expression, "a perfect man," one in whom God hath fulfilled His faithful word, "From all your filthiness and from all your idols I will cleanse you: I will also save you from all your uncleannesses." We understand hereby, one whom God hath "sanctified throughout, in body, soul, and spirit"; one who "walketh in the light as He is in the light; in whom is no darkness at all: the blood of Jesus Christ His Son having cleansed him from all sin."

This man can now testify to all mankind, "I am crucified with Christ: nevertheless I live; yet not I, but Christ liveth in me." He is "holy as God who called him is holy," both in heart and "in all manner of conversion." He "loveth the Lord his God with all his heart," and serveth Him with "all his strength." He "loveth his neighbour," every man, "as himself"; "yea," as Christ "loveth us"; them in particular that "despitefully use him, and persecute him, because they know not the Son, neither the Father." Indeed his soul is all love; filled with "bowels or mercies, kindness, meekness, gentleness, long-suffering." And his life agreeth thereto, full of "the work of faith, the patience of hope, the labour of love." "And whatsoever he doeth, either in word or deed, he doeth it all in the name," in the love and power, "of the Lord Jesus." In a word, he doeth "the will of God on earth, as it is done in heaven."

This it is to be a perfect man, to be "sanctified throughout"; even "to have a heart so all-flaming with the love of God" (to use Archbishop Usher's word), "as continually to offer up every thought, word, and work, as a spiritual sacrifice, acceptable to God, through Christ"; in every thought of our hearts, in every word of our tongues, in every work of our hands, to "show forth His praise, who hath called us out of darkness into His marvellous light." Oh that both we, and all who seek the Lord Jesus in sincerity, may thus be made perfect in one!

This it is to be a perfect man, to be "sanctified throughout"; even to which we preach at this day. Indeed, by viewing it in every point of light, and comparing it again and again with the word of God on the one hand, and the experience of the children of God on the other, we saw farther into the nature and properties of Christian perfection. But still there is no contrariety at all between our first and our last sentiments. Our first conception of it was, It is to have 'the mind which was in Christ,' and to 'walk as He walked'; to have all the mind that was in Him, and always to walk as He walked: in other words, to be inwardly and outwardly devoted to God; all devoted in heart and life. And we have the same conception of it now, without either addition or diminution.

In the year 1764, upon a review of the whole subject, I wrote down the sum of what I had observed in the following short propositions:—

1. There is such a thing as perfection; for it is again and again mentioned in Scripture.

2. It is not so early as justification; for justified persons are to "go on unto perfection" (Heb. vi. I).

3. It is not so late as death; for St. Paul speaks of living men that were perfect (Phil. iii. 15).

4. It is not absolute. Absolute perfection belongs not to man, nor to angels, but to God alone.

5. It does not make a man infallible; none is infallible while he remains in the body.

6. Is it sinless? It is not worth while to contend for a term. It is "salvation from sin."

7. It is "perfect love" (I John iv. 18). This is the essence of it: its properties, or inseparable fruits, are, rejoicing evermore, praying without ceasing, and in everything giving thanks (I Thess. v. 16, etc.).

8. It is improvable. It is so far from lying in an indivisible point,

from being incapable of increase, that one perfected in love may grow in grace far swifter than he did before.

9. It is amissible, capable of being lost; of which we have numerous instances. But we were not thoroughly convinced of this till five or six years ago.

10. It is constantly both preceded and followed by a gradual work.

11. But is it in itself instantaneous or not? In examining this, let us go on step by step.

An instantaneous change has been wrought in some believers; none can deny this.

Since that change they enjoy perfect love; they feel this, and this alone; they "rejoice evermore, pray without ceasing, and in everything give thanks." Now, this is all that I mean by perfection, therefore, these are witnesses of the perfection which I preach.

"But in some this change was not instantaneous." They did not perceive the instant when it was wrought. It is often difficult to perceive the instant when a man dies; yet there is an instant in which life ceases. And if ever sin ceases, there must be a last moment of its existence, and a first moment of our deliverance from it.

"But if they have this love now, they will lose it." They may; but they need not. And whether they do or no, they have it now; they now experience what we teach. They now are all love; they now rejoice, pray, and praise without ceasing.

"However, sin is only suspended in them; it is not destroyed." Call it which you please. They are all love to-day; and they take no thought for the morrow.

"But this doctrine has been much abused." So has that of justification by faith. But that is no reason for giving up either this or any other scriptural doctrine.

"When you wash your child," as one speaks, "throw away the water; but do not throw away the child."

"But those who think they are saved from sin say they have no need of the merits of Christ." They say just the contrary. Their language is—"Every moment, Lord, I want The merit of Thy death!" They never before had so deep, so unspeakable a conviction of the need of Christ in all His offices, as they have now.

Therefore, all our preachers should make a point of preaching perfection to believers constantly, strongly, and explicitly; and all believers should mind this one thing, and continually agonise for it.

I have now done what I proposed. I have given a plain and simple account of the manner wherein I first received, and wherein I do receive and teach it to this day. I have declared the whole and every part of what I mean by that scriptural expression. I have drawn the picture of it at full length, without either disguise or covering. And I would now ask any impartial person, What is there so frightful therein? Whence is all this outcry, which for these twenty years and upwards has been made throughout the kingdom; as if all Christianity were destroyed, and all religion torn up by the roots? Why is it that the very name of perfection has been cast out of the mouth of Christians; yea, exploded and abhorred, as if it contained the most pernicious heresy? Why have the preachers of it been hooted at, like mad dogs, even by men that fear God; nay, and by some of their own children; some whom they, under God, had begotten through the Gospel? What reason is there for this, or what pretence? Reason, sound reason, there is none; it is impossible there should be.

But pretences there are, and those in great abundance. Indeed, there is ground to fear that, with some who treat us thus, it is mere pretence; that it is no more than a copy of their countenance, from the beginning to the end. They wanted, they sought, occasion against me; and here they found what they sought. 'This is Mr. Wesley's doctrine! He preaches perfection!' He does: yet this is not his doctrine any more than it is yours, or any one else's, that is a minister of Christ. For it is His doctrine, peculiarly, emphatically His! It is the doctrine of Jesus Christ. Those are His words, not mine: "Ye shall therefore be perfect as your Father who is in heaven is perfect." And who says ye shall not; or, at least, not till your soul is separated from the body? It is the doctrine of St. Paul, the doctrine of St. James, of St. Peter, and St. John; and no otherwise Mr. Wesley's than as it is the doctrine of every one who preaches the pure and the whole gospel. I tell you, as plain as I can speak, where and when I found this. I found it in the oracles of God, in the Old and New Testaments; when I read them with no other view or desire but to save my own soul. But whosesoever this doctrine is, I pray you what harm is there in it?

Look at it again; survey it on every side, and that with the closest attention. In one view, it is purity of intention, dedicating all the life to God. It is the giving to God all our hearts: it is one desire and design ruling all our tempers. It is the devoting, not a part, but all our soul, body, and substance to God. In another view, it is all the mind which was in Christ, enabling us to walk as Christ walked. It is the circumcision of the heart from all filthiness, all inward as well as outward pollution. It is a renewal of the heart in the whole image of God, the full likeness of Him that created it. In yet another, it is the loving God with all our heart, and our neighbour as ourselves. Now, take it in which of these views you please (for there is no material difference), and this is the whole and sole perfection, as a train of writings proved to a demonstration, which I have believed and taught for these forty years, from the year 1725 to the year 1765.

Now, let this perfection appear in its native form, and who can speak one word against it? Will any dare to speak against loving the Lord our God with all our heart, and our neighbour as ourselves? Against a renewal of heart, not only in part, but in the whole image of God? Who is he that will open his mouth against being cleansed from all pollution both of flesh and spirit; or against having all the mind that was in Christ, and walking in all things as Christ walked? What man, who calls himself a Christian, has the hardiness to object to the devoting, not a part, but all our soul, body, and substance to God? What serious man would oppose the giving to God all our heart, and the having one design ruling all our tempers?

I say again, let this perfection appear in its own shape, and who will fight against it? It must be disguised before it can be opposed. It must be covered with a bear-skin first, or even the wild beasts of the people will scarce be induced to worry it. But whatever these do, let not the children of God any longer fight against the image of God. Let not the members of Christ say anything against having the whole mind that was in Christ. Let not those who are alive to God oppose the dedicating all our life to Him. Why should you who have His love shed abroad in your heart withstand the giving Him all your heart? Does not all that is within you cry out, 'Who that loves can love enough?'

What pity that those who desire and design to please Him should have any other design or desire! much more, that they should dread, as a fatal delusion, yea abhor, as an abomination to God, the having this one desire and design ruling every temper! Why should devout men be afraid of devoting all their soul, body, and substance to God? Why should those who love Christ count it a damnable error to think we may have all the mind that was in Him? We allow, we contend, that we are justified freely through the righteousness and the blood of Christ. And why are you so hot against us, because we expect likewise to be sanctified wholly through His Spirit?

We look for no favour either from the open servants of sin, or from those who have only the form of religion. But how long will you who worship God in spirit, who are 'circumcised with the circumcision not made with hands,' set your battle in array against those who seek an entire circumcision of heart, who thirst to be cleansed 'from all filthiness of flesh and spirit,' and to 'perfect holiness in the fear of God'?

Nay, we are your brethren, your fellow-labourers in the vineyard of our Lord, your companions in the kingdom and patience of Jesus. Although this we confess (if we are fools therein, yet as fools bear with us), we do expect to love God with all our heart, and our neighbour as ourselves. Yea, we do believe that He will in this world so 'cleanse the thoughts of our hearts by the inspiration of His Holy Spirit, that we shall perfectly love Him, and worthily magnify His holy name.'

THE HOLINESS TRADITION IN AMERICA

There are too many denominations in the Holiness movement to quote even the majority of their doctrinal statements. It is not necessary either, because most of them are so closely related as to be indistinguishable except for the accident of having a different founder and different historical beginnings.

Five churches have been chosen as representative of two divergent aspects of the Holiness tradition in Wesleyanism: those which omit or prescind from such extraordinary signs of the Holy Spirit as the gift of tongues, and those which include the charismata as characteristic of true conversion. The Nazarenes and Salvationists are typical of the first group, and the Pentecostals, Assemblies of God and the Churches of God are classified in the second.

The Church of the Nazarene was established in 1908 by a merger of the Pentecostal, Nazarene and Holiness Churches. In 1919 the word "Pentecostal" was dropped from the name to disclaim any connection with the more extreme forms of the Holiness movement. Its doctrine is built around sanctification as a second definite work of grace subsequent to justification. All clergymen and church officials are expected to have undergone the experience. Church polity is essentially Methodist, with stress on divine healing which does not, however, exclude recourse to medical agencies.

Salvationists are not commonly associated with the Holiness tradition; yet their distinctive theology is in the Wesleyan emphasis on man's cooperation with grace and the need for God's intervention to complete a person's sanctification. William Booth, founder of the Salvation Army, was an ordained minister in the Methodist New Connexion body in England. He left the active

Methodist ministry only when he felt that, like Wesley, he had a special mission to sinners and the neglected people of the Church. Though he dropped the sacraments in his later writings on essential Christianity, he insisted on holiness as the culmination of God's work in the life of a believing Christian who gives himself generously to the practice of the counsels.

Pentecostalism is such an inclusive term it is impossible to classify all the churches which profess to believe that in the life of every man who turns to Christ there occurs a second Pentecost. Not unlike the blessings received by the first Christians, the same outpouring of "the second rain" comes down on the faithful today. Most churches of the Pentecostal type are directly in the Holiness family; others have a Baptist background, but with a modern Pentecostalism in England, among the Irvingites, where the first dramatic outburst of tongues took place at Port Glasgow in Scotland in 1830. American Pentecostals say the birthday was December 31, 1900, at Topeka, Kansas, where the Methodist preacher Charles Fox Parham brought the gifts of the Spirit by laying hands on Agnes Ozman. Immediately she began to speak in a strange tongue.

The Assemblies of God are basically Pentecostals who formed a single larger body in 1914 in order to make their preaching and missionary crusade more effective. Started at Hot Springs, Arkansas, they have since spread into every state of the union and engage in extensive evangelism overseas. They are specially insistent that baptism in the Holy Spirit is shown by speaking in tongues and claim that all the gifts of the Spirit, enumerated in the New Testament, should be in evidence among churches that are faithful to the teachings of Christ.

Some two hundred independent religious denominations in the United States bear the name Church of God, with or without other qualifying terms. The largest of these, located in Tennessee and Arkansas, are specifically Pentecostal. They do not differ, except in accidentals, from other bodies in the same tradition. Like the Pentecostals properly so-called and the Assemblies, the Churches of God have made numerous converts north of the Mason-Dixon line. Their principal appeal has not changed, though; it is mainly directed to the socially underprivileged across the spectrum of racial and ethnic differences in the population.

Pentecostal groups in every denomination are commonly described as fundamentalist, which means the acceptance of the Trinity and belief in the divinity of Christ. This generalization should be carefully qualified because one of the largest bodies, the United Pentecostal Church, is officially Unitarian.

CONSTITUTION AND SPECIAL RULES
CHURCH OF THE NAZARENE

In order that we may preserve our God-given heritage, the faith once delivered to the saints, especially the doctrine and experience of sanctification as a second work of grace, and also that we may cooperate effectual with other branches of the Church of Jesus Christ in advancing God's kingdom among men, we the ministers and lay members of the Church of the Nazarene, in accordance with the principles of constitutional legislation established among us, do hereby ordain, adopt, and set forth as the fundamental law or constitution of the Church of the Nazarene the Articles of Faith, the General Rules, and the Articles of Organization and Government here following to wit:

I. *The Triune God.* We believe in one eternally existent, infinite God, Sovereign of the universe; that He only is God, creative and administrative, holy in nature, attributes, and purpose; that He, as God, is Triune in essential being, revealed as Father, Son, and Holy Spirit.

II. *Jesus Christ.* We believe in Jesus Christ, the Second Person of the Triune Godhead; that He was eternally one with the Father; that He became incarnate by the Holy Spirit and was born of the Virgin Mary, so that two whole and perfect natures, that is to say the Godhead and manhood, are thus united in one person very God and very man, the God-man.

We believe that Jesus Christ died for our sins, and that He truly arose from the dead and took again His body, together with all things appertaining to the perfection of man's nature, wherewith He ascended into heaven and is there engaged in intercession for us.

III. *The Holy Spirit.* We believe in the Holy Spirit, the Third Person of the Triune Godhead, that He is ever present and efficiently active in and with the Church of Christ, convincing the world of sin, regenerating those who repent and believe, sanctifying believers, and guiding into all truth as it is in Jesus.

IV. *The Holy Scriptures.* We believe in the plenary inspiration of the Holy Scriptures, by which we understand the sixty-six books of the Old and New Testaments given by divine inspiration, inerrantly revealing the will of God concerning us in all things necessary to our salvation, so that whatever is not contained therein is not to be enjoined as an article of faith.

V. *Original Sin, or Depravity.* We believe that original sin, or depravity, is that corruption of the nature of all the offspring of Adam by reason of which every one is very far gone from original righteousness or the pure state of our first parents at the time of their creation, is averse to God, is without spiritual life, and inclined to evil, and that continually. We further believe that original sin continues to exist with the new life of the regenerate, until eradicated by the baptism with the Holy Spirit.

VI. *Atonement.* We believe that Jesus Christ, by His sufferings, by the shedding of His own blood, and by His meritorious death on the Cross, made a full atonement for all human sin, and that this atonement is the only ground of salvation, and that it is sufficient for every individual of Adam's race. The atonement is graciously efficacious for the salvation of the irresponsible and for the children in innocency, but is efficacious for the salvation of those who reach the age of responsibility only when they repent and believe.

VII. *Free Agency.* We believe that man's creation in God-likeness included ability to choose between right and wrong, and that thus he was made morally responsible; that through the fall of Adam he became depraved so that he cannot now turn and prepare himself by his own natural strength and works to faith and calling upon God. But we also believe that the grace of God through Jesus Christ is freely bestowed upon all men, enabling all who will to turn from sin to righteousness, believe on Jesus Christ for pardon and cleansing from sin, and follow good works pleasing and acceptable in His sight.

We believe that man, though in the possession of the experience of regeneration and entire sanctification, may fall from grace and apostatize and, unless he repent of his sin, be hopelessly and eternally lost.

VIII. *Repentance.* We believe that repentance, which is a sincere and thorough change of the mind in regard to sin, involving a sense of personal guilt and a voluntary turning away from sin, is demanded of all who have by act or purpose become sinners against God. The Spirit of God gives to all who will repent the gracious help of penitence of heart and hope of mercy, that they may believe unto pardon and spiritual life.

IX. *Justification, Regeneration, and Adoption.* 1. We believe that

Justification is that gracious and judicial act of God, by which He grants full pardon of all guilt and complete release from the penalty of sins committed, and acceptance as righteous, to all who believe on Jesus Christ and receive Him as Lord and Saviour.

2. We believe that regeneration, or the new birth, is that gracious work of God whereby the moral nature of the repentant believer is spiritually quickened and given a distinctively spiritual life, capable of faith, love, and obedience.

3. We believe that adoption is that gracious act of God by which the justified and regenerated believer is constituted a son of God.

4. We believe that justification, regeneration, and adoption are simultaneous in the experience of seekers after God and are obtained upon the condition of faith, preceded by repentance; and that to this work and state of grace the Holy Spirit bears witness.

X. *Entire Sanctification.* We believe that entire sanctification is that act of God, subsequent to regeneration, by which believers are made free from original sin, or depravity, and brought into a state of entire devotement to God, and the holy obedience of love made perfect.

It is wrought by the baptism with the Holy Spirit, and comprehends in one experience the cleansing of the heart from sin and the abiding indwelling presence of the Holy Spirit, empowering the believer for life and service.

Entire sanctification is provided by the blood of Jesus, is wrought instantaneously by faith, preceded by entire consecration; and to this work and state of grace the Holy Spirit bears witness.

This experience is also known by various terms representing its different phases, such as "Christian Perfection," "Perfect Love," "Heart Purity," "The Baptism with the Holy Spirit," "The Fullness of the Blessing," and "Christian Holiness."

XI. *Second Coming of Christ.* We believe that the Lord Jesus Christ will come again; that we who are alive at His coming shall not precede them that are asleep in Christ Jesus; but that, if we are abiding in Him, we shall be caught up with the risen saints to meet the Lord in the air, so that we shall ever be with the Lord.

XII. *Resurrection, Judgment, and Destiny.* 1. We believe in the resurrection of the dead, that the bodies both of the just and of the unjust shall be raised to life and united with their spirits—"they that have done good, unto the resurrection of life; and they that have done evil, unto the resurrection of damnation."

2. We believe in future judgment in which every man shall appear before God to be judged according to his deeds in this life.

3. We believe that glorious and everlasting life is assured to all who savingly believe in, and obediently follow, Jesus Christ our Lord; and that the finally impenitent shall suffer eternally in hell.

XIII. *Baptism.* We believe that Christian baptism is a sacrament signifying acceptance of the benefits of the atonement of Jesus Christ, to be administered to believers as declarative of their faith in Jesus Christ as their Saviour, and full purpose of obedience in holiness and righteousness.

Baptism being the symbol of the New Testament, young children may be baptized, upon request of parents or guardians who shall give assurance for them of necessary Christian training.

Baptism may be administered by sprinkling, pouring, or immersion, according to the choice of the applicant.

XIV. *The Lord's Supper.* We believe that the Memorial and Communion Supper instituted by our Lord and Saviour Jesus Christ is essentially a New Testament sacrament, declarative of His sacrificial death, through the merits of which believers have life and salvation and promise of all spiritual blessings in Christ. It is distinctively for those who are prepared for reverent appreciation of this significance and by it they show forth the Lord's death till He come again. It being the Communion feast, only those who have faith in Christ and love for the saints should be called to participate therein.

XV. *Divine Healing.* We believe in the Bible doctrine of divine healing and urge our people to seek to offer the prayer of faith for the healing of the sick. Providential means and agencies when deemed necessary should not be refused.

PRINCIPAL DOCTRINES
OF THE SALVATION ARMY

I. *We believe* that the Scriptures of the Old and New Testaments were given by inspiration of God and that they only constitute the divine rule of Christian faith and practice.

II. *We believe* there is only one God who is infinitely perfect the Creator Preserver and Governor of all things and who is the only proper object of religious worship.

III. *We believe* that there are Three Persons in the Godhead—the Father the Son and the Holy Ghost—undivided in essence and co-equal in power and glory.

IV. *We believe* that in the person of Jesus Christ the Divine and human natures are united so that He is truly and properly God and truly and properly man.

V. *We believe* that our first parents were created in a state of innocency but by their disobedience they lost their purity and happiness and that in consequence of their fall all men have become sinners totally depraved and as such are justly exposed to the wrath of God.

VI. *We believe* that the Lord Jesus Christ has by His suffering and death made an atonement for the whole world so that whosoever will may be saved.

VII. *We believe* that repentance toward God, faith in our Lord Jesus Christ and regeneration by the Holy Spirit are necessary to Salvation.

VIII. *We believe* that we are justified by grace through faith in our Lord Jesus Christ and that he that believeth hath the witness in himself.

IX. *We believe* that continuance in a state of Salvation depends upon continued obedient faith in Christ.

X. *We believe* that it is the privilege of all believers to be 'wholly sanctified' and that 'their whole spirit and soul and body' may be 'preserved blameless unto the coming of our Lord Jesus Christ.' 1 Thess. v. 23.

XI. *We believe* in the immortality of the soul in the resurrection of the body in the general judgment at the end of the world in the eternal happiness of the righteous and in the endless punishment of the wicked.

AN OFFICER'S ENGAGEMENTS WITII THE SALVATION ARMY

An Officer is accepted as such upon condition that, when filling up the Candidate's Application Form, he makes certain promises and declarations. Briefly stated, there are:

I. *Life-long Salvationism.* He intends to live and die in the ranks of The Salvation Army.

II. *Acceptance of S.A. doctrine.* He has read and accepts the principal doctrines taught by The Army.

III. *Non-use of drink, tobacco, drugs, jewellery.* He has given up the use of intoxicating drink, tobacco, and pernicious drugs; also the wearing of jewellery, other than a simple engagement or marriage ring.

IV. *Observance of Regulations.* He pledges himself to study and carry out the Orders and Regulations of The Army.

V. *Uniform wearing.* He will wear uniform, and dress in every way in accordance with the direction of Headquarters.

VI. *Minimum daily service.* He will spend not less than nine hours every day in the active service of The Army, of which, in the case of a Corps Officer, not less than an average of three hours every week-day, or eighteen hours weekly, shall be devoted to visitation.

VII. *Record-keeping.* He will keep truthful records of his work, filling up, for the inspection of his Superior Officer, the required forms and books; and he will confess, so far as he is concerned, and report, so far as he may see in others, any neglect or variation from the orders or directions of his leaders.

VIII. *Acceptance of comrade Officer.* He promises to accept cheerfully the decision of Headquarters as to the person chosen from time to time as his Assistant or Commanding Officer.

IX. *No injury to The Army.* He will never, on any consideration, do anything calculated to injure The Salvation Army, neither will he take part in or attend any Meeting or Service held, or countenance any step taken, in opposition to The Army.

X. *No guaranteed salary.* He understands that no salary or allowance is guaranteed, and that he will have no claim against The Salvation Army, or against any one connected therewith, on account of monetary allowance not received by him.

XI. *No unauthorized remuneration.* He will not receive any gift or remuneration from any source other than is approved by Headquarters.

XII. *Presentations and testimonials.* He will comply with the Order which states that 'Officers are expected to refuse absolutely, and to prevent, if possible, even the proposal of, any presentation or testimonial to themselves.'

XIII. *No unauthorized publishing.* He will not publish any books, songs, or music, except for the benefit of The Salvation Army, and then only with the consent of Headquarters.

XIV. *No supplementary earnings.* He will not engage in any trade, profession, or money-making occupation, except for the benefit of The Salvation Army, and then only with the consent of Headquarters.

XV. *Personal expenses.* He is aware that Officers are responsible for all personal expenses, including medical attention, unless their Superior Officer arranges otherwise.

XVI. *Training.* He is willing to enter Training, and, should Headquarters conclude that he has not the necessary qualifications for Officership, he pledges himself to return home and work in his Corps without creating dissatisfaction.

XVII. *If unsuitable.* He understands that The Army does not undertake to employ or to retain in its service any one who is not fitted for the work or faithful and successful in it; and he solemnly pledges himself quietly to leave any appointment to which he may be sent, without making any attempt to disturb or annoy The Army in any way, should his responsible leader, on behalf of the General, desire him to do so.

XVIII. *Army not liable for loss.* He understands that a trial is necessary for the purpose of testing his suitability for the work of Salvation Army Officership, and that the General will not be responsible in any way for any loss he may suffer in consequence of his being dismissed during trial or afterward. Also he discharges The Army and the General from all liability, and pledges himself to make no claim on account of any situation, property, or interest he may give up in order to secure an engagement in The Army.

XIX. *Courting.* He is, or is not, courting as the case may be.

XX. *Service previous to courtship.* If not courting, he promises to refrain from anything of the kind while he is a Candidate (without first consulting his Leaders), during the first year of Training.

XXI. *Engagement and Marriage Regulations.* He agrees to comply with The Army's Regulations with respect to Engagement and Marriage, as set forth in Part II, Chapter VI, Section 2.

XXII. *Filling of Candidate's Form.* He declares that the answers given on his Candidate's Form appear to him to express fully the truth as to the questions put to him, and he knows of no other facts which would be likely to prevent his acceptance by the General, were such facts known to him.

CONFESSION OF FAITH
PENTECOSTAL CHURCH OF GOD

I. *The Scriptures.* The Scriptures of the Old and New Testaments are the inspired Word of God (II Timothy 3:15) presenting to us the complete revelation of His will for the Salvation of men, and constituting the Divine and only rule of Christian faith and practice (II Peter 1:21).

II. *The Godhead.* Our God is a trinity in unity, manifested in three persons: the Father, the Son, and the Holy Spirit. God is infinitely perfect, being in His three persons co-existent, co-equal, and co-eternal.

God the Father is greater than all (John 14:28); the source of the Word (LOGOS) and the Begetter (John 16:28; John 1:14).

The Son was the begotten of the Father, accepting earthly limitations, true God and true man; conceived by the Holy Ghost and born of the Virgin Mary. He died upon the cross, the Just for the unjust as a substitutionary sacrifice, and all who believe in Him are justified on the grounds of His shed blood. He arose from the dead according to the Scriptures. He is now at the right hand of the Majesty on High as our great High Priest, and He will return again to establish His kingdom of righteousness and justice.

The Holy Spirit is a Divine Person, Executive of the Godhead on earth, the Comforter sent by the Lord Jesus Christ to indwell, to guide, and to teach the believer, and to convince the world of sin, of righteousness, and of judgment.

III. *Man, His Fall and Redemption.* Man is a created being, made in the likeness and the image of God, but through Adam's transgression and fall sin came into the world. (Romans 5:12). "All have sinned and come short of the glory of God." (Romans 3:23). "As it is written, there is none righteous, no not one." (Romans 3:10). Jesus Christ, the Son of God, was manifested to undo the work of the devil and gave His life and shed His blood to redeem and restore man back to God. (I John 3:8).

Salvation is the gift of God to man, separate from works and the Law, and is made operative by grace through faith in Jesus Christ, producing works acceptable to God. (Eph. 2:8).

IV. *Salvation.* Salvation is made possible through the meritorious work of Jesus Christ on the cross and through Holy Spirit conviction. Godly sorrow works repentance and makes possible the experience of the new birth, and Christ formed within us is the gift of eternal life. (Tit. 2:11; Rom. 10:13-15; Luke 24:47; Tit. 3:5-7).

V. *Church.* The true Church is the Body of Jesus Christ (Colossians 1:18; Eph. 4:15), He being the Head. Its earthly consituents are all true believers, born again by the Spirit (John 3:6) and by the Word (I Peter 1:23).

To it is delegated the various gifts and offices of the Holy Spirit (I Corinthians 12:7-11 and 27, 28) necessary for the successful fulfillment of Christ's Great Commission to the Church, as given to the disciples in Matthew 28:19 and Mark 16:15-20.

VI. *Ministry.* God, through the Holy Spirit, definitely calls such as He desires to serve as evangelists, pastors and teachers, and specifically endues the one called with the talents and gifts peculiar to that office or offices (Eph. 4:11-13). Under no circumstances should anyone be ordained or set apart to any such office unless the calling is distinct and evident.

VII. *Water Baptism.* Baptism in water is by immersion, and is a direct commandment of our Lord (Matt. 28:19), and is for believers only. The ordinance is a symbol of the Christian's identification with Christ in His death, burial and resurrection. (Rom. 6:4; Colossians 2:12; Acts 8:36-39).

The following recommendation regarding the Water Baptismal formula is adopted, to wit:

"On the confession of your faith in the Lord Jesus Christ, the Son of God, and by His authority, I baptize you in the name of the Father, and of the Son, and of the Holy Ghost. Amen."

VIII. *Baptism of the Holy Ghost.* The Baptism of the Holy Ghost and fire (Matt. 3:11), is a gift from God, as promised by the Lord Jesus Christ to all believers in this dispensation, and is received subsequent to the new birth. (John 14:16-17; Acts 1:8; 2:4, 38-39; 10:44-48). The Baptism of the Holy Ghost is accompanied with the speaking in other tongues as the Holy Spirit Himself gives utterance as the initial physical sign and evidence. (Acts 2:4).

IX. *Sanctification.* The Bible teaches that without holiness no man can see the Lord. (Heb. 12:14). We believe in the doctrine of sanctification as a definite, yet progressive, work of grace, commencing at the time of regeneration and continuing until the consummation of Salvation. (Heb. 13:12; II Thess. 2:13; I Peter 1:2; Eph. 5:26; I Cor. 6:11; John 17:17; I Thess. 5:23).

X. *Lord's Supper.* The ordinance of the Lord's Supper is a commandment of our Saviour; and being a memorial to His death and resurrection is strictly limited to Christian believers (I Cor. 1:27). Its time and frequency of observance is left to the discretion of each congregation. (I Cor. 11:26).

Only unfermented grape juice, the fruit of the vine, as recommended by our Lord (Matt. 26:29; Mark 14:22; Luke 22:18) shall be used in connection therewith.

XI. *Foot Washing.* Foot washing is recognized among many believers as a Christian practice, and the time, manner and frequency of its observance is left to the discretion of each local congregation (John 13).

XII. *Divine Healing.* Healing is for the physical ills of the human body and is wrought by the power of God, through the prayer of faith, and by the laying on of hands (Mark 16:18; James 5:14-15); it is provided for the atonement of Christ, and is available to all who truly believe.

XIII. *Resurrection of the Just.* The Bible promises, "This same Jesus shall so come in like manner." (Acts 1:11). His coming is imminent; when He comes, "The dead in Christ shall rise first: then we which are alive and remain shall be caught up together with them in the clouds to meet the Lord in the air." (I Thess. 4:16-17). Following the tribulation, He shall return to earth, as King of Kings, and Lord of lords, and together with His saints, who shall be kings and priests, He shall reign a thousand years. (Rev. 20:6).

XIV. *Setting a Time for the Lord's Return.* It is unwise to teach that the Lord will come at some specified time, thereby setting a date for His appearing, and it is also unwise to teach, preach or publish visions of numbers and dates which would tend to fix the time of the second coming of the Lord. (Mark 13:32, 33).

XV. *The Coming of the Lord.* The Pentecostal Church of God of America has declared itself that it holds to the belief in the imminent coming of the Lord as the blessed hope of the Church.

Whereas, the teaching that the Church must go through the tribulation tends to bring confusion and division among the saints; therefore, we recommend that all our ministers teach the imminent coming of Christ, warning all men to be prepared for that coming, which may occur at any time, and not lull their minds into insecurity by any teaching that would cause them to feel that certain events must occur before the rapture of the Church.

Furthermore, we recommend that should any of our ministers hold to the post-tribulation doctrine, they refrain from preaching and teaching it. Should they persist in emphasizing this doctrine to the point of making it an issue, their standing in the fellowship will be seriously affected.

XVI. *Hell and Eternal Retribution.* The one who physically dies in his sins without Christ is hopelessly and eternally lost in the lake of fire, and therefore has no further opportunity of hearing the Gospel or for repentance (Heb. 9:27). The lake of fire is literal (Rev. 19:20). The terms "eternal" and "everlasting" used in describing the duration of the punishment of the damned (Matthew 25:41-46) in the lake of fire, carry the same thought and meaning of endless existence, as used in denoting the duration of joy and ecstacy of saints in the presence of God.

XVII. *Relation to War.* Whereas, we believe that our government is ordained of God, and whereas, we are thankful to the government of the United States of America for the freedom to worship God according to the dictates of our own conscience, and

Whereas, our religion teaches us, "Thou shalt not kill;" therefore, be it resolved, that in the time of war, we shall be glad to be of service to our government in any way consistent with non-combative service.

XVIII. *Tithes.* We recognize the Scriptural duty of all our people, as well as ministers, to pay tithes as unto the Lord. (Heb. 7:8).

Tithes should be used for the support of the active ministry and for the propagation of the Gospel and work of the Lord in general and not given to charity or used for other purposes. (Malachi 3:7-11; Heb. 7:2; I Cor. 9:7-11; 16:2).

STATEMENT OF FUNDAMENTAL TRUTHS
ASSEMBLIES OF GOD

The Bible is our all-sufficient rule for faith and practice. This Statement of Fundamental Truths is intended simply as a basis of fellowship among us (i.e., that we all speak the same thing, I Cor. 1:10; Acts 2:42). The phraseology employed in this Statement is not inspired or contended for, but the truth set forth is held to be essential to a full Gospel ministry. No claim is made that it contains all Biblical truth, only that it covers our need as to these fundamental doctrines.

I. *The Scriptures Inspired.* The Scriptures, both the Old and New Testaments, are verbally inspired of God and are the revelation of God to man, the infallible, authoritative rule of faith and conduct.

II. *The One True God.* The one true God has revealed Himself as the eternally self-existent "I AM," the Creator of heaven and earth and the Redeemer of mankind. He has further revealed Himself as embodying the principles of relationship and association as Father, Son and Holy Ghost.

THE ADORABLE GODHEAD

(a) *Terms Defined*

The terms "Trinity" and "persons," as related to the Godhead, while not found in the Scriptures, are words in harmony with Scripture, whereby we may convey to others our immediate understanding of the doctrine of Christ respecting the Being of God, as distinguished from "gods many and lords many." We therefore may speak with propriety of the Lord our God, who is One Lord, as a trinity or as one Being of three persons, and still be absolutely Scriptural.

(b) Distinction and Relationship in the Godhead

Christ taught a distinction of Persons in the Godhead which He expressed in specific terms of relationship, as Father, Son, and Holy Ghost, but that this distinction and relationship, as to its mode is *inscrutable* and *incomprehensible*, because *unexplained.*

(c) Unity of the One Being of Father, Son and Holy Ghost

Accordingly, therefore, there is *that* in the Son which constitutes Him *the Son* and not the Father; and there is *that* in the Holy Ghost which constitutes Him *the Holy Ghost* and not either the Father or the Son. Wherefore the Father is the Begetter, the Son is the Begotten; and the Holy Ghost is the one proceeding from the Father and the Son. Therefore, because these three persons in the Godhead are in a state of unity, there is but one Lord God Almighty and His name one.

(d) Identity and Co-operation in the Godhead

The Father, the Son and the Holy Ghost are never *identical* as to *Person;* nor *confused* as to *relation;* nor *divided* in respect to the Godhead; nor *opposed* as to *co-operation.* The Son is *in* the Father and the Father is *in* the Son as to relationship. The Son is *with* the Father and the Father is *with* the Son, as to fellowship. The Father is not *from* the Son, but the Son is *from* the Father, as to authority. The Holy Ghost is *from* the Father and the Son proceeding, as to nature, relationship, co-operation and authority. Hence, neither Person in the Godhead either exists or works separately or independently of the others.

(e) The Title, Lord Jesus Christ

The appellation, "Lord Jesus Christ," is a proper name. It is never applied, in the New Testament, either to the Father or to the Holy Ghost. It therefore belongs exclusively to the *Son of God.*

(f) The Lord Jesus Christ, God with us

The Lord Jesus Christ, as to His divine and eternal nature, is the proper and only Begotten of the Father, but as to His human nature, He is the proper Son of Man. He is, therefore, acknowledged to be both of God and man; who because He is God and man, is "Immanuel," God with us.

(g) The title, Son of God

Since the name "Immanuel" embraces both God and man in the one Person, our Lord Jesus Christ, it follows that the title, Son of God, describes His proper deity, and the title Son of Man, His proper humanity. Therefore, the title, Son of God, belongs to the *order of eternity,* and the title, Son of Man, to the *order of time.*

(h) Transgression of the Doctrine of Christ

Wherefore, it is a transgression of the Doctrine of Christ to say that

Jesus Christ derived the title, Son of God, solely from the fact of the incarnation, or because of His relation to the economy of redemption. Therefore, to deny that the Father is a real and eternal Father, and that the Son is a real and eternal Son, is a denial of the distinction and relationship in the Being of God; a denial of the Father and the Son; and a displacement of the truth that Jesus Christ is come in the flesh.

(i) *Exaltation of Jesus Christ as Lord*

The Son of God, our Lord Jesus Christ, having by Himself purged our sins, sat down on the right hand of the Majesty on high; angels and principalities and powers having been made subject unto Him. And having been made both Lord and Christ, He sent the Holy Ghost that we, in the name of Jesus, might bow our knees and confess that Jesus Christ is Lord to the glory of God the Father until the end, when the Son shall become subject to the Father that God may be all in all.

(j) *Equal Honor to the Father and to the Son*

Wherefore, since the Father has delivered all judgment unto the Son, it is not only the *express duty* of all in heaven and on earth to bow the knee, but it is an *unspeakable* joy in the Holy Ghost to ascribe unto the Son all the attributes of Deity, and to give Him all the honor and glory contained in all the names and titles of the Godhead (except those which express relationship. See paragraphs, *b*, *c*, and *d*), and thus honor the Son even as we honor the Father.

III. *The Deity of the Lord Jesus Christ.* The Lord Jesus Christ is the eternal Son of God. The Scriptures declare:

(a) His virgin birth.

(b) His sinless life.

(c) His miracles.

(d) His substitutionary work on the cross.

(e) His bodily resurrection from the dead.

(f) His exaltation to the right hand of God.

IV. *The Fall of Man.* Man was created good and upright; for God said, "Let us make man in our image, after our likeness." However, man by voluntary transgression fell and thereby incurred not only physical death but also spiritual death, which is separation from God.

V. *The Salvation of Man.* Man's only hope of redemption is through the shed blood of Jesus Christ the Son of God.

(a) *Conditions to Salvation*

Salvation is received through repentance toward God and faith toward the Lord Jesus Christ. By the washing of regeneration and renewing of the Holy Ghost, being justified by grace through faith, man becomes an heir of God according to the hope of eternal life.

(b) *The Evidence of Salvation*

The inward evidence of salvation is the direct witness of the Spirit. The outward evidence to all men is a life of righteousness and true holiness.

VI. *The Ordinances of the Church.*

(a) *Baptism in Water*

The ordinance of baptism by immersion is commanded in the Scriptures. All who repent and believe on Christ as Saviour and Lord are to be baptized. Thus they declare to the world that they have died with Christ and that they also have been raised with Him to walk in newness of life.

(b) *Holy Communion*

The Lord's Supper, consisting of the elements—bread and the fruit of the vine—is the symbol expressing our sharing the divine nature of our Lord Jesus Christ; a memorial of His suffering and death; and a prophecy of His second coming; and is enjoined on all believers "till He come!"

VII. *The Baptism in the Holy Ghost.* All believers are entitled to and should ardently expect and earnestly seek the promise of the Father, the baptism in the Holy Ghost and fire, according to the command of our Lord Jesus Christ. This was the normal experience of all in the early Christian Church. With it comes the enduement of power for life and service, the bestowment of the gifts and their uses in the work of the ministry. This experience is distinct from and subsequent to the experience of the new birth. With the baptism in the Holy Ghost come such experiences as an overflowing fullness of the Spirit, a deepened reverence for God, an intensified consecration to God and dedication to His work, and a more active love for Christ, for His Word and for the lost.

VIII. *The Evidence of the Baptism in the Holy Ghost.* The Baptism of believers in the Holy Ghost is witnessed by the initial physical sign of speaking with other tongues as the Spirit of God gives them utterance. The speaking in tongues in this instance is the same in essence as the gift of tongues, but different in purpose and use.

IX. *Sanctification.* Sanctification is an act of separation from that which is evil, and of dedication unto God. The Scriptures teach a life of "holiness without which no man shall see the Lord." By the power of the Holy Ghost we are able to obey the command: "Be ye holy, for I am holy."

X. *The Church.* The Church is the Body of Christ, the habitation of God through the Spirit, with divine appointments for the fulfillment of her great commission. Each believer, born of the Spirit, is an integral part of the General Assembly and Church of the First-born, which are written in heaven.

XI. *The Ministry.* A divinely called and scripturally ordained ministry has been provided by our Lord for a twofold purpose: 1) The evangelization of the world, and 2) The edifying of the Body of Christ.

XII. *Divine Healing.* Divine healing is an integral part of the gospel. Deliverance from sickness is provided for in the atonement, and is the privilege of all believers.

XIII. *The Blessed Hope.* The resurrection of those who have fallen asleep in Christ and their translation together with those who are alive and remain unto the coming of the Lord is the imminent and blessed hope of the Church.

XIV. *The Millennial Reign of Christ.* The second coming of Christ includes the rapture of the saints, which is our blessed hope, followed by the visible return of Christ with His saints to reign on the earth for one thousand years. This millennial reign will bring the salvation of national Israel and the establishment of universal peace.

XV. *The Final Judgment.* There will be a final judgment in which the wicked dead will be raised and judged according to their works. Whosoever is not found written in the Book of Life, together with the devil and his angels, the beast and the false prophet, will be consigned to everlasting punishment in the lake which burneth with fire and brimstone, which is the second death.

XVI. *The New Heavens and the New Earth.* "We, according to His promise, look for new heavens and a new earth, wherein dwelleth righteousness."

TEACHINGS OF THE CHURCH OF GOD

I. *Repentance.* Mark 1:15; Luke 13:3; Acts 3:19.

II. *Justification.* Rom. 5:1-9; Titus 3:7.

III. *Regeneration.* Matt. 19:28; Titus 3:5

IV. *Born Again.* John 3:3; I Peter 1:23; I John 3:9.

V. *Sanctification Subsequent to Justification.* Rom. 5:2; I Cor. 1:30; I Thess. 4:3; Heb. 13:12; I John 1:9.

VI. *Holiness.* Luke 1:74, 75; I Thess. 4:7; Heb. 12:14.

VII. *Water Baptism.* Matt. 28:19; Mark 1:8-10; John 3:22, 23; Acts 8:12, 36-38; 10:47, 48; 16:33; 19:3-5.

VIII. *Baptism with the Holy Ghost Subsequent to Cleansing; the Enduement of Power for Service.* Matt. 3:11; Luke 24:49-53; Acts 1:4-8.

IX. *The Speaking in Tongues as the Evidence of the Baptism with the Holy Ghost.* John 15:26; Acts 2:4; 10:44-46; 19:6.

X. *The Full Restoration of the Gifts to the Church.* I Cor. 12:1, 7-10, 28, 31; I Cor. 14:1.

XI. *Signs following Believers.* Mark 16:17-20; Rom. 15:18, 19; Heb. 2:4.

XII. *Fruit of the Spirit.* Rom. 6:22; Gal. 5:22, 23; Eph. 5:9; Phil 1:11.

XIII. *Divine Healing Provided for All in the Atonement.* Psa. 103:3; Isa. 53:4, 5; Matt. 8:17; James 5:14-16; I Peter 2:24.

XIV. *The Lord's Supper.* Luke 22:17-20; I Cor. 11:23-33.

XV. *Washing the Saints' Feet.* John 13:4-17; I Tim. 5:10.

XVI. *Tithing and Giving.* Gen. 14:18-20; 28:20-22; Mal. 3:10; Matt. 23:23; Luke 11:42; I Cor. 16:2; II Cor. 9:6-9; Heb. 7:1-21.

XVII. *Restitution Where Possible.* Matt. 3:8; Luke 19:8, 9; Rom. 13:8.

XVIII. *Pre-millennial Second Coming of Jesus.* First—To resurrect the dead saints and to catch away the living saints to meet Him in the air—Matt. 24:27, 28; I Cor. 15:51, 52; I Thess. 4:15-17.

Second—To reign on earth a thousand years—Zech. 14:4, 5; Luke 1:32; I Thess. 4:14; II Thess. 1:7-10; Jude 14, 15; Rev. 5:10; 19:11-21; 20:4-6.

XIX. *Resurrection.* Isa 26:19; Dan. 12:2; John 5:28, 29; Acts 24:15; Rev. 21:5, 6.

XX. *Eternal Life for the Righteous.* Matt. 25:46; Luke 18:30; John 10:28; Rom. 6:22; I John 5:11-13.

XXI. *Eternal Punishment for the Wicked.* No liberation nor Annihilation—Matt. 25:41-46; Mark 3:29; II Thess. 1:8, 9; Rev. 20:10-15; 21:8.

XXII. *Total Abstinence From All Liquor or Strong Drinks.* Prov. 20:1; 23:29-32; Isa. 28:7; I Cor. 5:11; 6:10; Gal. 5:21.

XXIII. *Against the Use of Tobacco in Any Form, Opium, Morphine, Etc.* Isa. 55:2; I Cor. 10:31, 32; II Cor. 7:1; Eph. 5:3-8; Jas. 1:21.

XXIV. *Meats and Drinks.* Rom. 14:2, 3, 17; I Cor. 8:8; I Tim. 4:1-5.

XXV. *The Sabbath.* Hosea 2:11; Rom. 13:1-2; Rom. 14:5, 6; Col. 2:16, 17.

XXVI. *Against Members Wearing Gold for Ornament or Decoration, such as Finger Rings, Bracelets, Ear Rings, Lockets, Etc.* Isa. 55:2; I Peter 3:3; I John 2:16.

XXVII. *Against Members Belonging to Lodges.* Matt. 5:34; John 18:20; II Cor. 6:14-17; Jas. 5:12.

XXVIII. *Against Members Swearing.* Matt. 5:34; Jas. 5:12.

XXIX. *Against the Divorce and Remarriage Evil.* Matt. 5:32; Matt. 19:3-12; Mark 10:12; Luke 16:18; Rom. 7:2, 3; I Cor. 5:1-5, 13; I Cor. 6:9, 13, 16-18; I Cor. 7:2, 10, 11; Rev. 2:20-22; Acts 15:28, 29; Matt. 14:3, 4.

6. The Free Church Tradition

The basic idea behind the Free Church Movement is nonconformity with established Protestant religions, which took different forms in different countries. On the continent the Anabaptists, Mennonites, and Brethren; in England the Separatists, including Quakers, Baptists and Congregationalists, professed the Free Church principle of dissociating from the doctrines, polity and discipline of the dominant Protestant body in their respective territory.

Continental Free Churchism began with the Anabaptists, the "rebaptizers" who refused to allow their children to be baptized and instituted the baptism of adult believers. They argued that the Reformers were unfaithful to their own tenet of *sola Scriptura* by allowing children to be baptized, since the Bible knows only the baptism of adults. Gradually the Protestant theory of private interpretation led to a cluster of other Anabaptist beliefs and practices which have remained in possession to modern times.

One of the earliest non-conformists was Thomas Munzer (1490-1525) and the Zwickau prophets who appeared at Wittenberg in 1521. Munzer favored the Peasants' Revolt (1525) and taught a doctrine of the Inner Light which reappeared later among the English Quakers. The Swiss Brethren reintroduced believer's baptism as a condition for church membership at Zurich in 1525, along with non-resistance and rejection of Christian participation in civil government. Soon these views spread throughout Switzerland and into Germany.

Communities that found asylum in Moravia, and led by Jacob Hutter (died 1536), founded settlements based on the idea of common property. After many wanderings and trials, the Hutterites became established in Central Europe or migrated to America. A group of Anabaptists in Munster attempted to form a Kingdom of the Saints, whose left-wing segment advocated polygamy. The idea was later revived among the American Mormons or Latter-Day Saints, under the reputed revelations of Joseph Smith (1805-1844). After the Munster episode, the Mennonites were reorganized in Holland and Friesland by Menno Simons (1496-1561), who first left the Catholic Church, joined the Anabaptists, and then founded his own denomination on the twin principle of independent church organization and no common doctrine.

The Anabaptists were vigorously denounced by Luther, Zwingli and Calvin, who encouraged their suppression by force of arms. Their influence on the English Separatists (Baptists, Congregationalists, and Quakers) places them in lineal relationship to the Free Church movement in Anglo-Saxon countries.

John Smyth (1570-1612), exiled Anglican minister, started the Baptists at Amsterdam in 1609, when he instituted the baptism of conscious believers as the basis of fellowship in a gathered church. Many Baptists were associated with the more radical spiritual and political movements in England in the seventeenth century. They were pioneers in pleas for freedom of conscience and religious liberty. John Bunyan (1628-1688), author of the *Pilgrim's Progress,* was an outstanding figure among them, not only because of his writings but because he advocated a Church community which should include Baptists and paedo-baptists (those who baptize infants).

Most of the Baptist population of the world (about ninety percent) is in the United States, divided into more than twenty bodies and following a modified Calvinism, tinged with Lutheran and Zwinglian elements. Since the stress is on baptism of believers, the attitude towards this sacrament is characteristic of Baptist theology as a whole. Baptism does not bring about the remission of sins or provide salvation. It is a symbol and "only a symbol of the blessed truths upon which remission of sins, salvation, and eternal life depend." There is nothing that comes after faith that is essential to salvation. With rare exception, baptism by immersion is considered essential.

In spite of their variety and individualism, most Baptists have remained strongly attached to the truths of evangelical Christianity. The popular evangelist, Billy Graham, became a Southern Baptist early in youth. Their worship is mainly in the Reformed tradition, and their church organization an American type of independency. Majority rule prevails in Baptist polity, "in accordance with the law of Christ." So that, "the will of the majority having been expressed, it becomes the minority to submit."

Congregationalism is that form of church structure which rests on the independence and autonomy of each local church. It professes to represent the principle of democracy in church government, said to have been the original type of organization founded by Christ recognizing only Him as its head. Since all the members of the Church are Christians, they are all equally priests unto God. He is in their midst, wherever two or three are gathered in His name; their thoughts and actions are led by His spirit and, with no authoritarian laws to bind them, they are nevertheless united in Christ with the Church Universal.

The beginnings of Congregationalism are commonly dated from the founding in 1581, of a church in Norwich, England, by Robert Browne, a Separatist Anglican minister. Browne was demoted from the ministry for teaching "seditious doctrines," notably that the basis of church membership was not submission to episcopal authority but acceptance of a covenant, to which a group of people gave their mutual consent. Pressure from the government forced Browne's followers to move to Holland, and then to America, where, as the Mayflower Pilgrims, they landed at Plymouth, Massachusetts, in 1620.

A few years later they were joined by a group of immigrant Puritans, with whom they signed a compact in 1629, and from whom they inherited a strong Calvinist creedalism that lasted almost two centuries. The Salem trials for witchcraft belong to the early period of New England Congregationalism. By 1730, however, the churches had become quite thoroughly secularized. This induced a reaction, called the Great Awakening, ushered in by Jonathan Edwards (1730-1758), pastor at Northampton, Massachusetts, who was consumed by the sovereignty of God, the fateful brevity of life and its eternal issues.

For more than two centuries, American Congregationalists were mainly concerned with higher education. Harvard was founded in 1636, Yale in 1701, to prepare students for the ministry. At present fifty-one colleges and universities in the United States have professedly Congregationalist affiliations. With expansion, however, came internal tension over doctrinal issues.

Two conflicting tendencies threatened to dissolve Congregationalism. By the middle of the last century, about two thousand churches, originally Congregationalist, became Presbyterian; they were looking for a more authoritative and dogmatic church polity. And during the same period a smaller, but even more influential, group of liberals seceded to form the American Unitarian Association.

The current history of Congregationalism has been largely a story of mergers and unitive movements. In 1925, the Protestant Evangelical Churches merged to form the Congregational Christian denomination, and in 1957, the Evangelical and Reformed entered into organic union to produce the United Church of Christ, leaving only a segment of less than a hundred thousand Congregationalists still dedicated to the full import of their doctrine of local church autonomy.

Congregationalism has given a major impulse to the ecumenical movement. The constitutional basis of the World Council of Churches as "fellowship of churches" whose function is to "offer counsel and provide opportunity of united action" among its constituents, is a paraphrase of Congregational principles expanded to global proportions.

Quakers are the most distinctive form of Free Church ideology extant in English-speaking countries. More commonly known as the Society of Friends, Quakers were organized as a separate Christian group in England in 1668, when George Fox (1624-1691) drew up his *Rule for the Management of Meetings*. They soon engaged in missionary work and in 1682 William Penn founded Pennsylvania on a Quaker basis.

The religious tenets of the Friends center around the idea of the Inner Light, first professed by George Fox and since become their focal doctrine. No Quaker has improved on the description of this Light given by Fox, and all Quakers subscribe to his definition.

> The Lord hath opened to me by His invisible power how that every man was enlightened by the divine Light of Christ; and I saw it shine through all; and that they that believed in it came out of condemnation and came to the Light of Life, and became the children of it; but they that hated it, and did not believe in it, were condemned by it, though they made a profession of

Christ. This I saw in the pure openings of the Light, without the help of any man, neither did I then know where to find it in the Scriptures, though afterwards, searching in the Scriptures, I found it. For I saw in that light and Spirit which was before the Scripture was given forth, and which led the holy men of God to give them forth, that all must come to that Spirit—if they would know God or Christ or the Scriptures aright—which they that gave them forth were led and taught by.*

According to the theory of the Light, its possession consists mainly in the sense of the Divine, and the direct working of God in the soul, by which a man is freed from sin, joined to Christ, and enabled to perform good works. From the paramount importance given to the Inner Light derives the Quaker rejection of the sacraments, the ministry, and all set forms of worship. Their meetings are ideally held in bare rooms and begin in silence, in "holy expectation before the Lord" until some member of the congregation feels inspired to speak.

Church organization is democratic, ranging from Preparative Meetings which consist of single congregations, to Yearly Meetings that comprise a whole country (as in England) or the Five Years' Meeting that forms one of several Quaker denominations in the United States.

The Quaker refusal to give military service and take oaths involved them in frequent conflict with civil authorities, more in Great Britain than America, and since the early nineteenth century the Friends have pioneered in promoting legislation in favor of conscientious objectors to war. Their devotion to social and educational work, as well as their high standards of personal integrity, has won popular support to their side and helped in the advancement of such humane movements as the elimination of slavery.

CONGREGATIONALISM

There are five principal American denominations in the Free Church tradition: the Congregationalists and Quakers from England, Baptists from England and the Continent, and the Men-

* George Fox, *Journal,* Cambridge University Press, 1952, p. 33.

nonites and Brethren almost exclusively from continental Europe. Each has a creedal history that would fill a volume, yet the number of typical doctrinal statements is relatively small—with the exception of the Baptists—as might be expected of churches which exclude, on principle, the acceptance of a binding creed as a condition for membership.

Throughout these documents is revealed the characteristic feature of this form of Protestantism, a grave concern for what is called "spiritual liberty," which means freedom from constraint or conformity to any human agency outside the immediate covenanted believers. There is another strain of tradition, however, that is less well known and therefore less often associated with the Free Churches: their desire to cooperate among themselves and with other religious bodies in the higher interests of total Christianity. If the first tendency comes closer to describing their historical image, the second becoming more significant as these churches enter the stream of the ecumenical movement.

FOUNDATIONS OF
AMERICAN CONGREGATIONALISM
THE CAMBRIDGE PLATFORM

Within a generation of their landing at Plymouth the Mayflower Pilgrims were faced with the necessity of identifying themselves in the practice of religion. What made the identification doubly necessary was their joining forces in 1629 with the Puritans from Salem, Massachusetts. Historians date the origins of American Congregationalism from that merger.

Their problem was to steer a middle course between two extremes, a negative Separatism on the left and full compliance with Presbyterianism on the right. After several unsuccessful attempts, due mainly to a raging epidemic in New England, a Synod met in the fall of 1648 at Cambridge and here drafted what has since come to be known as The Cambridge Platform, rightly considered "one of the greatest creations of the founding fathers," and, into modern times, the ranking statement of Congregational polity in the United States.

The Platform was written by several hands, but the main author was certainly Richard Mather of Dorchester. Its principal concern is to spell out the Congregational idea of church government, while leaving other doctrinal matters to be drawn from the Westminster Confession. This correlation of Congregational ecclesiology and Presbyterian theology has remained substantially unchanged, and explains, in part, the later mergers of American Congregationalists with churches in the Calvinist tradition.

Chapter I.
OF THE FORM OF CHURCH-GOVERNMENT; AND THAT IT IS ONE, IMMUTABLE, AND PRESCRIBED IN THE WORD OF GOD.

Ecclesiastical Polity or Church Government, or discipline is nothing else, but that Form and order that is to be observed in the Church of Christ upon earth, both for the Constitution of it, and all the Administrations that therein are to be performed.

2. Church-Government is Considered in a double respect either in regard of the parts of Government themselves, or necessary Circumstances thereof. . . .

3. The parts of Church-Government are all of them exactly described in the word of God being parts or means of Instituted worship according to the second Commandment; and therefore to continue one and the same, unto the appearing of our Lord Jesus Christ as a kingdom that cannot be shaken, until he shall deliver it up unto God, even the Father. So that it is not left in the power of men, officers, Churches, or any state in the world to add, or diminish, or alter any thing in the least measure therein.

4. The necessary circumstances, as time and place & belonging unto order and decency, are not so left unto men as that under pretence of them, they may thrust their own Inventions upon the Churches: Being Circumscribed in the word with many General limitations. . . .

Chapter II.
OF THE NATURE OF THE CATHOLIC CHURCH IN GENERAL AND IN SPECIAL, OF A PARTICULAR VISIBLE CHURCH.

The Catholic Church, is the whole company of those that are elected, redeemed, and in time effectually called from the state of sin and death unto a state of Grace, and salvation in Jesus Christ.

2. This church is either Triumphant, or Militant. Triumphant, the number of them who are Glorified in heaven: Militant, the number of them who are conflicting with their enemies upon earth.

3. This Militant Church is to be considered as Invisible, and Visible. Invisible, in respect of their relation wherein they stand to Christ, as a body unto the head, being united unto him, by the spirit of God, and faith in their hearts: Visible, in respect of the profession of their faith, in their persons, and in particular Churches: and so there may be acknowledged an universal visible Church.

4. The members of the Militant visible Church, considered either as not yet in church-order, or as walking according to the church-order of the Gospel. In order, and so besides the spiritual union, and communion, common to all believers, they enjoy more over an union and communion ecclesiastical-political: So we deny an universal visible church.

5. The state the members of the Militant visible church walking in order, was either before the law, Oeconomical, that is in families; or under the law, National: or, since the coming of Christ, only congregational: (The term Independent, we approve not:) Therefore neither national, provincial, nor classical.

6. A Congregational-church, is by the institution of Christ a part of the Militant-visible-church, consisting of a company of Saints by calling, united into one body, by a holy covenant, for the public worship of God, and the mutual edification one of another, in the Fellowship of the Lord Jesus.

Chapter III.
OF THE MATTER OF THE VISIBLE CHURCH BOTH IN RESPECT OF QUALITY AND QUANTITY.

The matter of a visible church are Saints by calling.

2. By Saints, we understand,

(1) Such, as have not only attained the knowledge of the principles of Religion, and are free from gross and open scandals, but also do together with the profession of their faith and Repentance, walk in blameless obedience to the word, so as that in charitable discretion they may be accounted Saints by calling, (though perhaps some or more of them be unsound, and hypocrites inwardly:) because the members of such particular churches are commonly by the holy ghost called Saints and faithful brethren in Christ, and sundry churches have been reproved for receiving, and suffering such persons to continue in fellowship amongst them, as have been offensive and scandalous: the name of God also by this means is Blasphemed: and the holy things of God defiled and Prophaned: the hearts of godly grieved: and the wicked themselves hardened: and helped forward to damnation: the example of such doth endanger the sanctity of others. A little Leaven Leaveneth the whole lump.

(2) The children of such, who are also holy.

3. The members of churches though orderly constituted, may in time degenerate, and grow corrupt and scandalous, which though they ought not to be tolerated in the church, yet their continuance therein, through the defect of the execution of discipline and Just censures, doth not immediately dissolve the being of the church, as appears in the church of Israel, and the churches of Galatia and Corinth, Pergamus, and Thyatira.

4. The matter of the Church in respect of its quantity ought not to be of greater number than may ordinarily meet together conveniently in one place: nor ordinarily fewer, than may conveniently carry to Church-work. . . .

5. Nor can it with reason be thought but that every church appointed and ordained by Christ, had a ministry ordained and appointed for the same: and yet plain it is, that there were no ordinary officers appointed by Christ for any other, than Congregational churches: Elders being appointed to feed, not all flocks, but the particular flock of God over which the holy Ghost had made them the overseers, and that flock they must attend, even the whole flock: and one Congregation being as much as any ordinary Elders can attend, therefore there is no greater Church than a Congregation, which may ordinarily meet in one place.

Chapter IV.
OF THE FORM OF A VISIBLE CHURCH
AND OF CHURCH COVENANT.

Saints by Calling, must have a Visible-Political-Union amongst themselves, or else they are not yet a particular church: as those similitudes hold forth, which Scripture makes use of, to show the nature of particular Churches: As a Body, A building, or House, Hands, Eyes, Feet, and other members must be united, or else, remaining separate are not a body. Stones, Timber, though squared, hewn and polished, are not an house, until they are compacted and united: so Saints or believers in judgment of charity, are not a church, unless Orderly knit together.

2. Particular churches cannot be distinguished one from another but by their forms. Ephesus is not Smyrna, and Pergamus Thyatira, but each one a distinct society of it self, having officers of their own, which had not the charge of others: Virtues of their own, for which others are not praised: Corruptions of their own, for which others are not blamed.

3. This Form is the Visible Covenant, Agreement, or consent whereby they give up themselves unto the Lord, to the observing of

the ordinances of Christ together in the same society, which is usually called the Church-Covenant; For we see not otherwise how members can have Church-power one over another mutually.

The Covenant, as it was that which made the Family of Abraham and children of Israel to be a church and people unto God, so it is that which now makes the several societies of Gentile believers to be churches in these days.

4. This Voluntary Agreement, Consent or Covenant (for all these are here taken for the same): Although the more express and plain it is, the more fully it puts us in mind of our mutual duty, and stirreth us up to it, and leaveth less room for the questioning of the Truth of the Church-estate of a Company of professors, and the Truth of member-ship of particular persons: yet we conceive, the substance of it is kept, where there is a real Agreement and consent, of a company of faithful persons to meet constantly together in one Congregation, for the public worship of God, and their mutual edification: which real agreement and consent they do express by their constant practice in coming to-gether for the public worship of God, and by their religious subjection unto the ordinances of God there: the rather, if we do consider how Scripture covenants have been entered into, not only expressly by word of mouth, but by sacrifice; by hand writing, and seal; and also some-times by silent consent, without any writing, or expression of words at all.

5. This form then being by mutual covenant, it followeth, it is not faith in the heart, nor the profession of that faith, nor cohabitation, nor Baptism; (1) not faith in the heart; because that is invisible: (2) not a bare profession; because that declareth them no more to be members of one church than of another: (3) not Cohabitation; Atheists or In-fidels may dwell together with believers: (4) not Baptism; because it presupposeth a church estate, as circumcision in the old Testament, which gave no being unto the church, the church being before it, and in the wilderness without it; seals presuppose a covenant already in being, one person is a complete subject of Baptism: but one person is incapable of being a church.

Chapter V.
OF THE FIRST SUBJECT OF CHURCH POWER OR, TO WHOM CHURCH POWER DOTH FIRST BELONG.

The first subject of church power, is either Supreme, or Subordinate, and Ministerial: The Supreme (by way of gift from the father) is the Lord Jesus Christ: The Ministerial, is either extraordinary; as the Apostles, Prophets, and Evangelists: or Ordinary; as every particular Congregational church.

2. Ordinary church power, is either the power of office that is such as is proper to the eldership: or, power of privilege, such as belongs unto the brotherhood. The latter is in the brethren formally, and immediately from Christ, that is, so as it may according to order be acted or exercised immediately by themselves: the former, is not in them formally or immediately, and therefore cannot be acted or exercised immediately by them, but is said to be in them, in that they design the persons unto office, who only are to act, or to exercise this power.

Chapter VI.
OF THE OFFICERS OF THE CHURCH, AND ESPECIALLY OF PASTORS AND TEACHERS.

A Church being a company of people combined together by covenant for the worship of God, it appeareth thereby, that there may be the essence and being of a church without any officers, seeing there is both the form and matter of a church, which is implied when it is said, the Apostles ordained elders in every church.

2. Nevertheless, though officers be not absolutely necessary, to the simple being of churches, when they be called: yet ordinarily to their calling they are, and to their well being: and therefore the Lord Jesus out of his tender compassion hath appointed, and ordained officers which he would not have done, if they had not been useful and needful for the church; yea, being Ascended into heaven, he received gifts for men, and gave gifts to men, whereof officers for the church are Justly accounted no small parts; they being to continue to the end of the world, and for the perfecting of all the Saints.

Chapter X.
OF THE POWER OF THE CHURCH, AND ITS PRESBYTERY.

Supreme and Lordly power over all the Churches upon earth, doth only belong unto Jesus Christ, who is King of the church, and the head thereof. He hath the Government upon his shoulders, and hath all power given to him, both in heaven and earth.

2. A Company of professed believers Ecclesiastically Confederate, as they are a church before they have officers, and without them; so even in that estate, subordinate Church-power under Christ delegated to them by him, doth belong to them, in such a manner as is before expressed. . . .

3. This Government of the church, is a mixed Government (and so

hath been acknowledged long before the term of Independency was heard of:) In respect of Christ, the head and King of the church, and the Sovereign power residing in him, and exercised by him, it is a Monarchy: In respect of the body, or Brotherhood of the church, and power from Christ granted unto them, it resembles a Democracy; in respect of the Presbytery and power committed to them, it is an Aristocracy.

4. The Sovereign power which is peculiar unto Christ, is exercised, I. In calling the church out of the world unto holy fellowship with himself. II. In instituting the ordinances of his worship, and appointing his ministers and officers for the dispensing of them. III. In giving laws for the ordering of all our ways, and the ways of his house. IV. In giving power and life to all his Institutions, and to his people by them. V. In protecting and delivering his church against and from all the enemies of their peace.

5. The power granted by Christ unto the body of the church and Brotherhood, is a prerogative or privilege which the church doth exercise: I. In Choosing their own officers, whether Elders, or Deacons. II. In admission of their own members and therefore, there is great reason they should have power to Remove any from their fellowship again. . . .

6. In case an Elder offend incorrigibly, the matter so requiring, as the church had power to call him to office, so they have power according to order (the counsel of other churches where it may be had) directing thereto to remove him from his Office: and being now but a member, in case he add contumacy to his sin, the Church that had power to receive him into their fellowship, had also the same power to cast him out, that they have concerning any other member.

7. Church-government, or Rule, is placed by Christ in the officers of the church, who are therefore called Rulers, while they rule with God: yet in case of mal-administration, they are subject to the power of the church, according as hath been said before. . . .

11. From the premises, namely, that the ordinary power of Government belonging only to the elders, power of privilege remaineth with the brotherhood, (as power of judgment in matters of censure, and power of liberty, in matters of liberty:) It followeth, that in an organic Church, and right administration; all church acts, proceed after the manner of a mixed administration, so as no church act can be consummated, or perfected without the consent of both.

Chapter XII.
OF ADMISSION OF MEMBERS INTO THE CHURCH.

The doors of the Churches of Christ upon earth, do not by God's appointment stand so wide open, that all sorts of people good or bad, may freely enter therein at their pleasure; but such as are admitted thereto, as members ought to be examined and tried first; whether they be fit and meet to be received into church-society, or not. The Eunuch of Ethiopia, before his admission was examined by Philip, whether he did believe on Jesus Christ with all his heart; the Angel of the church at Ephesus is commended, for trying such as said they were Apostles and were not. There is like reason for trying of them that profess themselves to be believers.

The officers are charged with the keeping of the doors of the Church, and therefore are in a special manner to make trial of the fitness of such who enter. Twelve Angels are set at the gates of the Temple, lest such as were Ceremonially unclean should enter thereinto.

2. The things which are requisite to be found in all church members, are, Repentance from sin, and faith in Jesus Christ. And therefore these are the things whereof men are to be examined, at their admission into the church and which then they must profess and hold forth in such sort, as may satisfy rational charity that the things are there indeed. . . .

3. The weakest measure of faith is to be accepted in those that desire to be admitted into the church: because weak christians if sincere, have the substance of that faith, repentance and holiness which is required in church members: and such have most need of the ordinances for their confirmation and growth in grace. . . .

4. In case any through excessive fear, or other infirmity, be unable to make their personal relation of their spiritual estate in public, it is sufficient that the Elders having received private satisfaction, make relation thereof in public before the church, they testifying their assents thereunto; this being the way that tendeth most to edification. But whereas persons are of better abilities, there it is more expedient, that they make their relations, and confessions personally with their own mouth, as David professeth of himself.

5. A personal and public confession, and declaring of God's manner of working upon the soul, is both lawful, expedient, and useful, in sundry respects, and upon sundry grounds. . . .

7. The like trial is to be required from such members of the church, as were born in the same, or received their membership, and were baptized in their infancy, or minority, by virtue of the covenant of their parents, when being grown up unto years of discretion, they shall desire to be made partakers of the Lord's supper: unto which, because holy things must not be given unto the unworthy, therefore it is requisite, that these as well as others, should come to their trial and examination, and manifest their faith and repentance by an open profession

thereof, before they are received to the Lord's supper, and otherwise not to be admitted there unto.

Yet these church-members that were so born, or received in their childhood, before they are capable of being made partakers of full communion, have many privileges which others (not church-members) have not: they are in covenant with God; have the seal thereof upon them, *viz.* Baptism; and so if not regenerated, yet are in a more hopeful way of attaining regenerating grace, and all the spiritual blessings both of the covenant and seal; they are also under Church-watch, and consequently subject, to the reprehensions, admonitions, and censures thereof, for their healing and amendment, as need shall require.

Chapter XV.
OF THE COMMUNION OF CHURCHES ONE WITH ANOTHER.

Although Churches be distinct, and therefore may not be confounded one with another: and equal, and therefore have not dominion one over another: yet all the churches ought to preserve Church-communion one with another, because they are all united unto Christ, not only as a mystical, but as a political head; whence is derived a communion suitable thereunto.

2. The communion of Churches is exercised sundry ways.

I. By way of mutual care in taking thought for one another's welfare.

II. By way of Consultation one with another, when we have occasion to require the judgment and counsel of other churches, touching any person, or cause wherewith they may be better acquainted than ourselves. . . .

III. A third way then of communion of churches is by way of admonition, to wit, in case any public offence be found in a church, which they either discern not, or are slow in proceeding to use the means for the removing and healing of. . . .

IV. A fourth way of communion of churches, is by way of participation: the members of one church occasionally coming unto another, we willingly admit them to partake with us at the Lord's table, it being the seal of our communion not only with Christ, nor only with the members of our own church, but also with all the churches of the saints: in which regard, we refuse not to baptize their children presented to us, if either their own minister be absent, or such a fruit of holy fellowship be desired with us. In like case such churches as are furnished with more ministers than one, do willingly afford one of their own ministers to supply the place of an absent or sick minister of another church for a needful season.

V. A fifth way of Church-communion is, by way of recommendation when a member of one church hath occasion to reside in another church; if but for a season, we commend him to their watchful fellowship by letters of recommendation; but if he be called to settle his abode there, we commit him according to his desire, to the fellowship of their covenant, by letters of dismission.

VI. A sixth way of Church-communion, is in case of Need, to minister relief and succour one unto another: either of able members to furnish them with officers; or of outward support to the necessities of poorer churches; as did the churches of the Gentiles contribute liberally to the poor saints at Jerusalem.

3. When a company of believers purpose to gather into church fellowship, it is requisite for their safer proceeding, and the maintaining of the communion of churches, that they signify their intent unto the neighbour-churches, walking according unto the order of the Gospel, and desire their presence, and help, right hand of fellowship which they ought readily to give unto them, when there is no just cause of excepting against their proceedings.

4. Besides these several ways of communion, there is also a way of propagation of churches; when a church shall grow too numerous, it is a way, and fit season, to propagate one Church out of another, by sending forth such of their members as are willing to remove, and to procure some officers to them, as may enter with them into church-estate amongst themselves: as Bees, when the hive is too full, issue forth by swarms, and are gathered into other hives, so the Churches of Christ may do the same upon like necessity; and therein hold forth to them the right hand of fellowship, both in their gathering into a church, and in the ordination of their officers.

Chapter XVI.

Synods orderly assembled, and rightly proceeding according to the pattern, Acts 15, we acknowledge as the ordinance of Christ: and though not absolutely necessary to the being, yet many times, through the iniquity of men, and perverseness of times, necessary to the well-being of churches, for the establishment of truth, and peace therein.

3. Magistrates, have power to call a Synod, by calling to the churches to send forth their Elders and other messengers, to counsel and assist them in matters of religion: but yet the constituting of a Synod, is a church act, and may be transacted by the churches, even when civil magistrates may be enemies to churches and to church assemblies.

4. It belongeth unto Synods and counsels, to debate and determine

controversies of faith, and cases of conscience; to clear from the word holy directions for the holy worship of God, and good government of the church; to bear witness against mal-administration and Corruption in doctrine or manners in any particular Church, and to give directions for the reformation thereof: Not to exercise Church-censures in way of discipline, nor any other act of church-authority or jurisdiction: which that presidential Synod did forbear.

5. The Synod's directions and determinations, so far as consonant to the word of God, are to be received with reverence and submission; not only for their agreement therewith (which is the principal ground thereof, and without which they bind not at all:) but also secondarily, for the power whereby they are made, as being an ordinance of God appointed thereunto in his word.

6. Because it is difficult, if not impossible, for many churches to come altogether in one place, in all their members universally: therefore they may assemble by their delegates or messengers, as the church of Antioch went not all to Jerusalem, but some select men for that purpose.

KANSAS CITY STATEMENT
CONGREGATIONAL CHURCHES
OF THE UNITED STATES

Although there were several minor adjustments in Congregational belief since the Cambridge Platform, the first major change occurred in 1913 when the National Council adopted a new statement of faith, polity and fellowship that has revolutionized this segment of Protestantism in the United States.

Called the Kansas City Statement from the place of its adoption, it opened the door for cooperation and eventual mergers that have deeply affected the ecumenical movement in America.

On the basis of its principles, Congregationalists have entered into organic union with the Protestant Evangelicals, then the Christian Churches, then the Evangelical and Reformed Church, and they are currently in the vanguard to advance the merger of more than half the Protestant bodies in the country. The operative passage in the Kansas City Creed states that, "we hold to the unity and catholicity of the Church of Christ, and will unite with all its branches in hearty cooperation, and will earnestly seek, so far as in us lies, that the prayer of our Lord for his disciples may be answered, that they all may be one." No single sentence in a profession of faith promises to have more influence on the future of American Protestantism.

The Congregational Churches of the United States, by delegates in National Council assembled, reserving all the rights and cherished memories belonging to this organization under its former constitution, and declaring the steadfast allegiance of the churches composing the Council to the faith which our fathers confessed, which from age to age has found its expression in the historic creeds of the Church universal and of this communion, and affirming our loyalty to the basic principles of our representative democracy, hereby set forth the things most surely believed among us concerning faith, polity, and fellowship.

Faith. We believe in God the Father, infinite in wisdom, goodness and love; and in Jesus Christ, his Son, our Lord and Savior, who for us and our salvation lived and died and rose again and liveth evermore; and in the Holy Spirit, who taketh of the things of Christ and revealeth them to us, renewing, comforting, and inspiring the souls of men. We are united in striving to know the will of God as taught in the Holy Scriptures, and to our purpose to walk in the ways of the Lord, made known or to be made known to us. We hold it to be the mission of the Church of Christ to proclaim the gospel to all mankind, exalting the worship of the one true God and laboring for the progress of knowledge, the promotion of justice, the reign of peace, and the realization of human brotherhood. Depending, as did our fathers, upon the continued guidance of the Holy Spirit to lead us into all truth, we work and pray for the transformation of the world into the kingdom of God; and we look with faith for the triumph of righteousness and the life everlasting.

Polity. We believe in the freedom and responsibility of the individual soul, and the right of private judgment. We hold to the autonomy of the local church and its independence of all ecclesiastical control. We cherish the fellowship of the churches, united in district, state, and national bodies, for council and co-operation in matters of common concern.

The Wider Fellowship. While affirming the liberty of our churches, and the validity of our ministry, we hold to the unity and catholicity of the Church of Christ, and will unite with all its branches in hearty co-operation, and will earnestly seek, so far as in us lies, that the prayer of our Lord for his disciples may be answered, that they all may be one.

STATEMENT OF FAITH
UNITED CHURCH OF CHRIST

When the United Church of Christ came into existence in June, 1957, as a result of the merger between the Congregational Christians and the Evangelical Reformed, its professed statement of doctrine was in marked contrast to previous confessions of faith.

From concern for the details of Christian belief found in the Cambridge Platform—and its companion document, the Westminster Confession—the present document is almost laconic in brevity and allows a maximum of creedal liberty to its constituent membership.

We believe in God, the Eternal Spirit, Father of our Lord Jesus Christ and our Father, and to his deeds we testify:

>He calls the worlds into being,
>>creates man in his own image,
>>and sets before him the ways of life and death.

>He seeks in holy love to save all people from aimlessness
>>and sin.

>In Jesus Christ, the man of Nazareth, our crucified and
>>risen Lord, he has come to us
>>and shared our common lot,
>>conquering sin and death
>>and reconciling the world to himself.

>He bestows upon us his Holy Spirit,
>>creating and renewing the Church of Jesus Christ,
>>binding in convenant faithful people of all ages,
>>tongues, and races.

>He calls us into his Church
>>to accept the cost and joy of discipleship,
>>to be his servants in the service of men,
>>to proclaim the gospel to all the world
>>and resist the powers of evil,
>>to share in Christ's baptism and eat at his table.
>>to join him in his passion and victory.

>He promises to all who trust him
>>forgiveness of sins and fullness of grace,
>>courage in the struggle for justice and peace,

his presence in trial and rejoicing,
and eternal life in his kingdom which has no end.
Blessing and honor, glory and power be unto him. Amen.

THE BAPTISTS

Baptists have been more concerned about doctrinal positions than Congregationalists, as witnessed by the variety of confessional documents. There are currently about thirty such statements, some running into several thousand words, one each for the principal Baptist denominations in the country.

Three of these documents are of great significance because they represent the creedal tradition of most American Baptists and, in the case of the first, stood the test of almost three centuries of acceptance by this branch of the Free Church movement in Protestantism.

THE PHILADELPHIA BAPTIST CONFESSION

The Philadelphia Confession of 1688 is the most generally accepted doctrinal statement among Baptists in England and the United States. It first appeared in London in 1671, under the title, "A Confession of Faith put forth by the Elders and Brethren of many Congregations of Christians, Baptized upon Profession of their Faith."

It was adopted in the eighteenth century by the Philadelphia Association of Baptist Churches, which accounts for the name.

As the document now stands, it is a slight modification of the Confession of the Westminster Assembly (1647) with changes to suit the Baptist views on church polity and the meaning of baptism.

Since the Westminster Confession has already been given, the confession which follows covers only those articles that differ from the Westminster formula.

Of the Church

1. The Catholic or Universal Church which (with respect to the internal work of the Spirit and truth of grace) may be called invisible, consists of the whole number of the elect, that have been, are, or shall be gathered into one, under Christ, the head thereof: and is the spouse, the body, the fullness of him that filleth all in all.

2. All persons throughout the world, professing the faith of the gospel, and obedience unto God by Christ according unto it, not destroying their own profession by any errors, everting the foundation, or unholiness of conversation, are and may be called visible saints; and of such ought all particular congregations to be constituted.

3. Their purest churches under heaven are subject to mixture and error; and some have so degenerated as to become no churches of Christ, but synagogues of Satan; nevertheless, Christ always hath had and ever shall have a kingdom in this world to the end thereof, of such as believe in him, and make professions of his name.

4. The Lord Jesus Christ is the head of the Church, in whom, by the appointment of the Father, all power for the calling, institution, order, or government of the Church is invested in a supreme and sovereign manner; neither can the Pope of Rome, in any sense, be head thereof, but is no other than Antichrist, that man of sin and son of perdition, that exalteth himself in the Church against Christ, and all that is called God: whom the Lord shall destroy with the brightness of his coming.

5. In the execution of this power wherewith he is so intrusted, the Lord Jesus calleth out of the world unto himself, through the ministry of his Word, by his Spirit, those that are given unto him by his Father, that they may walk before him in all the ways of obedience which he prescribeth to them in his Word. Those thus called he commandeth to walk together in particular societies or churches, for their mutual edification, and the due performance of that public worship which he requireth of them in the world.

6. The members of these churches are saints by calling, visibly manifesting and evidencing (in and by their profession and walking) their obedience unto that call of Christ; and do willingly consent to walk together according to the appointment of Christ, giving up themselves to the Lord and one to another, by the will of God, in the professed subjection to the ordinances of the gospel.

7. To each of these churches thus gathered, according to his mind declared in his Word, he hath given all that power and authority which is any way needful for their carrying on that order in worship and discipline which he hath instituted for them to observe, with commands and rules for the due and right exerting and executing of that power.

8. A particular church gathered and completely organized, according to the mind of Christ, consists of officers and members; and the officers appointed by Christ to be chosen and set apart by the Church (so-called and gathered) for the peculiar administration of ordinances,

and execution of power and duty, which he intrusts them with or calls them to, to be continued to the end of the world, are bishops or elders and deacons.

9. The way appointed by Christ for the calling of any person, fitted and gifted by the Holy Spirit, unto the office of bishop or elder in the church is that he be chosen thereunto by the common suffrage of the church itself, and solemnly set apart by fasting and prayer, with imposition of hands of the eldership of the church, if there be any before constituted therein and of a deacon, that he be chosen by the like suffrage, and set apart by prayer, and the like imposition of hands.

10. The work of pastors being constantly to attend the service of Christ in his churches, in the ministry of the Word and prayer, with watching for their souls, as they that must give an account to him, it is incumbent on the churches to whom they minister, not only to give them all due respect, but also to communicate to them of all their good things, according to their ability, so as they may have a comfortable supply, without being themselves entangled with secular affairs; and may also be capable of exercising hospitality towards others; and this is required by the law of nature, and by the express order of our Lord Jesus, who hath ordained that they that preach the gospel should live of the gospel.

11. Although it be incumbent on the bishops or pastors of the churches to be instant in preaching the Word by way of office, yet the work of preaching the Word is not so peculiarly confined to them but that others also, gifted and fitted by the Holy Spirit for it, and approved and called by the Church, may and ought to perform it.

12. As all believers are bound to join themselves to particular churches, when and where they have opportunity so to do, so all that are admitted unto the privileges of a church are also under the censures and government thereof, according to the rule of Christ.

13. No church members, upon any offense taken by them, having performed their duty required of them towards the person they are offended at, ought to disturb any church order, or absent themselves from the assemblies of the church or administration of any ordinances upon the account of such offense at any of their fellow-members, but to wait upon Christ in the further proceeding of the church.

14. As each church, and all the members of it, are bound to pray continually for the good and prosperity of all the churches of Christ, in all places, and upon all occasions to further it (every one within the bounds of their places and callings, in the exercise of their gifts and graces), so the churches (when planted by the providence of God so as

they may enjoy opportunity and advantage for it) ought to hold communion among themselves for their peace, increase of love, and mutual edification.

15. In cases of difficulties or differences, either in point of doctrine or administration, wherein either the churches in general are concerned or any one church, in their peace, union, and edification; or any member or members of any church are injured, in or by any proceedings in censures not agreeable to truth and order: it is according to the mind of Christ that many churches, holding communion together, do by their messengers meet to consider and give their advice in or about that matter in difference, to be reported to all the churches concerned; howbeit these messengers assembled are not intrusted with any church power properly so called, or with any jurisdiction over the churches themselves, to exercise any censures either over any churches or persons, to impose their determination on the churches or officers.

Of Baptism and the Lord's Supper

1. Baptism and the Lord's Supper are ordinances of positive and sovereign institution, appointed by the Lord Jesus, the only Law-giver, to be continued in his Church to the end of the world.

2. These holy appointments are to be administered by those only who are qualified, and thereunto called, according to the commission of Christ.

Of Baptism

1. Baptism is an ordinance of the New Testament ordained by Jesus Christ to be unto the party baptized a sign of his fellowship with him in his death and resurrection; of his being engrafted into him; of remission of sins; and of his giving up unto God, through Jesus Christ, to live and walk in newness of life.

2. Those who do actually profess repentance towards God, faith in and obedience to our Lord Jesus, are the only proper subjects of this ordinance.

3. The outward element to be used in this ordinance is water, wherein the party is to be baptized in the name of the Father, and of the Son, and of the Holy Spirit.

4. Immersion, or dipping of the person in water, is necessary to the due administration of this ordinance.

NEW HAMPSHIRE CONFESSION OF FAITH

The New Hampshire Baptist Convention appointed a committee in 1830 to prepare a statement of faith, which was published by the Board of the Convention in 1833.

Widely circulated among all Baptist groups in the country, it reflects a mild Calvinism that reacted against the extreme positions of the European Reformed Churches. It appears as the standard profession of belief in Baptist Church manuals and comes nearest to a comprehensive summary of doctrine among the religious descendants of John Smyth.

Its most noteworthy feature is silence on the idea of a universal church, which has made it especially attractive to those groups who emphasized the local congregation and strictly covenanted-believers' theology.

I. *Of the Scriptures.* We believe (that) [1] the Holy Bible was written by men divinely inspired, and is a perfect treasure of heavenly instruction; that it has God for its author, salvation for its end, and truth, without any mixture of error, for its matter; that it reveals the principles by which God will judge us; and therefore is, and shall remain to the end of the world, the true centre of Christian union, and the supreme standard by which all human conduct, creeds, and opinions should be tried.

II. *Of the True God.* (We believe) That there is one, and only one, living and true God, an infinite, intelligent Spirit, whose name is JEHOVAH, the Maker and Supreme Ruler of heaven and earth; inexpressibly glorious in holiness; and worthy of all possible honor, confidence, and love; revealed under the personal and relative distinctions of the Father, the Son, and the Holy Spirit; equal in every divine perfection, and executing distinct but harmonious offices in the great work of redemption.

III. *Of the Fall of Man.* (We believe) That man was created in a state of holiness, under the law of his Maker; but by voluntary transgression fell from that holy and happy state; in consequence of which all mankind are now sinners, not by constraint but choice, being by nature utterly void of that holiness required by the law of God, wholly given to the gratification of the world, of Satan, and of their own sinful passions, therefore under just condemnation of eternal ruin, without defense or excuse.

IV. *Of the Way of Salvation.* (We believe) That the salvation of sinners is wholly of grace; through the Mediatorial Offices of the Son of God, who (by the appointment of the Father, freely) took upon him our nature, yet without sin; honored the (divine) law by his personal

[1] Additions made by J. Newton Brown in 1853 are enclosed in parentheses.

obedience, and made atonement for our sins by his death; being risen from the dead he is now enthroned in heaven; and uniting in his wonderful person the tenderest sympathies with divine perfections, (he) is every way qualified to be a suitable, a compassionate, and an all-sufficient Saviour.

V. *Of Justification.* (We believe) That the great Gospel blessing which Christ of his fulness bestows on such as believe in Him, is Justification; that Justification consists in the pardon of sin and the promise of eternal life, on principles of righteousness; that it is bestowed not in consideration of any works of righteousness which we have done, but solely through His own redemption and righteousness, (by virtue of which faith his perfect righteousness is freely imputed to us of God;) that it brings us into a state of most blessed peace and favor with God, and secures every other blessing needful to time and eternity.

VI. *Of the Freeness of Salvation.* (We believe) That the blessings of salvation are made free to all by the Gospel; that it is the immediate duty of all to accept them by a cordial, (penitent) and obedient faith; and that nothing prevents the salvation of the greatest sinner on earth except his own (inherent depravity and) voluntary refusal to submit to the Lord Jesus Christ, which refusal will subject him to an aggravated condemnation.

VII. *Of Grace in Regeneration.* (We believe) That in order to be saved, we must be regenerated or born again; that regeneration consists in giving a holy disposition to the mind; and is effected in a manner above our comprehension or calculation, by the power of the Holy Spirit, (in connection with divine truth,) so as to secure our voluntary obedience to the Gospel; and that its proper evidence is found in the holy fruit which we bring forth to the glory of God.

VIII. *Of Repentance and Faith.* (This article added in 1853.) We believe that Repentance and Faith are sacred duties, and also inseparable graces, wrought in our souls by the regenerating Spirit of God; whereby being deeply convinced of our guilt, danger, and helplessness, and of the way of salvation by Christ, we turn to God with unfeigned contrition, confession, and supplication for mercy; at the same time heartily receiving the Lord Jesus Christ as our Prophet, Priest, and King, and relying on him alone as the only and all-sufficient Saviour.

IX. *Of God's Purpose of Grace.* (We believe) That Election is the gracious purpose of God, according to which he (graciously) regenerates, sanctifies, and saves sinners; that being perfectly consistent with the free agency of man, it comprehends all the means in connection with the end; that it is a most glorious display of God's sovereign goodness, being infinitely (free,) wise, holy, and unchangeable; that it utterly excludes boasting, and promotes humility, (love,) prayer, praise, trust in God, and active imitation of his free mercy; that it encourages the use of means in the highest degree; that it is ascertained by its effects in all who (truly) believe the gospel; (that it) is the foundation of Christian assurance; and that to ascertain it with regard to ourselves, demands and deserves our utmost diligence.

X. *Of Sanctification.* (Added in 1853.) We believe that Sanctification is the process by which, according to the will of God, we are made partakers of his holiness; that it is a progressive work; that it is begun in regeneration; and that it is carried on in the hearts of believers by the presence and power of the Holy Spirit, the Sealer and Comforter, in the continual use of the appointed means—especially the Word of God, self-examination, self-denial, watchfulness and prayer.

XI. *Of the Perseverance of Saints.* (We believe) That such only are real believers as endure unto the end; that their persevering attachment to Christ is the grand mark which distinguishes them from mere professors; that a special Providence watches over their welfare; and (that) they are kept by the power of God through faith unto Salvation.

XII. (*Of the*) *Harmony of the Law and the Gospel.* (We believe) That the Law of God is the eternal and unchangeable rule of his moral government; that it is holy, just, and good; and that the inability which the Scriptures ascribe to fallen men to fulfill its precepts, arises entirely from their love of sin; to deliver them from which, and to restore them through a Mediator to unfeigned obedience to the holy law, is one great end of the Gospel, and of the means of grace connected with the establishment of the visible Church.

XIII. *Of a Gospel Church.* (We believe) That a visible Church of Christ is a congregation of baptized believers, associated by covenant in the faith and fellowship of the Gospel; observing the ordinances of Christ; governed by his laws; and exercising the gifts, rights, and privileges invested in them by his word; that its only proper officers are Bishops or Pastors, and Deacons, whose qualifications, claim, and duties are defined in the Epistles to Timothy and Titus.

XIV. *Of Baptism and the Lord's Supper.* (We believe) That Christian Baptism is the immersion of a believer in water, in the name of the Father (and) Son, and Spirit, to show forth in a solemn and beautiful emblem, our faith in a crucified, buried, and risen Saviour, with its purifying power; that it is a prerequisite to the privileges of a church

282 THE FREE CHURCH TRADITION

relation; and to the Lord's Supper, in which the members of the church, by the (sacred) use of bread and wine, are to commemorate together the dying love of Christ; preceded always by solemn self-examination.

XV. *Of the Christian Sabbath.* (We believe) That the first day of the week is the Lord's-Day, or Christian Sabbath; and is to be kept sacred to religious purposes, by abstaining from all secular labor and (sinful) recreations; by the devout observance of all the means of grace, both private and public; and by preparation for that rest which remaineth for the people of God.

XVI. *Of Civil Government.* (We believe) That civil government is of divine appointment, for the interests and good order of human society; and that magistrates are to be prayed for, conscientiously honored, and obeyed, except (only) in things opposed to the will of our Lord Jesus Christ, who is the only Lord of the conscience, and the Prince of the kings of the earth.

XVII. *Of the Righteous and the Wicked.* (We believe) That there is a radical and essential difference between the righteous and the wicked; that such only as through faith and justified in the name of the Lord Jesus, and sanctified by the Spirit of our God, are truly righteous in his esteem; while all such as continue in impenitence and unbelief are in his sight wicked, and under the curse; and this distinction holds among men both in and after death.

XVIII. *Of the World to Come.* (We believe) That the end of this world is approaching: that at the last day, Christ will descend from heaven, and raise the dead from the grave to final retribution; that a solemn separation will then take place; that the wicked will be adjudged to endless punishment, and the righteous to endless joy; and that this judgment will fix forever the final state of men in heaven or hell, on principles of righteousness.

SOUTHERN BAPTISTS: ABSTRACT OF PRINCIPLES

Southern Baptists have a history all their own. They were founded in 1845 when a large segment withdrew from the General Missionary Convention over the question of slavery. Since then they have grown in numbers and influence beyond anything comparable with their coreligionists in other denominations, due mainly to their doctrinal conservatism, their strong sense of church loyalty, and their aloofness from the ecumenical policies of other Baptist bodies in the United States.

Without repudiating the two historic Baptist confessions of faith, the Philadelphia and New Hampshire statements, Southern Baptists have formulated two of their own: the Abstract of Principles and the Report on Baptist Faith and Message. Both have had much to do with developing the solidarity and independence of the Southern Baptist Convention.

The Abstract of Principles was adopted by the Southern Baptist Seminary, in Louisville, in 1859, and by the Southeastern Baptist Theological Seminary (Wake Forest, North Carolina) and from them has deeply affected the belief and ritual practice of the whole Baptist community belonging to the Southern Convention.

Where the Abstract of Principles was drafted in relative calm, the Statement of Baptist Faith and Message arose from the controversies of the time, and still remains a bulwark of Baptist defense against the inroads of modernism. Its basis is the New Hampshire document, but with noteworthy modifications: stressing the need for a clear position in the church when threatened with heterodoxy, explanation of the origin of man, Mary's virginity, and a long declaration of principles on Church and State.

I. *The Scriptures*. The Scriptures of the Old and New Testaments were given by inspiration of God, and are the only sufficient, certain and authoritative rule of all saving knowledge, faith and obedience.

II. *God*. There is but one God, the Maker, Preserver and Ruler of all things, having in and of himself, all perfections, and being infinite in them all; and to Him all creatures owe the highest love, reverence and obedience.

III. *The Trinity*. God is revealed to us as Father, Son and Holy Spirit each with distinct personal attributes, but without division of nature, essence or being.

IV. *Providence*. God from eternity decrees or permits all things that come to pass, and perpetually upholds, directs and governs all creatures and all events; yet so as not in any wise to be the author or approver of sin nor to destroy the free will and responsibility of intelligent creatures.

V. *Election*. Election is God's eternal choice of some persons unto everlasting life—not because of foreseen merit in them, but of His mere mercy in Christ—in consequence of which choice they are called, justified and glorified.

VI. *The Fall of Man.* God originally created man in His own image, and free from sin; but through the temptation of Satan, he transgressed the command of God, and fell from his original holiness and righteousness; whereby his posterity inherit a nature corrupt and wholly opposed to God and His law, are under condemnation, and as soon as they are capable of moral action, become actual transgressors.

VII. *The Mediator.* Jesus Christ, the only begotten Son of God, is the divinely appointed mediator between God and man. Having taken upon Himself human nature, yet without sin, He perfectly fulfilled the law, suffered and died upon the cross for the salvation of sinners. He was buried, and rose again the third day, and ascended to His Father, at whose right hand He ever liveth to make intercession for His people. He is the only Mediator, the Prophet, Priest and King of the Church, and Sovereign of the Universe.

VIII. *Regeneration.* Regeneration is a change of heart, wrought by the Holy Spirit, who quickeneth the dead in trespasses and sins, enlightening their minds spiritually and savingly to understand the Word of God, and renewing their whole nature, so that they love and practice holiness. It is a work of God's free and special grace alone.

IX. *Repentance.* Repentance is an evangelical grace, wherein a person being, by the Holy Spirit, made sensible of the manifold evil of his sin, humbleth himself for it, with godly sorrow, detestation of it, and self-abhorrence, with a purpose and endeavor to walk before God so as to please Him in all things.

X. *Faith.* Saving faith is the belief, on God's authority, of whatsoever is revealed in His Word concerning Christ; accepting and resting upon Him alone for justification and eternal life. It is wrought in the heart by the Holy Spirit, and is accompanied by all other saving graces, and leads to a life of holiness.

XI. *Justification.* Justification is God's gracious and full acquital of sinners, who believe in Christ, from all sin, through the satisfaction that Christ has made; nor for anything wrought in them or done by them; but on account of the obedience and satisfaction of Christ, they receiving and resting on Him and His righteousness by faith.

XII. *Sanctification.* Those who have been regenerated are also sanctified, by God's word and Spirit dwelling in them. This sanctification is progressive through the supply of Divine strength, which all saints seek to obtain, pressing after a heavenly life in cordial obedience to all Christ's commands.

XIII. *Perseverance of the Saints.* Those whom God hath accepted in the Beloved, and sanctified by His Spirit, will never totally nor finally fall away from the state of grace, but shall certainly persevere to the end; and though they may fall, through neglect and temptation, into sin, whereby they grieve the Spirit, impair their graces and comforts, bring reproach on the Church, and temporal judgments on themselves, yet they shall be renewed again unto repentance, and be kept by the power of God through faith unto salvation.

XIV. *The Church.* The Lord Jesus is the Head of the Church, which is composed of all His true disciples, and in Him is invested supremely all power for its government. According to His commandment, Christians are to associate themselves into particular societies or churches; and to each of these churches He hath given needful authority for administering that order, discipline and worship which He hath appointed. The regular officers of a Church are Bishops or Elders, and Deacons.

XV. *Baptism.* Baptism is an ordinance of the Lord Jesus, obligatory upon every believer, wherein he is immersed in water in the name of the Father, and of the Son, and of the Holy Spirit, as a sign of his fellowship with the death and resurrection of Christ, of remission of sins, and of his giving himself up to God, to live and walk in newness of life. It is prerequisite to church fellowship, and to participation in the Lord's Supper.

XVI. *The Lord's Supper.* The Lord's Supper is an ordinance of Jesus Christ to be administered with the elements of bread and wine, and to be observed by His churches till the end of the world. It is in no sense a sacrifice, but is designed to commemorate His death, to confirm the faith and other graces of Christians, and to be a bond, pledge and renewal of their communion with Him, and of their church fellowship.

XVII. *The Lord's Day.* The Lord's day is a Christian institution for regular observation, and should be employed in exercises of worship and spiritual devotion, both public and private, resting from worldly employments and amusements, works of necessity and mercy only excepted.

XVIII. *Liberty of Conscience.* God alone is Lord of the conscience; and He hath left it free from the doctrines and commandments of men, which are in anything contrary to His word, or not contained in it. Civil magistrates being ordained of God, subjection in all lawful things commanded by them ought to be yielded by us in the Lord, not only for wrath, but also for conscience sake.

XIX. *The Resurrection.* The bodies of men after death return to dust, but their spirits return immediately to God—the righteous to rest with

Him; the wicked, to be reserved under darkness to the judgment. At the last day, the bodies of all the dead, both just and unjust will be raised.

XX. *The Judgment.* God hath appointed a day, wherein He will judge the world by Jesus Christ, when everyone shall receive according to his deeds: the wicked shall go into everlasting punishment; the righteous, into everlasting life.

STATEMENT OF (SOUTHERN) BAPTIST
FAITH AND MESSAGE

Your committee beg leave to report as follows:

Your committee recognize that they were appointed "to consider the advisability of issuing another statement of the Baptist Faith and Message, and to report at the next Convention."

In pursuance of the instructions of the Convention, and in consideration of the general denominational situation, your committee have decided to recommend the New Hampshire Confession of Faith, revised at certain points, and with some additional articles growing out of present needs, for approval by the Convention, in the event a statement of the Baptist faith and message is deemed necessary at this time.

The present occasion for a reaffirmation of Christian fundamentals is the prevalence of naturalism in the modern teaching and preaching of religion. Christianity is supernatural in its origin and history. We repudiate every theory of religion which denies the supernatural elements in our faith.

As introductory to the doctrinal articles, we recommend the adoption by the Convention of the following statement of the historic Baptist conception of the nature and function of confessions of faith in our religious and denominational life, believing that some such statements will clarify the atmosphere and remove some causes of misunderstanding, friction, and apprehension. Baptists approve and circulate confessions of faith with the following understanding, namely:

1. That they constitute a consensus of opinion of some Baptist body, large or small, for the general instruction and guidance of our own people and others concerning those articles of the Christian faith which are most surely held among us. They are not intended to add anything to the simple conditions of salvation revealed in the New Testament, viz., repentance towards God and faith in Jesus Christ as Saviour and Lord.

2. That we do not regard them as complete statements of our faith,

having any quality of finality or infallibility. As in the past so in the future Baptists should hold themselves free to revise their statements of faith as may seem to them wise and expedient at any time.

3. That any group of Baptists, large or small, have the inherent right to draw up for themselves and publish to the world a confession of their faith whenever they may think it advisable to do so.

4. That the sole authority for faith and practice among Baptists is the Scriptures of the Old and New Testaments. Confessions are only guides in interpretation, having no authority over the conscience.

5. That they are statements of religious convictions, drawn from the Scriptures, and are not to be used to hamper freedom of thought or investigation in other realms of life.

I. *The Scriptures.* We believe that the Holy Bible was written by men divinely inspired and is a perfect treasure of heavenly instruction; that it has God for its author, salvation for its end, and truth, without any mixture of error, for its matter; that it reveals the principles by which God will judge us; and therefore is, and will remain to the end of the world, the true center of Christian union, and the supreme standard by which all human conduct, creeds and religious opinions should be tried.

II. *God.* There is one and only one living and true God, an intelligent, spiritual and personal Being, the Creator, Preserver and Ruler of the universe, infinite in holiness and all other perfections, to whom we owe the highest love, reverence and obedience. He is revealed to us as Father, Son and Holy Spirit, each with distinct personal attributes, but without division of nature, essence or being.

III. *The Fall of Man.* Man was created by the special act of God, recorded in Genesis. Gen. 1:27; Gen. 2:7. He was created in a state of holiness under the law of his maker, but, through the temptation of Satan he transgressed the command of God and fell from his original holiness and righteousness; whereby his posterity inherit a nature corrupt and in bondage to sin, are under condemnation, and as soon as they are capable of moral action, become actual transgressors.

IV. *The Way of Salvation.* The salvation of sinners is wholly of grace, through the mediatorial office of the Son of God, who by the Holy Spirit was born of the Virgin Mary and took upon him our nature, yet without sin; honored the divine law by his personal obedience, and made atonement for our sins by his death. Being risen from the dead, he is now enthroned in heaven, and, uniting in his person the tenderest sympathies with divine perfections, he is in every way qualified to be a compassionate and all-sufficient Saviour.

V. *Justification.* Justification is God's gracious and full acquittal upon principles of righteousness of all sinners who believe in Christ. This blessing is bestowed, not in consideration of any works of righteousness which we have done, but through the redemption which is in and through Jesus Christ. It brings us into a state of most blessed peace and favor with God, and secures every other needed blessing.

VI. *The Freeness of Salvation.* The blessings of salvation are made free to all by the Gospel. It is the duty of all to accept them by penitent and obedient faith. Nothing prevents the salvation of the greatest sinner except his own voluntary refusal to accept Jesus Christ as teacher, Saviour and Lord.

VII. *Regeneration.* Regeneration or the new birth is a change of heart wrought by the Holy Spirit, whereby we become partakers of the divine nature and a holy disposition is given, leading to the love and practice of righteousness. It is a work of God's free grace conditioned upon faith in Christ and made manifest by the fruit which we bring forth to the glory of God.

VIII. *Repentance and Faith.* We believe that repentance and faith are sacred duties, and also inseparable graces, wrought in our souls by the regenerating Spirit of God; whereby being deeply convinced of our guilt, danger, and helplessness, and of the way of salvation by Christ, we turn to God with unfeigned contrition, confession, and supplication for mercy; at the same time heartily receiving the Lord Jesus Christ as our Prophet, Priest and King and relying on him alone as the only and all-sufficient Saviour.

IX. *God's Purpose of Grace.* Election is the gracious purpose of God, according to which he regenerates, sanctifies and saves sinners. It is perfectly consistent with the free agency of man, and comprehends all the means in connection with the end. It is a most gracious display of God's sovereign goodness, and is infinitely wise, holy and unchangeable. It excludes boasting and promotes humility. It encourages the use of means in the highest degree.

X. *Sanctification.* Sanctification is the process by which the regenerate gradually attain to moral and spiritual perfection through the presence and power of the Holy Spirit dwelling in their hearts. It continues throughout the earthly life, and is accomplished by the use of all the ordinary means of grace, and particularly by the Word of God.

XI. *Perseverance.* All real believers endure to the end. Their continuance in well-doing is the mark which distinguishes them from mere professors. A special Providence cares for them, and they are kept by the power of God through faith unto salvation.

XII. *A Gospel Church.* A church of Christ is a congregation of baptized believers, associated by covenant in the faith and fellowship of the gospel; observing the ordinances of Christ, governed by his law, and exercising the gifts, rights and privileges invested in them by his word, and seeking to extend the Gospel to the ends of the earth. Its Scriptural officers are bishops or elders and deacons.

XIII. *Baptism and the Lord's Supper.* Christian baptism is the immersion of a believer in water in the name of the Father, the Son, and the Holy Spirit. The act is a symbol of our faith in a crucified, buried and risen Saviour. It is prerequisite to the privileges of a church relation and to the Lord's Supper, in which the members of the church, by the use of bread and wine, commemorate the dying love of Christ.

XIV. *The Lord's Day.* The first day of the week is the Lord's day. It is a Christian institution for regular observance. It commemorates the resurrection of Christ from the dead, and should be employed in exercises of worship and spiritual devotion, both public and private, and by refraining from worldly amusements, and resting from secular employments, works of necessity and mercy only excepted.

XV. *The Righteous and the Wicked.* There is a radical and essential difference between the righteous and the wicked. Those only who are justified through the name of the Lord Jesus Christ and sanctified by the Holy Spirit are truly righteous in his sight. Those who continue in impenitence and unbelief are in his sight wicked and are under condemnation. This distinction between the righteous and the wicked holds in and after death, and will be made manifest at the judgment when final and everlasting awards are made to all men.

XVI. *The Resurrection.* The Scriptures clearly teach that Jesus rose from the dead. His grave was emptied of its contents. He appeared to his disciples after his resurrection in many convincing manifestations. He now exists in his glorified body at God's right hand. There will be a resurrection of the righteous and the wicked. The bodies of the righteous will conform to the glorious spiritual body of Jesus.

XVII. *The Return of the Lord.* The New Testament teaches in many places the visible and personal return of Jesus to this earth. "This same Jesus which is taken up from you into Heaven, shall so come in like manner as ye have seen him go into Heaven." The time of his coming is not revealed (Matt. 24:36). It is the duty of all believers to live in readiness for his coming and by diligence in good works to make manifest to all men the reality and power of their hope in Christ.

XVIII. *Religious Liberty.* God alone is Lord of the conscience, and he has left it free from the doctrines and commandments of men which are contrary to his word or not contained in it. Church and state should be separate. The state owes to the church protection and full freedom in the pursuit of its spiritual ends. In providing for such freedom no ecclesiastical group or denomination should be favored by the state more than others. Civil government being ordained of God, it is the duty of Christians to render loyal obedience thereto in all things not contrary to the revealed will of God. The church should not resort to the civil power to carry on its work. The Gospel of Christ contemplates spiritual means alone for the pursuit of its ends. The state has no right to impose penalties for religious opinions of any kind. The state has no right to impose taxes for the support of any form of religion. A free church in a free state is the Christian ideal, and this implies the right of free and unhindered access to God on the part of all men, and the right to form and propagate opinions in the sphere of religion without interference by the civil power.

XIX. *Peace and War.* It is the duty of Christians to seek peace with all men on principles of righteousness. In accordance with the spirit and teachings of Christ they should do all in their power to put an end to war.

The true remedy for the war spirit is the pure gospel of our Lord. The supreme need of the world is the acceptance of his teachings in all affairs of men and nations, and the practical application of his law of love.

We urge Christian people throughout the land to pray for the reign of the Prince of Peace, and to oppose everything likely to provoke war.

XX. *Education.* Christianity is the religion of enlightenment and intelligence. In Jesus Christ are hidden all the treasures of wisdom and knowledge. All sound learning is therefore a part of our Christian heritage. The new birth opens all human faculties and creates a thirst for knowledge. An adequate system of schools is necessary to a complete spiritual program for Christ's people. The cause of education in the Kingdom of Christ is co-ordinate with the causes of missions and general benevolence, and should receive along with these the liberal support of the churches.

XXI. *Social Service.* Every Christian is under obligation to seek to make the will of Christ regnant in his own life and in human society; to oppose in the spirit of Christ every form of greed, selfishness and vice;

to provide for the orphaned, the aged, the helpless, and the sick; to seek to bring industry, government and society as a whole under the sway of the principles of righteousness, truth and brotherly love; to promote these ends Christians should be ready to work with all men of good will in any good cause, always being careful to act in the spirit of love without compromising their loyalty to Christ and his truth. All means and methods used in social service for the amelioration of society and the establishment of righteousness among men must finally depend on the regeneration of the individual by the saving grace of God in Christ Jesus.

XXII. *Co-operation.* Christ's people should, as occasion requires, organize such associations and conventions as may best secure co-operation for the great objects of the Kingdom of God. Such organizations have no authority over each other or over the churches. They are voluntary and advisory bodies designed to elicit, combine and direct the energies of our people in the most effective manner. Individual members of New Testament churches should co-operate with each other, and the churches themselves should co-operate with each other in carrying forward the missionary, educational and benevolent program for the extension of Christ's Kingdom. Christian unity in the New Testament sense is spiritual harmony and voluntary co-operation for common ends by various groups of Christ's people. It is permissible and desirable as between the various Christian denominations, when the end to be attained is itself justified, and when such co-operation involves no violation of conscience or compromise of loyalty to Christ and his Word as revealed in the New Testament.

XXIII. *Evangelism and Missions.* It is the duty of every Christian man and woman, and the duty of every church of Christ, to seek to extend the gospel to the ends of the earth. The new birth of man's spirit by God's Holy Spirit means the birth of love for others. Missionary effort on the part of all rests thus upon a spiritual necessity of the regenerate life. It is also expressly and repeatedly commanded in the teachings of Christ. It is the duty of every child of God to seek constantly to win the lost to Christ by personal effort and by all other methods sanctioned by the Gospel of Christ.

XIV. *Stewardship.* God is the source of all blessings, temporal and spiritual; all that we have and are we owe to him. We have a spiritual debtorship to the whole world, a holy trusteeship in the Gospel, and a binding stewardship in our possessions. We are therefore under obligation to serve him with our time, talents and material possessions; and should recognize all these as entrusted to us to use for the glory of God and helping others. Christians should cheerfully, regularly, systematically, proportionately, and liberally contribute of their means to advancing the Redeemer's cause on earth.

XV. *The Kingdom.* The Kingdom of God is the reign of God in the heart and life of the individual in every human relationship, and in every form and institution of organized society. The chief means for promoting the Kingdom of God on earth are preaching the Gospel of Christ, and teaching the principles of righteousness contained therein. The Kingdom of God will be complete when every thought and will of man shall be brought into captivity to the will of Christ. And it is the duty of all Christ's people to pray and labor continually that his Kingdom may come and his will be done on earth as it is in heaven.

THE QUAKERS
THEOLOGICAL THESES OF ROBERT BARCLAY

While George Fox was the founder of the Society of Friends, and Quakers still look to him for inspiration, his contemporary and disciple, Robert Barclay (1610-1686), formulated what has since become known as the *Theological Theses of Quakerism.*

Barclay had been educated at the Roman Catholic Scottish College in Paris. When his father joined the Society of Friends, Robert followed him and soon became the Quakers' stoutest champion against their critics in the established churches.

His great familiarity with the principles of scholastic theology gave precision to his ideas and a logic that opponents found irrefutable, once he was granted certain basic premises. In 1673 he published his *Catechism and Confession of Faith,* and three years later appeared his principal work, the *Apology* to defend the fifteen Quaker *Theses Theologiae* which he had propounded at Aberdeen and circulated in English, Latin, French, and Dutch.

The impressive and eloquent defense of the doctrine of the Inner Light against the sufficiency of external authorities, including the Bible, made it the classical exposition of Quaker principles.

Through the good graces of James II, Barclay became of service to William Penn in his foundation of Pennsylvania and in 1683 was himself appointed governor of East New Jersey, which was given a constitution on Quaker principles.

Robert Barclay, a Servant of the Lord God, and one of those who in derision are called Quakers, wisheth unfeigned repentance, unto the knowledge of the Truth.

Friends,—Unto you these following propositions are offered; in which, they being read and considered in the fear of the Lord, you may perceive that simple, naked truth, which man by his wisdom hath rendered so obscure and mysterious that the world is even burthened with the great and voluminous tractates which are made about it, and by their vain jangling and commentaries, by which it is rendered a hundredfold more dark and intricate than of itself it is: which great learning, so accounted of—to wit, your school divinity, which taketh up almost a man's whole lifetime to learn, brings not a whit nearer to God, neither makes any man less wicked, or more righteous than he was. Therefore hath God laid aside the wise and learned, and the disputers of this world; and hath chosen a few despicable and unlearned instruments, as to a letter-learning, as he did fishermen of old, to publish his pure and naked truth, and to free it of those mists and fogs wherewith the clergy hath clouded it, that the people might admire and maintain them. And among several others, whom God hath chosen to make known these things—seeing I also have received, in measure, grace to be a dispenser of the same gospel—it seemed good unto me, according to my duty, to offer unto you these propositions; which, though short, yet are weighty, comprehending much, and declaring what the true ground of knowledge is, even of that knowledge which leads to Life Eternal; which is here witnessed of, and the testimony thereof left unto the Light of Christ in all your consciences.

Farewell,   R. B.

The First Proposition.
Concerning the true Foundation of Knowledge.

Seeing the height of all happiness is placed in the true knowledge of God ('This is life eternal, to know thee the only true God, and Jesus Christ whom thou hast sent'), the true and right understanding of this foundation and ground of knowledge is that which is most necessary to be known and believed in the first place.

The Second Proposition.
Concerning Immediate Revelation.

Seeing 'no man knoweth the Father but the Son, and he to whom the Son revealeth him;' and seeing the revelation of the Son is in and by the Spirit; therefore the testimony of the Spirit is that alone by which the true knowledge of God hath been, is and can be only revealed;

who as, by the moving of his own Spirit, he converted the chaos of this world into that wonderful order wherein it was in the beginning, and created man a living soul, to rule and govern it, so by the revelation of the same Spirit he hath manifested himself all along unto the sons of men, both patriarchs, prophets, and apostles; which revelation of God by the Spirit, whether by outward voices and appearances, dreams, or inward objective manifestations in the heart, were of old the formal object of their faith, and remain yet so to be; since the object of the saints' faith is the same in all ages, though set forth under divers administrations. Moreover, these divine inward revelations, which we make absolutely necessary for the building up of true faith, neither do nor can ever contradict the outward testimony of the Scriptures, or right and sound reason. Yet from hence it will not follow that these divine revelations are to be subjected to the examination, either of the outward testimony of the Scriptures or of the natural reason of man, as to a more noble or certain rule or touchstone; for this divine revelation and inward illumination is that which is evident and clear of itself, forcing, by its own evidence and clearness, the well-disposed understanding to assent, irresistibly moving the same thereunto; even as the common principles of natural truths move and incline the mind to a natural assent: as, that the whole is greater than its part; that two contradictory sayings can not be both true, nor both false: which is also manifest, according to adversaries' principle, who—supposing the possibility of inward divine revelation—will nevertheless confess with us that neither Scripture nor sound reason will contradict it: and yet it will not follow, according to them, that the Scripture or sound reason should be subjected to the examination of the divine revelations in the heart.

The Third Proposition.
Concerning the Scriptures.

From these revelations of the Spirit of God to the saints have proceeded the Scriptures of truth, which contain: 1. A faithful historical account of the actings of God's people in divers ages, with many singular and remarkable providences attending them. 2. A prophetical account of several things, whereof some are already past, and some yet to come. 3. A full and ample account of all the chief principles of the doctrine of Christ, held forth in divers precious declarations, exhortations, and sentences, which, by the moving of God's Spirit, were at several times, and upon sundry occasions, spoken and written unto some churches and their pastors: nevertheless, because they are only a declaration of the fountain, and not the fountain itself, therefore they are not to be esteemed the principal ground of all truth and knowledge, nor yet the adequate primary rule of faith and manners. Nevertheless, as that which giveth a true and faithful testimony of the first foundation, they are and may be esteemed a secondary rule, subordinate to the Spirit, from which they have all their excellency and certainty; for as by the inward testimony of the Spirit we do alone truly know them, so they testify that the Spirit is that guide by which the saints are led into all truth: therefore, according to the Scriptures, the Spirit is the first and principal Leader. And seeing we do therefore receive and believe the Scriptures, because they proceeded from the Spirit, therefore also the Spirit is more originally and principally the rule, according to that received maxim in the schools, *Propter quod unumquodque est tale, illud ipsum est magis tale.* Englished thus: 'That for which a thing is such, that thing itself is more such.'

The Fourth Proposition.
Concerning the Condition of Man in the Fall.

All Adam's posterity, or mankind, both Jews and Gentiles, as to the first Adam, or earthly man, is fallen, degenerated, and dead, deprived of the sensation or feeling of this inward testimony or seed of God, and is subject unto the power, nature, and seed of the Serpent, which he sows in men's hearts, while they abide in this natural and corrupted state; from whence it comes that not their words and deeds only, but all their imaginations are evil perpetually in the sight of God, as proceeding from this depraved and wicked seed. Man, therefore, as he is in this state, can know nothing aright; yea, his thoughts and conceptions concerning God and things spiritual, until he be disjoined from this evil seed, and united to the Divine Light, are unprofitable both to himself and others: hence are rejected the Socinian and Pelagian errors, in exalting a natural light; as also of the Papists, and most Protestants, who affirm that man, without the true grace of God, may be a true minister of the gospel. Nevertheless, this seed is not imputed to infants, until by transgression they actually join themselves therewith; for they are by nature the children of wrath, who walk according to the power of the prince of the air.

The Fifth and Sixth Propositions.
Concerning the Universal Redemption by Christ,
and also the Saving
and Spiritual Light, wherewith every man is enlightened.

The Fifth Proposition

God, out of his infinite love, who delighteth not in the death of a sinner, but that all should live and be saved, hath so loved the world that he hath given his only Son a Light, that whosoever believeth in him should be saved; who enlighteneth every man that cometh into the world, and maketh manifest all things that are reprovable, and teacheth all temperance, righteousness, and godliness: and this Light enlighteneth the hearts of all in a day, in order to salvation, if not resisted: nor is it less universal than the seed of sin, being the purchase of his death, who tasted death for every man; 'for as in Adam all die, even so in Christ shall all be made alive.'

The Sixth Proposition.

According to which principle (or hypothesis), all the objections against the universality of Christ's death are easily solved; neither is it needful to recur to the ministry of angels, and those other miraculous means which, they say, God makes use of, to manifest the doctrine and history of Christ's passion unto such, who, living in those places of the world where the outward preaching of the gospel is unknown have well improved the first and common grace; for hence it well follows, that as some of the old philosophers might have been saved, so also may now some—who by providence are cast into those remote parts of the world where the knowledge of the history is wanting—be made partakers of the divine mystery, if they receive and resist not that grace, 'a manifestation whereof is given to every man to profit withal.' This certain doctrine then being received, to wit, that there is an evangelical and saving light and grace in all, the universality of the love and mercy of God towards mankind—both in the death of his beloved Son the Lord Jesus Christ, and in the manifestation of the light in the heart—is established and confirmed against all the objection of such as deny it. Therefore 'Christ hath tasted death for every man:' of all kinds of men, as some vainly talk, but for every one, of all kinds; the benefit of whose offering is not only extended to such, who have the distinct outward knowledge of his death and sufferings, as the same is declared in the Scriptures, but even unto those who are necessarily excluded from the benefit of this knowledge by some inevitable accident; which knowledge we willingly confess to be very profitable and comfortable, but not absolutely needful unto such, from whom God himself hath withheld it; yet they may be made partakers of the mystery of his death—though ignorant of the history—if they suffer his seed and light—enlightening their hearts—to take place; in which light communion with the Father and Son is enjoyed, so as of wicked men to become holy, and lovers of that power by whose inward and secret touches they feel themselves turned from the evil to the good, and learn to do to others as they would be done by; in which Christ himself affirms all to be included. As they then have falsely and erroneously taught who have denied Christ to have died for all men, so neither have they sufficiently taught the truth, who, affirming him to have died for all, have added the absolute necessity of the outward knowledge thereof in order to the obtaining its saving effect; among whom the Remonstrants of Holland have been chiefly wanting, and many other asserters of Universal Redemption, in that they have not placed the extent of this salvation in that divine and evangelical principle of light and life wherewith Christ hath enlightened every man that comes into the world, which is excellently and evidently held forth in these Scriptures: Gen. vi. 3; Deut. xxx. 14; John i 7-9; Rom. x. 8; Titus ii. 11.

The Seventh Proposition.
Concerning Justification.

As many as resist not this light, but receive the same, in them is produced an holy, pure, and spiritual birth, bringing forth holiness, righteousness, purity, and all those other blessed fruits which are acceptable to God; by which holy birth, to wit, Jesus Christ formed within us, and working his works in us, as we are sanctified, so we are justified in the sight of God, according to the apostle's words, 'But ye are washed, but ye are sanctified, but ye are justified, in the name of the Lord Jesus, and by the Spirit of our God.' Therefore it is not by our works wrought in our will, nor yet by good works, considered of themselves, but by Christ, who is both the gift and the giver, and the cause producing the effects in us; who, as he hath reconciled us while we were enemies, doth also in his wisdom save us, and justify us after this manner, as saith the same apostle elsewhere, 'According to his mercy he saved us, by the washing of regeneration, and the renewing of the Holy Ghost.'

The Eighth Proposition.
Concerning Perfection.

In whom this holy and pure birth is fully brought forth the body of death and sin comes to be crucified and removed, and their hearts united and subjected unto the truth, so as not to obey any suggestion or temptation of the evil one, but to be free from actual sinning and transgressing of the law of God, and in that respect perfect. Yet doth this perfection still admit of a growth; and there remaineth a possibility of sinning where the mind doth not most diligently and watchfully attend unto the Lord.

The Ninth Proposition.
Concerning Perseverance,
and the Possibility of Falling from Grace.

Although this gift and inward grace of God be sufficient to work out salvation, yet in those in whom it is resisted it both may and doth become their condemnation. Moreover, in whom it hath wrought in part, to purify and sanctify them, in order to their further perfection, by disobedience such may fall from it, and turn it to wantonness, making shipwreck of faith; and 'after having tasted of the heavenly gift, and been made partakers of the Holy Ghost, again fall away.' Yet such an increase and stability in the truth may in this life be attained, from which there can not be a total apostasy.

The Tenth Proposition.
Concerning the Ministry.

As by this gift, or Light of God, all true knowledge in things spiritual is received and revealed; so by the same, as it is manifested and received in the heart, by the strength and power thereof, every true minister of the gospel is ordained, prepared, and supplied in the work of the ministry; and by the leading, moving, and drawing hereof ought every evangelist and Christian pastor to be led and ordered in his labor and work of the gospel, both as to the place where, as to the persons to whom, and as to the times when he is to minister. Moreover, those who have this authority may and ought to preach the gospel, though without human comission or literature; as, on the other hand, those who want the authority of this divine gift, however learned or authorized by the commissions of men and churches, are to be esteemed but as deceivers, and not true ministers of the gospel. Also, who have received this holy and unspotted gift, 'as they have freely received, so are they freely to give,' without hire or bargaining, far less to use it as a trade to get money by it: yet if God hath called any from their employments or trades, by which they acquire their livelihood, it may be lawful for such, according to the liberty which they feel given them in the Lord, to receive such temporals—to wit, what may be needful to them for meat and clothing—as are freely given them by those to whom they have communicated spirituals.

The Eleventh Proposition.
Concerning Worship.

All true and acceptable worship to God is offered in the inward and immediate moving and drawing of his own Spirit, which is neither limited to places, times, or persons; for though we be to worship him always, in that we are to fear before him, yet as to the outward significcation thereof in prayers, praises, or preachings, we ought not to do it where and when we will, but where and when we are moved thereunto by the secret inspirations of his Spirit in our hearts, which God heareth and accepteth of, and is never wanting to move us thereunto, when need is, of which he himself is the alone proper judge. All other worship them, both praises, prayers, and preachings, which man sets about in his own will, and at his own appointment, which he can both begin and end at his pleasure, do or leave undone, as himself sees meet, whether they be a prescribed form, as a liturgy, or prayers conceived extemporarily, by the natural strength and faculty of the mind, they are all but superstitions, will-worship, and abominable idolatry in the sight of God; which are to be denied, rejected, and separated from, in this day of his spiritual arising: however it might have pleased him—who winked at the times of ignorance, with respect to the simplicity and integrity of some, and of his own innocent seed, which lay as it were buried in the hearts of men, under the mass of superstition—to blow upon the dead and dry bones, and to raise some breathings, and answer them, and that until the day should more clearly dawn and break forth.

The Twelfth Proposition.
Concerning Baptism.

As there is one Lord and one faith, so there is 'one baptism; which is not the putting away the filth of the flesh, but the answer of a good conscience before God, by the resurrection of Jesus Christ.' And this baptism is a pure and spiritual thing, to wit, the baptism of the Spirit and fire, by which we are buried with him, that, being washed and purged from our sins, we may 'walk in newness of life;' of which the baptism of John was a figure, which was commanded for a time, and not to continue forever.

As to the baptism of infants, it is a mere human tradition, for which neither precept nor practice is to be found in all the Scripture.

The Thirteenth Proposition.
Concerning the Communion, or Participation of the Body and Blood of Christ.

The communion of the body and blood of Christ is inward and spiritual, which is the participation of his flesh and blood, by which the inward man is daily nourished in the hearts of those in whom Christ dwells; of which things the breaking of bread by Christ with his disciples was a figure, which they even used in the Church for a time, who had received the substance, for the cause of the weak; even as 'abstaining from things strangled, and from blood;' the washing one another's feet, and the anointing of the sick with oil; all which are commanded with no less authority and solemnity than the former; yet seeing they are but the shadow of better things, they cease in such as have obtained the substance.

The Fourteenth Proposition.
Concerning the Power of the Civil Magistrate, in matters purely religious, and pertaining to the conscience.

Since God hath assumed to himself the power and dominion of the conscience, who alone can rightly instruct and govern it, therefore it is not lawful for any whatsoever, by virtue of any authority or principality they bear in the government of this world, to force the consciences of others; and therefore all killing, banishing, fining, imprisoning, and other such things, which men are afflicted with, for the alone exercise of their conscience, or difference in worship or opinion, proceedeth from the spirit of Cain, the murderer, and is contrary to the truth; provided always that no man, under the pretense of conscience, prejudice his neighbor in his life or estate, or do any thing destructive to, or inconsistent with, human society; in which case the law is for the transgressor, and justice to be administered upon all, without respect of persons.

The Fifteenth Proposition
Concerning Salutations and Recreations, etc.

Seeing the chief end of all religion is to redeem man from the spirit and vain conversation of this world, and to lead into inward communion with God, before whom, if we fear always, we are accounted happy, therefore all vain customs and habits thereof, both in word and deed, are to be rejected and forsaken by those who come to this fear; such as the taking off the hat to a man, the bowings and cringings of the body, and such other salutations of that kind, with all the foolish and superstitious formalities attending them; all which man has invented in his degenerate state, to feed his pride in the vain pomp and glory of this world; as also the unprofitable plays, frivolous recreations, sportings, and gamings, which are invented to pass away the precious time, and divert the mind from the witness of God in the heart, and from the living sense of his fear, and from that evangelical Spirit wherewith Christians ought to be leavened, and which leads into sobriety, gravity, and godly fear; in which, as we abide, the blessing of the

Lord is felt to attend us in those actions in which we are necessarily engaged, in order to the taking care for the sustenance of the outward man.

MENNONITE CONFESSION OF FAITH

The Mennonites are perhaps the least known descendants of the Free Church movement on the continent, more commonly called the Anabaptists. Yet their influence on world Protestantism has been immense, and in the United States their courageous stand on religious liberty (as regards parental rights to educate their children) is only now making juridical history.

Until very recently Mennonite theology was crystallized in the Confession of Dortrecht (Holland), formulated in 1632 and generally accepted throughout the world.

In 1963, however, the Mennonite General Conference adopted a new confession of faith. It represents the first major revision of doctrinal teaching since 1725, when the Dortrecht statement was officially accepted by the Pennsylvania Mennonites. There was an interim document in 1921, but nothing like the present declaration of faith and practice which restates "the doctrinal position of the church in terms relevant to today's issues" and incorporates the insights of several decades of dogmatic pronouncements by the Mennonite General Conference. It is, in a true sense, the Mennonite counterpart of the Second Vatican Council's Constitution on the Church.

The Mennonite Church, begun in Switzerland in 1525, was a part of the Reformation which attempted to restore the New Testament church. We conceive the church to be a body of regenerated believers, a fellowship of holy pilgrims baptized upon confession of faith in Christ. As committed believers we seek to follow the way of Christian love and non-resistance, and to live separate from the evil of the world. We earnestly endeavor to make Christian disciples of all the nations.

In its beliefs the Mennonite Church is bound ultimately to the Holy Scriptures, not to any human formulation of doctrine. We regard this present confession as a restatement of the Eighteen Articles adopted at Dortrecht in the Netherlands in 1632 and of the other statements adopted by our church. In this expression of our faith we sincerely accept the lordship of Jesus Christ and the full authority of the written Word of God, the Bible, and seek to promote the unity of the brotherhood, to safe-guard sound doctrine and life, and to serve as a testimony to others.

ARTICLE I. GOD AND HIS ATTRIBUTES

We believe in almighty God, the eternal Spirit who is infinite in His attributes of holiness, love, righteousness, truth, power, goodness, and mercy. This one and only God has revealed Himself as existing eternally as Father, Son, and Holy Spirit.

The Father

We believe that God is the Creator of all things, a God of providence, and the Author of our salvation through Christ. Although He is too great to be comprehended by the human mind, through Christ we can truly know Him. In redeeming love He entered into a covenant relationship with Abraham, later with the people of Israel, and has now made through Christ an eternal covenant in which He offers to the human race the forgiveness of sins and the blessings of divine sonship to those who will repent and believe.

The Son

We believe in Jesus Christ the divine Son of God, who was with the Father from all eternity, who for our salvation took upon Himself human nature, and who by His redemptive death and resurrection conquered the forces of sin and Satan and atoned for the sins of mankind. He was conceived by the Holy Spirit, born of the Virgin Mary, lived a sinless life, and in God's redemptive purpose was crucified. He rose from the dead, ascended into heaven, and now as Lord and Christ at the right hand of the Father intercedes for the saints. He is the Lord and Saviour of all Christian believers, and the coming judge of the living and the dead. We believe in His full deity and full humanity according to the Scriptures.

The Holy Spirit

We believe in the Holy Spirit, who was sent by the Father and the Son to bring to individuals the redemption of Christ. We believe in His personality as set forth in the Scriptures: that He loves, searches, testifies, guides, empowers, and intercedes for the Saints.

ARTICLE II. DIVINE REVELATION

We believe that the God of creation and redemption has revealed Himself and His will for men in the Holy Scriptures, and supremely and finally in His incarnate Son, the Lord Jesus Christ. God's purpose in this revelation is the salvation of all men. Although God's power and deity are revealed in His creation, so that the nations are without excuse, this knowledge of Him cannot save men, for it cannot make Christ known. God revealed Himself in saving word and deed to Israel as recorded in the Old Testament; He fulfilled this revelation of Himself in the word and deed of Christ as recorded in the New Testament. We believe that all Scripture is given by the inspiration of God, that men moved by the Holy Spirit spoke from God. We accept the Scriptures as the authoritative Word of God, and through the Holy Spirit as the infallible Guide to lead men to faith in Christ and to guide them in the life of Christian discipleship.

We believe that the Old Testament and the New Testament together constitute the Word of God, that the Old Covenant was preparatory, that its institutions were temporary in character, and that the New Covenant in Christ is the fulfillment of the Old. We believe that the Old Testament writings are inspired and profitable, and as the divine word of promise are to be interpreted in conjunction with the divine act of fulfillment recorded in the New. Christian doctrine and practice are based upon the whole Word of God, the word of promise of the Old Covenant as fulfilled in the New.

The message of the Bible points to the Lord Jesus Christ. It is to Him that the Scriptures of the Old Testament bear witness, and He is the One whom the Scriptures of the New Testament proclaim. He is the key to the proper understanding of the entire Bible.

ARTICLE III. GOD'S CREATION AND PROVIDENCE

We believe that in the beginning God created all things by His Son, and that all existence is therefore finite and dependent upon God, the Source and End of all things visible and invisible. He created man in His own image, which set man apart from the animal creation. In free will, moral character, superior intellect, and spiritual nature, man bore the image of his Creator.

In His providence God is concerned with the lives of His children, and in everything works for their eternal good. He hears and answers their prayers. By Jesus Christ He upholds the entire creation. He is Sovereign over all things, but He is not the author of sin. He has endowed man with the power of self-determination, and He holds him responsible for his moral choices.

ARTICLE IV. MAN AND HIS SIN

We believe that God created man sinless and holy, and subjected man to a moral test as a means of bringing him to full spiritual maturity. Man yielded, however, to the temptation of Satan and by willful disobedience to God failed to maintain that holy condition in which he had been created. This sin brought depravity and death to the race. Although men are sinners by nature because of Adam's fall, they are not guilty of his sin. Those who perish eternally do so only because of their own sin. The most grievous sin is the stubborn refusal to acknowledge Jesus Christ as Saviour and Lord. As a fallen creature man is self-centered, self-willed, rebellious toward God, unwilling to yield to Christ, unable to break with sin, and under divine judgment.

We believe that children are born with a nature which will manifest itself as sinful as they mature. When they come to know themselves to be responsible to God, they must repent and believe in Christ in order to be saved. Before the age when children are accountable to God, their sins are atoned for through the sacrifice of Christ. Jesus Himself assured us that children are in the kingdom of God.

ARTICLE V. CHRIST, THE SAVIOUR FROM SIN

We believe that there is one Mediator between God and men, the Man Christ Jesus. The purpose of the incarnation of God's eternal Son was to redeem men from sin and death, to destroy the power and works of the devil, and to reconcile men to God. As a prophet, the Lord Jesus not only proclaimed God's Word; He was in His very person the Word of God. As a priest, He Himself was the sacrifice for sin, and now makes intercession with the Father for the saints. As our risen Lord and King He is vested with all authority in heaven and on earth.

In His life the Lord Jesus demonstrated perfectly the will of God. Although tempted in all points as we are, yet He never sinned. Through the shedding of His blood He inaugurated the New Covenant, broke the power of sin for those who exercise faith in Him, and triumphed over Satan. By His resurrection from the dead, Christ accomplished the full justification of those who believe in Him. By faith each believer is united with the risen and glorified Christ, the Lord of glory.

ARTICLE VI. SALVATION BY GRACE THROUGH FAITH

We believe that men are saved, not by character, law, good works, or ceremonies, but by the grace of God. The merits of the death and resurrection of Christ are adequate for the salvation of all men, are offered to all, and are intended for all. Salvation is appropriated by faith in Christ. From all eternity God knew who would be the believers in Christ, and these persons foreknown as believers are elect according to the foreknowledge of God. Those who repent and believe in Christ as Saviour and Lord receive the gift of righteousness, are born again, and are adopted into the family of God. Saving faith involves the giving of the self to Christ, a full surrender of the will, a confident trust in Him, a joyful obedience to His Word as a faithful disciple, and an attitude of love to all men. It is the privilege of every believer to have the assurance of salvation. The God who saves is also able to keep each believer unto a happy end in Christ. As long as the believer lives, he stands in need of the forgiveness, cleansing, and grace of Christ.

ARTICLE VII. THE HOLY SPIRIT AND THE CHRISTIAN LIFE

We believe that Christ as Lord and Saviour does His work through the Holy Spirit. The Holy Spirit convicts of sin. Through the Holy Spirit those who believe are born again. The supreme ministry of the Spirit is to lead men to Christ and His salvation. As Christians yield to Christ and obey His Word, the Holy Spirit transforms them into the spiritual image of Jesus Christ, and enables perseverance in faith and holiness. He empowers them as effective witnesses to Christ and His salvation, fills their hearts with love for all men, and moves them to practice Christian discipleship. The Holy Spirit bestows upon each believer such gifts as He wills for the building up of the body of Christ. The indwelling of the Holy Spirit is God's seal of ownership of the Christian believer. He is God's guarantee that He will also redeem the bodies of believers on the day of Christ.

ARTICLE VIII. THE CHURCH OF CHRIST

Nature

We believe that God's redemptive work in history has led to the establishment of the Christian church. Christ established His church when He poured out His Spirit on the day of Pentecost. In preparation for this church He entered into covenant relationships with Abraham and his seed. Today the spiritual "seed of Abraham" are those who have faith in Christ, the people of God, the body of Christ, composed of believers from all races and nations. The church is the fellowship of those who are in the kingdom of Christ, the assembly of those who believe in Him, the brotherhood of the saints. The church is corporately the dwelling place of God in the Spirit, His holy temple. It is the visible body of those who are Christian disciples. Membership in the church is dependent upon a voluntary response to God's offer of salvation in Christ.

The primary unit of the church is the local assembly of believers. It is in the congregation that the work of teaching, witnessing, and disciplining is carried on. In order to maintain the unity of the church it is Scriptural and profitable for congregational representatives to meet together in conferences. The concern for the welfare of the whole church calls for Spirit-led conferences to assist local congregations in maintaining Biblical standards of faith, conduct, stewardship, and missions. The decisions of such conferences should be respected by the individual congregations and members.

Function

It is the function of the church to demonstrate to the world the will of God, to witness to all men of the saving power and intention of God in Christ, and to make disciples of all the nations. The church seeks to lead all men to the obedience of faith. Believers unite in the church for instruction and nurture, for worship, for inclusion in the witnessing and evangelizing body of Christ, for the observance of the ordinances, for Christian fellowship, and for the discipline of the Word and the Spirit of God. The Spirit leads the church to discover the gifts which He has bestowed upon the members for the building up of the body. The church has the obligation to speak authoritatively on God's will. It shall listen to the Word of God and obey it in the moral and spiritual conflicts of each era of history.

The church is called to be a brotherhood under the lordship of Jesus Christ, a loving fellowship of brethren and sisters who are concerned for the total welfare, both spiritual and material, of one another. This concern results in the attempt to help the erring brother find the right path; it includes sharing generously both financial aid and the word of encouragement, and a willingness to give and receive counsel.

Discipline

We believe that the Lord Jesus has given authority to His church to exercise discipline. The purposes of discipline are to lead each member to full stature in Christ, to restore to full fellowship the members who fall into sin, to clarify for all members the meaning of Christian discipleship, to promote the purity of the church, to warn the weak and immature of the serious character of sin and disobedience to God's Word, and to maintain the good name and witness of the church before the world. In this work the church employs public teaching, private counseling, intercessory prayer, earnest warning and rebuke, and sympathetic encouragement. If disobedience persists, the church may withhold the right to commune until the individual repents. And the church must, with a deep sense of loss, recognize that the one who goes on to full apostasy and spiritual ruin has severed his relation with

Christ and His body. The standard in church discipline is the Word of God as interpreted by the brotherhood. The entire congregation should share in the work of discipline and seek earnestly to win the fallen member.

Ceremonies and Practices

The Lord Jesus and His apostles instituted ordinances for the church to observe permanently as symbols of Christian truths. The apostolic church literally observed them. Among these are baptism with water, the communion of the Lord's Supper, the washing of the saints' feet, the holy kiss, the laying-on of hands in ordination, the veiling of Christian women, the anointing of the sick with oil, and the institution of Christian marriage. When the church observes ordinances as expressions of a heart of faith, divine blessings are received, and a Christian witness is given.

Since the Lord Jesus arose from the dead on the first day of the week, the Christian church, following apostolic precedent, observes the first day of each week in memory of the Lord's resurrection.

The Church and Healing

We believe that the church should exercise a ministry of prayer for those who are in need. Prayer for the sick may be accompanied by a symbolic anointing with oil by the elders of the church. In response to the prayer of faith, and in accordance with His will, God heals in various ways, through the use of the healing arts, or by direct intervention. When healing does not occur, we believe that God's grace is sufficient. The full redemption of the body will come only at the return of Christ.

ARTICLE IX. THE MISSION OF THE CHURCH TO SOCIETY

We believe that Christ has commissioned the church to go into all the world and make disciples of all the nations, baptizing them, and teaching them to observe His commandments. Jesus entrusted to the church the stewardship of the Gospel, and promised the power of the Holy Spirit for the work of evangelism and missions. This ministry of reconciliation is inherent in the very nature of the church. The church is interested not only in the spiritual welfare of men but in their total well-being. Jesus Himself fed the hungry, healed the sick, and had compassion on the poor. The church should likewise minister to those who are in physical or social need and to those who are physically or emotionally ill. The church should witness against racial discrimination, economic injustice, and all forms of human slavery and moral degradation.

ARTICLE X. THE MINISTERS OF THE CHURCH

We believe that it is the intention of Christ that there should be shepherds in His congregations to feed the flock, to serve as leaders, to expound the Word of God, to administer the ordinances, to exercise, in co-operation with the congregation, a Scriptural church discipline, and in general to function as servants of the church. Ordination is accompanied by a laying-on of hands, symbolic of the church assigning responsibility and of God imparting strength for the assignment. In addition to the primary office of apostle, in the New Testament church there were such gifts as prophets, evangelists, pastors, and teachers. The early church had regional overseers such as Timothy, and bishops (pastors) and deacons in the local congregations. Upon the pastors lay the responsibility for the leadership and pastoral care of the congregations, and the deacons served as their helpers. In each era of the life of the church, Christ through His Spirit seeks to lead the church to adapt its organization to the needs of time and place. The church is a brotherhood, and its organizational structure should insure the full participation of the members with their spiritual gifts in its life and discipline. It is the duty of the church to give financial support to those whom it asks to serve as evangelists, pastors, and teachers.

ARTICLE XI. CHRISTIAN BAPTISM

We believe in obeying the instruction of the Lord Jesus to baptize believers with water in the name of the Father and of the Son and of the Holy Spirit. In order to qualify for baptism one must repent, turn to Christ in sincere faith, and accept Him as Lord. We regard water baptism as an ordinance of Christ which symbolizes the baptism of the Holy Spirit, divine cleansing from sin and its guilt, identification with Christ in His death and resurrection, and the commitment to follow Him in a life of faithful discipleship. Since baptism with the Holy Spirit is a pouring out, we generally practice pouring as our mode of water baptism.

ARTICLE XII. THE LORD'S SUPPER

We believe in observing the communion of the Lord's Supper as an ordinance instituted by Jesus Christ to symbolize the New Covenant. We recognize the bread and the cup as symbols commemorating Christ's broken body and shed blood, of our spiritual life in Him, and of the spiritual unity and fellowship of the body of Christ. Each believer shall examine himself so as not to partake of the sacred emblems carelessly or while living in sin. The church shall invite to the Lord's table only those who have peace with God and with their fellow men, and who share the faith of the church. The Lord's Supper shall be observed faithfully until the Lord comes.

ARTICLE XIII. SYMBOLS OF CHRISTIAN BROTHERHOOD

We believe in the observance of the washing of the saints' feet as an ordinance instituted by the Lord Jesus. By His example Christ rebuked the pride and rivalry of the apostles and showed them that Christian discipleship involves obedience to His lordship and loving service. This ordinance reminds us of the brotherhood character of the church, of our mutual duty to serve and admonish one another, and of our need for continuous cleansing in our daily walk. In the New Testament the holy kiss and the right hand of fellowship are also symbols of Christian love in the church of Christ.

ARTICLE XIV. SYMBOLS OF CHRISTIAN ORDER

We believe that in their relation to the Lord men and women are equal, for in Christ there is neither male nor female. But in the order of creation God has fitted man and woman for differing functions; man has been given a primary leadership role, while the woman is especially fitted for nurture and service. Being in Christ does not nullify these natural endowments, either in the home or in the church. The New Testament symbols of man's headship are to be his short hair and uncovered head while praying or prophesying, and the symbols of woman's role are her long hair and her veiled head. The acceptance by both men and women of the order of creation in no way limits their rightful freedom, but rather ensures their finding the respective role in which they can most fruitfully and happily serve.

ARTICLE XV. MARRIAGE AND THE HOME

We believe that at the beginning of human history God instituted marriage. He ordained that a man shall leave his father and mother and cleave to his wife, and that the two shall become one in love and mutual submission. It is God's will that marriage be a holy state, monogamous, and for life. It is also fully acceptable to God to serve Christ unmarried. Marriage was instituted for the happiness of the husband and wife and for the procreation and Christian nurture of children. Christians shall marry only in the Lord, and for the sake of spiritual unity in the home they should become members of the same congregation. The Christian home ought regularly to have family worship, to seek faithfully to live according to the Word of God, and to support loyally the church in its mission. We believe it is appropriate for parents to pledge themselves to the faithful Christian nurture of their children.

ARTICLE XVI. DISCIPLESHIP AND NONCONFORMITY

We believe that there are two opposing kingdoms to which men give their spiritual allegiance, that of Christ and that of Satan. Those who belong to Satan's kingdom live for sin and self, and refuse the obedience of faith. The kingdom of Christ is composed of those who have been born again and who have entered into a faith union with the Lord Jesus Christ. In them the fruit of the Spirit is in evidence. They recognize the lordship of Christ, and perform all manner of good works. They seek for holiness of heart, life, and speech, and refuse any unequal yoke with unbelievers. They manifest only love towards those of other races, cultures, and economic levels. They regard their bodies as temples of the Holy Spirit and crucify their flesh with its affections and lusts. They therefore avoid such things as harmful drugs, beverage alcohol, and tobacco. We believe that their adornment should be a beauty of spirit, expressed in attire that is modest, economical, simple, and becoming to those professing Christian faith. They should seek to be Christian in their stewardship of money and possessions. Their recreational life should be consistent with the Christian walk. Through the Spirit they should put off the old man and put on the new.

ARTICLE XVII. CHRISTIAN INTEGRITY

We believe that it is a major Christian obligation to be strictly truthful and transparent in life and doctrine, with no secrecy or hypocrisy. The Lord Jesus Christ has forbidden to His followers the use of any and all oaths, because of the finite limitations of human beings, and the obligation always to speak the truth. In legal matters we therefore simply affirm the truth. We are opposed to membership in secret societies or lodges, because such membership would involve an unequal yoke with unbelievers, and because these organizations employ hierarchical titles, require oaths, stand for organized secrecy, and may offer salvation on grounds other than faith in the Lord Jesus Christ. We believe that it is in the church that we should find love, fellowship, and security.

ARTICLE XVIII. LOVE AND NONRESISTANCE

We believe that it is the will of God for His children to follow Christian love in all human relationships. Such a life of love excludes retaliation and revenge. God pours His love into the hearts of Christians so that they desire the welfare of all men. The supreme example of nonresistance is the Lord Jesus Himself. The teaching of Jesus not to resist him who is evil requires the renunciation by His disciples of all violence in human relations. Only love must be shown to all men. We believe that this applies to every area of life: to personal injustice, to situations in which people commonly resort to litigation, to industrial strife, and to international tensions and wars. As nonresistant Christians we cannot serve in any office which employs the use of force. Nor can we participate in military service, or in military training, or in the voluntary financial support of war. But we must aggressively, at the risk of life itself, do whatever we can for the alleviation of human distress and suffering.

ARTICLE XIX. THE CHRISTIAN AND THE STATE

We believe that the state is ordained of God to maintain law and order. We seek to obey the New Testament commands to render honor to the authorities, to pay our taxes, to obey all laws which do not conflict with the higher law of God, and to pray for our rulers. The church should also witness to the authorities of God's redeeming love in Christ, and of His sovereignty over all men. In law enforcement the state does not and cannot operate on the nonresistant principles of Christ's kingdom. Therefore, nonresistant Christians cannot undertake any service in the state or in society which would violate the principles of love and holiness as taught by Christ and His inspired apostles.

ARTICLE XX. THE FINAL CONSUMMATION

We believe that in addition to the physical order with which our senses are related, there also exists an eternal spiritual order, the realm of God, of Christ, of the Holy Spirit, of the angels, and of the church triumphant. We believe that at death the righteous enter at once into conscious joy and fellowship with Christ, while the wicked are in a state of conscious suffering. The church militant lives and witnesses in this present evil world, a world in which apostasy from God is to become even more pronounced. The church also looks forward with hope to the day of the Lord, to the personal return of Christ, and the glorious future of the kingdom of God. In His triumphant Second Coming Christ will judge Satan, and usher in the consummation of all things. His coming will introduce the resurrection, the transformation of the living saints, the judgment of the just and the unjust, and the fulfillment of His glorious reign. He will deliver the kingdom to God the Father, cleanse the world by fire, create new heavens and a new earth, consign unbelievers to eternal punishment, and usher His children into the eternal bliss of the world to come.

May God enable us all to attain His eternal kingdom prepared for us from the foundation of the world, that with His blessed Son we may enjoy fullness of life for ever and ever.

CHURCH OF THE BRETHREN
DENOMINATIONAL STATEMENT

The Church of the Brethren began in 1708 when their society was founded in Schwarzenau, Germany. In 1719 Peter Becker brought a group of the Brethren to America to settle in the free lands offered them by the Quaker, William Penn. Their first American foundation was at Germantown, Pennsylvania, where they were joined in 1729 by Alexander Mack, the patriarch of Brethrenism in the United States.

Given the openness that characterized the Brethren from the beginnings of their history, it is not surprising that they have suffered more than most other churches in the Anabaptist tradition from schisms and departures from their ranks. In 1728 a group under Conrad Beissel left the parent body to start the Seventh Day Baptists; in 1848 another group left to form the Church of God (New Dunkers); in 1881 still another schism resulted in the origins of the Old German Baptist Brethren (Old Order Dunkers); a year later came the worst split in their history, when the Brethren Church (Progressive Brethren) came into being; and in 1926 a body of conversatives departed for the opposite reason, to establish the Dunkard Brethren Church.

The original denomination has nevertheless prospered, and has entered more actively into the ecumenical movement than any other group of like size in the Free Church affiliation. Unlike other churches with the same history, the Church of the Brethren has not yet adopted a formal confessional statement with binding authority on its membership. Yet leading spokesmen in the church have at various times expressed what the denomination considers an authentic understanding of Brethren faith and polity. The most representative (and authoritative) was presented in 1950 as a position document for the theological commission of the World Council of Churches.

I. Christ founded the Church in the sense that He created a fellowship of men and women who had attached themselves to Him in faith, and this fellowship was perpetuated in the historical Church. He commissioned them to carry on the work of proclaiming the Gospel, and He empowered them for the task by giving them the Spirit. Though He thought of the Church as primarily a spiritual organism, He was not unmindful of certain outward aspects of its corporate life. In the appointment of the Twelve He contemplated activities beyond His lifetime and certain of His instructions had to do with this later period. He also instituted two sacraments.

II. The Brethren do not hold that one form of organisation is right to the exclusion of all others, but they have always insisted that their own organisation be simple, attempting to preserve the spirit of humility and service which marked the leadership of the Early Church. The only permanent officials are elders, ministers, and deacons, who are elected by the several congregations, and are inducted into office by the laying-on of hands. In the case of elders, this ceremony is called ordination. The polity of the Brethren tends to the Congregational type. There is a general conference, but its decisions are regarded as advisory rather than mandatory.

III. The Church is the fellowship of the 'Saints', attached by bonds of devotion to their Lord and to one another. This fellowship exhibits a spirit of mutual respect which abolishes distinctions based on wealth, class or cultural advantage. Membership in the Church is based on the individual's faith in Christ as Saviour and Lord, repentance from sin, and Baptism, and is marked by devotion, purity of life and service. In a broader sense, the Church includes the people of the Old Covenant who have fulfilled its conditions. The Church looks forward to its fulfillment in 'heaven'; the 'invisible Church' includes all who 'die in the Lord'. The Church as a close-knit community has authority on earth from Christ to admit to its membership and to exclude from it.

IV. Christ is the Lord of the Church, in that He founded it and is the source of its life. The attitude of the Church to Him is one of faith and obedience; faith in Him as Lord and Saviour, obedience to His commandments. The Church is more than a 'voluntary association'; although men enter the Church by their own choice, the impulse comes through the Holy Spirit, and thus, the whole process is a work of grace.

The term 'continuation of the incarnation' is not a familiar phrase among the Brethren. Certainly the Church carries on the work of evangelism which Christ began, but it is only the channel of His redemptive power, and the authority does not pass to the Church but remains in Him.

V. The message of the Church is Jesus Christ, the perfect revelation of God to the world. It is a gospel of God's redemptive grace, offered to all men in their sins, an offer of pardon and of acceptance into the family of God. The mission of the Church is to proclaim this message, a message of judgment and of salvation. The spoken message is to be reinforced by the influence of lives of purity and service, promoting the Kingdom of God in every area of human life with all the spiritual resources of the Church.

VI. (a) There is a line of cleavage between the Church and the world, based on the spiritual nature and higher ethics of the Church. Yet the world is the object of the concern of the Church. Christ commands His Church to make disciples of all the nations; His followers have caught something of His compassion for the lost, and desire to share their blessings with those who are outside. Though the Church is not of the world, it is ever seeking to win the world.

(b) In the matter of Church and State, the Brethren have regarded the State as 'having been ordained of God'. The State has its separate function, to set up and enforce regulations in the economic, political, and material spheres of life. On the other hand, due to its insistence on separation of Church and State, and partly due to the influence of its pietistic background, the Brethren Church has, in the past, stood against participation in political matters, even advising against voting. As a pacifist Church throughout its history it has had to resist the demands of the State to support war. But it attempts to create character in its membership which makes for good citizenship and thus promotes in society those agencies which conserve human values.

(c) With regard to the Church and the Kingdom of God, the Church is both the end and the means. The spiritual values of the Kingdom begin to be realised in the Church, and in turn the Church is the means toward the realisation of the Kingdom in its ultimate fullness.

VII. The Brethren believe that the maintenance of the 'continuity of the true Church of Christ' is a spiritual process. Though they cannot claim 'apostolic succession' as understood by the Roman Church, they do claim that they are in the line of the successors of the apostles by preaching the Word and administering the sacraments. But this succession is not through the ordained ministry but through the brotherhood of believers in Christ, of which the ministers are the servants.

VIII. The Brethren have turned from the isolation which marked their history after the Revolutionary War to a larger participation in community life, and to more cordial relations with other denominations. They have revived an earlier interest in education, both secular and theological. The membership is no longer wholly rural. The Church is moving toward a paid and educated ministry. The Brethren stress less than formerly the control of the individual conscience by the Church, attempting to secure character and growth through fostering a spirit of devotion to Christ and the Church. They implemented their peace testimony in the last war by taking an active part in the promotion of Civilian Public Service for all conscientious objectors.

IX. The Brethren have never claimed to possess Christian virtues above their fellow denominations. They share a common faith in Christ, a common responsibility to preach the Gospel, a common hope. While attempting to hold to a balanced program, there are certain special emphases which they hold as a heritage. They insist that trine immersion on confession of faith is in accord with the practice of the Early Church. They are a people of the Book, interpreting it rather literally. This is shown in their refusal to take the oath, and in their upholding of pacifism. They practise foot washing and the anointing of the sick with oil. They have always stressed the importance of wholesome family life and have opposed divorce except on scriptural grounds. They have been marked for their close community spirit and their emphasis on the simple, yet withal the good life.

We of the Brethren Church are coming to feel the need of a more cooperative fellowship with other communions. We need to give more attention to worship, and to cultivate the aesthetic in our corporate church life. We have neglected the formulation of our doctrinal beliefs and would do well to clarify our thinking and teaching in the field of Christian doctrine.

PART TWO

CHURCHES OF
AMERICAN ORIGIN

PART TWO

CHURCHES OF
AMERICAN ORIGIN

It would have been strange if a nation like the United States, with its heritage of freedom, had not given birth to new religious movements. In fact the number and variety of distinctively American religious creations is unique in Western Christianity.

Historians point out that the principle of religious liberty granted by the American Constitution subtly predisposed the people to assume that the formation of a new church was not only legally irreproachable but could be religiously approved. What is certain is the rise of church bodies that somehow had their roots in the Reformation but that, for all practical purposes, were native products that came into full being on American soil.

There is no easy way of deciding what constitutes a native American religion, since every denomination in the country may be called American at least by reason of geographical distinction. A workable norm might include one or more of several factors: native origin of its founder, positive reaction against its European ancestry, and (hardest to define) characteristic American features of its teaching and polity.

Even to classify all the sectarian groups that rise and disappear in the United States is impossible. And for our purpose it is not necessary. Less than fifteen of these indigenous American religions are sufficiently large or influential to deserve special consideration in this volume.

7. *Unitarianism*

Although Unitarianism as a denial of the Trinity may be found in the first century of the Christian era, the actual beginnings of a denomination by that name go back less than two hundred years.

Historically the origins of Unitarianism can be traced to the liberal reaction against Calvinism as understood by the Congregational churches in colonial New England. Under the influence of deistic ideas imported from England, liberal-minded Congregationalists began publicly to preach doctrines that contradicted the Calvinist elements in their church's confession.

Born as a secessionist movement in the Congregational Church, American Unitarianism took root as early as 1802, when the oldest Pilgrim Church, founded at Plymouth in 1620, became Unitarian. Within a short time, twenty out of the original twenty-five churches in Massachusetts became Unitarian.

Two landmarks in Unitarian history which laid down the principles for future development were the Baltimore Sermon in 1819 of William Ellery Channing, outstanding Congregational preacher, and the address delivered by Ralph Waldo Emerson at the graduation exercises of Harvard Divinity School in 1838.

Channing had graduated from Harvard, became regent there, and was appointed pastor of the Congregational Church in Boston in 1803. During the schism between the liberals and conservatives, he sided with the former until gradually he came to espouse fully the idea that the Trinity, Atonement and Total Depravity had no biblical foundation. What gave Channing such weight was the stress he placed on equating the Calvinism against which he reacted with the supernaturalism of Christianity as a whole. Kindred spirits who were uncomfortable with Total Depravity and Absolute Predestination accepted Channing's naturalism as the price of rejecting Calvinism.

321

Among the converts to Unitarianism that Channing attracted to "rational Christianity," undoubtedly the most famous was Thomas Jefferson, then living at Monticello. His letter to a friend, Timothy Pickering, is part of Unitarian history and sheds considerable light on the status of religion in the first generation of the new republic; it also helps to explain what Unitarianism had to offer a critical mind that was dissatisfied with traditional Protestantism. Jefferson's second letter, to Benjamin Waterhouse, is equally revealing, and accounts for the fact that the author of the Declaration of Independence is commonly regarded by modern Unitarians as one of the co-founders of their religion, along with Channing and Emerson.

WILLIAM ELLERY CHANNING
BALTIMORE SERMON OF 1819

There are two natural divisions under which my thoughts will be arranged. I shall endeavour to unfold: 1st, The principles which we adopt in interpreting the Scriptures. And 2dly, Some of the doctrines, which the Scriptures, so interpreted, seem to us clearly to express.

I. We regard the Scriptures as the records of God's successive revelations to mankind, and particularly of the last and most perfect revelation of his will by Jesus Christ. Whatever doctrines seem to us to be clearly taught in the Scriptures, we receive without reserve or exemption. We do not, however, attach equal importance to all the books in this collection. Our religion, we believe, lies chiefly in the New Testament. The dispensation of Moses, compared with that of Jesus, we consider as adapted to the childhood of the human race, a preparation for a nobler system, and chiefly useful now as serving to confirm and illustrate the Christian Scriptures. Jesus Christ is the only master of Christians, and whatever he taught, either during his personal ministry, or by his inspired apostles, we regard as of divine authority, and profess to make the rule of our lives. . . .

Our leading principle in interpreting Scripture is this, that the Bible is a book written for men, in the language of men, and that its meaning is to be sought in the same manner, as that of other books. We believe that God, when he speaks to the human race, conforms, if we may so say, to the established rules of speaking and writing. How else would the Scriptures avail us more, than if communicated in an unknown tongue?

Now all books, and all conversation, require in the reader or hearer the constant exercise of reason; or their true import is only to be obtained by continual comparison and inference. Human language, you very well know, admits various interpretations; and every word and every sentence must be modified and explained according to the subject which is discussed, according to the purposes, feelings, circumstances and principles of the writer, and according to the genius and idioms of the language which he uses. These are acknowledged principles in the interpretation of human writings; and a man, whose words we should explain without reference to these principles, would reproach us justly with a criminal want of candor, and an intention of obscuring or distorting his meaning. . . .

Enough has been said to show, in what sense we make use of reason in interpreting Scripture. From a variety of possible interpretations, we select that, which accords with the nature of the subject and the state of the writer, with the connexion of the passage, with the general strain of Scripture, with the known character and will of God, and with the obvious and acknowledged laws of nature. In other words, we believe that God never contradicts, in one part of Scripture, what he teaches in another; and never contradicts, in revelation, what he teaches in his works and providence. And we, therefore, distrust every interpretation, which, after deliberate attention, seems repugnant to any established truth. We reason about the Bible precisely as civilians do about the constitution under which we live; who, you know, are accustomed to limit one provision of that venerable instrument by others, and to fix the precise import of its parts, by inquiring into its general spirit, into the intentions of its authors, and into the prevalent feelings, impressions, and circumstances of the time when it was framed. Without these principles of interpretation, we frankly acknowledge, that we cannot defend the divine authority of the Scriptures. Deny us this latitude, and we must abandon this book to its enemies.

We do not announce these principles as original, or peculiar to ourselves. All Christians occasionally adopt them, not excepting those, who most vehemently decry them, when they happen to menace some favorite article of their creed. All Christians are compelled to use them in their controversies with infidels. All sects employ them in their warfare with one another. All willingly avail themselves of reason, when it can be pressed into the service of their own party, and only complain of it, when its weapons wound themselves. None reason more frequently than those from whom we differ. It is astonishing what a fabric they rear from a few slight hints about the fall of our first parents; and how ingeniously they extract, from detached passages, mysterious doctrines about the divine nature. We do not blame them for reasoning so abundantly, but for violating the fundamental rules of reasoning, for sacrificing the plain to the obscure, and the general strain of Scripture to a scanty number of insulated texts.

We object strongly to the contemptuous manner in which human reason is often spoken of by our adversaries, because it leads, we believe, to universal scepticism. If reason be so dreadfully darkened by the fall, then its most decisive judgments on religion are unworthy of trust, then Christianity, and even naturally theology, must be abandoned; for the existence and veracity of God, and the divine original of Christianity, are conclusions of reason, and must stand or fall with it. If revelation be at war with this faculty, it subverts itself, for the great question of its truth is left by God to be decided at the bar of reason. . . .

II. Having thus stated the principles according to which we interpret Scripture, I now proceed to the second great head of this discourse, which is, to state some of the views, which we derive from that sacred book, particularly those which distinguish us from other Christians.

1. In the first place, we believe in the doctrine of GOD'S UNITY, or that there is one God, and one only. To this truth we give infinite importance, and we feel ourselves bound to take heed, lest any man spoil us of it by vain philosophy. The proposition, that there is one God, seems to us exceedingly plain. We understand by it, that there is one being, one mind, one person, one intelligent agent, and one only, to whom underived and infinite perfection and dominion belong. We conceive, that these words could have conveyed no other meaning to the simple and uncultivated people, who were set apart to be the depositaries of this great truth, and who were utterly incapable of understanding those hair-breadth distinctions between being and person, which the sagacity of latter ages has discovered. We find no intimation, that this language was to be taken in an unusual sense, or that God's unity was a different thing from the oneness of other intelligent beings.

We object to the doctrine of the Trinity, that whilst acknowledging in words, it subverts in effect, the unity of God. According to this doctrine, there are three infinite and equal persons, possessing supreme divinity, called the Father, Son, and Holy Ghost. Each of these persons, as described by theologians, has his own particular consciousness, will, and perceptions. They love each other, converse with each other, and delight in each other's society. They perform different parts in man's redemption, each having his appropriate office, and neither doing the work of the other. The Son is mediator and not the Father. The Father sends the Son, and is not himself sent; nor is he conscious, like the Son, of taking flesh. Here then, we have three intelligent agents, possessed of different consciousnesses, different wills, and different perceptions, performing different acts, and sustaining different relations; and if these things do not imply and constitute three minds or beings, we are utterly at a loss to know how three minds or beings are to be formed. It is difference of properties, acts, and consciousness, which leads us to the belief of different intelligent beings, and if this mark fails us, our whole knowledge falls; we have no proof, that all the agents and persons in the universe are not one and the same mind. When we attempt to conceive of three Gods, we can do nothing more, than represent to ourselves three agents, distinguished from each other by similar marks and peculiarities to those, which separate the persons of the trinity; and when common Christians hear these persons spoken of as conversing with each other, loving each other, and performing different acts, how can they help regarding them as different beings, different minds? . . . .

This doctrine, were it true, must, from its difficulty, singularity, and importance, have been laid down with great clearness, guarded with great care, and stated with all possible precision. But where does this statement appear? From the many passages which treat of God, we ask for one, one only, in which we are told, that he is a threefold being, or, that he is three persons, or that he is Father, Son, and Holy Ghost. On the contrary in the New Testament, where, at least, we might expect many express assertions of this nature, God is declared to be one, without the least attempt to prevent the acceptation of the words in their common sense; and he is always spoken of and addressed in the singular number, that is, in language which was universally understood to intend a single person, and to which no other idea could have been attached, without an express admonition. So entirely do the Scriptures abstain from stating the trinity, that when our opponents would insert it into their creeds and doxologies, they are compelled to leave the bible, and to invent forms of words altogether unsanctioned by scriptural phraseology.

2. Having thus given our views of the unity of God, I proceed in the second place to observe, that we believe in the unity of Jesus Christ. We believe that Jesus is one mind, one soul, one being, as truly one as we are, and equally distinct from the one God. We complain of the doctrine of the trinity, that not satisfied with making God three beings, it makes Jesus Christ two beings, and thus introduces infinite confusion

into our conception of his character. This corruption of Christianity, alike repugnant to common sense, and to the general strain of scripture, is a remarkable proof of the power of a false philosophy in disfiguring the simple truth of Jesus.

According to this doctrine, Jesus Christ, instead of being one mind, one conscious intelligent principle, whom we can understand, consists of two souls, two minds; the one divine, the other human; the one weak, the other almighty; the one ignorant, the one omniscient. Now we maintain, that this is to make Christ two beings. To denominate him one person, one being, and yet to suppose him made up of two minds, infinitely different from each other, is to abuse and confound language, and to throw darkness over all our conceptions of intelligent natures. According to the common doctrine, each of these two minds in Christ has its own consciousness, its own will, its own perceptions. They have in fact no common properties. The divine mind feels none of the wants and sorrows of the human, and the human is infinitely removed from the perfection and happiness of the divine. Can you conceive of two beings in the universe more distinct? We have always thought that one person was constituted and distinguished by one consciousness. The doctrine, that one, and the same person should have two consciousnesses, two wills, two souls, infinitely different from each other, this we think an enormous tax on human credulity. . . .

Trinitarians profess to derive some important advantages from their mode of viewing Christ. It furnishes them, they tell us, with an infinite atonement, for it shows them an infinite being, suffering for their sins. The confidence with which this fallacy is repeated astonishes us. When pressed with the question, whether they really believe, that the infinite and unchangeable God suffered and died on the cross, they acknowledge that this is not true, but that Christ's human mind alone sustained the pains of death. How have we then an infinite sufferer? This language seems to us an imposition on common minds, and very derogatory to God's justice, as if this attribute could be satisfied by a sophism and a fiction.

We are also told, that Christ is a more interesting object, that his love and mercy are more felt, when he is viewed as the Supreme God, who left his glory to take humanity and to suffer for men. That Trinitarians are strongly moved by this representation, we do not mean to deny; but we think their emotions altogether founded on a misapprehension of their own doctrines. They talk of the second person of the trinity's leaving his glory and his Father's bosom, to visit and save the world. But this second person, being the unchangeable and infinite

God, was evidently incapable of parting with the least degree of his perfection and felicity. At the moment of his taking flesh, he was as intimately present with his Father as before, and equally with his Father filled heaven, and earth, and immensity. This Trinitarians acknowledge; and still they profess to be touched and overwhelmed by the amazing humiliation of this immutable being! But not only does their doctrine, when fully explained, reduce Christ's humiliation to a fiction, it almost wholly destroys the impressions with which his cross ought to be viewed. According to their doctrine, Christ was, comparatively, no sufferer at all. It is true, his human mind suffered; but this, they tell us, was an infinitely small part of Jesus, bearing no more proportion to his whole nature, than a single hair of our heads to the whole body, or than a drop to the ocean. The divine mind of Christ, that which was most properly himself, was infinitely happy, at the very moment of the suffering of his humanity. Whilst hanging on the cross, he was the happiest being in the universe, as happy as the infinite Father; so that his pains, compared with his felicity, were nothing. This Trinitarians do, and must acknowledge. It follows necessarily from the immutableness of the divine nature, which they ascribe to Christ; so that their system, just viewed, robs his death of interest, weakens our sympathy with his sufferings, and is, of all others most unfavorable to a love of Christ, founded on a sense of his sacrifices for mankind. We esteem our own views to be vastly more affecting. It is our belief, that Christ's humiliation was real and entire, that the whole Saviour, and not a part of him, suffered, that his crucifixion was a scene of deep and unmixed agony. As we stand round his cross, our minds are not distracted, nor our sensibility weakened, by contemplating him as composed of incongruous and infinitely differing minds, and as having a balance of infinite felicity. We recognize in the dying Jesus but one mind. This, we think renders his sufferings, and his patience and love in bearing them, incomparably more impressive and affecting, than the system we oppose.

3. Having thus given our belief on two great points, namely, that there is one God, and that Jesus Christ is a being distinct from, and inferior to God, I now proceed to another point on which we lay still greater stress. We believe in the *moral perfection of God*. We consider no part of theology so important as that which treats of God's moral character; and we value our views of Christianity chiefly, as they assert his amiable and venerable attributes. . . .

We believe that God is infinitely good, kind, benevolent, in the proper sense of these words; good in disposition, as well as in act;

good, not to a few, but to all; good to every individual, as well as to the general system.

We believe, too, that God is just; but we never forget, that his justice is the justice of a good being, dwelling in the same mind, and acting in harmony with perfect benevolence. . . .

To give our views of God, in one word, we believe in his Parental character. We ascribe to him, not only the name, but the dispositions and principles of a father. We believe that he has a father's concern for his creatures, a father's desire for their improvement, a father's equity in proportioning his commands to their powers, a father's joy in their progress, a father's readiness to receive the penitent, and a father's justice for the incorrigible. We look upon this world as a place of education, in which he is training men by prosperity and adversity, by aids and obstructions, by conflicts of reason and passion, by motives to duty and temptations to sin, by a various discipline suited to free and moral beings, for union with himself, and for a sublime and ever growing virtue in heaven.

Now we object to the systems of religion, which prevail among us, that they are adverse, in a greater or less degree, to these purifying, comforting, and honorable views of God, that they take from us our Father in heaven, and substitute for him a being, whom we cannot love if we would, and whom we ought not to love if we could. We object, particularly on this ground, to that system, which arrogates to itself the name of Orthodoxy, and which is now industriously propagated through our country. This system indeed takes various shapes, but in all it casts dishonor on the Creator. According to its old and genuine form, it teaches, that God brings us into life wholly depraved, so that under the innocent features of our childhood, is hidden a nature averse to all good and propense to all evil, a nature, which exposes us to God's displeasure and wrath, even before we have acquired power to understand our duties, or to reflect upon our actions. According to a more modern exposition, it teaches, that we came from the hands of our Maker with such a constitution and are placed under such influences and circumstances, as to render certain and infallible the total depravity of every human being, from the first moment of his moral agency; and it also teaches, that the offence of the child, who brings into life this ceaseless tendency to unmingled crime, exposes him to the sentence of everlasting damnation. Now, according to the plainest principles of morality, we maintain, that a natural constitution of the mind, unfailingly disposing it to evil and to evil alone, would absolve it from guilt; that to give existence under this condition would argue unspeakable cruelty, and that to punish the sin of this unhappily constituted child with endless ruin, would be a wrong unparalleled by the most merciless despotism.

This system also teaches, that God selects from this corrupt mass a number to be saved, and plucks them, by a special influence, from the common ruin; that the rest of mankind, though left without that special grace which their conversion requires, are commanded to repent under penalty of aggravated woe; and that forgiveness is promised them on terms, which their very constitution infallibly disposes them to reject, and in rejecting which they awfully enhance the punishments of hell. These proffers of forgiveness and exhortations of amendment, to beings born under a blighting curse, fill our minds with a horror, which we want words to express. . . .

The false and dishonorable views of God, which have now been stated, we feel ourselves bound to resist unceasingly. Other errors we can pass over with comparative indifference. But we ask our opponents to leave to us a GOD, worthy of our love and trust, in whom our moral sentiments may delight, in whom our weakness and sorrows may find refuge. We cling to the divine perfections. We meet them everywhere in creation, we read them in the scriptures, we see a lovely image of them in Jesus Christ; and gratitude, love and veneration call on us to assert them. Reproached, as we often are, by men, it is our consolation and happiness, that one of our chief offences is the zeal with which we vindicate the dishonored goodness and rectitude of God.

4. Having thus spoken of the unity of God; of the unity of Jesus, and his inferiority to God; and of the perfections of the divine character; I now proceed to give our views of the mediation of Christ and of the purposes of his mission. With regard to the great object, which Jesus came to accomplish, there seems to be no possibility of mistake. We believe, that he was sent by the Father to effect a moral, or spiritual deliverance of mankind; that is, to rescue men from sin and its consequences, and to bring them to a state of everlasting purity and happiness. We believe, too, that he accomplishes this sublime purpose by a variety of methods; by his instructions respecting God's unity, parental character, and moral government, which are admirably fitted to reclaim the world from idolatry and impiety, to the knowledge, love, and obedience of the Creator; by his promise of pardon to the penitent, and of divine assistance to those, who labor for progress in moral excellence; by the light which he has thrown on the path of duty; by his own spotless example, in which the loveliness and sublimity of virtue shines forth to warm and quicken, as well as guide us to perfec-

tion; by his threatenings against incorrigible guilt; by his glorious dis-coveries of immortality; by his sufferings and death; by that signal event, the resurrection, which powerfully bore witness to his divine mission, and brought down to men's senses a future life; by his con-tinual intercession, which obtains for us spiritual aid and blessings; and by the power with which he is invested of raising the dead, judging the world, and conferring the everlasting rewards, promised to the faithful.

We have no desire to conceal the fact, that a difference of opinion exists among us, in regard to an interesting part of Christ's mediation; I mean, in regard to the precise influence of his death, on our forgive-ness. Many suppose, that this event contributes to our pardon, as it was a principal means of confirming his religion, and of giving it a power over the mind; in other words, that it procures forgiveness by leading to that repentance and virtue, which is the great and only condition on which forgiveness is bestowed. Many of us are dissatisfied with this explanation, and think that the scriptures ascribe the remission of sins to Christ's death, with an emphasis so peculiar, that we ought to con-sider this event as having a special influence in removing punishment, though the scriptures may not reveal the way, in which it contributes to this end.

Whilst, however, we differ in explaining the connexion between Christ's death and human forgiveness, a connexion, which we all grate-fully acknowledge, we agree in rejecting many sentiments, which pre-vail in regard to his mediation. The idea, which is conveyed to common minds by the popular system, that Christ's death has an influence in making God placable or merciful, in awakening his kindness toward men, we reject with strong disapprobation. . . . We earnestly maintain, that Jesus, instead of calling forth in any way or degree, the mercy of the Father, was sent by that mercy, to be our Saviour; that he is noth-ing to the human race, but what he is by God's appointment; that he communicates nothing but what God empowers him to bestow; that our Father in heaven is originally, essentially and eternally placable, and disposed to forgive; and that his unborrowed, underived, and un-changeable love, is the only fountain of what flows to us through his Son. . . .

We believe too, that this system is unfavorable to the character. It naturally leads men to think, that Christ came to change God's mind, rather than their own; that the highest object of his mission, was to avert punishment, rather than to communicate holiness; and that a large part of religion consists in disparaging good works and human virtue, for the purpose of magnifying the value of Christ's vicarious sufferings. In this way, a sense of the infinite importance and indispensable necessity of personal improvement is weakened, and high sounding praises of Christ's cross seem often to be substituted for obedience to his precepts. For ourselves, we have not so learned Jesus. Whilst we gratefully acknowledge, that he came to rescue us from punishment, we believe, that he was sent on a still nobler errand, namely, to deliver us from sin itself, and to form us to a sublime and heavenly virtue. We regard him as a Saviour, chiefly as he is the light, physician, and guide of the dark, diseased, and wandering mind. . . .

5. Having thus stated our views of the highest object of Christ's mission, that it is the recovery of men to virtue, or holiness, I shall now, in the last place, give our views of the nature of christian virtue, or true holiness. We believe that all virtue has its foundation in the moral nature of man, that is, in conscience, or his sense of duty, and in the power of forming his temper and life according to conscience. We believe that these moral faculties are the grounds of responsibility, and the highest distinctions of human nature, and that no act is praiseworthy, any farther than it springs from their exertion. We believe, that no dispositions infused into us without our own moral activity, are of the nature of virtue, and therefore, we reject the doctrine of irresistible divine influence on the human mind, moulding it into goodness, as marble is hewn into a statue. Such goodness, if this word may be used, would not be the object of moral approbation, any more than the instinctive affections of inferior animals, or the constitutional amiableness of human beings. . . .

Among the virtues, we give the first place to the love of God. We believe, that this principle is the true end and happiness of our being, that we were made for union with our Creator, that his infinite perfection is the only sufficient object and true resting place for the insatiable desires and unlimited capacities of the human mind, and that without him, our noblest sentiments, admiration, veneration, hope, and love, would wither and decay. We believe too, that the love of God is not only essential to happiness, but to the strength and perfection of all virtues; that conscience, without the sanction of God's authority and retributive justice, would be a weak director; that benevolence, unless nourished by communion with his goodness, and encouraged by his smile, could not thrive amidst the selfishness and thanklessness of the world; and that self-government, without a sense of the divine inspection, would hardly extend beyond an outward and partial purity. God, as he is essentially goodness, holiness, justice, and virtue, so he is the life, motive and sustainer of virtue in the human soul. . . .

Another important branch of virtue, we believe to be love to Christ. The greatness of the work of Jesus, the spirit with which he executed it, and the sufferings which he bore for our salvation, we feel to be strong claims on our gratitude and veneration. We see in nature no beauty to be compared with the loveliness of his character, nor do we find on earth a benefactor, to whom we owe an equal debt. We read his history with delight, and learn from it the perfection of our nature. We are particularly touched by his death, which was endured for our redemption, and by that strength of charity, which triumphed over his pains. His resurrection is the foundation of our hope of immortality. His intercession gives us boldness to draw nigh to the throne of grace, and we look up to heaven with new desire, when we think, that if we follow him here, we shall there see his benignant countenance and enjoy his friendship forever.

THOMAS JEFFERSON
UNITARIAN PRINCIPLES

To Timothy Pickering, Esquire

Monticello, February 27, 1821

I have received, Sir, your favor of the 12th, and I assure you I received it with pleasure. It is true, as you say, that we have differed in political opinions; but I can say with equal truth, that I never suffered a political to become a personal difference. I have been left on this ground by some friends whom I dearly loved, but I was never the first to separate. With some others, of politics different from mine, I have continued in the warmest friendship to this day, and to all, and to yourself particularly, I have ever done a moral justice.

I thank you for Mr. Channing's discourse, which you have been so kind as to forward me. It is not yet at hand, but is doubtless on its way. I had received it through another channel, and read it with high satisfaction. No one sees with greater pleasure than myself the progress of reason in its advances towards rational Christianity. When we shall have done away the incomprehensible jargon of the Trinitarian arithmetic, that three are one, and one is three; when we shall have knocked down the artificial scaffolding, reared to mask from view the simple structure of Jesus; when, in short, we shall have unlearned everything which has been taught since His day, and got back to the pure and simple doctrines He inculcated, we shall then be truly and worthily His disciples; and my opinion is that if nothing had ever been added to what flowed purely from His lips, the whole world would at this day have been Christian. I know that the case you cite, of Dr. Drake, has been a common one. The religion-builders have so distorted and deformed the doctrines of Jesus, so muffled them in mysticisms, fancies and falsehoods, have caricatured them into forms so monstrous and inconceivable, as to shock reasonable thinkers, to revolt them against the whole, and drive them rashly to pronounce its Founder an impostor. Had there never been a commentator, there never would have been an infidel. In the present advance of truth, which we both approve, I do not know that you and I may think alike on all points. As the Creator has no two faces alike, so no two minds, and probably no two creeds. We well know that among Unitarians themselves there are strong shades of difference, as between Doctors Price and Priestly, for example. So there may be peculiarities in your creed and in mine. They are honestly formed without doubt. I do not wish to trouble the world with mine, nor to be troubled for them. These accounts are to be settled only with Him who made us; and to Him we leave it, with charity for all others, of whom, also, He is the only rightful and competent Judge. I have little doubt that the whole of our country will soon be rallied to the unity of the Creator, and, I hope, to the pure doctrines of Jesus also.

In saying to you so much, and without reserve, on a subject on which I never permit myself to go before the public, I know that I am safe against the infidelities which have so often betrayed my letters to the strictures of those for whom they were not written, and to whom I never mean to commit my peace. To yourself I wish every happiness, and will conclude, as you have done, in the same simple style of antiquity, *da operam ut valeas; hoc mihi gratius facere nibil potes.*

To Doctor Benjamin Waterhouse

Monticello, June 26, 1822

Dear Sir,

I have received and read with thankfulness and pleasure your denunciation of the abuses of tobacco and wine. Yet, however sound in its principles, I expect it will be but a sermon to the wind. You will find it is as difficult to inculcate these sanative precepts on the sensualities of the present day, as to convince an Athanasian that there is but one God. I wish success to both attempts, and am happy to learn from you that the latter, at least, is making progress, and the more rapidly in proportion as our Platonizing Christians make more stir and noise about it. The doctrines of Jesus are simple, and tend all to the happiness of man.

1. That there is one only God, and He all perfect.

2. That there is a future state of rewards and punishments.

3. That to love God with all thy heart and thy neighbor as thyself, is the sum of religion. These are the great points on which He endeavored to reform the religion of the Jews. But compare with these the demoralizing dogmas of Calvin.

1. That there are three Gods.

2. That good works, or the love of our neighbor, are nothing.

3. That faith is everything, and the more incomprehensible the proposition, the more merit in its faith.

4. That reason in religion is of unlawful use.

5. That God, from the beginning, elected certain individuals to be saved, and certain others to be damned; and that no crime of the former can damn them; no virtues of the latter save.

Now, which of these is the true and charitable Christian? He who believes and acts on the simple doctrines of Jesus? Or the impious dogmatists, as Athanasius and Calvin? Verily I say these are the false shepherds foretold as to enter not by the door into the sheepfold, but to climb up, some other way. They are mere usurpers of the Christian name, teaching a counter-religion made up of the *deliria* of crazy imaginations, as foreign from Christianity as that of Mahomet. Their blasphemies have driven thinking men into infidelity, who have too hastily rejected the supposed Author himself, with the horrors so falsely imputed to Him. Had the doctrines of Jesus been preached always as pure as they came from his lips, the whole civilized world would now have been Christian. I rejoice that in this blessed country of free inquiry and belief, which has surrendered its creed and conscience to neither kings nor priests, the genuine doctrine of one only God is reviving, and I trust that there is not a *young man* now living in the United States who will not die an Unitarian.

But much I fear, that when this great truth shall be reestablished, its votaries will fall into the fatal error of fabricating formulas of creed and confessions of faith, the engines which so soon destroyed the religion of Jesus, and made of Christendom a mere Aceldama; that they will give up morals for mysteries, and Jesus for Plato. How much wiser are the Quakers, who, agreeing in the fundamental doctrines of the Gospel, schismatize about no mysteries, and, keeping within the pale of common sense, suffer no speculative differences of opinion, any more than of feature, to impair the love of their brethren. Be this the wisdom of Unitarians, this the holy mantle which shall cover within its charitable circumference all who believe in one God, and who love their neighbor! I conclude my sermon with sincere assurances of my friendly esteem and respect.

RALPH WALDO EMERSON
TRANSCENDENTAL UNITARIANISM

Emerson, unlike Channing, did not react against Calvinist Congregationalism. The son of a Unitarian minister in Boston, he attended Harvard and was ordained as a Unitarian clergyman.

His address to the Harvard Divinity School complements Channing's ideas to a point that between the two men Unitarians have a complete spectrum of natural religion, minus miracles and revelation and ultimately based on reason alone.

Emerson's religion is really a profound faith in Transcendentalism, that is, the doctrine that "the highest revelation is that God is in every man." Consequently man contains all that is needful in himself and everything that happens to him has its origin within man.

The introduction and conclusion of Emerson's discourse have been omitted from the following text. They are diffuse and have little bearing on the essentials of Unitarianism beyond what he said in his two main criticisms of established Christianity.

Jesus Christ belonged to the true race of prophets. He saw with open eye the mystery of the soul. Drawn by its severe harmony, ravished with its beauty, he lived in it, and had his being there. Alone in all history he estimated the greatness of man. One man was to what is in you and me. He saw that God incarnates himself in man, and evermore goes forth anew to take possession of his World. He said, in this jubilee of sublime emotion, "I am divine. Through me, God acts; through me, speaks. Would you see God, see me; or see thee, when thou also thinkest as I now think." But what a distortion did his doctrine and memory suffer in the same, in the next, and the following ages! There is no doctrine of the Reason which will bear to be taught by the Understanding. The understanding caught this high chant from the poet's lips, and said, in the next age, "This was Jehovah come down out of heaven. I will kill you, if you say he was a man." The idioms of his language and the figures of his rhetoric have usurped the place of his truth; and churches are not built on his principles, but on his tropes. Christianity became a Mythus, as the poetic teachings of Greece and of Egypt, before. He spoke of miracles; for he felt that man's life was a miracle, and all that man doth, and he knew that this daily miracle shines as the character ascends. But the word Miracle, as pronounced by Christian churches, gives a false impression; it is Monster. It is not one with the blowing clover and the falling rain.

He felt respect for Moses and the prophets, but no unfit tenderness at postponing their initial revelations to the hour and the man that now is; to the eternal revelation in the heart. Thus was he a true man. Having seen that the law in us is commanding, he would not suffer it to be commanded. Boldly, with hand, and heart, and life, he declared it was God. Thus is he, as I think, the only soul in history who has appreciated the worth of man.

1. In this point of view we become sensible of the first defect of historical Christianity. Historical Christianity has fallen into the error that corrupts all attempts to communicate religion. As it appears to us, and as it has appeared for ages, it is not the doctrine of the soul, but an exaggeration of the personal, the positive, the ritual. It has dwelt, it dwells, with noxious exaggeration about the *person* of Jesus. The soul knows no persons. It invites every man to expand to the full circle of the universe, and will have no preferences but those of spontaneous love. But by this eastern monarchy of a Christianity, which indolence and fear have built, the friend of man is made the injurer of man. The manner in which his name is surrounded with expressions which were once sallies of admiration and love, but are now petrified into official titles, kills all generous sympathy and liking. All who hear me, feel that the language that describes Christ to Europe and America is not the style of friendship and enthusiasm to a good and noble heart, but is appropriated and formal,—paints a demigod, as the Orientals or the Greeks would describe Osiris or Apollo. Accept the injurious impositions of our early catechetical instruction, and even honesty and self-denial were but splendid sins, if they did not wear the Christian name. One would rather be

"A pagan, suckled in a creed outworn,"

than to be defrauded of his manly right in coming into nature and finding not names and places, not land and professions, but even virtue and truth foreclosed and monopolized. You shall not be a man even. You shall not own the world; you shall not dare and live after the infinite Law that is in you, and in company with the infinite Beauty which heaven and earth reflect to you in all lovely forms; but you must accept our interpretations, and take his portrait as the vulgar draw it.

That is always best which gives me to myself. The sublime is excited in me by the great stoical doctrine, Obey thyself. That which shows God in me, fortifies me. That which shows God out of me, makes me a wart and a wen. There is no longer a necessary reason for my being. Already the long shadows of untimely oblivion creep over me, and I shall decrease forever.

The divine bards are the friends of my virtue, of my intellect, of my strength. They admonish me that the gleams which flash across my mind are not mine, but God's; that they had the like, and were not disobedient to the heavenly vision. So I love them. Noble provocations go out from them, inviting me to resist evil; to subdue the world; and to Be. And thus, by his holy thoughts, Jesus serves us, and thus only. To aim to convert a man by miracles is a profanation of the soul. A true conversion, a true Christ, is now, as always, to be made by the reception of beautiful sentiments. It is true that a great and rich soul, like his, falling among the simple, does so preponderate, that, as his did, it names the world. The world seems to them to exist for him, and they have not yet drunk so deeply of his sense as to see that only by coming again to themselves, or to God in themselves, can they grow forevermore. It is a low benefit to give me something; it is a high benefit to enable me to do somewhat of myself. The time is coming when all men will see that the gift of God to the soul is not a vaunting, overpowering, excluding sanctity, but a sweet, natural goodness like thine and mine, and that so invites thine and mine to be and to grow.

The injustice of the vulgar tone of preaching is not less flagrant to Jesus than to the souls which it profanes. The preachers do not see that they make his gospel not glad, and shear him of the locks of beauty and the attributes of heaven. When I see a majestic Epaminondas, or Washington; when I see among my contemporaries a true orator, an upright judge, a dear friend; when I vibrate to the melody and fancy of a poem; I see beauty that is to be desired. And so lovely, and with yet more entire consent of my human being, sounds in my ear the severe music of the bards that have sung of the true God in all ages. Now do not degrade the life and dialogues of Christ out of the circle of this charm, by insulation and peculiarity. Let them lie as they befell, alive and warm, part of human life and of the landscape and of the cheerful day.

2. The second defect of the traditionary and limited way of using the mind of Christ is a consequence of the first; this, namely; that the Moral Nature, that Law of laws whose revelation introduce greatness —yea, God himself—into the open soul, is not explored as the fountain of the established teaching in society. Men have come to speak of the revelation as somewhat long ago given and done, as if God were dead. The injury to faith throttles the preacher; and the goodliest of institutions becomes an uncertain and inarticulate voice.

It is very certain that it is the effect of conversation with the beauty of the soul, to beget a desire and need to impart to others the same knowledge and love. If utterance is denied, the thought lies like a burden on the man. Always the seer is a sayer. Somehow his dream is told; somehow he publishes it with solemn joy: sometimes with pencil on canvas, sometimes with chisel on stone, sometimes in towers and aisles of granite, his soul's worship is builded; sometimes in anthems of indefinite music, but clearest and most permanent, in words.

The man enamored of this excellency becomes its priest or poet. The office is coeval with the world. But observe the condition, the spiritual limitation of the office. The spirit only can teach. Not any profane man, not any sensual, not any liar, not any slave can teach, but only he can give, who has; he only can create, who is. The man on whom the soul descends, through whom the soul speaks, alone can teach. Courage, piety, love, wisdom, can teach; and every man can open his door to these angels, and they shall bring him the gift of tongues. But the man who aims to speak as books enable, as synods use, as the fashion guides, and as interest commands, babbles. Let him hush.

To this holy office you propose to devote yourselves. I wish you may feel your call in throbs of desire and hope. The office is the first in the world. It is of that reality that it cannot suffer the deduction of any falsehood. And it is my duty to say to you that the need was never greater of new revelation than now. From the views, I have already expressed, you will infer the sad conviction, which I share, I believe, with numbers, of the universal decay and now almost death of faith in society. The soul is not preached. The Church seems to totter to its fall, almost all life extinct. On this occasion, any complaisance would be criminal which told you, whose hope and commission it is to preach the faith of Christ, that the faith of Christ is preached.

It is time that this ill-suppressed murmur of all thoughtful men against the famine of our churches;—this moaning of the heart because it is bereaved of the consolation, the hope, the grandeur that come along out of the culture of the moral nature,—should be heard through the sleep of indolence, and over the din of routine. This great and perpetual office of the preacher is not discharged. Preaching is the expression of the moral sentiment in application to the duties of life. In how many churches, by how many prophets, tell me, is man made sensible that he is an infinite Soul; that the earth and heavens are passing into his mind; that he is drinking forever the soul of God? Where now sounds the persuasion, that by its very melody imparadises my heart, and so affirms its own origin in heaven? Where shall I hear words such as in elder ages drew men to leave all and follow,—father and mother, house and land, wife and child? Where shall I hear these august laws of moral being so pronounced as to fill my ear, and I feel ennobled by the offer of my uttermost action and passion?

UNITARIAN UNIVERSALIST ASSOCIATION:

When the Unitarians and Universalists joined forces in 1961 to establish the Unitarian Universalist Association, they brought together two streams of American religious thought that had been converging for over a century.

If the basic doctrine of Unitarianism is the denial of a Trinity of persons in God, the fundamental tenet of the Universalists is the denial of eternal punishment.

Universalism in Christianity has been traced to the writings of men like Clement of Alexandria, Origen and Theodore of Mopsuestia. Those who favored universalism in the early Church claimed that all of God's punishments are remedial, so that eternal loss of beatitude is fictitious. They were condemned by the Church as heretical.

The modern phase of Universalism was a strong reaction to Calvin's theory of predestinarianism. John Murray is credited with having brought the Universalist position to America in 1770. Hosea Ballou gave it a systematic form in 1805 with the publication of his *Treatise of the Atonement.*

Like the Unitarians, Universalists made their first inroads among the churches in New England, notably among the Congregational, Episcopalian and Anabaptist bodies. Gradually the movement spread throughout the country.

As Universalist churches became Unitarian in their attitude towards the Trinity and the Incarnation, they found themselves cooperating more and more with the American Unitarian Association. The eventual merger gave this long-standing collaboration juridical form.

In the absence of a confession of faith, ruled out in the nature of the case, the Unitarian Universalist Association has drafted a position statement. When this is taken along with its Constitution, it becomes very clear what the Association stands for—a religion without acceptance of a mandatory creed or obedience to ecclesiastical authority that claims to have been sanctioned by God.

If the Association is limited in the number of active members, less than many denominations of Protestant lineage, the principles it proclaims are implicitly followed by millions of Americans. Some would say that the largest single group in the United States—over fifty million—are practical Unitarian Universalists. They attend no church or synagogue, profess no allegiance to a body of revealed truths and, in general, subscribe to what their more hardy confreres in the Association call "the religion of reason."

POSITION STATEMENT

The Role of Tradition. Every individual and every institution, the church included, must come to terms with its own past. To the extent that our thoughts and actions are motivated by an attempt to reject what has preceded us, we are as yoked to the past as though we obeyed its dictates blindly.

To be sure in all human institutions, and in the church, perhaps more than any, tradition tends to harden, to become fixed and unchangeable. Ours is a fellowship which consciously and continually resists this tendency. The issue comes to focus for us just now in the debate over whether we are or are not Christian. Of course the only sensible answer to the question is the exasperating one: It depends on who is talking and what *he* thinks Christianity is.

But we are not primarily concerned with whether we are Christian; we are concerned with whether we are right. We are not concerned whether we hold to the teaching of the elders; we are concerned whether the tradition to which we hold is good. Our attitude toward tradition is neither to embrace it completely nor to reject it completely. We wish to keep whatever in the past is valid, while letting go whatever is not.

Our position in this respect is summed up in the following observation of Robert Oppenheimer. He wrote: "Tradition is thus what makes it possible for us to deal as sentient and thinking beings with our experiences, to cope with our sorrows, to limit and ennoble our joys, to understand what happens to us, to talk with one another, to find themes which organize experience and give it meaning, to see the relevance of one thing to another . . . It is also the matrix which makes discovery, in an important sense, possible."

It is folly to exhaust ourselves in an attempt to decide how far we have retained Christianity and how far we have rejected it. Acknowledging the fact that we are the product of all the traditions that they have converged to make us and our churches what they are, we rejoice in the very broadness of our common heritage, which includes the Christian, but also the Jewish, Greek, Roman, scientific, Catholic, Protestant, and secular. As we become aware of the influences of oriental religions, to some degree the Buddhist, Shintoist, Confucian, and Taoist also become part of our heritage. Who can say what we are in this respect or what we are not? Who can predict what we will become? As Emerson said, "A man is a bundle of relations, a knot of roots, whose flower and fruitage is the world." This is no less true of our denomination.

Our genius lies, not in a particular break with a particular tradition, but in a constant willingness to break with whatever elements of tradition threaten to bind us. Whenever our practice ceases to reflect the highest aims we can imagine and seek to serve, whenever our worship is of something less than we conceive to be the Most High, we are compelled to make a break with the past through gradual reform, if possible, but if not, by revolt—even by the formation of a new church.

Our churches are distinguished from others not so much by the rejection of all tradition as sacred simply because people immersed in that tradition believe it to be sacred. We do not believe that any particular tradition may claim allegiance to the exclusion of all others. We do not assume in advance that truth may come only from one source and not from any other; from this prophet but not from that. Our ideal is an openness that does not exclude anything that may be illuminating—from the Old Testament to today's newspaper. We seek to approach all possible sources of truth with the same inquiring and searching mind. We are ready to receive new truth from whencesoever it may come. We are prepared to break with every orthodoxy including our own.

The Free Spirit. One of the most distinctive aspects of our movement is our acceptance of open questions. We do not claim to be the only church to hold this view, but we find our identity in the degree to which we insist that the spirit must be unfettered in all its expressions. This principle can be stated negatively: that truth cannot be reduced to a creed. But it can also be stated positively: that ours is a church in which creedal matters are purposely kept open. We formulate our convictions as clearly as we can, but we regard our formulation as neither closed nor complete.

Individual members of many of the other denominations as they wrestle with theological problems also look upon theological problems as open rather than closed. They, no less than we, find themselves in a quandary as to how they are to be resolved. But there is a difference which is fundamental. In most other churches, theological quandary is personal. It is not institutional. It is the individual who wrestles with these problems, but the church as a church usually does not. Normally a church has a faith which it states officially in its creeds and offers to the individual member. He in turn must struggle with that faith and come to terms with it in his own way. As a result of his difficulties with the official teachings of his church, he may remain in a quandary and often does. He may state his personal faith in terms of questions. But his church does not. Its faith is clear, and its statement is not in terms of questions but of answers.

With us, on the contrary, theological quandary is not personal, it is institutional. We have set at the heart of our church, not a creed or a statement of faith, but the principle that theological questions shall be kept open. We, therefore, have no creed and can have none.

As a result of the freedom which is ours, our members reach many different conclusions on theological and other questions. But these differences do not divide us. They vitalize us. Our ideal is that each shall be given full opportunity to express his views; that none shall submit to the dominance of those whose views are different; but also that none shall go his schismatic way alone. We do not merely tolerate differing opinions, we encourage them and look upon them as the most likely source of new and better understanding. With us the heretic is the man who insists upon having his own way, who says, "Play my way or I won't play at all." The real opposite of liberalism is not a traditional set of theological opinions but the dogmatic insistence that a particular set of opinions is right.

Does it not follow then, that there are as many opinions among us as there are individual members? In one sense, yes. But it is the experience of all of us to find across the country Unitarians and Universalists very much alike—interested in the same ideas, fighting for the same causes, although sometimes asserting, "We don't have to believe anything to be what we are." Our commitments and activities belie this statement. To speak of the church of the free spirit is to proclaim a principle of a very clear and precise character.

Congregational Polity. A third distinctive characteristic of our fellowship is its democratic form of church government. Known in ecclesiastical circles as "congregational polity," it is the conscious application within a human institution of belief in the free spirit.*

Although this form of organization is not unique with us, our allegiance to it grows increasingly distinctive, as other denominations,

---

* Many who gladly support a democratic civil government, think that the risks and burdens of democracy are too great to be assumed in matters of religion. We think the church is too important to trust to anything else.

once as congregational as we, move under various pressures toward more centralized authoritarian structures. Our form of government is one of the tests of our commitment to the principle of freedom. There is no point at which our most profoundly held insights and convictions as to the nature of man ought to find clearer expression than in our religious communities and organizations.

Congregational polity is based upon these principles:

1. That a local congregation is a complete church with all the powers of a church;

2. That its being and powers rest upon the free, deliberate consent of the individual members; and

3. That all business shall be conducted within the church in accordance with accepted rules of order.

Because congregationalism rests upon free individual consent, it requires disciplined individuals to make it work. They covenant to abide by the rules, but they reserve the right to criticize both the rules and the authority that enforces them. They may even change the structure of that authority itself.

CONSTITUTION

I. *Name.* The name of this organization shall be Unitarian Universalist Association.

II. *Purposes and Objectives.*

Section 1. The Unitarian Universalist Association is an incorporated organization which by consolidation has succeeded to the charter powers of the American Unitarian Association, incorporated in 1847 and the Universalist Church of America, incorporated in 1869, by virtue of legislation enacted by the The Commonwealth of Massachusetts and the State of New York, respectively.

The Unitarian Universalist Association is empowered to, and shall devote its resources to and exercise its corporate powers for, religious, educational and charitable purposes. It is further empowered: to solicit and receive funds separately or with others to support its work; to make appropriations to carry on its work including appropriations to its associate members and to other organizations to enable them to assist the Unitarian Universalist Association in carrying on its work; and without limitation as to amount, to receive, hold, manage, invest, reinvest and distribute any real and personal property for the foregoing purposes.

Section 2. In accordance with these corporate purposes, the

members of the Unitarian Universalist Association, dedicated to the principles of a free faith, unite in seeking:

(1) To strengthen one another in a free and disciplined search for truth as the foundation of our religious fellowship;

(2) To cherish and spread the Universal truths taught by the great prophets and teachers of humanity in every age and tradition, immemorially summarized in the Judeo-Christian heritage as love to God and love to man;

(3) To affirm, defend and promote the supreme worth of every human personality, the dignity of man, and the use of the democratic method in human relationships;

(4) To implement our vision of one world by striving for a world community founded on ideals of brotherhood, justice and peace;

(5) To serve the needs of member churches and fellowships, to organize new churches and fellowships, and to extend and strengthen liberal religion;

(6) To encourage cooperation with men of good will in every land.

Section 3. The Unitarian Universalist Association hereby declares and affirms the independence and autonomy of local churches, fellowships and associate members; and nothing in this Constitution or in the By-Laws of the Association shall be deemed to infringe upon the congregational polity of churches and fellowships, nor upon the exercise of direct control by their memberships of associate member organizations, nor upon the individual freedom of belief which is inherent in the Universalist and Unitarian heritages. No minister shall be required to subscribe to any particular interpretation of religion, or to any particular religious belief or creed to obtain and hold Fellowship with the Unitarian Universalist Association.

III. *Membership.*

Section 1. All churches and fellowships which are members of the American Unitarian Association and all churches and fellowships which are members of or in full fellowship with The Universalist Church of America on the effective date of this Constitution shall be members of the Unitarian Universalist Association.

Section 2. Those individuals who, on the effective date of this Constitution, were Life Members of the American Unitarian Association and were so constituted on or before May 1, 1925, shall be Life Members of the Unitarian Universalist Association and shall have all the rights and privileges of membership, including the right to vote at meetings of the Association. Those individuals who, on the effective date of this Constitution, have served as President of The Universalist Church of America shall be Life Members of the Unitarian Universalist Association and shall have all the rights and privileges of membership, including the right to vote at meetings of the Association.

Section 3. A church or fellowship may become a member of the Association upon acceptance by the Board of Trustees of the Association of a written application for membership stating that it subscribes to the purpose and objectives of the Association and pledges itself to support the Association.

8. Church of Jesus Christ of Latter-Day Saints

The founder of Mormonism was Joseph Smith, a farmer's son, born at Sharon, Vermont in 1805. He died in 1844 with his brother Hyrum at Carthage, Illinois, both victims of opposition to the rapid growth of the Church of the Latter-Day Saints in its movement across the country.

Joseph Smith is said to have received a series of divine communications which began at Manchester (near Palmyra), New York, in 1820, and continued until shortly before his death. The most important of these communications concerned a long-lost set of plates that were later translated into the Mormon Bible. Equally essential is the *Doctrine and Covenants,* which gives Smith's private revelations from angelic sources. A third part of the Mormon sacred writings is called the *Pearl of Great Price,* containing the translations by Joseph Smith of sections from the Bible and from the apocryphal Books of Moses and Abraham.

After the death of Smith, the Mormons divided into several factions which have not been reunited to the present day. The largest group, known as the Church of Jesus Christ of Latter-Day Saints, was led by Brigham Young to Utah, where they founded Salt Lake City in 1847. A smaller body protested Brigham Young's assumption of authority, claiming that Joseph Smith's son had sole title to leadership. Young was also charged with having been the first to sanction polygamy. Led by Joseph Smith III, the Reorganized Church of Jesus Christ of Latter Day Saints settled at Independence, Missouri, where the "gathering of Zion" is expected to take place before the second coming of Christ.

Other splinter groups with a negligible membership were further organized in protest against either Brigham Young or Joseph Smith's son.

The total content of Mormon sacred literature is monumental. Out of this have been chosen certain writings that are most representative and historically significant: Joseph Smith's own account of his revelation, from the *Pearl of Great Price;* his thirteen articles of the Mormon faith which are accepted by all branches of the Latter Day Saints; the prophet's twelve principles for guiding his people in their relation with the civil government; and the verses from the *Doctrine and Covenants* that Utah Mormons believe were revealed to Smith regarding plural marriages.

Following this basic documentation is the crucial passage from the Missouri version of the *Doctrine and Covenants* respecting the valid succession of authority from Joseph Smith.

JOSEPH SMITH'S
AUTOBIOGRAPHY OF REVELATIONS

Joseph Smith's own account of the revelations he received about the Latter-Day Saints is part of the Mormon faith. Certainly written by Smith and detailed in narrative, this account forms the basis of Mormon theology. Its principal claim is that after His Ascension, Jesus Christ organized a nascent Church among the Nephites in America; that after the passing of the Nephites a race of believers would arise as the Latter-Day Saints, blessed with the gift of revelation and prophecy and inaugurating an age of unparalleled prosperity among all nations. Underlying this mission of the Saints was the conviction that God did not intend fully to establish the true Church in Palestine at the time of Christ, but in America at the present (latter) day. All preceding events, for example, the revival of learning, the Reformation, the discovery of the new world, the landing of the Pilgrims, American independence and leadership in world affairs, were a prologue to the destiny in store for the American nation, of which the Mormons are divinely chosen prophets.

Early in 1842, Joseph Smith was asked to publish a summary of the Mormon religion. He prepared a list of thirteen articles of faith, issued on March 1, 1842, which have since become the standard of orthodoxy.

According to his followers, these articles were given by inspira-

tion, and form a simple, comprehensive declaration of many doctrines of the Church which have since been accepted by the vote
of the Latter-Day Saints as a basic epitome of belief.

1. Owing to the many reports which have been put in circulation by
evil-disposed and designing persons, in relation to the rise and progress
of the Church of Jesus Christ of Latter-day Saints, all of which have
been designed by the authors thereof to militate against its character as
a Church and its progress in the world—I have been induced to write
this history, to disabuse the public mind, and put all inquirers after
truth in possession of the facts, as they have transpired, in relation both
to myself and the Church, so far as I have such facts in my possession.

2. In this history I shall present the various events in relation to this
Church, in truth and righteousness, as they have transpired, or as they
at present exist, being now the eighth year since the organization of the
said Church.

3. I was born in the year of our Lord one thousand eight hundred
and five, on the twenty-third day of December, in the town of Sharon,
Windsor county, State of Vermont. . . . My father, Joseph Smith, Sen.,
left the State of Vermont, and moved to Palmyra, Ontario (now
Wayne) county, in the State of New York, when I was in my tenth
year, or thereabouts. In about four years after my father's arrival in
Palmyra, he moved with his family into Manchester in the same county
of Ontario—

4. His family consisting of eleven souls, namely, my father, Joseph
Smith; my mother, Lucy Smith (whose name, previous to her marriage, was Mack, daughter of Solomon Mack); my brothers, Alvin (who
died November 19th, 1824, in the 27th year of his age), Hyrum, myself, Samuel Harrison, William, Don Carlos; and my sisters, Sophronia,
Catherine, and Lucy.

5. Some time in the second year after our removal to Manchester,
there was in the place where we lived an unusual excitement on the
subject of religion. It commenced with the Methodists, but soon became general among all the sects in that region of country. Indeed, the
whole district of country seemed affected by it, and great multitudes
united themselves to the different religious parties, which created no
small stir and division amongst the people, some crying, "Lo, here!"
and others, "Lo, there!" Some were contending for the Methodist faith,
some for the Presbyterian, and some for the Baptist.

6. For, notwithstanding the great love which the converts to these
different faiths expressed at the time of their conversion, and the great

zeal manifested by the respective clergy, who were active in getting up and promoting this extraordinary scene of religious feeling, in order to have everybody converted, as they were pleased to call it, let them join what sect they pleased; yet when the converts began to file off, some to one party and some to another, it was seen that the seemingly good feelings of both the priests and the converts were more pretended than real; for a scene of great confusion and bad feeling ensued—priest contending against priest, and convert against convert; so that all their good feelings one for another, if they ever had any, were entirely lost in a strife of words and a contest about opinions.

7. I was at this time in my fifteenth year. My father's family was proselyted to the Presbyterian faith, and four of them joined that church, namely, my mother, Lucy; my brothers Hyrum and Samuel Harrison; and my sister Sophronia.

8. During this time of great excitement my mind was called up to serious reflection and great uneasiness; but though my feelings were deep and often poignant, still I kept myself aloof from all these parties, though I attended their several meetings as often as occasion would permit. In process of time my mind became somewhat partial to the Methodist sect, and I felt some desire to be united with them; but so great were the confusion and strife among the different denominations, that it was impossible for a person young as I was, and so unacquainted with men and things, to come to any certain conclusion who was right and who was wrong.

9. My mind at times was greatly excited, the cry and tumult were so great and incessant. The Presbyterians were most decided against the Baptists and Methodists, and used all the powers of both reason and sophistry to prove their errors, or, at least, to make the people think they were in error. On the other hand, the Baptists and Methodists in their turn were equally zealous in endeavoring to establish their own tenets and disprove all others.

10. In the midst of this war of words and tumult of opinions, I often said to myself: What is to be done? Who of all these parties are right; or, are they wrong together? If any one of them be right, which is it, and how shall I know it?

11. While I was laboring under the extreme difficulties caused by the contests of these parties of religionists, I was one day reading the Epistle of James, first chapter and fifth verse, which reads: *If any of you lack wisdom, let him ask of God, that giveth to all men liberally, and upbraideth not; and it shall be given him.*

12. Never did any passage of scripture come with more power to the

heart of man than this did at this time to mine. It seemed to enter with great force into every feeling of my heart. I reflected on it again and again, knowing that if any person needed wisdom from God, I did; for how to act I did not know, and unless I could get more wisdom than I then had, I would never know; for the teachers of religion of the different sects understood the same passages of scripture so differently as to destroy all confidence in settling the question by an appeal to the Bible.

13. At length I came to the conclusion that I must either remain in darkness and confusion, or else I must do as James directs, that is, ask of God. I at length came to the determination to "ask of God," concluding that if he gave wisdom to them that lacked wisdom, and would give liberally, and not upbraid, I might venture.

14. So, in accordance with this, my determination to ask of God, I retired to the woods to make the attempt. It was on the morning of a beautiful, clear day, early in the spring of eighteen hundred and twenty. It was the first time in my life that I had made such an attempt, for amidst all my anxieties I had never as yet made the attempt to pray vocally.

15. After I had retired to the place where I had previously designed to go, having looked around me, and finding myself alone, I kneeled down and began to offer up the desire of my heart to God. I had scarcely done so, when immediately I was seized upon by some power which entirely overcame me, and had such an astonishing influence over me as to bind my tongue so that I could not speak. Thick darkness gathered around me, and it seemed to me for a time as if I were doomed to sudden destruction.

16. But, exerting all my powers to call upon God to deliver me out of the power of this enemy which had seized upon me, and at the very moment when I was ready to sink into despair and abandon myself to destruction—not to an imaginary ruin, but to the power of some actual being from the unseen world, who had such marvelous power as I had never before felt in any being—just at this moment of great alarm, I saw a pillar of light exactly over my head, above the brightness of the sun, which descended gradually until it fell upon me.

17. It no sooner appeared than I found myself delivered from the enemy which held me bound. When the light rested upon me I saw two Personages, whose brightness and glory defy all description, standing above me in the air. One of them spake unto me, calling me by name and said, pointing to the other—*This is My Beloved Son. Hear Him!*

18. My object in going to inquire of the Lord was to know which of all the sects was right, that I might know which to join. No sooner, therefore, did I get possession of myself, so as to be able to speak, than I asked the Personages who stood above me in the light, which of all the sects was right—and which I should join.

19. I was answered that I must join none of them, for they were all wrong; and the Personage who addressed me said that all their creeds were an abomination in his sight; that those professors were all corrupt; that: "they draw near to me with their lips, but their hearts are far from me, they teach for doctrines the commandments of men, having a form of godliness, but they deny the power thereof."

20. He again forbade me to join with any of them; and many other things did he say unto me, which I cannot write at this time. When I came to myself again, I found myself lying on my back, looking up into heaven. When the light had departed, I had no strength; but soon recovering in some degree, I went home. And as I leaned up to the fireplace, mother inquired what the matter was. I replied, "Never mind, all is well—I am well enough off." I then said to my mother, "I have learned for myself that Presbyterianism is not true." It seems as though the adversary was aware, at a very early period of my life, that I was destined to prove a disturber and an annoyer of his kingdom; else why should the powers of darkness combine against me? Why the opposition and persecution that arose against me, almost in my infancy?

21. Some few days after I had this vision, I happened to be in company with one of the Methodist preachers, who was very active in the before mentioned religious excitement; and, conversing with him on the subject of religion, I took occasion to give him an account of the vision which I had had. I was greatly surprised at his behavior; he treated my communication not only lightly, but with great contempt, saying it was all of the devil, that there were no such things as visions or revelations in these days; that all such things had ceased with the apostles, and that there would never be any more of them.

22. I soon found, however, that my telling the story had excited a great deal of prejudice against me among professors of religion, and was the cause of great persecution, which continued to increase; and though I was an obscure boy, only between fourteen and fifteen years of age, and my circumstances in life such as to make a boy of no consequence in the world, yet men of high standing would take notice sufficient to excite the public mind against me, and create a bitter

persecution; and this was common among all the sects—all united to persecute me.

23. It caused me serious reflection then, and often has since, how very strange it was that an obscure boy, of a little over fourteen years of age, and one, too, who was doomed to the necessity of obtaining a scanty maintenance by his daily labor, should be thought a character of sufficient importance to attract the attention of the great ones of the most popular sects of the day, and in a manner to create in them a spirit of the most bitter persecution and reviling. But strange or not, so it was, and it was often the cause of great sorrow to myself.

24. However, it was nevertheless a fact that I had beheld a vision. I have thought since, that I felt much like Paul, when he made his defense before King Agrippa, and related the account of the vision he had when he saw a light, and heard a voice; but still there were but few who believed him; some said he was dishonest, others said he was mad; and he was ridiculed and reviled. But all this did not destroy the reality of his vision. He had seen a vision, he knew he had, and all the persecution under heaven could not make it otherwise; and though they should persecute him unto death, yet he knew, and would know to his latest breath, that he had both seen a light and heard a voice speaking unto him, and all the world could not make him think or believe otherwise.

25. So it was with me. I had actually seen a light, and in the midst of that light I saw two Personages, and they did in reality speak to me; and though I was hated and persecuted for saying that I had seen a vision, yet it was true; and while they were persecuting me, reviling me, and speaking all manner of evil against me falsely for so saying, I was led to say in my heart: Why persecute me for telling the truth? I have actually seen a vision; and who am I that I can withstand God, or why does the world think to make me deny what I have actually seen? For I had seen a vision; I knew it, and I could not deny it, neither dared I do it; at least I knew that by so doing I would offend God, and come under condemnation.

26. I had now got my mind satisfied so far as the sectarian world was concerned—that it was not my duty to join with any of them, but to continue as I was until further directed. I had found the testimony of James to be true—that a man who lacked wisdom might ask of God, and obtain and not be upbraided.

27. I continued to pursue my common vocations in life until the twenty-first of September, one thousand eight hundred and twenty-

three, all the time suffering severe persecution at the hands of all classes of men, both religious and irreligious, because I continued to affirm that I had seen a vision.

28. During the space of time which intervened between the time I had the vision and the year eighteen hundred and twenty-three—having been forbidden to join any of the religious sects of the day, and being of very tender years, and persecuted by those who ought to have been my friends and to have treated me kindly, and if they supposed me to be deluded to have endeavored in a proper and affectionate manner to have reclaimed me—I was left to all kinds of temptations; and, mingling with all kinds of society, I frequently fell into many foolish errors, and displayed the weakness of youth, and the foibles of human nature; which, I am sorry to say, led me into divers temptations, offensive in the sight of God. In making this confession, no one need suppose me guilty of any great or malignant sins. A disposition to commit such was never in my nature. But I was guilty of levity, and sometimes associated jovial company, etc., not consistent with that character which ought to be maintained by one who was called of God as I had been. But this will not seem very strange to any one who recollects my youth, and is acquainted with my native cheery temperament.

29. In consequence of these things, I often felt condemned for my weakness and imperfections; when, on the evening of the above-mentioned twenty-first of September, after I had retired to my bed for the night, I betook myself to prayer and supplication to Almighty God for forgiveness of all my sins and follies, and also for a manifestation to me, that I might know of my state and standing before him; for I had full confidence in obtaining a divine manifestation, as I previously had one.

30. While I was thus in the act of calling upon God, I discovered a light appearing in my room, which continued to increase until the room was lighter than at noonday, when immediately a personage appeared at my bedside, standing in the air, for his feet did not touch the floor.

31. He had on a loose robe of most exquisite whiteness. It was a whiteness beyond anything earthly I had ever seen; nor do I believe that any earthly thing could be made to appear so exceedingly white and brilliant. His hands were naked, and his arms also, a little above the wrist; so, also, were his feet naked, as were his legs, a little above the ankles. His head and neck were also bare, I could discover that he

had no other clothing on but his robe, as it was open, so that I could see into his bosom.

32. Not only was his robe exceedingly white, but his whole person was glorious beyond description, and his countenance truly like lightning. The room was exceedingly light, but not so very bright as immediately around his person. When I first looked upon him, I was afraid; but the fear soon left me.

33. He called me by name, and said unto me that he was a messenger sent from the presence of God to me, and that his name was Moroni; that God had a work for me to do; and that my name should be had for good and evil among all nations, kindreds, and tongues, or that it should be both good and evil spoken of among all people.

34. He said there was a book deposited, written upon gold plates, giving an account of the former inhabitants of this continent, and the source from whence they sprang. He also said that the fulness of the everlasting Gospel was contained in it, as delivered by the Savior to the ancient inhabitants;

35. Also, that there were two stones in silver bows—and these stones, fastened to a breastplate, constituted what is called the Urim and Thummim—deposited with the plates; and the possession and use of these stones were what constituted "seers" in ancient or former times; and that God had prepared them for the purpose of translating the book.

36. After telling me these things, he commenced quoting the prophecies of the Old Testament. He first quoted part of the third chapter of Malachi; and he quoted also the fourth or last chapter of the same prophecy, though with a little variation from the way it reads in our Bibles. Instead of quoting the first verse as it reads in our books, he quoted it thus:

37. *For behold, the day cometh that shall burn as an oven, and all the proud, yea, and all that do wickedly shall burn as stubble; for they that come shall burn them, saith the Lord of Hosts, that it shall leave them neither root nor branch.*

38. And again, he quoted the fifth verse thus: *Behold, I will reveal unto you the Priesthood, by the hand of Elijah the prophet, before the coming of the great and dreadful day of the Lord.*

39. He also quoted the next verse differently: *And he shall plant in the hearts of the children the promises made to the fathers, and the hearts of the children shall turn to their fathers. If it were not so, the whole earth would be utterly wasted at his coming.*

40. In addition to these, he quoted the eleventh chapter of Isaiah, saying that it was about to be fulfilled. He quoted also the third chapter of Acts, twenty-second and twenty-third verses, precisely as they stand in our New Testament. He said that that prophet was Christ; but the day had not yet come when "they who would not hear his voice should be cut off from among the people," but soon would come.

41. He also quoted the second chapter of Joel, from the twenty-eighth verse to the last. He also said that this was not yet fulfilled, but was soon to be. And he further stated that the fulness of the Gentiles was soon to come in. He quoted many other passages of scripture, and offered many explanations which cannot be mentioned here.

42. Again, he told me, that when I got those plates of which he had spoken—for the time that they should be obtained was not yet fulfilled —I should not show them to any person; neither the breastplate with the Urim and Thummim; only to those to whom I should be commanded to show them; if I did I should be destroyed. While he was conversing with me about the plates, the vision was opened to my mind that I could see the place where the plates were deposited, and that so clearly and distinctly that I knew the place again when I visited it.

43. After this communication, I saw the light in the room begin to gather immediately around the person of him who had been speaking to me, and it continued to do so until the room was again left dark, except just around him; when, instantly I saw, as it were, a conduit open right up into heaven, and he ascended till he entirely disappeared, and the room was left as it had been before this heavenly light had made its appearance.

44. I lay musing on the singularity of the scene, and marveling greatly at what had been told to me by this extraordinary messenger; when, in the midst of my meditation, I suddenly discovered that my room was again beginning to get lighted, and in an instant, as it were, the same heavenly messenger was again by my bedside.

45. He commenced, and again related the very same things which he had done at his first visit, without the least variation; which having done, he informed me of great judgments which were coming upon the earth, with great desolations by famine, sword, and pestilence; and that these grievous judgments would come on the earth in this generation. Having related these things, he again ascended as he had done before.

46. By this time, so deep were the impressions made on my mind, that sleep had fled from my eyes, and I lay overwhelmed in astonish-

ment at what I had both seen and heard. But what was my surprise when again I beheld the same messenger at my bedside, and heard him rehearse or repeat over again to me the same things as before; and added a caution to me, telling me that Satan would try to tempt me (in consequence of the indigent circumstances of my father's family), to get the plates for the purpose of getting rich. This he forbade me, saying that I must have no other object in view in getting the plates but to glorify God, and must not be influenced by any other motive than that of building his kingdom; otherwise I could not get them.

47. After this third visit, he again ascended into heaven as before, and I was again left to ponder on the strangeness of what I had just experienced; when almost immediately after the heavenly messenger had ascended from me for the third time, the cock crowed, and I found that day was approaching, so that our interviews must have occupied the whole of that night.

48. I shortly after arose from my bed, and, as usual, went to the necessary labors of the day; but, in attempting to work as at other times, I found my strength so exhausted as to render me entirely unable. My father, who was laboring along with me, discovered something to be wrong with me, and told me to go home. I started with the intention of going to the house; but, in attempting to cross the fence out of the field where we were, my strength entirely failed me, and I fell helpless on the ground, and for a time was quite unconscious of anything.

49. The first thing that I can recollect was a voice speaking unto me, calling me by name. I looked up, and beheld the same messenger standing over my head, surrounded by light as before. He then again related unto me all that he had related to me the previous night, and commanded me to go to my father and tell him of the vision and commandments which I had received.

50. I obeyed; I returned to my father in the field, and rehearsed the whole matter to him. He replied to me that it was of God, and told me to go and do as commanded by the messenger. I left the field, and went to the place where the messenger had told me the plates were deposited; and owing to the distinctness of the vision which I had had concerning it, I knew the place the instant that I arrived there.

51. Convenient to the village of Manchester, Ontario county, New York, stands on a hill of considerable size, and the most elevated of any in the neighborhood. On the west side of this hill, not far from the top, under a stone of considerable size, lay the plates, deposited in a stone box. This stone was thick and rounding in the middle on the upper

edges, so that the middle part of it was visible above the ground, but the edge all around was covered with earth.

52. Having removed the earth, I obtained a lever, which I got fixed under the edge of the stone, and with a little exertion raised it up. I looked in, and there indeed did I behold the plates, the Urim and Thummim, and the breastplate, as stated by the messenger. The box in which they lay was formed by laying stones together in some kind of cement. In the bottom of the box were laid two stones crossways of the box, and on these stones lay the plates and the other things with them.

53. I made an attempt to take them out, but was forbidden by the messenger, and was again informed that the time for bringing them forth had not yet arrived, neither would it, until four years from that time; but he told me that I should come to that place precisely in one year from that time, and that he would there meet with me, and that I should continue to do so until the time should come for obtaining the plates.

54. Accordingly, as I had been commanded, I went at the end of each year, and at each time I found the same messenger there, and received instruction and intelligence from him at each of our interviews, respecting what the Lord was going to do, and how and in what manner his kingdom was to be conducted in the last days.

55. As my father's wordly circumstances were very limited, we were under the necessity of laboring with our hands, hiring out by day's work and otherwise, as we could get opportunity. Sometimes we were at home, and sometimes abroad, and by continuous labor were enabled to get a comfortable maintenance.

56. In the year 1824 my father's family met with a great affliction by the death of my eldest brother, Alvin. In the month of October, 1825, I hired with an old gentleman by the name of Josiah Stoal, who lived in Chenango county, State of New York. He had heard something of a silver mine having been opened by the Spaniards in Harmony, Susquehanna county, State of Pennsylvania; and had, previous to my hiring to him, been digging, in order, if possible, to discover the mine. After I went to live with him, he took me, with the rest of his hands, to dig for the silver mine, at which I continued to work for nearly a month without success in our undertaking, and finally I prevailed with the old gentleman to cease digging after it. Hence arose the very prevalent story of my having been a money-digger.

57. During the time that I was thus employed, I was put to board with a Mr. Isaac Hale, of that place; it was there I first saw my wife

(his daughter), Emma Hale. On the 18th of January, 1827, we were married, while I was yet employed in the service of Mr. Stoal.

58. Owing to my continuing to assert that I had a vision, persecution still followed me, and my wife's father's family were very much opposed to our being married. I was, therefore, under the necessity of taking her elsewhere; so we went and were married at the house of Squire Tarbill, in South Bainbridge, Chenango county, New York. Immediately after my marriage, I left Mr. Stoal's, and went to my father's, and farmed with him that season.

59. At length the time arrived for obtaining the plates, the Urim and Thummim, and the breastplate. On the twenty-second day of September, one thousand eight hundred and twenty-seven, having gone as usual at the end of another year to the place where they were deposited, the same heavenly messenger delivered them up to me with this charge: that I should be responsible for them; that if I should let them go carelessly, or through any neglect of mine, I should be cut off; but that if I would use all my endeavors to preserve them, until he, the messenger, should call for them, they should be protected.

60. I soon found out the reason why I had received such strict charges to keep them safe, and why it was that the messenger had said that when I had done what was required at my hand, he would call for them. For no sooner was it known that I had them, then the most strenuous exertions were used to get them from me. Every stratagem that could be invented was resorted to for that purpose. The persecution became more bitter and severe than before, and multitudes were on the alert continually to get them from me if possible. But by the wisdom of God, they remained safe in my hands, until I had accomplished by them what was required at my hand. When, according to arrangements, the messenger called for them, I delivered them up to him; and he has them in his charge until this day, being the second day of May, one thousand eight hundred and thirty-eight.

61. The excitement, however, still continued, and rumor with her thousand tongues was all the time employed in circulating falsehoods about my father's family, and about myself. If I were to relate a thousandth part of them, it would fill up volumes. The persecution, however, became so intolerable that I was under the necessity of leaving Manchester, and going with my wife to Susquehanna county, in the State of Pennsylvania. While preparing to start—being very poor, and the persecution so heavy upon us that there was no probability that we would ever be otherwise—in the midst of our afflictions we found a

friend in a gentleman by the name of Martin Harris, who came to us and gave me fifty dollars to assist us on our journey. Mr. Harris was a resident of Palmyra township, Wayne county, in the State of New York, and a farmer of respectability.

62. By this timely aid was I enabled to reach the place of my destination in Pennsylvania; and immediately after my arrival there I commenced copying the characters off the plates. I copied a considerable number of them, and by means of the Urim and Thummim I translated some of them, which I did between the time I arrived at the house of my wife's father, in the month of December, and the February following.

63. Sometime in this month of February, the aforementioned Mr. Martin Harris came to our place, got the characters which I had drawn off the plates, and started with them to the city of New York. For what took place relative to him and the characters, I refer to his own account of the circumstances, as he related them to me after his return, which was as follows:

64. "I went to the city of New York, and presented the characters which had been translated, with the translation thereof, to Professor Charles Anthon, a gentleman celebrated for his literary attainments. Professor Anthon stated that the translation was correct, more so than any he had before seen translated from the Egyptian. I then showed him those which were not yet translated; and he said they were Egyptian, Chaldaic, Assyriac, and Arabic; and he said they were true characters. He gave me a certificate, certifying to the people of Palmyra that they were true characters, and that the translation of such of them as had been translated was also correct. I took the certificate and put it into my pocket, and was just leaving the house, when Mr. Anthon called me back, and asked me how the young man found out that there were gold plates in the place where he found them. I answered that an angel of God had revealed it unto him." '

65. "He then said to me, 'Let me see that certificate.' I accordingly took it out of my pocket and gave it to him, when he took it and tore it to pieces, saying that there was no such thing now as ministering of angels, and that if I would bring the plates to him he would translate them. I informed him that part of the plates were sealed, and that I was forbidden to bring them. He replied, 'I cannot read a sealed book.' I left him and went to Dr. Mitchell, who sanctioned what Professor Anthon had said respecting both the characters and the translation."

66. On the 5th day of April, 1829, Oliver Cowdery came to my house, until which time I had never seen him. He stated to me that

having been teaching school in the neighborhood where my father resided, and my father being one of those who sent to the school, he went to board for a season at his house, and while there the family related to him the circumstance of my having received the plates, and accordingly he had come to make inquiries of me.

67. Two days after the arrival of Mr. Cowdery (being the 7th of April) I commenced to translate the Book of Mormon, and he began to write for me.

68. We still continued the work of translation, when, in the ensuing month (May, 1829), we on a certain day went into the woods to pray and inquire of the Lord respecting baptism for the remission of sins, that we found mentioned in the translation of the plates. While we were thus employed, praying and calling upon the Lord, a messenger from heaven descended in a cloud of light, and having laid his hands upon us, he ordained us, saying:

69. *Upon you my fellow servants, in the name of Messiah, I confer the Priesthood of Aaron, which holds the keys of the ministering of angels, and of the gospel of repentance, and of baptism by immersion for the remission of sins; and this shall never be taken again from the earth until the sons of Levi do offer again an offering unto the Lord in righteousness.*

70. He said this Aaronic Priesthood had not the power of laying on hands for the gift of the Holy Ghost, but that this should be conferred on us hereafter; and he commanded us to go and be baptized, and gave us directions that I should baptize Oliver Cowdery, and that afterwards he should baptize me.

71. Accordingly we went and were baptized. I baptized him first, and afterwards he baptized me—after which I laid my hands upon his head and ordained him to the Aaronic Priesthood, and afterwards he laid his hands on me and ordained me to the same Priesthood—for so we were commanded.

72. The messenger who visited us on this occasion and conferred this Priesthood upon us, said that his name was John, the same that is called John the Baptist in the New Testament, and that he acted under the direction of Peter, James and John, who held the keys of the Priesthood of Melchizedek, which Priesthood, he said, would in due time be conferred on us, and that I should be called the first Elder of the Church, and he (Oliver Cowdery) the second. It was on the fifteenth day of May, 1829, that we were ordained under the hand of this messenger, and baptized.

73. Immediately on our coming up out of the water after we had

been baptized, we experienced great and glorious blessings from our Heavenly Father. No sooner had I baptized Oliver Cowdery, than the Holy Ghost fell upon him, and he stood up and prophesied many things which should shortly come to pass. And again, so soon as I had been baptized by him, I also had the spirit of prophecy, when, standing up, I prophesied concerning the rise of this Church, and many other things connected with the Church, and this generation of the children of men. We were filled with the Holy Ghost, and rejoiced in the God of our salvation.

74. Our minds being now enlightened, we began to have the scriptures laid open to our understandings, and the true meaning and intention of their more mysterious passages revealed unto us in a manner which we never could attain to previously, nor ever before had thought of. In the meantime we were forced to keep secret the circumstances of having received the Priesthood and our having been baptized, owing to a spirit of persecution which had already manifested itself in the neighborhood.

75. We had been threatened with being mobbed, from time to time, and this, too, by professors of religion. And their intentions of mobbing us were only counteracted by the influence of my wife's father's family (under Divine providence), who had become very friendly to me, and who were opposed to mobs, and were willing that I should be allowed to continue the work of translation without interruption; and therefore offered and promised us protection from all unlawful proceedings, as far as in them lay.

MORMON ARTICLES OF FAITH

1. We believe in God, the Eternal Father, and in His Son, Jesus Christ, and in the Holy Ghost.

2. We believe that men will be punished for their own sins, and not for Adam's transgression.

3. We believe that through the Atonement of Christ, all mankind may be saved, by obedience to the laws and ordinances of the Gospel.

4. We believe that the first principles and ordinances of the Gospel are: first, Faith in the Lord Jesus Christ; second, Repentance; third, Baptism by immersion for the remission of sins; fourth, Laying on of hands for the gift of the Holy Spirit.

5. We believe that a man must be called of God, by prophecy, and

by the laying on of hands, by those who are in authority to preach the Gospel and administer in the ordinances thereof.

6. We believe in the same organization that existed in the Primitive Church, viz., apostles, prophets, pastors, teachers, evangelists, etc.

7. We believe in the gift of tongues, prophecy, revelation, visions, healing, interpretation of tongues, etc.

8. We believe the Bible to be the word of God as far as it is translated correctly; we also believe the Book of Mormon to be the word of God.

9. We believe all that God has revealed, all that He does now reveal, and we believe that He will yet reveal many great and important things pertaining to the Kingdom of God.

10. We believe in the literal gathering of Israel and in the restoration of the Ten Tribes; that Zion will be built upon this (the American) continent; that Christ will reign personally upon the earth; and, that the earth will be renewed and receive its paradisiacal glory.

11. We claim the privilege of worshiping Almighty God according to the dictates of our own conscience, and allow all men the same privilege, let them worship how, where, or what they may.

12. We believe in being subject to kings, presidents, rulers, and magistrates, in obeying, honoring, and sustaining the law.

13. We believe in being honest, true, chaste, benevolent, virtuous, and in doing good to all men; indeed, we may say that we follow the admonition of Paul—We believe all things, we hope all things, we have endured many things, and hope to be able to endure all things. If there is anything virtuous, lovely, or of good report or praiseworthy, we seek after these things.

Joseph Smith.

TWELVE PRINCIPLES
FOR DEALING WITH THE GOVERNMENT

1. We believe that governments were instituted of God for the benefit of man; and that he holds men accountable for their acts in relation to them, both in making laws and administering them, for the good and safety of society.

2. We believe that no government can exist in peace, except such laws are framed and held inviolate as will secure to each individual the

free exercise of conscience, the right and control of property, and the protection of life.

3. We believe that all governments necessarily require civil officers and magistrates to enforce the laws of the same; and that such as will administer the law in equity and justice should be sought for and upheld by the voice of the people if a republic, or the will of the sovereign.

4. We believe that religion is instituted of God; and that men are amenable to him, and to him only, for the exercise of it, unless their religious opinions prompt them to infringe upon the rights and liberties of others; but we do not believe that human law has a right to interfere in prescribing rules of worship to bind the consciences of men, nor dictate forms for the public or private devotion; that the civil magistrate should restrain crime, but never control conscience; should punish guilt, but never suppress the freedom of the soul.

5. We believe that all men are bound to sustain and uphold the respective governments in which they reside, while protected in their inherent and inalienable rights by the laws of such governments; and sedition and rebellion are unbecoming every citizen thus protected, and should be punished accordingly; and that all governments have a right to enact such laws as in their own judgments are best calculated to secure the public interest; at the same time, however, holding sacred the freedom of conscience.

6. We believe that every man should be honored in his station, rulers and magistrates as such, being placed for the protection of the innocent and the punishment of the guilty; and that to the laws all men owe respect and deference, as without them peace and harmony would be supplanted by anarchy and terror; human laws being instituted for the express purpose of regulating our interests as individuals and nations, between man and man; and divine laws given of heaven, prescribing rules on spiritual concerns, for faith and worship, both to be answered by man to his Maker.

7. We believe that rulers, states, and governments have a right, and are bound to enact laws for the protection of all citizens in the free exercise of their religious belief; but we do not believe that they have a right in justice to deprive citizens of this privilege, or proscribe them in their opinions, so long as a regard and reverence are shown to the laws and such religious opinions do not justify sedition nor conspiracy.

8. We believe that the commission of crime should be punished according to the nature of the offense; that murder, treason, robbery, theft, and the breach of the general peace, in all respects should be

punished according to their criminality and their tendency to evil among men, by the laws of that government in which the offense is committed; and for the public peace and tranquility all men should step forward and use their ability in bringing offenders against good laws to punishment.

9. We do not believe it just to mingle religious influence with civil government, whereby one religious society is fostered and another proscribed in its spiritual privileges, and the individual rights of its members, as citizens, denied.

10. We believe that all religious societies have a right to deal with their members for disorderly conduct, according to the rules and regulations of such societies; provided that such dealings be for fellowship and good standing; but we do not believe that any religious society has authority to try men on the right of property or life, to take from them this world's goods or to put them in jeopardy of either life or limb, or to inflict any physical punishment upon them. They can only excommunicate them from their society, and withdraw from them their fellowship.

11. We believe that men should appeal to the civil law for redress of all wrongs and grievances, where personal abuse is inflicted or the right of property or character infringed, where such laws exist as will protect the same; but we believe that all men are justified in defending themselves, their friends and property, and the government, from the unlawful assaults and encroachments of all persons in times of exigency, where immediate appeal cannot be made to the laws, and relief afforded.

12. We believe it just to preach the gospel to the nations of the earth, and warn the righteous to save themselves from the corruption of the world; but we do not believe it right to interfere with bond-servants, neither preach the gospel to, nor baptize them contrary to the will and wish of their master, nor to meddle with or influence them in the least to cause them to be dissatisfied with their situations in this life, thereby jeopardizing the lives of men; such interference we believe to be unlawful and unjust, and dangerous to the peace of every government allowing human beings to be held in servitude.

JOSEPH SMITH'S
REVELATION ON PLURAL MARRIAGES

There are two versions of the Mormon doctrine on plural marriages: that of the Church in Utah which believes that polygamy is divinely sanctioned, although legally prohibited in the United States, and that of the Reorganized Church in Missouri which claims that plural marriages were never revealed to Joseph Smith (nor practiced by him) but were introduced later on by his followers.

In the passages which are here quoted from the *Doctrine and Covenants,* Smith is reported to have received a heavenly communication in favor of plural marriages, consistent with the belief and practice of the Jews in the Old Testament. The conflicts which this doctrine have brought into Mormon history were finally resolved juridically by a famous proclamation, dated October 6, 1890, in which the general conference of the Latter-Day Saints submitted to a federal law forbidding polygamy. Mormon President, Wilford Woodruff, had drafted the submissive declaration.

> Inasmuch as laws have been enacted by Congress, which laws have been pronounced constitutional by the court of last resort, I hereby declare my intention to submit to these laws, and to use my influence with the members of the church over which I preside to have them do likewise.
>
> And now I publicly declare that my advice to the Latter Day Saints is to refrain from contracting any marriage forbidden by the law of the land.*

Although legally outlawed, plural marriages remain, in principle, a part of the revealed faith of the Church of Jesus Christ of Latter-Day Saints.

1. Verily, thus saith the Lord unto you my servant Joseph, that inasmuch as you have inquired of my hand to know and understand wherein I, the Lord, justified my servants Abraham, Isaac, and Jacob, as also Moses, David and Solomon, my servants, as touching the principle and doctrine of their having many wives and concubines—

2. Behold, and lo, I am the Lord thy God, and will answer thee as touching this matter.

3. Therefore, prepare thy heart to receive and obey the instructions which I am about to give unto you; for all those who have this law revealed unto them must obey the same.

4. For behold, I reveal unto you a new and everlasting covenant;

* Wilford Woodruff, quoted by Joseph Fielding Smith, *Essentials in Church History,* Salt Lake City: Deseret News Press, 1950, pp. 607-608.

and if ye abide not that covenant, then are ye damned; for no one can reject this covenant and be permitted to enter into my glory.

5. For all who will have a blessing at my hands shall abide the law which was appointed for that blessing, and the conditions thereof, as were instituted from before the foundation of the world.

6. And as pertaining to the new and everlasting covenant, it was instituted for the fulness of my glory; and he that receiveth a fulness thereof must and shall abide the law, or he shall be damned, saith the Lord God.

7. And verily I say unto you, that the conditions of this law are these: All covenants, contracts, bonds, obligations, oaths, vows, performances, connections, associations, or expectations, that are not made and entered into and sealed by the Holy Spirit of promise, of him who is anointed, both as well for time and for all eternity, and that too most holy, by revelation and commandment through the medium of mine anointed, whom I have appointed on the earth to hold this power (and I have appointed unto my servant Joseph to hold this power in the last days, and there is never but one on the earth at a time on whom this power and the keys of this priesthood are conferred), are of no efficacy, virtue, or force in and after the resurrection from the dead; for all contracts that are not made unto this end have an end when men are dead.

8. Behold, mine house is a house of order, saith the Lord God, and not a house of confusion.

9. Will I accept of an offering, saith the Lord, that is not made in my name?

10. Or will I receive at your hands that which I have not appointed?

11. And will I appoint unto you, saith the Lord, except it be by law, even as I and my Father ordained unto you, before the world was?

12. I am the Lord thy God; and I give unto you this commandment —that no man shall come unto the Father but by me or by my word, which is my law, saith the Lord.

13. And everything that is in the world, whether it be ordained of men, by thrones, or principalities, or powers, or things of name, whatsoever they may be, that are not by me or by my word, saith the Lord, shall be thrown down, and shall not remain after men are dead, neither in nor after the resurrection, saith the Lord your God.

14. For whatsoever things remain are by me; and whatsoever things are not by me shall be shaken and destroyed.

15. Therefore, if a man marry him a wife in the world, and he marry

her not by me nor by my word, and he covenant with her so long as he is in the world and she with him, their covenant and marriage are not of force when they are dead, and when they are out of the world; therefore, they are not bound by any law when they are out of the world.

16. Therefore, when they are out of the world they neither marry nor are given in marriage; but are appointed angels in heaven; which angels are ministering servants, to minister for those who are worthy of a far more, and an exceeding, and an eternal weight of glory.

17. For these angels did not abide my law; therefore, they cannot be enlarged, but remain separately and singly, without exaltation, in their saved condition, to all eternity; and from henceforth are not gods, but are angels of God forever and ever.

18. And again, verily I say unto you, if a man marry a wife, and make a covenant with her for time and for all eternity, if that covenant is not by me or by my word, which is my law, and is not sealed by the Holy Spirit of promise, through him whom I have anointed and appointed unto this power, then it is not valid neither of force when they are out of the world, because they are not joined by me, saith the Lord, neither by my word; when they are out of the world it cannot be received there, because the angels and the gods are appointed there, by whom they cannot pass; they cannot, therefore, inherit my glory; for my house is a house of order, saith the Lord God.

19. And again, verily I say unto you, if a man marry a wife by my word, which is my law, and by the new and everlasting covenant, and it is sealed unto them by the Holy Spirit of promise, by him who is anointed, unto whom I have appointed this power and the keys of this priesthood; and It shall be said unto them—Ye shall come forth in the first resurrection; and if it be after the first resurrection, in the next resurrection; and shall inherit thrones, kingdoms, principalities, and powers, dominions, all heights and depths—then shall it be written in the Lamb's Book of Life, that he shall commit no murder whereby to shed innocent blood, and if ye abide in my covenant, and commit no murder whereby to shed innocent blood, it shall be done unto them in all things whatsoever my servant hath put upon them, in time, and through all eternity; and shall be of full force when they are out of the world; and they shall pass by the angels, and the gods, which are set there, to their exaltation and glory in all things, as hath been sealed upon their heads, which glory shall be a fulness and a continuation of the seeds forever and ever.

20. Then shall they be gods, because they have no end; therefore

shall they be from everlasting to everlasting, because they continue; then shall they be above all, because all things are subject unto them. Then shall they be gods, because they have all power, and the angels are subject unto them.

21. Verily, verily, I say unto you, except ye abide my law ye cannot attain to this glory.

22. For strait is the gate, and narrow the way that leadeth unto the exaltation and continuation of the lives, and few there be that find it, because ye receive me not in the world neither do ye know me.

23. But if ye receive me in the world, then shall ye know me, and shall receive your exaltation; that where I am ye shall be also.

24. This is eternal lives—to know the only wise and true God, and Jesus Christ, whom he hath sent. I am he. Receive ye, therefore, my law.

25. Broad is the gate, and wide the way that leadeth to the deaths; and many there are that go in thereat, because they receive me not, neither do they abide in my law.

26. Verily, verily, I say unto you, if a man marry a wife according to my word, and they are sealed by the Holy Spirit of promise, according to mine appointment, and he or she shall commit any sin or transgression of the new and everlasting covenant whatever, and all manner of blasphemies, and if they commit no murder wherein they shed innocent blood, yet they shall come forth in the first resurrection, and enter into their exaltation; but they shall be destroyed in the flesh, and shall be delivered unto the buffetings of Satan unto the day of redemption, saith the Lord God.

27. The blasphemy against the Holy Ghost, which shall not be forgiven in the world nor out of the world, is in that ye commit murder wherein ye shed innocent blood, and assent unto my death, after ye have received my new and everlasting covenant, saith the Lord God; and he that abideth not this law can in nowise enter into my glory, but shall be damned, saith the Lord.

28. I am the Lord thy God, and will give unto thee the law of my Holy Priesthood, as was ordained by me and my Father before the world was.

29. Abraham received all things, whatsoever he received, by revelation and commandment, by my word, saith the Lord, and hath entered into his exaltation and sitteth upon his throne.

30. Abraham received promises concerning his seed, and of the fruit of his loins—from whose loins ye are, namely, my servant Joseph—

which were to continue so long as they were in the world; and as touching Abraham and his seed, out of the world they should continue; both in the world and out of the world should they continue as innumerable as the stars; or, if ye were to count the sand upon the seashore ye could not number them.

31. This promise is yours also, because ye are of Abraham, and the promise was made unto Abraham; and by this law is the continuation of the works of my Father, wherein he glorifieth himself.

32. Go ye, therefore, and do the works of Abraham; enter ye into my law and ye shall be saved.

33. But if ye enter not into my law ye cannot receive the promise of my Father, which he made unto Abraham.

34. God commanded Abraham, and Sarah gave Hagar to Abraham to wife. And why did she do it? Because this was the law; and from Hagar sprang many people. This, therefore, was fulfilling, among other things, the promises.

35. Was Abraham, therefore, under condemnation? Verily I say unto you, Nay; for I, the Lord commanded it.

36. Abraham was commanded to offer his son Isaac; nevertheless, it was written: Thou shalt not kill. Abraham, however, did not refuse, and it was accounted unto him for righteousness.

37. Abraham received concubines, and they bore him children; and it was accounted unto him for righteousness, because they were given unto him, and he abode in my law; as Isaac also and Jacob did none other things than that which they were commanded; and because they did none other things than that which they were commanded, they have entered into their exaltation, according to the promises, and sit upon thrones, and are not angels but are gods.

38. David also received many wives and concubines, and also Solomon and Moses my servants, as also many others of my servants, from the beginning of creation until this time; and in nothing did they sin save in those things which they received not of me.

39. David's wives and concubines were given unto him of me, by the hand of Nathan, my servant, and others of the prophets who had the keys of this power; and in none of these things did he sin against me save in the case of Uriah and his wife; and, therefore he hath fallen from his exaltation, and received his portion; and he shall not inherit them out of the world, for I gave them unto another, saith the Lord.

40. I am the Lord thy God, and I gave unto thee, my servant Joseph, an appointment, and restore all things. Ask what ye will, and it shall be given unto you according to my word.

41. And as ye have asked concerning adultery, verily, verily, I say unto you, if a man receiveth a wife in the new and everlasting covenant, and if she be with another man, and I have not appointed unto her by the holy anointing, she hath committed adultery and shall be destroyed.

42. If she be not in the new and everlasting covenant, and she be with another man, she has committed adultery.

43. And if her husband be with another woman, and he was under a vow, he hath broken his vow and hath committed adultery.

44. And if she hath not committed adultery, but is innocent and hath not broken her vow, and she knoweth it, and I reveal it unto you, my servant Joseph, then shall you have power, by the power of my Holy Priesthood, to take her and give her unto him that hath not committed, adultery but hath been faithful; for he shall be made ruler over many.

45. For I have conferred upon you the keys and power of the priesthood, wherein I restore all things, and make known unto you all things in due time.

46. And verily, verily, I say unto you, that whatsoever you seal on earth shall be sealed in heaven; and whatsoever you bind on earth, in my name and by my word, saith the Lord, it shall be eternally bound in the heavens; and whosesoever sins you remit on earth shall be remitted eternally in the heavens; and whosesoever sins you retain on earth shall be retained in heaven.

47. And again, verily I say, whomsoever you bless I will bless, and whomsoever you curse I will curse, saith the Lord; for I, the Lord, am thy God.

48. And again, verily I say unto you, my servant Joseph, that whatsoever you give on earth, and to whomsoever you give any one on earth, by my word and according to my law, it shall be visited with blessings and not cursings, and with my power, saith the Lord, and shall be without condemnation on earth and in heaven.

49. For I am the Lord thy God, and will be with thee even unto the end of the world, and through all eternity; for verily I seal upon you your exaltation, and prepare a throne for you in the kingdom of my Father, with Abraham your father.

50. Behold, I have seen your sacrifices, and will forgive all your sins; I have seen your sacrifices in obedience to that which I have told you. Go, therefore, and I make a way for your escape, as I accepted the offering of Abraham of his son Isaac.

51. Verily, I say unto you: A commandment I give unto mine hand-

maid, Emma Smith, your wife, whom I have given unto you, that she stay herself and partake not of that which I commanded you to offer unto her; for I did it, saith the Lord, to prove you all, as I did Abraham, and that I might require an offering at your hand, by covenant and sacrifice.

52. And let mine handmaid, Emma Smith, receive all those that have been given unto my servant Joseph, and who are virtuous and pure before me; and those who are not pure, and have said they were pure, shall be destroyed, saith the Lord God.

53. For I am the Lord thy God, and ye shall obey my voice; and I give unto my servant Joseph that he shall be made ruler over many things; for he hath been faithful over a few things, and from henceforth I will strengthen him.

54. And I command mine handmaid, Emma Smith, to abide and cleave unto my servant Joseph, and to none else. But if she will not abide this commandment she shall be destroyed, saith the Lord; for I am the Lord thy God, and will destroy her if she abides not in my law.

55. But if she will not abide this commandment, then shall my servant Joseph do all things for her, even as he hath said; and I will bless him and multiply him and give unto him an hundred-fold in this world, of fathers and mothers, brothers and sisters, houses and lands, wives and children, and crowns of eternal lives in the eternal world.

56. And again, verily I say, let mine handmaid forgive my servant Joseph his trespasses; and then shall she be forgiven her trespasses, wherein she has trespassed against me; and I, the Lord thy God, will bless her, and multiply her, and make her heart to rejoice.

57. And again, I say, let not my servant Joseph put his property out of his hands, lest an enemy come and destroy him; for Satan seeketh to destroy; for I am the Lord thy God, and he is my servant; and behold, and lo, I am with him, as I was with Abraham, thy father, even unto his exaltation and glory.

58. Now, as touching the law of the priesthood, there are many things pertaining thereunto.

59. Verily, if a man be called of my Father, as was Aaron, by mine own voice, and by the voice of him that sent me, and I have endowed him with the keys of the power of this priesthood, if he do anything in my name, and according to my law and by my word, he will not commit sin, and I will justify him.

60. Let no one, therefore, set on my servant Joseph; for I will justify

him; for he shall do the sacrifice which I require at his hands for his transgressions, saith the Lord your God.

61. And again, as pertaining to the law of the priesthood—if any man espouse a virgin, and desire to espouse another, and the first give her consent, and if he espouse the second, and they are virgins, and have vowed to no other man, then is he justified; he cannot commit adultery for they are given unto him; for he cannot commit adultery with that that belongeth unto him and to no one else.

62. And if he have ten virgins given unto him by this law, he cannot commit adultery, for they belong to him, and they are given unto him; therefore is he justified.

63. But if one or either of the ten virgins, after she is espoused, shall be with another man, she has committed adultery, and shall be destroyed; for they are given unto him to multiply and replenish the earth, according to my commandment, and to fulfil the promise which was given by my Father before the foundation of the world, and for their exaltation in the eternal worlds, that they may bear the souls of men; for herein is the work of my Father continued, that he may be glorified.

64. And again, verily, verily, I say unto you, if any man have a wife, who holds the keys of this power, and he teaches unto her the law of my priesthood, as pertaining to these things, then shall she believe and administer unto him, or she shall be destroyed, saith the Lord your God; for I will destroy her; for I will magnify my name upon all those who receive and abide in my law.

65. Therefore, it shall be lawful in me, if she receive not this law, for him to receive all things whatsoever I, the Lord his God, will give unto him, because she did not believe and administer unto him according to my word; and she then becomes the transgressor; and he is exempt from the law of Sarah, who administered unto Abraham according to the law when I commanded Abraham to take Hagar to wife.

66. And now, as pertaining to this law, verily, verily, I say unto you, I will reveal more unto you, hereafter; therefore, let this suffice for the present. Behold, I am Alpha and Omega. Amen.

REORGANIZED CHURCH OF JESUS CHRIST OF LATTER DAY SAINTS

The Reorganized Church of Jesus Christ of Latter Day Saints is completely distinct from the larger and better known denomination centered in Salt Lake City. It is also much smaller than the Mormon body founded in Utah by Brigham Young. Yet its doctrinal position has a permanent place in the religious history of Mormonism.

Like the Utah body it also subscribes verbatim to the same thirteen articles of faith composed by Joseph Smith. It also derives its belief and ritual from the revelation which the prophet is said to have experienced. In many other ways the two institutions overlap. But they differ radically on the right of succession to final authority in the church, and consequently also on the validity of certain teachings as these depend on authoritative action within the denomination. The most interesting, if not most practically important, historical difference concerns polygamy—which the Reorganized Church absolutely denies was ever part of the Mormon creed.

In the following passage from the Reorganized version of Smith's *Doctrine and Covenants,* the Missouri segment of Mormonism finds validation for its claim to lineal descent from Joseph Smith as a divinely revealed condition for the transmission of authority to Smith's successors. Since, it is argued, the Utah group lacks this kind of descent in its leadership, it therefore lacks divine authorization for its teaching.

DOCTRINE AND COVENANTS
RIGHT OF SUCCESSION TO JOSEPH SMITH

1. O hearken, ye elders of my church, and give ear to the words which I shall speak unto you: for, behold, verily, verily I say unto you, that ye have received a commandment for a law unto my church, through him whom I have appointed unto you, to receive commandments and revelations from my hand. And this ye shall know assuredly, that there is none other appointed unto you to receive commandments and revelations until he be taken, if he abides in me.

2. But verily, verily I say unto you, that none else shall be appointed unto this gift except it be through him, for if it be taken from him he shall not have power, except to appoint another in his stead; and this shall be a law unto you, that ye receive not the teachings of any that shall come before you as revelations, or commandments; and this I give unto you, that you may not be deceived, that you may know they are

not of me. For verily I say unto you, that he that is ordained of me, shall come in at the gate and be ordained as I have told you before, to teach those revelations which you have received, and shall receive through him whom I have appointed.

3. And now, behold, I give unto you a commandment, that when ye are assembled together, ye shall instruct and edify each other, that ye may know how to act and direct my church how to act upon the points of my law and commandments, which I have given; and thus ye shall become instructed in the law of my church, and be sanctified by that which ye have received, and ye shall bind yourselves to act in all holiness before me, that inasmuch as ye do this, glory shall be added to the kingdom which ye have received. Inasmuch as ye do it not, it shall be taken, even that which ye have received. Purge ye out the iniquity which is among you; sanctify yourselves before me, and if ye desire the glories of the kingdom, appoint ye my servant Joseph Smith, jr., and uphold him before me by the prayer of faith. And again, I say unto you, that if ye desire the mysteries of the kingdom, provide for him food and raiment and whatsoever thing he needeth to accomplish the work, wherewith I have commanded him; and if ye do it not, he shall remain unto them that have received him, that I may reserve unto myself a pure people before me.

4. Again I say, hearken ye elders of my church whom I have appointed: ye are not sent forth to be taught, but to teach the children of men the things which I have put into your hands by the power of my Spirit; and ye are to be taught from on high. Sanctify yourselves and ye shall be endowed with power, that ye may give even as I have spoken.

5. Hearken ye, for, behold, the great day of the Lord is nigh at hand. For the day cometh that the Lord shall utter his voice out of heaven; the heavens shall shake and the earth shall tremble, and the trump of God shall sound both long and loud, and shall say to the sleeping nations: Ye saints arise and live: Ye sinners stay and sleep until I shall call again: wherefore gird up your loins, lest ye be found among the wicked. Lift up your voices and spare not. Call upon the nations to repent, both old and young, both bond and free; saying, Prepare yourselves for the great day of the Lord: for if I, who am a man, do lift up my voice and call upon you to repent, and ye hate me, what will ye say when the day cometh when the thunders shall utter their voices from the ends of the earth, speaking to the ears of all that live, saying: Repent, and prepare for the great day of the Lord; yea, and again, when the lightnings shall streak forth from the east unto the

west, and shall utter forth their voices unto all that live, and make the ears of all tingle, that hear, saying these words: Repent ye, for the great day of the Lord is come.

6. And again, the Lord shall utter his voice out of heaven, saying: Hearken, O ye nations of the earth, and hear the words of that God who made you. O, ye nations of the earth, how often would I have gathered you together as a hen gathereth her chickens under her wings, but ye would not? How oft have I called upon you by the mouth of my servants, and by the ministering of angels, and by mine own voice, and by the voice of thunderings, and by the voice of lightnings, and by the voice of tempests, and by the voice of earthquakes, and great hailstorms, and by the voice of famines and pestilences of every kind, and by the great sound of a trump, and by the voice of judgment, and by the voice of mercy all the day long, and by the voice of glory and honor, and the riches of eternal life, and would have saved you with an everlasting salvation, but ye would not? Behold, the day has come, when the cup of the wrath of mine indignation is full.

7. Behold, verily I say unto you, that these are the words of the Lord your God; wherefore, labor ye, labor ye in my vineyard for the last time: for the last time call upon the inhabitants of the earth, for in my own due time will I come upon the earth in judgment; and my people shall be redeemed and shall reign with me on earth; for the great millennial, which I have spoken by the mouth of my servants, shall come; for Satan shall be bound; and when he is loosed again, he shall only reign for a little season, and then cometh the end of the earth; and he that liveth in righteousness, shall be changed in the twinkling of an eye; and the earth shall pass away so as by fire; and the wicked shall go away into unquenchable fire; and their end no man knoweth on earth, nor ever shall know, until they come before me in judgment.

8. Harken ye to these words, behold, I am Jesus Christ, the Savior of the world. Treasure these things up in your hearts, and let the solemnities of eternity rest upon your minds. Be sober. Keep all my commandments. Even so. Amen.

9. *American Adventism*

While Adventism as a religious phenomenon has been found in every period of Christian history, the existing Adventist churches in America trace their origin to the preaching of William Miller, a Baptist minister, who predicted the end of the world in the early eighteen-forties.

Miller's studies of the Book of Daniel led him to expect the early second coming of Christ. When the parousia did not occur as predicted, the Millerite movement divided into three main segments. A small group remained faithful to Miller and organized as the American Millenial Association (later the Evangelical Adventists) which dissolved as a separate denomination in 1926. Another section was rallied by Jonathan Cummings and came to be known as the Advent Christian Church.

The most important offshoot of the Millerites, the present Seventh-Day Adventists, owes its inception and remarkable development to the mystical experiences attributed to a woman disciple of William Miller, Ellen Harmon, later Mrs. James White.

In December, 1844, at the age of seventeen, she reported her first heavenly vision, predicting the growth of Adventism. Though she had never studied theology, her output of religious literature was enormous: twenty volumes and about three thousand articles dealing with every phase of exegesis, morals, doctrine and church organization.

Early in the beginnings of Adventism, some leaders urged the biblical obligation of keeping the Sabbath instead of Sunday as the Lord's Day. The issue was finally settled by a vision of Mrs. White's: she saw the tables of the Law and "the fourth [Catholic third] commandment with a soft halo of light encircling it." She was told by the angel in the vision that "it is the only one of the ten which defines the living God." And "if the true Sabbath had been kept, there would never had been an infidel or atheist."

Gradually this doctrine was accepted as co-essential with the imminent second coming. The name, Seventh-Day Adventists, was officially adopted in 1860.

Few denominations publish more extensively than the Adventists, in almost every language of modern times. Yet all the literature is somehow connected with their *Fundamental Beliefs,* concisely reduced to twenty-two principles in official publications, and summarizing all the writings of Ellen G. White.

Strong on eschatology, these documents also show that Adventism believes in God's continued revelation of Himself to chosen souls. If the Bible is somehow normative, it is not exhaustive of divine communication to His people. In the words of the prophetess, "after the close of the canon of Scripture, the Holy Spirit was still to continue its work, to enlighten, warn, and comfort the children of God."

FUNDAMENTAL BELIEFS
SEVENTH-DAY ADVENTISTS

Seventh-day Adventists hold certain fundamental beliefs, the principal features of which, together with a portion of the scriptural references upon which they are based, may be summarized as follows:

1. That the Holy Scriptures of the Old and New testaments were given by inspiration of God, contain an all-sufficient revelation of His will to men, and are the only unerring rule of faith and practice. 2 Tim. 3:15-17.

2. That the Godhead, or Trinity, consists of the Eternal Father, a personal, spiritual Being, omnipotent, omnipresent, omniscient, infinite in wisdom and love; the Lord Jesus Christ, the Son of the Eternal Father, through whom all things were created and through whom the salvation of the redeemed hosts will be accomplished; the Holy Spirit, the third person of the Godhead, the great regenerating power in the work of redemption. Matt. 28:19.

3. That Jesus Christ is very God, being of the same nature and essence as the Eternal Father. While retaining His divine nature He took upon Himself the nature of the human family, lived on the earth as a man, exemplified in His life as our Example the principles of righteousness, attested His relationship to God by many mighty miracles, died for our sins on the cross, was raised from the dead, and

ascended to the Father, where He ever lives to make intercession for us. John 1:1, 14; Heb. 2:9-18; 8:1, 2; 4:14-16; 7:25.

4. That every person in order to obtain salvation must experience the new birth; that this comprises an entire transformation of life and character by the recreative power of God through faith in the Lord Jesus Christ. John 3:16; Matt. 18:3; Acts 2:37-39.

5. That baptism is an ordinance of the Christian church, and should follow repentance and forgiveness of sins. By its observance faith is shown in the death, burial, and resurrection of Christ. That the proper form of baptism is by immersion. Rom. 6:1-6; Acts 16:30-33.

6. That the will of God as it relates to moral conduct is comprehended in His law of ten commandments; that these are great moral, unchangeable precepts, binding upon all men, in every age. Ex. 20:1-17.

7. That the fourth commandment of this unchangeable law requires the observance of the seventh-day Sabbath. This holy institution is at the same time a memorial of creation and a sign of sanctification, a sign of the believer's rest from his own works of sin, and his entrance into the rest of soul which Jesus promises to those who come to Him. Gen. 2:1-3; Ex. 20:8-11; 31:12-17; Heb. 4:1-10.

8. That the law of ten commandments points out sin, the penalty of which is death. The law cannot save the transgressor from his sin, nor impart power to keep him from sinning. In infinite love and mercy, God provides a way whereby this may be done. He furnishes a substitute, even Christ the Righteous One, to die in man's stead, making "Him to be sin for us, who knew no sin; that we might be made the righteousness of God in Him." 2 Cor. 5:21. That one is justified, not by obedience to the law, but by the grace that is in Christ Jesus. By accepting Christ, man is reconciled to God, justified by His blood for the sins of the past, and saved from the power of sin by His indwelling life. Thus the gospel becomes "the power of God unto salvation to everyone that believeth." Rom. 1:16. This experience is wrought by the divine agency of the Holy Spirit, who convinces of sin and leads to the Sin-Bearer, inducting the believer into the new covenant relationship, where the law of God is written on his heart, and through the enabling power of the indwelling Christ, his life is brought into conformity to the divine precepts. The honor and merit of this wonderful transformation belong wholly to Christ. 1 John 2:1, 2; 3:4; Rom. 3:20; 5:8-10; 7:7; Eph. 2:8-10; 3:17; Gal. 2:20; Heb. 8:8-12.

9. That God "only hath immortality." 1 Tim. 6:15. Mortal man possesses a nature inherently sinful and dying. Eternal life is the gift of God through faith in Christ. Rom. 6:23. "He that hath the Son hath

life." 1 John 5:12. Immortality is bestowed upon the righteous at the second coming of Christ, when the righteous dead are raised from the grave and the living righteous translated to meet the Lord. Then it is that those accounted faithful "put on immortality." 1 Cor. 15:51-55.

10. That the condition of man in death is one of unconsciousness. That all men, good and evil alike, remain in the grave from death to the resurrection. Eccl. 9:5, 6; Ps. 146:3, 4; John 5:28, 29.

11. That there shall be a resurrection both of the just and of the unjust. The resurrection of the just will take place at the second coming of Christ; the resurrection of the unjust will take place a thousand years later, at the close of the millennium. John 5:28, 29; I Thess. 4:13-18; Rev. 20:5-10.

12. That the finally impenitent, including Satan, the author of sin, will, by the fires of the last day be reduced to a state of nonexistence, becoming as though they had not been, thus purging God's universe of sin and sinners. Rom. 6:23; Mal. 4:1-3; Rev. 20:9, 10; Obadiah 16.

13. That no prophetic period is given in the Bible to reach the second advent, but that the longest one, the 2300 days of Dan. 8:14, terminated in 1844, and brought us to an event called the cleansing of the sanctuary.

14. That the true sanctuary, of which the tabernacle on earth was a type, is the temple of God in Heaven, of which Paul speaks in Hebrews 8 and onward, and of which the Lord Jesus, as our great high priest, is minister; and that the priestly work of the Jewish priests of the former dispensation; that this heavenly sanctuary is the one to be cleansed at the end of the 2300 days of Daniel 8:14; its cleansing being, as in the type, a work of judgment, beginning with the entrance of Christ as the high priest upon the judgment phase of His ministry in the heavenly sanctuary foreshadowed in the earthly service of cleansing the sanctuary on the day of atonement. This work of judgment in the heavenly sanctuary began in 1844. Its completion will close human probation.

15. That God, in the time of the judgment and in accordance with His uniform dealing with the human family in warning them of coming events vitally affecting their destiny (Amos 3:6, 7), sends forth a proclamation of the approach of the second advent of Christ; that this work is symbolized by the three angels of Revelation 14; and that their threefold message brings to view a work of reform to prepare a people to meet him at His coming.

16. That the time of the cleansing of the sanctuary, synchronizing with the period of the proclamation of the message of Revelation 14, is a time of investigative judgment, first with reference to the dead, and

secondly, with reference to the living. This investigative judgment determines who of the myriads sleeping in the dust of the earth are worthy of a part in the first resurrection, and who of its living multitudes are worthy of translation. I Peter 4:17, 18; Dan. 7:9, 10; Rev. 14:6, 7; Luke 20:35.

17. That the followers of Christ should be a godly people, not adopting the unholy maxims nor conforming to the unrighteous ways of the world, not loving its sinful pleasures nor countenancing its follies. That believers should recognize their bodies as the temple of the Holy Spirit, and that therefore they should clothe that body in neat, modest, dignified apparel. Further, that in eating and drinking and in their entire course of conduct, they should shape their lives as becometh followers of the meek and lowly Master. Thus the followers of Christ will be led to abstain from all intoxicating drinks, tobacco, and other narcotics, and to avoid every body and soul defiling habit and practice. I Cor. 3:16, 17; 9:25; 10:31; I Tim. 2:9, 10; I John 2:6.

18. That the divine principle of tithes and offerings for the support of the gospel is an acknowledgment of God's ownership in our lives, and that we are stewards who must render account to Him of all that He has committed to our possession. Lev. 27:30; Mal. 3:8-12; Matt. 23:23; I Cor. 9:9-14; 2 Cor. 9:6-15.

19. That God has placed in His church the gifts of the Holy Spirit, as enumerated in 1 Corinthians 12 and Ephesians 4. That these gifts operate in harmony with the divine principles of the Bible, and are given for the perfecting of the saints, the work of the ministry, the edifying of the body of Christ. Rev. 12:17; 19:10; 1 Cor. 1:5-7. That the gift of the Spirit of prophecy is one of the identifying marks of the remnant church. 1 Cor. 1:5, 7; 12:1, 28; Rev. 12:17; 19:10; Amos. 3:7; Hosea 12:10, 13. They recognize that this gift was manifested in the life and ministry of Ellen G. White.

20. That the second coming of Christ is the great hope of the church, the grand climax of the gospel and plan of salvation. His coming will be literal, personal, and visible. Many important events will be associated with His return, such as the resurrection of the dead, the destruction of the wicked, the purification of the earth, the reward of the righteous, the establishment of His everlasting kingdom. The almost complete fulfillment of various lines of prophecy, particularly those found in the books of Daniel and the Revelation, with existing conditions in the physical, social, industrial, political, and religious worlds, indicates that Christ's coming "is near, even at the doors." Matt. 24:33. The exact time of the event has not been foretold. Be-

lievers are exhorted to be ready, for "in such an hour as ye think not the Son of man" (Matt. 24:44) will be revealed. Luke 17:26-30; 21:25-27; John 14:1-3; Acts 1:9-11; Rev. 1:7; Heb. 9:28; James 5:1-8; Joel 3:9-16; 2 Tim. 3:1-5; Dan. 7:27; Matt. 24:36, 44.

21. That the millennial reign of Christ covers the period between the first and the second resurrections, during which time the saints of all ages will live with their blessed Redeemer in Heaven. At the end of the millennium, the Holy City with all the saints will descend to the earth. The wicked, raised in the second resurrection, will go up on the breadth of the earth with Satan at their head to compass the camp of the saints, when fire will come down from God out of Heaven and devour them. In the conflagration which destroys Satan and his host, the earth itself will be regenerated and cleansed from the effects of the curse. Thus the universe of God will be purified from the foul blot of sin. Rev. 20; Zech. 14:1-4; 2 Peter 3:7-10.

22. That God will make all things new. The earth, restored to its pristine beauty, will become forever the abode of the saints of the Lord. The promise of Abraham, that through Christ he and his seed should possess the earth throughout the endless ages of eternity, will be fulfilled. "The kingdom and dominion, and the greatness of the kingdom under the whole heaven will be given to the people of the saints of the Most High, whose kindgom is an everlasting kingdom, and all dominions shall serve and obey Him." Dan. 7:27. Christ, the Lord, will reign supreme, and every creature which is in heaven and on the earth and under the earth, and such as are in the sea will ascribe "blessing, and honor, and glory, and power," unto "Him that sitteth upon the throne, and unto the Lamb forever and ever." Gen. 13:14-17; Rom. 4:13; Heb. 11:8-16; Matt. 5:5; Isa. 35; Rev. 21:1-7; 5:13; Dan. 7:27.

ADVENT CHRISTIAN CHURCH

Adventism in the United States is not limited to the Seventh Day Adventists. During the crucial years after the Millerites became the American Millenial Association, the Adventist Christian Church was formed, between 1854 and 1860, in protest over the doctrine of immortality.

While the Christian Adventists have not enjoyed the growth and influence of the more prosperous Seventh Day Adventists, their distinctive beliefs and policy reflect a tradition that is only lately coming to be recognized.

They are authentic Adventists in professing faith in the early second coming of Christ, that "he is near, even at the doors."

They further believe in "conditional immortality," of body and soul, so that, unless a person has faith and dies in the friendship of God, he will not live into eternity.

Most significantly, they do not subscribe to the strongly held position of the Sabbatarian branch of the Adventists, that the Christian Church has changed the mandate of the Old Law and wrongly substituted Sunday for Saturday as the Day of the Lord. Hence the characteristic absence of the term, "Seventh Day," from their name, and the insistence that they are in the full Christian tradition which traces the first (and not seventh) day of the week as specially dedicated to the worship of God.

DECLARATION OF PRINCIPLES

I. *We believe* that the Bible is the inspired Word of God, being in its entirety a revelation given to man under Divine inspiration and providence; that its historic statements are correct, and that it is the only Divine and infallible standard of faith and practice. Romans 15:4; 2 Timothy 3:15, 16; John 17:17.

II. *We believe,* as revealed in the Bible—

1. In one God, our Father, eternal, and infinite in his wisdom, love, and power, the Creator of all things, "in whom we live, and move, and have our being." Genesis 1:1; Isaiah 40:28; Matthew 6:6.

2. And in Jesus Christ, our Lord, the only begotten Son of God, conceived of the Holy Spirit, born of the Virgin Mary; who came into our world to seek and to save that which was lost; who died for our sins, who was raised bodily from the dead for our justification; who ascended into heaven as our High Priest and Mediator, and who will come again in the end of this age, to judge the living and the dead, and to reign forever and ever. 1 Timothy 3:16.

3. And in the Holy Spirit, the Comforter, sent from God to convince the world of sin, of righteousness and of judgment, whereby we are sanctified and sealed unto the day of redemption. John 14:16, 26; 16:7-11; Ephesians 1:13.

III. *We believe* that man was created for immortality, but that through sin he forfeited his Divine birthright; that because of sin, death entered into the world, and passed upon all men; and that only through faith in Jesus Christ, the divinely ordained Life-giver, can men become "partakers of the divine nature," and live forever. 2 Timothy 1:10; Romans 2:7; 1 Corinthians 15:22, 51-54.

IV. *We believe* that death is a condition of unconsciousness to all persons, righteous and wicked; a condition which will remain unchanged until the resurrection at Christ's second coming, at which time the righteous will receive everlasting life while the wicked will be "punished with everlasting destruction"; suffering complete *extinction of being*. Ecclesiastes 9:5; Job 14:14; John 5:28, 29; Matthew 10:28.

V. *We believe* that salvation is free to all those who, in this life and in this age, accept it on the conditions imposed, which conditions are simple and inflexible; namely, turning from sin, repentance toward God, faith in the Lord Jesus Christ, and a life of consecration to the service of God; thus excluding all hope of a future probation, or of universal salvation. John 3:16; 2 Corinthians 6:2; Luke 13:25-28.

VI. *We believe* that Jesus Christ, according to his promise, will come again to this earth, even "in like manner" as he went into heaven—personally, visibly and gloriously—to reign here forever; and that this coming is the hope of the Church, inasmuch as upon that coming depend the resurrection and the reward of the righteous, the abolition of sin and its consequences, and the renewal of the earth—now marred by sin—to become the eternal home of the redeemed, after which event the earth will be forever free from sin and death. Acts 1:11; 1 Thessalonians 4:16, 17; Revelation 22:12, 20.

VII. *We believe* that Bible prophecy has indicated the approximate time of Christ's return; and comparing its testimony with the signs of our times, we are confident that he is near, "even at the doors," and we believe that the great duty of the hour is the proclamation of this soon-coming redemption, the defense of Bible authority, inspiration and truth, and the salvation of lost men. 2 Peter 1:19-21; Matthew 24:42-45; Revelation 22:17.

VIII. *We believe* the Church of Christ is an institution of Divine origin, which includes all true Christians, of whatever name; but that local church organizations should be independent of outside control, congregational in government, and subject to no dictation of priest, bishop, or pope—although true fellowship and unity of action should exist between all such organizations. Matthew 16:18; Ephesians 5:25; Ephesians 4:15.

IX. *We believe* that the only ordinances of the Church of Christ are Baptism and the Lord's Supper; immersion being the only true baptism. Matthew 28:19; Romans 6:3-5; 1 Corinthians 11:23-26.

X. *We believe* that the first day of the week, as the day set apart by the early Church in commemoration of Christ's resurrection, should be observed as the Christian Sabbath, and used as a day of rest and religious worship. Psalm 118:22-24; Luke 24:1-12; 1 Corinthians 16:2.

XI. *We believe* that war is contrary to the spirit and teachings of our Lord and Master, Jesus Christ; that it is contrary to the spirit of true brotherhood, and inimical to the welfare of humanity. We believe that Christ's followers are under obligation to use their influence against war; that they are justified in refusing to bear arms for conscience' sake in loyalty to their divine Master.

10. Spiritualism

Spiritualism as an organized religion dates from the experiences of the Fox sisters at Hydesville, New York, in 1848. They heard strange knockings in their home, first at Hydesville and later in Rochester, which they interpreted as signals from the spirit world. They worked out a system of communication. A year before, Andrew Jackson Davis had published *Nature's Divine Revelations,* stating the basic principles that have since become the accepted philosophy of Spiritualism.

At first spiritualist societies were small groups of interested persons who met regularly at seances and were united only by their common attachment to a particularly successful medium. A national society was organized in 1863, but it lasted only nine years. In 1893 the National Spiritualist Association was established in Chicago, and is today the largest autonomous group among kindred bodies. Finally in 1936 an International General Assembly of Spiritualists was formed, with headquarters in Norfolk, Virginia, as a cooperative federation whose primary purpose is to charter Spiritualist churches throughout the world.

The national office publishes position statements that represent as authoritatively as possible the creedal principles of Spiritualism.

DECLARATION OF PRINCIPLES

I. We believe in Infinite Intelligence.

II. We believe that the phenomena of nature, both physical and spiritual, are the expression of Infinite Intelligence.

III. We affirm that a correct understanding of such expression and living in accordance therewith constitute true religion.

IV. We affirm that the existence and personal identity of the individual continue after the change called death.

V. We affirm that communication with the so-called dead is a fact, scientifically proven by the phenomena of Spiritualism.

VI. We believe that the highest morality is contained in the Golden Rule: "Whatsoever ye would that others should do unto you, do ye also unto them."

VII. We affirm the moral responsibility of the individual, and that he makes his own happiness or unhappiness as he obeys or disobeys Nature's physical and spiritual laws.

VIII. We affirm that the doorway to reformation is never closed against any human soul or hereafter.

IX. We affirm that the precept of Prophecy contained in the Bible is a divine attribute proven through Mediumship.

DEFINITIONS
Adopted by the
National Spiritualist Association of Churches

1. Spiritualism is the Science, Philosophy and religion of continuous life, based upon the demonstrated fact of communication, by means of mediumship, with those who live in the Spirit World.

2. A Spiritualist is one who believes, as the basis of his or her religion, in the communication between this and the spirit world by means of mediumship, and who endeavors to mould his or her character and conduct in accordance with the highest teachings derived from such communion.

3. A Medium is one whose organism is sensitive to vibrations from the spirit world through whose instrumentality intelligences in that world are able to convey messages and produce the phenomena of Spiritualism.

4. A Spiritualist Healer is one who, either through his own inherent powers or through his mediumship, is able to impart vital, curative force to pathologic conditions.

5. The Phenomena of Spiritualism consist of Prophecy, Clairvoyance, Clairaudience, Gift of Tongues, Laying on of Hands, Healing, Visions, Trance, Apports, Revelation, Levitation, Raps, Automatic and Independent Writing and Paintings, Photography, Materialization, Psychometry, Voice and any other manifestation proving the continuity

of life as demonstrated through the physical and Spiritual Senses and faculties of man.

"Spiritualism Is a Science" because it investigates, analyzes and classifies facts and manifestations demonstrated from the spirit side of life.

"Spiritualism Is a Philosophy" because it studies the laws of nature both on the seen and unseen sides of life and bases its conclusions upon present observed facts. It accepts statements of observed facts of past ages and conclusions drawn therefrom, when sustained by reason and by results of observed facts of the present day.

"Spiritualism Is a Religion" because it strives to understand and to comply with the Physical, Mental and Spiritual Laws of Nature, "which are the laws of God."

WHAT SPIRITUALISM IS AND DOES

It teaches personal responsibility.

It removes all fear of death, which is really the portal of the spirit world.

It teaches that death is not the cessation of life, but mere change of condition.

It teaches, not that a man has a soul, but that man is a soul and has a body.

That man is a spiritual being now, even while encased in flesh.

That as man sows on earth he reaps in the life to come.

That those who have passed on are conscious—not asleep.

That communion between the living and the "dead" is scientifically proved.

It teaches that the spark of divinity dwells in all.

That as a flower gradually unfolds in beauty, so the spirit of man unfolds and develops in the spirit spheres.

Spiritualism is God's message to mortals, declaring that There Is No Death. That all who have passed on still live. That there is hope in the life beyond for the most sinful.

That every soul will progress through the ages to heights, sublime and glorious, where God is Love and Love is God.

It is a manifestation, a demonstration, and a proof of the continuity of life and of the truth of the many Spirit manifestations recorded in the Bible.

It demonstrates the many Spiritual gifts with which mankind is endowed but which through want of knowledge have been allowed to lie dormant or through prejudice have been violently and unjustly suppressed.

SPIRITUAL HEALING

The results of Spiritual Healing are produced in several ways to wit:

1. By the spiritual influences working through the body of the medium and thus infusing curative, stimulating and vitalizing fluids and energies into the diseased parts of the patient's body.

2. By the spiritual influences illuminating the brain of the healing medium so that the cause, nature and seat of the disease in the patient become known to the medium.

3. Through the application of absent treatments whereby spiritual beings combine their own healing forces with the magnetism and vitalizing energy of the medium and convey them to the patient who is distant from the medium and cause them to be absorbed by the system of the patient.

SPIRITUAL HEALING is recognized by the New Testament. It has been a tenet of ancient and modern religions and is now a tenet of modern spiritualism practiced by our healers.

Spiritualism does not deny that physicians and surgeons are quite necessary. We cooperate with them at all times.

OBJECTS OF SPIRITUALISM

The objects of the organized movement of Spiritualism may be stated in part as follows:

To teach the truths and principles expressed in the Declaration of Principles and in the Definitions of "SPIRITUALISM," "A SPIRITUALIST," "A MEDIUM," and "A SPIRITUALIST HEALER," as adopted by the National Spiritualist Association of the United States of America.

To teach and proclaim the science, philosophy and religion of modern Spiritualism, to encourage lectures on all subjects pertaining to the Spiritual and Secular welfare of mankind. To protest against every attempt to compel mankind to worship God in any particular or prescribed manner. To advocate and promote spiritual healing and to protect and encourage spiritual teachers and mediums in all laudable efforts in giving evidence or proof to mankind of a continued intercourse and relationship between the living and the so-called dead. To encourage every person in holding present beliefs always open to restatement as growing thought and investigation reveal new truth, thereby leaving every individual free to follow the dictates of reason and conscience in spiritual as in secular affairs.

11. Disciples and Christians

The founder of the Disciples of Christ was Thomas Campbell, born in Ireland in 1763. His father had been a Roman Catholic. The young Thomas began as an Anglican but withdrew from the English Church in protest against what he considered its excessive ritualism. As a Presbyterian he worked for union in his own church and among other denominations, but with little success.

Discouraged by the opposition his efforts met in Ireland, he came to the United States in 1807 and began his ministry in Philadelphia as a Presbyterian. Within two years the presbyteries resisted him openly, especially after he published his outspoken *Declaration and Address,* issued "to all that love our Lord Jesus Christ in all sincerity, throughout all the churches."

The *Declaration and Address* corresponds in importance to the Augsburg Confession of the Lutheran Churches and the Westminster Confession of the Presbyterians. It is a synthesis of religious principles for the Disciples of Christ and the Churches of Christ, whose impact on American thought and institutions has been immense and whose vigorous ecumenism has much to do with the progress of Christian unity in the United States.

As originally formulated, the document was a statement of principles for the Christian Association of Washington. Dated September 7, 1809, it was a pamphlet of fifty-six pages containing four parts: first a Declaration (three pages) stating briefly the reasons for the organization, its central ideas and purposes; second, an Address (eighteen pages) signed by Thomas Campbell, amplifying the argument for the unity of all Christians and developing in some detail the means by which it could be attained; third, an Appendix (thirty-one pages) which answered actual or expected criticisms and explained several points in the Address; and fourth a Postscript (three pages), written three months later, suggesting immediate steps to be taken for the advancement of the enterprise.

In the citations which follow, the Declaration is given entire, but the Address is slightly abbreviated, with the omitted portions (mainly repetitions) indicated.

A third document has been added to the two basic statements of the founder of the Disciples and Christians. Drafted for the Theological Commission of the World Council of Churches, it is the most definitive confession of faith for present-day Disciples of Christ and illustrates their lineal continuity with the original Campbellites.

Although both the Disciples of Christ and Christians are derived from Campbellites, and both subscribe to the principles of their founder, they are now juridically distinct denominations. Their main division occurred in 1906, occasioned by different interpretations of Thomas Campbell. The Disciples are more ecumenical, homogeneous, and less literal in their understanding of Campbell. They are also more influential in American religious thought. Their creedal positions may therefore be taken as typical of this indigenous form of American Free-Church Protestantism.

THE DECLARATION OF THOMAS CAMPBELL

From the series of events which have taken place in the churches for many years past, especially in this Western Country, as well as from what we know in general of the present state of things in the christian world; we are persuaded that it is high time for us not only to think, but also to act, for ourselves; to see with our own eyes, and to take all our measures directly and immediately from the Divine Standard; to this alone we feel ourselves divinely bound to be conformed; as by this alone we must be judged. We are also persuaded that as no man can be *judged* for his brother, so no man can *judge* for his brother: every man must be allowed to judge for himself, as every man must bear his own judgment;—must give account of himself to God—We are also of opinion that as the divine word is equally binding upon all so all lie under an equal obligation to be bound by it, and it alone; and not by any human interpretation of it and that therefore no man has a right to judge his brother, except in so far as he manifestly violates the express letter of the law. That every such judgment is an express violation of the law of Christ, a daring usurpation of his throne, and a gross intrusion upon the rights and liberties of his subjects. We are therefore of opinion that we should beware of such things; that we should keep at the utmost distance from every thing of this nature; and, that, knowing the judgment of God against them that commit such things; we should neither do the same ourselves, nor take pleasure in them that do them. Morever, being well aware, from sad experience, of the heinous nature, and pernicious tendency of religious controversy among christians; tired and sick of the bitter jarrings and janglings of a party spirit, we would desire to be at rest; and, were it possible; we would also desire to adopt and recommend such measures, as would give rest to our brethren throughout all the churches;—as would restore unity, peace, and purity, to the whole church of God. This desirable rest, however, we utterly despair either to find for ourselves, or to be able to recommend to our brethren, by continuing amidst the diversity and rancour of party contentions, the veering uncertainty and clashings of human opinions: nor, indeed, can we reasonably expect to find it any where, but in Christ and his simple word; which is the same yesterday, today, and for ever. Our desire, therefore, for ourselves and our brethren would be, that rejecting human opinions and the inventions of men, as of any authority, or as having any place in the church of God, we might forever cease from farther contentions about such things; returning to, and holding fast by, the original standard; taking the divine word alone for our rule; the Holy Spirit for our teacher and guide, to lead us into all truth; and Christ alone as exhibited in the word for our salvation—that, by so doing, we may be at peace among ourselves, follow peace with all men, and holiness, without which no man shall see the Lord.—Impressed with these sentiments, we have resolved as follows:

I. That we form ourselves into a religious association under the denomination of the Christian Association of Washington—for the sole purpose of promoting simple evangelical christianity, free from all mixture of human opinions and inventions of men.

II. That each member, according to ability, cheerfully and liberally subscribe a certain specified sum to be paid half yearly, for the purpose of raising a fund to support a pure Gospel Ministry, that shall reduce to practice that whole form of doctrine, worship, discipline, and government, expressly revealed and enjoined in the word of God. And also for supplying the poor with the Holy Scriptures.

III. That this society consider it a duty; and shall use all proper means in its power, to encourage the formation of similar associations;

and shall for this purpose hold itself in readiness, upon application, to correspond with, and render all possible assistance to, such as may desire to associate for the same desirable and important purposes.

IV. That this society by no means considers itself a church, nor does at all assume to itself the powers peculiar to such a society; nor do the members, as such, consider themselves as standing connected in that relation: nor as at all associated for the peculiar purposes of church association;—but merely as voluntary advocates for church reformation; and, as possessing the powers common to all individuals, who may please to associate in a peaceable and orderly manner, for any lawful purpose: namely, the disposal of their time, counsel, and property, as they may see cause.

V. That this society, formed for the sole purpose of promoting simple evangelical christianity, shall, to the utmost of its power, countenance and support such ministers, and such only, as exhibit a manifest conformity to the original standard in conversation and doctrine, in zeal and diligence;—only such as reduced to practice that simple original form of christianity, expressly exhibited upon the sacred page; without attempting to inculcate anything of human authority, of private opinion, or inventions of men, as having any place in the constitution, faith, or worship, of the christian church—or, any thing, as matter of christian faith, or duty, for which there cannot be expressly produced a thus saith the Lord either in express terms, or by approved precedent.

VI. That a standing committee of twenty-one members of unexceptionable moral character, inclusive of the secretary and treasurer, be chosen annually to superintend the interests, and transact the business, of the society. And that said committee be invested with full powers to act and do, in the name and behalf of their constituents, whatever the society had previously determined, for the purpose of carrying into effect the entire object of its institution—and that in case of any emergency, unprovided for in the existing determinations of the society, said committee be empowered to call a special meeting for that purpose.

VII. That this society meet at least twice a year, viz. On the first Thursday of May, and of November, and that the collectors appointed to receive the half-yearly quotas of the promised subscriptions, be in readiness, at or before each meeting, to make their returns to the treasurer, that he may be able to report upon the state of the funds. The next meeting to be held at Washington on the first Thursday of November next.

VIII. That each meeting of the society be opened with a sermon, the constitution and address read, and a collection lifted for the benefit of the society—and that all communications of a public nature be laid before the society at its half-yearly meetings.

IX. That this society, relying upon the all-sufficiency of the Church's Head; and, through His grace, looking with an eye of confidence to the generous liberality of the sincere friends of genuine christianity; holds itself engaged to afford a competent support to such ministers, as the Lord may graciously dispose to assist, at the request, and by invitation of, the society, in promoting a pure evangelical reformation, by the simple preaching of the everlasting gospel, and the administration of its ordinances in an exact conformity to the Divine Standard as afore-said—and, that therefore, whatever the friends of the institution shall please to contribute towards the support of ministers in connexion with this society who may be sent forth to preach at considerable distances, the same shall be gratefully received and acknowledged as a donation to its funds.

THE ADDRESS OF THOMAS CAMPBELL

That it is the grand design and native tendency of our holy religion to reconcile and unite men to God, and to each other, in truth and love, to the glory of God, and their own present and eternal good, will not, we presume, be denied, by any of the genuine subjects of Christianity. The nativity of its Divine author was announced from heaven, by a host of angels, with high acclamations of "Glory to God in the highest, and on earth peace and good-will toward men." The whole tenor of that Divine book which contains its institutes, in all its gracious decla-rations, precepts, ordinances, and holy examples, most expressively and powerfully inculcates this. In so far, then as this holy unit and una-nimity in faith and love is attained, just in the same degree is the glory of God and the happiness of men promoted and secured. Impressed with those sentiments, and at the same time, grievously affected with those sad divisions which have so awfully interfered with the benign and gracious intention of our holy religion, by exciting its professed subjects to bite and devour one another, we cannot suppose ourselves justifiable in witholding the mite of our sincere and humble endeavors to heal and remove them. . . .

Dearly beloved brethren, why should we deem it a thing in-credible that the Church of Christ, in this highly favored country, should resume that original unity, peace, and purity which belong to its constitution, and constitute its glory? Or, is there anything that can be justly deemed necessary for this desirable purpose, both to conform to the model and adopt the practice of the primitive Church, expressly exhibited in the New Testament? Whatever alterations this might produce in any or in all of the Churches, should, we think, neither be deemed inadmissible nor ineligible. Surely such alteration would be every way for the better, and not for the worse, unless we should suppose the divinely inspired rule to be faulty, or defective. Were, we, then, in our Church constitution and managements, to exhibit a complete conformity to the apostolic Church, would we not be, in that respect, as perfect as Christ intended we should be? And should not this suffice us?

It is, to us, a pleasing consideration that all the Churches of Christ which mutually acknowledge each other as such, are not only agreed as to the positive ordinances of the Gospel institution; so that our differences, at most, are about the things in which the kingdom of God does not consist, that is, about matters of private opinion or human invention. What a pity that the kingdom of God should be divided about such things! Who, then, would not be the first among us to give up human inventions in the worship of God, and to cease from imposing his private opinions upon his brethren, that our breaches might thus be healed? Who would not willingly conform to the original pattern laid down in the New Testament, for this happy purpose? Our dear brethren of all denominations will please to consider that we have our educational prejudices and particular customs to struggle against as well as they. But this we do sincerely declare, that there is nothing we have hitherto received as matter of faith or practice, which is not expressly taught and enjoined in the word of God, either in express terms or approved precedent, that we would not heartily relinquish, so that we might return to the original constitutional unity of the Christian Church; and in this happy unity, enjoy full communion with all our brethren in peace and charity. The like dutiful condescension we candidly expect of all that are seriously impressed with a sense of the duty they owe to God, to each other, and to their perishing brethren of mankind. To this we call, we invite, our dear brethren of all denominations, by all the sacred motives which we have avouched as the impulsive reasons of our thus addressing them.

You are all, dear brethren, equally included as the objects of our esteem and love. With you all we desire to unite in the bonds of an entire Christian unity—Christ alone being the head, the center, his word the rule; an explicit belief of, and manifest conformity to it, in all things—the terms. More than this, you will not require of us; and less we cannot require of you; nor, indeed, can you reasonably suppose any would desire it, for what good purpose would it serve? We dare neither assume nor propose the trite, indefinite distinction between essentials and non-essentials, in matters of revealed truth and duty; firmly persuaded, that, whatever may be their comparative importance, simply considered, the high obligation of the Divine authority revealing, or enjoining them, renders the belief or performance of them absolutely essential to us, in so far as we know them. And to be ignorant of anything God has revealed can neither be our duty nor our privilege. We humbly presume, then, dear brethren, you will have no relevant objection to meet us upon this ground. And, we again beseech you, let it be known that it is the invitation of but few; by your accession we shall be many; and whether few, or many, in the first instance, it is all one with respect to the event which must ultimately await the full information and hearty concurrence of all. Besides, whatever is done, must begin, some time, some where; and no matter where, nor by whom, if the Lord puts his hand to the work, it must surely prosper. And has he not been graciously pleased, upon many signal occasions, to bring to pass the greatest events from very small beginnings, and even by means the most unlikely! Duty then if ours; but events belong to God.

We hope, then, what we urge will neither be deemed an unreasonable nor an unseasonable undertaking. Why should it be thought unreasonable? Can any time be assigned, while things continue as they are, that would prove more favourable for such an attempt, or what could be supposed to make it so? Might it be the approximation of parties to a greater nearness, in point of public profession, and similarity of customs? Or might it be expected from a gradual decline of bigotry? As to the former, it is a well-known fact that where the difference is least, the opposition is always managed with a degree of vehemence inversely proportioned to the merits of the cause. With respect to the latter, though, we are happy to say, that in some cases and places, and, we hope, universally, bigotry is upon the decline; yet we are not warranted, either by the past or present, to act upon that supposition. We have, as yet, by this means seen no such effect produced; nor indeed could we reasonably expect it; for there will always be multitudes of weak persons in the Church, and these are generally the most subject to bigotry; add to this, that while divisions exist, there will always be found interested men who will not fail to support them; nor can we at all suppose that Satan will be idle to improve an advantage so important to the interests of his kingdom. And, let it be further observed upon the whole, that, in matters of similar importance to our secular interests, we would by no means content ourselves with such kind of reasoning. We might further add, that the attempt here suggested, not being of a partial, but of general nature, it can have no just tendency to excite the jealousy, or hurt the feelings of any party. On the contrary, every effort toward a permanent Scriptural unity among the churches, upon the solid basis of universally acknowledged and self-evident truths, must have the happiest tendency to enlighten and conciliate, by thus manifesting to each other their mutual charity and zeal for the truth: "Whom I love in the truth," saith the apostle, "and not I only, but also all they that have known the truth; for truth's sake, which is in us, and shall be with us forever." Indeed, if no such Divine and adequate basis of union can be fairly exhibited, as will meet the approbation of every upright and intelligent Christian, nor such mode of procedure adopted in favour of the weak as will not oppress their consciences, then the accomplishment of this grand object upon principle must be forever impossible. There would, upon this supposition, remain no other way of accomplishing it, but merely by voluntary compromise, and good-natured accomodation. That such a thing, however, will be accomplished, one way or the other, will not be questioned by any that allow themselves to believe that the commands and prayers of our Lord Jesus Christ will not utterly prove ineffectual. Whatever way, then, it is to be effected, whether upon the solid basis of Divinely revealed truth, or the good-natured principle of Christian forbearance and gracious condescension, is it not equally practicable, equally eligible to us, as ever it can be to any; unless we should suppose ourselves destitute of that Christian temper and discernment which is essentially necessary to qualify us to do the will of our gracious Redeemer, whose express command to his people is, that there be "no divisions among them; but that they all walk by the same rule, speak the same thing, and be perfectly joined together in the same mind, and in the same judgment?" We believe then it is as practicable as it is eligible. Let us attempt it. "Up, and be doing, and the Lord will be with us." . . . For certainly the collective graces that are conferred upon the Church, if duly united and brought to bear upon any point of commanded duty, would be amply sufficient for the right and successful performance of it. "For to one is given by the Spirit the word of wisdom; to another the word of knowledge by the same Spirit; to another faith by the same Spirit; to another the discerning of spirits, but the manifestation of the Spirit is given to every man to profit withal. As every man, therefore, hath received the gift, even so minister the same one to another as good stewards of the manifold grace of God." In the face, then, of such instructions, and with such assurances of an all-sufficiency of Divine grace, as the Church has received from her exalted Head, we can neither justly doubt the concurrence of her genuine members; nor yet their ability, when dutifully acting together, to accomplish anything that is necessary for his glory, and their own good; and certainly their visible unity in truth and holiness, in faith and love, is, of all things, the most conducive to both these, if we may credit the dying commands and prayers of our gracious Lord. In a matter, therefore, of such confessed importance, our Christian brethren, however unhappily distinguished by party names, will not, cannot, withhold their helping hand. We are as heartily willing to be their debtors, as they are indispensably bound to be our benefactors. Come, then, dear brethren, we most humbly beseech you, cause your light to shine upon our weak beginnings, that we may see to work by it. Evince your zeal for the glory of Christ, and the spiritual welfare of your hearty and zealous co-operation to promote the unity, purity, and prosperity of his Church.

Let none imagine that the subjoined propositions are at all intended as an overture toward a new creed or standard for the Church, or as in any wise designed to be made a term of communion; nothing can be further from our intention. They are merely designed for opening up the way, that we may come fairly and firmly to original ground upon clear and certain premises, and take up things just as the apostles left them, that thus disentangled from the accruing embarrassments of the intervening ages, we may stand with evidence upon the same ground on which the Church stood at the beginning. Having said so much to solicit attention and prevent mistake, we submit as follows:

Prop. 1. That the Church of Christ upon earth is essentially, intentionally, and constitutionally one; consisting of all those in every place that profess their faith in Christ and obedience to him in all things according to the Scriptures, and that manifest the same by their tempers and conduct, and of none else; as none else can be truly and properly called Christians.

2. That although the Church of Christ upon earth must necessarily exist in particular and distinct societies, locally separate one from another, yet there ought to be no schisms, no uncharitable divisions among them. They ought to receive each other as Christ Jesus hath also received them, to the glory of God. And for this purpose they ought all to walk by the same rule, to mind and speak the same thing; and to be perfectly joined together in the same mind, and in the same judgment.

3. That in order to do this, nothing ought to be inculcated upon Christians as articles of faith; nor required of them as terms of communion, but what is expressly taught and enjoined upon them in the word of God. Nor ought anything to be admitted, as of Divine obligation, in

their Church constitution and managements, but what is expressly enjoined by the authority of our Lord Jesus Christ and his apostles upon the New Testament Church; either in express terms or by approved precedent.

4. That although the Scriptures of the Old and New Testaments are inseparably connected, making together but one perfect and entire revelation of the Divine will, for the edification and salvation of the Church, and therefore in that respect cannot be separated; yet as to what directly and properly belongs to their immediate object, the New Testament is as perfect a constitution, for the worship, discipline, and government of the New Testament Church, and as perfect a rule for the particular duties of its members, as the Old Testament was for the worship, discipline, and government of the Old Testament Church, and the particular duties of its members.

5. That with respect to the commands and ordinances of our Lord Jesus Christ, where the Scriptures are silent as to the express time or manner of performance, if any such there be, no human authority has power to interfere, in order to supply the supposed deficiency by making laws for the Church; nor can anything more be required of Christians in such cases, but only that they so observe these commands and ordinances as will evidently answer the declared and obvious end of their institution. Much less has any human authority power to impose new commands or ordinances upon the Church, which our Lord Jesus Christ has not enjoined. Nothing ought to be received into the faith or worship of the Church, or to be made a term of communion among Christians, that is not as old as the New Testament.

6. That although inferences and deductions from Scripture premises, when fairly inferred, may be truly called the doctrine of God's holy word, yet are they not formally binding upon the consciences of Christians farther than they perceive the connection, and evidently see that they are so; for their faith must not stand in the wisdom of men, but in the power and veracity of God. Therefore, no such deductions can be made terms of communion, but do properly belong to the after and progressive edification of the Church. Hence, it is evident that no such deductions or inferential truths ought to have any place in the Church's confession.

7. That although doctrinal exhibitions of the great system of Divine truths, and defensive testimonies in opposition to prevailing errors, be highly expedient, and the more full and explicit they be for these purposes, the better; yet, as these must be in a great measure the effect of human reasoning, and of course must contain many inferential

truths, they ought not to be made terms of Christian communion; unless we suppose, what is contrary to fact, that none have a right to the communion of the Church, but such as possess a very clear and decisive judgment, or are come to a very high degree of doctrinal information; whereas the Church from the beginning did, and ever will, consist of little children and young men, as well as fathers.

8. That as it is not necessary that persons should have a particular knowledge or distinct apprehension of all Divinely revealed truths in order to entitle them to a place in the Church; neither should they, for this purpose, be required to make a profession more extensive than their knowledge; but that, on the contrary, their having a due measure of Scriptural self-knowledge respecting their lost and perishing condition by nature and practice, and of the way of salvation through Jesus Christ, accompanied with a profession of their faith in and obedience to him, in all things, according to his word, is all that is absolutely necessary to qualify them for admission into his Church.

9. That all that are enabled through grace to make such a profession, and to manifest the reality of it in their tempers and conduct, should consider each other as the precious saints of God should love each other as brethren, children of the same family and Father, temples of the same Spirit, members of the same body, subjects of the same grace, objects of the same Divine love, bought with the same price, and joint-heirs of the same inheritance. Whom God hath thus joined together no man should dare to put asunder.

10. That division among the Christians is a horrid evil, fraught with many evils. It is antichristian, as it destroys the visible unity of the body of Christ; as if he were divided against himself, excluding and excommunicating a part of himself. It is antiscriptural, as being strictly prohibited by his sovereign authority; a direct violation of his express command. It is antinatural, as it excites Christians to condemn, to hate, and oppose one another, who are bound by the highest and most endearing obligations to love each other as brethren, even as Christ has loved them. In a word, it is productive of confusion and of every evil work.

11. That (in some instances) a partial neglect of the expressly revealed will of God, and (in others) an assumed authority for making the approbation of human opinions and human inventions a term of communion, by introducing them into the constitution, faith, or worship of the Church, are, and have been, the immediate, obvious, and universally acknowledged causes of all the corruptions and divisions that ever have taken place in the Church of God.

12. That all that is necessary to the highest state of perfection and purity of the Church upon earth is, first, that none be received as members but such as having that due measure of Scriptural self-knowledge described above, do profess their faith in Christ and obedience to Him in all things according to the Scriptures; nor, secondly, that any be retained in her communion longer than they continue to manifest the reality of their profession by their tempers and conduct. Thirdly, that her ministers, duly and Scripturally qualified, inculcate none other things than those very articles of faith and holiness expressly revealed and enjoined in the word of God. Lastly, that in all their administrations they keep close by the observance of all Divine ordinances, after the example of the primitive Church, exhibited in the New Testament; without any additions whatsoever of human opinions or inventions of men.

13. Lastly. That if any circumstantials indispensably necessary to the observance of Divine ordinances be not found upon the page of express revelation, such, and such only, as are absolutely necessary for this purpose should be adopted under the title of human expedients, without any pretence to a more sacred origin, so that any subsequent alteration or difference in the observance of these things might produce no contention nor division in the Church.

From the nature and construction of these propositions, it will evidently appear, that they are laid in a designed subserviency to the declared end of our association; and are exhibited for the express purpose of performing a duty of previous necessity, a duty loudly called for in existing circumstances at the hand of every one that would desire to promote the interests of Zion; a duty not only enjoined, as has been already observed from Isiah lvii: 14, but which is also there predicted of the faithful remnant as a thing in which they would voluntarily engage. "He that putteth his trust in me shall possess the land, and shall inherit my holy mountain; and shall say Cast ye up, cast ye up, prepare the way; take up the stumbling-block out of the way of my people." To prepare the way for a permanent Scriptural unity among Christians, by calling up to their consideration fundamental truths, directing their attention to first principles, clearing the way before them by removing the stumbling blocks—the rubbish of ages, which has been thrown upon it, and fencing it on each side, that in advancing toward the desired object they may not miss the way through mistake or inadvertency, by turning aside to the right hand or to the left, is at least, the sincere intention of the above propositions. It remains with our brethren now to say, how far they go toward answering this intention. . . .

DENOMINATIONAL STATEMENT
DISCIPLES OF CHRIST

1. Disciples generally hold that the Church came into existence on the day of Pentecost. This is not to deny that there was a 'people of God' under the earlier dispensation, or that the coming of Christ was the realisation of a Messianic expectation, or that the Law and Prophets constituted a significant preparation. All these things are parts of the total history of God's dealings with men, the redemptive process and the Kingdom of God; but they are not parts of the history of the Christian Church, which is specifically based upon the life, teaching, death and resurrection of Jesus Christ. Since these facts about Jesus Christ, including His death, are essential to the existence of a Christian Church, it would be more accurate to say that Disciples consider Christ the foundation rather than the founder of the Church. ('Other foundation can no man lay . . .' (I Cor. e. II), 'a chief cornerstone' (I Peter 2. 6).

Nevertheless, most Disciples would answer Yes to the question, Did Christ found the Church? It was His expectation and intention that there should be a Church. Presumably He gave His Apostles some instructions as to its nature and perhaps its structure. It has generally been held that the teachings and actions of the Apostles, as related to the formation of the Church, to evidently represent the mind of Christ that they are to be received as normative.

2. It has been the historic claim of Disciples of Christ (as of many other bodies) that their polity and practice are essentially a 'restoration of primitive Christianity' as recorded in the New Testament. While the Roman Catholic Church claims to prepetuate primitive Christianity uncorrupted (though with its germinal truths and cultus properly developed), and practically every reformer has sought to restore what seemed to him the essential features of a lost primitive purity. Disciples of Christ have so generally made 'restoration' their slogan that many of them do not know that anybody else ever thought of it before Barton W. Stone and Alexander Campbell. The extent to which there was an exact pattern to be restored has been the occasion of no little internal controversy among them and of one major division.

Some have held, and an increasing number now hold, that the New Testament does not reflect a uniform type of church organisation. But generally they have regarded congregational independency as supported by Apostolic teaching and precedent, and quite unanimously they have denied any such authority for either a presbyterial or an episcopal form of government. The unity of the Church, which they have always sought to stress and if possible restore, has always been conceived as a unity of spirit and purpose, of devotion to a common Master, of voluntary co-operation in carrying on His work, and of free fellowship among all His disciples; never as an organisational unity held together by submission to the authority of any body of general officials or higher clergy, or even of any democratically based general organisation exercising control over the constituent congregations.

3. Even the most rigid and conservative Disciples of Christ have never thought of the Church as limited to their own communion, but have considered it as including all who, throughout the ages, have sought to follow Christ and have allied themselves with any group that claimed to be Christian. Their constant plea for the union of all Christians has carried the implication that the members of the divided Church were Christians and that the separated communions were genuine, though erring and fragmented, parts of the one Church. This implication has been recognised and, with negligible exceptions, universally accepted. It has been a familiar and standard statement that 'Disciples of Christ are neither *the* Church nor *a* Church, but are a movement within the Church'. The phrase, 'Our movement', is their own most common designation for the whole group; 'our church' is never used in that sense by those even moderately well informed.

As a movement within the Church, the purpose has been to promote the reunion of the divided Church by restoring and practising what are believed to be the original and simple conditions of admission to Christian fellowship—i.e. faith in Jesus Christ as Son of God and Saviour, repentance of past sins, and the Baptism (immersion) of the penitent believer. There has been no disposition to 'damn the unimmersed', even though they have not generally (not at all until recently) been admitted to membership. They have, if otherwise qualified, been regarded as Christians and brothers in Christ, even if not admissable as members of a movement to unite the Church on the basis indicated.

In recent years there have come to be many Disciples—a growing and influential minority—who think that Baptism should be regarded as in the category of 'opinion', since competent and devout scholars with equal access to the same historical data actually do have different opinions as to the mind of Christ on this subject, and who would therefore leave Baptism to the option of the individual. Others, who would not do this, are fully persuaded that it should be left to the individual congregation without prejudice to the unity of the fellowship.

4. The Church is held to be a voluntary society in the sense that it should include in its membership only those who voluntarily join it. This does not mean that the Church was brought into existence by the will of man. Disciples are averse to any conception or practice which

would make the Church an institution in which membership is gained by the accident of birth or by any process (such as the Baptism of infants) in which the person concerned is not a participant by his own conscious choice, or a society—whether or not State sponsored—which is presumed to be coextensive with the total community. Though opposed to sectarianism and ardent for unity, their view of the Church is distinctly in accordance with Troeltsch's 'sect-type church', composed of those who have made a personal commitment to Christ and His cause, in contrast with the more inclusive 'church-type church'. The Christian nurture which it is the duty of parents and of the Church to give to the young is viewed as preparing the young to make their own personal commitment to Christ and thus become members of the Church rather than as implying their prior membership.

If the definition of the Church as 'a continuation of the incarnation' were used at all—as it is not, though I think there would be no objection to it unless perhaps on the ground that it sounds like a fourth-century (or later) rather than a first-century definition—it would be understood as a figure of speech. Like such phrases as 'the body of Christ', 'members of his body', and 'the head of the body, the Church' (I Cor. 12. 27; Eph. 4. 12, 5. 30; Col. I. 18), it would be regarded as a vivid, but figurative, expression of the intimate spiritual relation between the living Christ and His disciples in and through the Church.

5. The message and mission of the Church are a projection of the message and mission of Christ. The function of the Church is to strengthen Christians in faith and character, to go into all the world and preach the Gospel to every creature, and to promote the realisation of the Kingdom of God by all means within its power. In this area, the ideas and attitudes of Disciples of Christ do not differ in principle from those of other Christian bodies.

6. Disciples do not, in general, take a pessimistic view of the world. The Church is an institution ordained by God to minister His grace to men. Since 'God so loved the world', it seems not too much to hope that eventually the world's evil ways may be changed into the ways of Christ. The Church as such has no relation to the State, except that it exists in areas in which States constitute the political organisation of society, and the members of the Church also owe allegiance to the State. If the Church wishes to own property, to become an employer, or otherwise to function as a secular corporation, it must do these things under the laws of the civil government. Neither its divine origin nor its sacred function can give to its human officers and agents any claim to a right to carry on secular operations independently of the State—even under the plea that these operations are essential to the

discharge of its spiritual ministry. But the message of the Church in-cludes a message of human freedom from every form of tyranny which infringes the rights and violates the dignity of man; and where such human freedom exists the Church also will be free.

The Church is an agency for the promotion of the Kingdom of God.

7. The concept of historical continuity is not deemed important. Any group of followers of Christ may constitute a congregation, or local church, which will be an authentic part of the Church. Its claim to a genuine part of the true Church is not invalidated by any lack of continuous ecclesiatical lineage. The only form of 'apostolic succession' that is deemed meaningful is that which is gained by saying essentially what the Apostles said and doing what the Apostles did.

8. In general, there has been a movement away from the conception of an authoritative pattern in detail for the Church and from an almost exclusive emphasis upon evangelism under the formula of 'faith, re-pentance and baptism', and toward a more fraternal co-operation with those who do not accept this formula in the sense in which Disciples have understood it. The watchword of 'restoration' has gained a more spiritual, more ethical, and less rigid meaning in the minds of many.

9. Disciples of Christ have emphasised, with varying success, the possibility of Christian fellowship and church union on a very simple and non-credal basis of agreement. Their distinction between 'faith' and 'opinion' (relegating to the latter category most of the dogmas about which theological controversy has raged) has made for unity with liberty for diverse views. They have not been free from the fault of treating some of their own opinions as though they were articles of faith. They have too much ignored the Christian heritage from the ages between the first century and the nineteenth. They have been so fiercely democratic and individualistic (or congregational) that they still have much to learn about effective co-operation among themselves and wider fellowship with the Christian world.

12. Christian Science

Christian Science is one of the most typically American religions. It was founded by Mrs. Mary Baker Eddy (1821-1910), a native of New Hampshire. Her early life was marked by long periods of sickness, owing to her naturally delicate temperament and nervous disposition. For several years she visited Phineas Parkhurst Quimby (1802-1866), mental healer and mesmerist, whose writings deeply influenced her.

Shortly after Quimby's death, she fell at her home in Lynn, Massachusetts, and suffered an injury that required medical care. According to Mrs. Eddy, the physician who treated her said she was injured beyond recovery. Awaiting a clergyman who was to prepare her for death, she began to read the Bible and came upon the words of Christ in Matthew's Gospel, addressed to the man sick with palsy. As she read, "Arise, take up thy bed," she realized that death is only a figment of the mind based on the error of duality in human nature. That moment marked the end of any idea she might have had that man was composed of a body that dies and a soul that lives on forever.

Quimby's manuscripts, to which his clients had ready access, abound in ideas and terms that have since become standard in Christian Science. As Quimby explained it, matter has no intelligence of its own, and to believe intelligence is in matter is the error which produces pain and inharmony of all sorts. If people could be convinced that they are a principle outside of matter, they would not be influenced by the opinions of man, but "held to the workings only of a principle, Truth, in which there are no inharmonies of sickness, pain or sin."

He further believed that he had come across the method so effectively used by Jesus in healing the sick, and was convinced that anyone who learned the secret could restore people to health no less than Jesus had done. The secret was to realize that "matter is an error," that "matter was but opinion that could be formed into any shape which the belief gave it," and therefore "to give intelligence to matter is an error which is sickness."

The ordinary name that Quimby gave to his discovery was the "Science of Health." At other times he called it the "Science of Christ," while he also used the name "Christian Science." *

One of the earliest biographers of Mrs. Eddy was her contemporary, Georgine Milmine, who summarized the doctrine taught by the foundress. The characterization is still widely current as based on the sources of Christian Science, notably *Science and Health with Key to the Scriptures,* first published in 1875.

> The Christian Science faith has, from the beginning, owed its growth to its radical principle that sickness of soul and body are delusions which can be dispelled at will, and that the natural state of the human creature is characterized by health, happiness and goodness. The message which Mrs. Eddy brought to Lynn was substantially that God is not only all-good, all-powerful, and all-present, but that there is nothing but God in all the Universe; that evil is a non-existent thing, a sinister legend which has been handed down from generation to generation until it has become a fixed belief. Mrs. Eddy's mission was to uproot this implanted belief and to emancipate the race from the terrors which had imprisoned it for so many thousands of years. "Ye shall know the Truth," she said, "and the Truth shall make you free." **

Essential to Mrs. Eddy's doctrine was the distinction between Christ and Jesus. The former is spiritual and divine; the latter is corporeal and human. It is quite possible for people since Christ to imitate His healing powers, provided they discover what He knew, that sickness and death are not real and that Truth can destroy their seeming reality.

A great deal has happened in Christian Science, however, since the death of Mary Baker Eddy. While remaining loyal to the memory of their foundress, the Scientists have naturally been affected by the American culture in which they live and are susceptible to the changes taking place in the national religious climate. Two of these changes are so significant that nothing else

* *The Quimby Manuscripts,* edited by Horatio W. Dresser, New York: Thomas Y. Crowell, 1921, pp. 249, 131, 388.
** Georgine Milmine, *The Life of Mary Baker G. Eddy and the History of Christian Science,* New York: Doubleday, Page and Co., 1909, p. 212.

in recent years can compare with them: the adoption of categories and forms of thought that belong to the mainstream of traditional Christianity, and the entrance of members of the Church of Christ Scientist into the ecumenical movement. Both developments may be seen in the two documents which follow.

These documents were presented in 1964 at the Ecumenical Institute in Geneva, under the auspices of the World Council of Churches. One is on *The Theology of Christian Science* and the other on *The Practice of Christian Science*. Together they constitute an authoritative statement of the basic religious position of Christian Science today. They have outstanding documentary value as being the first formal presentation of the principles of Christian Science to an ecumenical body. Moreover, both quote extensively from the writings of Mary Baker Eddy, and one of them includes the tenets of Christian Science as set down by Mrs. Eddy in *Science and Health*.

THE THEOLOGY OF CHRISTIAN SCIENCE

We can probably all agree that whatever we say about God in human language is in some degree symbolic. No one word can convey to human sense the essence of God, for God transcends all human categories. Jesus of Nazareth spoke of Him constantly as Father—his Father and our Father—and Christian Scientists use that word to express their sense of God's intimate relationship with His creation. They supplement it with the word Mother, for they understand God to be the source of all the qualities of being which are ordinarily called feminine, as well as those which are called masculine.

In the sublimely simple words of Genesis, "God created man in his own image . . . male and female created he them." *Gen. 1:27.* As Father-Mother, God is the sole source of being, the I AM revealed to Moses at the burning bush, the nourishing power revealed to Isaiah in the divine promise: "As one whom his mother comforteth, so will I comfort you, and ye shall be comforted in Jerusalem." *Isa. 66:13.*

We know that there are many other definitions or disclosures of God in the Bible. He is defined as Life, as Truth, as Love, and as Spirit. All these terms are used in Christian Science as synonyms of God. When they are so used they are always capitalized in order to differentiate them from the lower meaning which is given to them in common speech. By implication He is also disclosed as Mind and Soul, as the conscious Being in whom we live and move and have our own true being.

Christian Scientists worship God by still another name, a name which is sometimes greatly misunderstood. That name is Principle. . . . We speak of God both as Person and as Principle, and feel no contradiction between the two. We do not say that He is *a* principle, any more than *a* person; but we say that He is Principle itself, *the* Principle of all true being, the source of all law and order, just as He is *the* infinite Person from whom proceed all particular identities. As human sense conceives the words "personal" and "impersonal," both are inadequate to express the allness of God, just as the words "transcendence" and "immanence" are inadequate of themselves to express the relation of God to His creation.

As the word Principle is used by Christian Scientists in relation to God, it certainly does not denote a *thing* to be used by mortals for their own purposes; rather, it expresses the sublimity of the conscious, creative, infinite power which is Love, upholding its whole creation through eternal, invariable law. As the Epistle of James puts it, "Every good gift and every perfect gift is from above, and cometh down from the Father of lights, with whom is no variableness, neither shadow of turning." *James 1:17.* If divine will and divine law are one and the same, then the conscious purpose of the creative Principle, Love, is carried out through universal law.

Some may think that this makes impossible in Christian Science the personal encounter with God, or the I-Thou relationship. But remember that Principle as a synonym for God can only be understood in conjunction with all the other revealed aspects of Deity. The God who is Life, Mind, Spirit, and Love is as near as breathing, as purposeful as thought, as instant as light, as compassionate as healing.

What might be called the formal definition of God is to be found in the Christian Science textbook, *Science and Health with Key to the Scriptures* by Mary Baker Eddy: "God is incorporeal, divine, supreme, infinite Mind, Spirit, Soul, Principle, Life, Truth, Love." *S&H p. 465.* The author then goes on to ask, "Are these terms synonymous?" and she answers: "They are. They refer to one absolute God. They are also intended to express the nature, essence, and wholeness of Deity."

Here you have the basis of Christian Science theology; but this definition is in fact more than formal, it is operational. The peculiarity of Truth is that it *acts*; it does not leave us where it found us. We grow into an understanding of God through revelation, reason, and what Christian Scientists call demonstration—that is, practical demonstration in actual living.

In one of her shorter works Mrs. Eddy writes, "As Christian Scientists you seek to define God to your own consciousness by feeling and applying the nature and practical possibilities of divine Love." *Message to the Mother Church for 1901, p. 1.* The same might be said of each of the other seven synonyms listed, and this is further brought out in another passage in *Science and Health* in regard to the man Jesus: "Through the magnitude of his human life, he demonstrated the divine Life. Out of the amplitude of his pure affection, he defined Love." *S&H p. 54.* Love here is capitalized to signify God. Love can be defined only by living, and Jesus is the supreme example of authentic living.

What, then, of man?

We read in Genesis 1 that God made man in His own image and likeness, and that He pronounced His whole creation to be very good. The image and likeness of Spirit must be spiritual. Perfect goodness in the image and likeness can no more include the capacity to sin than perfect goodness in God can include the capacity to sin. According to this reasoning, man's true freedom and dignity lie in his likeness to God, not in a supposed ability to be unlike God. Man as God conceives him and as he exists in the divine Mind must express the intelligence and dominion of that Mind. In fact, the whole universe of Mind must express the sublimity, beauty, and purity with which creative Love has endowed it.

This is the state of being which the Bible calls the kingdom of heaven. It is not a state of being to be achieved only after death, for it is eternal and ever present; it is here now, to the degree that it is recognized, accepted, and lived. Jesus said, "The kingdom of God is within you," *Luke 17:21*—within you and among you. The reality of God's perfect spiritual universe lies at the very heart of experience, as holy and shining as it emerges from the creative will of God.

Man as a citizen of this heavenly kingdom is what Christian Science means by the real or true man and what Paul described as the new man "which after God is created in righteousness and true holiness." *Eph. 4:24.* This is the man of whom we read in the First Epistle of John: "Whosoever is born of God doth not commit sin; for his seed remaineth in him: and he cannot sin, because he is born of God." *I John 3:9.* This is the man who was brought to light through Jesus Christ, the man who is truly the son of God, the man who was given dominion over all the earth.

But of course a very different picture from this presents itself to us in daily experience. The man we find in matter is the unlikeness rather than the likeness of God. Biological man, economic man, the man of anthropology and psychology, even religious man—what an infinite distance away from God he seems. Sin and mortality are written into the very basis of his existence; frustration and despair seem to dog his every footstep. Where is the evidence of divine Love in the hideous suffering with which an innocent child may be burdened? Is the congenital idiot or the deliberate connoisseur of evil a citizen of the kingdom of God?

Christian Scientists believe that evil needs to be faced as evil and not idealized or rationalized as good. Long before the existential crisis of today, Mrs. Eddy called in question the nineteenth-century optimism which believed in inevitable progress under the direction of human reason. In *Science and Health* she wrote:

> A mortal sinner is not God's man. Mortals are the counterfeits of immortals. They are the children of the wicked one, or the one evil, which declares that man begins in dust or as a material embryo. . . . Mortals are not fallen children of God. They never had a perfect state of being, which may subsequently be regained. They were, from the beginning of mortal history, "conceived in sin and brought forth in iniquity." . . . Learn this, O mortal, and earnestly seek the spiritual status of man, which is outside of all material selfhood. Remember that the Scriptures say of mortal man: "As for man, his days are as grass: as a flower of the field, so he flourisheth. For the wind passeth over it, and it is gone; and the place thereof shall know it no more." *S&H pp. 475, 476.*

What Christian Science says is that the man described in these words is not really man but a mortal and material misconception of man. This misconception is the product of what Christian Science calls "mortal mind" and what Paul called the "carnal mind," which is "enmity against God." Mortal mind is the opposite of divine Mind, or God, and mortal man is a lie, a false representation of God's man. Jesus said of the devil or the carnal mind which is enmity against God: "He was a murderer from the beginning, and abode not in the truth, because there is no truth in him. When he speaketh a lie, he speaketh of his own: for he is a liar, and the father of it." *John 8:44.*

To Christian Scientists the second creation account, in Genesis 2, is a remarkable allegory exposing the falsity of a material concept of creation. The Adam and Eve who are formed from the dust are far from being the male and female created in God's spiritual likeness. They are fallible from the beginning, lacking the wisdom and purity of intention that would enable them unerringly to resist evil. They are supposed to have a power which God has not—the power to err. This power is of course a weakness, but it is a weakness which, according to the story, has been built into their nature by Jehovah, who must therefore take ultimate responsibility for the evil he allows to come into existence. The Jehovah of Genesis 2 is the sort of God to be deduced from the sin and misery of mortal life, and in a sense he is made in the image and likeness of mortal man. He is the necessary hypothesis for a universe that includes famine, war, and holocaust.

It was Jehovah, you remember, who cast Adam into a deep sleep. Christian Scientists sometimes speak of mortal existence as the Adam-dream, a dream which can all too easily turn into a nightmare. The whole problem of mortal existence, as they see it, is to awake to the reality of being, to find man's true spiritual status "outside of all material selfhood." It is to exchange the Adam-man for the Christ man, dream for reality, sin for holiness, death for life.

Paul writes in Ephesians: "Awake thou that sleepest, and arise from the dead, and Christ shall give thee light." *Eph. 5:14.*

It is interesting that Jesus himself described death as a state of sleep from which we need to be awakened. When Lazarus died, the Saviour said to his disciples, "Our friend Lazarus sleepeth; but I go, that I may awake him out of sleep." *John 11:11.* In a larger sense the whole of mortal existence is a sleep or death from which the Christ awakens and rescues us.

In Christian Science a distinction is always observed in the use of the words "Jesus" and "Christ." Jesus is understood as the name of the historic figure who was born of a virgin, lived in the flesh, healed, taught, suffered, was crucified, rose from the grave, and finally rose entirely beyond the material perception of his followers. He is viewed as God's highest earthly representative, the "only immaculate," the Exemplar and Master of all Christians throughout all time. Though his bodily presence is no longer with us, the Truth he embodied in all that he said and did is forever with us, and this Truth is what Christian Scientists call the Christ.

In *Science and Health* Mrs. Eddy writes: "The Christ was the Spirit which Jesus implied in his own statements: 'I am the way, the truth, and the life;' 'I and my Father are one.' This Christ, or divinity of the man Jesus, was his divine nature, the godliness which animated him."

To Christian Scientists the historic Jesus is inseparable from the eternal Christ, yet the Christ is not confined to Jesus. Another passage in *Science and Health* explains it this way:

> The advent of Jesus of Nazareth marked the first century of the Christian era, but the Christ is without beginning of years or end

of days. Throughout all generations both before and after the Christian era, the Christ, as the spiritual idea,—the reflection of God,—has come with some measure of power and grace to all prepared to receive Christ, Truth. Abraham, Jacob, Moses, and the prophets caught glorious glimpses of the Messiah, or Christ, which baptized these seers in the divine nature, the essence of Love. The divine image, idea, or Christ was, is, and ever will be inseparable from the divine Principle, God.

You will see that this quotation contains terms unfamiliar to traditional Christianity, although we consider them to be implicit in Biblical theology. Just as the Christian Scientist's use of the word "Principle" in relation to Deity needs to be properly understood, so does the word "idea" in relation to Christ.

We speak of man himself as an idea in the divine Mind, and by this we certainly do not mean anything insubstantial or abstract, a merely intellectual concept. Each individual conceived by Mind exists as concrete, substantial reality—far more concrete and substantial than a material body could ever be. The body of St. Paul, for instance, is today nonexistent, yet the tremendous power and vision of his Epistle to the Romans reveal him to us as a living identity, and we catch at least a glimpse of the Paul whom God must know, the Paul who exists eternally in Mind. It is this spiritual expression or manifestation that we describe as idea—not man's idea but God's idea.

This is far removed from Platonic or Hegelian idealism, for it cannot be understood as a mere philosophical abstraction or intellectual concept; it must be felt as the Christ-power. Paul himself wrote, "Henceforth know we no man after the flesh: yea, though we have known Christ after the flesh, yet now henceforth know we him no more," *II Cor. 5:16* and he spoke of "Christ the power of God, and the wisdom of God." *I Cor. 1:24.*

The Christ, as the idea or Son of God, is equally available to all men who are willing to lay down their mortal sense of selfhood and to follow the Master in his demonstration of divine Life. It has long been an embarrassment to Christians that he should have demanded, "Be ye therefore perfect, even as your Father which is in heaven is perfect." *Matt. 5:48.* Imperfect mortals obviously cannot be perfect. But the Christ, as Christian Scientists understand it, comes to reveal that in reality we are not imperfect mortals but the spiritual sons of God who must necessarily be as perfect as their divine Father. This understanding enables us step by step to put off the old man and to put on the new man "which is renewed in knowledge after the image of him that created him." *Col. 3:10.*

This transformation may be most visibly evident in the sign of healing, about which my colleague is going to speak to you. But I should like to point out that the theology of Christian Science cannot be separated from its healing, nor its healing from its theology. This fact separates Christian Science not only from all forms of philosophical idealism but also from all forms of gnostic heresy. Jesus himself said, "It is the spirit that quickeneth; the flesh profiteth nothing," *John 6:63* but he nevertheless redeemed and healed the flesh, and even resurrected it from the grave, in preparation for that final transformation in which all fleshliness will be dropped forever and man's true spiritual being be brought fully to light.

There is a cross to be taken up in this great work, and this cross is the denial of the material selfhood which seems to obscure our spiritual sonship with God. In the last analysis, however, it is the redemption, not merely the sacrifice—the resurrection, not merely the crucifixion—which reveals the full glory of divine Love. It was the risen Lord which was the good news of primitive Christianity, and Christian Science in a similar way emphasizes the triumph of the resurrection. For here is the proof of eternal Life, of the reality of Spirit and the powerlessness of matter, sin, and death to blot out God's likeness. We share in the resurrection in proportion as we awake from the Adam-dream to the perfect universe and perfect man of God's creating.

The Church of Christ, Scientist, is described by its founder, Mary Baker Eddy, as a church without creeds. She does, however, list its religious tenets briefly in *Science and Health:*

1. As adherents of Truth, we take the inspired Word of the Bible as our sufficient guide to eternal Life.

2. We acknowledge and adore one supreme and infinite God. We acknowledge His Son, one Christ; the Holy Ghost or divine Comforter, and man in God's image and likeness.

3. We acknowledge God's forgiveness of sin in the destruction of sin and the spiritual understanding that casts out evil as unreal. But the belief in sin is punished so long as the belief lasts.

4. We acknowledge Jesus' atonement as the evidence of divine, efficacious Love, unfolding man's unity with God through Christ Jesus the Way-shower; and we acknowledge that man is saved through Christ, through Truth, Life, and Love as demonstrated by the Galilean Prophet in healing the sick and overcoming sin and death.

5. We acknowledge that the crucifixion of Jesus and his resurrection served to uplift faith to understand eternal Life, even the allness of Soul, Spirit, and the nothingness of matter.

6. And we solemnly promise to watch, and pray for that Mind to be in us which was also in Christ Jesus; to do unto others as we would have them do unto us; and to be merciful, just, and pure.

On the basis of these tenets it may be easier to understand the Christian Science view of the sacraments. Both baptism and holy communion are a part of its faith and worship, but they are interpreted spiritually. There is no water, no visible element of bread or wine. Baptism is defined in *Science and Health* as, "Purification by Spirit; submergence in Spirit," *S&H p. 581* and it is looked upon as a daily process of regeneration. In the chapter "Atonement and Eucharist" in the same book, the Lord's Supper is also lifted to its spiritual significance in the daily life of the individual. Mrs. Eddy writes:

If Christ, Truth, has come to us in demonstration, no other commemoration is requisite, for demonstration is Immanuel, or *God with us;* and if a friend be with us, why need we memorials of that friend? . . . If all who seek his commemoration through material symbols will take up the cross, heal the sick, cast out evils, and preach Christ, or Truth, to the poor,—the receptive thought,— they will bring in the millennium.

Christian Scientists recognize the deep spiritual significance which the sacraments have in the life of the traditional churches, and without doubt we can all unite at that deepest level of experience in recognizing the sacramental nature of all true living. The healing which results from overcoming the alienation of thought from God is in itself profoundly sacramental in character. In healing, the Word is renewedly made flesh and Truth is once more tested against experience.

THE PRACTICE OF CHRISTIAN SCIENCE

The increasing frequency of actual verifiable healings of sick people today, brought about through prayer, serves to throw an especially vivid light on the references to healing in the New Testament. These present-day experiences recall the emphasis our Saviour laid on healing —for example, his answer when John the Baptist sent messengers asking whether he was indeed the Christ: "Go and shew John again those things which ye do hear and see: the blind receive their sight, and the lame walk, the lepers are cleansed, and the deaf hear, the dead are raised up, and the poor have the gospel preached to them." *Matt. 11:4,5.*

These modern experiences also bring to mind the accounts given us in the New Testament, and in early Christian writings, of cures accomplished through prayer. Our Master evidently foresaw the possibility of his followers' being able to heal the sick by spiritual means, for he said, "He that believeth on me, the works that I do shall he do also." *John 14:12.* And again, "These signs shall follow them that believe; in my name shall they cast out devils; . . . they shall lay hands on the sick, and they shall recover." *Mark 16:17–19.* Even if this last verse from Mark be looked on as a later emendation, it shows the tradition of the early Church in respect to healing.

The present-day developments in the realm of spiritual healing also throw an interesting light on the point of view presented by Christian Science. The fact is that Christian Science is probably best known for its stress upon Christian healing. This has been the case for many decades, even though healing the sick is regarded in Christian Science as only one of the signs of the continuing presence of the Christ among men. Actually, healing is not the whole nor even the major purpose of the practice of Christian Science, which is more deeply concerned with the regeneration of human character and the full salvation of human beings. Yet healing is a natural, inherent part, a vital part, of the work of Christ in human hearts and lives, even as Jesus himself indicated on so many occasions.

Perhaps it is natural that healing is so generally associated with Christian Science. Healing marked the beginnings of this religious movement in America nearly one hundred years ago. The history of Christian Science in the intervening years has been marked by thousands of healings of disease of every sort, often when no other remedy had proved effectual, and frequently under conditions of scrutiny by observers which left no room for reasonable doubt. An important characteristic of these healings is that, like those of earliest Christian times, they have been brought about entirely by spiritual means—that is, by prayer alone rather than by depending partly or wholly on material remedies. . . .

It is the view of Christian Science that as human consciousness comes into closer communion with God, into obedience to His holy law, the divine influence more and more takes precedence in our lives, and physical discords disappear. In the words of Mary Baker Eddy in *Science and Health with Key to the Scriptures,* "It is our ignorance of God, the divine Principle, which produces apparent discord, and the right understanding of Him restores harmony." *S&H p. 390.*

A statement of this sort implies that the healing in Christian Science is inseparable from its theology, and that is indeed the case. Christ came preaching the kingdom of God and healing the sick, and as we see it the two are interrelated. Neither sin nor suffering can find a foothold in the heavenly kingdom, the kingdom which our Master said is really at hand and within us. It is the teaching of Christian Science that insofar as we learn to understand and know this heavenly kingdom, this divine state of consciousness or being, we experience the spiritual transfiguration which Paul alluded to when he wrote to the Romans: "The law of the Spirit of life in Christ Jesus hath made me free from the law of sin and death." *Rom. 8:2.*

Another way of saying this is that in Christian Science the healing of physical, mental, and moral sickness is accomplished through deep and earnest prayer which brings one into harmony with God. Not prayer which entreats but prayer which acknowledges. This is not a prayer in which we plead with God for a special favor, as we might plead with a human judge or ruler. Rather it is a prayer in which we acknowledge the infinite goodness and absolute perfection of the divine Principle, Love. We acknowledge, also, that in God's sight everything that He has created expresses His perfection, harmony, and omnipotent government. We acknowledge that His nature includes no taint or breath of evil; that He is not the originator of disease or death because these have no foothold in absolute Love.

It is true that human affliction is a self-imposed penalty for disobedience or sin or ignorance of God; in other words, it is the end result of the perversity of the carnal mind which is enmity against God. One might draw a parallel, in a certain sense, to what happens when one disobeys or is ignorant of the rules of mathematics, and so finds himself in a wilderness of confusion. He suffers the consequences of his folly until he thoroughly corrects his way of thinking and brings his conduct into harmony with mathematical principles, which are right at hand. Christian Science teaches that the divine Principle, Love, is also right at hand, and that its laws can be known and understood and obeyed. This is what deep and earnest prayer helps us to do. Mrs. Eddy expresses the underlying thought when she writes: "Prayer cannot change the Science of being, but it tends to bring us into harmony with it." *S&H p. 2.*

Prayer as we understand it in Christian Science is not in any way a focusing of the human will, or the practice of suggestion, in an effort to exorcise disease. Rather it is a deep-felt agreeing with and acceptance of the divine will, which is the will and the law of perfect Love. This calls for a sincere effort to sacrifice the arrogance, rebellion, and disobedience of the human mind, to lay aside human will, and to lay hold of the spirit and power of the Christ which is Truth. In the measure that we are successful in doing this we find that the Christ is awakening us spiritually; we are becoming aware of the nature of God and His presence; and sin, sickness, discord are correspondingly blotted out of our consciousness and our lives.

The Christian Science textbook, *Science and Health,* contains a chapter entitled "Christian Science Practice" which is especially devoted to the subject of healing. The opening pages of this chapter comprise a discussion of the mental qualities which open the way for experiencing the healing and saving power of Christ. I say "mental qualities" and it is evident from these pages that this means spiritual qualities, that is, those pure elements of thought which come to us from God. It is plain from the explanations here that it is actually *living* in accord with the spirit and precepts of Christ which opens the way for healing. It is not a theory or a juggling of intellectual or philosophical concepts, but a deep Christianity of thought and desire.

Turning these pages one finds it emphasized that self-righteousness cannot heal. Hypocrisy, pride, envy, lust, selfishness, dishonesty, worldliness—these would only choke out the spirit of Christ and block the way of healing. Shining through the discussion is the central message that it is divine Love that heals. The content of these opening pages is aptly summarized in these words: "If the Scientist has enough Christly affection to win his own pardon, and such commendation as the Magdalen gained from Jesus, then he is Christian enough to practise scientifically and deal with his patients compassionately; and the result will correspond with the spiritual intent." *S&H p. 365.*

The extent of the healing work of Christian Science has sometimes led inquirers to ask if there is something more, some secret, perhaps, which accounts for the results. It is true that a generalized virtue or a vague and undefined awareness of God would not by itself be enough. But there is no secret. Great stress is laid, in Christian Science, on systematic examining of thought for the purpose of bringing our thoughts and actions into better accord with the Christlike way of life which is our goal. As a means of this examination of thought, Christian Science sets forth many rules and precepts which, as we see it, are implicit in the Scriptures but which need to be learned specifically and permitted to govern our thoughts and acts.

An important fundamental is that all disease is basically mental. A diseased physical condition is an expression of diseased thinking. This may mean ungodlike thinking done consciously or unconsciously on the part of the victim, or it may mean the unconscious acceptance of the general atmosphere of human thinking, with its widely felt fears and conflicts, its biases and antagonisms. Indeed, from the viewpoint of Christian Science, matter itself is a false form of thinking. This is another way of saying that existence is a mental experience. Indeed a subjective experience. Change the subjective mental state by an influx of divine light, and disease is healed.

To elaborate this point a little further, Mrs. Eddy writes in *Science and Health:* "The procuring cause and foundation of all sickness is fear, ignorance, or sin. . . . Disease is an image of thought externalized." *S&H p. 411.* And it may be noted that both fear and sin are forms of ignorance of God. It is the position of Christian Science that in every case every form of disease is—in the deepest sense and from beginning to end—entirely the outcome of fear, ignorance, or sin. Not just partially but wholly.

The remedy is the Christ-power, made active within our lives by means of an enlightened understanding of God. This power destroys the mental states which are at fault by awakening us to the presence of God and the omnipotent power of divine Love. Let me stress that something more than human faith or human belief is involved here. Faith is a necessary element but by itself it is not enough, any more than faith alone can solve a problem in geometry. What is needed also is an uncovering of the thinking which is causing the trouble and the casting out of it through understanding. As Mrs. Eddy writes, "The remedy consists in probing the trouble to the bottom, in finding and casting out by denial the error of belief which produces a mortal disorder, never honoring erroneous belief with the title of law nor yielding obedience to it." *S&H p. 184.* And again: "The anatomy of Christian Science teaches when and how to probe the self-inflicted wounds of selfishness, malice, envy, and hate. It teaches the control of mad ambition. It unfolds the hallowed influences of unselfishness, philanthropy, spiritual love." *S&H p. 462.*

Healing may involve much humble and patient searching of one's thoughts and correction of them step by step. But this particular process is not always necessary. On many occasions an individual has gained through prayer so clear and vivid a sense of God's presence that a deep-seated change of thought has taken place immediately and the physical healing has been instantaneous. But whether the healing work comes about slowly or quickly, it does require a regeneration of thought. We feel that the deep and indeed the systematic effort to spiritualize our thoughts and motives has the authority of a Scriptural demand upon us, for as Paul said: "The weapons of our warfare are not carnal, but mighty through God to the pulling down of strongholds; casting down imaginations, and every high thing that exalteth itself against the knowledge of God, and bringing into captivity every thought to the obedience of Christ." *II Cor. 10:4,5.*

This approach to healing rests squarely on the basis that all disease is mental and therefore amenable to a change of consciousness brought about through spiritual power. The Christian Science approach to healing is rooted in the awareness that Christ Jesus never depended wholly or partially on a drug or a material remedy but accomplished his healings solely through spiritual power.

In this connection we may note that when the disciples asked Jesus why they could not heal the epileptic boy whom he had healed after their efforts had failed, our great Master referred to prayer as the remedy, even for this difficult case. According to the traditional wording, he said, "This kind goeth not out but by prayer and fasting." *Matt. 17:21.*

Seen from the standpoint of Christian Science, he referred here to an entirely mental and spiritual process. The fasting would include abstaining from every thought arrayed against the supremacy of divine Principle, God; the prayer would include the deep and sincere acknowledgment of God's love, power, presence; both prayer and fasting so fervently and faithfully maintained as to bring about a deep change in human consciousness—not a superficial change but one that goes to the very roots of one's being.

. . . the healing of physical disease is not the entire or even the chief concern of Christian Science. We have considered it here because of the insights it yields into the nature of the religious teachings and because it is an aspect of the Christian ministry particularly identified with Christian Science. From our viewpoint, healing is a necessary and requisite part of the Christian way of life.

. . . From our point of view, physical healing through prayer is only a token of the deeper and greater work of the power of the Christ in human hearts, which is the reformation of human character, the spiritualization of human thought—in a word, the cleansing of sin and the redemption of society.

As stated in *Science and Health:* "To-day the healing power of Truth is widely demonstrated as an immanent, eternal Science, instead of a phenomenal exhibition. Its appearing is the coming anew of the gospel of 'on earth peace, good-will toward men.' This coming, as was promised by the Master, is for its establishment as a permanent dispensation among men; but the mission of Christian Science now, as in the time of its earlier demonstration, is not primarily one of physical healing. Now, as then, signs and wonders are wrought in the metaphysical healing of physical disease; but these signs are only to demonstrate its divine origin,—to attest the reality of the higher mission of the Christ-power to take away the sins of the world."

13. Jehovah's Witnesses

The Jehovah's Witnesses were founded in Pittsburgh in 1872 by Charles Taze Russell, former Congregationalist. They have been known, in sequence, as the Russelites, the Millenial Dawnists and the International Bible Students. In 1931 they became the Witnesses of Jehovah to symbolize their belief that each member is a personal witness to God in a godless world.

At his death in 1961, Russell was succeeded by Judge J. F. Rutherford, a Missouri lawyer who had defended Russell in his several conflicts with civil authorities. During his almost forty years of presidency, the Witnesses developed their present hierarchical system and highly centralized form of government.

A relative consistency in doctrine is maintained by means of a strict centrality of organization in which the writings of Russell and Rutherford are accepted without question.

Theocracy, or the rule of God, is the foundation of the Witnesses faith and practice. According to Rutherford, when Lucifer rebelled he became ruler of the world, and from then on the human race has followed his lead. Satan remained in heaven until he was driven out by Christ in 1914, reflected on earth in the calamities of the First World War. But Lucifer is still master on earth, where he organized the visible part of his empire by founding churches, the great capitalistic organizations and civil societies. The great tragedy of history is that Satan has forced mankind to practice religion through this triple alliance of ecclesiastical, commercial and political powers.

Since 1914 Christ is said to have been fighting Satan invisibly, and will finally defeat him at Armageddon, annihilating the army of the devil with the help of a host of angels. This will usher in the millennium, a thousand years of earthly happiness for all the righteous who will be resurrected. The wicked will not rise from the dead. After the millennium, Satan will appear again for a short time, only to be utterly destroyed so that even his memory will be removed. At the same time the righteous begin to live forever in peace and blessedness.

Among Rutherford's writings is a volume on *Government*, in which he lays the doctrinal basis for the society he helped to found. His principles on the role of the Witnesses in the world are the mainstay of their faith and the explanation of their astounding zeal to extend the Kingdom of Jehovah to the ends of the earth.

JOSEPH F. RUTHERFORD
PROCLAMATIONS

Jehovah is now doing a marvelous work among the people. That work he long ago foretold by his prophet and gave the reason for doing it. "Wherefore the Lord said, Forasmuch as this people draw near me with their mouth, and with their lips they honour me, but have removed their hearts far from me, and their fear toward me is taught by the precept of men; therefore, behold, I will proceed to do a marvelous work among this people, even a marvelous work and a wonder: for the wisdom of their wise men shall perish, and the understanding of their prudent men shall be hid." (Isa. 29:13, 14)

That prophecy had a miniature fulfillment when Jesus was on earth. It is having a broader and complete fulfillment now since he has come to his temple. In the former days the Jewish clergy, made up of the Pharisees and their allies, caused the people to draw near to the Lord with their mouths, but their hearts were far removed from him. Today the denominational systems, following their leaders the clergy, draw near to God with their mouths, sing songs apparently to his praise, have prayers offered by some clergyman in the legislative bodies as well as in the church buildings, but the hearts of those who engage therein are not near the Lord. The precepts of men are followed and the Word of God is ignored.

God has given much outward evidence, that all who study his Word might understand that his kingdom is here; but this evidence is ignored by the clergy and their allies and they turn the people away therefrom. The clergy are deceiving many people, but of course they are not deceiving God nor retarding the marvelous work that the Lord is doing. The time is here to do his work, and even though he employs the weakest instruments for his visible servants there is no power that can prevent that work from going on.

Included in that marvelous work is the giving of the witness to the peoples of the earth concerning Jehovah and his righteous government that is now being set up. So far as the visible work that is being done is concerned, it is not being done by those of any great reputation amongst men but, on the contrary, by the meek and lowly of heart. God has not committed his work to the great and honorable clergy, but he has committed it to a little company of despised ones in the world whose devotion is entirely to him. That makes it the more marvelous, because it is by the power of God manifested through imperfect men that results are being accomplished.

It was in 1914 that the great prophecy uttered by Jesus concerning the end of the world began to have its fulfillment. The World War, famine, pestilence, revolutions, and earthquakes coming one after the other, furnished good news to the faithful followers of Jesus. How could such terrible things be good news? Of course the suffering of the people brought no joy; but these things coming to pass as they had been foretold furnished the proof conclusive that the world had ended and the time had come for Christ, whose right it is, to begin his reign.

That constituted the good news that gladdened the hearts of the faithful watchers. That was the beginning of the most momentous event of human history, because God's government of righteousness had begun. It was the event for which the true followers of Jesus had been looking for more than 1800 years and about which the holy prophets had testified more than 4000 years ago. To those followers of Jesus who saw the meaning of the events that began to transpire in 1914 it was a time to laugh and dance for joy and to sing with grateful hearts the praise of God Almighty and the praise of his beloved Son who is earth's rightful Governor. That song of gladness then begun by the faithful continues with increased fervency.

Not until after Jesus Christ came to his temple did even his most devoted followers have a clear vision concerning what they should do. It was in 1918 that the World War ceased, and the same year the Lord came to his temple. To those whom the Lord found faithful, and whom he constituted the "faithful and wise servant," he gave flashes of lightning from the temple, that they might have a better understanding of what was expected of them.

The wonderful things that had come to pass since 1914 furnished such great and good news to the faithful watchers that the words of Jesus came to them with a clearer understanding than ever before. The Lord stopped the World War for a purpose, and that purpose was to furnish the opportunity to the faithful to give proclamation of this good news to the people before the final end. Jesus said: "This gospel of the kingdom shall be preached in all the world for a witness unto all nations; and then shall the end come." (Matt. 24:14) The real meaning of these words of the Anointed One could not be understood until after he came to his temple. When he said "this gospel," he meant the good news furnished by the fact that the world had ended and the time had come for Jehovah's righteous government to be put in operation.

Here the Prince of Peace gave to his younger brethren the positive command that must be obeyed, and all who love him and love God will keep this commandment and, keeping it, will have God's special favor. (John 14:21) The keeping of this commandment means to engage in the great and wonderful work which God is doing in the earth. Of what does that work consist? Jesus answers that it is good news that must be told to the people and nations of the earth as a witness to them. That means of course that somebody must testify before the peoples and rulers of the earth that Jehovah is the only true God and that he is the source of life and blessings. Notice must be served upon the rulers of the earth that the time has come for God's government to take charge of the affairs of men. The "prisoners" in the various denominational systems must have an opportunity to hear the message of truth, that their hearts may be made glad. The people must have an opportunity to hear; and to this end the standard must be lifted up to them that they may understand that there are better conditions awaiting them in the very near future; and all this must be done before the "great day of God Almighty" in which Satan's organization must go down.

THE PEOPLE

Jehovah established the jubilee system amongst the Israelites. That jubilee foreshadowed his kingdom or righteous government, when all the oppressed ones must be relieved and have a fair opportunity to start in the way of righteousness. At the opening of the jubilee year the law required the trumpet to be sounded to inform the people that the jubilee year had arrived. (Lev. 25:9, 10) Thereby the Lord foreshadowed that he would have the people informed concerning the establishment of his righteous government through which man shall be returned unto all of his possessions originally intended for him. For this reason Jesus declared that the good news of the kingdom must be given to all nations as a witness before the final sorrows should come upon Satan's organization in which his evil organization will be overthrown. Through his prophet God said to his anointed remnant, his witnesses: "Go through, go through the gates; prepare ye the way of the people; cast up, cast up the highway; gather out the stones; lift up a standard for the people. Behold, the Lord hath proclaimed unto the end of the world, Say ye to the daughter of Zion, Behold, thy salvation cometh; behold, his reward is with him, and his work before him."—Isa. 62:10, 11.

A "gate", as here used, is a symbol of an entrance into the kingdom. The remnant, being now in the temple, are therefore entering the gates of the kingdom. As God's witnesses they are commanded to prepare the way for the people by pointing them to his righteous government. They are told to remove the stumbling stones, which are the false doctrines and theories by which the people have been blinded. They are told to lift up a standard for the people, which means to point the people to the fact that God's righteous government is the standard to which they must rally. This is a part of the work that the Lord God is having done in the earth at this time, and only those who are unselfishly devoted to him are participating in that work.

The only active enemies of Satan now on the earth are those who are joyfully announcing the fact that God has placed his King upon his throne. These must be obedient to God's commands as his witnesses to do his work and finish it before the Lord dashes to pieces Satan's organization in the final time of trouble which Christ Jesus pointed out is now impending. (Matt. 24:14, 21, 22) It is to be expected that Satan, that old Dragon, is exceedingly angry at the faithful witnesses of the Lord and will do everything within his power to destroy them. The Lord said that this is what he would do: "And the dragon was wroth with the woman, and went to make war with the remnant of her seed, which keep the commandments of God, and have the testimony of Jesus Christ."—Rev. 12:17.

Through the clergy and the principal of their flocks Satan presses his warfare against the remnant of God because of their faithfulness. But the enemy can not prevail, for the reason it is written: "And they overcame him by the blood of the Lamb, and by the word of their testimony; and they loved not their lives unto the death."—Rev. 12:11.

The faithful remnant, trusting in the blood of Christ, anointed by the spirit of Jehovah, counting not their lives dear unto them, are joyfully giving the testimony and by the Lord's grace they will overcome the enemy. On they go in the work with joy and singing. They press the battle to the very gate of Satan's organization, and while so doing fear no evil because they are in the secret place of the Most High. (Ps. 91:1-15) Foreseeing this day of his wonderful work God through his prophet says to the remnant: "In that day shall the Lord of hosts be for

a crown of glory, and for a diadem of beauty, unto the residue (remnant) of his people, and for a spirit of judgment to him that sitteth in judgment, and for strength to them that turn the battle to the gate."
—Isa. 28:5, 6.

Many Christians have deceived themselves into believing that God is trying to have them develop a beautiful and sweet character that they might go to heaven and there sing and enjoy ease and comfort forever. The true remnant class realize that in order to be of the heavenly government class they must do some singing while on earth and do it to the praise of Jehovah's name. They must be witnesses that he is the Mighty God. They are called out of darkness into the marvelous light that they might show forth his praises while on earth. (1 Pet. 2:9, 10) God will take into his government and make official members thereof only those who prove that they love him and his King more than their own lives. Perfect love has no fear of man or Devil, but he who has perfect love and absolute confidence in the Lord boldly makes proclamation of the truth as a witness in the name of the Lord.—I John 4:17, 18.

LEADER OF THE PEOPLE

When Jesus accepted the call and received the anointing of the holy spirit he became the heir of David the king, and the everlasting covenant applied to him from that time forward. Why was the covenant made? Among other reasons God's prophet answers: "Behold, I have given him for a witness to the people, a leader and commander to the people." (Isa. 55:4) God made the everlasting covenant with Jesus for a throne, and immortality, which included all the interests of his righteous government on earth. The kingdom interests required him to be a witness to the name of Jehovah. Pilate said to Jesus: "Art thou a king?" The answer of Jesus was: "Thou sayest that I am a king. To this end was I born, and for this cause came I into the world, that I should bear witness unto the truth. Every one that is of the truth heareth my voice." (John 18:36, 37) This is proof conclusive that one of the conditions of the everlasting covenant was that he should bear witness to the name of Jehovah. To his faithful followers Jesus said: "And I covenant for you, even as my Father has covenanted for me, a kingdom." Just so surely as Jesus must bear witness to the truth, even so must every one who is in that covenant bear witness to the truth. This is especially true after the Lord comes to his temple. By that covenant Jesus was made the leader of the people. It also follows that all who are taken into that covenant must become leaders of the people under the direction of the

Head. That leading of the people must be in the way of God's righteousness. To be a leader each one must be a faithful witness as opportunity affords. It means also that such leaders must be entirely out of accord with the evil world and its god the Devil. Jesus refused to compromise with the Devil. His followers must do the same thing. As Jesus forgot self and did only as his Father commanded, even so those who are taken into the covenant must forget self and joyfully obey the commandments of the Lord.

In this day of distress and perplexity, when the people are suffering under the burdens of unrighteous governments and know not which way to turn, never was there such a blessed opportunity as that given now to the true followers of Jesus to lead the people in the way of righteousness by pointing them to God's kingdom. It is that righteous government that shall bring relief and everlasting joy to mankind. Some of the anointed ones for a time neglected the privilege of being such witnesses. The Scriptures show that some of these become aware of their negligence and awake to their privileges and then take a part in proclaiming the glad message; and so doing, God bestows upon them his everlasting blessings. (Isa. 59:20, 21) While the Lord progresses with the establishment of his government, he says to those whom he has chosen for his witnesses: "I have put my words in thy mouth, and I have covered thee in the shadow of mine hand, that I may plant the heavens, and lay the foundations of the earth, and say unto Zion, Thou art my people."—Isa. 51:16.

The fact that he has put his message in the mouth of these witnesses is conclusive proof that they must be proclaiming his name and his government to those who have hearing ears. This is the part of such in the planting of the invisible, as well as the visible, part of God's government. It is their privilege and duty to tell the people what the present events mean and how the Lord will establish for them a government that will bring them peace and blessings. In so doing, these associates with Christ Jesus constitute leaders for the people.

VENGEANCE

The anointed ones of the Lord now on earth are commanded to declare the day of the vengeance of God. (Isa. 61:1, 2) The vengeance of Jehovah is not expressed against individuals, but against Satan and his wicked organization by which he oppresses and blinds the people, and against the instruments that he uses for that purpose. Jehovah's purpose is to destroy Satan's wicked works and his organization, and he is now having the witness given making known that fact to the nations. For this reason he discloses to those of the temple class what constitutes the Devil's organization. It is seen to be a powerful and dreadfully wicked organization which the Lord alone can and will destroy. He lays upon his servants the obligation of declaring his purpose to destroy it. Jesus states that after the good news of the kingdom has been declared to the people there shall come upon the nations of the earth a time of trouble the like of which was never known and that it will be the last. That will be the expression of God's indignation against the evil one and his system. (Matt. 24:21, 22) The period of time from the cessation of hostilities in the world to the time of the final trouble is reserved specifically for the giving of the witness of and concerning God's purposes.

Through his prophet Jehovah declares that he has a controversy with the nations that make up Satan's organization and that he will destroy such. Having already ousted Satan from heaven and destroyed his rule there, we may know that God will destroy his rule and influence on earth. Such is one of the preliminary works of God's righteous government. (Jer. 25:29-36) In that work of destruction Jesus Christ leads the assault. This he does as the mighty Executive Officer of Jehovah. (Ps. 110:5, 6) Christ alone is the wine-press that crushes the life out of the evil organization. (Isa. 63:3-5) The part in this great work that is performed by the faithful followers of Christ on earth is that of process servers. They serve notice by telling the rulers and peoples of earth of Jehovah's purpose through Christ to destroy the evil organization. (I John 3:8) Of course Satan knows that the great fight is approaching, but he is so self-centered that he believes he will win that fight. Knowing that the time is short for him to prepare for it, he hastens to gather the nations and rulers of earth into a condition for the great battle, in which great battle Satan's organization will fall, never to rise again; and the name of Jehovah God shall be everlastingly exalted.—Rev. 12:12; 16:13-16.

AMBASSADORS

The faithful remnant of the followers of Christ Jesus now on earth are ambassadors of God and his King. These are in the world to represent the Lord. To some it may seem to be inconsistent for these ambassadors to be in the world and yet proclaiming the truth concerning what is about to befall the world. It may be argued that ambassadors are in a country only when both countries involved are at peace and that when war is declared the ambassador withdraws; whereas God's government is not at peace with Satan's organization. Such is the rule that obtains in the divisions of the government controlled by Satan. Such is not the rule of the Lord. The Scriptures show that the Lord's ambassadors are sent to the rulers when hostilities exist. Satan's organization is hostile to God's organization and God has declared his purpose to destroy Satan's organization. Christ is God's Ambassador to bring reconciliation between the people and God because hostilities do exist.

The members of the body of Christ are ambassadors participating in that work of reconciliation because the people are hostile to God. In no other way can the words of the Apostle Paul be properly understood. (II Cor. 5:19, 20) The ambassadors of the Lord are now in the world but not of it. They are authorized to declare in denunciatory terms that which God's Word says concerning his purpose of manifesting his indignation against the evil system which Satan has builded up. This system being an oppressor of the people, God will relieve the people therefrom and wills that they shall be so told. Paul spoke of himself as an "ambassador in bonds," and his bonds were placed upon him by Satan's organization. (Eph. 6:20) All the ambassadors of Christ on earth would now be in bonds except that God has put his hand over them and by his power shields them until the work committed to them is done. When that work of proclaiming his name and purposes is done, then God will take the ambassadors away.

JOY OF THE LORD

While these ambassadors of the Lord are in the world they have much tribulation, even as Jesus foretold. (John 16:33) Their tribulation is caused by the opposers of the message they are bringing and the work they are doing. These faithful ones, however, like Paul, "rejoice in tribulation" because such is a token to them from God that they are his anointed saints. (Phil. 1:28, 29; Rom. 12:12; Acts 14:22) Those of the remnant class have entered into the joy of the Lord because they see that the time has come for God to vindicate his holy name, to overthrow the oppressor, and to bring peace and righteousness to the earth through his anointed King. When, at the end of the long period of waiting, Jesus received the command from His Father to arise and take action against the enemy, that was a time of great joy to Christ the Lord. When he came to his temple and found some whom he approved because of their faithfulness, he invited them to enter into his joy. Those who since that time have seen and appreciated that the kingdom is here and that the time has come to vindicate Jehovah's name, and who continue to love the Lord, have gone forward to their work abounding in the joy of the Lord.

14. Ethical Culture

The term "Ethical Culture" is commonly applied to a movement started by Felix Adler (1851-1933) of New York City in 1876. It has since come to be applied also to the societies which owe their origin to the principles of Ethical Culture, even though some statisticians fail to include these societies among the religious denominations.

Felix Adler, the founder of Ethical Culture, was an immigrant from the Rhineland who came to the United States as a child and after graduation from Columbia became teacher of Oriental literature at Cornell University. His religious background was Jewish and he was to have succeeded his father as rabbi of Temple Emmanuel in New York City. The struggle that Adler underwent in conflict with traditional Judaism resulted in his revolt against the synagogue. At first only a few friends joined him, but soon a coterie of followers pledged themselves "to assert the supreme importance of the ethical factor in all relations of life, personal, social, national and international, apart from any theological or metaphysical considerations."

Among the formative factors to which Adler attributed his discovery of Ethical Culture, the moral teachings of Jesus were of paramount importance. Christian ethics, he said, has promoted the moral development of mankind in a thousand ways. It has emphasized the inner springs of conduct. Nevertheless, "like every product of the mind and aspirations of man, it exhibits the limitations of the time and of the social conditions under which it arose. The conditions have since changed."

It was Adler's contention that with the help of Christianity a philosophy of life can be developed that will dispense with the theology of the Gospels and bring up to date the ethical ideals of Jesus of Nazareth. Adler believed that he could improve on the teachings of Christ, and Ethical Culture is still based on the same premises.

Ethical Culture societies in the major cities, for example, New York, Chicago and St. Louis, are affiliated in the American Ethical Union (1889), which publishes as its organ *The Standard* and which coordinates the far-reaching educational and social activities of the local branches. Their "leaders" perform the usual functions of ordained ministers in conducting marriage and funeral services, and membership is open in the societies to all persons who accept the single doctrine of the ethical aim as the supreme purpose of life, without regard for individual opinions about the existence of God or the immortality of the soul.

Public services are extremely simple, consisting of music, inspirational readings and the ethical address or "sermon." A number of societies have introduced congregational singing and responsive readings. But they have generally been reluctant to copy the ritual programs of established churches.

Someone has described Ethical Culture as "Unitarian Moralism," and the designation is apt because it specifies the two principal foci of this religious movement: the exclusion of revelation as a necessary foundation of faith, and the preoccupation with moral issues as the mainstay of human life.

Adler's writings in both areas are normative for the Ethical Culture societies. His *Ethical Philosophy of Life* is the nearest approximation to a doctrinal standard recognized by his followers.

Within the *Ethical Philosophy*, Adler synthesized his entire position and gave Ethical Culturists their organizational structure in the document here quoted, on "Religious Fellowship as the Culminating Social Institution."

This document is more than the basis of an American religious body. It has deeply influenced national thought through men like David Muzzey, the historian, and organizations like the Child Study Association of America, originally a group of mothers in the Ethical Culture Society.

FELIX ADLER
RELIGIOUS FELLOWSHIP
AS THE CULMINATING SOCIAL INSTITUTION

The religious society is the last term in the series of social institutions, and its peculiar office is to furnish the principle for the successive transformation of the entire series. It is to be the laboratory in which the ideal of the spiritual universe is created and constantly recreated, the womb in which the spiritual life is conceived. No single religious society can adequately fulfill this purpose. The spiritual ideal itself must necessarily be conceived differently by different minds; but the great general purpose will be the same, despite variations in shades of meaning and points of view.

The fellowship of the religious society must be based on the voluntary principle; membership must be a matter of free choice. In antiquity the boundaries of the political and religious organizations coincided. The citizen was under obligations as a part of his civic duty to worship the divinities of the state. In modern times a state church is still maintained in some countries and supported out of the public funds, while dissenting and noncomformist bodies exist more or less on sufferance at its side. But this arrangement is harmful, especially so to those whom it seems to favor. Erastianism paralyzes religious spontaneity. The state, it is true, is profoundly interested in the flourishing of ethical idealism, and in the constant rebirth in its midst of spiritual ideals. But it is not competent to determine what the character of these ideals shall be. The moment they cease to be freely produced they lose their life-giving power. The state within limits may enforce action; it may not even attempt to enforce beliefs.

On the other hand, the "secularization of the state" has given rise to the deplorable impression that the state exists only for so-called secular purposes, and has stripped the idea of the state of the lofty attributes with which the great thinkers of antiquity had clothed it. It is the function of the religious society, dwelling uncoerced in the midst of the state, to reinvest the state with the sacred character that belongs to it. . . . The object of religious devotion is the infinite holy community, the spiritual universe. The function of the religious society is to generate the ideal of the infinite holy community, of the spiritual universe. The family, the vocation, the nation, are sub-groups of this, lesser entities. Even mankind itself is but a province of the ideal spiritual commonwealth that extends beyond it. To concentrate worship upon the state or nation as some propose, would be to usurp for the part the piety that belongs to the whole.

In describing a religious society three main aspects are to be borne in mind:

The teaching, the organization, the worship.

The Teaching. In the religious society as here conceived there is to be worked out a body of doctrine, and there is to be a body of specially designated teachers. An ethico-religious society cannot ignore or dispense with a general philosophy of life and statements of belief. It cannot restrict itself to encouraging practical morality without regard to what are called metaphysical subtleties. A moral society of this kind would soon become ossified. On the contrary, an ethico-religious society should excel in the fertility with which it gives rise to new metaphysical constructions and original formulations of ethical faith. The will cannot be divorced from the intellect. The active volitional life cannot be successfully stimulated and guided without the assistance of the mind as well as of the imagination.

But the relation between philosophy and formulas of belief on the one hand and volitional experience on the other should be the reverse of what it has been in the past. Here there must be a new departure. The doctrine, the formulations, whatever they may be, must not be dogmatic but flexible. Growing originally out of ethical experience, they must ever prove themselves apt to enlarge and deepen ethical experience. By this test they will be judged and they must therefore ever be subject to revision and correction. Every dogma, every philosophic or theological creed, was at its inception a statement in terms of the intellect of a certain inner experience. But then it claimed for itself eternal validity, compressing the spiritual life within its mold, and checking further development. The body of doctrine . . . will likewise be an interpretation of ethical experience, intended to make explicit the fundamental principles implicit in ethical experience, and thereby clarifying it, and assisting its further unfolding. But it is not and should never be allowed to become dogmatic. The difference . . . is plain: in the one case experience contracted in procrustean fashion into a rigid formula, in the other case an elastic formula adapted to and subordinated to the experience.

Thus much for the body of teachings. There should also be a body of teachers. A teacher in an ethico-religious society will retain something of the character of his predecessors—priest, prophet, rabbi, pastor. The priest is the mediator of grace; the prophet is the seer of visions; the rabbi is learned in the Divine law, and the pastor is the helper of the individual in securing his individual salvation. But these functions will now be seen in an altered light, and will be radically modified in their exercise. The magical attribute of the priest disappears. The confident prediction of future events, based on the assumption that the moral order is to be completely realized in human society, has ceased to be convincing. The Divine law is no longer identical with the Law revealed in the Scriptures and their commentaries, and the salvation of the individual is to be accomplished by other means.

The religious teacher of the new kind is to resemble his predecessors in being a specialist. The word specialist in this connection may, perhaps, awaken misgivings, and these must be removed. He is not a specialist in the sense of having a conscience unlike that of others, or in being the keeper of other men's consciences. Nor shall he impose his philosophy of life or his belief authoritatively, but propose it suggestively. His best results will be gained if he succeeds in so stimulating those whom he influences that they will attain an individualized spiritual outlook of their own, consonant with their own individual nature and need. But specialists of this kind are indispensable. The generality of men have neither the time nor the mental equipment to think out the larger problems of life without assistance, and the attempt on their part to do so leads to crudities and eccentricities of which one meets nowadays with many pathetic examples among those who have severed their connection with traditional faiths, and have tried in their groping fashion to invent a metaphysic or a creed of their own.

The preparation of the ethical teacher for his special task consists in making himself thoroughly acquainted with the great religious systems of the past, in which much that is of permanent spiritual value is enshrined. He is to fit himself to revitalize what is vital, not to repristinate what is obsolete. There is required of him a first-hand knowledge of the great ethical systems, and of their philosophical backgrounds: furthermore acquaintance, so far as it is as yet accessible, with the moral history of mankind, as distinguished from the history of ethical thinking; in addition, he should intensively study the economic, social and political problems of the time from the ethical point of view, and the psychology both of individual and national character, so far as that fascinating and difficult subject has been opened up by competent writers. Apprenticeship in the social reform movements of the day, direct touch with the inner life of people, on its healthful as well as on its sick side, is also presupposed.

Since no single person can be adequately prepared in these various subjects, and since a variety of gifts and talents is demanded, it follows that the teaching function shall be exercised by a body or group of teachers, not by a single pastor at whose feet the congregation are supposed to sit. Some of the persons engaged in this work will excel as public speakers, others as writers, others as teachers of the young, others as leaders of vocational groups. But all these different functionaries must learn to work, not only in harmony, but in organic, reciprocal support, themselves illustrating in their group life the spiritual relation, the knowledge and the practice of which they are to carry out into the world. The guild or group idea must be applied to the religious teachers of the future.

The Organization. Every religion exhibits a certain form of organization peculiar to itself and derived from its controlling idea. The organization of the Buddhist fellowship is dependent on the Buddhist ideal of preparation for absorption in Nirvana. The constitution of the Jewish synagogue reflects the conception of the relation of the Chosen People, as an *elite* corps of the divinity. The organization of the Christian church is characterized by its bifurcation into an *ecclesia militans* and an *ecclesia triumphans,* and further by the idea of incorporation into the body of Christ, a difficult mystical conception as of a typical divine individual including with his body a multitude of other individuals.

The organization of the ethico-religious society has been foreshadowed in the chapter on the vocations. The society is to be divided into vocational groups. In each vocational group is to be worked out the specific ethical ideal of that vocation. In the groups the general ethical philosophy of life is to be applied, tested and enriched. The so-called ethical teachers will here come into fruitful contact with those who are in touch at first hand with actual conditions, and are cognizant of the difficulties to be surmounted in ethicizing vocational standards. The members of the groups in democratic fashion will contribute to the advancement, not only of ethical practice, but of ethical knowledge, and thus become on their side teachers of the teachers. The danger of the formation of an ethical clergy will be averted. The teachers will be in certain respects the pupils of the taught, and the relation be reciprocal, that is, ethical.

Among the groups the vocational group of Mothers will occupy the central place. The influence of women, especially of the mother group, must penetrate the religious society through and through, for the purpose of drawing the entire fellowship together into a coherent unity. Women henceforth will take a deeper interest in the ethical development of human society. A main factor, if not the only factor in the ethical development of human society, is the elevation of the vocational standards. The group of mothers will therefore be in close touch with the other vocational groups in order to gain a knowledge of the higher standards therein proposed, in order to appraise them, and to inspire the growing generation with the devoted purpose to carry these standards out in practice.

The Worship or Public Manifestation of Religion. The ideal of worship likewise must undergo transformation. It has meant an act of homage toward a superior or supreme individual; it has meant eulogistic affirmation of the power, wisdom, goodness, of that individual; it has meant prayer or petition for help from that individual. It has also meant spiritual edification.

In all these various modes, religious worship heretofore has focused attention on a single individual deity as one who embodies in himself the sum of perfection. In thus presenting the ideal of perfection, it has encouraged preference for unity at the expense of plurality. The salient feature of the spiritual ideal sketched in this volume is the affirmation, on ethical grounds, that plurality is of equal dignity with unity, and hence that the divine ideal is to be represented not as One, but as manifold; not as an individual, however supereminent, but as an infinite holy community,—every human being being in his essential nature a member of that community.

But can worship be offered to the members of a holy community? In a certain sense one might say, Yes, preeminently so, since worship may be taken to mean Worthship, and the worth intrinsic in our fellowmen is the object of our unceasing homage. At the same time very different associations have gathered about the word. Public worship consists largely of eulogistic singing, prayer, adoration, genuflexion, and these are appropriate only to deity conceived as an individual. We cannot even say with the Psalmist "the heavens declare the glory of God, and the firmament showeth his handiwork." For though the beauty and order apparent in Nature is one aspect of nature on which we delight to dwell, yet we cannot disingenuously suppress the counter evidence of disorder, ugliness and suffering which Nature no less obtrudes on our sight. The argument from design implied in the Pslamist's words is no longer tenable. Certainly we cannot any longer pray for material assistance as our forefathers did, or invoke supernatural intervention in situations where human science and human helpfulness are impotent. But worship also aims at ethical edification, by holding up to the mind the moral ideal as an object of imitation, and as a rebuke to man's shortcomings. This indeed is its highest function. Nevertheless the moral ideal, as we conceive it, is incapable of being presented in the guise of an individual being, no matter by what superlative language the limitation inseparable from individuality be concealed. The bare attributes of omniscience and omnipotence are abstract and convey no positive meaning whatever. In actual worship a concrete image is invariably associated with the notion of the individualized Deity, such as the Father image or the Christ image. And as soon as this is done, the vast ethical ideal tends to shrink to the dimensions of a human image; and instead of the ideal in its fullness, only certain selected but inadequate aspects of ethical excellence are presented to the worshiper.

And yet in an ethico-religious society also the public manifestation of religion is indispensable. Of what elements shall it consist?

First, there are to be the public addresses by the teachers, having for their main object to arouse or intensify a certain kind of spiritual distress, and then as far as possible to appease it. Every religion . . . originates in a particular kind of anguish, and is an attempt to assuage it. The spiritual distress in which the ethico-religious society has its origin is the agonizing consciousness of tangled relations with one's fellow-beings, and the inexpressible longing to come into right relations with them. He is fit to be a public teacher of this religion who profoundly experiences this distress, who desires nothing so much as to cease to be, for his part, a thorn in his neighbor's side. We are that, each of us, inevitably. The more this feeling is strong in him the more will he arouse similar feelings in others, and thus awaken those who are spiritually asleep, the self-righteous, the self-satisfied, and he will then indicate to the utmost of his power, the way of relief.

The specific ethical ideals of life are also to be presented in public assemblies—the ideals of private ethics, of marriage, friendship, and the rest. These expressions of the specific ideals, charged with feeling, and taking on appropriate imagery, will gradually attain a certain classical fitness—classical at least for a time—and may be used as public readings.

But is there a substitute for prayer?

Among the advantages of prayer is often mentioned this: that in it the soul reaches out towards its source, and in so doing wonderfully recruits its spiritual energy. It finds, ethically speaking, its second wind. It reaches down beneath its utmost strength to find an increment of strength not previously at its disposal. The question is whether this increment of strength cannot be obtained more surely and to better purpose in another way, namely, by concentrating attention on the spiritual need of the fellow-being with whom we are in daily touch, and by becoming aware to what an extent the finer nature imprisoned in them is dependent for its release upon our exertions. The appeal of the God in our neighbor is the substitute for the appeal in prayer to the God in heaven, the call of the stifled spiritual nature in the men and women at our side, is to draw out of us our utmost latent force, the strengths underneath the strength.

The common life we share with our fellow-members in the religious society demands expression in song and in responsive services. The high wave of this common life welling up in us, rising to the surface, makes the glow of religious meeting, gives them fervor, and a touch of rapture, not indeed the common life conceived as a uniform life, but as the life we live in others, and they in us.

The addresses that awaken and appease spiritual pain, the presentation of the various modes of right living, the songs that lift the individual above his private self and help him to live, not indeed submerged, but rather spiritually accentuated in the life of the whole, these are the public manifestations of ethical religion. . . . They will contribute to make of the society itself the symbol of its ethical faith. We shall not have an external symbol like the cross: the fellowship itself will be our symbol.

There will also be festivals. Every religion must have its festivals. In place of Baptism the solemn taking of responsibility for the spiritual development of the child. A festival of vocational initiation, like the ancient assumption of the *toga*. Festivals of citizenship, inspired by the ideal of the national character as one to be spiritually transformed. Festivals of humanity in connection with commemoration of great events in the history of our race and of great leaders who were inspired in some degree by the ideal task of humanity. Festivals of the seasons, deriving their significance from the spiritual interpretation of the corresponding seasons of human life,—youth, middle age, old age. And a solemn though not mournful festival in commemoration of the departed.

The religious assembly should itself be organized; the members of the different vocational groups should be allocated to different parts of the meeting hall, as were the Guilds in certain of the mediaeval cathedrals.

Besides the public manifestations, the private religion will receive attention. The religious society as a whole is to be the microcosm of the spiritual macrocosm, a miniature model of the ideal society, but care must also be taken for the private communion of the individual with the spiritual presences which the ideal evokes. There should be a special breviary for the sick, a Book of Consolation for the bereaved, a Book of Friendship, a Book of direction for those who pass through the experience of sin, and a book of preparation for those who face the end.

15. *Unity School of Christianity*

The Unity School of Christianity describes itself as a religious educational institution devoted to demonstrating that the teaching of Jesus Christ is a practical seven-days-a-week way of life. Because of its non-denominational stress on Christian teaching and healing, it prefers to be called a school rather than a church, yet "prepared through its activities to help anyone, regardless of church affiliation, to find health, peace, joy and plenty through his day-by-day practice of Christian principles."

The Unity movement out of which the School grew, was founded in Kansas City, Missouri, on December 7, 1892, the day that Charles Fillmore and his wife Myrtle wrote their *Dedication and Covenant*. They declared:

> We, Charles Fillmore and Myrtle Fillmore, husband and wife, hereby dedicate ourselves, our time, our money, all we have and all we expect to have, to the Spirit of Truth, and through it, to the Society of Silent Unity.
>
> It being understood and agreed that the Savior's Spirit of Trust shall render unto us an equivalent for this dedication, in peace of mind, health of body, wisdom, understanding, love, life, and an abundant supply of all things necessary to meet every want without our making any of these things the object of our existence.*

Two things led the Fillmores to make this dedication: their several years' experience with Christian Science and the wife's unexpected cure of an inherited tuberculosis. The Fillmores parted company with the Christian Scientists over several doctrinal positions, notably the acceptance of the reality of the material world. Sin, sickness and death, according to the Fillmores, are real, but they can be overcome, and Unity possesses the means by which they may be overcome.

* *Blessings From the Unity Household,* Lee's Summit, Missouri, 1967, p. 4.

While differing substantially from Christian Science, Unity also differs from New Thought, with which it was associated originally and is still sometimes mistakenly confused.

The final breach with New Thought came in 1922, when the directors of Unity voted unanimously to retire from the New Thought Alliance. They disagreed with the Alliance on the question of eternal life. According to Unity, eternal life is to be won here and now by the process of body refinement, and body refinement can be achieved by mental realization of oneness with the Absolute, together with the renunciation (if possible) of all pleasures that exalt sense above the soul. Thus man can overcome death—whereas most New Thought groups believed that death was the entrance into a higher life.

The Unity School of Christianity carries on an extensive correspondence with its affiliates and publishes a wide variety of books and pamphlets directed to the cultivation of peace of mind and health of body, through adjustment of soul to the Divine Mind. One of its most popular forms of prayerful communication is Silent Unity, expressed in the promise that "through faithful practice of the presence of God man can be healed of illness, lack, or any other inharmonious condition besetting him."

Its most authoritative creedal declaration is *Unity's Statement of Faith,* issued by the national headquarters of the Unity School of Christianity.

UNITY'S STATEMENT OF FAITH

1. We believe in God, the one and only omnipotent, omniscient, and omni-present Spirit-mind.

2. We believe in Christ, the Son of God, in whom is imaged the ideal creation, with perfect man on the throne of dominion.

3. We believe in Christ Jesus, the Son of God made manifest in Jesus of Nazareth, who overcame death, and who is now with us in His perfect body as the Way-shower in regeneration for all men.

4. We believe in the Holy Spirit, which baptizes the universe and man with the thoughts of God and perpetually establishes the divine law in all manifestation.

5. We believe in the supremacy and the eternity of the good, as the one and only objective of man and of all things visible and invisible.

6. We believe in the twelve disciples, the twelve powers of man, going forth into mind and body with power and authority to teach, preach, heal, and wholly save man and the world from sin, sickness and death.

7. We believe that "God is spirit," as Jesus taught, and that all of His Spirit is with us at all times, supplying every need.

8. We believe that divine intelligence is present in every atom of man and matter, and that the more abundant life, which Jesus promised, is flooding the world and quickening the minds and the bodies of men everywhere.

9. We believe that the original authority and dominion given to man was over his own thoughts, emotions, feelings, and passions, and that, in the lawful exercise of this authority, he will harmonize all discords within and without and restore the kingdom of God on earth.

10. We believe in the creative power of thoughts and words; that they do accomplish that whereto they are sent and that all men are held accountable for even their lightest words.

11. We believe that through indulgence in sense consciousness men fell into the belief in the reality of matter and material conditions. We believe that the "kingdom of God" can be attained here and now by overcoming the world, the flesh and the Adversary through Jesus Christ.

12. We believe in the at-one-ment that Jesus re-established between God and man, and that through Jesus we can regain our original estate as sons of God.

13. We believe that the prayer of faith will save the sick, resurrect the body from "trespasses and sins," and finally overcome the last enemy, death.

14. We believe that Jesus Christ, the Son of God, is alive and in the world today. We believe that the more abundant life, which Jesus promised, is poured into the race stream as a vitalizing energy, and that, when accepted in faith, it purifies the life-flow in our bodies and makes us immune to all diseased thoughts and germs.

15. We believe that sense consciousness may be lifted up, "as Moses lifted up the serpent in the wilderness," and that all men may be again restored to paradise through faith, understanding, and practice of the divine law, as Jesus Christ taught and demonstrated.

16. We believe that creative Mind, God, is masculine and feminine, and that these attributes of Being are fundamental in both natural and spiritual man. "And God created man in his own image, in the image of God created he him; male and female created he them."

17. We believe that we live, move, and have our being in God-Mind; also that God-Mind lives, moves, and has being in us, to the extent of our consciousness.

18. We believe that the body of man is the highest-formed manifestation of creative Mind and that it is capable of unlimited expression of that Mind. "Know ye not that your body is a temple of the Holy Spirit?"

19. We believe that through conscious union with Jesus in the regeneration, man can transform his body and make it perpetually healthy, therefore immortal, and that he can attain eternal life in this way and in no other way.

20. We believe that the blood of Jesus represents eternal life, that the body of Jesus represents incorruptible substance. We believe that these are original elements in Being and that they can be appropriated by all who, through faith and understanding, attain the Christ standard of spirituality.

21. We believe that spirit, soul, and body are a unit, and that any separation of these three is transgression of the divine law. We believe that the death that came into the world through the Adamic man resulted in body dissolution and that the restoration of the lost Eden is already begun, in the demonstration over the death of the body, as shown in the resurrection of Jesus Christ.

22. We believe that the dissolution of spirit, soul, and body, caused by death, is annulled by rebirth of the same spirit and soul in another body here on earth. We believe the repeated incarnations of man to be a merciful provision of our loving Father to the end that all may have opportunity to attain immortality through regeneration, as did Jesus. "This corruptible must put on incorruption."

23. We believe that the kingdom of heaven or harmony is within man and that through man the law and order existing in Divine Mind are to be established on the earth.

24. We believe that the "second coming" of Jesus Christ is now being fulfilled, that His Spirit is quickening the whole world. "For as the lightning cometh forth from the east, and is seen even unto the west; so shall be the coming of the Son of man."—"Watch therefore; for yet know not on what day your Lord cometh."

25. We believe that the Golden Rule, "Do unto others as you would have them do unto you," should be the standard of action among men.

26. We believe that Jehovah God is incarnate in Jesus Christ and that all men may attain the Christ perfection by living the righteous life. "Ye therefore shall be perfect, as your heavenly Father is perfect."

27. We believe that the Word of God is the thought of God expressed in creative ideas and that these ideas are the primal attributes of all enduring entities in the universe, visible and invisible. The Logos of the first chapter of the Gospel of John is the God idea or Christ that produced Jesus, the perfect man. We believe that the Scriptures are the testimonials of men who have in a measure apprehended the divine Logos but that their writings should not be taken as final.

28. We believe in the final resurrection of the body, through Christ. We believe that we do free our minds and resurrect our bodies by true thoughts and words and that this resurrection is being carried forward daily and will ultimate in a final purification of the body from all earthly errors. Through this process we shall be raised to the consciousness of continuous health and eternal life here and now, following Jesus Christ in the regeneration or "new birth."

29. We believe all the doctrines of Christianity spiritually interpreted.

30. Almighty Father-Mother, we thank Thee for this vision of Thine omnipotence, omniscience, and omnipresence in us and in all that we think and do, in the name of Jesus Christ. Amen.

HEALING MINISTRY INSTRUCTIONS

It is a joy to welcome you to the ministry of this center. Jesus Christ is the head of our work, and it is in His name and through His power that you are blessed and lifted up. Christ's healing, prospering, harmonizing presence is within you, and it is our purpose to assist you to realize this presence consciously.

United Prayer. The name Unity implies not only oneness with the Spirit but also a co-operative action. We pray with you in the joyous faith that sees you bringing forth the Father's vision of you, the fulness of life, joy, and plenty, but only as you diligently seek to develop your indwelling possibilities can you fulfill this vision. Our desire is that through prayer we may point the way to your Christ perfection.

In order that this desire may be speedily accomplished we ask that you join us each day in the prayer given to you. Think about the words until you understand their full meaning and feel their quickening power within you. Let them steady your mind and free you from all fear or doubt as you go about your activities. Great importance is attached to the matter of your regular and faithful co-operation, and much emphasis is placed upon it, for it is in this manner that a channel is formed for the Father's rich blessings to come through you and to you.

Reports. Besides praying regularly with us we request a report from you within two weeks, or the time agreed upon. This request has a twofold purpose, and is for your benefit as well as ours. First, sending a good report is something for you to look forward to; and secondly, this report keeps us who are vitally interested in you informed of your progress. We shall rejoice in a good report from you, or we shall consider it a privilege to continue praying with you until your demonstration is complete.

Compensation. The union established between the center ministry and student is an eternal bond, and each contributes to the other. The ministry freely and generously given you touches the chord of grateful receiving in your consciousness. The grateful heart is a giving heart and desires to share of its good. Therefore your thoughts of love, your prayerful attitude, and your love offerings are very welcome. Our center ministry is sustained by prayer and the freewill offerings and tithes of those interested in the work.

Your trust in God and your belief in the power of prayer has made you a strengthening part of our work. Your faith has widened the circle of our spiritual service, strengthened our consciousness of Truth, and brought us all nearer to the establishment of God's kingdom in the earth.

16. New Thought

As a religious movement, New Thought is any form of modern belief in mental healing other than the practices associated with traditional Christianity. The name came into vogue in 1895 and was used as the title of a magazine published for a time in Melrose, Massachusetts, to describe a "new thought" about life based on the premise that knowledge of the real world of ideas has marvelous power to relieve people of various ills.

The movement began with the work of Phineas P. Quimby (1802-1866) of Portland, Maine, who practiced mental and spiritual healing for over twenty years and greatly influenced Mrs. Mary Baker Patterson, better known as Mary Baker Eddy, foundress of Christian Science.

Quimby organized no society, but the persons whom he had helped adapted his methods and passed them on to others, though not without additions and changes of their own. Two of his followers, Warren F. Evans and Julius A. Dresser, coordinated the master's ideas and reduced them to systematic form. They are regarded as the intellectual founders of New Thought and its allied movements.

Evans published six books on the subject, of which the most significant were *The Mental Cure* (1869), *Mental Medicine* (1872) and *Soul and Body* (1875). According to Evans, disease has its roots in wrong belief. Once that is changed, disease is cured. A devoted Swedenborgian, he had long been familiar with the writings of Berkeley and other idealists. His own character and personal experiences further led him to a point where he was ready to apply an extreme form of idealism to the healing of disease.

Julius Dresser was cured by Quimby in 1860, but his major work in mental healing was not started until 1882, in Boston, where Dresser and his wife Annetta were competing with Mrs.

451

Baker Eddy. Dresser's clients were also instructed in a series of twelve class lectures, which included a study of divine immanence and a consideration that the spiritual life is continuous, that men already live in eternity. "To realize that our real life is spiritual," he said, "was to overcome the illusions of sense experience with its manifold bondages." Dresser's son and biographer popularized his father's teaching.

Evans and Dresser remained faithful to the memory of Quimby, whereas Mrs. Eddy disclaimed all dependence on the New England healer. Her followers became organized in a tightly-knit society, the Church of Christ, Scientist; the disciples of Quimby founded numerous small groups under different names like Divine Science, Unity, Practical Christianity, Home of Truth, and the Church of the Higher Life.

Before the turn of the century, these came to be known as New Thought and in 1894 the first national convention was held. In 1908 the name, National New Thought Alliance, was adopted, and six years later the organization became international. Its membership now extends to all the major countries of the world.

New Thought has not substantially changed since Quimby or Evans and Dresser. There has been an expansion of scope, however, to cover a broader perspective than healing sickness. The Declaration of Principles, adopted by the International Alliance in 1917, allows a wide range of belief among its membership.

DECLARATION OF PRINCIPLES
INTERNATIONAL NEW THOUGHT ALLIANCE

We affirm the freedom of each soul as to choice and as to belief, and would not, by the adoption of any declaration of principles, limit such freedom. The essence of the New Thought is Truth, and each individual must be loyal to the Truth he sees. The windows of his soul must be kept open at each moment for the higher light, and his mind must be always hospitable to each new inspiration.

We affirm the Good. This is supreme, universal and everlasting. Man is made in the image of the Good, and evil and pain are but the tests and correctives that appear when his thought does not reflect the full glory of this image.

We affirm health, which is man's divine inheritance. Man's body is his holy temple. Every function of it, every cell of it, is intelligent, and is shaped, ruled, repaired, and controlled by mind. He whose body is full of light is full of health. Spiritual healing has existed among all races in all times. It has now become a part of the higher science and art of living the life more abundant.

We affirm the divine supply. He who serves God and man in the full understanding of the law of compensation shall not lack. Within us are unused resources of energy and power. He who lives with his whole being, and thus expresses fullness, shall reap fullness in return. He who gives himself, he who knows and acts in his highest knowledge, he who trusts in the divine return, has learned the law of success.

We affirm the teaching of Christ that the Kingdom of Heaven is within us, that we are one with the Father, that we should not judge, that we should love one another, that we should heal the sick, that we should return good for evil, that we should minister to others, and that we should be perfect even as our Father in Heaven is perfect. These are not only ideals, but practical, everyday working principles.

We affirm the new thought of God as Universal Love, Life, Truth and Joy, in whom we live, move, and have our being, and by whom we are held together; that His mind is our mind now, that realizing our oneness with Him means love, truth, peace, health and plenty, not only in our own lives but in the giving out of these fruits of the Spirit to others.

We affirm these things, not as a profession, but practice, not on one day of the week, but in every hour and minute of every day, sleeping and waking, not in the ministry of a few, but in a service that includes the democracy of all, not in words alone, but in the innermost thoughts of the heart expressed in living the life. "By their fruits ye shall know them."

We affirm Heaven here and now, the life everlasting that becomes conscious immortality, the communion of mind with mind throughout the universe of thoughts, the nothingness of all error and negation, including death, the variety in unity that produces the individual expressions of the One-Life, and the quickened realization of the indwelling God in each soul that is making a new heaven and earth.

We affirm that the universe is spiritual and we are spiritual beings. This is the Christ message to the twentieth century, and it is a message not so much of words as of works. To attain this, however, we must be clean, honest and trustworthy and uphold the Jesus Christ standards as taught in the Four Gospels. We now have the golden opportunity to form a real Christ movement. Let us build our house upon this rock, and nothing can prevail against it. This is the vision and mission of the Alliance.

17. Community Churches

A typically American development of Protestantism is the rise of Community Churches, so called because they grow out of the life of a community. They offer religious services that are designed to satisfy the needs and aspirations of all who participate without contradicting the beliefs of any.

Individual Community Churches may belong to one or more denominations (such as Methodist, Baptist or Presbyterian) or have no denominational affiliation but operate entirely on their own. For this reason, it is said that the true Community Church can be recognized by the spirit in which it conducts its life and work, rather than by its relationship to any Protestant denomination.

Freedom of belief and the absence of any mandatory creed are the individualist side of Community Churches; mutual respect and friendly cooperation are the social balance to individuality. Together they form what some would consider "the grass roots level of the ecumenical movement," where the desire for Christian reunion is put into immediate practice. The basic principle is that Christians may and ought to worship and serve the Lord together despite differences of theological opinion and biblical interpretation.

The National Council of Community Churches was organized in 1950, and in the same year the International Council of Community Churches was formed. Centered in the United States, both organizations aim to broaden their respective fellowships to include community-centered churches of every race and nation throughout the world. They are officially known as The Council of Community Churches and have a constitution which corresponds to a formal profession of faith.

Not unlike a convention of Baptist churches, the council is not an authoritative body prescribing to the member churches any

455

matter of policy, doctrine or program. It is a free and democratic society in which each church agrees to share the best that has come to it with others in a religious democracy. It proposes to make available to all the spiritual possessions of each, over every barrier of race, color and creed.

CONSTITUTION
OF THE
COUNCIL OF COMMUNITY CHURCHES

Preamble. Confessing that we are members of ecumenically-minded churches, finding that it is possible here and now to have united churches at the local level, and longing for a comprehensive united church that will answer Jesus' prayer "that they all may be one," we herewith provide an instrument through which community-minded and freedom loving churches can cooperate in making a united contribution toward a united church.

Purpose. The Council of Community Churches is a fellowship that seeks to realize Christian unity in local, national and world relations. Believing that communities require united churches, the Council is committed to Christian unity, and works toward a united church, a church as comprehensive as the spirit and teachings of Christ and as inclusive as the love of God. It welcomes all churches that seek to make the church an instrument for discovering and putting into practice the will of God in community life.

The Council approaches the task of the church in the community in terms of the community's needs.

The Constitution is an instrument to aid in harmonious cooperation in the Kingdom of God. It gives no authority to elected and appointed officers for dictation of method or program over the churches which are affiliated with the Council.

Objectives. Upon invitation this Council will help communities without any church to form one all-inclusive church that is free to provide all Christian forms of religious expression.

Upon invitation this Council will help over-churched communities to federate and unite into one community-centered church.

This Council will encourage denominations to set up procedures to alleviate over-churched situations through their cooperative agencies and upon invitation will cooperate with them.

This Council will help churches requesting such help to find community-minded ministers. The decision rests with the minister and the local church. The Council prepares itself for this service by: a) Encouraging young people of community churches to dedicate themselves to the Christian ministry, b) Discovering community-minded ministers, and c) Thorough investigation of all applicants so that the highest educational, moral and ethical standards shall prevail in our ministry.

This Council will seek to stimulate giving to community churches, ecumenical and other missionary projects and will encourage member churches to develop a ministry to the neglected and depressed people of the world.

This Council will create and distribute literature which will set forth the concepts and the techniques of the community-centered unity on local, national and world levels.

This Council will cooperate with and foster movements for a united church in every way possible; and nourish the growth of church unity on local, national and world levels.

And finally, this Council will urge its churches to merge themselves with other followers of our Lord, as soon as a significant proportion of Protestantism, in obedience of Him, unites to form one holy church.

Acknowledgments

The author is grateful to the following publishers and writers for permission to use selections from copyright material. In each case, the selections are faithfully reprinted from the original. The sequence follows the order in the book, classified under the respective denominational tradition.

LUTHERANISM

Augsburg Confession, *The Book of Concord*, Theodore G. Tappert editor, Fortress Press, Philadelphia, 1959, pp. 27-96.
Luther's Small Catechism, *Ibid.*, pp. 337-356.

CALVINISM AND THE REFORMED TRADITION

The Heidelberg Catechism, *The Heidelberg Catechism, 1563-1963* (400th Anniversary Edition), United Church Press, Philadelphia, 1962. Used by permission of the publisher.
The Belgic Confession, *Doctrinal Standards of the Christian Reformed Church*, Publication Committee of the Christian Reformed Church, Grand Rapids, 1962, pp. 2-21.
Canons of Dort, *The Doctrinal Standards of the Reformed Church in America*, The Board of Education, New York, 1965, pp. 38-47.
Westminster Confession, *The Creeds of the Evangelical Protestant Churches*, Philip Schaff, editor, Hodder and Stoughton, London, 1877, pp. 600-673.
Presbyterian Confession of 1967, *Presbyterian Confessions: A Guide to the Book of Confessions of the United Presbyterian Church in the U.S.A.*, Edward A. Dowey, editor, Westminster Press, Philadelphia, 1967.

ANGLICANISM

Thirty-Nine Articles, *The Book of Common Prayer*, Church Pension Fund, New York, 1965, pp. 603-611.
Episcopalian Catechism, *Ibid.*, pp. 577-583.
The Lambeth-Chicago Quadrilateral, *The Episcopal Church in the*

United States 1789-1931 by James Thayer Addison, Charles Scribner's Sons, New York, 1951, pp. 273-274.

Anglican Ordinal, *The Book of Common Prayer*, pp. 529, 536-548.

Anglo-Catholicism, "How to Worship at the Eucharist," *The People's Anglican Missal in the American Edition*, Frank Gavin Liturgical Foundation, New York, 1962, pp. 241-250.

METHODISM

John Wesley's Articles of Religion, *Doctrines and Discipline of The Methodist Church*, The Methodist Publishing House, Nashville, 1964, pp. 36-43.

Evangelical United Brethren Confession of Faith, *The Constitution for The United Methodist Church with Enabling Legislation and Other Historic Documents*, Lovick Pierce and Donald A. Theuer, publishers, 1967, pp. 30-34.

Methodist Social Creed, *Ibid.*, pp. 38-44.

THE HOLINESS MOVEMENT

John Wesley's *A Plain Account of Christian Perfection*, Epworth Press, London, 1952, pp. 28-30, 106-111.

Constitution of the Church of the Nazarene, *Manual of the Church of the Nazarene*, Nazarene Publishing House, Kansas City, Missouri, 1964, pp. 25-32.

Principal Doctrines of the Salvation Army, *Orders and Regulations for Officers of The Salvation Army*, International Headquarters, London, 1950, pp. 43-44.

An Officer's Engagements with the Salvation Army, *Ibid.*, 1960 edition, pp. 555-557.

Confession of Faith—The Pentecostal Church of God, *Constitution and By-Laws of the Pentecostal Church of God*, General Headquarters, Joplin, Missouri, 1967, pp. 1-6.

Statement of Fundamental Truths—Assemblies of God, *Constitution: General Council of the Assemblies of God*, 1967, pp. 1-4.

Teachings of the Church of God. U.S.A. Headquarters, Queens Village, New York, 1967.

THE FREE CHURCH TRADITION

Congregationalism

The Cambridge Platform, *American Christianity: An Historical Interpretation with Representative Documents* by H. Shelton Smith, Robert T. Handy and Lefferts A. Loetscher, vol. I, Charles Scribner's Sons, New York, 1960, pp. 129-140.

Kansas City Statement, *History of American Congregationalism* by Gaius Glenn Atkins and Frederick L. Fagley, Pilgrim Press, Boston, 1942, pp. 404-405.

Statement of Faith—United Church of Christ, *United Church of Christ, History and Program,* Division of Publication, New York, 1966, p. 36.

The Baptists

Philadelphia Baptist Confession, *The Creeds of the Evangelical Protestant Churches,* pp. 738-741.

New Hampshire Confession of Faith, *Ibid.,* pp. 742-748.

Southern Baptists—Abstract of Principles, *Southeastern Baptist Theological Seminary Bulletin,* Tenth Catalog, May 1961, vol. 10, no. 3, pp. 74-76.

The Baptist Faith and Message: A Statement Adopted by the Southern Baptist Convention, Sunday School Board, Southern Baptist Convention, Nashville, 1965.

The Quakers: Theological Theses of Robert Barclay, *An Apology for the True Christian Divinity being an Explanation and Vindication of the Principles and Doctrines of the People Called Quakers* by Robert Barclay, Samuel Wood and Sons, New York, 1832, pp. 1-14.

Mennonite Confession of Faith (Adopted by Mennonite General Conference, August 22, 1963), Herald Press, Scottdale, Pa., 1966.

Church of the Brethren: Denomination Statement, *The Nature of the Church* (Papers Presented to the Theological Commission of the World Conference on Faith and Order), edited by R. Newton Flew, Harper, New York, 1952, pp. 298-302.

UNITARIANISM

From William Ellery Channing, *Unitarian Christianity and Other Essays,* edited by Irving H. Bartlett, copyright © 1957, Liberal Arts Press, Inc., reprinted by the permission of the Liberal Arts Division of The Bobbs-Merrill Company, Inc.

Thomas Jefferson: Unitarian Principles (Letters to Timothy Pickering and Benjamin Waterhouse), *The Writings of Thomas Jefferson,* edited by Andrew A. Lipscomb and Albert E. Bergh, The Thomas Jefferson Memorial Association, Washington, 1903-4, vol. XV, pp. 322-324, 383-385.

Ralph Waldo Emerson: Transcendental Unitarianism (Harvard Divinity School Address), *The Complete Works of Ralph Waldo Emerson,* Houghton Mifflin, Boston, 1903-4, vol. I, pp. 127-151.

Position Statement—Unitarian Universalist Association, *The Free Church: Its Nature, Nurture, Character,* Boston, 1965.

Constitution of the Unitarian Universalist Association, Boston, 1965.

CHURCH OF JESUS CHRIST OF LATTER-DAY SAINTS

Joseph Smith's Autobiography of Revelations, *The Pearl of Great Price* by Joseph Smith, The Church of Jesus Christ of Latter-Day Saints, Salt Lake City, 1952, pp. 46-57.

Mormon Articles of Faith, *Ibid.,* p. 59.

Twelve Principles for Dealing with the Government, "A Declaration of Belief regarding Governments and Laws in general, adopted by unanimous vote at a general assembly of the Church of Jesus Christ of Latter-Day Saints, held at Kirtland, Ohio, August 17, 1835," *The Doctrine and Covenants of the Church of Jesus Christ of Latter-Day Saints,* Salt Lake City, 1952, Section 134, pp. 250-252.

Joseph Smith's Revelation on Plural Marriages, *Ibid.,* Section 132, pp. 239-245.

Right of Succession to Joseph Smith, *Book of Doctrine and Covenants,* "A Revelation given February, 1831," used by permission of the Board of Publication of the Reorganized Church of Jesus Christ of Latter Day Saints, Independence, Missouri (1966, Section 43, pp. 101-104).

AMERICAN ADVENTISM

Fundamental Beliefs—Seventh-Day Adventists, *Seventh-Day Adventist Yearbook,* Review and Herald Publishing Association, Washington, 1967, pp. 5-6.

Declaration of Principles of the Advent Christian Church, *The Advent Christian Manual,* Advent Christian General Conference, Aurora, Illinois, 1963, pp. 100-101.

SPIRITUALISM

Declaration of Principles Adopted by the National Spiritualist Association of Churches U.S.A., National Spiritualist Association, Milwaukee, 1967.

Definitions Adopted by the National Spiritualist Association, *Ibid.*

Spiritual Healing, *The National Spiritualist,* Cassadaga, Florida, 1967.

Objects of Spiritualism, National Spiritualist Association, *Ibid.*

DISCIPLES AND CHRISTIANS

The Declaration of Thomas Campbell, *Disciples of Christ—A History,* by Winfred E. Garrison and Alfred T. DeGroot, Christian Board of Publication, The Bethany Press, St. Louis, 1954, pp. 146-148.

The Address of Thomas Campbell, *Historical Documents Advocating Christian Union* by Charles A. Young, Christian Century Co., Chicago, 1904, pp. 79-80, 92-99, 105-115.

CHRISTIAN SCIENCE

The Theology of Christian Science (Robert Peel), Copyright 1968, The Christian Science Board of Directors, All rights reserved.

The Practice of Christian Science (DeWitt John), Copyright 1968, The Christian Science Board of Directors, All rights reserved.

JEHOVAH'S WITNESSES

Proclamations of Joseph F. Rutherford, *Government* by Joseph F. Rutherford, Watch Tower Bible and Tract Society, Brooklyn, N.Y., 1928, "Proclamation," pp. 201-204; "The People," pp. 218-221; "Leader of the People," pp. 221-223; "Vengeance," pp. 228-229; "Ambassadors," pp. 229-230; "Joy of the Lord," p. 231.

ETHICAL CULTURE

Religious Fellowship As the Culminating Social Institution, *An Ethical Philosophy of Life Presented in Its Main Outlines* by Felix Adler, Appleton and Co., New York, 1920, pp. 341-353.

UNITY SCHOOL OF CHRISTIANITY

Unity's Statement of Faith, Unity School of Christianity (Original Publisher), Lee's Summit, Missouri, 1967.

Healing Ministry Instructions, Ibid.

NEW THOUGHT

Declaration of Principles: International New Thought Alliance, *Mind Remakes Your World*, Dodd, Mead and Co., New York, 1944, p. xi.

COMMUNITY CHURCHES

Constitution of the Council of Community Churches, The Council of Community Churches, Columbus, Ohio, 1966.

Confessional Index of the Protestant Churches of America

The following is a complete list of all the religious bodies in America that somehow qualify as Protestant. Each denomination is identified, in parentheses, with one or more confessional statements as found in the book. Where the document is not in italics, it is specifically the church's teaching; italics mean that it substantially represents the church's position.

Moreover, each body is further described in concise terms that distinguish it from other denominations in the same religious tradition.

The composite information gives an accurate picture of the doctrines and practices of all the Protestant Churches of America.

Key	Confessional Statement	Pages
AC	Augsburg Confession (Lutheran)	12
ACC	Advent Christian Church: Declaration and Principles	382
AG	Assemblies of God: Statement of Fundamental Truths	250
AO	Anglican Ordinal (Episcopalian)	191
ATC	Address of Thomas Campbell (Disciples and Christians)	397
BC	Belgic Confession (Reformed)	87
CB	Church of the Brethren: Denominational Statement	312
CCC	Constitution of Community Churches	456
CD	Canons of Dort (Reformed and Mennonite)	107
CG	Church of God—Teachings	255
CP	Cambridge Platform (Congregational, United Church of Christ)	262
CSH	Christian Science Healing	418
CST	Christian Science Theology	411
DCR	Doctrine and Covenants of Reorganized Church of Latter-Day Saints	374
DCS	Disciples of Christ Statement	405

Key	Confessional Statement	Pages
UUS	Unitarian Universalist Statement of Belief	340
WAR	Wesley's Articles of Religion (Methodist, Holiness, Pentecostal)	215
WC	Westminster Confession (Presbyterian, Baptist)	123
WEC	William Ellery Channing (Unitarian Christianity)	322
WPA	Wesley's Plain Account of Christian Perfection (Methodist, Holiness, Pentecostal)	232

Adventist Bodies

Advent Christian Church (ACC)
Sunday observance, conditional immortality, pacifism, congregational polity

Church of God (Abrahamic Faith) (*SDA*)
Restoration of Israel, premillennial, death unconsciousness, congregational

Primitive Advent Christian Church (*SDA*)
Conservative Adventism, Advent Christian Church derivative

Seventh-day Adventists (SDA)
Sabbatarian, vegetarian, abstinence, early Parousia, premillennial, missions

African Orthodox Church (*AO, EC, LQ, PAM, TNA*)
Negro, Episcopalian origin, Anglican-Greek-Roman Liturgy, no divorce

Amana Church Society (*MC*)
German pietistic origin, communal living, continued inspiration, no oaths

American Evangelical Christian Churches (CCC)
Also called American Bible Churches, Community Churches, conservative theology

American Rescue Workers (SA)
Salvation Army principles, believe in Baptism and Eucharist

Apostolic Faith (*PC*, WPA)
Wesleyan doctrine, Presbyterian polity, Arminian, no worldly amusements

Apostolic Overcoming Holy Church of God (*CG*, WPA)
Methodist origin, name changed from "Ethiopian," Pentecostal, foot washing

Assemblies of God, General Council (AG)
Pentecostal, Trinitarian, Arminian, pacifist, Presbyterian-Congregational polity

Baptist Bodies

American Baptist Association (NHC, PBC)
Landmarkers, absolute local church autonomy, pre-Reformation faith and polity

American Baptist Convention (NHC, PBC)
  Formerly Northern Baptist Convention, liberal, ecumenical, open Communion
Baptist General Conference (NHC, PBC)
  Swedish origin, Lutheran pietism, conservative theology, youth missionaries
Bethel Baptist Assembly (NHC, PBC)
  Originally Evangelistic Ministerial Alliance, Sabbath schools
Christian Unity Baptist Association (NHC, PBC)
  Open Communion, universal atonement, foot washing, revivals, strictly congregational
Conservative Baptist Association of America (NHC, PBC)
  Originally Fundamentalist Fellowship, against Modernism, not denomination
Duck River (and Kindred) Associations of Baptists (NHC, PBC)
  Theology between Particular (Calvinist) and General (Arminian) Baptists
Free Will Baptists (NHC, PBC)
  Welsh origin, Arminian (free will) against Calvinism, open Communion, foot washing
General Association of Regular Baptist Churches (NHC, PBC)
  Left the American Baptists, antimodernist, premillennial, civil authority divine
General Baptists (NHC, PBC)
  English-Dutch origin, Arminian, Presbyterian polity, foot washing, anti-Calvinist
General Conference of the Evangelical Baptist Church, Inc. (NHC, PBC)
  Formerly Full Gospel Inc., associated with Free Will Baptists, Arminian
General Six-Principle Baptists (NHC, PBC)
  Arminian, Creed: repentance, faith, Baptism, laying on hands, resurrection, hell
Independent Baptist Church of America (NHC, PBC)
  Originally Swedish Free Baptists, pacifist, admission by laying on hands
National Baptist Convention of America (NHC, PBC)
  Negro, formerly part of National Baptist Convention U.S.A., schism in 1915
National Baptist Convention U.S.A., Inc. (NHC, PBC)
  More Calvinistic than Arminian, largest Negro denomination in America
National Baptist Evangelical Life and Soul Saving Assembly of U.S.A. (NHC, PBC)
  Negro, formerly National Baptists of America, evangelism, relief work
National Primitive Baptist Convention in the U.S.A. (NHC, PBC)
  Negro, segregated after Civil War, Sunday schools, aid societies, Calvinistic
North American Baptist Association (NHC, PBC)
  Militant fundamentalist, publication emphasis, mission stress on Latin America

North American Baptist General Conference (NHC)
  German origin, Winebrennarian-United Brethren ancestry, mission emphasis
Primitive Baptists (NHC, PBC)
  Calvinist, antimission, "Hard Shell," no central administration, no Sunday schools
Progressive National Baptist Convention, Inc. (NHC, PBC)
  Negro, seceded (1961) from National Baptists U.S.A. over election procedure
Regular Baptists (NHC, PBC)
  Midway Calvinist and Arminian, regional groups without general organization
Separate Baptists in Christ (NHC, PBC)
  No creeds, annual confessions of faith, now General Association of Separate Baptists
Seventh Day Baptist General Conference (NHC, PBC)
  Saturday as Christian Sabbath, formerly Sabbatarian Baptists of England
Seventh Day Baptists (German, 1728) (NHC, PBC)
  German Brethren origin, founded Ephrata community, Dunker doctrines
Southern Baptist Convention (NHC, SBA, SBS)
  Centralized organization, national scope, Calvinistic, publications, missions
Two-Seed-in-the Spirit Predestinarian Baptists (NHC, PBC)
  Absolute predestinarianism: either God's or devil's seed in man from birth
United Baptists (NHC, PBC)
  Total depravity, theology between Calvinism and Arminianism
United Free Will Baptist Church (NHC, PBC)
  Strong anti-Calvinism congregational polity

Bible Protestant Church (*WAR, WPA*)
  Refused Methodist Church merger (1939), conservative Wesleyanism, premillennial

Bible Way Churches of Our Lord Jesus Christ World Wide, Inc. (*PC*)
  Left the Church of Apostolic Faith (1957), Pentecostal, congregational polity

Brethren (German Baptists)
  Brethren Church (Ashland, Ohio) (*CB*)
    Left the Brethren Church (Progressive Dunkers) in 1939, Arminian stress
  Church of the Brethren (CB)
    Doctrine of brotherhood, pacifism, abstinence, noncreedal, no oaths, ecumenism
  National Fellowship of Brethren Churches (*CB*)
    Formerly Brethren Church (Progressive), Arminian, foot washing, anointing

Old German Baptist Brethren (*CB*)
   Left the German Baptist Brethren (1881), conservative, pacifist, no
   Sunday schools

Plymouth Brethren (*ATC, DTC*)
   English and Irish Separatist origin, no creeds, no ordination, no
   organization

Brethren (River)
   Brethren in Christ (*WAR, WPA*)
      Revivalist origin (Susquehanna River), Holiness, Arminian, imminent
      Parousia
   Old Order River Brethren, or Yorker (*WAR, WPA*)
      Nonresistance, no conformity to world, no church edifices, ritual in
      homes
   United Zion Church (*WAR, WPA*)
      Derived from Brethren of Christ, foot washing, women veiled, modest
      attire

Christadelphians (*WEC*)
   Unitarian, Adventist, millennium from Canaan, no angels, only saved
   immortal

Christian and Missionary Alliance (*WC*)
   Presbyterian origins, missionary emphasis, separation from world,
   premillennial

Christian Churches (Disciples of Christ, International Convention) (*ATC,
   DCS, DTC*)
   No creeds, Holiness, congregational polity, denominations unbiblical,
   ecumenical

Christian Union (*CP*)
   Basic principle: no controversy over any issue, complete local church
   autonomy

Christ's Sanctified Holy Church (*WAR, WPA*)
   Methodist, Holiness stress, interracial origins, no tobacco or alcohol

Church of Christ (Holiness) U.S.A. (*WAR, WPA*)
   Baptist origins, Episcopalian polity, divine healing, foot washing,
   Holiness

Church of Christ, Scientist (CSH, CST)
   God is all, nothingness of matter, sickness-sin-death unreal, worldwide
   publication

Churches of God
   Church of God (Anderson, Indiana) (*CG*)
      Holiness, unstructured church, no millennium, foot washing, no formal
      membership
   Church of God (Cleveland, Tennessee) (*CG*)
      Lutheran theology, Wesleyan morality, Pentecostal, centralized govern-
      ment
   Church of God (Seventh Day), Salem, West Virginia (*CG*)

Saturday Sabbath, Jewish dietary laws, derived from Seventh-Day Adventists

The (Original) Church of God, Inc. (CG)
Lutheran Soteriology, Pentecostal, creeds unbiblical, foot washing

The Church of God (CG)
Over 200 denominations with this name, Pentecostal, Episcopal polity, healing

The Church of God (Seventh Day), Denver (CG)
Saturday Sabbath, earthly Paradise, abstinence, premillennial, split from Millerites

Church of God by Faith (CG)
Isolation of sinners, Eucharist as preaching, Baptism with fire, Episcopal polity

Church of God of Prophecy (CG, WPA)
Pentecostal, formerly Tomlinson Church of God, related to Church of God of all Nations

Church of God as Organized by Christ (CG, MC)
Mennonite origins, opposed to Protestant ecclesiasticism, ordination by Christ

Church of God and Saints of Christ (CG)
Jewish stress, church built on patriarchs, Decalogue only code, no legalism

Church of God in Christ (CG)
Pentecostal, Episcopal polity, Holiness for salvation, split from Baptists

Churches of God, Holiness (CG, WPA)
Baptist origins, Episcopalian structure, Pentecostal practices, sanctification

Churches of God in North America (General Eldership) (CG, CB)
Winebrenner origins, revivalist stress, no creeds, Bible only guide

The Church of Illumination (TRB, USF)
Gnostic ancestry, reincarnation, Apocalypse to be unsealed, equality of men and women

Church of the Living God (CG)
Freemason religion, fraternal structure, foot washing, "Christian Workers Fellowship"

Church of Nazarene (NC)
Sanctification after regeneration, abstinence, divine healing, not Pentecostal

Church of Our Lord Jesus Christ of the Apostolic Faith, Inc. (CG)
No creeds, Pentecostal, premillennial, foot washing, founded on Pentecost

Churches of Christ (ATC, DTC)
Separated (1906) from Disciples of Christ, strictly congregational, 20,000 groups

Churches of Christ in Christian Union (PC, WPA)
Pentecostal, evangelistic, camp meetings, soul-winning campaigns, nonritual

Churches of the New Jerusalem
  General Church of the New Jerusalem (*NSA, UUS*)
    Emanuel Swedenborg founder (1688-1772), basis for Spiritualism, Christ is Trinity
  General Convention of the New Jerusalem in the U.S.A. (*NSA, UUS*)
    Swedenborg founder, basis for Spiritualism, Trinity is Christ, liturgical

Community Churches
  Council of Community Churches (CCC)
    Noncreedal, nondenominational, community-centered, (sub)urban, ecumenical
  Federated Churches (*CCC, CP*)
    Quasi-denominational, rural (village) Baptist-Methodist-Presbyterian-United cooperatives

Congregational Churches
  Christian Church of North America, General Council (*CP, PC*)
    Merger of Italian Christians and Italian Pentecostals, Latin American missions
  The Christian Congregation (*ATC, CP, DTC*)
    Basic creed: John 13:34-45, congregational polity, ethical activism, undenominational
  Congregational Christian Churches, National Association (CP, KCS)
    Organized 1955 against United Church merger, strict local church autonomy
  Congregational Holiness Church (CP, KCS, *PC*)
    Pentecostal, democratic polity, abstinence, foot washing, nonconformity to world
  Conservative Congregational Christian Conference (CP, KCS)
    Founded 1948 against United Church merger, historic congregationalism, biblical

Ethical Culture (ECP)
    Jewish origins, antidoctrinal, antistructural, freedom of thought, social action

Evangelical Churches
  Evangelical Congregational Church (*EUB, WAR*)
    Methodist polity, Arminian, evangelistic, congregational spirit, pastors annual
  The Evangelical Covenant Church of America (AC, LC)
    Swedish Lutheran State Church origins, personal freedom, pietistic, nonconfessional
  The Evangelical Free Church of America (AC, LC, *CP*)
    Lutheran origins, congregational doctrine and polity, Swedish orientation
  Evangelical United Brethren Church (EUB, WAR, WPA)
    Arminian, evangelistic, merger (1968) with Methodists, Eucharist Calvinistic

Holiness Churches
  Apostolic Christian Church (Nazarean) (*CP, MC,* WPA)

Mennonite origin, Swiss and German orientation, entire sanctification, congregational

Apostolic Christian Churches of America (WPA)
Swiss-German background, life of godliness, unpaid ministry, pacifism

Church of Daniel's Band (WAR, WPA)
Methodist origins, evangelistic, primitive Wesleyanism, strongly perfectionist

Fire Baptized Holiness Church (*PC*, WAR, WPA)
Negro, Pentecostal orientation, divine healing, premillennial, episcopal polity

Fire Baptized Holiness Church (Wesleyan) (WAR, WPA)
Dissenters from Methodism, primitive Wesleyanism, strong evangelism, sanctification

Free Christian Zion Church of Christ (WAR, WPA)
Negro, Methodist doctrine and polity, relief activity, some Baptist elements

The Holiness Church of God, Inc. (CG, WPA)
Pentecostal orientation, mainly in North Carolina, Episcopalian structure

The Metropolitan Church Association (WAR, WPA)
Methodist revival origin, strong Wesleyan theology, evangelism of the poor

Pillar of Fire (*PC*, WAR, WPA)
Formerly Pentecostal Union, four classes: probationary, associate, regular, full

House of David (*MC*, *NC*)
"Descendants of Lost Tribes of Israel," communal property, vegetarian, no shaving

House of God, Pillar and Ground of Truth, Inc. (CG)
Operative Masonry in three degrees: Baptism, Eucharist, Foot Washing, fraternalism

Independent Churches
Independent Churches (CCC)
Same as Community Churches

Independent Assemblies of God, International (*AG*)
Fellowship of Pentecostal ministers, Swedish connection, main Protestants in Brazil

Independent Christian Churches (ATC, *DCS*, DTC)
Not denomination but brotherhood, conservative theology, no formal organization

Independent Fundamental Churches of America (ATC, *CG*, DTC)
Organized to safeguard fundamentalist doctrines, evangelistic, creedal position

Independent Negro Churches (*CCC*, *CG*, *CP*)
Community churches generally of Baptist, Methodist or Pentecostal orientation

International Church of the Foursquare Gospel (*CG*, *PC*)
Aimee McPherson founder, Adventist, fundamentalist, Pentecostal, healing, missions

Jehovah's Witnesses (JWP)
> Rule of God, all other churches false, allies of Satan: churches, state, business

Kodesh Church of Immanuel (EC, WAR, WPA)
> Formerly African Methodist Episcopal Zion Church, Wesleyan, Arminian, healing

Latter Day Saints
Church of Christ (Temple Lot) (JSA, MAF)
> Remnant founded by Joseph Smith, land at Independence, Missouri, for Lord's temple-to-come

The Church of Jesus Christ (JSA, MAF)
> Bickertonites, vs polygamy and polytheism, own *Book of Mormon*, vs Brigham Young

Church of Jesus Christ (Cutlerites) (JSA, MAF)
> Iowa segment, vs Brigham Young, lineage from Alpheus Cutler—Joseph Smith's friend

Church of Jesus Christ of Latter-Day Saints (JSA, MAF, MGA, MPM)
> Largest Mormon body, Utah group founded by Brigham Young, worldwide missions

Church of Jesus Christ of Latter-Day Saints (Strangites) (JSA, MAF)
> Wisconsin segment, Unitarian, vs polytheism, Saturday Sabbath, vs Brigham Young

Reorganized Church of Jesus Christ of Latter-Day Saints (DCR, JSA, MAF)
> Independence, Mo., claim only valid descent from Joseph Smith, vs polygamy

Lutherans
Lutheran Council in the U.S.A.
American Lutheran Church (AC, LC)
> Merger (1960-3) of American-Evangelical-Free-United Evangelical Lutherans

Lutheran Church in America (AC, LC)
> Merger (1963) of American Evangelical-Augustana-Finnish-United Lutherans

Lutheran Church, Missouri Synod (AC, LC)
> German origin, Reformation loyalty, extensive church-related school system

Synod of Evangelical Lutheran Churches (AC, LC)
> Formerly Slovak Evangelical Lutheran, collaboration with Missouri Synod

Other Lutheran Bodies
Apostolic Lutheran Church of America (AC, LC)
> Finnish origins, spiritual experience required, public confession of sins

Church of the Lutheran Brethren of America (AC, LC)
> Personal experience of salvation, nonliturgical worship, free prayer

Evangelical Lutheran Church in America (Eielsen Synod) (AC, LC)
> Norwegian origin, proof of conversion for membership, lay trustees

Evangelical Lutheran Synod (AC, LC)

Norwegian origin, separated over dispute on predestination and grace, congregational

Protestant Conference (Lutheran) (AC, LC)

Separated from Wisconsin synod, stress on forgiveness of sin through Christ

Wisconsin Evangelical Lutheran Synod (AC, LC)

German origin, vs Lutheran ecumenism without doctrinal unity, parochial schools

Mennonites

Beachy Amish Mennonite Churches (CD, *MC*)

Left Old Order Amish, milder discipline, church buildings, Sunday schools, missions

Church of God in Christ (Mennonite) (CD, *MC*)

Holy Spirit Baptism, apostates avoided, nonconformity to world, mode form of Baptism

Conference of the Evangelical Mennonite Church (CD, *MC*)

Formerly Defenseless Mennonite Church, stress on regeneration and nonresistance

Conservative Mennonite Conference (CD, MC)

Formerly Conservative Amish, favors meetinghouses, English ritual, Sunday schools

Evangelical Mennonite Brethren (CD, *MC*)

Formerly Conference of Defenseless Mennonites, Russian origins, overseas missions

General Conference, Mennonite Church (CD, MC)

Federation of Mennonite congregations, local church autonomy, liberal orientation

Hutterian Brethren (CD, *MC*)

Austrian origins, Amish stress, common property, day schools, absolute nonconformity

Mennonite Brethren Church of North America (CD, *MC*)

Russian origins, rigid enforcement of ban, stress on prayer and Bible study

Mennonite Church (CD, *MC*)

Canons of Dort primary, milder ban, includes Amish, German origins, evangelism

Old Order Amish Mennonite Church (CD, *MC*)

Strict observance, worship in homes, old forms of attire, vs centralized schools

Old Order (Wisler) Mennonite Church (CD, *MC*)

Left Mennonite Church protesting vs English ritual and Sunday schools

Reformed Mennonite Church (CD, *MC*)

Strict discipline, ban enforced, no written rules, vs missions, entire nonresistance

Unaffiliated Conservative and Amish Mennonite Churches (CD, *MC*)

No written statement of general principles, wide variety of faith and polity

Methodists
African Methodist Episcopal Church (EC, WAR, WPA)
    Negro, left Methodist Episcopal over discrimination, African-West Indies missions
African Methodist Episcopal Zion Church (*EC*, WAR, WPA)
    Negro, separated over discrimination, evangelism, Africa-South America missions
African Union First Colored Methodist Protestant Church, Inc. (WAR, WPA)
    Negro, no bishops, clergy and laity equal authority, no foreign missions
Christian Methodist Episcopal Church (*EC*, WAR, WPA)
    Formerly (1954) the Colored Methodist Episcopal Church, college of bishops
Congregational Methodist Church (CP, WAR, WPA)
    Left Methodist Episcopalians vs bishops' authority, local churches call pastors
Congregational Methodist Church of U.S.A. (CP, WAR, WPA)
    Left Methodist Episcopalians, democratic church structure, vs episcopal authority
Cumberland Methodist Church (WAR, WPA)
    Withdrew from Congregational Methodist Church over doctrine and polity, Tennessee
Evangelical Methodist Church (WAR, WPA)
    Arminian, fundamental in doctrine, evangelistic in program, congregational polity
Free Methodist Church of North America, (*NC*, WAR, WPA)
    Experience of forgiveness required, Holiness orientation, strict Wesleyanism
Fundamental Methodist Church, Inc. (*NC*, WAR, WPA)
    Protest vs Methodist Church merger (1939), no bishops, primitive Wesleyanism
Holiness Methodist Church (*NC*, WAR, WPA)
    Two bodies: North Carolina and North Dakota, witness of Spirit, home missions
Independent African Methodist Episcopal Church (WAR, WPA)
    Distinct Book of Discipline, formerly part of African Methodist Episcopalians
Lumber River Annual Conference of the Holiness Methodist Church (WAR, WPA)
    Formerly Holiness Methodists, North Carolina
The United Methodist Church (MSC, WAR, WPA)
    Largest Methodist group, merger (1939) of Methodist Episcopal-Protestant-South, merger (1968) with Evangelical United Brethren
New Congregational Methodist Church (CP, *WAR*, WPA)
    Left Methodist Episcopalians, episcopacy rejected, foot washing, congregational
Primitive Methodist Church U.S.A. (CP, WAR, WPA)
    Camp-meeting origins, no bishops or superintendents, Africa-South America missions

Reformed Methodist Union Episcopal Church (WAR, WPA)
   Left African Methodist Episcopal Church, class meetings, love feasts
Reformed Zion Union Apostolic Church (WAR, WPA)
   Negro, left African Methodist Zion Church over discrimination, elders
   are ministers
Southern Methodist Church (WAR, WPA)
   Opposed merger (1939) of Methodist Church, no bishops, segregation
   biblical
Union American Methodist Episcopal Church (WAR, WPA)
   Negro, formerly Union Church of Africans, rare meeting of general
   conference
Wesleyan Methodist Church of America (WAR, WPA)
   Strong Wesleyanism, membership conditions: abstinence, no tobacco,
   sanctification
Missionary Church Association (CG, CP)
   Local churches independent, conservative doctrine, evangelism, South
   America missions
New Thought Alliance (NTA, RWE, WEC)
   Based on principles of Channing-Emerson-Swedenborg, mind over
   matter gives health
Open Bible Standard Churches, Inc. (ATC, CG, DTC, PC, WPA)
   Fundamentalist, evangelistic, Pentecostal, premillennial, sanctification,
   healing
Pentecostal Churches
   Calvary Pentecostal Church, Inc. (CG, PC, WPA)
      Ministerial fellowship, relief of weak churches, Presbyterian polity,
      home missions
   Elim Missionary Assemblies (CG, CP, PC, WPA)
      Stress on foreign missions, Congregational polity, belong to Pentecostal
      Fellowship
   Emmanuel Holiness Church (CG, PC, WPA)
      Left Pentecostal Fire Baptized Holiness Church (1953), vs authori-
      tarianism
   International Pentecostal Assemblies (CG, PC, WPA)
      Absolute pacifism, African missions, anointing of sick, foot washing
      optional
   Pentecostal Assemblies of the World, Inc. (CG, PC, WPA)
      Originally interracial, Methodist polity, vs Unitarian trend in Pente-
      costalism
   Pentecostal Church of Christ (CG, PC, WPA)
      Stress on Holiness, divine healing typical, ecumenical among Pente-
      costal bodies
   Pentecostal Church of God of America, Inc. (CG, PC, WPA)
      Formerly Pentecostal Assemblies of the U.S.A., liberal orientation,
      missions
   Pentecostal Evangelical Church of God, National and International, Inc.
   (CG, PC, WPA)
      Progressive sanctification, stress on use of Bible, missionary program

Pentecostal Fire Baptized Holiness Church (*CG, PC,* WPA)
  Left Pentecostal Holiness (1918), spontaneous worship, vs jesting, jewelry
Pentecostal Free-Will Baptist Church, Inc. (*CG,* NHC, PBC, *PC,* WPA)
  Doctrine mixture of Baptist and Pentecostal, Arminian, sanctification
Pentecostal Holiness Church, Inc. (*CG, PC, WAR,* WPA)
  Basically Methodist doctrine, three experiences: justification, holiness, tongues
United Pentecostal Church, Inc. (UUS, *WPA*)
  Unitarian, largest American Pentecostal body, Baptism in the name of Jesus

Pilgrim Holiness Church (CP, *NC, PC,* WPA)
  Close to Nazarenes in doctrine and polity, Arminian, Congregational-Episcopal forms

Presbyterians
Associate Presbyterian Church of North America (WC)
  Scottish origins, left United Presbyterian Church of North America, Psalms exclusive in worship
Associate Reformed Presbyterian Church (General Synod) (WC)
  Covenanter origins, grace of salvation offered to all, Communion to sick
Cumberland Presbyterian Church (WC)
  Revivalist origin, vs fatality doctrine of Westminster Confession, missions
Orthodox Presbyterian Church (WC)
  J. Gresham Machen founder, principles normative for all American Fundamentalists
Presbyterian Church in the United States (WC)
  Popular name "Southern Presbyterians," Calvinistic, conservative theology, missions
Presbyterian Church in the United States of America (WC)
  Merged (1958) with United Presbyterian of North America, now United Presbyterian Church U.S.A.
Reformed Presbyterian Church, Evangelical Synod (WC)
  Merger (1965) of conservative bodies, vs Modernism-Pacifism-Communism, Calvinistic
Reformed Presbyterian Church of North America (Old School) (WC)
  No general assembly, no voting or holding public office, vs New Light (Evang. Synod)
Second Cumberland Presbyterian Church in the United States (WC)
  Negro, Arminian, no hell, formerly Colored Cumberland Presbyterian Church
The United Presbyterian Church in the United States (UP, WC)
  Largest Presbyterian body in America, liberal orientation, social concern, education
United Presbyterian Church of North America (UP, WC)
  Merged (1958), now United Presbyterian Church U.S.A., Arminian orientation

Protestant Episcopal Church (AO, EC, LCQ, PAM, TNA)
Clergy oath: ". . . to conform to the doctrine, discipline and worship of the Prot. Ep. Ch."

Reformed Churches
Christian Reformed Church (BC, CD, HC)
Formerly Holland Reformed Church, Calvinistic, conservative, parochial schools
Hungarian Reformed Church in America (BC, CD, HC)
Polity a combination of Episcopal and Presbyterian elements, ecumenical
Netherlands Reformed Congregations (BC, CD, HC)
Secession from state church of Holland, Calvinistic, similar to Christian Reformed
Protestant Reformed Churches of America (BC, CD, HC)
Strict predestinarians, left Christian Reformed (1926), Presbyterian government
Reformed Church in America (BC, CD, HC)
Oldest Reformed body in America, liberal orientation, liturgical forms optional
Reformed Church in the United States (HC)
Formed in protest of merger with Evangelical and Reformed (1934), Calvinistic
Reformed Episcopal Church (*HC*, TNA)
Left Protestant Episcopal Church (1873), vs ritualism and ecclesiasticism, no priests

Salvation Army (SA)
Methodist origin, formerly Christian Mission, social rehabilitation, no sacraments

Schwenkfelder Church (CP, *TRB*, *UUS*)
Indwelling Word, congregational polity, Christ's divinity progressive, Eucharist symbolic

Social Brethren (*NHC, PBC, WPA*)
Conservative theology, polity a fusion of Baptist and Methodist structure, social work

Society of Friends (Quakers)
Central Yearly Meeting of Friends (TRB)
Evangelical and fundamental in doctrine, mission work in South America
Friends United Meeting (Five Years Meeting of Friends) (TRB)
Largest body of Quakers in the country, loose federation of Yearly Meetings
Ohio Yearly Meetings of Friends (TRB)
Also called Evangelical Friends Alliance, fundamentalist, stress primitive Christianity
Oregon Yearly Meeting of Friends Church (TRB)

Originally part of Society of Friends (Five Years Meeting), more structured polity

Pacific Yearly Meeting of Friends (TRB)
No ordained clergy having charges, Sunday schools, founded (1947) at Palo Alto

Religious Society of Friends, Conservative (TRB)
Wilburites, no creed but immediate revelation, silent Quaker meetings, no ritual

Religious Society of Friends, General Conference (*RWE, TRB, UUS, WEC*)
Hicksites, Unitarian, formed (1900) along liberal and rationalist lines, social concern

Religious Society of Friends, Kansas City Yearly Meeting (TRB)
History of conflict between Orthodox (Fox) and Methodist (Wesley) type of Quakerism

Spiritualists

International General Assembly of Spiritualists (NSA)
Founded (1936) to charter new churches, cooperative body to unify Spiritualism

The National Spiritual Alliance of the United States of America (*NSA*)
Founded (1913), believes in supernormal manifestations and inter-communion with spirits

National Spiritualist Association of Churches (NSA)
Orthodox Spiritualism as science, religion and philosophy based on facts

Triumph the Church and Kingdom of God in Christ (*CG*, WPA)
Holiness tradition, Baptism by fire, entire sanctification, early Second Coming

Unitarian Universalist Association (RWE, TJP, UUC, UUS, WEC)
No supernatural revelation, Christ only man, no creeds, Deism, social concern

United Brethren

Evangelical Church of North America (EUB)
Formed (1968) by Evangelical United Brethren vs merger of United Methodist Church

United Brethren in Christ, Old Constitution (*EUB*)
Methodist and Evangelical origins, conservative, abstinence, pacifist, missions

United Christian Church (ATC, DTC, *EUB*)
Formerly Hoffmanites, Campbellite orientation, fundamentalist, evangelistic

United Seventh Day Brethren (*EUB, SDA*)
Merger (1947), evangelical, Sabbatarian, premillennial, in Arizona and Nebraska

United Church of Christ (CP, KCS, UCC)
Merger (1961) of Evangelical and Reformed with Congregational Christian Church

United Holy Church of America, Inc. (CG, *PC*)
   Negro Pentecostal body, Sabbath observance, sanctification immediately after conversion

United Missionary Church (*CD, MC*)
   Formerly (1947) Mennonite Brethren, Wesleyan-Arminian holiness, millennium

Unity School of Christianity (UHM, USF)
   No real death, increasingly better states until a man becomes as Christ, mail order

Universalist Church of America (RWE, TJP, UUC, UUS, WEC)
   Merged (1961) to form Unitarian Universalist Association

Universal Orthodox Christian Spiritual Faith and Church of All Nations (CG, *PC*)
   Baptist origin, Pentecostal doctrine and polity, Episcopal structure, interracial

Volunteers of America (*SA*)
   Founded (1896) by Booth Jr., son of Salvation Army founder, sacraments, democratic

Analytic Index

Aaronic priesthood, Mormons, 361

Absolution of sin, Augsburg Confession, 17

Luther, 55-56

Abstinence—strong drink, Church of God, 255-256

Actions of unregenerate sinful, Westminster Confession, 140

Actual sin, Westminster Confession, 132

Adam-Dream as mortality, Christian Science, 415

Additions to sacraments, Belgic Confession, 105

Address of Thomas Campbell: biblical deductions not binding, 402-403

bigotry and disunity, 399-400

Christ only head, 398-399

Church as one, 401

Church not only for learned, 402, 403

disunity sinful, 397, 403

dogmatic faith unnecessary, 402-403

human inventions cause disunity, 397-398

means to unity, 404

no creeds, 401-402

orthodoxy and excommunication, 403-404

return to Bible, 398

unity through love, 403

unity through Scripture, 399-400

Adler, Felix, founder of Ethical Culture, 435-436

Adultery dissolves marriage, Westminster Confession, 148-149

Adventists, American history, 377-378

African Methodist Episcopal Church, origins, 213

African Methodist Episcopal Zion Church, origins, 213

Alcohol problems, Methodist Social Creed, 227-228

Alcoholic beverages, Methodist prohibition, 212

and tobacco forbidden, Adventist, 381

All disease mental, Christian Science, 421-422

Ambassadors of God, Jehovah's Witnesses, 432-433

Amen, Luther's meaning, 53

America—the Promised Land, Mormonism, 363

American Ethical Union, origins, 435-436

American Free Church tradition, characteristics, 261-262

American Millennial Association, Adventists origin, 377

American Presbyterianism, history, 156-158

American Protestantism, characteristics, 319

American Unitarian Association, Congregationalist, 259-260

Anabaptists: condemned in Belgic Confession, 103-104

Free Church Tradition, 257

ministry opposed, Augsburg Confession, 16

Angel guardians, Belgic Confession, 92

Anglicanism: confessional statements, 169-172

orders, meaning and grades, 193-194

Ordinal, history of, 191-193

Anglo-Catholicism: analysis, 200-202

early Christian worship, 202

Eucharistic sacrifice, 204-205

Real Presence in, 207

liturgical prayer, 202

participation in Mass, 205-207

ritual of, 203-204

Prayer Book ritual, 202-203

Anointing of sick, Church of the Brethren, 315

Anthon, Charles, in Mormon history, 360-361

483

baptism by immersion, 352-363
Book of Mormon equal to Bible, 363
Church and State separation, 365
civil authority from God, 363-364
civil disobedience to be punished, 364-365
concept of God, 362
concubines of Abraham and David approved, 370-371
conditions for valid marriage, 368
freedom of conscience, 363-364
history, 347-348
liberty of conscience, 363-364
marriage covenant, 367-369
miraculous gifts of, 363
no evangelism with force, 365
polygamy, and federal law, 366
  history of doctrine on, 365-366
  Old Testament basis, 366-367
  priests' rights to several wives, 372-373
  revelation of, 366-373
  right to, 372-373
religious freedom demanded, 365
self-defense apart from State, 369
sin against Holy Spirit, 369
succession, Joseph Smith's revelation, 374-376
Morning and evening prayers, Luther, 57
Moroni, Mormon revelation from angel, 354-355
Mortification and self-denial, Baptist New Hampshire Confession, 281
Munzer, Thomas, and Inner Light, 257
Music in Lutheranism, 10-11
Muzzy, David, Ethical Culturist, 436
Mystery of God's operation in soul, Canons of Dort, 116
  of predestination taught with prudence, Westminster Confession, 130

National Council of Community Churches, history, 455-456
National security, United Presbyterians, willingness to risk, 165
National Spiritualists Association of Churches, definitions of, 388-389
National Youth Thought Alliance, origin, 452
Nature of God, Belgic Confession, 88
Nazarene Church: baptism, meaning—effects, 243
  Christ, divinity and humanity, 240

on second coming of, 242
entire sanctification defined, 242
eschatology, 242-243
Eucharist as memorial and meal, 243
healing ministry, 243
Holy Spirit, role of, 240
inerrancy of Scripture, 240-241
justification as regeneration—adoption, 241-242
man free though depraved, 241
original sin—total depravity, 240-241
predestination, atonement for all, 241
Trinity, doctrine on, 240
Virgin birth of Christ, 240
voluntary repentance, 241-242
Necessity, of Church for salvation, Westminster Confession, 149
  of prayer, Heidelberg Catechism, 85
Nephites, predecessors of Mormons, 348
Netherland Reformed confession of faith, *Confessio Belgica*, 63
New earth after last day, Adventist, 382
New Hampshire Confession of Faith, history, 278-279
New kingdom to be established, Jehovah's Witnesses, 429
New life in Christ, United Presbyterians, 161-162
New Testament, Westminster Confession, covenant of grace, 133
New Thought: body cells intelligent, 452-453
heaven on earth, 453
history, 451-452
man, one with God, 453
spiritual healing universal, 452-453
Swedenborgian origins, 451
universe spiritual, 453
New York City, Ethical Culture's origins, 435
Nicaea, Augsburg Confession, 14-15
Nicene and Apostles' Creeds, Thirty-Nine Articles, 176
Non-Christian religions, Unitarians part of, 340-341
  United Presbyterians on, 164-165
Non-Christians are not saved, Westminster Confession, 136
Nonresistance respected by State, Mennonites, 311
Norfolk, Virginia, Spiritualist headquarters, 387
Nothing happens by chance, Belgic Confession, 93

Reformed Church in America: basic confessions of faith, 65
origins and spirit, 65
Reformed and Lutheran confessions of faith compared, 60-64
Reformed Protestantism: attitude toward Thirty-Nine Articles, 123
baptism's effects, 61
and Canons of Dort, 107-108
distinctive features, 60-62
Eucharistic doctrine, 61
Evangelical comparison, 60-64
five fundamental doctrines, 108
founded by John Knox, Scotland, 60
God's sovereignty stressed, 60-61
Lutheran comparison, 59
predestination, doctrinal defense, Canons of Dort, 121-122
and election, 60-61
principal confessions of faith, 65
sources, 59-60
Reformed Protestantism in Flanders and Netherlands, Belgic Confession, 87-88
Regeneration of sinner, Canons of Dort, 116-117
Regulations of Church adjusted to times, Augsburg Confession, 42-43
Reincarnation, Unity, 448
Religion, as feeling, Schleiermacher on, 11-12
as subjective experience in Lutheranism, 11-12
Religious freedom: Southern Baptists, 290
instruction, Luther—method, 46
life as escape from world, Augsburg Confession, 41
vows null and void, 35
worship, Westminster Confession, 144-145
Remission of sins through Eucharist, Luther, 56-57
Remonstrance of Arminian Calvinists, 63-64
Reorganized Church of Latter Day Saints: challenges Utah Mormons, 374-375
divine justice for disobedience, 375-376
eschatology, 376
history, 347-348

Joseph Smith's revelation on succession, 374-376
valid ordination only through, 374
Repentance: Augsburg Confession, 17
and conversion compared, Heidelberg Catechism, 80-81
after death, Spiritualists, 388
Westminster Confession as unto life, 138-139
Reprobation of the non-elect, Canons of Dort, 109
fear caused by, 112
Resurrection, of the body, Heidelberg Catechism, 74-75
Westminster Confession on, 155-156
of Christ, Heidelberg Catechism's purpose of, 73
of dead, Belgic Confession, 106-107
Revelation immediate, Quaker teaching, 293-294
Reward through grace not merit, Heidelberg Catechism, 75
Righteousness only from Christ, Heidelberg Catechism, 69
as only by faith, 75-76
originally due to nature, Luther, 5
Roman Catholicism as false Church, Belgic Confession, 101
Russell, Charles Taze, founder of Jehovah's Witnesses, 425
Rutherford, Joseph F., Organizer of Jehovah's Witnesses, 425

Sabbath sanctified, Westminster Confession, 195
Sacrament: of altar, Luther, 56-57
definition, Belgic Confession, 102-103
efficacy, Augsburg Confession, 16-17
and meaning, Episcopalian Catechism, 186-187
and number, Thirty-Nine Articles, 179
only for predestined, Reformed Protestantism, 61
explanation, Heidelberg Catechism, 76
Luther's commentary, 53-57
meaning and number, Westminster Confession, 150-151
necessity, Augsburg Confession, 17-18
as spiritual, Christian Science, 418
substantially same—Old and New